Program Form

```pascal
PROGRAM Demo (input, output);
CONST
  Skip = ' ';
VAR
  Count : integer;
  Score1, Score2 : real;
  Average : real;
BEGIN
  Count := 0;
  readln (Score1, Score2);
  Average := (Score1 + Score2) / 2;
  Count := Count + 1;
  writeln ('Average', Average:8:2)
END.
```

Functions

```pascal
FUNCTION Cube (X : integer) : integer;
  BEGIN
    Cube := X * X * X
  END;  { of FUNCTION Cube  }
```

call by
```pascal
Y := Cube(X);
```
or
```pascal
writeln (Cube (X));
```

Selection Statements

```pascal
IF Num > 0 THEN
  BEGIN
    PosCount := PosCount + 1;
    X := sqrt(Num)
  END;

IF Num >= 0 THEN
  BEGIN
    NonNegCount := NonNegCount + 1;
    X := sqrt(Num)
  END
ELSE
  BEGIN
    NegCount := NegCount + 1;
    X := abs(Num)
  END;

CASE GasType OF
  'R' : writeln ('Regular');
  'U' : writeln ('Unleaded');
  'S' : writeln ('SuperUnleaded')
END;  { of CASE GasType  }
```

Procedures

```pascal
PROCEDURE GetData (VAR Amount : AmountList;
                   VAR Count : integer);
  BEGIN
    Count := 0;
    WHILE NOT eof DO
      BEGIN
        Count := Count + 1;
        readln (Amount[Count])
      END
  END;  { of PROCEDURE GetData  }
```

call by
```pascal
GetData (Amount, Count);
```

Repetition Statements

```pascal
FOR J := 1 TO 20 DO
  writeln (J:5, J*J:5, J*J*J:5);

WHILE NOT eof Do
  BEGIN
    Count := Count + 1;
    readln (Score);
    Total := Total + Score
  END;

REPEAT
  A := 2 * A;
  B := sqrt(A)
UNTIL B > 1000;
```

Using Arrays

```pascal
Total := 0;
J := 0;
WHILE NOT eof DO
  BEGIN
    J := J + 1;
    readln (Donation[J]);
    Total := Total + Donation[J]
  END;
Count := J;
Average := Total / Count;
FOR K := 1 TO Count DO
  writeln ('$':10, Donation[K]:8:2);
writeln;
writeln ('Average', Average:11:2);
```

Type Definitions

```
TYPE
   String20 = PACKED ARRAY [1..20] OF char;
   NameList = ARRAY [1..ClassSize] OF String20;
   AmountList = ARRAY [1..MaxSize] OF real;
   CurrentYears = 1950..2000;
   WeatherType = (Cloudy, Sunny, Rain, Snow, Balmy);
```

Record Definition

```
TYPE
   String20 = PACKED ARRAY [1..20] OF char;
   PatientInfo = RECORD
                    Name : String20;
                    Age : 0..100;
                    Weight : 0..300
                 END;  {  of RECORD PatientInfo  }
   PatientList = ARRAY [1..100] OF PatientInfo;
VAR
   Patient : PatientList;
```

Using Records

```
FOR J := 1 TO NumPatients DO
   BEGIN
      WITH Patient[J] DO
         BEGIN
            writeln (Name:30);
            writeln (Age:10, Weight:10)
         END;
      writeln; writeln
   END;  {  of FOR...TO loop  }
```

File Definition

```
TYPE
   String20 = PACKED ARRAY [1..20] OF char;
   PatientInfo = RECORD
                    Name : String20;
                    Age : 0..100;
                    Weight : 0..300
                 END;  {  of RECORD PatientInfo  }
   PatientFile = FILE OF PatientInfo;
VAR
   Patient : PatientFile;
   TempRec : PatientInfo;
```

Using Files

```
rewrite (Patient);
WHILE NOT eof(input) DO
   BEGIN
      GetData (Patient^);
      Process (Patient^);
      put (Patient)
   END;
```

Pascal: Understanding Programming and Problem Solving, Third Edition
Douglas W. Nance
© 1992 West Publishing Company

Pascal: Understanding Programming and Problem Solving

THIRD EDITION

TO THE STUDENT

There is a student solutions manual available with complete, step-by-step solutions to selected end-of-section exercises in this text, as well as complete, documented programs for two programming problems at the end of each chapter. Students can purchase the solutions from the local bookstore under the title *Student's Solutions Manual for Pascal: Understanding Programming and Problem Solving,* Third edition, prepared by Douglas Nance and James Cowles.

Pascal:

Understanding

Programming and

Problem Solving

THIRD EDITION

Douglas W. Nance
CENTRAL MICHIGAN UNIVERSITY

WEST PUBLISHING COMPANY

ST. PAUL   NEW YORK   LOS ANGELES   SAN FRANCISCO

To Helen

Copyeditor and Indexer: Janet Hunter
Interior design: Paula Schlosser, Lucy Lesiak, and John Rokusek
Illustrations: Randy Miyake
Composition: Carlisle Communications
Production, PrePress, Printing and Binding:
  West Publishing Company

WEST'S COMMITMENT TO THE ENVIRONMENT
In 1906, West Publishing Company began recycling materials left over from the production of books. This began a tradition of efficient and responsible use of resources. Today, up to 95 percent of our legal books and 70% of our college texts are printed on recycled, acid-free stock. West also recycles nearly 22 million pounds of scrap paper annually—the equivalent of 181,717 trees. Since the 1960s, West has devised ways to capture and recycle waste inks, solvents, oils, and vapors created in the printing process. We also recycle plastics of all kinds, wood, glass, corrugated cardboard, and batteries, and have eliminated the use of styrofoam book packaging. We at West are proud of the longevity and the scope of our commitment to our environment.

Printed in the United States of America
99 98 97 96 95 94 93 92   8 7 6 5 4 3 2 1 0

Library of Congress Cataloging-in-Publication Data

Nance, Douglas W.
    Pascal: understanding programming and problem solving / Douglas
    W. Nance.— 3rd ed.
        p. cm.
      Includes index.
      ISBN 0−314−90877−3
      1. Pascal (Computer program language) I. Title.
    QA76.73.P2N35   1991
005.13′3 —dc20   91−27770

  CIP

⊞ Contents

CHAPTER   **3 ▪** Arithmetic, Variables, Input, Constants, and Standard Functions   53

CHAPTER

6 ▪ Repetition Statements   207

CHAPTER

7 ▪ Subprograms: Writing Procedures and Functions   279

CHAPTER

8 ▪ Subprograms: Using Procedures and Functions   329

CHAPTER

9 ∎ Text Files and Enumerated Data Types   381

CHAPTER   **10** ∎ One-Dimensional Arrays   419

CHAPTER   **11** ∎ Arrays of More Than One Dimension   487

CHAPTER   **14** ■ Sorting and Merging   627

CHAPTER   **15** ■ Sets   647

⊞ Preface

Those who teach entry-level courses in computer science are familiar with the problems that beginning students encounter. Initially, students can get so involved in learning a language that they may fail to grasp the significance of using the language to solve problems. Conversely, it is possible to emphasize problem solving to the extent that using a particular language to solve problems becomes almost incidental. The intent of this text is to be somewhere between these two extremes. Besides providing a complete, one semester course in Pascal, the broader goals are for students to understand language concepts and subsequently be able to use them to solve problems.

Overview and Organization

As with the second edition, the material in Chapters 1–4 is presented at a deliberate pace. If students in the class have already had some programming experience, these chapters may be covered rapidly. However, students must be able to solve problems using top-down design with stepwise refinement. If this is overlooked, students will have difficulty designing solutions to more complex problems later.

Throughout the text, I have attempted to explain and develop concepts carefully. These are illustrated by frequent examples and diagrams. New concepts are then used in complete programs to show how they aid in solving problems. An early and consistent emphasis has been placed on good writing habits and on producing neat, attractive output. I firmly believe program documentation and readability are important. Thus, I frequently discuss them in the text, and I offer style tips where appropriate.

There are at least three general scenarios for which this text would be appropriate.

1. A deliberately paced, thorough presentation of concepts would allow you to get through records and/or files in a one-semester course.
2. An accelerated pace with students who have previous computing experience would allow you to get into Chapter 16 in a one-semester course.

3. A deliberate pace with a thorough presentation would allow you to present the material in Chapters 1–16 in a two-quarter sequence.

Subprograms (procedures and functions) are presented in Chapters 7 and 8, after students have become familiar with the concepts of selection and repetition. Many students find working with procedures more difficult than working with decision or looping statements. Thus, it is to their advantage to become comfortable with some basic concepts in Pascal before encountering the slightly more difficult concepts associated with writing subprograms. At this stage, students are better able to understand the use of parameters. All subsequent work utilizes subprograms in problem solution and program design.

In this edition, Chapter 9 presents text files as well as user-defined data types. Since larger data sets are typically used with arrays and files, it is assumed that most data will be read from data files (rather than entered interactively) after this chapter.

Chapters 10 and 11 develop arrays. Due to the significance of this concept, these chapters contain numerous examples, illustrations, and applications. A selection sort has been used to sort array elements. However, a bubble sort and an insertion sort are developed in Chapter 14, and either could be used in place of the sorting algorithm presented in Section 10.3. Records and files are discussed in Chapters 12 and 13, respectively. Their placement there is traditional. These chapters, combined with Chapters 10 and 11, present a detailed treatment of static data structures.

Chapter 14 is an optional chapter that discusses sorting and merging. For advanced classes, material in this chapter could be used to motivate additional work with data structures. It is possible to use this material with preceding chapters. For example, sorting could be discussed in conjunction with Chapter 10, and merging with Chapter 13.

Chapter 15, Sets, could be presented any time after Chapter 9. Although a full chapter has been devoted to this topic, a working knowledge could be given to students in one or two days. Dynamic variables and data structures are introduced in Chapter 16. A reasonable discussion and development of pointers, linked lists, and binary trees is included. However, a full development of these concepts would have to come from a second course with a different text.

$\boxed{T}$
Pascal statements in this text conform to standard Pascal. Due to the increasing use of Turbo Pascal with personal computers, Turbo Pascal references are included in the margins to indicate where Turbo differs from standard Pascal. Both interactive and batch mode examples are used in this text. Interactive examples are indicated by a logo in the left margin, as shown here.

Features

This text has a number of noteworthy pedagogical features.

- Objectives—a concise list of topics and learning objectives in each section.
- Style tips—suggestions for programming style, intended to enhance readability.
- Exercises—short-answer questions at the end of each section.

- Programming problems and projects—starting with Chapter 4, lengthy lists of suggestions for complete programs and projects given at ends of chapters.
- Module specifications for program modules.
- Structure charts to reflect modular development. These include use of data flow arrows to emphasize transmission of data to and/or from each module. This sets the stage for understanding use of value and variable parameters when procedures are introduced.
- Notes of Interest—tidbits of information intended to create awareness of and interest in various aspects of computer science.
- Suggestions for test programs—ideas included in exercises that encourage the student to use the computer to determine answers to questions and to see how to implement concepts in short programs.
- Focus on Program Design—when appropriate, a complete program at the end of the chapter that illustrates utilization of concepts developed within the chapter.
- Running and debugging hints preceding each summary and programming problems set at the ends of chapters.
- New terms are italicized when first introduced.

In the back of the book there is a complete glossary, as well as appendixes on reserved words, standard identifiers, syntax diagrams, character sets, compiler error messages, Turbo Pascal references, the **GOTO** statement, and packing and unpacking. The final section of back matter provides answers to selected exercises.

Changes for the Third Edition

The first edition of this text carefully presented and illustrated new concepts. It was assumed that users had little or no experience in computer science; hence, a deliberate approach emphasizing language constructs was used.

As the discipline of computer science evolves, there are two issues that its textbook authors must address. First, students of Pascal have increasing experience and sophistication with computers. Second, the nature of an entry-level course should reflect current trends and meet current needs. These issues shaped the changes made in the second edition.

This edition maintains the philosophy that computer science is a dynamic discipline. Although Pascal is still the language most used in entry-level courses, many concepts are presented in a language-independent manner. Thus, learning a language for the sake of learning the language is frequently deemphasized in favor of emphasizing concepts and problem-solving skills. Further, there is an increasing need for students to see both interactive and batch mode programs. These environments, coupled with popular nonstandard versions of Pascal (Turbo, for example), dictate greater flexibility in text preparation.

Consistent with the philosophy that Pascal is evolving as an introductory course in computer science, this third edition features the following:

- Continuing emphasis on the design of solutions to problems.
- Graphic documentation to illustrate how sections of code work.
- Two sections on using assertions.

- A section on software engineering and subsections throughout the text indicating how new concepts relate to software engineering.
- A section on the software system life cycle.
- Significantly more material on abstraction, including subsections on procedural abstraction, data abstraction, and abstract data types.
- More rigor in the development and use of current terminology associated with subprograms, including discussions of cohesion, encapsulation, and interface.
- New material emphasizing communication in computer science. This includes text references and exercises in every chapter designed to allow students to interview people, write reports, give oral reports, and write program specifications without writing code.
- Graphic documentation of some algorithms has been included to enable students to more easily understand code by using visual illustrations.
- Continuing use of interactive and batch mode examples in the first half of the text.
- Occasional use of photographs to clarify and enhance presentations.
- Comments about Turbo Pascal in the text and in the Turbo Appendix are appropriate for all versions of Turbo.
- A significant increase in mathematical examples and programming problems.
- Of the thirty-six Notes of Interest, twenty-one are new and ten have been updated since the last edition to reflect the changing scene of computer use and growth.

All of these changes have been made with two thoughts prevalent in my mind. It is essential that this edition reflect current trends and future directions of computer science. It is also essential that concepts continue to be presented in such a manner that beginning students understand a concept and see how it can be used to design a solution to solving some problem. In this regard, every attempt has been made to retain the pedogogical features that have proven to be the trademark of the first two editions. These include frequent use of examples, clear exposition of new concepts, use of test programs, and varied exercises with every section.

Ancillaries

It is our belief that a broad based teaching support package is essential for an introductory course in Pascal. Thus, the following ancillary materials are available from West Publishing Company:

1. Laboratory Manuals—In keeping with our intent to provide a modern approach and to meet the growing need for laboratory experience as put forth by the new ACM Curriculum Guidelines, there are two laboratory manuals (one for standard Pascal and one for Turbo users) that are tied closely to the text's pedogogy. Authored by Carol Wilson, (Western Kentucky University) and class-tested with students at two universities, both provide excellent sets of lab exercises to promote students' understanding.
2. A Student's Solutions Manual—This contains solutions to all exercises at the end of each section. Explanation and development are

given for appropriate problems. Complete solutions for two programming problems are included for each chapter.

3. An Instructor's Manual—This manual contains the following for each chapter:
   a. outline
   b. teaching test questions
   c. chapter test questions
   d. answers to test questions
4. A Set of Transparency Masters—More than 75 transparency masters are available to adopters of the text. These include figures, tables, and selected other material from the text.
5. Software with Machine-readable Programming Problems—This software contains at least four complete programming problem solutions in each chapter and the complete Focus on Program Design problem. This software will run on IBM-PCs and compatibles, Apple MacIntoshes, and DEC Baxes. It is available in both standard and Turbo Pascal.
6. A Computerized Test Bank—Adopters of this edition will receive a computerized test-generation system. This provides a test-bank system that allows you to edit, add, or delete as you wish.

West Publishing Company recognizes the growing need for an integrated full-year textbook for computer science students. Consequently, this text has been used as the basis for the first part of *Introduction to Computer Science: Programming, Problem Solving, and Data Structures,* which I co-authored with Tom Naps. The full-year text would be appropriate for a two-semester or three-quarter course (with generic titles of CS1 and CS2) which presents Pascal as the programming language in the first term. Contact West Publishing Company for examination copies.

Each program and program segment in the text and all ancillaries have been compiled and run. Hence, original versions were all working. Unfortunately, the publication process does allow errors in code to occur after a program has been run. Every effort has been made to produce an error-free text, although this is virtually impossible. I assume full responsibility for all errors and omissions. If you detect any, please be tolerant and notify me or West Publishing Company so they can be corrected in subsequent printings and editions.

Acknowledgments

I would like to take this opportunity to thank those who in some way contributed to the completion of this text. Several reviewers contributed significant constructive comments during various phases of manuscript development for this third edition. They include:

Anthony Q. Baxter
University of Kentucky

Sid Bradley
McNeese State University

Thomas J. Cheatham
Western Kentucky University

David Cordes
David University of Alabama

Lee D. Cornell
Mankato State University

A. Downing
University of Western Ontario

George Friedman
University of Illinois at
Urbana-Champaign

Hugh Garraway
University of Southern Mississippi

Linda Hayden
Elizabeth City State University

Michael Jenkin
York University

William C. Jones, Jr.
Central Connecticut State University

Debbie C. Kaneko
Hampton University

Angela R. Kcith
Elizabethtown Community College

S. B. Khleif
Tennessee Technological University

Danny Kopec
University of Maine

Kurk Lew
New River Community College

Doris K. Lidtke
Towson State University

Ronald Mann
University of Louisville

William A. Moy
University of Wisconsin-Parkside

William C. Nico
California State-Hayward

Lynne O'Hanlon
Los Angeles Pierce College

Joshua Panar
Ryerson Polytechnical Institute

Sue Pilgreen
McNeese State University

Ingrid F. Russell
University of Hartford

James A. Schaefer
Rhode Island College

Paul S. Schnare
Eastern Kentucky University

Kay G. Schulze
United States Naval Academy

Patricia A. Slaminka
Auburn University

David J. Thuente
Indiana-Purdue University at Ft. Wayne

Debra Trantina
Arizona State University

Winnie Y. Yu
Southern Connecticut State University

Jim Cowles, Ohio University in Lancaster, has done yeoman's work in preparing many of the ancillaries. Carol Wilson, Western Kentucky University, contributed two Notes of Interest and prepared a Laboratory Manual that can be used with this text. Marilyn Jussell, Kearney State College, revised the Turbo Pascal Notes (Appendix 6) to make this text more practical for classroom use when Turbo is being used by students in the class. Tom Naps, Lawrence University in Wisconsin, contributed many helpful suggestions and recommendations.

Three other people deserve special mention because, without their expertise, this book would not exist. They are:

Janet Hunter, copyeditor. This is my sixth book with Janet. Once again, she rearranged her schedule to accommodate our deadlines. She is an outstanding copyeditor, but more importantly, she is a nice person with an excellent sense of humor.

Lynette D'Amico, production assistant. Lynette has done a remarkable job of coordinating work on four related texts simultaneously. She is precise, prompt, and understanding. It is a pleasure to work with her.

Jerry Westby, Manager, College Editorial. This is our eighth book together, and my respect for Jerry keeps increasing. He has an excellent sense for what makes a book useful. Most of the special features of this text are the result of Jerry's suggestions. He has offered constant support and invaluable suggestions.

My family and friends deserve special mention for their support and patience. Most of my recent spare time and energy have been devoted to this project. This would not have been possible without their encouragement and understanding.

Finally, there is one person without whose help this project would not have been possible. Helen, who was a student in my first Pascal class, has been of tremendous assistance since the inception of this effort. She prepared every part of the manuscript on her word processor. She served as an "in-house" copyeditor and made many helpful suggestions regarding presentation of the material.

This is the sixth text for which she has done all of the above. Her unfailing patience and support were remarkable. Fortunately for me, she has been my wife and best friend for more than thirty years.

Douglas W. Nance

Computer Science, Computer Architecture, and Computer Languages

This chapter provides a quick introduction to computer science, computer architecture, and computer languages. Section 1.1 provides a preview of the study of computer science. Section 1.2 examines the structure and parts of a computer and introduces the idea of computer software. Section 1.3 analyzes how computer languages are used to make a computer run.

As you read this chapter, do not be overly concerned about the introduction and early use of terminology. All terms will be subsequently developed. A good approach to an introductory chapter like this is to reread it periodically. This will help you maintain a good perspective as to how new concepts and techniques fit in the broader picture of using computers. Finally, remember that learning a language that will make a computer work can be exciting; being able to control such a machine can lead to quite a sense of power.

■ 1.1
Computer Science:
A Preview

Computer science is a very young discipline. Electronic computers were initially developed in the 1940s. Those who worked with computers in the 1940s and 1950s often did so by teaching themselves about computers; most schools did not then offer any instruction in computer science. However, as these early pioneers in computers learned more about the machines they were using, a collection of principles began to evolve into the discipline we now call computer science. Because it emerged from the efforts of people

1

OBJECTIVES

■ to understand that computer science is not computer literacy
■ to understand that computer science is:
Objectives continued.
a. mathematics and logic
b. science
c. engineering
d. communication
e. interdisciplinary

using computers in a variety of disciplines, the influence of these disciplines can often be seen in computer science. With that in mind, in the next sections I will briefly define what computer science is (and what it is not).

Computer Science Is Not Computer Literacy

In the 1990s, computer literate people will know how to use a variety of computer software to make their professional lives and home lives more productive and easier. This software includes, for instance, word processors for writing and data management systems for storing every conceivable form of information (from address lists to recipes).

However, knowing how to use specific pieces of computer software is not the same as acquiring an understanding of computer science, just as being able to drive a car does not qualify you as an expert mechanic. The user of computer software must merely be able to follow instructions about how to use the software. On the other hand, the modern computer scientist must, more than anything else, be a skillful problem-solver. The collection of problems that computer science encompasses and the techniques used to solve those problems are the real substance of this rapidly expanding discipline.

Computer Science Is Mathematics and Logic

The problem-solving emphasis of computer science borrows heavily from the areas of mathematics and logic. Faced with a problem, computer scientists must first formulate a solution. This method of solution, or *algorithm* as it is often called in computer science, must be thoroughly understood before the computer scientists make any attempt to implement the solution on the computer. Thus, at the early stages of problem solution, computer scientists work solely with their minds and do not rely upon the machine in any way.

Once the solution is understood, computer scientists must then state the solution to this problem in a formal language called a *programming language.* This parallels the fashion in which mathematicians or logicians must develop a proof or argument in the formal language of mathematics. This formal solution as stated in a programming language must then be evaluated in terms of its correctness, style, and efficiency. Part of this evaluation process involves entering the formally stated algorithm as a programmed series of steps for the computer to follow.

Another part of the evaluation process is distinctly separate from a consideration of whether or not the computer produces the "right answer" when the program is executed. Indeed, one of the main areas of emphasis throughout this book is in developing well-designed solutions to problems and in recognizing the difference between such solutions and ones that work, but inelegantly. True computer scientists seek not just solutions to problems, but the best possible solutions.

Computer Science Is Science

Perhaps nothing is as intrinsic to the scientific method as the formulation of hypotheses to explain phenomena and the careful testing of these hypotheses to prove them right or wrong. This same process plays an integral role in the way computer scientists work.

Upon observing a problem, such as a long list of names that we would like arranged in alphabetical order, computer scientists formulate a hypothesis in the form of an algorithm that they believe will effectively solve the problem. Using mathematical techniques, they can make predictions about how such a proposed algorithm will solve the problem. But because the problems facing computer scientists arise from the world of real applications, predictive techniques relying solely upon mathematical theory are not sufficient to prove an algorithm correct. Ultimately, computer scientists must implement their solutions on computers and test them in the complex situations that originally gave rise to the problems.

Only after thorough testing can the hypothetical solutions be declared right or wrong. Moreover, just as many scientific principles are not 100 percent right or wrong, the hypothetical solutions posed by computer scientists are often subject to limitations. An understanding of those limitations—of when the method is appropriate and when it is not—is a crucial part of the knowledge that computer scientists must have. This is analogous to the way in which any scientist must be aware of the particular limitations of a scientific theory in explaining a given set of phenomena.

Do not forget the experimental nature of computer science as you study this book. You must participate in computer science to truly learn it. Although a good book can help, *you* must solve the problems, implement those solutions on the computer, and then test the results. View each of the problems you are assigned as an experiment for which you are to propose a solution and then verify the correctness of your solution by testing it on the computer. If the solution does not work exactly as you hypothesized, do not become discouraged. Instead, ask yourself why it did not work; by doing so you will acquire a deeper understanding of the problem and your solution. In this sense, the computer represents the experimental tool of the computer scientist. Do not be afraid to use it for exploration.

Computer Science Is Engineering

Whatever the area of specialization, an engineer must neatly combine a firm grasp of scientific principles with implementation techniques. Without knowledge of the principles, the engineer's ability to creatively design models for a problem's solution is severely limited. Such model-building is crucial to the engineering design process. The ultimate design of a bridge, for instance, is the result of the engineer's considering many possible models of the bridge and then selecting the best one. The transformation of abstract ideas into models of a problem's solution is thus central to the engineering design process. The ability to generate a variety of models that can be explored is the hallmark of creative engineering.

Similarly, the computer scientist is a model-builder. Faced with a problem, the computer scientist must construct models for its solution. Such models take the form of an information structure to hold the data pertinent to the problem and the algorithmic method to manipulate that information structure to actually solve the problem. Just as an engineer must have an in-depth understanding of scientific principles to build a model, so must a computer scientist. With these principles, the computer scientist may conceive of models that are elegant, efficient, and appropriate to the problem at hand.

An understanding of principles alone is not sufficient for either the engineer or the computer scientist. Experience in the actual implementation of hypothetical models is also necessary. Without such experience, you can have only very limited intuition about what is feasible and how a large-scale project should be organized to reach a successful conclusion. Ultimately, computers are used to solve problems in the real world. There, you will need to design programs that come in on time, that are within (if not under) the budget, and that solve all aspects of the original problem. The experience you acquire in designing problem solutions and then implementing them is vital to your being a complete computer scientist. Hence, remember that you cannot actually study computer science without actively doing it. To merely read about computer science techniques will leave you with an unrealistic perspective of what is possible.

Computer Science Is Communication

As the discipline of computer science continues to evolve, communication is assuming a more significant role in the undergraduate curriculum. The Association for Computing Machinery, Inc. Curriculum Guidelines for 1991 state, ". . . undergraduate programs should prepare students to . . . define a problem clearly; . . . document that solution; . . . and to communicate that solution to colleagues, professionals in other fields, and the general public."

It is no longer sufficient to be content with a program that runs correctly. Extra attention should be devoted to the communication aspects associated with such a program. For instance, you might be asked to submit a written proposal prior to designing a solution, or to carefully and completely document a program as it is being designed, or to write a follow-up report after a program has been completed.

These are some ways in which communication can be emphasized as an integral part of computer science. Several opportunities will be provided in the Exercises and problem lists of this text for you to focus on the communication aspects associated with computer science.

Computer Science Is Interdisciplinary

The problems solved by computer scientists come from a variety of disciplines—mathematics, physics, chemistry, biology, geology, economics, business, engineering, linguistics, and psychology, to name a few. As a computer scientist working on a problem in one of these areas, you must be a quasi-expert in that discipline as well as in computer science. For instance, you cannot write a program to manage the checking account system of a bank unless you thoroughly understand how banks work and how that bank runs its checking accounts. At minimum, you must be literate enough in other disciplines to converse with the people for whom you are writing programs and to learn precisely what it is they want the computer to do for them. Since such people are often very naive about the computer and its capabilities, you will have to possess considerable communication skills as well as a knowledge of that other discipline.

Are you beginning to think that a computer scientist must be knowledgeable about much more than just the computer? If so, you are correct. Too often, computer scientists are viewed as technicians, tucked away in their own little worlds and not thinking or caring about anything other than computers. Nothing could be further from the truth. The successful computer scientist must be able to communicate, to learn new ideas quickly, and to adapt to ever-changing conditions. Computer science is emerging from its early dark ages into a mature process, one that I hope you will find rewarding and exciting. In studying computer science, you will be developing many talents; this text can get you started on the road to that development process.

1.2 Computer Architecture

OBJECTIVES

- to understand the historical development of computers
- to know what constitutes computer hardware
- to know what constitutes computer software
- to understand the various levels of computer languages

This section is intended to provide you with a brief overview of what computers are and how they are used. Although there are various sizes, makes, and models of computers, you will see that they all operate in basically the same straightforward manner. Whether you work on a personal computer that costs a few hundred dollars or on a mainframe that costs in the millions, the principles of making the machine work are essentially the same.

Modern Computers

The search for aids to perform calculations is almost as old as number systems. Early devices include the abacus, Napier's bones, the slide rule, and mechanical adding machines. More recently, calculators have changed the nature of personal computing as a result of their availability, low cost, and high speed. The development of computers over time is highlighted in Figure 1.1. For more complete information, see *People and Computers, Partners in Problem Solving*, by John F. Vinsonhaler, Christian C. Wagner, and Castelle G. Gentry, West Publishing Company, 1989.

The last few decades have seen the most significant change in computing machines in the world's history as a result of improvements that have led to modern computers. As recently as the 1960s, a computer required several rooms because of its size. However, the advent of silicon chips has reduced the size and increased the availability of computers so that parents are able to purchase personal computers as presents for their children. These computers are more powerful than the early behemoths.

What is a computer? According to *Webster's New World Dictionary of the American Language* (2nd College Edition), a computer is "an electronic machine which, by means of stored instructions and information, performs rapid, often complex calculations or compiles, correlates, and selects data." Basically, a computer can be thought of as a machine that manipulates information in the form of numbers and characters. This information is referred to as *data*. What makes computers remarkable is the extreme speed and precision with which they can store, retrieve, and manipulate data.

Several types of computers currently are available. An oversimplification is to categorize computers as mainframe, minicomputer, or microcomputer. In this grouping, *mainframe* computers are the large machines used by major companies, government agencies, and universities. They have the capability of being used by as many as 100 or more people at the same time and can cost millions of dollars. *Minicomputers,* in a sense, are smaller versions of large computers. They can be used by several people at once but have less storage capacity and cost far less. *Microcomputers* are frequently referred to as personal computers. They have limited storage capacity (in a relative sense), are generally used by one person at a time, and can be purchased for as little as a few hundred dollars.

As you begin your work with computers, you will hear people talking about *hardware* and *software*. Hardware refers to the actual machine and its support devices. Software refers to programs that make the machine do something. Many software packages exist for today's computers. They include word processing, data-base programs, spreadsheets, games, operating

FIGURE 1.1
Development of computers

Era	Early Computing Devices		Mechanical Computers	Electro-mechanical Computers
Year	1000 B.C. A.D. 1614	1650	1900	1945
Development	Abacus Napier's bones		Adding machine Slide rule Difference engine Analytic engine	Cogged wheels Instruction register Operation code Address Plug board Harvard Mark I Tabulating machine

systems, and compilers. You can (and will!) learn to create your own software. In fact, that is what this book is all about.

A *program* can be thought of as a set of instructions that tells the machine what to do. When you have written a program, the computer will behave exactly as you have instructed it. It will do no more or no less than what is contained in your specific instructions. For example,

```
PROGRAM ComputeAverage (input, output);

VAR
   A, B, C : integer;
   Average : real;

BEGIN
   read (A, B, C);
   Average := (A + B + C) / 3;
   writeln (Average:20:3)
END.
```

is a Pascal program that causes a computer to get three integers (the data) from an input device, computes their average, and then prints the result. Do not be concerned about specific parts of this program. It is intended only to illustrate the idea of a set of instructions. Very soon, you will be able to write significantly more sophisticated programs.

Learning to write programs requires two skills.

1. You need to be able to use specific terminology and punctuation that can be understood by the machine: you need to learn a programming language.
2. You need to be able to develop a plan for solving a particular problem. Such a plan is often referred to as an algorithm. This is a sequence of steps that, when followed, will lead to a solution of the problem.

Noncommercial Electronic Computers	Batch Processing	Time-Sharing Systems	Personal Computers
1945 1950	1965	1975	Present
First-generation computers Vacuum tubes Machine language programming ENIAC	Second-generation computers Transistors Magnetic core memory Assemblers Compilers UNIVAC I IBM 704	Third-generation computers Integrated circuit technology Operating system software Teleprocessing	Fourth-generation computers Fifth-generation computers (supercomputers) Microprocessors Workstations

Initially, you may think that learning a language is the more difficult task because your problems will have relatively easy solutions. Nothing could be further from the truth! **The single most important thing you can do as a student of computer science is to develop the skill to solve problems.** Once you have this skill, you can learn to write programs in several different languages.

Computer Hardware

Let's take another look at the question: What is a computer? Our previous answer indicated it is a machine. Although there are several forms, names, and brands of computers, each consists of a *main unit* that is subsequently connected to peripheral devices. The main unit of a computer consists of a *central processing unit (CPU)* and *main (primary) memory*. The CPU is the "brain" of the computer. It contains an *arithmetic/logic unit (ALU)*, which is capable of performing arithmetic operations and evaluating expressions to see if they are true or false, and the *control unit*, which controls the action of remaining components so your program can be followed step-by-step, or *executed*.

Main memory can be thought of as mailboxes in a post office. It is a sequence of locations where information representing instructions, numbers, characters, and so on can be stored. It is usable while the computer is turned on. The program being executed and the data it is manipulating are stored in main memory.

As you develop a greater appreciation of how the computer works, you might wonder: How are data stored in memory? Each memory location has an address and is capable of holding a sequence of *binary* (0 or 1) *digits*, which are commonly referred to as *bits*. Instructions, symbols, letters, numbers, and so on are translated into an appropriate pattern of binary digits and then stored in various memory locations. These are retrieved, used, and changed according to instructions in your program. In fact, the program itself is similarly translated and stored in part of main memory. Main memory can be envisioned as in Figure 1.2, and the main unit can be envisioned as in Figure 1.3.

FIGURE 1.2
Main memory

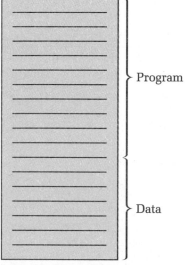

FIGURE 1.3
Main unit

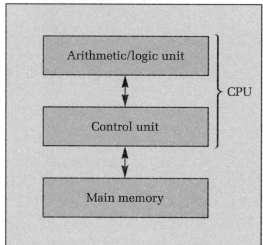

FIGURE 1.4
Keyboard

Peripherals can be divided into three categories: *input devices, output devices,* and *secondary (auxiliary) memory devices.* Input devices are necessary to give information to the computer. One input device, a typical keyboard, is shown in Figure 1.4. Whatever input device you use, your program will be entered through it, and the program statements will be translated and stored as previously indicated.

Output devices are necessary to show the results of your programs. These are normally in the form of a screen, line printer, impact printer, or laser printer (Figure 1.5). Input and output devices are frequently referred to as *I/O devices.*

Secondary (auxiliary) memory devices are used if additional memory is needed. On small computers, these secondary memory devices could be floppy disks or hard disks (Figure 1.6), magnetic tapes, or magnetic bubbles.

FIGURE 1.5
(a) Screen, (b) line printer (mainframe), (c) impact printer (microcomputer), and (d) laser printer

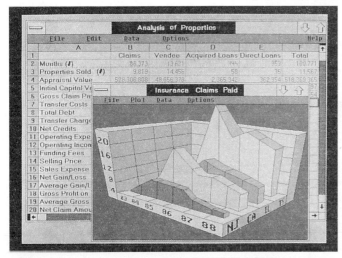

(a)

(b)

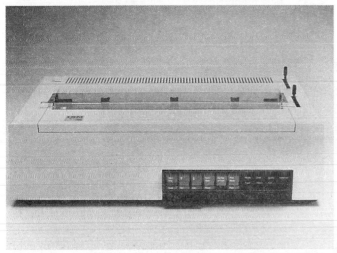

(c)

(d)

FIGURE 1.6
(a) Disk drive, and (b) microcomputer with hard disk

(a)

(b)

Programs and data waiting to be executed are kept "waiting in the wings" in secondary memory.

Communication between components of a computer is frequently organized around a group of wires called a *bus.* The relationship between a bus and various computer components can be envisioned as in Figure 1.7.

FIGURE 1.7
Illustration of a bus

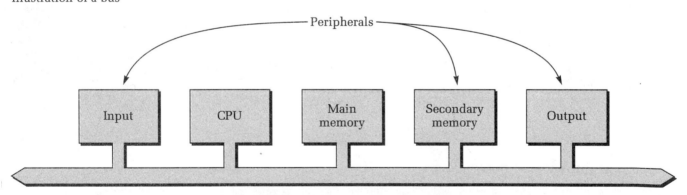

A photograph of a bus is shown in Figure 1.8. What appear to be lines between the slots are actually wires imprinted upon the underlying board. Boards with wires connected to peripheral devices may be inserted into the slots.

Computer Software

As previously stated, software refers to programs that make the machine do something. Software consists of two kinds of programs: *system software* and *applications software.*

System software includes what is often called the *operating system.* (You may have heard reference to DOS, which is an acronym for Disk Operating

FIGURE 1.8
Bus

System.) The operating system for a computer is a large program and is usually supplied with a computer. This program allows the user to communicate with the hardware. More specifically, an operating system might control computer access (via passwords), allocate peripheral resources (perhaps with a printer queue), schedule shared resources (for CPU use), or control execution of other programs.

Applications software consists of programs designed for a specific use. Examples of applications software include programs for word processing, text editing, simulating spreadsheets, playing games, designing machinery, and figuring payrolls. Most computer users work with applications software and have little need for learning a computer language; the programs they require have already been written to accomplish their tasks.

■ 1.3
Computer Languages

What is a computer language? All data transmission, manipulation, storage, and retrieval is actually done by the machine using electrical pulses generated by sequences of binary digits. If eight-digit binary codes are used, there

Data Loss on Floppy Disks

Why is it important to keep the dust covers on your diskettes? Look at the figure shown here. It illustrates how some very small particles look huge in comparison to the distance between the surface of a diskette and the read/write head. If these particles become lodged between the head and the surface of the diskette, the surface may be scratched, resulting in data loss. So consider yourself warned; handle your disks carefully.

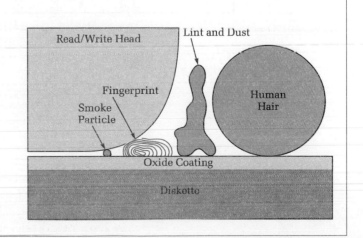

are 256 numbered instructions from 00000000 to 11111111. Instructions for adding two numbers would consist of a sequence of these eight-digit codes.

Instructions written in this form are referred to as *machine language*. It is possible to write an entire program in machine language. However, this is very time consuming and difficult to read and understand.*

Therefore, the next level of computer language allows words and symbols to be used in an unsophisticated manner to accomplish simple tasks. For example, the machine code for adding two integers might be

01000011001110100011110101000001001010101101000010

This is replaced by

    LOAD A
    ADD B
    STORE C

This causes the number in A to be added to the number in B and the result to be stored for later use in C. This computer language is an *assembly language*, which is generally referred to as a *low-level language*. What actually happens is that words and symbols are translated into appropriate binary digits and the machine uses the translated form.

Although assembly language is an improvement on machine language for readability and program development, it is still a bit cumbersome. Consequently, many *high-level languages* have been developed; these include Pascal, PL/I, FORTRAN, BASIC, COBOL, C, Ada, Modula-2, Logo, and others. These languages simplify even further the terminology and symbolism necessary for directing the machine to perform various manipulations of data. For example, the task of adding two integers would be written as

    C := A + B;   (Pascal)
    C = A + B;   (PL/I)
    C = A + B   (FORTRAN)
    C = A + B   (BASIC)
    ADD A,B GIVING C   (COBOL)
    C = A + B;   (C)
    C := A + B;   (Ada)
    C := A + B;   (Modula-2)
    MAKE "C :A + :B   (Logo)

A high-level language makes it easier to read, write, and understand a program. This book develops the concepts, symbolism, and terminology necessary for using Pascal as a programming language for solving problems. After you have become proficient in using Pascal, you should find it relatively easy to learn the nuances of other high-level languages.

For a moment, let's consider how an instruction such as

    C := A + B;

gets translated into machine code. The actual bit pattern for this code varies according to the machine and software version. As previously indicated, it could be

01000011001110100011110101000001001010101101000010

In order for this to happen, a special program called a *compiler* "reads" the high-level instructions and translates them into machine code. This com-

A NOTE OF INTEREST

Why Learn Pascal?

From the point of view of many potential users, Pascal's major drawback is that it is a compiled rather than an interpreted language. This means that developing and testing a small Pascal program can take a lot longer and involve many more steps than it would with an interpreted language like BASIC. The effect of this drawback has been lessened recently with the development of interpretor programs for Pascal. [For example, some current versions of Pascal, such as Turbo Pascal, are easy to use, have quick compilation, and are as easy to use as most interpreted languages.] Even so, most programs written by users of personal computers are small ones designed for quick solutions to particular problems, and the use of Pascal for such programs may be a form of overkill.

Ironically, the characteristics of Pascal that make it relatively unsuited for small programs are a direct consequence of its strengths as a programming language. The discipline imposed by the language makes it easier to understand large programs, but it may be more than a small program demands. For serious development of large programs or for the creation of tools that will be used over and over again (and require modifications from time to time), Pascal is clearly superior.

Experts generally consider Pascal an important language for people who are planning to study computer science or to learn programming. Indeed, the College Entrance Examination Board has designated Pascal as the required language for advanced-placement courses in computer science for high school students. While it is true that an experienced programmer can write clearly structured programs in any language, learning the principle of structured programming is much easier in Pascal.

Is Pascal difficult to learn? We don't think so, but the question is relative and may depend on which language you learn first. Programmers become accustomed to the first language they learn, making it the standard by which all others are judged. Even the poor features of the familiar language come to be seen as necessities, and a new language seems inferior. Don't let such subjective evaluations bar your way to learning Pascal, a powerful and elegant programming language.

---

piled version is then run using some appropriate data. The results are then presented through some form of output device. As previously indicated, the special programs that activate the compiler, run the machine-code version, and cause output to be printed are examples of system programs (software). The program you write is a *source program,* and the machine-code version is an *object program* (also referred to as *object code*).

As you will soon see, the compiler does more than just translate instructions into machine code. It also detects certain errors in your source program and prints appropriate messages. For example, if you write the instruction

    C := (A + B;

where a parenthesis is missing, when the compiler attempts to translate this line into machine code, it will detect that ")" is needed to close the parenthetical expression. It will then give you an error message such as

    ERROR IN VARIABLE

You will then need to correct the error (and any others) and recompile your source program before running it with the data.

Before leaving this introductory chapter, let's consider the question: Why study Pascal? Various languages have differing strengths and weaknesses. Pascal's strong features include the following:

1. It incorporates program structure in a reasonable approximation of English. For example, if a certain process is to be repeated until some condition is met, this could be written in the program as

REPEAT

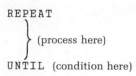 (process here)

UNTIL (condition here)

2. It allows the use of descriptive words for variables and data types. Thus, programs for computing payrolls could use words like Hours-Worked, StateTax, FICA, TotalDeductions, and GrossPay.
3. It facilitates good problem-solving habits; in fact, many people consider this to be Pascal's main strength. As previously noted, developing the skill to solve a problem using a computer program is the most important trait to develop as a beginning programmer. Pascal is structured in such a manner that it encourages—indeed, almost requires—good problem-solving skills.

You are now ready to begin a detailed study of Pascal. You will undoubtedly spend much time and encounter some frustration during the course of your work. I hope your efforts result in an exciting and rewarding learning experience. Good luck.

■ Summary

Key Terms

algorithm	executed	object program
applications software	hardware	operating system
arithmetic/logic unit (ALU)	high-level language	output device
	input device	program
assembly language	I/O devices	programming language
binary digits	low-level language	secondary (auxiliary) memory devices
bits	machine language	
bus	mainframe	software
central processing unit (CPU)	main (primary) memory	source program
	main unit	system software
compiler	microcomputer	
control unit	minicomputer	
data	object code	

Writing Your First Programs

Chapter 1 presented an overview of computers and computer languages. We are now ready to examine problems that computers can solve. First we need to know how to solve a problem and then we need to learn how to use a programming language to implement our solution on the computer.

Before looking at problem solving and writing programs for the computer, we should consider some psychological aspects of working in computer science. Studying computer science can cause a significant amount of frustration because

1. Planning is a critical issue. You must plan to develop instructions to solve your problem and translate those instructions into code before you sit down at the keyboard. You should not attempt to type in code "off the top of your head."
2. Time is a major problem. Writing programs is not like completing other assignments. You cannot expect to complete a programming assignment by staying up late the night before it is due. You must begin early and expect to make several revisions before your final version will be ready.
3. Successful problem solving and programming require extreme precision. Generally, concepts in computer science are not difficult; however, implementation of these concepts allows no room for error. For example, one misplaced semicolon in a 1,000-line program could prevent the program from working.

In other words, you must be prepared to plan well, start early, be patient, handle frustration, and work hard to succeed in computer science. If you cannot do this, you will probably neither enjoy computer science nor be successful at it.

■ 2.1
Program Development— Top-Down Design

The key to writing a successful program is planning. Good programs do not just happen; they are the result of careful design and patience. Just as an artist commissioned to paint a portrait would not start out by shading in the lips and eyes, a good computer programmer would not attack a problem by immediately trying to write code for a program to solve the problem. Writing a program is like writing an essay: an overall theme is envisioned, an outline of major ideas is developed, each major idea is subdivided into several parts, and each part is developed using individual sentences.

Six Steps to Good Programming Habits

In developing a program to solve a problem, six steps should be followed: analyze the problem, develop an algorithm, write code for the program, run the program, test the results, and document the program. These steps will help develop good problem-solving habits and, in turn, solve programming problems correctly. A brief discussion of each of these steps follows:

Step 1. Analyze the Problem. This is not a trivial task. Before you can do anything, you must know exactly what it is you are to do. You must be able to formulate a clear and precise statement of what is to be done. You should understand completely what data are available and what may be assumed. You should also know exactly what output is desired and the form it should take.

Step 2. Develop an Algorithm. An algorithm is a finite sequence of effective statements that, when applied to the problem, will solve it. An *effective statement* is a clear, unambiguous instruction that can be carried out. Each algorithm you develop should have a specific beginning; at the completion of one step, have the next step uniquely determined; and have an ending that is reached in a reasonable amount of time.

Step 3. Write Code for the Program. When the algorithm correctly solves the problem, you can think about translating your algorithm into a high-level language. An effective algorithm will significantly reduce the time you need to complete this step.

Step 4. Run the Program. After writing the code, you are ready to run the program. This means that, using an editor, you type the program code into the computer, compile the program, and run the program. At this point, you may discover errors that can be as simple as typing errors or that may require a reevaluation of all or parts of your algorithm. The probability of having to make some corrections or changes is quite high.

Step 5. Test the Results. After your program has run, you need to be sure that the results are correct, that they are in a form you like, and that your program produces the correct solution in all cases. To be sure the results are correct, you must look at them and compare them with what you expect. In the case of using a program with arithmetic operations, this means checking some results with pencil and paper. Often you will need to make revisions and return to Step 4.

Step 6. Document the Program. It is very important to completely document a working program. The writer knows how the program works; if others are to modify it, they must know the logic used. As you develop the ability to write programs to solve more complex problems, you will find it helpful to include documentation in Step 3 as you write the code.

Developing Algorithms

Algorithms for solving a problem can be developed by stating the problem and then subdividing the problem into major subtasks. Each subtask can then be subdivided into smaller tasks. This process is repeated until each remaining task is one that is easily solved. This process is known as *top-down design,* and each successive subdivision is referred to as a *stepwise refinement.* Tasks identified at each stage of this process are called *modules.* The relationship between modules can be shown graphically in a *structure chart* (see Figure 2.1).

FIGURE 2.1
Structure chart illustrating top-down design

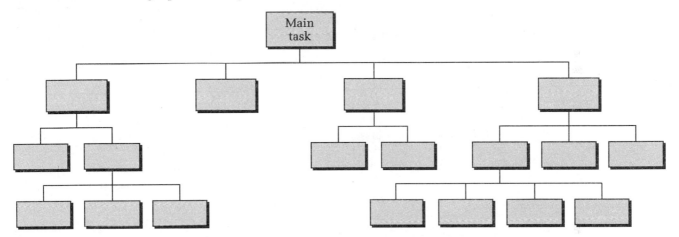

To illustrate developing an algorithm, we'll use the problem of updating a checkbook after a transaction has been made. A first-level refinement is shown in Figure 2.2.

An arrow pointing into a module means information is needed before the task can be performed. An arrow pointing out of a module means the module task has been completed and information required for subsequent work is available. Each of these modules could be further refined as shown in Figure 2.3. Finally, one of the last modules could be refined as shown in Figure 2.4. The complete top-down design could then be envisioned as illustrated in Figure 2.5. Notice that each remaining task can be accomplished in a very direct manner.

FIGURE 2.2
First-level refinement

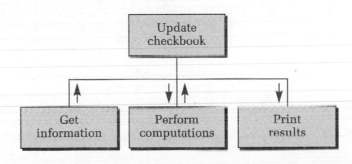

FIGURE 2.3
Second-level refinement

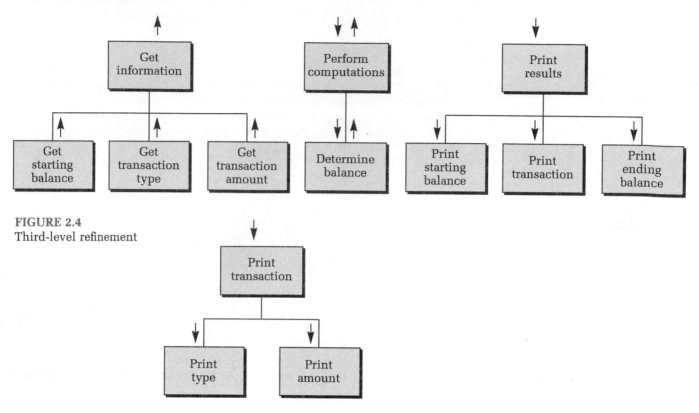

FIGURE 2.4
Third-level refinement

FIGURE 2.5
Structure chart for top-down design

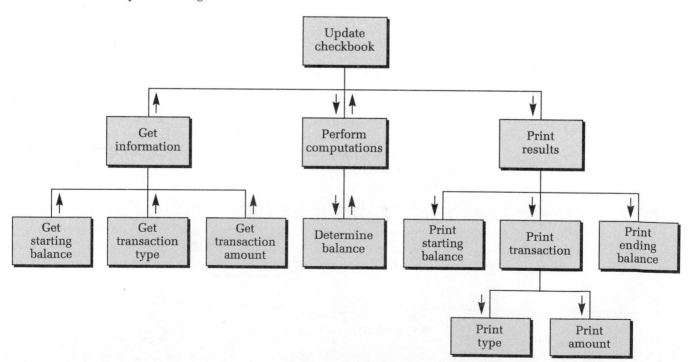

As a further aid to understanding how data are transmitted, we will list *module specifications* for each main (first-level) module. Each module specification includes a description of data received, information returned, and logic used in the module. Module specifications for the Get Information module are

Get Information Module
Data received: None
Information returned: Starting balance
                      Transaction type
                      Transaction amount
Logic: Have the user enter information from the keyboard.

For the Update checkbook problem, complete module specifications are

1. Get Information Module
   Data received: None
   Information returned: Starting balance
                         Transaction type
                         Transaction amount
   Logic: Have the user enter information from the keyboard.

2. Perform Computations Module
   Data received: Starting balance
                   Transaction type
                   Transaction amount
   Information returned: Ending balance
   Logic: If transaction is a deposit, add it to the starting balance; otherwise, subtract it.

3. Print Results Module
   Data received: Starting balance
                   Transaction type
                   Transaction amount
                   Ending balance
   Information returned: None
   Logic: Print results in a readable form.

At least two comments should be made about top-down design. First, different people can (and probably will) have different designs for the solution of a problem. However, each good design will have well-defined modules with functional subtasks. Second, the graphic method just used helps to formulate general logic for solving a problem but is somewhat awkward for translating to code. Thus, we will use a stylized, half-English, half-code method called *pseudocode* to illustrate stepwise refinement in such a design. This will be written in English, but the sentence structure and indentations will suggest Pascal code. Major tasks will be numbered with whole numbers and subtasks with decimal numbers. First-level pseudocode for the checkbook-balancing problem is

1. Get information
2. Perform computations
3. Print results

A second-level pseudocode development produces

1. Get information
   1.1 get starting balance
   1.2 get transaction type
   1.3 get transaction amount
2. Perform computations
   2.1 **IF** deposit **THEN**
       add to balance
       ELSE
         subtract from balance
3. Print results
   3.1 print starting balance
   3.2 print transaction
   3.3 print ending balance

Finally, step 3.2 of the pseudocode is subdivided as previously indicated into

3.2 print transaction
    3.2.1 print transaction type
    3.2.2 print transaction amount

Two final comments are in order. First, each module developed should be tested with data for that module. Once you are sure each module does what you want, the whole program should work when the modules are used together. Second, the process of dividing a task into subtasks is especially suitable for writing programs in Pascal.

A Pascal program for this problem follows:

```
PROGRAM Checkbook (input, output);

VAR
  StartingBalance,
  EndingBalance,
  TransAmount : real;
  TransType : char;

BEGIN  {  Main Program  }

  {  Module for getting the data  }

  writeln ('Enter the starting balance and press <RETURN>.');
  readln (StartingBalance);
  writeln ('Enter the transaction type (D) deposit or (W) withdrawal');      1*
  writeln ('and press <RETURN>.');
  readln (TransType);
  writeln ('Enter the transaction amount and press <RETURN>.');
  readln (TransAmount);

  {  Module for performing computations  }

  IF TransType = 'D' THEN
    EndingBalance := StartingBalance + TransAmount                           2
  ELSE
    EndingBalance := StartingBalance - TransAmount;
```

*These numbers refer to the modules previously developed with module specifications.

```
{  Module for printing results  }                              ⎫
                                                               ⎪
writeln;                                                       ⎪
writeln ('Starting Balance          $', StartingBalance:8:2);  ⎬  3
writeln ('Transaction               $', TransAmount:8:2, TransType:2);
writeln ('---------':33);                                      ⎪
writeln ('Ending Balance            $', EndingBalance:8:2)     ⎪
END.  {  of main program  }                                    ⎭
```

Notice how sections of the program correspond to module specifications. Sample runs of the program produce the output

```
Enter the starting balance and press <RETURN>.
235.16
Enter the transaction type (D) deposit or (W) withdrawal
and press <RETURN>.
D
Enter the transaction amount and press <RETURN>.
75.00

Starting Balance          $  235.16
Transaction               $   75.00 D
                             ---------
Ending Balance            $  310.16

Enter the starting balance and press <RETURN>.
310.16
Enter the transaction type (D) deposit or (W) withdrawal
and press <RETURN>.
W
Enter the transaction amount and press <RETURN>.
65.75

Starting Balance          $  310.16
Transaction               $   65.75 W
                             ---------
Ending Balance            $  244.41
```

You probably would not use the power of a computer for something as simple as this program. You could just press a few calculator keys instead. However, as you will see, the language supports development of subprograms for specific subtasks. You will, for example, soon be able to enhance this program to check for overdrafts, save the new balance for later use, and repeat the process for several transactions. Learning to think in terms of modular development now will aid you not just in creating algorithms to solve problems, but it will aid you in writing programs to solve problems.

Software Engineering

The phrase *software engineering* is used to refer to the process of developing and maintaining very large software systems. Before becoming engrossed in the specifics of solving problems and writing relatively small programs, it is instructive to consider the broader picture faced by those who develop software for "real world" use.

It is not unusual for software systems to be programs that, if written in this size type, would require between 100 and 150 pages of text. These systems must be reliable, economical, and subject to use by a diverse audience. Because of these requirements, software developers must be aware of and practice certain techniques.

A NOTE OF INTEREST

Software Verification

Sitting 70 kilometers east of Toronto on the shore of Lake Ontario, the Darlington Nuclear Generating Station looks much like any other large nuclear power plant of the Canadian variety. Behind its ordinary exterior lies an unusual design feature.

Darlington is the first Canadian nuclear station to use computers to operate the two emergency shutdown systems that safeguard each of its four reactors. In both shutdown systems, a computer program replaces an array of electrically operated mechanical devices—switches and relays—designed to respond to sensors monitoring conditions critical to a reactor's safe operations, such as water levels in boilers.

When completed in 1992, Darlington's four reactors will supply enough electricity to serve a city of 2 million people. Its Toronto-based builder, Ontario Hydro, opted for sophisticated software rather than old-fashioned hardware in the belief that a computer-operated shutdown system would be more economical, flexible, reliable and safe than one under mechanical control.

But that approach carried unanticipated costs. To satisfy regulators that the shutdown software would function as advertised, Ontario Hydro engineers had to go through a frustrating but essential checking process that required nearly three years of extra effort.

"There are lots of examples where software has gone wrong with serious consequences," says engineer Glenn H. Archinoff of Ontario Hydro. "If you want a shutdown system to work when you need it, you have to have a high level of assurance."

The Darlington experience demonstrates the tremendous effort involved in establishing the correctness of even relatively short and straightforward computer programs. The 10,000 "lines" of instructions, or code, required for each shutdown system pale in comparison with the 100,000 lines that constitute a typical word-processing program or the millions of lines needed to operate a long-distance telephone network or a space shuttle.

As you might imagine, such large programs are not the work of a single individual but are developed by teams of programmers. Issues such as communication, writing style, and technique become as important as developing algorithms to solve particular parts of the problem. Management, coordination, and design are major considerations that need resolution very early in the process. Although you will not face these larger organizational issues in this course, you will see how some of what you learn has implications for larger design issues.

Software engineering has been so titled because techniques and principles from the more established engineering disciplines are used to guide the large-scale development required in major software. To illustrate, consider the problems faced by an engineer who is to design and supervise construction of a bridge. This analysis was presented by Alfred Spector and David Gifford in an article entitled "A Computer Science Perspective on Bridge Design" published in *Communications of the ACM* (April 1986).

Engineers designing a bridge view it first as a hierarchy of substructures. This decomposition process continues on the substructures themselves until a level of very fundamental objects (such as beams and plates) ultimately is reached. This decomposition technique is similar to the stepwise refinement technique used by software designers, who break a complex problem down into a hierarchy of subproblems each of which ultimately can be solved by a relatively simple algorithm.

Engineers build conceptual models before actually constructing a bridge. This model-building allows them to evaluate various design alternatives in a way which eventually leads to the best possible design for the application being considered. This process is analogous to the way in which a skilled software designer builds models of a software system using structure charts and first-level pseudocode descriptions of modules. The designer then studies these conceptual models and eventually chooses the most elegant and efficient model for the application.

By the fashion in which engineers initially break down the bridge design, they insure that different aspects of the design can be addressed by different subordinate groups of design engineers working in a relatively independent fashion. This is similar to the goal of a software designer who oversees a program development team. The design of the software system must insure that individual components may be developed simultaneously by separate groups whose work will not have harmful side effects when the components are finally pulled together.

This overview is presented to give you a better perspective on how developments in this text are part of a greater whole. As you progress through your study of Pascal, you will see specific illustrations of how concepts and techniques can be viewed as part of the software engineering process.

Software System Life Cycle

Software engineering is the process by which large software systems are produced. As you might imagine, these systems need to be maintained and modified; ultimately, they are replaced with other systems. This entire process parallels that of an organism. That is, there is a development, maintenance, and subsequent demise. Thus, this process is referred to as the *software system life cycle.* Specifically, a system life cycle can be viewed in the following phases:

1. Analysis
2. Design
3. Coding
4. Testing/verification
5. Maintenance
6. Obsolescence

It probably comes as a surprise that computer scientists view this process as having a phase that precedes the design phase. However, it is extremely critical that a problem be completely understood before any attempt is made to design a solution. The analysis phase is complicated by the fact that potential users may not supply enough information when describing their intended use of a system. Analysis requires careful attention to items such as exact form of input, exact form of output, how data entry errors (there will be some) should be handled, how large the data bases will become, how much training in using the system will be provided, and what possible modifications might be required as the intended audience increases/decreases. Clearly, the analysis phase requires an experienced communicator.

The design phase is what much of this book is about. This is where the solution is developed using a modular approach. Attention must be paid to techniques which include communication, algorithm development, writing style, team work, and so on.

Coding closely follows design. Unfortunately, many beginning students want to write code too quickly. This can be a painful lesson if you have to scrap several days of work because your original design was not sufficient. You are encouraged to make sure your designs are complete before writing any code. In the real world, teams of designers work many hours before programmers ever get a chance to start writing code.

The testing phase of a large system is a significant undertaking. Early testing is done on individual modules to get them running properly. Larger data sets must then be run on the entire program to make sure the modules interact properly with the main program. When the system appears ready to the designers, it is usually field tested by selected users. Each of these testing levels is likely to require changes in the design and coding of the system.

Finally, the system is released to the public and the maintenance phase begins. This phase lasts throughout the remainder of the program's useful life. During this phase, we are concerned with repairing problems that arise with the system after it has been put into use. These problems are not necessarily bugs introduced during the coding phases. More often they are the result of user needs that change over time. For instance, annual changes in the tax laws necessitate changes in even the best payroll programs. Or problems may be due to misinterpretation of user needs during the early analysis phase. Whatever the reason, we must expect that a program will have to undergo numerous changes during its lifetime. During the maintenance phase, the time spent documenting the original program will be repaid many times over. One of the worst tasks imaginable in software development is to be asked to maintain an undocumented program. Undocumented code can quickly become virtually unintelligible, even to the program's original author. Indeed, one of the measures of a good program is how well it stands up to the maintenance phase.

Of course, no matter how good a program may be, it will eventually become obsolete. At that time, the system life cycle starts all over again with the development of a new system to replace the obsolete one. Hence, the system life cycle is never-ending, being itself part of a larger repetitive pattern that continues to evolve with changing user needs and more powerful technology.

Exercises 2.1

1. Which of the following can be considered effective statements; that is, clear, unambiguous instructions that can be carried out? For each statement, explain why it is effective or why it is not.

   a. Pay the cashier $9.15.

   b. Water the plants a day before they die.

   c. Determine all positive prime numbers less than 1,000,000.

   d. Choose X to be the smallest positive fraction.

   e. Invest your money in a stock that will increase in value.

2. What additional information must be obtained in order to understand each of the following problems?

   a. Find the largest number of a set of numbers.

   b. Alphabetize a list of names.

   c. Compute charges for a telephone bill.

3. Outline the main tasks for solving each of the following problems.

   a. Write a good term paper.

   b. Take a vacation.

   c. Choose a college.

   d. Get a summer job.

   e. Compute the semester average for a student in a computer science course and print all pertinent data.

4. Refine the main tasks in each part of Exercise 3 into a sufficient number of levels so that the problem can be solved in a well-defined manner.

5. Use pseudocode to write a solution for each of the following problems. Indicate each stage of your development.

   a. Compute the wages for two employees of a company. The input information will consist of the hourly wage and the number of hours worked in one week. The output should contain a list of all deductions, gross pay, and net pay. For this problem, assume deductions are made for federal withholding taxes, state withholding taxes, social security, and union dues.

   b. Compute the average test score for five students in a class. Input for this problem will consist of five scores. Output should include each score and the average of these scores.

6. Develop an algorithm to find the total, average, and largest number in a given list of 25 numbers.

7. Develop an algorithm for finding the greatest common divisor (GCD) of two positive integers.

8. Develop an algorithm for solving the system of equations

   $$ax + by = c$$
   $$dx + cy = f$$

9. Draw a structure chart and write module specifications for each of the following exercises.

   a. Exercise 5a.

   b. Exercise 5b.

   c. Exercise 6.

10. Discuss how the top-down design principles of software engineering are similar to the design problems faced by a construction engineer for a building. Be sure to include anticipated work with all subcontractors.

11. Using the construction analogy of Exercise 10, give an example of some specific communication required between electricians and the masons who finish the interior walls. Discuss why this information flow should be coordinated by a construction engineer.

12. State the phases of the software system life cycle.

13. Contact some company or major user of a software system to see what kinds of modifications might be required in a system after it has been released to the public. (Your own computer center might be sufficient.)

■ ■ ■ ■

■ 2.2
Writing Programs

- to be able to recognize reserved words and predefined standard identifiers
- to be able to recognize and declare valid identifiers
- to know the three basic components of a program
- to understand the basic structure of a Pascal program

Words in Pascal

Consider the following complete Pascal program.

```
PROGRAM Example (input, output);

CONST
  Skip = ' ';

VAR
  J, X, Sum : integer;
  Average : real;

BEGIN
  Sum := 0;
  FOR J := 1 TO 30 DO
    BEGIN
      read (X);
      Sum := Sum + X
    END;
  Average := Sum / 30;
  writeln;
  writeln (Skip:10, 'The average is', Average:8:2);
  writeln;
  writeln (Skip:10, 'The number of scores is', 30:3)
END.
```

This program—and most every programming language—requires the use of words when writing code. In Pascal, words that have a predefined meaning that cannot be changed are called *reserved words*. Some other predefined words (*standard identifiers*) can have their meanings changed if the programmer has strong reasons for doing so. Other words (programmer-supplied *identifiers*) must be created according to a well-defined set of rules, but can have any meaning, subject to those rules.

In the body of this text, reserved words are capitalized and in bold type; standard identifiers are lowercase and in bold type. Reserved words used in the text's example programs are capitalized and standard identifiers are lowercase. This convention is not required by the language.

Reserved Words

In Pascal, reserved words are predefined and cannot be used in a program for anything other than the purpose for which they are reserved. Some examples are **AND, OR, NOT, BEGIN, END, IF,** and **FOR.** As you continue in Pascal, you will learn where and how these words are used. At this time, however, you need only become familiar with the reserved words in Table 2.1; they are also listed in Appendix 1.

TABLE 2.1
Reserved words

AND	ELSE	IF	OR	THEN
ARRAY	END	IN	PACKED	TO
BEGIN	FILE	LABEL	PROCEDURE	TYPE
CASE	FOR	MOD	PROGRAM	UNTIL
CONST	FORWARD	NIL	RECORD	VAR
DIV	FUNCTION	NOT	REPEAT	WHILE
DO	GOTO	OF	SET	WITH
DOWNTO				

Standard Identifiers

A second set of predefined words, standard identifiers, can have their meanings changed by the programmer. For example, if you could develop a better algorithm for the trigonometric function **sin,** you could then substitute it in the program. However, these words should not be used for anything other than their intended use. This list will vary somewhat from computer to computer, so you should obtain a list of standard identifiers used in your local implementation of Pascal. Some standard identifiers are listed in Table 2.2 and in Appendix 2. The term *keywords* is used to refer to both reserved words and standard identifiers in subsequent discussions.

TABLE 2.2
Standard identifiers

Data Types	Constants	Functions	Procedures	Files
boolean	false	abs	dispose	input
char	maxint	arctan	get	output
integer	true	chr	new	
real		cos	pack	
text		eof	page	
		eoln	put	
		exp	read	
		ln	readln	
		odd	reset	
		ord	rewrite	
		pred	unpack	
		round	write	
		sin	writeln	
		sqr		
		sqrt		
		succ		
		trunc		

Syntax and Syntax Diagrams

Syntax refers to the rules governing construction of valid statements. This includes the order in which statements occur, together with appropriate punctuation. *Syntax diagramming* is a method to describe formally the legal syntax of language structures. Syntax diagrams show the permissible alternatives for each part of each kind of sentence and where the parts may appear. The symbolism we use is shown in Figure 2.6. A combined listing of syntax diagrams is contained in Appendix 3.

FIGURE 2.6
Symbols used in syntax diagrams

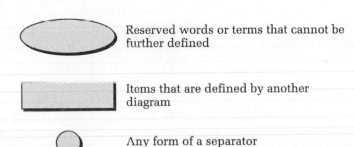

Reserved words or terms that cannot be further defined

Items that are defined by another diagram

Any form of a separator

Arrows are used to indicate possible alternatives. To illustrate, a syntax diagram for forming words in the English language is

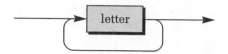

If the word must start with a vowel, the diagram is

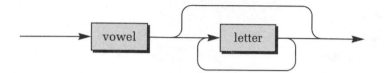

where vowel and letter are defined in a manner consistent with the English alphabet. Syntax diagrams are used throughout the text to illustrate formal constructs. You are encouraged to become familiar with them.

Identifiers

Reserved words and standard identifiers are restricted in their use. Most Pascal programs require other programmer-supplied identifiers; the more complicated the program, the more identifiers needed. A valid identifier must start with a letter of the alphabet and must consist only of letters and digits. A syntax diagram for forming identifiers is

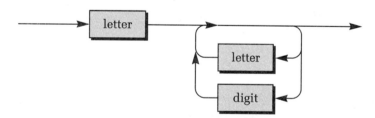

Table 2.3 gives some valid and invalid identifiers along with the reasons for those that are invalid. A valid identifier can be of any length. However, some versions of Pascal recognize only the first part of a long identifier, for example, the first eight or the first ten characters. Therefore, identifiers such as MathTestScore1 and MathTestScore2 might be the same identifier to a computer and could not be used as different identifiers in a program. Thus, you should learn what restrictions are imposed by your compiler.

TABLE 2.3
Valid and invalid identifiers

Identifier	Valid	If Invalid, Reason
Sum	Yes	
X + Y	No	"+" is not allowed
Average	Yes	
Text1	Yes	
1stNum	No	Must start with a letter
X	Yes	
K mart	No	Spaces are not allowed
ThisIsaLongOne	Yes	

The most common use of identifiers is to name the variables to be used in a program. Recall from algebra that variables such as *x, y,* and *z* are frequently used in functional relationships; these could also be used as identifiers in a Pascal program. However, we should generally use names that are more descriptive. A detailed explanation of the use of variables is given in Chapter 3.

Another use of identifiers is to name symbolic constants to be used in a program; for example, to identify a certain name or date to be used repeatedly. A third use of identifiers is to name the program. Every program requires a name, and the name must be a valid identifier. Identifiers are also needed to name new data types and subprograms, but don't worry; we'll get to that in later chapters.

It is important to develop the habit of using appropriate descriptive identifiers in your programs. For example, if you are using scores in a program, identifiers like Score1, Score2, and Score3 are better than X, Y, and Z. Similarly, use descriptive identifiers like Sum, Average, Balance, or Hours when appropriate. Initially, you may not think this important, but as programs get longer and more complex, you will appreciate the fact that descriptive identifiers make a program easier to read.

Basic Program Components

A program in Pascal consists of three components: a *program heading,* an optional *declaration section,* and an *executable section.* These three components are illustrated in the program shown in Figure 2.7.

FIGURE 2.7
Components of a program

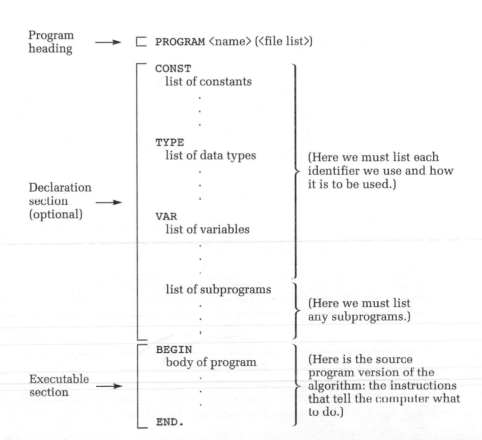

The syntax diagram for a program is

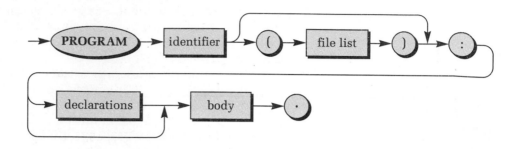

Figure 2.8 illustrates the program components of the sample program (**PROGRAM** Example) that started this section.

FIGURE 2.8
Components of **PROGRAM**
Example

Program heading ⟶

```
PROGRAM Example (input, output);
```

Declaration section ⟶

```
CONST
  Skip = ' ';

VAR
  J, X, Sum : integer;
  Average : real;
```

Executable section ⟶

```
BEGIN
  Sum := 0;
  FOR J := 1 TO 30 DO
    BEGIN
      read (X)
      Sum := Sum + X
    END;
  Average := Sum / 30;
  writeln;
  writeln (Skip:10, 'The average is', Average:8:2);
  writeln;
  writeln (Skip:10, 'The number of scores is', 30:3)
END.
```

The program heading is the first statement of any Pascal program. It is usually one line and must contain the reserved word **PROGRAM**; the program name, which must be a valid identifier; a list of files used; and a semicolon at the end. The respective parts of a program heading are

PROGRAM ⟨name⟩ (⟨file list⟩);

In standard Pascal, the file list must include the files **input** and/or **output**. Some other versions, for example Turbo Pascal, do not have this requirement. *Note:* The symbol T appears in the margin to alert you to cases in which Turbo differs from standard Pascal. These differences are explained in Appendix 6.

The template or fill-in-the-blanks form just presented is used throughout this book. Reserved words and standard identifiers are shown. You must use identifiers to replace the words in lowercase letters and enclosed in arrowheads "⟨ ⟩". Thus,

> **PROGRAM** ⟨name⟩ (⟨file list⟩);

could become

```
PROGRAM Rookie (input, output);
```

Examples of program headings include

```
PROGRAM FirstOne (<file list>);
PROGRAM FindSum (input, output);
PROGRAM Checkbook (input, output);
PROGRAM Number1 (output);
```

You need not be concerned about **input** and **output** files in the file list at this point. Merely be aware that if a program is producing some output (and what program wouldn't?), **output** may be required. If data are to be read into a program, **input** (or a similar file) may also be required. Any list has its parts separated by commas. However, many current versions of Pascal (Apple, Turbo, and UCSD, for example) do not require such a list.

A syntax diagram for a program heading follows:

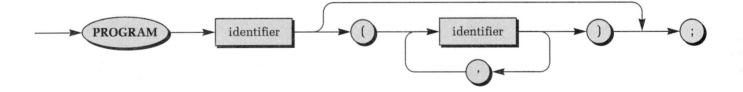

The remainder of the program is sometimes referred to as the *main block*; major divisions are the declaration section and the executable section. The declaration section is used to declare (name) all symbolic constants, data types, variables, and subprograms that are necessary to the program. All constants named in the declaration section are normally referred to as being defined. Thus, we generally say variables are declared and constants are defined.

When constants are defined, they appear in the *constant definition* portion of the declaration section after the reserved word **CONST.** The form for defining a constant is

> **CONST**
> ⟨identifier1⟩ = ⟨value 1⟩;
> ⟨identifier2⟩ = ⟨value 2⟩;
> .
> .
> .
> ⟨identifier$n$⟩ = ⟨value n⟩;

The syntax diagram for this part is

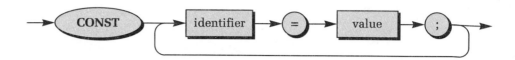

Values of constant identifiers cannot be changed during program execution.

If a value is one character or a string of characters, it must be enclosed in single quotation marks (apostrophes). For example,

```
CONST
  Date = 'July 4, 1776';
```

Any number of constants may be defined in this section. Maximum readability is achieved when the constants are listed consecutively and aligned down the page. A typical constant definition portion of the declaration section could be

```
CONST
  Skip = ' ';
  Name = 'George Washington';
  Date = 'July 4, 1776';
  Splats = '***************************';
  Line = '-----------------------------';
  ClassSize = 35;
  SpeedLimit = 65;
  CmToInches = 0.3937;
```

The **TYPE** portion of the declaration section will be explained in Section 8.1. For now, we assume all data used in a Pascal program must be one of the four *standard simple types:* **integer, real, char,** or **boolean.** Discussion of types **integer, real,** and **char,** is in Section 2.3; discussion of **boolean** is in Section 5.1.

The *variable declaration* portion of the declaration section must be listed after the **TYPE** portion, if present, and must begin with the reserved word **VAR.** This section must contain all identifiers for variables to be used in the program; if a variable is used that has not been declared, an error will occur when the program is compiled. As with constants, variables must be valid identifiers and are usually listed down the page to enhance readability.

The form required for declaring variables is somewhat different from that used for defining constants: it requires a colon instead of an equal sign and specific data types. The simplest correct form is

```
VAR
  ⟨identifier1⟩ : ⟨data type 1⟩;
       .
       .
       .
  ⟨identifiern⟩ : ⟨data type n⟩;
```

The syntax diagram is

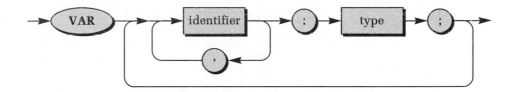

The reserved word **VAR** may appear only once in a program (exceptions will be noted when subprograms are developed). If no variables are to be used, a variable declaration section is not needed; however, this seldom happens. A typical variable declaration section could look like this:

```
VAR
   Sum : integer;
   Average : real;
   I, J, K : integer;
   Ch : char;
```

Four other examples of permissible methods of writing this declaration section are

```
VAR
   I : integer;
   J : integer;
   K : integer;
   Sum : integer;
   Ch : char;
   Average : real;

VAR
   I, J, K, Sum : integer;
   Ch : char;
   Average : real;

VAR
   I,
   J,
   K,
   Sum : integer;
   Ch : char;
   Average : real;

VAR
   I, J,
   K, Sum : integer;
   Ch : char;
   Average : real;
```

The third basic program component is the executable section. This section contains the statements that cause the computer to do something. It must start with the reserved word **BEGIN** and conclude with the reserved word **END.** Also, a period must follow the last **END** in the executable section. The syntax diagram is

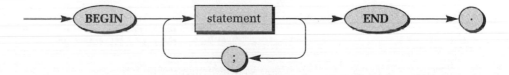

Writing Code in Pascal

We are now ready to examine the use of the executable section of a program. In Pascal, the basic unit of grammar is an *executable statement,* which consists of valid identifiers, standard identifiers, reserved words, numbers, and/or characters together with appropriate punctuation.

One of the main rules for writing code in Pascal is that a semicolon is used to separate executable statements. For example, if the statement

```
writeln ('The results are':20, Sum:8, ' and', Aver:6:2)
```

were to be used in a program, it would (almost always) require a semicolon between it and the next executable statement. Thus, it should be

```
writeln ('The results are':20, Sum:8, ' and', Aver:6:2);
```

One instance exists where an executable statement does not need a following semicolon. When a statement is followed by the reserved word **END,** a semicolon is not required. This is because **END** is not a statement by itself, but part of a **BEGIN . . . END** pair. However, if a semicolon is included, it will not affect the program.

Although you are not currently familiar with many executable statements, you can visualize the executable section as shown in Figure 2.9.

FIGURE 2.9
Executable section

```
            ┌─ BEGIN
            │     ⟨statement 1⟩;
            │     ⟨statement 2⟩;
Executable ─┤         .
section     │         .
            │         .
            │     ⟨statement n − 1⟩;
            │     ⟨statement n⟩
            └─ END.
```

Two comments are now in order. First, Pascal does not require that each statement be on a separate line. Actually, you could write a program as one long line (which would wrap around to fit the screen) if you wish; however, it would be very difficult to read. Compare, for example, the readability of the following two programs.

```
PROGRAM ReadCheck (output); CONST Name = 'George';
Age = 26; VAR J, Sum : integer; BEGIN Sum := 0;
FOR J := 1 TO 10 DO Sum := Sum + J; writeln
('My name is ':28, Name); writeln ('My age is ':27, Age);
writeln; writeln ('The sum is ':28, Sum) END.

PROGRAM ReadCheck (output);

CONST
  Name = 'George';
  Age = 26;

VAR
  J, Sum : integer;
```

Blaise Pascal

Blaise Pascal (1623–1662) began a spectacular, if short, mathematical career at a very early age. He was a brilliant child. As a youngster of 14, he attended meetings of senior French mathematicians. At age 16, he had so impressed the famous mathematician Descartes with his writings that Descartes refused to believe the author could be so young.

Two years later, Pascal invented a calculating machine, the Pascaline, (shown at right) that stands as the very remote predecessor of the modern computer. The Pascaline could add and subtract; it functioned by a series of eight rotating gears, similar to an automobile's odometer. Pascal's machine was opposed by tax clerks of the era who viewed it as a threat to their jobs. Pascal presented his machine to Queen Christina of Sweden in 1650; it is not known what she did with it.

In spite of his obvious talent for mathematics, Pascal devoted most of this adult life to questions of theology;

his work in this area is still regularly studied. A man who often perceived omens in events around him, Pascal concluded that God's plan for him did not include mathematics and dropped the subject entirely. However, while experiencing a particularly nagging toothache when he was 35, Pascal let his thoughts wander to mathematics, and the pain disappeared.

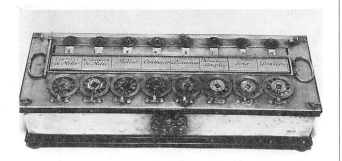

He took this as a heavenly sign and made a quick but intensive return to mathematical research. In barely a week, he managed to discover the fundamental properties of the cycloid curve. With that, Pascal again abandoned mathematics, and in 1662, at the age of 39 he died.

```
BEGIN
  Sum := 0;
  FOR J := 1 TO 10 DO
    Sum := Sum + J;
  writeln ('My name is ':28, Name);
  writeln ('My age is ':27, Age);
  writeln;
  writeln ('The sum is ':28, Sum)
END.
```

You are not expected to know what the statements mean at this point, but it should be obvious that the second program is much more readable than the first. In addition, it is easier to change if corrections are necessary.

Second, Pascal ignores extra spaces and line boundaries. This explains why the two programs are identical. For example, in a program heading, the following are equivalent:

```
PROGRAM ExtraBlanks (output);

PROGRAM ExtraBlanks(output);

PROGRAM ExtraBlanks  (  output  );
```

A good principle to follow is to use spacing to enhance readability. Decide on a style you like (and your instructor can tolerate) and use it consistently. Most programmers, however, include a space before a left parenthesis and after a right parenthesis when appropriate but no spaces immediately inside parentheses; for example.

```
PROGRAM LooksNice (input, output);
```

Exercises 2.2

1. List the rules for forming valid identifiers.

2. Which of the following are valid identifiers? Give an explanation for those that are invalid.

    a. 7Up   g. 1a
    b. Payroll   h. Time&Place
    c. Room222   i. CONST
    d. Name List   j. X*Y
    e. A   k. ListOfEmployees
    f. A1   l. Lima,Ohio

3. Which of the following are valid program headings? Give an explanation for those that are invalid.

    a. PROGRAM Rookie (output)
    b. PROGRAM Pro (input, output);
    c. TestProgram (input, output);
    d. PROGRAM (output);
    e. PROGRAM GettingBetter (output);
    f. PROGRAM Have Fun (input, output);
    g. PROGRAM 2ndOne (output);

4. Name the three main sections of a Pascal program.

5. Write constant definition statements for the following:

    a. your name
    b. your age
    c. your birth date
    d. your birthplace

6. Find all errors in the following definitions and declarations:

    a. CONST
          Company : 'General Motors';
       VAR
          Salary : real;
    b. VAR
          Age = 25;

```
c. VAR
     Days : integer;
     Ch : char;
   CONST
     Name = 'John Smith';
d. CONST
     Car : 'Cadillac';
e. CONST
     Score : integer;
f. VAR
     X, Y, Z : real;
     Score,
     Num : integer;
```

7. Discuss the significance of a semicolon in writing Pascal statements. Include an explanation of when semicolons are not required in a program.

■ ■ ■ ■

■ 2.3
Data Types and Output

OBJECTIVES

- to understand and be able to use the data types **integer, real,** and **char**
- to understand the difference between floating-point form and fixed-point form of decimal numbers
- to understand the syntax for and use of **write** and **writeln** for output
- to be able to format output

Type integer

Pascal requires that all data used in a program be given a *data type.* Since numbers in some form will be used in computer programs, we will first look at numbers of type **integer,** which are integers that are positive, negative, or zero.

Some rules that must be observed when using integers are

1. Plus "+" signs do not have to be written before a positive integer. For example, +283 and 283 have the same value and both are allowed.
2. Minus "−" signs must be written when using a negative number.
3. Leading zeros are ignored. For example, 00073, +073, 0073, and 73 all have the same value.
4. Decimal points cannot be used when writing integers. Although 14 and 14.0 have the same value, 14.0 is not of type **integer.**
5. Commas cannot be used when writing integers. 271,362 is not allowed; it must be written as 271362.

The syntax diagram for an integer is

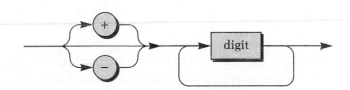

There is a limit on the largest and the smallest integer constant. The largest such constant is **maxint** and the smallest is usually −**maxint** or (−**maxint** − 1). **maxint** and −**maxint** are recognized by every version of Pascal; however, different machines have different values for them. This section ends with a program that enables you to discover the value of **maxint** on your computer. Operations with integers will be examined in the next section and integer variables will be discussed in Chapter 3.

Type real

Working with real numbers is more complicated than working with integers. When using decimal notation, numbers of type **real** must be written with a decimal point "." with at least one digit on each side of the decimal. Thus, .2 is not a valid **real** but 0.2 is.

Plus " + " and minus " − " signs for data of type **real** are treated exactly as with integers. When working with reals, however, both leading and trailing zeros are ignored. Thus, + 23.45, 23.45, 023.45, 23.450, and 0023.45000 have the same value.

All reals seen thus far have been in *fixed-point* form. The computer will also accept reals in *floating-point* or exponential form. Floating-point form is an equivalent method for writing numbers in scientific notation to accommodate numbers that may have very large or very small values. The difference is, instead of writing the base decimal times some power of 10, the base decimal is followed by E and the appropriate power of 10. For example, 231.6 in scientific notation would be 2.316×10^2 and in floating-point form would be 2.316E2. Table 2.4 sets forth several fixed-point decimal numbers with the equivalent scientific notation and floating-point form. Floating-point form for real numbers does not require exactly one digit on the left of the decimal point. In fact, it can be used with no decimal points written. To illustrate, 4.16E1, 41.6, 416.0E-1, and 416E-1 have the same value and all are permissible. However, it is not a good habit to use floating-point form for decimal numbers unless exactly one digit appears on the left of the decimal. In most other cases, fixed-point form is preferable.

TABLE 2.4
Forms for equivalent numbers

Fixed-point	Scientific Notation	Floating-point
46.345	4.6345×10	4.6345E1
59214.3	5.92143×10^4	5.92143E4
0.00042	4.2×10^{-4}	4.2E − 4
36000000000.0	3.6×10^{10}	3.6E10
0.000000005	5.0×10^{-9}	5.0E − 9
− 341000.0	-3.41×10^5	− 3.41E5

The syntax diagram for a floating-point number is

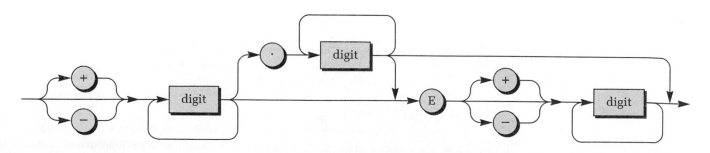

When using reals in a program, you may use either fixed-point or floating-point form. But the computer prints out reals in floating-point form unless you specify otherwise. Formatting output is discussed later in this section.

Type char

Another data type available in Pascal is **char,** which is used to represent character data. In standard Pascal, data of type **char** can be only a single character (which could be a blank space). These characters come from an available character set that differs somewhat from computer to computer, but always includes the letters of the alphabet (uppercase and lowercase); the digits 0, 1, 2, 3, 4, 5, 6, 7, 8, and 9; and special symbols such as #, &, !, +, −, *, /, and so on. Two common character sets are given in Appendix 4.

Character constants of type **char** must be enclosed in single quotation marks when used in a program. Otherwise, they will be treated as variables and subsequent use will cause a compilation error. Thus, to use the letter A as a constant, you would type 'A'. The use of digits and standard operation symbols as characters is also permitted; for example, '7' would be considered a character, but 7 is an integer.

If a word of one or more characters is used as a constant in a program, it is referred to as a *string constant.* String constants, generally called *strings,* may be defined in the **CONST** portion of the declaration section. The entire string must be enclosed in single quotation marks. Some sample definitions are

```
CONST
  Name = 'John Q. Public';
  Date = 'July 4, 1776';
  Splats = '************************';
```

Students with experience in using BASIC usually expect the equivalent of a string variable for storing names, and other information. A string is not a standard Pascal data type; standard Pascal does not have such a feature. However, an analogous feature, packed arrays of characters, is presented in Section 9.5.

When a single quotation mark is needed within a string, it is represented by two single quotation marks. For example, if the name desired was O'Malley, it would be represented by

```
'O''Malley'
```

When a single quotation mark is needed as a single character, it can be represented by placing two single quotation marks within single quotation marks. When typed, this appears as ''''. Note that these are all single quotation marks; use of the double quotation mark character here will not produce the desired result.

Type string (Optional: nonstandard)

As previously mentioned, standard Pascal does not provide for a **string** data type. However, since many versions of Pascal (particularly Turbo) do contain a **string** data type, we have decided to include mention of this data type in this edition of this book.

Having the data type **string** available allows a programmer to design programs that are capable of using strings of characters as well as numeric data. This is particularly useful when using names of people and companies, for example. Later we will see how such strings can be incorporated into a program; for now it is sufficient that you be aware that several versions of nonstandard Pascal provide a **string** data type.

Output

The goal of most programs is to print something. What gets printed (either on paper or on a screen) is referred to as output. The two program statements that produce output are **write** and **writeln** (pronounced "write line"). They are usually followed by character strings, numbers, numerical expressions, or variable names enclosed in parentheses. The general form is

---

write (⟨expression 1⟩, ⟨expression 2⟩, . . . , ⟨expression n⟩)

or

writeln (⟨expression 1⟩, ⟨expression 2⟩, . . . , ⟨expression n⟩)

A simplified syntax diagram for **write** (applicable also for **writeln**) is

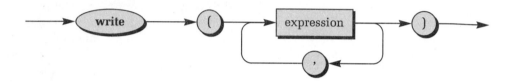

For more information on syntax diagrams for **write** and **writeln**, see Appendix 3.

A **writeln** can also be used as a complete statement.

```
writeln;
```

causes a blank line to be printed. This technique is frequently used to produce more readable output.

The **write** statement causes subsequent output to be on the same line; **writeln** causes the next output to be on the next line. This is because **writeln** is actually a **write** statement followed by a line feed. To illustrate,

```
write ('This is a test.');
writeln ('How many lines are printed?');
```

causes the output

```
This is a test.How many lines are printed?
```

whereas,

```
writeln ('This is a test.');
writeln ('How many lines are printed?');
```

causes the output

```
This is a test.
How many lines are printed?
```

When output is to a monitor, **writeln** causes the cursor to move to the next line for the next I/O operation.

Note:

1. Some printers reserve the first column for carriage control. Thus, the first character in a string on the left side of a page would not be printed.

2. Some implementations use a buffer to gather output from **write** statements and then print the gathered line when a **writeln** is encountered.
3. Some implementations require a **writeln** for the last output statement. Otherwise, output gathered in a buffer does not get printed.

You should check with your instructor concerning these features.

As indicated, character strings can be printed by enclosing the string in single quotation marks within the parentheses. Numerical data can be printed by including the desired number or numbers within the parentheses. Thus,

```
writeln (100)
```

produces

```
      100
```

and

```
writeln (100, 87, 95)
```

produces

```
      100        87        95
```

The spaces at the beginning of the lines and between the numbers are caused by a default field width. Many implementations of Pascal use a predetermined field width for output. This predetermined default width will be used unless output is controlled by the programmer. Methods for controlling field width of output will be examined shortly.

■ **EXAMPLE 2.1**

Let's write a complete Pascal program to print the address

> 1403 South Drive
> Apartment 3B
> Pittsburgh, PA   15238

A complete program to print this is

```
PROGRAM Address (output);

BEGIN
   writeln ('1403 South Drive');
   writeln ('Apartment 3B');
   writeln ('Pittsburgh, PA', 15238)
END.
```

When this program is run on a computer, you may get

```
1403 South Drive
Apartment 3B
Pittsburgh, PA        15238
```

■ **EXAMPLE 2.2**

Let's now combine various methods of using **writeln** to write a complete Pascal program that may produce the following output:

```
COMPUTER SCIENCE 150
--------------------

TEST SCORES:
        100        98        93
         89        82        76
         73        64
```

The program would be

```
PROGRAM PrintScores (output);

BEGIN
  writeln;
  writeln ('COMPUTER SCIENCE 150');
  writeln ('--------------------');
  writeln;
  writeln ('TEST SCORES:');
  writeln (100, 98, 93);
  writeln (89, 82, 76);
  writeln (73, 64);
  writeln
END.
```

When designing a program to solve a problem, you should constantly be aware of how the output should appear. The spacing of output on a line can be controlled by formatting expressions in **write** and **writeln** statements.

Formatting Integers

If the programmer does not control the output, each integer will be printed in a predetermined field width (unless the integer exceeds the field width). This is referred to as a default field width. This width depends on the machine and version of Pascal being used. In this text, we will assume a width of ten spaces. Negative signs occupy one position in the field and plus signs are not printed. Spacing of output on a page will frequently be denoted by an underscore for each blank space. Some **writeln** statements and their output with a default field width of ten follow.

Program Statement	Output
`writeln (123);`	`_____123`
`writeln (+5062);`	`_____5062`
`writeln (-12);`	`_____-12`
`writeln (0);`	`_____0`

A complete Pascal program to illustrate the field width for these integers is

```
PROGRAM PrintInteger (output);

BEGIN
  writeln;
  writeln (123);
  writeln (+5062);
  writeln (-12);
  writeln (0);
  writeln
END.
```

Controlling output is referred to as *formatting*. It is relatively easy to format output for integers. Using a **writeln** statement, the desired field width is designated by placing a colon ":" after the integer (or identifier) and then an integer specifying the field width. The integer printed will be right justified in the specified field. The general form for formatting integers is

writeln (⟨integer⟩:⟨*n*⟩);

Some illustrations for formatting integer output are

Program Statement	Output
`writeln (123:6);`	`___123`
`writeln (15, 10:5);`	`_____15___10`
`writeln (-263:7, 21:3);`	`___-263_21`
`writeln (+5062:6);`	`__5062`
`writeln (65221:3);`	`65221`

Note that, in line five, an attempt is made to specify a field width smaller than the number of digits contained in the integer. Most versions of Pascal will automatically print the entire integer; however, some versions will print only in the specified width. The following program will enable you to find out exactly what your machine will do.

```
PROGRAM FieldWidth (output);

BEGIN
  writeln;
  writeln ('This program will check field width.');
  writeln ('         1         2         3');
  writeln ('123456789012345678901234567890');
  writeln;
  writeln (123:5);
  writeln (12345:3);
  writeln (1);
  writeln (-12345:4)
END.
```

When this program is run on a VAX 8530 with a VMS operating system, the output is

```
This program will check field width.
          1         2         3
1234567890123456789012345678490

  123
12345
          1
-12345
```

When this program is run on an IBM PC using Turbo 5.0, the output is

```
This program will check field width.
          1         2         3
1234567890123456789012345678490

  123
12345
1
-12345
```

Formatting Reals

As with data of type **integer,** data of type **real** can be used in **writeln** statements. If no formatting is used, the output will be in floating-point form. Different machines and different versions of Pascal produce a variety of default field widths. For example, some use a standard field width of 16 and some use a standard width of 22. Assuming a field width of 22, the program

```
PROGRAM UnformattedReals (output);

BEGIN
  writeln;
  writeln (231.45);
  writeln (0.00456);
  writeln (4.0);
  writeln (-526.1E5);
  writeln (0.91E-8);
  writeln
END.
```

produces

```
__2.3145000000000E+002
__4.5600000000000E-003
__4.0000000000000E+000
__-5.2610000000000E+007
__9.1000000000000E-009
```

Most programs using data of type **real** require a neater method of expressing the output. This can be accomplished by formatting. To format reals you must specify both the field width and the number of decimal places to the right of the decimal. This is done by writing the real, followed by a colon ":", followed by an integer, followed by a colon and another integer. For example, if you are writing a program that prints wages of workers, you could get a field width of eight with two places to the right of the decimal as follows:

```
writeln (231.45:8:2);
```

231.45 is the computed wage, 8 specifies the field width, and 2 specifies how many digits appear to the right of the decimal. The output for this statement is

```
__231.45
```

The general form for formatting reals is

> **writeln** ($\langle$real$\rangle$:$\langle n1 \rangle$:$\langle n2 \rangle$);

Use of this formatting procedure causes the following to happen:

1. The decimal uses one position in the specified field width.
2. Leading zeros are not printed.
3. Trailing zeros are printed to the specified number of positions to the right of the decimal.
4. Leading plus "+" signs are omitted.
5. Leading minus "−" signs are printed and use one position of the specified field.
6. Digits appearing to the right of the decimal have been rounded rather than truncated.

As with integers, if a field width is specified that is too small, most versions of Pascal will default to the minimum width required to present all digits to the left of the decimal as well as the specified digits to the right of the decimal. The following table illustrates how output using data of type **real** can be formatted.

Program Statement	Output
`writeln (765:432:10:3)`	`___765.432`
`writeln (023.14:10:2)`	`_____23.14`
`writeln (65.50:10:2)`	`_____65.50`
`writeln (+341.2:10:2)`	`____341.20`
`writeln (-341.2:10:2)`	`___-341.20`
`writeln (16.458:10:2)`	`_____16.46`
`writeln (0.00456:10:4)`	`____0.0046`
`writeln (136.51:4:2)`	`____136.51`

Reals in floating-point form can also be used in a formatted **writeln** statement. Output from the following complete program

```
PROGRAM FormatReals (output);

BEGIN
  writeln;
  writeln (1.234E2:10:2);
  writeln (-723.4E-3:10:5);
  writeln (-723.4E-3:10:3);
  writeln (6.435E2:10:2, 2.3145E2:10:2);
  writeln
END.
```

is

```
____123.40
__-0.72340
_____-0.720
____643.50____231.45
```

Formatting Strings

Strings and string constants can be formatted using a single colon ":" followed by a positive integer "n" to specify field width. The general form for formatting strings is

> **writeln** ('⟨string⟩':⟨n⟩);

The string will be right justified in the field. Unlike reals, strings are truncated when necessary. The following program illustrates string formatting.

```
PROGRAM StringFormat (output);

CONST
  Indent = ' ';

BEGIN
  writeln;
  writeln (Indent:4, 'Note the strings below.');
  writeln (Indent:4, '-----------------------');
  writeln;
  writeln ('This is a sample string.':35);
  writeln ('This is a sample string.':30);
  writeln ('This is a sample string.':25);
  writeln ('This is a sample string.':20);
  writeln
END.
```

The output from this program would be

```
    Note the strings below.
    -----------------------

              This is a sample string.
         This is a sample string.
    This is a sample string.
This is a sample string.
```

Note the use of the constant "Indent" in the last program. This is used to control indented output. Since Pascal does not have a tabbing or spacing command, you might want to also define something like

```
Skip = ' ';
```

in the **CONST** section. Thus, you would have

```
CONST
  Indent = ' ';
  Skip = ' ';
```

You could then use

```
Indent:n
```

for indenting and

```
Skip:n
```

for spacing on a line.

Test Programs

Programmers should develop the habit of using *test programs* to improve their knowledge and programming skills. Test programs should be relatively short and written to provide an answer to a specific question. For example, **maxint** was discussed earlier in this section. It was mentioned that the value of **maxint** depended upon the machine being used. You could use a test program to discover what your computer uses for **maxint**. A complete program that accomplishes this is

```
PROGRAM TextMax (output);

BEGIN
  writeln ('Maxint is ', maxint)
END.
```

Notice that a brief message, "Maxint is", is included to explain the output. Such a message (or output label) is almost always desirable.

Test programs allow you to play with the computer. You can answer "What if . . ." questions by adopting a "try it and see" attitude. This is an excellent way to become comfortable with your computer and the programming language you are using. For example, you might change the previous test program to

```
PROGRAM TestMax (output);

BEGIN
  writeln ('Maxint is ', maxint);
  writeln ('TooMuch is ', maxint + 1)
END.
```

Exercises 2.3

1. Which of the following are valid integers? Explain why the others are invalid.
   a. 521
   b. −32.0
   c. 5,621
   d. +00784
   e. +65
   f. 6521492183
   g. −0

2. Which of the following are valid reals? Explain why the others are invalid.
   a. 26.3
   b. +181.0
   c. −.14
   d. 492.
   e. +017.400
   f. 43E2
   g. −0.2E−3
   h. 43,162.3E5
   i. −176.52E+1
   j. 1.43000E+2

3. Change the following fixed-point decimals to floating-point decimals with exactly one nonzero digit to the left of the decimal.
   a. 173.0
   b. 743927000000.0
   c. −0.000000023
   d. +014.768
   e. −5.2

4. Change the following floating-point decimals to fixed-point decimals.
   a. −1.0046E+3
   b. 4.2E−8
   c. 9.020E10
   d. −4.615230E3
   e. −8.02E−3

5. Indicate the data type for each of the following:

   a. −720   e. '150'

   b. −720.0   f. '23.4E2'

   c. 150E3   g. 23.4E−2

   d. 150

6. Write and run test programs for each of the following:

   a. Examine the output for a decimal number without field width specified; for example,

      ```
      writeln (2.31)
      ```

   b. Try to print a message without using quotation marks for a character string; for example,

      ```
      writeln (Hello);
      ```

7. For each of the following, write a program that would produce the indicated output.

   a. Score   b. Price
      -----   -------
         86                            $ 19.94
         82                            $100.00
         79                            $ 58.95
      where "S" is in column 10.   where "P" is in column 50.

8. Assume the hourly wages of five student employees are

   3.65
   4.10
   2.89
   5.00
   4.50

   Write a program that will produce this output, where the "E" of Employee is in column 20.

   ```
   -----------------------
   Employee    Hourly Wage
   -----------------------
      1           $ 3.65
      2           $ 4.10
      3           $ 2.89
      4           $ 5.00
      5           $ 4.50
   -----------------------
   ```

9. What is the output from the following segment of code on your printer or terminal?

   ```
   writeln ('My test average is', 87.5);
   writeln ('My test average is':20, 87.5:10);
   writeln ('My test average is':25, 87.5:10:2);
   writeln ('My test average is':25, 87.5:6:2);
   ```

10. Write a program that will produce the following output. Start Student in column 20 and Test in column 40.

    ```
    Student Name          Test Score

    Adams, Mike               73
    Conley, Theresa           86
    Samson, Ron               92
    O'Malley, Colleen         81
    ```

11. The Great Lakes Shipping Company is going to use a computer program to generate billing statements for their customers. The heading of each bill is to be

```
          GREAT LAKES SHIPPING COMPANY
            SAULT STE. MARIE, MICHIGAN
--------------------------------------------------
    Thank you for doing business with our company.
    The information listed below was used to
    determine your total cargo fee. We hope you
    were satisfied with our service.
--------------------------------------------------
  CARGO        TONNAGE       RATE/TON        TOTAL DUE
```

Write a complete Pascal program that will produce this heading.

12. What output is produced by each of the following statements or sequence of statements when executed by the computer?

   a. `writeln (1234, 1234:8, 1234:6);`

   b. `writeln (12:4, -21:4, 120:4);`

   c. `writeln ('FIGURE   AREA   PERIMETER');`
      `writeln ('----------------------');`
      `writeln;`
      `writeln ('SQUARE', 16:5, 16:12);`
      `writeln;`
      `writeln ('RECT ', 24:5, 20:12);`

13. Write a complete program that will produce the following table:

```
WIDTH         LENGTH        AREA
  4             2             8
 21             5            105
```

14. What output is produced when each of the following is executed?

   a. `writeln (2.134:15:2);`

   b. `writeln (423.73:5:2);`

   c. `writeln (-42.1:8:3);`

   d. `writeln (-4.21E3:6:2);`

   e. `writeln (10.25);`

   f. `writeln (1.25, 1.25:6:2, 1.25:6:1);`

15. Write a complete program that produces the following output:

```
Hourly Wage        Hours Worked        Total
     5.0               20.0            100.00
     7.50              15.25           114.375
```

16. What type of data would be used to print each of the following?

   a. your age

   b. your grade point average

   c. your name

   d. a test score

   e. the average test score

   f. your grade

■ ■ ■ ■

■ Summary

Key Terms

constant definition
data type
declaration section
effective statement
executable section
executable statement
fixed point
floating point
formatting
identifier
keyword

main block
module
module specifications
program heading
pseudocode
reserved word
software engineering
software system life
  cycle
standard identifier

standard simple type
stepwise refinement
string
string constant
structure chart
syntax
syntax diagram
test program
top-down design
variable declaration

Keywords

BEGIN
char
CONST
END
input

integer
maxint
output
PROGRAM
real

VAR
write
writeln

Key Concepts

- Six steps in problem solving include: analyze the problem, develop an algorithm, write code for the program, run the program, test the results against answers manually computed with paper and pencil, and document the program.
- Top-down design is a process of dividing tasks into subtasks until each subtask can be readily accomplished.
- Stepwise refinement refers to refinements of tasks into subtasks.
- A structure chart is a graphic representation of the relationship between modules.
- Software engineering is the process of developing and maintaining large software systems.
- The software system life cycle consists of the following phases:
  1. Analysis
  2. Design
  3. Coding
  4. Testing/verification
  5. Maintenance
  6. Obsolescence
- Valid identifiers must begin with a letter and they can contain only letters and digits.
- The three components of a Pascal program are program heading, declaration section, and executable section.
- Semicolons are used to separate executable statements.
- Extra spaces and blank lines are ignored in Pascal.
- Output is generated by using **write** or **writeln.**
- Strings are formatted using a single colon followed by a positive integer that specifies the total field width, for example

```
writeln ('This is a string,':30);
```

- The following table summarizes the use of the data types **integer, real,** and **char.**

Data Type	Permissible Data	Formatting
integer	numeric	one colon; for example `writeln (25:6);`
real	numeric	two colons; for example `writeln (1234.5:8:2);`
char	character	one colon; for example `writeln ('A':6);`

■ Programming Problems and Projects

Write and run a short program for each of the following:

1. A program to print your initials in block letters. Your output could look like

```
JJJJJ            A              CC
    J           A A           C    C
    J          A   A         C
    J          AAAAA         C
J   J          A   A          C    C
 JJ            A   A           CC
```

2. Design a simple picture and print it out using **writeln** statements. If you plan the picture using a sheet of graph paper, keeping track of spacing will be easier.

3. A program to print out your mailing address.

4. Our Lady of Mercy Hospital prints billing statements for patients when they are ready to leave the hospital. Write a program that prints a heading for each statement as follows:

```
//////////////////////////////////////////////
/                                            /
/        Our Lady of Mercy Hospital          /
/        --------------------------          /
/                                            /
/             1306 Central City              /
/            Phone (416) 333-5555            /
/                                            /
//////////////////////////////////////////////
```

5. Your computer science instructor wants course and program information included as part of every assignment. Write a program that can be used to print this information. Sample output is

```
*******************************************
*                                         *
*      Author:        Mary Smith          *
*      Course:        CPS-150             *
*      Assignment:    Program #3          *
*      Due Date:      September 18         *
*      Instructor:    Mr. Samson          *
*                                         *
*******************************************
```

6. As part of a programming project that will compute and print grades for each student in your class, you have been asked to write a program

that produces a heading for each student report. The columns in which the various headings should be are as follows:

- the border for the class name starts in column 30
- Student Name starts in column 20
- Test Average starts in column 40
- Grade starts in column 55

Write a program to print the heading as follows:

```
                             *************************
                             *                       *
                             *    CPS 150     Pascal  *
                             *                       *
                             *************************

     Student Name                Test Average    Grade
     ------------                ------------    -----
```

Arithmetic, Variables, Input, Constants, and Standard Functions

In this chapter we will discuss arithmetic operations, using data in a program, obtaining input, and using constants and variables. We will also discuss the use of functions to perform standard operations such as finding the square root or absolute value of a number.

■ 3.1
Arithmetic in Pascal

OBJECTIVES

- to be able to evaluate arithmetic expressions using data of type **integer**
- to be able to evaluate arithmetic expressions using data of type **real**
- to understand the order of operations for evaluating expressions
- to be able to identify mixed-mode expressions
- to be able to distinguish between valid and invalid mixed-mode expressions
- to be able to evaluate mixed-mode expressions ☐T☐

Basic Operations for Integers

Integer arithmetic in Pascal allows the operations of addition, subtraction, and multiplication to be performed. The notation for these operations is

Symbol	Operation	Example	Value
+	Addition	3 + 5	8
−	Subtraction	43 − 25	18
*	Multiplication	4 * 7	28

Noticeably absent from this list is a division operation. This is because *integer arithmetic operations* are expected to produce integer answers. Since division problems might not produce integers, Pascal provides two operations, **MOD** and **DIV**, to produce integer answers.

In a standard division problem, there is a quotient and remainder. In Pascal, **DIV** produces the quotient and **MOD** produces the remainder when the first operand is positive. For example, in the problem 17 divided by 3, 17 **DIV** 3 produces 5, and 17 **MOD** 3 produces 2. Avoid using **DIV** 0 (zero) and **MOD** 0 (zero). A precise description of how **MOD** works is given on page 39 of the *Second Draft ANSI Standard for Pascal* as: "A term of the form *i* mod

53

j shall be an error if j is zero or negative, otherwise the value of i mod j shall be that value of $(i - (k * j))$ for integral k such that $0 <= i$ mod $j < j$."

Several integer expressions and their values are shown in Table 3.1. Notice that when 3 is multiplied by -2, the expression is written as $3 * (-2)$ rather than $3 * -2$. This is because consecutive operators cannot appear in an arithmetic expression. However, this expression could be written as $-2 * 3$.

TABLE 3.1
Values of integer expressions

Expression	Value
-3 + 2	-1
2 - 3	-1
-3 * 2	-6
3 * (-2)	-6
-3 * (-2)	6
17 DIV 3	5
17 MOD 3	2
17 DIV (-3)	-5
-17 DIV 3	-5
-17 MOD 3	1
-17 DIV (-3)	5

Order of Operations for Integers

Expressions involving more than one operation are frequently used when writing programs. When this happens, it is important to know the order in which these operations are performed. The priorities for these are

1. All expressions within a set of parentheses are evaluated first. If there are parentheses within parentheses (the parentheses are nested), the innermost expressions are evaluated first.
2. The operations *, **MOD,** and **DIV** are evaluated next in order from left to right.
3. The operations + and - are evaluated last from left to right.

These operations are the operations of algebra and are summarized in Table 3.2.

TABLE 3.2
Integer arithmetic priority

Expression or Operation	Priority
( )	1. Evaluate from inside out
*, MOD, DIV	2. Evaluate from left to right
+, -	3. Evaluate from left to right

To illustrate how expressions are evaluated, consider the values of the expressions listed in Table 3.3.

As expressions get more elaborate, it can be helpful to list partial evaluations in a manner similar to the order in which the computer performs the evaluations. For example, suppose the expression

    (3 - 4) + 18 DIV 5 + 2

is to be evaluated. If we consider the order in which subexpressions are evaluated, we get

```
(3 - 4)  +  18 DIV 5 + 2
   ↓
  -1     +  18 DIV 5 + 2
              ↓
  -1     +     3      + 2
        ↓
        2            + 2
              ↓
              4
```

TABLE 3.3
Priority of operations

Expression	Value
3 - 4 * 5	-17
3 - (4 * 5)	-17
(3 - 4) * 5	-5
3 * 4 - 5	7
3 * (4 - 5)	-3
17 - 10 - 3	4
17 - (10 - 3)	10
(17 - 10) - 3	4
-42 + 50 MOD 17	-26

Using MOD and DIV

MOD and **DIV** can be used when it is necessary to perform conversions within arithmetic operations. For example, consider the problem of adding two weights given in units of pounds and ounces. This problem can be solved by converting both weights to ounces, adding the ounces, and then converting the total ounces to pounds and ounces. The conversion from ounces to pounds can be accomplished by using **MOD** and **DIV**. If the total number of ounces is 243, then

> 243 **DIV** 16

yields the number of pounds (15), and

> 243 **MOD** 16

yields the number of ounces (3).

Basic Operations for Reals

The operations of addition, subtraction, and multiplication are the same for data of type **real** as for integers. Additionally, division is now permitted. Since **MOD** and **DIV** are restricted to data of type **integer,** the symbol for division of data of type **real** is "/". The *real arithmetic operations* are as follows:

Symbol	Operation	Example	Value
+	Addition	4.2 + 19.36	23.56
−	Subtraction	19.36 - 4.2	15.16
*	Multiplication	3.1 * 2.0	6.2
/	Division	54.6 / 2.0	27.3

Division is given the same priority as multiplication when arithmetic expressions are evaluated by the computer. The rules for order of operation are the same as those for evaluating integer arithmetic expressions. A summary of these operations is shown in Table 3.4.

TABLE 3.4
Real arithmetic priority

Expression or Operation	Priority
( )	1. Evaluate from inside out
*, /	2. Evaluate from left to right
+, −	3. Evaluate from left to right

Some example calculations using data of type **real** are

Expression	Value
-1.0 + 3.5 + 2.0	4.5
-1.0 + 3.5 * 2.0	6.0
2.0 * (1.2 - 4.3)	−6.2
2.0 * 1.2 - 4.3	−1.9
-12.6 / 3.0 + 3.0	−1.2
-12.6 / (3.0 + 3.0)	−2.1

As with integers, consecutive operations signs are not allowed. Thus, if you want to multiply 4.3 by −2.0, you can use −2.0 * 4.3 or 4.3 * (−2.0), but you cannot use 4.3 * −2.0. As expressions get a bit more complicated, it is again helpful to write out the expression and evaluate it step by step. For example,

```
18.2 + (-4.3) * (10.1 + (72.3 / 3.0 - 4.5))
                               ↓
18.2 + (-4.3) * (10.1 +    (24.1    - 4.5))
                                       ↓
18.2 + (-4.3) * (10.1 +           19.6)
                           ↓
18.2 + (-4.3) *           29.7
                ↓
18.2 +           -127.71
        ↓
     -109.51
```

Note that exponentiation has not been listed as an available operation for either integers or reals. Pascal does not have an exponentiation operator. A method of overcoming this problem is presented in Section 7.2.

Overflow and Underflow

Arithmetic operations with computers have some limitations. One of these is the problem of *overflow*. Integer overflow occurs when an integer expression exceeds the absolute value of **maxint**. Thus, an attempt to use (**maxint** + 1) or (− **maxint** − 1) causes an overflow problem. Ideally, an error message would be printed when such a situation arises. Some systems do print a message such as ARITHMETIC OVERFLOW when this occurs; however, other systems merely assign a meaningless value and continue with the program. In Section 5.3 we discuss how to protect a program against this problem.

Real overflow occurs when the absolute value of a **real** is too large to fit into a memory location. Similar to the case for integer overflow, some systems do not print an error message when this occurs, but the manual for your system should include information on the limitations regarding storage of **real** numbers.

A second problem occurs when working with reals. If a real number is too small to be represented, it is replaced by zero. This is called *underflow*. Thus, your computations may produce a real of the magnitude $1.0 * 10^{-100}$, but your system could replace this with a zero.

In general, underflow is less of a problem than overflow; however, it cannot be completely ignored. Some mathematical approximations require use of numbers as they approach zero. Some financial calculations (such as computing interest) also require the use of very small numbers. If your computations do not require use of small numbers, you can ignore underflow. However, if you do use such numbers, you must know the system limitations before writing programs that need them. Consult your system manual to find the limitations of your system. Figure 3.1 illustrates the overflow and underflow possibilities.

FIGURE 3.1
Overflow and underflow

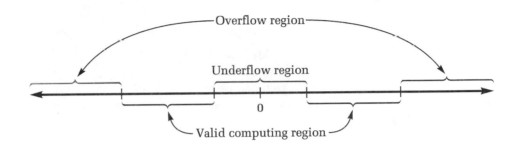

Mixed Expressions

We have seen examples of arithmetic expressions using data of types **integer** and **real.** What happens if both **integer** and **real** data types are used in the same expression?

It is possible for some expressions to contain data of both types. These are called *mixed-mode* expressions. All of the operations studied thus far except **MOD** and **DIV** will allow operands of both types. However, when any operand in a simple arithmetic expression is of type **real,** the value of the expression will be given as a real and not as an integer. For example, 4 + 3.0 will be the real 7.0 rather than the integer 7. It is permissible to use data of type **integer** with the real number operation, division "/"; when this happens, the answer is given as a real number. For example, 6/3 will be the real 2.0 rather than the integer 2. However, when data of type **real** is used with either **MOD** or **DIV,** an error message will occur. Several examples of valid and invalid mixed-mode expressions are shown in Table 3.5.

TABLE 3.5
Mixed-mode arithmetic priority

Expression	Valid	Data Type
-2.0 * 17	Yes	**real**
13.1 - 22	Yes	**real**
14 / 7	Yes	**real**
14 / 7.0	Yes	**real**
10.0 MOD 2	No	
10 MOD 2.0	No	
-15 DIV 3	Yes	**integer**
-15 DIV 3.0	No	
32.0 DIV 4.0	No	
7 + 5.0	Yes	**real**

Evaluation of mixed-mode expressions is similar to evaluating either real or integer arithmetic expressions. If an expression is valid, the order of operations for evaluating the expression is the same as that used for the data type of the value of the expression. As an example, consider the evaluation of the expression $(-4.2 + 17 \text{ DIV } 3 * 2.1) / 2$. Within the parentheses, 17 **DIV** 3 has first priority, hence the operation is valid. The sequential evaluation is given by

```
(-4.2 + 17 DIV 3 * 2.1) / 2
              ↓
(-4.2 +      5    * 2.1) / 2
                    ↓
(-4.2 +          10.5)    / 2
        ↓
      6.3                 / 2
                   ↓
                 3.15
```

Mixed-mode expressions can be used in **writeln** statements. The programmer must be careful, however, when formatting output. Only data of type **real** can be formatted using two colons (:8:3). If this method of formatting is used on other data types, an error will result. However, reals can be formatted with a single colon. For example,

```
writeln (18.5:8);
```

is a valid statement. This produces 18.5 in floating-point form in a total field width of eight columns, as 1.850E+1. However, this is usually not a desirable practice.

Some valid and invalid statements using formatted output are

Statement	Valid	Output
writeln (-7.0:8:2)	Yes	___-7.00
writeln (187:6)	Yes	___187
writeln (187:6:2)	No	
writeln (-9.0:8)	Yes	_-9.0E+0
writeln (-9.0:6:2)	Yes	_-9.00
writeln (-80:8:3)	No	

Now that you have some degree of familiarity with mixed-mode expressions, you should know that, if possible, you should avoid them. There are at least three good reasons for not using them: invalid expressions may be obtained (10 **MOD** 2.0); improper formatting could result; and improper assignment statements could result (see Section 3.2).

Exercises 3.1

1. Find the value of each of the following expressions:
   a. 17 - 3 * 2
   b. -15 * 3 + 4
   c. 123 MOD 5
   d. 123 DIV 5
   e. 5 * 123 DIV 5 + 123 MOD 5
   f. -21 * 3 * (-1)
   g. 14 * (3 + 18 DIV 4) - 50
   h. 100 - (4 * (3 + 2)) * (-2)
   i. -56 MOD 3
   j. 14 * 8 MOD 5 - 23 DIV (-4)

2. Find the value of each of the following expressions:

   a. `3.21 + 5.02 / 6.1`

   b. `6.0 / 2.0 * 3.0`

   c. `6.0 / (2.0 + 3.0)`

   d. `-20.5 * (2.1 + 2.0)`

   e. `-2.0 * ((56.8 / 4.0 + 0.8) + 5.0)`

   f. `1.04E2 * 0.02E3`

   g. `800.0E-2 / 4.0 + 15.3`

3. Which of the following are valid expressions? For those that are, indicate whether they are of type **integer** or **real**.

   a. `18 - (5 * 2)`   f. `28 / 7`

   b. `(18 - 5) * 2`   g. `28.0 / 4`

   c. `18 - 5 * 2.0`   h. `10.5 + 14 DIV 3`

   d. `25 * (14 MOD 7.0)`   i. `24 DIV 6 / 3`

   e. `1.4E3 * 5`   j. `24 DIV (6 / 3)`

4. Evaluate each of the valid expressions in Exercise 3.

5. What is the output produced by the following program?

```
PROGRAM MixedMode (output);

BEGIN
  writeln;
  writeln ('   Expression      Value');
  writeln ('   ----------      -----');
  writeln;
  writeln ('   10 / 5' , 10/5:12:3);
  writeln ('   2.0+7*(-1)', 2.0 + 7 * (-1));
  writeln
END.
```

6. Find all errors in the following Pascal statements:

   a. `writeln (-20 DIV 4.0 :8:3);`

   b. `writeln (-20 DIV 4 :8:3);`

   c. `writeln (-20 DIV 4 :8);`

   d. `writeln (8 - 3.0 * 5 :6);`

   e. `writeln (7 * 6 DIV 3 / 2:6:2);`

   f. `writeln (-17.1 + 5 * 20.0 :8:3);`

■ ■ ■ ■

■ 3.2
Using Variables

Memory Locations

It is frequently necessary to store values for later use. This is done by putting the value into a *memory location* by using a symbolic name to refer to this location. If the contents of the location are to be changed during a program, the symbolic name is referred to as a *variable;* if the contents are not to be changed, it is referred to as a *constant.*

A graphic way to think about memory locations is to envision them as boxes; each box is named and a value is stored inside. For example, suppose a program is written to add a sequence of numbers. If we name the memory location to be used Sum, initially we have

```
┌──────────┐
│          │
└──────────┘
   Sum
```

which depicts a memory location that has been reserved and can be accessed by a reference to Sum. If we then add the integers 10, 20, and 30 and store them in Sum, we have

```
┌──────────┐
│    60    │
└──────────┘
   Sum
```

It is important to distinguish between the name of a memory location (Sum) and the value or contents of a memory location (60). The name does not change during a program, but the contents can be changed as often as necessary. (Contents of memory locations which are referred to by constants cannot be changed.) If 30 were added to the contents in the previous example, the new value stored in Sum could be depicted as

```
┌──────────┐
│    90    │
└──────────┘
   Sum
```

Those symbolic names representing memory locations whose values will be changing must be declared in the **VAR** section of the program (as indicated in Section 2.2); for example,

```
VAR
   Sum : integer;
```

Those that represent memory locations whose values will not be changing must be declared in the **CONST** section.

Assignment Statements

Let's now examine how the contents of variables are manipulated. A value may be put into a memory location with an *assignment statement* in the form of

```
┌─────────────────────────────────────────────────┐
│  ⟨variable name⟩ := ⟨value (or expression)⟩ ;    │
└─────────────────────────────────────────────────┘
```

where "variable name" is the name of the memory location. For example, if Sum had no value, then

```
   Sum := 30;
```

changes

```
┌──────┐        ┌──────┐
│  ?   │   to   │  30  │
└──────┘        └──────┘
  Sum             Sum
```

The syntax diagram for this is

Some important rules concerning assignment statements are

1. The assignment is always made from right to left (←).
2. The syntax for assigning requires a colon followed immediately by an equal sign (:=).

3. Only one variable can be on the left of the assignment symbol.
4. Constants cannot be on the left of the assignment symbol.
5. The expression may be a constant, a constant expression, a variable that has previously been assigned a value, or a combination of variables and constants.
6. Values on the right side of the assignment symbol are not changed by the assignment.
7. The variable and expression must match in data type.

Two common errors that beginners make are trying to assign from left to right and forgetting the colon when using an assignment statement.

Repeated assignments can be made. For example, if Sum is an integer variable, the statements

```
Sum := 50;
Sum := 70;
Sum := 100;
```

produce first 50, then 70, and finally 100 as shown.

```
50 70 100
    Sum
```

In this sense, memory is destructive in that it retains only the last value assigned.

Pascal variables are symbolic addresses that can hold values. When a variable is declared, the type of values it will store must be specified (declared). Storing a value of the wrong type in a variable leads to a program error. This means that data types must match when using assignment statements: reals must be assigned to **real** variables, integers to **integer** variables, and characters to **char** variables. The only exception is that an integer can be assigned to a **real** variable; however, the integer is then converted to a real. If, for example, Average is a **real** variable and the assignment statement

```
Average := 21;
```

is made, the value is stored as the real 21.0.

Assignments to a character variable require that the constant be enclosed in single quotation marks. For example, if Letter is of type **char** and you want to store the letter C in Letter, use the assignment statement

```
Letter := 'C';
```

This could be pictured as

```
C
Letter
```

Furthermore, only one character can be assigned or stored in a character variable at a time.

To illustrate working with assignment statements, assume that the variable declaration portion of the program is

```
VAR
   Sum : integer;
   Average : real;
   Letter : char;
```

Examples of valid and invalid assignment statements using the variable declarations just declared are shown in Table 3.6.

TABLE 3.6
Assignment statements

Statement	Valid	If Invalid, Reason
`Sum := 50;`	Yes	
`Sum := 10.5;`	No	Data types do not match
`Average := 15.6;`	Yes	
`Average := 33;`	Yes	
`Letter := 'A';`	Yes	
`Letter := 'HI';`	No	Not a single character
`Letter := 20;`	No	Data types do not match
`Letter := 'Z';`	Yes	
`Letter := A;`	?	Valid if A is a variable or constant of type **char**
`Sum := 7;`	Yes	
`Letter := '7';`	Yes	
`Letter := 7;`	No	Data types do not match
`Sum := '7';`	No	Data types do not match

Expressions

Actual use of variables in a program is usually more elaborate than what we have just seen. Variables may be used in any manner that does not violate their type declarations. This includes both arithmetic operations and assignment statements. For example, if Score1, Score2, Score3, and Average are **real** variables,

```
Score1 := 72.3;
Score2 := 89.4;
Score3 := 95.6;
Average := (Score1 + Score2 + Score3) / 3.0;
```

is a valid fragment of code.

Let's now consider the problem of accumulating a total. Assuming NewScore and Total are integer variables, the following code is valid.

```
Total := 0;
NewScore := 5;
Total := Total + NewScore;
NewScore := 7;
Total := Total + NewScore;
```

As this code is executed, the values of memory locations for Total and NewScore could be depicted as

	Total	NewScore
`Total := 0;`	0	
`NewScore := 5;`	0	5
`Total := Total + NewScore;`	5	5
`NewScore := 7;`	5	7
`Total := Total + NewScore;`	12	7

Output

Variables and variable expressions can be used when creating output. When used in a **writeln** statement, they perform the same function as a constant. For example, if the assignment statement

```
Age := 5;
```

has been made, these two statements

```
writeln (5);
writeln (Age);
```

produce the same output. If Age1, Age2, Age3, and Sum are integer variables and the assignments

```
Age1 := 21;
Age2 := 30;
Age3 := 12;
Sum := Age1 + Age2 + Age3;
```

are made,

```
writeln ('The sum is ', 21 + 30 + 12);
writeln ('The sum is ', Age1 + Age2 + Age3);
writeln ('The sum is ', Sum);
```

all produce the same output.

Formatting variables and variable expressions in **writeln** statements follows the same rules that were presented in Chapter 2 for formatting constants. The statements needed to write the sum of the problem we just saw in a field width of four are

```
writeln ('The sum is ', (21 + 30 + 12):4);
writeln ('The sum is ', (Age1 + Age2 + Age3):4);
writeln ('The sum is ', Sum:4);
```

■ **EXAMPLE 3.1**

Suppose you want a program to print data about the cost of three textbooks and the average price of the books. The variable declaration section could include:

```
VAR
   MathText, BioText,
   CompSciText,
   Total, Average : real;
```

A portion of the program could be

```
MathText := 23.45;
BioText := 27.50;
CompSciText := 19.95;
Total := MathText + BioText + CompSciText;
Average := Total / 3;
```

The output could be created by

```
writeln;
writeln ('Text              Price');
writeln ('----              -----');
writeln;
writeln ('Math', MathText:18:2);
writeln ('Biology', BioText:15:2);
writeln ('CompSci', CompSciText:15:2);
writeln;
```

```
writeln ('Total', Total:17:2);
writeln;
writeln ('The average price is', Average:7:2);
```

The output would be

```
Text              Price
----              -----

Math              23.95
Biology           27.50
CompSci           19.95

Total             71.40

The average price is   23.80
```

Software Engineering

The communication aspect of software engineering can be simplified by judicious choices of meaningful identifiers. Systems programmers must be aware that over time many others will need to read and analyze the code. Some extra time spent thinking about and using descriptive identifiers provides great timesavings during the testing and maintenance phases. Code that is written using descriptive identifiers is referred to as *self-documenting code.*

Exercises 3.2

1. Assume the variable declaration section of a program is

```
VAR
  Age, IQ : integer;
  Income : real;
```

Indicate which of the following are valid assignment statements. Give the reason for each that is invalid.

a. `Age := 21;`

b. `IQ := Age + 100;`

c. `IQ := 120.5;`

d. `Age + IQ := 150;`

e. `Income := 22000;`

f. `Income := 100 * (Age + IQ);`

g. `Age := IQ / 3;`

h. `IQ := 3 * Age;`

2. Write and run a test program to illustrate what happens when values of one data type are assigned to variables of another type.

3. Suppose A, B, and Temp have been declared as integer variables. Indicate the contents of A and B at the end of each sequence of statements.

```
a. A := 5;          b. A := 31;
   B := -2;            B := 26;
   A := A + B;         Temp := A;
   B := B - A;         A := B;
                       B := Temp;
```

c.
```
A := 0;
B := 7;
A := A + B Mod 2 * (-3);
B := B + 4 * A;
```

d.
```
A := -8;
B := 3;
Temp := A + B;
A := 3 * B;
B := A;
Temp := Temp + A + B;
```

4. Suppose X and Y are real variables and the assignments

```
X := 121.3;
Y := 98.6;
```

have been made. What **writeln** statements would cause the following output?

a. The value of X is   121.3

b. The sum of X and Y is   219.9

c.
```
X =       121.3
Y =        98.6
      -----
Total = 219.9
```

5. Assume the variable declaration section of a program is

```
VAR
   Age, Height : integer;
   Weight : real;
   Gender : char;
```

What output would be created by the following program fragment?

```
Age := 23;
Height := 73;
Weight := 186.5;
Gender := 'M';
writeln ('Gender', Gender:10);
writeln ('Age', Age:14);
writeln ('Height', Height:11, ' inches');
writeln ('Weight', Weight:14:1, ' lbs');
```

6. Write a complete program that allows you to add five integers and then print

a. The integers.

b. Their sum.

c. Their average.

7. Assume Ch and Age have been appropriately declared. What output is produced by the following?

```
Ch := 'M';
Age := 21;
writeln ('*****************************':40);
writeln ('*':11, '*':29);
write ('*':11, 'Name':7, 'Age':9);
writeln ('Gender':6, '*':4);
writeln ('*':11, '____':7, '___':9, '___':9, '*':4);
writeln;
write ('*':11, 'Jones':8, Age:8, Ch:9, '*':4);
writeln;
writeln ('*':11, '*':29);
writeln ('*************************************':40);
```

8. Assume the variable declaration section of a program is

```
VAR
   Weight1, Weight2 : integer;
   AverageWeight : real;
```

and the following assignment statements have been made:

```
Weight1 := 165;
Weight2 := 174;
AverageWeight := (Weight1 + Weight2) / 2;
```

a. What output would be produced by the following section of code?

```
writeln ('Weight');
writeln ('_____');
writeln;
writeln (Weight1);
writeln (Weight2);
writeln;
writeln ('The average weight is',
(Weight1 + Weight2) / 2);
```

b. Write a segment of code to produce the following output (use AverageWeight).

```
        Weight
        ------

        165
        174
        ---
Total   339
```

```
The average weight is 169.5 pounds.
```

9. Assume the variable declaration section of a program is

```
VAR
   Letter : char;
```

and the following assignment has been made:

```
Letter := 'A';
```

What output is produced from the following segment of code?

```
writeln ('This reviews string formatting,':40);
writeln ('When a letter', Letter, 'is used,');
writeln ('Oops!':14, 'I forgot to format.':20);
writeln ('When a letter':22, Letter:2, 'is used,':9);
writeln ('it is a string of length one.':38);
```

■ ■ ■ ■

OBJECTIVES

- to be able to use **read** and **readln** to get data for a program
- to understand the difference between interactive input and batch input
- to understand the concept of end-of-line markers
- to understand the concept of end-of-file markers

Earlier, "running a program" was subdivided into the three general categories of getting the data, manipulating it appropriately, and printing the results. Our work thus far has centered on creating output and manipulating data. We are now going to focus on how to get data for a program.

Input Statements

Data for a program are usually obtained from an input device, which can be a keyboard, terminal, card reader, disk, or tape. When such data are obtained, the standard file **input** must be included in the file list of the program heading. (Some interactive systems use a different method. Check with your instructor.) Your program heading will (probably) have the form

PROGRAM ⟨program name⟩ (**input, output**);

The Pascal statements used to get data are **read** and **readln;** they are analogous to **write** and **writeln** for output. General forms for these input statements are

> **read** (⟨variable name⟩);
> **read** (⟨variable 1⟩, ⟨variable 2⟩, . . . , ⟨variable *n*⟩);
> **readln** (⟨variable name⟩);
> **readln** (⟨variable 1⟩, ⟨variable 2⟩, . . . , ⟨variable *n*⟩);
> **readln;**

A simplified syntax diagram for **read** and **readln** statements is

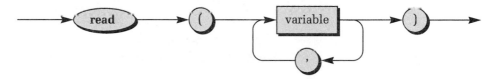

See Appendix 3 for a more detailed diagram.

When **read** or **readln** is used to get data, the value of the data item is stored in the indicated memory location. Data read into a program must match the type of variable in the variable list. To illustrate, if a variable declaration section includes

```
VAR
   Age : integer;
   Wage : real;
```

and the data items are

```
21          5.25
```

then

```
read (Age, Wage);
```

results in

21		5.25
Age		Wage

[T] To illustrate the difference between **read** and **readln,** we must first learn about a line of data. Whether from the terminal or from a text file, numeric data items are entered on a line with blanks separating items. When you are through creating a data line, you press "return" on the keyboard. This causes the computer to create a special symbol it recognizes as an *end-of-line marker* **(eoln).** If we use the symbol ▮ to represent this, two lines of integer data could be shown by

> 89 93 78 ▮

> 95 84 100 68 ▮

When either **read** or **readln** is first used, a data pointer is positioned at the beginning of the first (perhaps only) line.

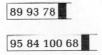 line 1

Pointer here

 line 2

As data items are read using **read,** the pointer moves to the first position past the last data item read. Thus, if Score1 and Score2 are declared as integer variables, the statement

```
read (Score1, Score2);
```

results in

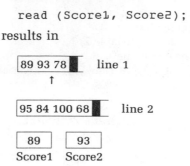

89 93 78 ▮   line 1
↑

95 84 100 68 ▮   line 2

┌────┐   ┌────┐
│ 89 │   │ 93 │
└────┘   └────┘
Score1   Score2

The **readln** statement works in the same manner, with an exception: after it has read a value for each variable in its list, it causes the pointer to skip over data items remaining on that line and go to the beginning of the next line. Thus, if the pointer is at the beginning of line 1,

```
readln (Score1, Score2);
```

results in

89 93 78 ▮   line 1

95 84 100 68 ▮   line 2
↑

┌────┐   ┌────┐
│ 89 │   │ 93 │
└────┘   └────┘
Score1   Score2

Variables in the variable list of **read** and **readln** can be listed singly or in any combination that does not result in a type conflict when data are read. For example, for the data line

89 93 78 ▮
↑

```
read (Score1, Score2);
```

could be replaced by

```
read (Score1);
read (Score2);
```

Interactive Input

If you are working on a system where input is expected from a keyboard—*interactive input*—**read** or **readln** causes the program to halt and wait for data items to be typed. After you enter the data and press "return," an end-of-line marker is placed after the last data entered. In this text, we use **readln** when getting input interactively. The difference between **read** and **readln** is that **readln** causes a line feed. This has two effects. First, all remaining (unread) data items on a line are skipped. Second, output from **write** or **writeln** statements will start on the next line rather than the same line. For example, when working interactively, consider the statements shown below:

```
read (A);
write (A);
```

and

```
readln (A);
write (A);
```

When these are executed and you enter the number 45 and press "return," the first may cause

```
4545
```

to appear on the screen and the second causes

```
45
45
```

if pressing "return" causes a line feed.

Consider the following program that will find the average of three integers.

```
PROGRAM Average (input, output);

CONST
  Skip = ' ';

VAR
  Num1, Num2, Num3 : integer;
  Aver : real;

BEGIN
  readln (Num1, Num2, Num3);
  Aver := (Num1 + Num2 + Num3) / 3;
  writeln;
  writeln (Skip:10, 'The numbers are', Num1:4, Num2:4, Num3:4);
  writeln;
  writeln (Skip:10, 'Their average is', Aver:8:2);
  writeln
END.
```

When this program is run, execution will halt at the line

```
readln (Num1, Num2, Num3);
```

and a *prompt* will appear on the screen. In this text, these prompts will be shown as ▯. At this point, you must enter at least three integers and press "return" (or some sequence of integers and "return" until at least three numbers are read in as data items). The remaining part of the program will then be executed and the output (using 20, −14, and 81 as input)

```
The numbers are 20 -14 81
Their average is   29.00
```

will be printed.

Normally, interactive programs require a prompting message to the user so the user can know what to do when the prompt is on the screen. For example, the previous example could be modified by the line

```
writeln ('Please enter 3 integers and press <RETURN>.');
```

and when the program is run, the screen will display the message

```
Please enter 3 integers and press <RETURN>.
?
```

Clearly stated screen messages to the person running a program are what make a program *user-friendly*. For long messages or several lines of output, you can use

---

A NOTE OF INTEREST

Ethics and Computer Science

Ethical issues in computer science are rapidly gaining public attention. As evidence, consider the following article from the *Washington Post*.

Should law-enforcement agencies be allowed to use computers to help them determine whether a person ought to be jailed or allowed out on bond? Should the military let computers decide when and on whom nuclear weapons should be used?

While theft and computer viruses have not gone away as industry problems, a group of 30 computer engineers and ethicists who gathered in Washington recently agreed that questions about the proper use of computers is taking center stage. At issue is to what degree computers should be allowed to make significant decisions that human beings normally make.

Already, judges are consulting computers, which have been programmed to predict how certain personality types will behave. Judges are basing their decisions more on what the computer tells them than on their own analysis of the arrested person's history. Computers are helping doctors decide treatments for patients. They played a major role in the July 1988 shooting of the Iranian jetliner by the USS Vincennes, and they are the backbone of this country's Strategic Defense Initiative ("Star Wars").

Representatives from universities, IBM Corp., the Brookings Institution, and several Washington theological seminaries [recently discussed] what they could do to build a conscience in the computer field.

The computer industry has been marked by "creativity and drive for improvement and advance-

ment," not by ethical concerns, said Robert Melford, chairman of the computing-ethics subcommittee of the Institute of Electrical and Electronics Engineers.

Computer professionals, Melford said, often spend much of their time in solitude, separated from the people affected by their programs who could provide valuable feedback.

Unlike hospitals, computer companies and most organized computer users have no staff ethicists or ethics committees to ponder the consequences of what they do. Few businesses have written policies about the proper way to govern computers. But there is evidence that technical schools, at least, are beginning to work an ethical component into their curricula.

[For example, in recent years,] all computer engineering majors at Polytechnic University in Brooklyn [have been required to take a course in ethics.] The Massachusetts Institute of Technology is considering mandating five years of study instead of the current four to include work in ethics.

Affirmation that such questions should be addressed by computer scientists is contained in the 1991 curriculum guidelines of the Association for Computing Machinery, Inc. These guidelines state that "Undergraduates should also develop an understanding of the historical, social, and ethical context of the discipline and the profession." You will see further Notes of Interest on this area of critical concern later in this book.

```
writeln ('Press <RETURN> to continue.');
readln;
```

as a complete statement to halt execution. When you press "return," the program will continue.

Note: Some users of this textbook will be working in an interactive environment, others will not be. Consequently, both interactive and noninteractive examples are included. A logo of a computer screen accompanies each interactive example.

■ **EXAMPLE 3.2**

Pythagorean triples are sets of three integers that satisfy the Pythagorean theorem. That is, integers a, b, and c such that $a^2 + b^2 = c^2$. 3, 4, 5 is such a triple because $3^2 + 4^2 = 5^2$. Formulas for generating Pythagorean triples are

$a = m^2 - n^2$, $b = 2mn$, and $c = m^2 + n^2$ where m and n are positive integers such that $m > n$. The following interactive program allows the user to enter values for m and n and then have the Pythagorean triple printed.

```
PROGRAM PythagoreanTriple (input, output);

VAR
  M, N, A, B, C : integer;

BEGIN
  writeln ('Enter a positive integer and press <RETURN>.');
  readln (N);
  write ('Enter a positive integer greater than ', N);
  writeln (' and press <RETURN>.');
  readln (M);
  A := (M * M) - (N * N);
  B := 2 * M * N;
  C := (M * M) + (N * N);
  writeln;
  writeln ('For M = ', M, ' and N = ', N);
  writeln ('the Pythagorean triple is ', A:5, B:5, C:5)
END.
```

Sample runs of this program (using data 1,2 and 2,5) produce the following:

```
Enter a positive integer and press <RETURN>.
?1
Enter a positive integer greater than 1 and press <RETURN>.
?2

For M = 2 and N = 1
the Pythagorean triple is     3    4    5

Enter a positive integer and press <RETURN>.
?2
Enter a positive integer greater than 2 and press <RETURN>.
?5
For M = 5 and N = 2
the Pythagorean triple is    21   20   29
```

Batch Input

Batch processing is a technique for executing programs and data without user interaction with the computer. If you are working on a system that uses batch processing, input data will have been previously entered in a file created by you or the instructor. Input in this form is referred to as *batch* or *stream input* and can be envisioned by lines listed consecutively separated by end-of-line markers. For example,

```
93 84 95 ▮ 87 80 73 91 ▮
```

represents two lines of data with three integers on the first line and four integers on the second line. When data are read from such an input file, a pointer is moved as previously indicated. One additional feature should be noted when using batch input. Since all data lines will have been previously entered, a special marker is inserted by the machine to indicate the end of the input file. This is referred to as an *end-of-file marker* (**eof**) and is represented in this text by the symbol ■. This is placed immediately following the last end-of-line marker. Thus, the previous input file would be illustrated by

Reading Numeric Data

Reading numeric data into a program is reasonably straightforward. At least one blank must be used to separate items on each data line and, since leading blanks are ignored, the statement

```
read (<variable name>);
```

will cause the next numeric value to be stored in the appropriate memory location. An end-of-line marker will be read as a blank, so even if the next item is on another line, it will be located and stored as desired. In each case, the pointer will be advanced as before.

Some caution should be exercised when both reals and integers are in the input file. As long as the variable data type matches the numeric data type, there will be no problem. Thus, if the variable declaration section is

```
VAR
  A : integer;
  X : real;
```

and a data line is

read (X, A) causes

```
  97.5        86
   X           A
```

However, **read** (A, X) would result in an error because A is of type **integer** and 97 is read into A. The pointer is then positioned at the decimal.

An attempt to read a value into X may then result in a type mismatch error.

One exception to type mismatch errors is that an integer value can be read into a variable of type **real**. However, it is then stored as a **real** and must be used accordingly.

Character Sets

Before we look at reading character data, we need to examine the way in which character data are stored. In the **char** data type, each character is associated with an integer. Thus, the sequence of characters is associated with a sequence of integers. The particular sequence used by a machine for this purpose is referred to as the *collating sequence* for that *character set.* Two such sequences currently in use are

1. American Standard Code for Information Interchange (ASCII) and
2. Extended Binary Coded Decimal Interchange Code (EBCDIC).

Each collating sequence contains an ordering of the characters in a character set and is listed in Appendix 4. For programs in this text, we use the ASCII code. As shown in Table 3.7, fifty-two of these characters are letters, ten are digits, and the rest are special characters.

TABLE 3.7
ASCII code

ƀ ! " # $ % & ' ( ) * + , − . / 0 1 2 3 4 5 6 7 8 9 : ; < = > ? @
A B C D E F G H I J K L M N O P Q R S T U V W X Y Z [\ ] ^ — '
a b c d e f g h i j k l m n o p q r s t u v w x y z {	} ~

Note: Of the special characters, ƀ is the symbol to denote a blank.

Reading Character Data

Reading characters is much different from reading numeric data. When using standard Pascal, the following features apply to reading character data from an input file.

1. Only one character can be read at a time.
2. Each blank is a separate character.
3. Each end-of-line marker is read as a blank.
4. If the pointer is positioned at a numeric data item and you read a character variable, the digit indicated by the pointer will be read as a character.
5. After the character has been read, the pointer is advanced one position.

To illustrate the features of reading character data, assume a variable declaration of

```
VAR
   Ch1, Ch2, Ch3 : char;
```

and a stream input of

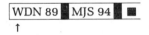

with the pointer positioned as indicated. Further, assume Ch1, Ch2, and Ch3 have not been assigned values, nor have they had values read into them. They can be visualized as

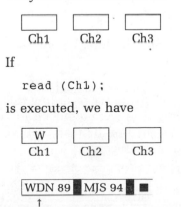

If

```
read (Ch1);
```

is executed, we have

W		
Ch1	Ch2	Ch3

If the line of code

```
read (Ch2, Ch3);
```

is then executed, we have

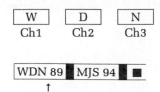

If the next **read** command in the program is

```
read (Ch1, Ch2, Ch3);
```

we obtain

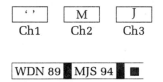

Since we are reading character variables, the blank is read as a character and the number 89 is read as two characters, '8' and '9'. Since these are read as characters, you cannot perform arithmetic operations with them.

The pointer is now positioned at an end-of-line marker and you may think that the three characters (MJS) can now be read by

```
read (Ch1, Ch2, Ch3);
```

However, this is incorrect because the end-of-line marker is read as a blank and you actually obtain

Some computers add a blank at the end of a data line in order to have an even number of character positions. Thus, you may want to have a data line be

but when you enter the line, it could be stored as

WN 89

Check with your instructor regarding this feature of your machine.

When reading data from a stream input, you eventually get the pointer positioned at the end-of-file marker. If you attempt to read more data, you may get an error message such as

```
PROGRAM TERMINATED AT LINE 5 IN PROGRAM PRAC.
TRIED TO READ DATA 41 PAST EOS/EOF.
                                --- PRAC ---
            A =        UNDEF
```

When you see such a message, check your **read** statements to see if you are trying to read past the end-of-file marker.

The material in Table 3.8 indicates what happens when an attempt is made to read data into a variable location where the data type is different from the data in the file.

TABLE 3.8
Results of reading data of varying types

Variable Type	Attempt to Read	Result
integer	integer	Will read as expected
	real	Will read integer portion of real
	character	Error message (unless the character is a blank)
real	integer	Will read the integer and convert it to a real
	real	Will read as expected
	character	Error message (unless the character is a blank)
char	integer	Will read one position as a character and advance the pointer one position
	real	Will read one position as a character and advance the pointer one position
	character	Will read as expected

Exercises 3.3

1. What must be included in the program heading in order to get data from an input file?

2. Write a test program that will enable you to determine whether or not your computer adds a blank at the end of a data line in order to have an even number of positions per line. (Hint: **read** and **write** characters from short lines of data.)

3. What is the difference between an end-of-line marker and an end-of-file marker?

4. Assume that a stream input is as illustrated

```
18  19M  −14.3  JO  142.1F  ■
```

and the variable declaration section of the program is

```
VAR
  A, B : integer;
  X, Y : real;
  Ch : char;
```

What output would be produced from each of the following segments of code? (Assume that the pointer is positioned at the beginning for each problem.)

a. ```
read (A);
read (B, Ch);
writeln (A:5, B:5, Ch:5);
```

b. ```
read (Ch);
write (Ch:10);
readln (Ch);
writeln (Ch);
read (Ch);
writeln (Ch:10);
```

```
c. read (A, B, Ch, X);
   writeln (A, B, Ch, X);
   writeln (A:5, B:5, Ch:5, X:10:2);
   read (Ch);
   writeln (Ch:5);
d. readln;
   read (Ch, Ch);
   readln (Y);
   writeln (Ch:5, Y:10:2);
```

5. Using the same stream input and variable declaration section as in Exercise 4, indicate the contents of each variable location and the position of the pointer after each segment of code is executed. Assume that the pointer is positioned at the beginning for each problem.

   a. `read (Ch, A);`

   b. `readln (Ch, A);`

   c. `readln;`

   d. `readln;`
   `readln;`

   e. `readln (A, B, Ch, X);`

   f. `read (A, B, Ch, Y);`

   g. `readln (A, Ch);`
   `readln (Ch, Ch, B);`

   h. `read (A, B, Ch, X, Ch);`

6. Using the same stream input and variable declaration section as in Exercise 4, indicate which of the following will produce an error. For those that do, explain why an error occurs.

   a. `read (X, Y);`

   b. `readln (A);`
   `read (B);`

   c. `readln (Ch);`
   `readln (Ch);`
   `readln (Ch);`

   d. `read (X, A, Ch, B, Ch);`

   e. `readln;`
   `read (Ch, Ch, A, Ch, B);`

7. Write a complete program that will read your initials and five test scores. Your program should then compute your test average and print out all information in a reasonable form with suitable messages.

■ ■ ■ ■

■ 3.4
Using Constants

OBJECTIVES
- to be aware of appropriate use of constants
- to be able to use constants in programs
- to be able to format constants

The word "constant" has several interpretations. In this section, it will refer to values defined in the **CONST** definition subsection of a program. Recall that a Pascal program consists of a program heading, a declaration section, and an executable section. The declaration section contains a variable declaration subsection, discussed in Section 3.2, and possibly a constant definition subsection. When both are used, the **CONST** subsection must precede the **VAR** subsection. We will now examine uses for constants defined in the **CONST** subsection.

Defined Constants and Space Shuttle Computing

An excellent illustration of the utilization of defined constants in a program was given by J. F. ("Jack") Clemons, former manager of avionics flight software development and verification for the space shuttle on-board computers. In an interview with David Gifford, editor for *Communications of the ACM*, Clemons was asked: "Have you tried to restructure the software so that it can be changed easily?"

His response was, "By changing certain data constants, we can change relatively large portions of the software on a mission-to-mission basis. For example, we've designed the software so that characteristics like atmospheric conditions on launch day or different lift-off weights can be loaded as initial constants into the code. This is important when there are postponements or last-minute payload changes that invalidate the original inputs."

Rationale for Uses

There are many reasons to use constants in a program. If a number is to be used frequently, the programmer may wish to give it a descriptive name in the **CONST** definition subsection and then use the descriptive name in the executable section, thus making the program easier to read. For example, if a program included a segment that computed a person's state income tax, and the state tax rate was 6.25 percent of taxable income, the **CONST** section might include:

```
CONST
   StateTaxRate = 0.0625;
```

This defines both the value and type for StateTaxRate. In the executable portion of the program, the statement

```
StateTax := Income * StateTaxRate;
```

computes the state tax owed. Or suppose you wanted a program to compute areas of circles. Depending upon the accuracy you desire, you could define pi "π" as

```
CONST
   Pi = 3.14159;
```

You could then have a statement in the executable section such as

```
Area := Pi * Radius * Radius;
```

where Area and Radius are appropriately declared variables.

Perhaps the most important use of constants is for values that are currently fixed but subject to change for subsequent runs of the program. If these are defined in the **CONST** section, they can be used throughout the program. If the value changes later, only one change need be made to keep the program current. This prevents the need to locate all uses of a constant in a program. Some examples might be

```
CONST
   MinimumWage = 4.25;
   SpeedLimit = 65;
   Price = 0.75;
   StateTaxRate = 0.0625;
```

Constants can also be used to name character strings that occur frequently in program output. Suppose a program needs to print two different company names. Instead of typing the names each time they are needed, the following definition could be used.

```
CONST
   Company1 = 'First National Bank of America';
   Company2 = 'Metropolitan Bank of New York';
```

Company1 and Company2 could then be used in **writeln** statements.

Another situation could call for a constant defined for later repeated use in making output more attractive. Included could be constants for underlining and for separating sections of output. Some definitions could be

```
CONST
   Underline = '_____';
   Splats = '**********************************';
```

To separate the output with asterisks, the statement

```
writeln (Splats, Splats);
```

could be used. In a similar fashion

```
writeln (Underline);
```

could be used for underlining.

Software Engineering

The appropriate use of constants is consistent with principles of software engineering. Communication between teams of programmers is enhanced when program constants have been agreed upon. Each team should have a list of these constants for use as they work on their part of the system.

The maintenance phase of the software system life cycle is also aided by use of defined constants. Clearly, a large payroll system is dependent upon being able to perform computations that include deductions for federal tax, state tax, FICA, Medicare, health insurance, retirement options, and so on. If appropriate constants are defined for these deductions, system changes are easily made as necessary. For example, the current salary limit for deducting FICA taxes is $53,400. Since this amount changes regularly, one could define

```
CONST
   FICALimit = 53400.00;
```

Program maintenance is then simplified by changing the value of this constant as the law changes.

Formatting Constants

Formatting numerical constants is identical to formatting reals and integers as discussed in Section 2.3. If the constant definition section contains

```
CONST
   Pi = 3.14159;
   SpeedLimit = 55;
```

then

```
writeln ('Pi is used as', Pi:10:5);
writeln ('Speed limit is', SpeedLimit:4);
```

produces

```
Pi is used as   3.14159
Speed limit is  55
```

When character strings are defined as constants, a single positive integer can be used for formatting. This integer establishes the field width for the character string and right justifies the character string in the output field. For example, suppose the constant definition section includes

```
CONST
  Company1 = 'First National Bank of America';
  Company2 = 'Metropolitan Bank of New York';
  Underline = '_____';
  Splats = '******************************************';
```

If the program contains the program fragment

```
writeln;
writeln (Splats:50);
writeln;
writeln (Company1:45);
writeln (Underline:45);
writeln;
writeln (Company2:44);
writeln (Underline:45);
writeln;
writeln (Splats:50);
```

these statements produce the output

```
******************************************

        First National Bank of America
        ------------------------------
        Metropolitan Bank of New York
        ------------------------------

******************************************
```

Exercises 3.4

1. One use of constants is for values that are used throughout a program but are subject to change over time (minimum wage, speed limit, and so on). List at least five items in this category that were not mentioned in this section.

2. Assume the **CONST** definition section of a program is

```
CONST
  CourseName = 'CPS 150';
  TotalPts = 100;
  Underline = '_____';
```

We want output as follows:

```
COURSE:         CPS 150      TEST #1
------------------------------------------

TOTAL POINTS    100
```

Fill in the appropriate formatting positions in the following **writeln** statements to produce the indicated output.

```
writeln ('COURSE:':7, CourseName:    , 'TEST #1':13);
writeln (Underline:    );
writeln;
writeln ('TOTAL POINTS':12, TotalPts:    );
```

3. Using the same **CONST** definition section as in Exercise 2, what output is produced by the following segment of code?

```
writeln;
writeln (CourseName:10, 'TEST #2':20);
writeln (Underline:40);
writeln;
writeln ('Total points':16, TotalPts:15);
writeln ('My score':12, 93:19);
writeln ('Class average':17, 82.3:14:1);
```

4. Use the constant definition section to define appropriate constants for the following:

a. Your name.

b. Today's date.

c. Your social security number.

d. Your age.

e. The name of your school.

f. The number of students in your class.

g. The average age of students in your class.

h. The average hourly wage of steelworkers.

i. The price of a new car.

■ ■ ■ ■

■ 3.5
Standard Functions

OBJECTIVES

- to understand reasons for having standard functions
- to be able to use standard functions in a program
- to be able to use appropriate data types for arguments of standard functions

Some standard operations required by programmers are squaring numbers, finding square roots of numbers, rounding numbers, and truncating numbers. Because these operations are so basic, Pascal provides *standard (built-in) functions* for them. Different versions of Pascal and other programming languages have differing standard functions available, so you should always check which functions can be used. Appendix 2 sets forth those available in most versions of Pascal.

A function can be used in a program if it appears in the following form.

⟨function name⟩ (⟨argument⟩)

where *argument* is a value or variable with an assigned value. When a function is listed in this manner, it is said to be *called* or *invoked*. A function is invoked by using it in a program statement. If, for example, you want to square the integer 5,

```
sqr(5)
```

produces the desired result.

The syntax diagram for this is

Many functions operate on numbers, starting with a given number and returning some associated value. Table 3.9 shows five standard functions, each with its argument type, data type of return, and an explanation of the value returned.

TABLE 3.9
Numeric function calls and return types

Function Call	Argument Type	Type of Return	Function Value
sqr(argument)	**real** or **integer**	Same as argument	Returns the square of the argument
sqrt(argument)	**real** or **integer** (nonnegative)	**real**	Returns the square root of the argument
abs(argument)	**real** or **integer**	Same as argument	Returns absolute value of the argument
round(argument)	**real**	**integer**	Returns value rounded to the nearest integer
trunc(argument)	**real**	**integer**	Returns value truncated to an integer

Several examples of specific function expressions together with the value returned by each expression are depicted in Table 3.10.

TABLE 3.10
Values of function expressions

Expression	Value
sqr(2)	4
sqr(2.0)	4.0
sqr(-3)	9
sqrt(25.0)	5.0
sqrt(25)	5.0
sqrt(0.0)	0.0
sqrt(-2.0)	Not permissible
abs(5.2)	5.2
abs(-3.4)	3.4
abs(-5)	5
round(3.78)	4
round(8.50)	9
round(-4.2)	-4
round(-4.7)	-5
trunc(3.78)	3
trunc(8.5)	8
trunc(-4.2)	-4
trunc(-4.7)	-4

Using Functions

When a function is invoked, it produces a value in much the same way that 3 + 3 produces 6. Thus, use of a function should be treated similarly to using constants or values of an expression. Since function calls are not complete Pascal statements, they must be used within some statement. Typical uses are in assignment statements,

```
X := sqrt(16.0);
```

output statements,

```
writeln (abs(-8):20);
```

or arithmetic expressions

```
X := round(3.78) + trunc(-4.1);
```

Arguments of functions can be expressions, variables, or constants. However, be sure the argument is always appropriate. For example,

```
A := 3.2;
X := sqrt(trunc(A));
```

is appropriate, but

```
A := -3.2;
X := sqrt(trunc(A));
```

produces an error since **trunc**(-3.2) has the value -3 and **sqrt**(-3) is not a valid expression.

The following example illustrates how functions can be used in expressions.

■ EXAMPLE 3.3

Find the value of the following expression:

```
4.2 + round(trunc(2.0 * 3.1) + 5.3) - sqrt(sqr(-4.1));
```

The solution is

```
4.2 + round(trunc(2.0 * 3.1) + 5.3) - sqrt(sqr(-4.1))
                       ↓                       ↓
4.2 +      round(trunc(6.2)      + 5.3) - sqrt(16.81)
                 ↓                            ↓
4.2 +          round(6.0         + 5.3) -      4.1
                           ↓
4.2 +              round(11.3)          -      4.1
                       ↓
4.2 +                  11.0             -      4.1
         ↓
       15.2                             -      4.1
                       ↓
                     11.1
```

■

Character Functions

Ordering a character set requires associating an integer with each character. Data types ordered in some association with the integers are known as *ordinal data types*. Each integer is the ordinal of its associated character. Integers are therefore considered to be an ordinal data type. Character sets are also considered to be an ordinal data type, as shown in Table 3.11. In each case, the ordinal of the character appears to the left of the character.

Using ASCII, as shown in Table 3.11, the ordinal of a capital a ('A') is 65, the ordinal of the character representing the arabic number one ('1') is 49, the ordinal of a blank ('Ƅ') is 32, and the ordinal of a lowercase a ('a') is 97.

Pascal provides several standard functions that have arguments of ordinal type. These are listed in Table 3.12 together with a related function **chr** that returns a character when called.

Again using the ASCII collating sequence shown in Table 3.11, we can determine the value of these functions as shown in Table 3.13.

TABLE 3.11
ASCII ordering of a character set

Ordinal	Character	Ordinal	Character	Ordinal	Character
32	ƀ	64	@	96	`
33	!	65	A	97	a
34	"	66	B	98	b
35	#	67	C	99	c
36	$	68	D	100	d
37	%	69	E	101	e
38	&	70	F	102	f
39	'	71	G	103	g
40	(	72	H	104	h
41	)	73	I	105	i
42	*	74	J	106	j
43	+	75	K	107	k
44	,	76	L	108	l
45	−	77	M	109	m
46	.	78	N	110	n
47	/	79	O	111	o
48	0	80	P	112	p
49	1	81	Q	113	q
50	2	82	R	114	r
51	3	83	S	115	s
52	4	84	T	116	t
53	5	85	U	117	u
54	6	86	V	118	v
55	7	87	W	119	w
56	8	88	X	120	x
57	9	89	Y	121	y
58	:	90	Z	122	z
59	;	91	[	123	{
60	<	92	\	124		
61	=	93	]	125	}
62	>	94	^	126	~
63	?	95	—		

Note: Codes 00−31 and 127 are nonprintable control characters.

TABLE 3.12
Function calls with ordinal arguments or character values

Function Call	Argument Type	Type of Result	Function Value
ord(argument)	Any ordinal type	**integer**	Ordinal corresponding to argument
pred(argument)	Any ordinal type	Same as argument	Predecessor of the argument
succ(argument)	Any ordinal type	Same as argument	Successor of the argument
chr(argument)	**integer**	**char**	Character associated with the ordinal of the argument

Herman Hollerith

Herman Hollerith (1860–1929) was hired by the United States Census Bureau in 1879 at the age of 19. Since the 1880 census was predicted to take a long time to complete (it actually took until 1887), Hollerith was assigned the task of developing a mechanical method of tabulating census data. He introduced his census machine in 1887. It consisted of four parts:

1. a punched paper card that represented data using a special code (Hollerith code),
2. a card punch apparatus,
3. a tabulator that read the punched cards,
4. a sorting machine with 24 compartments.

The punched cards used by Hollerith were the same size as cards still used today.

Using Hollerith's techniques and equipment, the 1890 census tabulation was completed in one-third the time required for the previous census tabulation. This included working with data for twelve million additional people.

Hollerith proceeded to form the Tabulating Machine Company (1896), which supplied equipment to census bureaus in the United States, Canada, and western Europe. After a disagreement with the census director, Hollerith began marketing his equipment in other commercial areas. Hollerith sold his company in 1911. It was later combined with twelve others to form the Computing-Tabulating-Recording Company, a direct ancestor of International Business Machines Corp.

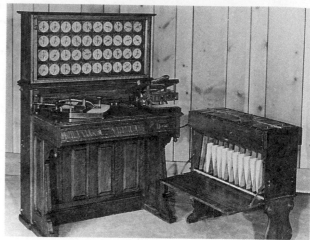

In the meantime, Hollerith's successor at the census bureau, James Powers, redesigned the census machines. He then formed his own company which subsequently became Remington Rand and Sperry Univac.

TABLE 3.13
Values of character functions

Expression	Value
ord('E')	69
ord('9')	57
ord(9)	9
ord('>')	62
pred('N')	M
pred('A')	@
succ('(')	)
succ('!')	"
chr(74)	J
chr(32)	␢
chr(59)	;
chr(114)	r

Variables and variable expressions can be used as arguments for functions. For example, if Ch is a **char** variable and the assignment statement

```
Ch := 'D';
```

is made, then **ord**(Ch) has the value 68.

Let's now consider a short program that allows the use of standard functions **ord, pred, succ,** and **chr.**

```
PROGRAM FunctionTest (output);

VAR
  Ch : char;

BEGIN
  Ch := 'C';
  writeln ('Ord of C is', ord(Ch):5);
  writeln ('Succ of C is', succ(Ch):4);
  writeln ('Pred of C is', pred(Ch):4);
  writeln ('Chr of 67 is', chr(67):4)
END.
```

When this program is run, the output is

```
Ord of C is  67
Succ of C is  D
Pred of C is  B
Chr of 67 is  C
```

You should obtain a complete list of characters available and their respective ordinals for your local system. Note particular features such as when using EBCDIC, **succ**('R') is not 'S'; and when using ASCII, **chr**(n) is nonprintable for $n < 32$ or $n > 126$.

One of the uses for functions **chr** and **ord** is to convert between uppercase and lowercase letters. Closely related is the conversion of a digit (entered as a **char** value) to its integer value. In the next example, we show how to convert an uppercase letter to lowercase. Other conversions are deferred to the exercises.

■ **EXAMPLE 3.4**

Show how functions **chr** and **ord** can be used to convert an uppercase letter to lowercase.

For purposes of illustration, let's assume that our task is to convert the letter 'H' into the letter 'h'. Using the ASCII chart shown in Table 3.11, we first note that the ordinal of 'H' is 72. We subtract the ordinal of 'A' from this to obtain

```
ord('H') - ord('A')
```

which is

```
72 - 65 - 7
```

We now add the ordinal of 'a' to get

```
ord('H') - ord('A') + ord('a')
```

which yields

```
72 - 65 + 97 = 104
```

This is the ordinal of 'h'. It can be converted to the letter by using **chr.** Thus,

```
chr(ord('H') - ord('A') + ord('a'))
```

produces the letter 'h'.

In general, the following is sufficient for converting from uppercase to lowercase:

```
Lowercase := chr(ord(Uppercase) - ord('A') + ord('a'));
```

Note that if you always use the same ASCII ordering, $-$ord('A') + ord('a') could be replaced by the constant 32. If you choose to do this, it should be done in the **CONST** section. A typical definition is

```
CONST
    UpperToLowerShift = 32;
```

You would then write the Lowercase conversion as

```
Lowercase := chr(ord(Uppercase) + UpperToLowerShift);
```

■   ■

Exercises 3.5

1. Find the value of each of the following expressions:
   a. `abs(-11.2) + sqrt(round(15.51))`
   b. `trunc(abs(-14.2))`
   c. `4 * 11 MOD (trunc(trunc(8.9) / sqrt(16)))`
   d. `sqr(17 DIV 5 * 2)`
   e. `-5.0 + sqrt(5 * 5 - 4 * 6) / 2.0`
   f. `3.1 * 0.2 - abs(-4.2 * 9.0 / 3.0)`

2. Write a test program that illustrates what happens when an inappropriate argument is used with a function. Be sure to include something like **ord**(15.3).

3. Two standard algebraic problems come from the Pythagorean theorem and the quadratic formula. Assume variables a, b, and c have been declared in a program. Write Pascal expressions that allow you to evaluate
   a. the length of the hypotenuse of a right triangle

   $$(\sqrt{a^2 + b^2})$$

   b. both solutions to the quadratic formula

   $$\frac{-b \pm \sqrt{b^2 - 4ac}}{2a}$$

4. Indicate whether the following are valid or invalid expressions. Find the value of those that are valid; explain why the others are invalid.
   a. `-6 MOD (sqrt(16))`
   b. `8 DIV (trunc(sqrt(65)))`
   c. `sqrt(63 MOD 2)`
   d. `abs(-sqrt(sqr(3) + 7))`
   e. `sqrt(16 DIV (-3))`
   f. `sqrt(sqr(-4))`
   g. `round(14.38 * 10) / 10`

5. The standard function **round** permits you to round to the nearest integer. Write an expression that permits you to round the real number X to the nearest tenth.

6. Using ASCII, find the values of each of the following expressions:
   a. `ord(13 + 4 MOD 3)`
   b. `pred(succ('E'))`
   c. `succ(pred('E'))`
   d. `ord(5)`
   e. `ord('5')`
   f. `chr(ord('+'))`
   g. `ord(chr(40))`

7. Assume the variable declaration section of a program is

```
VAR
  X : real;
  A : integer;
  Ch : char;
```

What output is produced by each of the following program fragments?

a. ```
X := -4.3;
writeln (X:6:2, abs(X):6:2, trunc(X):6, round(X):6);
```

b. ```
X := -4.3;
A := abs(round(X));
writeln (ord(A));
writeln (ord('A'));
```

c. ```
Ch := chr(76);
writeln (Ch:5, pred(Ch):5, succ(Ch):5);
```

8. Write a complete program to print each uppercase letter of the alphabet and its ordinal in the collating sequence used by your machine's version of Pascal.

9. Using ASCII, show how each of the following conversions can be made.

a. A lowercase letter converted into its uppercase equivalent.

b. A digit entered as a **char** value into its indicated numeric value.

■ ■ ■ ■

Writing styles and suggestions are gathered for quick reference in the following style tip summary. These tips are intended to stimulate rather than terminate your imagination.

**STYLE TIP**
■ ■ ■ ■ ■ ■ ■ ■ ■ ■ ■

1. Use descriptive identifiers. Words—Sum, Score, Average—are easier to understand than letters—A, B, C or X, Y, Z.

2. Constants can be used to create neat, attractive output. For example,

```
CONST
  Splats = '******************************************';
  Underline = '_____';
  Border = '*                                      *';
```

3. Use the constant definition section to define an appropriately named blank and use it to control line spacing for output. Thus, you could have

```
CONST
  Skip = ' ';
  Indent = ' ';
```

and then output statements could be

```
writeln (Skip:20, <message>, Skip:10, <message>);
```

or

```
writeln (Indent:20, <message>, Skip:10, <message>);
```

4. As you write Pascal statements, use blanks for line spacing within the program. Spacing between words and expressions should resemble typical English usage. Thus,

```
PROGRAM EarlyBird (input, output);
```

is preferable to

```
PROGRAM   EarlyBird   (   input,      output   );
```
```

5. Output of a column of reals should have decimal points in a line.

```
 14.32
181.50
 93.63
```

6. Output can be made more attractive by using columns, left and right margins, underlining, and blank lines.
7. Extra **writelns** at the beginning and end of the executable section will separate desired output from other messages.

```
BEGIN
  writeln;
         .
         .(program body here)
         .
  writeln
END.
```

■ Summary

Key Terms

argument
assignment statement
batch processing
batch (stream) input
character set
collating sequence:
   ASCII, EBCDIC
constant
end-of-file marker **(eof)**
end-of-line marker **(eoln)**

input
integer arithmetic
   operations: +, −, *,
   MOD, DIV
interactive input
invoke (call)
memory location
mixed-mode expression
ordinal data type
overflow

prompt
real arithmetic
   operations: +, −, *, /
self-documenting code
standard (built-in)
   function
underflow
user-friendly
variable

Keywords

abs	**MOD**	**round**
chr	**ord**	**sqr**
DIV	**pred**	**sqrt**
eof	**read**	**succ**
eoln	**readln**	**trunc**

Key Concepts

■ Operations and priorities for data of type **integer** and **real** are summarized as follows:

Data Type	Operations	Priority
integer	*, **MOD, DIV**	1. Evaluate in order from left to right
	+, −,	2. Evaluate in order from left to right
real	*, /	1. Evaluate in order from left to right
	+, −	2. Evaluate in order from left to right

■ Mixed-mode expressions return values of type **real**.
■ Priority for order of operations on mixed-mode expressions is
  1. *, /, **MOD, DIV** in order from left to right
  2. +, − in order from left to right
■ Overflow is caused by a value too large for computing on a particular machine.

- Underflow is caused by a value too small (close to zero) for computing. These numbers are automatically replaced by zero.
- A memory location can have a name which can be used to refer to the contents of the location.
- The name of a memory location is different from the contents of the memory location.
- Self-documenting code is code that is written using descriptive identifiers.
- Assignment statements are used to assign values to memory locations, for example

```
Sum := 30 + 60;
```

- Variables and variable expressions can be used in output statements.
- **read(ln)** is used to get data from an input file; correct form is

  read(ln) (⟨variable name⟩),
  read(ln) (⟨variable 1⟩, ⟨variable 2⟩, . . . , ⟨variable n⟩);

- **read** (⟨variable name⟩) causes a value to be transferred to the variable location and the input file pointer to be advanced to the first position following the data item.
- **readln** is used similarly to **read** except that it causes the input file pointer to advance to the beginning of the next line of data after data have been read.
- End-of-line markers are inserted at the end of each line of data (when "return" is pressed).
- An end-of-file marker is inserted after the end-of-line marker for the last line of data.
- Interactive input expects data items to be entered from the keyboard at appropriate times during execution of the program.
- Batch input expects data to be read from a file previously created.
- Data types for variables in a **read** or **readln** statement should match data items in the input file.
- Appropriate uses for constants in the **CONST** definition section include frequently used numbers; current values subject to change over time, for example, (MinimumWage = 4.25); and character strings for output.
- Character strings are formatted using a single colon.
- Five standard numeric functions available in Pascal are **sqr, sqrt, abs, round,** and **trunc.**
- Functions can be used in assignment statements, for example

```
X := sqrt(16.0);
```

  in output statements

```
writeln (abs(-8):20);
```

  and in arithmetic expressions

```
X := round(3.78) + trunc(-4.1);
```

- Four standard character functions available in Pascal are **ord, pred, succ,** and **chr.**

■ Programming Problems and Projects

Write a complete Pascal program for each of the following problems. Each program should use one or more **read** or **readln** statements to obtain necessary values. For interactive programs, each **read** or **readln** should be preceded by an appropriate prompting message.

1. Susan purchases a computer for $985. The sales tax on the purchase is 5.5 percent. Compute and print the total purchase price.

2. Find and print the area and perimeter of a rectangle that is 4.5 feet long and 2.3 feet wide. Print both rounded to the nearest tenth of a foot.

3. Compute and print the number of minutes in a year.

4. Light travels as $3*10^8$ meters per second. Compute and print the distance that a light beam would travel in one year. (This is called a light year.)

5. The 1927 New York Yankees won 110 games and lost 44. Compute their winning percentage and print it rounded to three decimal places.

6. A 10 kilogram object is traveling at 12 meters per second. Compute and print its momentum (momentum is mass times velocity).

7. Convert 98.0 degrees Fahrenheit to degrees Celsius.

8. Given a positive number, print its square and square root.

9. The Golden Sales Company pays its salespeople $.27 for each item they sell. Given the number of items sold by a salesperson, print the amount of pay due.

10. Given the length and width of a rectangle, print its area and perimeter.

11. The kinetic energy of a moving object is given by the formula:

    $$KE = (1/2)mv^2$$

    Given the mass (m) and the speed (v) of an object, find its kinetic energy.

12. Miss Lovelace wants a program to enable her to balance her checkbook. She wishes to enter a beginning balance, five letters for an abbreviation for the recipient of the check, and the amount of the check. Given this information, write a program that will find the new balance in her checkbook.

13. A supermarket wants to install a computerized weighing system in its produce department. Input to this system will consist of a three-letter identifier for the type of produce, the weight of the produce purchase (in pounds), and the cost per pound of the produce. A typical input screen would be

```
Enter each of the following:

Description <RETURN>
?ABC
Weight <RETURN>
?2.0
Price/lb. <RETURN>
?1.98
```

Print a label showing the input information along with the cost of the purchase. The label should appear as follows:

```
%%%%%%%%%%%%%%%%%%%%%%%%%%%%%%%%%%%%%%%%%%%%%%%%

          Penny Spender Supermarket
              Produce Department

   ITEM        WEIGHT        COST/lb       COST
   ABC         2.0 lb         $1.98        $3.96

              Thank You!

%%%%%%%%%%%%%%%%%%%%%%%%%%%%%%%%%%%%%%%%%%%%%%%%
```

14. The New-Wave Computer Company sells its product, the NW-.
$675. In addition, they sell memory expansion cards for $69.95, disk
drives for $198.50, and software for $34.98 each. Given the number of
memory cards, disk drives, and software packages desired by a customer purchasing an NW-PC, print out a bill of sale that appears as
follows:

```
***************************
     New Wave Computers

    ITEM               COST
 1  NW-PC            $675.00
 2  Memory card       139.90
 1  Disk Drive        198.50
 4  Software          139.92
                     --------
        TOTAL       $1153.32
```

15. Write a test program that allows you to see the characters contained
within the character set of your computer. Given a positive integer,
you can use the **chr** function to determine the corresponding character. On most computers, only integers less than 255 are valid for this.
Also, remember that most character sets contain some unprintable
characters such as ASCII values less than 32. Print your output in the
form:

```
Character number nnn is x.
```

16. Mr. Vigneault, a coach at Shepherd High School, is working on a program that can be used to assist cross-country runners in analyzing
their times. As part of the program, a coach enters elapsed times for
each runner given in units of minutes, seconds, and hundredths. In a
5000 meter (5K) race, elapsed times are entered at the one-mile and
two-mile marks. These elapsed times are then used to compute
"splits" for each part of the race; that is, how long did it take a runner to run each of the three race segments.

Write a complete program that will accept as input three times
given in units of minutes, seconds, and hundredths and then produce
output that includes the split for each segment. Typical input would
be

```
Runner number            234
Mile times:        1    5:34.22
                   2   11:21.67
Finish time:           17:46.85
```

Typical output would be

```
Runner number         234
Split one            5:34.22
Split two            5:47.45
Split three          6:25.18
Finish time         17:46.85
```

17. Many (but not all) instructors in beginning computer science courses
encourage their students to use meaningful identifiers in writing code.
It is natural to wonder to what extent this practice is followed outside
the educational world. Investigate this issue by contacting several programmers who work for nearby companies. Prepare a complete written report of your conversations for distribution to class members. Include charts that summarize your findings.

C H A P T E R 4

Designing and Writing Complete Programs

We are now at the stage where we can begin a thorough look at writing more elaborate programs. Chapter 2 gave us the three basic components of a program: program heading, declaration section, and executable section. Chapter 3 provided some additional tools for use in constructing programs, specifically, the use of variables, input, constants, and standard functions. Before using these ideas to write programs to solve problems, however, we need to look at the method in which programs should be constructed. Oversimplified, but absolutely essential, the idea is to design the program and write code for the program. You should never start writing code to solve a problem until you have an adequately designed solution. In this chapter, we will see how the writing of code follows in a natural fashion from a carefully designed algorithm. We will then look at typical errors, which include both mechanical errors (syntax, declaration, assignment, and so on) and logic errors (why your program doesn't solve the problem).

OBJECTIVES

- to be able to write code from pseudocode
- to be able to use program comments
- to be able to use indenting and blank lines to enhance readability

Writing Code from Pseudocode

The process of writing statements that are part of a program to solve a problem is referred to as writing code. This expression is commonly used and we will use it throughout the text. To illustrate the idea of writing actual code to solve a problem from an algorithm developed using pseudocode, consider the problem of computing your bowling score for an evening. Assume you are to read in three integer scores, compute their average, and print out the scores together with the average. A design for this problem is shown in Figure 4.1.

FIGURE 4.1
Top-down design

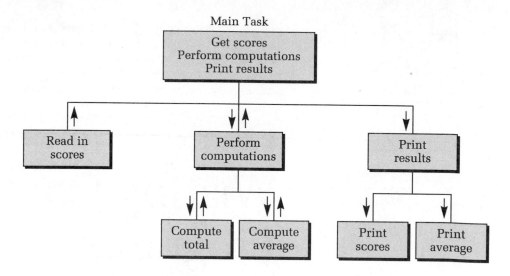

Corresponding pseudocode is

1. Read in Score1, Score2, and Score3
2. Compute
    2.1 let Sum = Score1 + Score2 + Score3
    2.2 let Average = Sum divided by 3
3. Print results
    3.1 print scores
    3.2 print average

Assuming Score1, Score2, and Score3 have been declared as **integer** variables, then

1. Read in Score1, Score2, Score3

is coded as

```
read (Score1, Score2, Score3);
```

Assuming Sum and Average have been declared as **integer** and **real** variables, respectively, then

    2.1 let Sum = Score1 + Score2 + Score3
    2.2 let Average = Sum divided by 3

is coded as

```
Sum := Score1 +Score2 +Score3;
Average := Sum / 3.0;
```

The third line of pseudocode,

3. Print results

requires us to know the desired form for the output. For example, assume we would like the following output produced:

```
Game        Score
----        -----
  1          150
  2          178
  3          162
Your series total is      490
The average score is   163.33
```

Before writing code for this you need to be aware of the significance of being able to produce attractive output. Many students feel that just getting the desired information printed is a sufficient accomplishment. This is not true! It is extremely important that you develop good habits with respect to producing clear, attractive output. Some ideas to consider include:

1. Use **writeln** to produce blank lines where appropriate.
2. Use **writeln** ('--------') with the appropriate number of underscores for underlining.
3. Move the output in from the left margin of the page.
4. Use appropriate left margins and columns for various sections of the output.
5. Use descriptive headings and messages.

Consider the problem of writing code for the problem just described. If the constant definition section includes

```
CONST
  Skip = ' ';
```

the output can be accomplished by using **writeln** statements as follows:

```
writeln (Skip:19, 'Game', Skip:6, 'Score');
writeln (Skip:19, '----', Skip:6, '-----');
writeln (1:22, Score1:11);
writeln (2:22, Score2:11);
writeln (3:22, Score3:11);
writeln;
writeln (Skip:19, 'Your series total is', Sum:8);
writeln (Skip:19, 'The average score is', Average:8:2);
writeln;
```

Each line of pseudocode has now been translated into Pascal statements, so we can write a complete program using five variables (Sum, Score1, Score2, Score3, and Average) to solve the problem. The program follows.

```
PROGRAM Bowling (input, output);

CONST
  Skip = ' ';

VAR
  Score1, Score2, Score3 : integer;
  Sum : integer;
  Average : real;

BEGIN
  read (Score1, Score2, Score3);
  Sum := Score1 + Score2 + Score3;
  Average := Sum / 3.0;
  writeln;
  writeln (Skip:19, 'Game', Skip:6, 'Score');
  writeln (Skip:19, '----', Skip:6, '-----');
  writeln (1:22, Score1:11);
  writeln (2:22, Score2:11);
  writeln (3:22, Score3:11);
  writeln;
  writeln (Skip:19, 'Your series total is', Sum:8);
  writeln (Skip:19, 'The average score is', Average:8:2);
  writeln
END.
```

When this program is run on the computer using input of 150, 178, and 162, we obtain the following output.

```
        Game        Score
        ----        -----
         1           150
         2           178
         3           162

        Your series total is       490
        The average score is    163.33
```

This output is a result of running the program in batch mode. If this were an interactive program, prompts would be required.

Program Comments

Programming languages typically include some provision for putting *comments* in a program. These comments are nonexecutable and are used to document and explain various parts of the program. In Pascal, the form for including comments in a program is either

```
    { . . . comment . . . }
or
    (* . . . comment . . . *)
```

You should check with your instructor to see which form is preferred.

As you write more sophisticated and complex programs, you will see the need for documentation and comments. Let's now go back to **PROGRAM** Bowling and see how comments could be used to enhance readability of the program.

The line of code

```
writeln;
```

causes the printer to skip one line; a line comment could be used to explain this. Thus, the line of code could be

```
writeln;  {  Skip one line  }
```

Since comments are nonexecutable, the output is not affected but the program is now more readable.

A second major use of comments is for program documentation. Suppose your instructor would like you to include the following as part of a program but not as part of the output.

Course number
Assignment number
Due date
Author
Instructor

This documentation is frequently included immediately after (or before) the program heading and could be written as either a single comment or a series of comments. A sample documentation section is

```
{          Course Number           CPS 150          }
{          Assignment              One              }
{          Due Date                Sept. 20         }
{          Author                  Mary Smith       }
{          Instructor              Dr. Jones        }
```

These comments do not affect the output; they merely enhance readability. You should try several ways to include comments within a program. You are limited only by your imagination and your instructor's wishes. Let's now rewrite **PROGRAM** Bowling using a documentation section and other comments within the program.

```
PROGRAM Bowling (input, output);
{          Course Number           CPS 150                              }
{          Assignment              One                                  }
{          Due Date                Sept. 20                             }
{          Author                  Mary Smith                           }
{          Instructor              Dr. Jones                            }
CONST
  Skip = ' ';
VAR
  Score1, Score2, Score3 : integer;
  Sum : integer;
  Average : real;
BEGIN  {  Main program  }
  read (Score1, Score2, Score3);                    {  Get the scores  }
  Sum := Score1 + Score2 + Score3;     {  Perform the computations  }
  Average := Sum / 3.0;
  writeln;
  writeln (Skip:19, 'Game', Skip:6, 'Score');       {  Print heading  }
  writeln (Skip:19, '----:, Skip:6, '-----');
  writeln (1:22, Score1:11);                        {  Print the results  }
  writeln (2:22, Score2:11);
  writeln (3:22, Score3:11);
  writeln;
  writeln (Skip:19, 'Your series total is', Sum:8);
  writeln (Skip:19, 'The average score is', Average:8:2);
  writeln
END.  {  of main program  }
```

Program Style

When writing a program, a major point to remember is to make your program easy to read. Three commonly used methods for doing this are indenting sections of code, using blank lines, and using program comments.

First, indenting is used to identify sections of code and should roughly correspond to the indenting implied by pseudocode. No standard exists regarding the number of spaces to use for indenting. However, we find that one space makes programs difficult to read, and four or more spaces sometimes does not leave sufficient space for complicated programs. All sample programs in this text will use two spaces for indenting.

Many programmers use the leftmost column for the reserved words **PROGRAM, CONST, VAR, BEGIN,** and **END** where **BEGIN** and **END** denote the start and finish of the executable portion of the program. Other statements are indented at least two spaces. This does not affect the program; it simply makes it easier to read.

A second stylistic technique is to use blank lines to separate sections of code. The use of blank lines is not standardized; it depends on your preference for readability. A note of caution, however; too many blank lines can be distracting. To illustrate how blank lines may be used, consider the following version of the previous program to compute bowling scores.

```
PROGRAM Bowling (input, output);
{          Course Number        CPS 150                    }
{          Assignment           One                        }
{          Due Date             Sept. 20                   }
{          Author               Mary Smith                 }
{          Instructor           Dr. Jones                  }

CONST
  Skip = ' ';

VAR
  Score1, Score2, Score3 : integer;
  Sum : integer;
  Average : real;

BEGIN  { Main program  }
  read (Score1, Score2, Score3);              { Get the scores  }

  Sum := Score1 + Score2 + Score3;   { Perform the computations  }
  Average := Sum / 3.0;

  writeln;
  writeln (Skip:19, 'Game', Skip:6, 'Score');  { Print heading  }
  writeln (Skip:19, '----', Skip:6, '-----');

  writeln (1:22, Score1:11);                 { Print the results  }
  writeln (2:22, Score2:11);
  writeln (3:22, Score3:11);
  writeln;
  writeln (Skip:19, 'Your series total is', Sum:8);
  writeln (Skip:19, 'The average score is', Average:8:2);
  writeln
END.  { of main program  }
```

Since this is such a short program, you may not see much difference in readability between this and the version before it; but blank lines have been used to separate all sections of the program and parts within the executable section.

A third method for enhancing readability is the use of program comments for program description, a variable dictionary, and section comments. Let's first consider the problem of describing the program. Each program should contain some description of what the program does. The program description generally follows the program heading. You will realize the necessity for such descriptions as you accumulate a group of programs. Using our bowling problem, a program description could be

```
{  This is one of our early complete Pascal   }
{  programs. It solves the problem of         }
{  listing bowling scores and computing the   }
{  total and average. In addition to this,    }
{  the final version will contain an initial  }
{  effort to develop a programming style      }
{  using                                      }
{        1.   Indenting                       }
{        2.   Blank lines                     }
{        3.   Program comments                }
```

Another relatively standard use of program comments is to establish a *variable dictionary*. In short programs, the need for this is not obvious; however, it is essential for longer programs.

Several styles are used for describing variables. One method is to use comments on the same line as the variables in the variable declaration section. For example, for the bowling problem, you might use

```
VAR
  Score1, Score2, Score3 : integer;   {  Scores for games  }
  Sum : integer;                      {  Sum of the scores  }
  Average : real;                     {  Average of game scores  }
```

A second method is to use a separate comment section preceding the variable declaration section, such as

```
{                Variable Dictionary        }
{                                           }
{      Average      Average game score       }
{      Score1       Score for game one       }
{      Score2       Score for game two       }
{      Score3       Score for game three     }
{      Sum          Sum of the scores        }
```

You are encouraged to try both styles of describing variables as well as any variation you might like.

Another use of program comments is to describe what a section of code is to do. In **PROGRAM** Bowling, the executable section consists of three sections: get data, perform computations, and produce output. A comment block could be used to describe what happens in each portion of the program.

```
{  Get the scores  }
            .
            .
            .
{  Perform the computations  }
            .
            .
            .
{  Print the heading  }
            .
            .
{  Print the results  }
            .
            .
```

At this stage, you may be thinking that developing a style for writing programs was the subject of Shakespeare's play *Much Ado About Nothing* since none of these suggestions has anything to do with whether or not a program runs. Not true. It is fairly easy to learn to write short programs. As you continue your study of computer science, you will accumulate programs that are progressively longer and more complex. Thus, you should begin now to develop a concise, consistent style for writing programs.

Now we will incorporate all the previous suggestions for writing style into **PROGRAM** Bowling.

```
PROGRAM Bowling (input, output);

{            Course Number        CPS 150           }
{            Assignment           One               }
```

```
{              Due Date          Sept. 20                    }
{              Author            Mary Smith                  }
{              Instructor        Dr. Jones                   }
{                                                            }
{                      Program Comments                      }
{                                                            }
{   This is one of our early complete Pascal programs.  It   }
{   solves  the  problem  of  listing  bowling  scores and   }
{   computing  the  total  and  average.  In addition, the   }
{   final version contains an initial effort to  develop a   }
{   programming style using                                  }
{                                                            }
{                      1.  Indenting                         }
{                      2.  Blank lines                       }
{                      3.  Program comments                  }

CONST
  Skip = ' ';

VAR                               {       Variable Dictionary   }
  Score1, Score2, Score3 : integer; {  Scores for three games   }
  Sum : integer;                    {  Sum of the three scores  }
  Average : real;                   {  Average game score       }

BEGIN {  Main program  }

  {  Get the scores   }

  read (Score1, Score2, Score3);

  {  Perform the computations  }

  Sum := Score1 + Score2 + Score3;
  Average := Sum / 3.0;

  {  Print a heading  }

  writeln;
  writeln (Skip:19, 'Game', Skip:6, 'Score');
  writeln (Skip:19, '----', Skip:6, '-----');

  {  Print the results  }

  writeln (1:22, Score1:11);
  writeln (2:22, Score2:11);
  writeln (3:22, Score3:11);
  writeln;
  writeln (Skip:19, 'Your series total is', Sum:8);
  writeln (Skip:19, 'The average score is', Average:8:2);
  writeln
END. {  of main program  }
```

When this program is run, the output is

```
                Game      Score
                ----      -----
                 1         150
                 2         178
                 3         162

         Your series total is     490
         The average score is   163.33
```

Software Engineering

Perhaps the greatest difference between beginning students in computer science and "real world" programmers is how they perceive the need for documentation. Typically, beginning students want to make a program run; they view anything that delays this process as an impediment. Thus, some students consider using descriptive identifiers, writing variable dictionaries, describing a problem as part of program documentation, and using appropriate comments throughout a program as a nuisance.

In contrast, system designers and programmers who write code for a living often spend up to 50 percent of their time and effort on documentation. There are at least three reasons for this difference in perspective.

First, real programmers work on large, complex systems with highly developed logical paths. Without proper documentation, even the person who developed an algorithm will have difficulty following the logic six months later. Second, communication between and among teams is required as systems are developed. Complete, clear statements about what the problems are and how they are being solved is essential. And third, programmers know they can develop algorithms and write subsequent code. They are trained so that problems of searching, sorting, and file manipulation are routine. Knowing that they can solve a problem thus allows them to devote more time and energy to documenting how the solution has been achieved.

■ EXAMPLE 4.1

Let's conclude this section by writing a program to assist the treasurer of the local chapter of Lions International, a civic organization dedicated to assisting those who have vision deficiencies. The treasurer would like help in computing and printing a monthly statement for each member.

To write the program, we need to know the following:

1. What regular charges should be included each month?
2. Will there be any miscellaneous charges?
3. How do members decrease the amount due?
4. What information needs to be included as part of the output?

We assume these questions are answered as follows:

1. Regular monthly charges are meals and dues. These will be defined in the **CONST** section.
2. There may be miscellaneous charges for club pins, guests for dinner meetings, and so on.
3. Members may decrease the amount due in two ways: they may pay all or part of the balance due, or they may have a credit toward their account by having purchased some supplies needed for a club activity.
4. The output should include the previous balance, all new charges, payments and credits toward the balance, and the new balance. Typical output for one club member could be

```
Please enter data for John Williams
Previous balance?  Press <RETURN> when finished.
?50
Amount of miscellaneous charges?
?3.00
Payments made during month?
?30
Amount of other credits toward account?
?2
```

```
                    Local Lions Club
                    September 1992

      Member name:  John Williams

      Previous balance due:              $ 50.00

      Meal charges:             11.00
      Dues:                      2.50
      Miscellaneous:             3.00
                                -------
      Total new charges:                 + 16.50

      Payments made:            30.00
      Other credits:             2.00
                                -------
      Total paid                         - 32.00
                                         -------

      New Balance due:                   $ 34.50
```

Algorithm Development

Now that the problem is sufficiently defined, we can develop an algorithm for its solution. We will continue using pseudocode with stepwise refinement in developing our algorithms. An initial algorithm for this problem is

1. Get information for one member
2. Compute total charges
3. Compute total payments and credits
4. Compute new balance
5. Print the monthly statement

Module specifications for the five main modules are

1. Get Data Module
   Data received: None
   Information returned: Previous balance
                        Miscellaneous charges
                        Payments made
                        Other credits
   Logic: Use **readln** statements to get data.

2. Compute Total Charges Module
   Data received: Meal charges
                  Dues
                  Miscellaneous charges
   Information returned: Total charges
   Logic: Sum all new charges.

3. Compute Total Payments Module
   Data received: Payments made
                  Credits
   Information returned: Total of payments and credits
   Logic: Sum payments made and credits.

4. Compute New Balance Module
   Data received: Previous balance
                   Total charges
                   Total payments
   Information returned: New balance
   Logic: Subtract total payments from the sum of the previous balance
           and total charges.

5. Print Statement Module
   Data received: Previous balance
                   All new charges
                   Total new charges
                   All payments and credits
                   Total payments/credits
                   New balance
   Information returned: None
   Logic: Use **writeln** statements to produce the desired output.

A structure chart for this problem is given in Figure 4.2.

FIGURE 4.2
Structure chart for Local Lions Club program

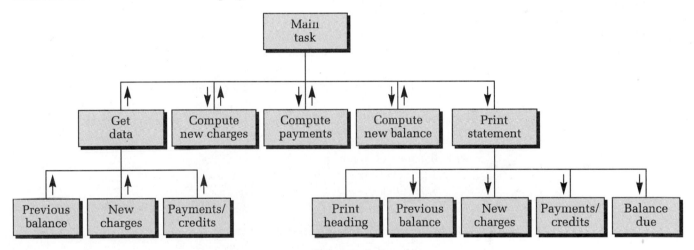

A second-level pseudocode solution is

1. Get information for one member
   1.1 previous balance
   1.2 miscellaneous charges
   1.3 payments/credits
2. Compute total charges
3. Compute total payments and credits
4. Compute new balance
5. Print statement
5.1 print a heading
5.2 print previous balance
5.3 list new charges
5.4 list payment/credits
5.5 print new balance

Communication Skills Needed

Emphasis on communication has been increasing in almost every area of higher education. Evidence of this is the current trend toward "writing across the curriculum" programs implemented in many colleges and universities in the 1980s. Indications that this emphasis is shared among computer scientists was given by Paul M. Jackowitz, Richard M. Plishka, and James R. Sidbury, University of Scranton, when they stated, "Make it possible to write programs in English, and you will discover that programmers cannot write in English."

All computer science educators are painfully aware of the truth of this old joke. We want our students to be literate. We want them to have well-developed writing skills and the capacity to read technical journals in our area. But too often we produce skilled programmers whose communication skills are poor and who have almost no research skills. We must alleviate this problem. Since the organizational techniques used to write software are the same ones that should be used to write papers, computing science students should have excellent writing skills. We should exploit this similarity in skills to develop better writers.

Further, Janet Hartman of Illinois State University and Curt M. White of Indiana-Purdue University at Fort Wayne noted: "Students need to practice written and oral communication skills, both in communications classes and computer classes. Students should write system specifications, project specifications, memos, users' guides or anything else which requires them to communicate on both a nontechnical and technical level. They should do presentations in class and learn to augment their presentations with audiovisual aids."

On a more general note, the need for effective communication skills in computer science has been acknowledged in the 1991 curriculum guidelines of the Association for Computing Machinery, Inc. These guidelines state that "undergraduate programs should prepare students to apply their knowledge to specific, constrained problems and produce solutions. This includes the ability to . . . communicate that solution to colleagues, professionals in other fields, and the general public."

We now need to decide if further refinement is needed. Since each pseudocode line can be implemented in a relatively direct fashion, some programmers might choose to make no further refinements. However, we will further refine step 5.3 to obtain

        5.3 list new charges
            5.3.1 meal costs
            5.3.2 dues
            5.3.3 miscellaneous

Assume data for one member are

Previous balance due	=	$50.00
Meal charges	=	$11.00
Dues	=	$ 2.50
Miscellaneous	=	$ 3.00
Payments made	=	$32.00
Other credits	=	$ 2.00

A program to solve this problem can now be written incorporating previous suggestions of writing style.

```
PROGRAM MonthlyStatement (input, output);

{  This program is designed to print a monthly statement for   }
{  members of Local Lions Club.  Information for a member is    }
{  obtained, subtotals are computed, the new balance is         }
{  computed, and all information is printed in a reasonable     }
{  manner.  Note the use of the CONST section to define values  }
{  that are currently stable but subject to change over time.   }
```

```
CONST
  ClubName = 'Local Lions Club';
  Month = 'September 1992';
  MemberName = 'John Williams';
  Underline = '-------';
  Indent = ' ';
  MealCharge = 11.00;
  Dues = 2.50;

VAR
  PreviousBalance,          {     Balance at end of last month  }
  Miscellaneous,            {              Nonstandard charges  }
  Payments,                 {                      Amount paid  }
  Credits,                  {             Credit toward account }
  MonthlyCharges,           {               Amount due for month }
  TotalPaid,                {     Sum of payments and credits   }
  NewBalance : real;        {                      Balance due  }

BEGIN  {  Main program  }

  {  Get data  }

  writeln ('Please enter data for ', MemberName);
  writeln ('Previous balance?  Press <RETURN> when finished.');
  readln (PreviousBalance);
  writeln ('Amount of miscellaneous charges?');
  readln (Miscellaneous);
  writeln ('Payments made during month?');
  readln (Payments);
  writeln ('Amount of other credits toward account?');
  readln (Credits);

  {  Compute total charges  }

  MonthlyCharges := MealCharge + Dues + Miscellaneous;

  {  Compute payments and credits  }

  TotalPaid := Payments + Credits;

  {  Compute new balance  }

  NewBalance := PreviousBalance + MonthlyCharges - TotalPaid;

  {  Now print all information  }

  writeln;
  writeln (Indent:9, ClubName);
  writeln (Indent:10, Month);
  writeln;
  writeln ('Member name:  ', MemberName);
  writeln;
  writeln ('Previous balance due:', '$':11, PreviousBalance:6:2);
  writeln;
  writeln ('Meal charges:', MealCharge:17:2);
  writeln ('Dues:', Dues:25:2);
  writeln ('Miscellaneous:', Miscellaneous:16:2);
  writeln (Underline:30);
  writeln ('Total new charges:', '+':14, MonthlyCharges:6:2);
  writeln;
  writeln ('Payments made:', Payments:16:2);
```

1

2

3

4

5

```
            writeln ('Other credits:', Credits:16:2);
            writeln (Underline:30);
            writeln ('Total paid', '-':22, TotalPaid:6:2);
            writeln (Underline:38);
            writeln;
            writeln ('New Balance due:', '$':16, NewBalance:6:2)

    END.
```

Output from this program is

```
Please enter data for John Williams
Previous balance?  Press <RETURN> when finished.
?50
Amount of miscellaneous charges?
?3.00
Payments made during month?
?30
Amount of other credits toward account?
?2


            Local Lions Club
            September 1992

Member name:  John Williams

Previous balance due:           $ 50.00

Meal charges:          11.00
Dues:                   2.50
Miscellaneous:          3.00
                       -------
Total new charges:              + 16.50

Payments made:         30.00
Other credits:          2.00
                       -------
Total paid                      - 32.00
                                -------

New Balance due:                $ 34.50
```

Exercises 4.1

1. Assume that each of the following are lines of pseudocode. Write Pascal statements for each.

   a. Add the scores from Test1, Test2, Test3, and Test4

   b. Let Average = Total divided by 4

   c. Let TotalIncome = Salary plus Tips

   d. Let Time = Distance divided by Rate

   e. Let Grade = TotalPoints divided by 6

   f. Write out your name, TotalPoints, and Grade

   g. Write out NumberAttending, TicketPrice, and TotalReceipts

2. Assume the output for a program to compute parking lot fees is to contain

   a. Vehicle type (car or truck)   d. Total time

   b. Time in   e. Parking fee

   c. Time out

   Use **writeln** statements to produce a suitable heading for this output.

3. Given the following algorithm in pseudocode form, write a complete program that will compute the volume of a box.

    1. Assign dimensions
    2. Compute volume
    3. Print results
        3.1   dimensions
        3.2   volume

4. List four uses for program comments.

5. Discuss variations in program writing styles for each of the following:

   a. Using blank lines.

   b. Using program comments.

   c. Writing variable dictionaries.

6. Use program comments to create a program description section that might be used to solve the problem of computing semester grades for a class.

7. Which of the following are valid forms for program comments?

```
a.  {             message here         }

b. (*                                  *)
   (*             message here         *)
   (*                                  *)

c. (*
                  message here
                                       *)

d.  *             message here         *)

e. {**************************
    *                         *
    *             message here *
    *                         *
    **************************}

f. (*                         *
   (*             message here *
   (*                         *)

g. (*                         *)
    *                         *)
    *             message here *)
    *                         *)
    *                         *)

h. {**************************}
   {*                        *}
   {*             message here *}
   {*                        *}
   {**************************}
```

■ ■ ■ ■

OBJECTIVES

- to be aware of typical errors caused by incorrect syntax
- to be aware of errors made in the declaration section of a program
- to be aware of typical errors made when using assignment statements
- to be aware of typical errors made when using **writeln** to produce output

What you learn in this chapter will help you avoid problems when first working with Pascal. You are now aware of the significance of carefully designing an algorithm to solve a problem before you attempt to write a program. Also, you are now able to write code to implement a simple algorithm via a Pascal program. Therefore, to help you avoid frustration, we will examine some typical errors made when writing code.

In an ideal situation, you would submit your program to the computer and it would run with no errors and produce exactly what you desire for output on the first attempt. Since this probably will not happen, you need to be aware of the kinds of errors that can occur. These fall into three general categories: *compilation errors, run-time errors,* and *design errors.*

Compilation errors are errors detected when the program is being compiled. These include *syntax errors,* which are errors in spelling, punctuation, or placement of certain key symbols in a program. Run-time errors are errors that are detected during execution of the program. Design errors are errors that occur in the design of the algorithm or in coding the program that implements the algorithm. These are also referred to as *logic errors.*

Syntax

In Section 2.2, it was stated that syntax refers to the rules governing construction of valid statements. This includes spelling, punctuation, and placement of certain key symbols. Errors made by improper use of syntax are usually easy to identify and correct.

First, let's examine uses of the semicolon. This is the fundamental punctuation mark in Pascal: it is used to separate statements. It first appears after the program heading statement and then *between* complete statements throughout the program. It may appear that semicolons are used at the end of each line. This is not true. In particular, certain keywords appear on a line but are not complete statements. Also, semicolons are not required between a statement and **END.**

To see how semicolons are needed, consider the example given in Table 4.1. The program to the left in this table has no semicolons; the one on the right has the minimum number of semicolons required to make the program run: four. These are explained as follows:

1. A semicolon must appear after the program heading.

   ```
   PROGRAM CheckSemi (output);
   ```

2. A semicolon must appear after each declaration list in the variable declaration section.

   ```
   A, B : real;
   ```

3. and **4.** A semicolon must appear between complete statements in the executable portion of the program.

   ```
   A := 3.0;
   B := 2 * A;
   ```

TABLE 4.1
Illustration of using semicolons

Incorrect Program		Correct Program
`PROGRAM CheckSemi (output)`	1.	`PROGRAM CheckSemi (output);`
`VAR`		`VAR`
`  A, B : real`	2.	`  A, B : real;`
`BEGIN`		`BEGIN`
`  A := 3.0`	3.	`  A := 3.0;`
`  B := 2 * A`	4.	`  B := 2 * A;`
`  writeln (A:5:2, B:5:2)`		`  writeln (A:5:2, B:5:2)`
`END.`		`END.`

Two comments are in order. First, since Pascal ignores extra blanks and line boundaries, the semicolons do not have to be written directly after the statements. Second, as we've seen before, the semicolon at the end of the last statement preceding the reserved word **END** is unnecessary.

A second syntax error results from using the symbol for equality "=" instead of the symbol for an assignment statement ":=". This is compounded by the fact that several programming languages use the equal sign to assign values to variables, and the equal sign is used to define values in the **CONST** section.

A third type of syntax error occurs when writing program comments. Most of these occur when a comment begins with "(*" and ends with "*)". As comments get longer and you attempt to produce attractive readable programs, you may produce some of the following errors.

1. Improper beginning
   (instead of (* or {
2. Improper ending
) instead of *) or }
   * instead of *)
   $) instead of *)
3. Extra blanks
   (*   comment   *   ) instead of (*   comment   *)
4. No close for a long comment (no ending parenthesis or brace)

```
{************************************
 *                                 *
 *   This is a long comment with   *
 *   improper closing punctuation. *
 *                                 *
 ************************************
```

A fourth type of syntax error results from omitting the period after **END** at the end of the executable portion of the program. This error will be detected by the compiler.

A fifth type of error that some computer programmers consider a syntax error is misspelling keywords. Table 4.2 sets forth a program with seven misspelled keywords. You may think the identifiers Inital and Scre are also misspelled keywords. But remember: they are not keywords and can be used as spelled in the program. It is not good practice to use identifiers like this,

TABLE 4.2
Spelling keywords
and identifiers

Incorrect Spelling	Correct Spelling
PROGRM Spelling (output);	PROGRAM
VR	VAR
Wage : reale;	real
Inital : chr;	char
Scre : interger;	integer
BEGN	BEGIN
Wage := 5.0;	
Inital := 'D';	
Scre := 75;	
writln (Wage:10:2, Inital:3, Scre:5)	writeln
END.	

however, since you could easily spell them differently throughout the program and they would not be recognized as variables by the compiler.

Declarations

Errors sometimes made when defining constants in the CONST section include:

1. Using an assignment statement rather than an equal sign

    Incorrect   *Correct*
    ```
    CONST                      CONST
      MaxScore := 100;           MaxScore = 100;
    ```

2. Omitting single quotation marks from string constants

    Incorrect   *Correct*
    ```
    CONST                      CONST
      Name = Mary Smith;         Name = 'Mary Smith';
      Letter = Z;                Letter = 'Z';
    ```

3. Using single quotation marks around numerical constants

    Incorrect   *Correct*
    ```
    CONST                      CONST
      MaxScore = '100';          MaxScore = 100;
    ```

The declaration

```
MaxScore = '100';
```

will not result in an error during compilation. Technically, it is not an error. However, this declaration makes MaxScore a string rather than the integer constant 100. Consequently, you could not assign MaxScore to an integer variable or use it in arithmetic computations.

More errors are usually made in the variable declaration section than in the constant definition section. Several illustrations of incorrect variable declarations and the corrected versions are shown in Table 4.3.

TABLE 4.3
Errors in declaration sections

Incorrect	Correct
```VAR A; B; C : real```	```VAR A, B, C : real;```
```VAR Age ; integer;```	```VAR Age : integer;```
```VAR Initial = char;```	```VAR Initial : char;```
```VAR Wage : real; Score Hours : integer;```	```VAR Wage : real; Score, Hours : integer;```

Assignment Statements

In Section 3.2 you learned to assign a value to a variable with a statement such as

```
Score := 87;
```

Some common mistakes in assignment statements are

1. Trying to put more than one variable on the left of an assignment statement

   Incorrect   *Correct*
   ```
   X + Y := Z;     Z := X + Y;
   A + 3 := B;     B := A + 3;
   ```

2. Trying to make an assignment from left to right

   Incorrect   *Correct*
   ```
   87 := Score;    Score := 87;
   ```

3. Trying to assign the value of one identifier (A) to another identifier (B) from left to right

   Incorrect   *Correct*
   ```
   A := B;         B := A;
   ```

   (This statement will not be detected as an error during compilation; thus, your program will run, but you will probably get incorrect results.)

4. Attempting to assign a value of one data type to a variable of another data type. If, for example, Score had been declared as an **integer** variable, each of the following would produce an error.

   a. `Score := 77.3;`
   b. `Score := 150 / 3;`
   c. `A := 18.6;`
   `    Score := A;`

   There is an exception to this rule. The value of an **integer** data type can be assigned to a variable of type **real.** For example, if Average is a **real,**

   ```
   Average := 43;
   ```

   is a valid assignment statement. However, 43 is then stored as the **real** 43.0 rather than the **integer** 43.

5. Attempting to use undeclared variables and constants. This error often results from listing the variables used in the program in the variable declarations section after the program has been written, and inadvertently omitting some variable from the list. During the compilation, you will get an error message something like "Identifier not declared" when the variable first appears in a line of code. This is easily corrected by adding the variable to the **VAR** section.

   This same error results from misspelling identifiers. For example, if the **VAR** section has

   ```
   VAR
      Initial : char;
   ```

   and you use the statement

   ```
   Inital := 'D';
   ```

in the executable section, you will get an error message. The error message will be the same as that for an undeclared identifier because the compiler did not find Inital in its list of previously declared identifiers. Misspellings are not obvious and are difficult to detect. This is another reason for using descriptive identifiers; they are common words and you are less likely to misspell them.

This is one of the advantages of Pascal as a programming language. Since you cannot use variables unless you declare them, misspelled variables are detected at compilation time. In some other languages (BASIC, for example), if you misspell a variable, create one unintentionally, or initialize one to zero, for example, the problem may not be discovered until after a sample run has been made.

Using writeln

The last general category of errors concerns statements used to create output. Section 2.3 discussed the use of **writeln** for creating a line of output. We have subsequently used this as part of executable statements in several examples. In an attempt to help you avoid making certain errors, we will examine common incorrect uses of **writeln.**

1. Format errors. When using format control with **writeln** statements, three errors are typical.
   a. Attempting to format an integer as a real

      Incorrect   *Correct*
      ```
      writeln (Score:20:2);    writeln (Score:20);
      ```

   b. Attempting to use a noninteger as a format control number

      Incorrect   *Correct*
      ```
      writeln (Average:20:2.0);    writeln (Average:20:2);
      ```

      (where Average is a **real** variable).

   c. Attempting to format a real as an integer. This will not cause a compilation error; your program will run, but you will get unexpected output. For example, suppose Average is a **real** variable whose value is 83.42 and you want a line of output to be

      ```
      The average score is:    83.42
      ```

      If you use the statement

      ```
      writeln ('The average score is:':30, Average:10);
      ```

      the output is

      ```
      The average score is:  8.3E+001
      ```

      Floating-point form is used for the real but the total field width is controlled by the use of ":10". This statement should be written

      ```
      writeln ('The average score is:':30, Average:10:2);
      ```

2. Inappropriate use of quotation marks. Errors of this type result from omitting needed single quotation marks or putting quotation marks where they are not needed. Remember that character strings must be enclosed in single quotation marks. For example, assume you want the output Hello.

      Incorrect   *Correct*
      ```
      writeln (Hello:20);    writeln ('Hello':20);
      ```

A more subtle problem arises when constants and variables have been declared in the **CONST** and **VAR** declaration sections. To illustrate, assume these sections are as follows:

```
CONST
   Name = 'Mary Smith';
   Age = 18;
VAR
   A : integer;
```

and consider the following program fragments.

a. `writeln ('My name is':20, Name:15);`

This is correct and produces

```
My name is      Mary Smith
```

b. `writeln ('My name is':20, 'Name':15);`

This format is also correct but produces

```
My name is                Name
```

This program runs, but you get incorrect output.

c. `writeln ('My age is':20, Age:4);`

This is correct and produces

```
My age is   18
```

d. Assume the assignment A := 10 has been made in the program and consider

```
writeln ('A':5, A:5);
```

This produces

```
     A   10
```

Note that using 'A' creates a character string of one character, but using A causes the contents of A to be printed. This suggests a method of obtaining descriptive output. If you want both the name of a variable and the value of a variable, you could use

```
writeln ('A =':5, A:5);
```

to obtain

```
   A =   10
```

3. Attempting to have an executable statement within the parentheses.

Incorrect	*Correct*
`writeln (A := B + C);`	`A := B + C;`
	`writeln (A);`
	or
	`writeln (B + C);`

Attempts to do this probably result from the fact that expressions can be used in a **writeln** statement. Assuming suitable declarations of variables, each of the following is correct.

```
writeln (A + B:15);
writeln ('Her IQ is':10, Age + 100:5);
writeln ('The total is':20, Average * 12:6:2);
```

In summary, you should now be aware of some errors you may make at some time during your programming career. They are easily corrected and you will make fewer of them as you write more programs.

Exercises 4.2

1. Find two syntax errors in the following program fragment.

```
X := 3 * Y
Y = 4 - 2 * Z;
writeln (X, Y);
```

2. Write a test program to illustrate what happens when extra semicolons are used in a program.

3. Add the minimum number of semicolons required to make the following program syntactically correct.

```
PROGRAM ExerciseThree (output)

CONST
  Name = 'Jim Jones'
  Age = 18

VAR
  Score : integer

BEGIN
  Score := 93
  writeln ('Name':13, Name:15)
  writeln ('Age':12, Age:16)
  writeln ('Score':14, Score:14)
END.
```

4. Find all incorrect uses of "=" and ":=" in the following program.

```
PROGRAM ExerciseFour (output);

CONST
  Name := 'Jim Jones';
  Age := 18;

VAR
  Score = integer;

BEGIN
  Score = 93;
  writeln (Name:10, Age:10, Score:10)
END.
```

5. Find and correct all misspelled keywords in the following program.

```
PROGRRAM ExercseFiv (output);

VAR
  X, Y : reals;
  Nam : chr;
  Scor : interger;

BEGIN
  X := 3.0;
  Y := X * 4.2;
  Nam := 'S';
  Scor := X + Y;
  writln (X:4:2, Y:4:2, Nam:3, Scor:4)
END.
```

6. Assume the variable declaration section of a program is

```
VAR
  A, Score : integer;
  X : real;
  Init : char;
```

Indicate which of the following assignment statements are valid and which are invalid. Give a reason for each that is invalid.

```
a. A := 4 * (-3);        f. A := X + A;
b. Score := 1 * 2.0;     g. Init := 'M';
c. A := Score MOD 8;     h. Init := A;
d. X := Score / 6;       i. Init := 'A';
e. X := X + A;           j. X := Init;
```

7. Assume the declaration section of a program is

```
CONST
  Name = 'John Harris';

VAR
  A, B : integer;
  Wages : real;
  CourseName : char;
```

Indicate which of the following statements are valid and which are invalid. Explain those that are invalid.

```
a. A := A + B;
b. A + B := A;
c. C := A - 2;
d. Wage := 5.75;
e. CourseName := 'C';
f. Wages := Hours * 6.0;
g. CourseName := Name;
h. Name := 'John Harris';
i. A := 2 * Wages;
```

8. Assume the declaration section of a program is the same as in Exercise 7. Label each of the following as valid or invalid. Correct those that are invalid.

```
a. writeln (Name);
b. writeln (Name:20);
c. writeln ('Name':20)
d. writeln (A, B);
e. writeln ('A', 'B');
f. writeln ('A = ', A);
g. writeln ('A = ':10, A:3, B = :10, B:3);
h. writeln ('A = ':10, 'A':3);
i. writeln (Wages, ' are wages');
j. writeln (' Wages are', Wages);
```

9. Find all errors in the following program.

```
PROGRAM Errors (output(;

(****************************************)
(*                                    *)
(*   There are thirteen errors.       $)
(*                                    *)
(****************************************

VAR
  Day : char;
  Percent : real
  A, B ; int:
```

```
BEGIN     (  Main program  )
  Day = 'M';
  Percentage := 72 / 10;
  A := 5;
  B := A * 3.2;
  writln (A, B:20);
  writeln (Day:10:2);
  writeln (A + B:8, Percent:8)
END
```

■ ■ ■ ■

Making a Program Run

- to be able to understand the difference between compilation errors, run-time errors, and design errors
- to be able to use the following error-correcting techniques: debugging, program walk-throughs, echo checking, short programs, and design error checking

Now that we have examined some typical errors, you may think all programs will run on the first try. Unfortunately, this is not true. All programmers eventually encounter problems when trying to make a program run. Although some short programs may run the first time and produce the desired output, you should always plan time for correcting your program. This is a normal part of a programmer's life and you should not get discouraged when you have to rework a program.

Compilation Errors

Compilation errors are errors detected when the program is being compiled; the printed error messages usually are sufficient to enable you to correct your program. As you gain experience, you will make fewer errors of this type. Your program will not run until all compilation errors are removed, so you must develop the ability to correct these errors.

Run-Time Errors

Run-time errors occur after your program has all compilation errors corrected, but when you run your program, you get partial output or error messages instead of output. A run-time error occurs in the following incorrect program.

```
PROGRAM RunError (output);

VAR
  A, B : integer;

BEGIN
  A := 3;
  B := 0;
  A := A DIV B;
  writeln (A, B)
END.
```

The compiler will not detect any errors, but when this is run, you will get a message something like the following (depending on your computer and version of Pascal).

```
Program terminated  at line 9 in program RunError.
Division by zero.
                        --- RunError ---
        A =        3                              B =        0
```

Another example of a run-time error is trying to read the value of a variable that has been declared as an **integer,** but is entered as the value of a different type (for example, **real** or **char**). As you develop more programming skills, you may encounter run-time errors involving the logical flow of your program that are generally more difficult to locate and correct.

Design or Logic Errors

Design (logic) errors occur after you have eliminated both compilation errors and run-time errors. At this stage, your program runs and produces output; however, when you examine the output, it is not what you want. The problems can include having columns incorrectly lined up, having incorrect values for the output, or not getting all of the output.

```
PROGRAM DesignError (output);

VAR
   Score : integer;

BEGIN
   writeln;
   writeln ('Scores':20);
   writeln ('------':25);
   Score := 87;
   writeln (Score);
   Score := 92;
   writeln (Score);
   writeln
END.
```

produces the output

```
           Scores
                 ------
   87
   92
```

instead of

```
           Scores
           ------
               87
               92
```

Therefore, the program should be modified as follows:

```
PROGRAM DesignError (output);

CONST
   LabelWidth = 20;

VAR
   Score : integer;

BEGIN
   writeln;
   writeln ('Scores':LabelWidth);
   writeln ('------':LabelWidth);
   writeln;
   Score := 87;
   writeln (Score:18);
   Score := 92;
   writeln (Score:18);
   writeln
END.
```

The remainder of this section covers techniques to help you detect and correct program errors. Programmers use many different techniques for doing this. We will examine some of the more common, helpful practices, which include *program walk-throughs (traces), echo checking,* and writing short programs.

Debugging Techniques

Debugging is a term loosely used to refer to the process of eliminating errors. (This term dates back to 1945. Computer scientists were working on the Mark II and suddenly something went wrong. During a check of the machine, someone found that a moth was caught in one of the relays. It was removed, and the first computer had been debugged. The term is now used in a somewhat broader sense.). When trying to debug a program, you can do several things. First, carefully reading the code will help you identify and eliminate many of the errors mentioned in the previous section, such as syntax errors, invalid identifiers, incorrect spelling, and incorrect use of **writeln** statements. This technique requires patience and thoroughness, but will save you time in the end by making your programs run sooner.

A second debugging technique is to use compiler error messages to help you correct errors you missed during your careful reading of code. Since these messages vary from machine to machine (they are implementation dependent), you will have to learn to interpret the messages printed by your machine. A list of typical messages is included in Appendix 5.

Errors causing compiler error messages are not always easy to find. Sometimes an error message on one line is the result of a previous error several lines earlier. For example, the program

```
PROGRAM CompileError (output);

{  This will detect a compilation error  $

CONST
  Name = 'Mary Smith';
  Indent = ' ';

VAR
  Age : integer;

BEGIN
  Age := 18;
  writeln (Indent:10, 'My name is', Name:15);
  writeln (Indent:10, 'My age is', Age:3)
END.
```

when compiled, may produce

```
*** Incomplete program.
Compiler error message(s).
```

We have been using constants Skip and Indent to control spacing of output. If some strings are to be right justified (abutting the right-hand margin), we can define a constant—as in **PROGRAM** DesignError—

```
CONST
  LabelWidth = 20;
```

and use it to format strings. For example,

```
writeln ('Score':LabelWidth);
writeln ('-----':LabelWidth);
```

This can be corrected by changing the comment line

```
{  This will detect a compilation error  $
```

to

```
{  This will detect a compilation error  }
```

Once you remove the syntax error ($), you should have an error-free compilation and be ready to run the program.

A third debugging technique can be utilized after you get an error-free compilation. Run the program and get a list of run-time error messages. (If you have been very careful, you may not have any run-time errors.) Consider the program

---

A NOTE OF INTEREST

A Software Glitch

The software glitch that disrupted AT&T's long-distance telephone service for nine hours in January 1990, dramatically demonstrates what can go wrong even in the most reliable and scrupulously tested systems. Of the roughly 100 million telephone calls placed with AT&T during that period, only about half got through. The breakdown cost the company more than $60 million in lost revenues and caused considerable inconvenience and irritation for telephone-dependent customers.

The trouble began at a "switch"—one of 114 interconnected, computer-operated electronic switching systems scattered across the United States. These sophisticated systems, each a maze of electronic equipment housed in a large room, form the backbone of the AT&T long-distance telephone network.

When a local exchange delivers a telephone call to the network, it arrives at one of these switching centers, which can handle up to 700,000 calls an hour. The switch immediately springs into action. It scans a list of 14 different routes it can use to complete the call, and at the same time hands off the telephone number to a parallel, signaling network, invisible to any caller. This private data network allows computers to scout the possible routes and to determine whether the switch at the other end can deliver the call to the local company it serves.

If the answer is no, the call is stopped at the original switch to keep it from tying up a line, and the caller gets a busy signal. If the answer is yes, a signaling-network computer makes a reservation at the destination switch and orders the original switch to pass along the waiting call—after that switch makes a final check to ensure that the chosen line is functioning properly. The whole process of passing a call down the network takes 4 to 6 seconds. Because the switches must keep in constant touch with the signaling network and its computers, each switch has a computer program that handles all the necessary communications between the switch and the signaling network.

AT&T's first indication that something might be amiss appeared on a giant video display at the company's network control center in Bedminster, N.J. At 2:25 P.M. on Monday, January 15, 1990, network managers saw an alarming increase in the number of red warning signals appearing on many of the 75 video screens showing the status of various parts of AT&T's world-wide network. The warnings signaled a serious collapse in the network's ability to complete calls within the United States.

To bring the network back up to speed, AT&T engineers first tried a number of standard procedures that had worked in the past. This time, the methods failed. The engineers realized they had a problem never seen before. Nonetheless, within a few hours, they managed to stabilize the network by temporarily cutting back on the number of messages moving through the signaling network. They cleared the last defective link at 11:30 that night.

Meanwhile, a team of more than 100 telephone technicians tried frantically to track down the fault. Because the problem involved the signaling network and seemed to bounce from one switch to another, they zeroed in on the software that permitted each switch to communicate with the signaling-network computers.

The day after the slowdown, AT&T personnel removed the apparently faulty software from each switch, temporarily replacing it with an earlier version of the communications program. A close examination of the flawed software turned up a single error in one line of the program. Just one month earlier, network technicians had changed the software to speed the processing of certain messages, and the change had inadvertently introduced a flaw into the system.

From that finding, AT&T could reconstruct what had happened.

```
PROGRAM RunTimeError (output);

Var
  A, B : integer;
  Average : real;

BEGIN
  A := 10;
  Average := (A + B) / 2.0;
  writeln ('The average is':20, Average:10:2)
END.
```

There are no compilation errors in the program, but the output is something equivalent to

```
Program terminated at line 9 in program RunTimeErr.
Integer larger than maxint.
                        --- RunTimeErr ---
    Average =    Undef                                    A =     10
          B =    Undef
```

and not the desired output because B has not been assigned a value.

Use these messages to analyze and correct your program. Remember, these messages are implementation dependent and it will take time before you can understand them.

Program Walk-Through

Program walk-through, sometimes referred to as a trace, is used to describe the process of using pencil and paper to carefully follow the steps the computer uses to solve the problem given in your program. Two types of walk-throughs are used by programmers. First, you follow the logical flow of your program. During this check, you are not looking for syntax errors; you are merely making sure that the order in which things are done is correct. This type of checking will be more efficient after you have written more programs. A second type of program walk-through (sometimes called hand execution) is to keep track of values of the variables on paper. The following example illustrates this idea.

■ **EXAMPLE 4.2**

Let's walk through the following program.

```
PROGRAM WalkThru (output);

VAR
  A, B :integer;
BEGIN
  A := 5;
  B := A + 4;
  A := B - 2;
  B := A * 5;
  B := B DIV 3;
  writeln (A:5, B:5)
END.
```

To walk through this program, we will list the variables and then proceed through the program one line at a time.

Statement	Value of A	Value of B
A := 5;	5	Undefined
B := A + 4;	5	9
A := B - 2;	7	9
B := A * 5;	7	35
B := B DIV 3;	7	11

At the end of the program, A has the value 7 and B has the value 11.

Echo Checking

Echo checking is a technique whereby you let the computer check the values of your variables and the data used in your program. When reading values or changing the value of a variable, you could use a **writeln** statement to immediately print out the new value with a short, descriptive message. To illustrate, consider the short **PROGRAM** WalkThru in Example 4.2. An echo check could be implemented by inserting **writeln** statements as follows:

```
PROGRAM WalkThru (output);

VAR
  A, B : integer;

BEGIN
  A := 5;
  writeln ('A =', A:3);
  B := A + 4;
  writeln ('B =', B:3);
  A := B - 2;
  writeln ('A =', A:3);
  B := A * 5;
  writeln ('B =', B:3);
  B := B DIV 3;
  writeln ('B =', B:3);
  writeln (A:5, B:5)
END.
```

The output for this program is

```
A =  5
B =  9
A =  7
B = 35
B = 11
    7   11
```

You can echo check input data similarly. For example, if an input statement is

```
read (A, B, C);
```

the values can be checked by inserting an output statement such as

```
writeln ('A = ', A, 'B = ', B, 'C = ', C);
```

You probably will not want to print each variable value in the final program. Therefore, once your program produces the desired output, remove the **writeln** statements used for checking and you have a working program.

Short Programs

Using short test programs is another technique for error checking. It is particularly effective on longer, more complex programs, but to illustrate we will consider the following short example.

■ **EXAMPLE 4.3**

Suppose you are writing a program and you want to exchange the values of variables A and B. You think this could be accomplished by

```
A := B;
B := A;
```

You could write a short program to check this as follows:

```
PROGRAM ExchangeCheck (output);

VAR
  A, B : integer;

BEGIN
  A := 5;
  B := 10;
  writeln ('A =', A:3, ' B =', B:3);

{  Now exchange  }

  A := B;
  B := A;
  writeln ('A =', A:3, ' B =', B:3)
END.
```

When you run this short program, the output

```
A =  5 B = 10
A = 10 B = 10
```

indicates your method of exchanging values did not work and you have to redesign your program. The exchange could be accomplished by declaring a third variable Temp and then using the code:

```
Temp := A;
A := B;
B := Temp;
```
■   ■

The example given is quite simple, but as you start writing programs to solve complex problems, you will find that using short programs is a very effective technique.

Exercises 4.3

1. Perform a program walk-through for the following program segment to determine the values of A, B, and C at the end of the segment.

```
A := 33;
B := -2;
A := A - 5;
B := A;
C := B + 2;
A := B;
```

```
C := A - B + 1;
A := A + 1;
```

2. Write a separate test program to illustrate what error messages appear for each of the following:

   a. division by zero.

   b. printing a variable that has not been assigned a value.

   c. using a variable that has not been assigned a value.

3. Correct all compilation errors for the following programs. Check your results by running each program exactly as it is written here and examining the compilation error messages.

   a.
   ```
   PROGRAM CompileErrors (output);

   CONST
     Max = 100.0 : real;

   VAR
     A, Sum : integer

   BEGIN
     A := 86.0;
     Sum := A + 0;
     A + Sum := Sum
     writeln (Sum:15:2)
   END.
   ```
   b.
   ```
   PROGRAM Compile Errors (output);

   VAR
     A : integer;
     Ch : char;

   BEGIN
     Ch := 'M';
     A := 83;
     B := A - 10;
     writeln (' The value of A is:20, A:6);
     writeln (Ch:20)
   END.
   ```

4. Suppose the output from a program is as follows:
   ```
   NameJohn    JohnsAge    18
     Test Scores
   -----
   73                 82                    96
   ```
   Indicate a more desirable form for the output and describe what changes could be made in the program to achieve those desired results.

5. Consider the program
   ```
   PROGRAM Donations (output);

   VAR
     Amount1, Amount2,
     Amount3, Amount4,
     Sum : real;
   ```

```
      BEGIN
        Amount1 := 100.0;
        Amount2 := 150.0;
        Amount3 := 75.0;
        Amount4 := 200.50;
        Sum := Amount1 + Amount2 + Amount3 + Amount4;
        writeln ('Donations':29);
        writeln (Amount1:28:2);
        writeln (Amount2:28:2);
        writeln (Amount3:28:2);
        writeln (Amount4:28:2);
        writeln ('------':28);
        writeln (Sum:28:2)
      END.
```

The output for this program is

```
              Donations
              100.00
              150.00
               75.00
              200.50
              ------
              525.50
```

Change the program so the output would be

```
              Donations
              ---------

           $ 100.00
           $ 150.00
           $  75.00
           $ 200.50
              ---------

Total      $ 525.50
```

6. The following program has no compilation errors. However, there are some run-time errors. Find them and indicate what could be done to correct them.

```
PROGRAM RunErrors (output);

VAR
  A : integer;
  X : real;
  Ch : char;

BEGIN
  A := 4;
  X := 100.0;
  Ch := 'F';
  X := X / (4 MOD 2);
  X := 3 * X;
  writeln (Ch:5, X:8:2, A:5)
END.
```

7. List three types of errors made by computer programmers. Discuss their differences and what methods may be used to correct them.

8. Use **writeln** statements in the following program to echo check the values of each of the variables. Indicate what the output would be when you run the echo-check version.

```
PROGRAM EchoCheck (output);

VAR
  Sum, Score, Count : integer;
  Average : real;

BEGIN
  Count := 0;
  Sum := 0;
  Score := 86;
  Sum := Sum + Score;
  Count := Count +1;
  Score := 89;
  Sum := Sum + Score;
  Count := Count + 1;
  Average := Sum / Count;
  writeln;
  writeln ('There were':20, Count:3, ' scores.');
  writeln;
  writeln ('The average is':24, Average:6:2)
END.
```

■ ■ ■ ■

■ 4.4
Writing a Complete Pascal Program

OBJECTIVE

■ to be able to write a complete Pascal program to solve a problem

By now you should be able to implement the five steps in problem solving. You should also be able to write complete programs that include the following features:

- clear program documentation and writing style
- the ability to get data from a data file
- correct, neat, attractive output

By way of example, we end this chapter with one complete program in which problem solving and these design features are demonstrated. Once you are comfortable that you can use these skills as illustrated, you can easily add new programming skills to your repertoire.

Dr. Lae Z. Programmer, teacher of computer science, wants a program that will allow him to give an individual progress report to each student in his computer science class. The report for each student should include the student's initials, three test scores, test average, five quiz scores, weighted quiz total, and final percentage. We will develop a program for this problem and test it by running it for two students. In Chapter 6, we will see how this program could be conveniently used for the entire class.

The first step in problem solving is to understand the problem. For this particular problem, we need to know what the stream input will look like, how quizzes are to be weighted, how final percentage is to be computed, and what form is desired for the output. Let us assume these questions have been asked and answered as follows:

1. Each line of data in the stream input will start with a student's initials followed by three test scores and then five quiz scores. Scores will be integers and will be separated by blanks. The test scores are based on 100 points each and the quiz scores are based on 10 points each. Thus, the data file for two students will look like

```
┌─────────────────────────┐ ┌─────────────────────────┐
│ MJS 91 87 79 8 10 10 9 7 ■│ │ JHJ 93 85 89 10 9 8 10 7 ■│
└─────────────────────────┘ └─────────────────────────┘
```

2. The quizzes are to be counted as the equivalent of one 100-point test. Thus, their total should be multiplied by two when computing the weighted total.

3. Final percentage is to be computed based on a total of 400 points: 100 for each test and 100 for the quiz total.

4. Each student's interim report should look like

```
         **********************
         *                    *
         *   Interim Report   *
         *   --------------    *
         *                     *
         **********************

Class:       Computer Science
Date:        October 15
Instructor:  Dr. Lae Z. Programmer

              Test      Test         Quiz          Quiz
Initials     Scores    Average      Scores         Total
-----------------------------------------------------------
  MJS       91 87 79   85.67      8 10 10  9  7     88

Final percentage =   86.25
-------------------------------
```

The second step in problem solving is to develop an algorithm. This will be done using stepwise refinement. As a first level of pseudocode, we have

1. Get data for first student
2. Perform computations
3. Print student report
4. Get data for second student
5. Perform computations
6. Print student report

Module specifications for the modules corresponding to steps 1, 2, and 3 are

1. <u>Get Data Module</u>
   Data received: None
   Information returned: Three initials
                         Five quiz scores
                         Three test scores
   Logic: Use **read** statements to get data.

2. <u>Perform Computations Module</u>
   Data received: Five quiz scores
                  Three test scores
   Information returned: Test average
                         Weighted quiz total
                         Final percentage
   Logic: Divide total of test scores by three.
           Multiply quiz total by two for weighting.
           Sum totals and divide by four for final average.

3.   Print Student Report Module
       Data received: All input data
                             Test average
                             Quiz total
                             Final percentage
     Information returned: None
     Logic: Use **writeln** statements to print information in desired format.

Since steps 4, 5, and 6 are repetitions of steps 1, 2, and 3, we will refine only the first three.

1.   Get data for first student
       1.1   get initials
       1.2   get test scores
       1.3   get quiz scores

Each of these lines could be refined further. For example, step 1.1 could be subdivided into

       1.1   get initials
               1.1.1   get first initial
               1.1.2   get second initial
               1.1.3   get third initial

At some stage, you have to decide what is a sufficient refinement when developing an algorithm. This will vary according to students and instructors. In general, when you have a clearly defined statement that can be accomplished by a single line of code, there is no need for subsequent refinement. In fact, a single line of pseudocode may require several lines of written code in a program. The important thing to remember is that algorithm development via pseudocode is only a step in helping solve a problem; it is not the solution itself.

Refining step 2, we could have

2.   Perform computations
       2.1   compute test average
       2.2   compute quiz total
       2.3   compute final percentage

This can be further refined to

2. Perform computations
    2.1   compute test average
        2.1.1   add test scores
        2.1.2   divide by three
    2.2   compute quiz total
        2.2.1   add quiz scores
        2.2.2   multiply by two
    2.3   compute final percentage
        2.3.1   add test totals to quiz total
        2.3.2   divide by four

A structure chart for one student with the second module developed through three levels is given in Figure 4.3.

Refining step 3 might result in

3. Print student report
    3.1   print report heading
    3.2   print student information

This can be further refined to

3. Print student report
    3.1   print report heading
        3.1.1   print title
        3.1.2   print class information
        3.1.3   print column headings
    3.2   print student information
        3.2.1   print initials
        3.2.2   print test scores
        3.2.3   print test average
        3.2.4   print quiz scores
        3.2.5   print quiz total
        3.2.6   print final percentage

Since a similar report is required for the second student, steps 4, 5, and 6 will be repetitions of steps 1, 2, and 3. Thus, the complete algorithm will be

1. Get data for first student
    1.1   get initials
        1.1.1   get first initial
        1.1.2   get second initial
        1.1.3   get third initial
    1.2   get test scores
    1.3   get quiz scores
2. Perform computations
    2.1   compute test average
        2.1.1   add test scores
        2.1.2   divide by three
    2.2   compute quiz total
        2.2.1   add quiz scores
        2.2.2   multiply by two
    2.3   compute final percentage
        2.3.1   add test totals to quiz total
        2.3.2   divide by four

FIGURE 4.3
Sturcture chart for Student Report

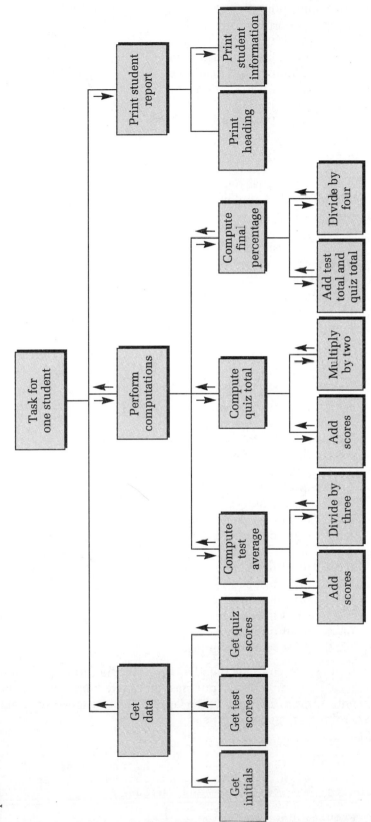

3. Print student report
  3.1 reprint report heading
      3.1.1 print title
      3.1.2 print class information
      3.1.3 print column headings
  3.2 print student information
      3.2.1 print initials
      3.2.2 print test scores
      3.2.3 print test average
      3.2.4 print quiz scores
      3.2.5 print quiz total
      3.2.6 print final percentage
4. Get data for second student
  4.1 get initials
      4.1.1 get first initial
      4.1.2 get second initial
      4.1.3 get third initial
  4.2 get test scores
  4.3 get quiz scores
5. Perform computations
  5.1 compute test average
      5.1.1 add test scores
      5.1.2 divide by three
  5.2 compute quiz total
      5.2.1 add quiz scores
      5.2.2 multiply by two
  5.3 compute final percentage
      5.3.1 add test totals to quiz total
      5.3.2 divide by four
6. Print student report
  6.1 print report heading
      6.1.1 print title
      6.1.2 print class information
      6.1.3 print column headings
  6.2 print student information
      6.2.1 print initials
      6.2.2 print test scores
      6.2.3 print test average
      6.2.4 print quiz scores
      6.2.5 print quiz total
      6.2.6 print final percentage

You may now write code for the algorithm. In the following version, an attempt to create presentable output has included boxed descriptions of headings, centering on the page when appropriate, underlining, skipping lines, and carefully created columns.

```
PROGRAM StudentReport (input, output);

{     This program is written for Dr. Lae Z. Programmer.  It    }
{     produces an interim progress report for two  students.    }
{     The following features have been included.                }
{                                                               }
{          1.  Program documentation                            }
{          2.  Writing style                                    }
```

```
{                3.   Procedure for a heading                        }
{                4.   Using a stream input                           }
{                5.   Descriptive variables                          }
{                6.   Neat, attractive output                        }

CONST
   Splats = '*********************';
   Edge =   '*                   *';
   Line = '------------------------------------------------------';
   Skip = ' ';

VAR
   FinalPercent : real;              {         Final class percentage }
   Init1, Init2, Init3 : char;       {     Initials for one student   }
   Quiz1, Quiz2, Quiz3,
   Quiz4, Quiz5 : integer;           { Quiz scores for one student    }
   QuizTotal : integer;              {         Sum of five quizzes    }
   Test1, Test2, Test3 : integer;    { Test scores for one student    }
   TestAverage : real;               {         Average of three tests }
   TestTotal : integer;              {         Sum of three test scores }


{****************************************************************** }


BEGIN  {  Program  }

   {  Get data for the first student  }

   read (Init1, Init2, Init3);
   read (Test1, Test2, Test3);
   readln (Quiz1, Quiz2, Quiz3, Quiz4, Quiz5);

   {  Perform necessary computations  }

   TestTotal := Test1 + Test2 + Test3;
   TestAverage := TestTotal / 3.0;
   QuizTotal := (Quiz1 + Quiz2 + Quiz3 + Quiz4 + Quiz5) * 2;
   FinalPercent := (TestTotal + QuizTotal) / 4.0;

   {  Print the title  }

   writeln;
   writeln (Skip:30, Splats);
   writeln (Skip:30, Edge);
   writeln (Skip:30, '*    Interim Report   * ');
   writeln (Skip:30, '*    -------------   * ');
   writeln (Skip:30, Edge);
   writeln (Skip:30, Splats);

   {  Print the class information  }

   writeln;
   writeln (Skip:15, 'Class:        Computer Science');
   writeln (Skip:15, 'Date:         October 15');
   writeln (Skip:15, 'Instructor:  Dr. Lae Z. Programmer');
   writeln;

   {  Print the column headings  }

   writeln (Skip:27, 'Test', 'Test':10, 'Quiz':14, 'Quiz':14);
   writeln (Skip:15, 'Initials', 'Scores':9, 'Average':11,
            'Scores':12, 'Total':13);
   writeln (Skip:15, Line);
```

```
{  Print the student information  }

write (Init1:18, Init2, Init3);
write (Test1:7, Test2:3, Test3:3);
write (TestAverage:8:2);
write (Quiz1:7, Quiz2:3, Quiz3:3, Quiz4:3, Quiz5:3);
writeln (QuizTotal:7);
writeln;
writeln (Skip:15, 'Final percentage = ', FinalPercent:7:2);
writeln (Skip:15, '----------------------');
```

3

```
{  Repeat process for the second student  }

read (Init1, Init2, Init3);
read (Test1, Test2, Test3);
readln (Quiz1, Quiz2, Quiz3, Quiz4, Quiz5);
```

1

```
{  Perform necessary computations  }

TestTotal := Test1 + Test2 + Test3;
TestAverage := TestTotal / 3.0;
QuizTotal := (Quiz1 + Quiz2 + Quiz3 + Quiz4 + Quiz5) * 2;
FinalPercent := (TestTotal + QuizTotal) / 4.0;
```

2

```
{  Print the title  }

writeln;
writeln (Skip:30, Splats);
writeln (Skip:30, Edge);
writeln (Skip:30, '*    Interim Report   *');
writeln (Skip:30, '*    -------------     *');
writeln (Skip:30, Edge);
writeln (Skip;30, Splats);

{  Print the class information  }

writeln;
writeln (Skip:15, 'Class:        Computer Science');
writeln (Skip:15, 'Date:         October 15');
writeln (Skip:15, 'Instructor:   Dr. Lae Z. Programmer');
writeln;

{  Print the column headings  }

writeln (Skip:27, 'Test', 'Test':10, 'Quiz':13, 'Quiz':14);
writeln (Skip:15, 'Initials', 'Scores':9, 'Average':11,
         'Scores':12, 'Total':13);
writeln (Skip:15, Line);

{  Print the student information  }

write (Init1:18, Init2, Init3);
write (Test1:7, Test2:3, Test3:3);
write (TestAverage:8:2);
write (Quiz1:7, Quiz2:3, Quiz3:3, Quiz4:3, Quiz5:3);
writeln (QuizTotal:7);
writeln;
writeln (Skip:15, 'Final percentage = ', FinalPercent:7:2);
writeln (Skip:15, '----------------------');
writeln
END.  {  of main program  }
```

3

■ Summary

Key Terms

comment
compilation error
debugging
design (logic) error

echo checking
program walk-through
    (trace)

run-time error
syntax error
variable dictionary

Key Concepts

- It is not sufficient to produce correct output; your output should also be clear, neat, and attractive.
- Attractive output is produced by using blank lines as appropriate, underlining, right- and left-hand margins, columns, and descriptive headings and messages.
- Program comments are nonexecutable statements that can be included in a program using the form

```
{  ...comment...  }
```

or

```
(*  ...comment...  *)
```

- Program readability is enhanced by indenting, using blank lines, and using program comments.
- Programs should be documented by using a comment section to describe the program and a variable dictionary.
- Common syntax errors result from inappropriate use of the semicolon, using "=" for assigning rather than ":=", incorrectly starting or ending comments, forgetting the period "." at the end of the program, or misspelling keywords.
- Other sources of errors for beginners include errors made in declarations, or assignment statements, or in using **writeln.**
- Program errors can be detected and eliminated by debugging, program walk-throughs, echo checking, using short programs, and design error checking.
- When writing a complete program, make sure you have answered all questions concerning input, processing, and output before you attempt to design the solution.
- After all questions are answered, design a solution to the problem; refine steps in the solution until you can easily write code for the program.
- When writing the program, use a neat, consistent, readable writing style.
- Your style should include documentation, including a program description section, a variable dictionary, and, when appropriate, comment sections and line comments. You should use consistent indenting, blank lines to separate code, and a procedure for the heading.
- The output for your program should be neat and readable; features should include use of the middle of the output page, appropriate titles and headings, columns where appropriate, blank lines, and underlining.

A NOTE OF INTEREST

Debugging or Sleuthing: Answers

1. "The problem was in the terminal's keyboard: the tops of two keys were switched. When the programmer was seated, he was a touch-typist and the problem went unnoticed, but when he stood, he was led astray by hunting and pecking."

2. "When [the programmers] observed the behavior more closely, they found that the problem occurred as they entered data for the country of Ecuador: when the user typed the name of the capital city (Quito), the program interpreted that as a request to quit the run!"

■ **Programming Problems and Projects**

Before going on, you should test your knowledge of the material by writing a complete program for some of the following problems. Each will require an input file. For each problem you solve, include an algorithm development with an accompanying structure chart. Write module specifications for each main module. Problems marked by a color square ■ left of the number will be referred to in later chapters.

1. The Roll-Em Lanes bowling team would like to have a computer program to print the team results for one series of games. The team consists of four members whose names are Weber, Fazio, Martin, and Patterson. Each person on the team bowls three games during the series; thus, the input will contain three lines, each with four integer scores. Your output should include all input data, individual series totals, game average for each member, team totals, and team average.
   Sample output is

```
Name              Game 1       Game 2       Game 3       Total       Average
----              ---- -       ---- -       ---- -       -----       -------
Weber              212          220          190
Fazio              195          235          210
Martin             178          190          206
Patterson          195          215          210

Team Total:

Team Average:
```

■ 2. The Natural Pine Furniture Company has recently hired you to help them convert their antiquated payroll system to a computer-based model. They know you are still learning, so all they want right now is a program that will print a one-week pay report for three employees. You should use the constant definition section for the following:
   a. Federal withholding tax rate   18%
   b. State withholding tax rate   4.5%
   c. Hospitalization $25.65
   d. Union dues $7.85

   Each line of input will contain
   a. Employee's initials
   b. Number of hours worked
   c. Hourly rate

   Your output should include a report for each employee and a summary report for the company files. A sample employee form follows:

```
Employee:      JTM
Hours Worked:  40.00
Hourly Rate:    9.75

    Total Wages:

    Deductions:
        Federal Withholding
        State Withholding
        Hospitalization
        Union Dues
            Total Deductions

Net Pay
```

Output for a summary report could be:

```
            Natural Pine Furniture Company
                   Weekly Summary

   Gross Wages:

   Deductions:
           Federal Withholding
           State Withholding
           Hospitalization
           Union Dues
                  Total Deductions

   Net Wages:
```

■ 3. The Child-Growth Encyclopedia Company wants a computer program that will print a monthly sales chart. Products produced by the company, prices, and sales commissions for each are

   a. Basic encyclopedia $325.00   22%
   b. Child educational supplement $127.50   15%
   c. Annual update book $ 18.95   20%

Write a program that will get the monthly sales data for two sales regions and produce the desired company chart. Each line of data will contain a two-letter code for the region followed by three integers representing number of products a, b, and c sold, respectively. The prices may vary from month to month and should be defined in the constant definition section. The commissions are not subject to change.

    Sample data lines are

```
MI 150 120 105   TX 225 200 150   ■
```

Typical output could be:

```
REGION                                    SALES
------                                    -----
                   (Encyclopedia)  Supplement)  (Update)

MI                      150            120         105
TX                      225            200         150

Total Sales:

Total Commission:
```

4. The Village Variety Store is having its annual Christmas sale. They would like you to write a program to produce a daily report for the store. Each item sold is identified by a code consisting of one letter followed by one digit. Your report should include data for three items. Each of the three lines of data will include item code, number of items sold, original item price, and reduction percentage. Your report should include a chart with the input data, sale price per item, and total amount of sales per item. You should also print a daily summary.

    Sample data lines are

```
A1 13 5.95 15   A2 24 7.95 20   A3 80 3.95 50   ■
```

Typical output form could be:

```
Item Code    #Sold   Original Price   Reductions   Sale Price   Income
---------    ------  ---------------   ----------   ----------   ------


   A1          13         $5.95           15%         $5.06      $65.78

Daily Summary
----- -------


   Gross Income:
```

5. The Holiday-Out Motel Company, Inc., wants a program that will print a statement for each overnight customer. Each line of input will contain room number (integer), number of nights (integer), room rate (real), telephone charges (real), and restaurant charges (real). You should use the constant definition section for the date and current tax rate. Each customer statement should include all input data, the date, tax rate and amount, total due, appropriate heading, and appropriate closing message. Test your program by running it for two customers. The tax rate applies only to the room cost.
A typical data line is

```
135 3 39.95 3.75 57.50 ▮
```

A customer statement form is

```
        Holiday-Out Motel Company, Inc.
        -------------------------------

Date: XX-XX-XX
Room #                      135
Room Rate:                $39.95
Number of Nights:            3

Room Cost:               $119.85
Tax: XXX%                   4.79
      Subtotal:                    $124.64

Telephone:                          3.75
Meals:                             57.50

   TOTAL DUE                       $185.89

    Thank you for staying at Holiday-Out
               Drive safely
            Please come again
```

6. As a part-time job this semester, you are working for the Family Budget Assistance Center. Your boss has asked you to write and execute a program that will analyze data for a family. Input for each family will consist of

Family ID number	**(integer)**
Number in family	**(integer)**
Income	**(real)**
Total debts	**(real)**

Output from your program should include the following:
a. An appropriate header.
b. The family's identification number, number in family, income, and total debts.

c. Predicted family living expenses ($3000 times the size of the family).
d. The monthly payment necessary to pay off the debt in one year (Debt / 12).
e. The amount the family should save (the family size times 2 percent of the income minus debt—FamSize * 0.02 (income − debt)).
f. Your service fee (.5 percent of the income).

Run your program for the following two families:

Identification Number	Size	Income	Debt
51	4	18000.00	2000.00
72	7	26000.00	4800.00

Output for the first family could be:

```
        Family Budget Assistance Center
                 March 1992
            Telephone: (800)555-1234

Identification number              51
Family size                         4
Annual income            $  18000.00
Total debt               $   2000.00
Expected living expenses $  12000.00
Monthly payment          $     166.67
Savings                  $    1280.00
Service fee              $      90.00
```

7. The Caswell Catering and Convention Service has asked you to write a computer program to produce customers' bills. The program should read in the following data.
   a. The number of children to be served.
   b. The number of adults to be served.
   c. The cost per adult meal.
   d. The cost per child's meal (60 percent of the cost of the adult's meal).
   e. The cost for dessert (same for adults and children).
   f. The room fee (no room fee if catered at the person's home).
   g. A percentage for tip and tax (not applied to the room fee).
   h. Any deposit should be deducted from the bill.

The following is sample data for this problem.

Data	Child Count	Adult Count	Adult Cost	Dessert Cost	Room Rate	Tip/Tax	Deposit
1	7	23	12.75	1.00	45.00	18%	50.00
2	3	54	13.50	1.25	65.00	19%	40.00
3	15	24	12.00	0.00	45.00	18%	75.00
4	2	71	11.15	1.50	0.00	6%	0.00

Data set 1 was used to produce the following sample output.

```
            Caswell Catering and Convention Service
                          Final Bill

                    Number of adults:            23
                  Number of children:             7
     Cost per adult without dessert:    $     12.75
     Cost per child without dessert:    $      7.65
                   Cost per dessert:    $      1.00
                          Room fee:    $     45.00
                  Tip and tax rate:           0.18

         Total cost for adult meals:    $    293.25
         Total cost for child meals:    $     53.55
            Total cost for dessert:    $     30.00
                  Total food cost:    $    376.80
               Plus tip and tax:    $     67.82
                  Plus room fee:    $     45.00
                                       ---------
                         Total due:    $    489.62

                     Less deposit:    $     50.00
                                       ---------
                     Balance due:    $    439.62
```

Write a program and test it using data sets 2, 3, and 4.

8. The Maripot Carpet Store has asked you to write a computer program
   to calculate the amount a customer should be charged. The president
   of the company has given you the following information to help in
   writing the program.
   a. The carpet charge is equal to the number of square yards pur-
      chased times the labor cost per square yard.
   b. The labor cost is equal to the number of square yards purchased
      times the cost per square yard. A fixed fee for floor preparation is
      added to some customers' bills.
   c. Large volume customers are given a percentage discount but the
      discount applies only to the carpet charge, not the labor costs.
   d. All customers are charged 4 percent sales tax on the carpet; there
      is no sales tax on the labor cost.

Sample data for this problem are

Customer	Sq. yds.	Cost per sq. yd.	Labor per sq. yd.	Prep. Cost	Discount
1	17	18.50	3.50	38.50	0.02
2	40	24.95	2.95	0.00	0.14
3	23	16.80	3.25	57.95	0.00
4	26	21.25	0.00	80.00	0.00

The data for customer 1 were used to produce the following sample
output.

```
Square yards purchased:        17
   Cost per square yard:  $   18.50
  Labor per square yard:  $    3.50
 Floor preparation cost:  $   38.50
        Cost for carpet:  $  314.50
         Cost for labor:  $   98.00
     Discount on carpet:  $    6.29
          Tax on carpet:  $   12.33
     Charge to customer:  $  418.54
```

Write a program and test it for customers 2, 3, and 4.

9. The manager of the Croswell Carpet Store has asked you to write a program to print customers' bills. The manager has given you the following information.
   a. The store expresses the length and width of a room in terms of feet and tenths of a foot. For example, the length might be reported as 16.7 feet.
   b. The amount of carpet purchased is expressed as square yards. It is found by dividing the area of the room (in square feet) by nine.
   c. The store does not sell a fraction of a square yard. Thus, square yards must always be rounded up.
   d. The carpet charge is equal to the number of square yards purchased times the carpet cost per square yard. Sales tax equal to 4 percent of the carpet cost must be added to the bill.
   e. All customers are sold a carpet pad at $2.25 per square yard. Sales tax equal to 4 percent of the pad cost must be added to the bill.
   f. The labor cost is equal to the number of square yards purchased times $2.40, which is the labor cost per square yard. No tax is charged on labor.
   g. Large volume customers may be given a discount. The discount may apply only to the carpet cost (before sales tax is added), only to the pad cost (before sales tax is added), only to the labor cost, or to any combination of the three charges.
   h. Each customer is identified by a five-digit number and that number should appear on the bill.
      The sample output follows:

```
        Croswell Carpet Store
              Invoice

     Customer number:      26817
              Carpet :     574.20
                 Pad :      81.00
               Labor :      86.40

            Subtotal :     741.60
     Less discount :        65.52

            Subtotal :     676.08
            Plus tax :      23.59

               Total :     699.67
```

Write the program and test it for the following three customers.

a. Mr. Wilson (customer 81429) ordered carpet for his family room, which measures 25 feet long and 18 feet wide. The carpet sells for $12.95 per square yard and the manager agreed to give him a discount of 8 percent on the carpet and 6 percent on the labor.

b. Mr. and Mrs. Adams (customer 04246) ordered carpet for their bedroom, which measures 16.5 feet by 15.4 feet. The carpet sells for $18.90 per square yard and the manager granted a discount of 12 percent of everything.

c. Ms. Logan (customer 39050) ordered carpet that cost $8.95 per square yard for her daughter's bedroom. The room measures 13.1 by 12.5 feet. No discounts were given.

10. Each week Abduhl's Flying Carpets pays its salespeople a base salary plus a bonus for each carpet they sell. In addition, they pay a commission of 10 percent of the total sales by each salesperson.

Write a program to compute a salesperson's salary for the month by inputting Base, Bonus, Quantity, and Sales, and making the necessary calculations. Use the following test data:

Salesperson	Base	Bonus	Quantity	Commission	Sales
1	250.00	15.00	20	10%	1543.69
2	280.00	19.50	36	10%	2375.90

The commission figure is 10 percent. Be sure you can change this easily if necessary. Sample output follows:

```
     Salesperson :    1
            Base :  250.00
           Bonus :   15.00
        Quantity :   20
     Total Bonus :  300.00
      Commission :   10%
           Sales : 1543.69
Total Commission :  154.37
             Pay :  704.37
```

11. Write a complete program to calculate and print the pay for a babysitter who gets $1.50 per hour between 6:00 P.M. and 10:00 P.M. and $2.50 per hour for each subsequent hour. Sample output is

```
Number of hours from 6:00 - 10:00 P.M.   3 @ 1.50 =  4.50
Number of hours after 10:00 P.M.          2 @ 2.50 =  5.00
                                                     -----
Total due                                            $9.50
```

Use the CONST section to define the hourly rates.

12. Cramer's Rule is a method for solving a system of linear equations. If you have two equations with variables x and y written as

$$ax + by = c$$
$$dx + ey = f$$

then the solution for x and y can be given as

$$x = \frac{\begin{vmatrix} c & b \\ f & e \end{vmatrix}}{\begin{vmatrix} a & b \\ d & e \end{vmatrix}} \quad , \quad y = \frac{\begin{vmatrix} a & c \\ d & f \end{vmatrix}}{\begin{vmatrix} a & b \\ d & e \end{vmatrix}}$$

Using this notation,

$$\begin{vmatrix} a & b \\ d & e \end{vmatrix}$$

is the determinant of the matrix

$$\begin{bmatrix} a & b \\ d & e \end{bmatrix}$$

and is equal to $ae - bd$.

Write a complete program that will solve a system of two equations using Cramer's Rule. Input will be all coefficients and constants in the system. Output will be the solution to the system. Typical output is

```
For the system of equations

    x +  2y = 5
   2x -   y = 0

we have the solution

    x = 1
    y = 2
```

Note: Do not allow the expression $(ae - bd)$ to equal zero. In the next chapter, we will see how to have the program guard against this possibility.

13. Contact a professional programmer and discuss the issue of program documentation. Find out what portion of that programmer's time is spent on documenting large programs. In general, how many lines of code does the programmer write compared to the number of lines of documentation. Are there certain documentation standards to which the programmer must adhere? Prepare a written report of your findings. Deliver an oral report to your class.

14. Contact instructors of computer science and discuss documentation issues with them. Prepare a written report describing both the similarities and differences in their philosophies about documentation. Deliver a five-minute report to your class. Include descriptive charts prepared for an overhead projector as part of your presentation.

15. Prepare to debate the issue of whether or not documentation standards should be adopted by an influential national group of computer scientists. What would be the advantages and disadvantages of having such standards? As part of the preparation for your debate, prepare your own set of documentation standards.

CHAPTER 5

Selection Statements

The previous four chapters set the stage for using computers to solve problems. You have seen how programs in Pascal can be used to get data, perform computations, and print results. You should be able to write complete, short programs, so it is now time to examine other aspects of programming.

A major feature of a computer is its ability to make decisions. For example, a condition is examined and a decision is made as to which program statement is next executed. Statements that permit a computer to make decisions are called *selection statements*. Selection statements are examples of *control structures* because they allow the programmer to control the flow of execution of program statements.

Before looking at decision making, we need to examine the logical constructs in Pascal, which include a new data type called **boolean.** This data type allows you to represent something as true or false. Although this sounds relatively simple (and it is), this is a very significant feature of computers.

■ 5.1
Boolean Expressions

The boolean Data Type

Thus far we have used only the three data types **integer, real,** and **char;** a fourth data type is **boolean.** A typical declaration of a Boolean variable is

```
VAR
    Flag : boolean;
```

In general, Boolean variables are declared by

> **VAR**
>   ⟨variable1⟩,
>   ⟨variable2⟩,
>   ·
>   ·
>   ·
>   ⟨variable *n*⟩ : **boolean;**

There are only two values for variables of the **boolean** data type: **true** and **false.** These are both constant standard identifiers and can only be used as Boolean values. When these assignments are made, the contents of the designated memory locations will be the assigned values. For example, if the declaration

```
VAR
    Flag1, Flag2 : boolean;
```

is made,

```
Flag1 := true;
Flag2 := false;
```

produces

As with other data types, if two variables are of type **boolean,** the value of one variable can be assigned to another variable as

```
Flag1 := true;
Flag2 := Flag1;
```

and can be envisioned as

true		true
Flag1		Flag2

Note that quotation marks are not used when assigning the values **true** or **false** since these are Boolean constants, not strings.

The **boolean** data type is an ordinal type. Thus, there is an order relationship between **true** and **false: false** < **true.** Furthermore, the **ord** function can be applied to the **boolean** values; **ord(false)** = 0 and **ord(true)** = 1.

Output of boolean

In standard Pascal, Boolean variables can be used as arguments for **write** and **writeln.** Thus,

```
Flag := true;
writeln (Flag);
```

produces

```
true
```

However, some versions will not support output of Boolean variables.

The field width for Boolean output varies with the machine being used. It can be controlled by formatting with a colon followed by a positive integer to designate the field width. The Boolean value will appear right justified in the field. To illustrate, if Flag is a Boolean variable with the value **false,** the segment of code

```
writeln (Flag:6);
writeln (Flag:8);
```

produces the output

```
_false
___false
```

Boolean constants **true** and **false** can also be used in **writeln** statements. For example,

```
writeln (true);
writeln (false);
writeln (true:6, false:6);
```

executed on a machine using a default field width of ten columns produces

```
_____true
_____false
__true_false
```

Although Boolean variables and constants can be assigned and used in output statements, they cannot be used in input statements in standard Pascal. Thus, if Flag is a Boolean variable, a statement such as

```
read (Flag);
```

produces an error. Instead, one would typically read some value and then use this value to assign an appropriate Boolean value to a Boolean variable. This technique will be illustrated later.

The Standard Identifiers eoln and eof as Functions

Section 3.3 introduced the concepts of end-of-line and end-of-file. These were presented as markers that were put in a stream input to separate lines and designate the end of a data file. Both **eoln** and **eof** are built-in Boolean functions that are used to indicate when the pointer is positioned at one of these markers. If the data pointer is positioned at an end-of-line marker, then **eoln** is **true;** otherwise, **eoln** is **false.** Similarly, if the pointer is positioned at the end-of-file marker, **eof** is **true;** otherwise, **eof** is **false.** An exception to the **eoln** value being **false** when the pointer is not at end-of-line marker is when the pointer is at an end-of-file marker. In this case, **eoln** may have the value **true** or may not be defined.

Since **eoln** and **eof** are built-in functions, they can be used in assignment statements. To illustrate, assume we have the data file

with the pointer positioned at the beginning of the file. Furthermore, assume the variable declaration section of a program includes

```
VAR
  A, B : integer;
  Ch1, Ch2 : char;
  EolnFlag, EofFlag : boolean;
```

If no previous assignments have been made, we have

```
[    ]   [    ]   [    ]   [    ]   [    ]   [    ]
  A        B       Ch1      Ch2    EolnFlag EofFlag
```

The assignments

```
EolnFlag := eoln;
EofFlag := eof;
```

might be envisioned as

```
[    ]   [    ]   [    ]   [    ]   [false]  [false]
  A        B       Ch1      Ch2    EolnFlag EofFlag
```

If the line of code

```
read (Ch1, Ch2);
```
is executed, the data pointer is

HI█22█13 −48█ ■
  ↑

and the assignment statements
```
EolnFlag := eoln;
EofFlag := eof;
```
result in

		H	I	**true**	**false**
A	B	Ch1	Ch2	EolnFlag	EofFlag

If the next three lines of code are
```
readln (A);
EolnFlag := eoln;
EofFlag := eof;
```
this produces

HI█22█13 −48█ ■
   ↑

22		H	I	**false**	**false**
A	B	Ch1	Ch2	EolnFlag	EofFlag

Then
```
read (A, B);
EolnFlag := eoln;
EofFlag := eof;
```
produces

HI█22█13 −48█ ■
    ↑

13	−48	H	I	**true**	**false**
A	B	Ch1	Ch2	EolnFlag	EofFlag

And finally
```
read (Ch1);
EolnFlag := eoln;
EofFlag := eof;
```
produces

HI█22█13 −48█ ■
    ↑

13	−48	␤	I	**true**	**true**
A	B	Ch1	Ch2	EolnFlag	EofFlag

Both **eoln** and **eof** can also be used in output statements. For example,
```
writeln (eoln, eof);
write (eoln:6, eof:6);
```
are appropriate statements.

The following example illustrates the use of **eoln** and **eof** in output statements and how their values change according to the data pointer for a stream input. (This example assumes input from a data file; interactive input would produce a different result.)

Let's write a short program that allows us to examine a line of data and the respective values of **eoln** and **eof.** Suppose the data file is

and you want to produce a chart that indicates the values after each character is read. The chart heading should include the character read, **eoln** value, and **eof** value. The code needed to produce one line of the chart is

```
read (Ch);
writeln (Ch:15, eoln:20, eof:20);
```

Since we can read four characters and two end-of-line markers from this data file, this segment of code needs to be executed six times. An attempt to **read** (Ch) seven times would produce an error since you would be trying to read past the end-of-file marker. The complete program for this example follows.

```
PROGRAM ReadCheck (input, output);

CONST
  Indent = ' ';

VAR
  Ch : char;

BEGIN  {  Program  }

  {  Print a heading for the output  }

  writeln;
  writeln (Indent:10, 'Character read', 'eoln value':17, 'eof value':19);
  writeln (Indent:10, '--------------', '----------':17, '---------':19);
  writeln;

  {  Now read the data file  }

  read (Ch);
  writeln (Indent:15, Ch, eoln:22, eof:20);
  read (Ch);
  writeln (Indent:15, Ch, eoln:22, eof:20);
  read (Ch);
  writeln (Indent:15, Ch, eoln:22, eof:20);
  read (Ch);
  writeln (Indent:15, Ch, eoln:22, eof:20);
  read (Ch);
  writeln (Indent:15, Ch, eoln:22, eof:20);
  read (Ch);
  writeln (Indent:15, Ch, eoln:22, eof:20);
  writeln
END.  {  of program  }
```

The output from this program is

```
Character read              eoln value              eof value
---------------             ----------              ---------
      A                        false                  false
      B                        true                   false
                               false                  false
      1                        false                  false
      2                        true                   false
                               true                   true
```

Relational Operators and Simple Boolean Expressions

In arithmetic, integers and reals can be compared using equalities (=) and inequalities(<, >, ≠, and so on). Pascal also provides for the comparison of numbers or values of variables. The operators used for comparison are called *relational operators* and there are six of them. Their arithmetic notation, Pascal notation, and meaning are given in Table 5.1.

Table 5.1
Relational operators

Arithmetic Operation	Relational Operator	Meaning
=	=	Is equal to
<	<	Is less than
>	>	Is greater than
≤	<=	Is less than or equal to
≥	>=	Is greater than or equal to
≠	<>	Is not equal to

The previous section indicated how Boolean values could be generated using the built-in functions **eoln** and **eof** when reading data. Let's now examine some other methods of generating Boolean values. This is necessary so we can control selection in a program.

When two numbers or variable values are compared using a single relational operator, the expression is referred to as a *simple Boolean expression*. Each simple Boolean expression has the Boolean value **true** or **false** according to the arithmetic validity of the expression. In general, only data of the same type can be compared; thus, integers must be compared to integers, reals must be compared to reals, and characters must be compared to characters. The usual exception can be applied here; that is, reals can be compared to integers. When comparing reals, however, the computer representation of a real number might not be the exact real number intended.

Table 5.2 sets forth several Boolean expressions and their respective Boolean values, assuming the assignment statements A := 3 and B := 4 have been made.

Arithmetic expressions can also be used in simple Boolean expressions. Thus,

```
4 < (3 + 2)
```

has the value **true.** When the computer evaluates this expression, the parentheses dictate that (3 + 2) be evaluated first and then the relational operator. Sequentially, this becomes

```
4 < (3 + 2)
4 <     5
true
```

TABLE 5.2
Values of simple Boolean
expressions

Simple Boolean Expression	Boolean Value
7 = 7	true
−3.0 = 0.0	false
4.2 > 3.7	true
−18 < −15	true
13 < 100	true
13 <= 100	true
13 <= 13	true
0.012 > 0.013	false
−17.32 <> −17.32	false
A <= B	true
B > A	true

What if the parentheses had not been used? Could the expression be evaluated? This type of expression necessitates a priority level for the relational operators and the arithmetic operators. A summary for the priority of these operations is

Expression	Priority
( )	1
*, /, **MOD, DIV**	2
+, −	3
=, <,>, <=, >=, <>	4

Thus, we see that the relational operators are evaluated last. As with arithmetic operators, these are evaluated in order from left to right. Thus, the expression

```
4 < 3 + 2
```

could be evaluated without parentheses and would have the same Boolean value.

The following example illustrates the evaluation of a somewhat more complex Boolean expression.

EXAMPLE 5.2

Indicate the successive steps in the evaluation of the Boolean expression

```
10 MOD 4 * 3 - 8 <= 18 + 30 DIV 4 - 20
```

The steps in this evaluation are

As shown in Example 5.2, even though parentheses are not required when using arithmetic expressions with relational operators, it is usually a good idea to use them to enhance the readability of the expression and to avoid using an incorrect expression.

Logical Operators and Compound Boolean Expressions

Boolean values may also be generated by using *logical operators* with simple Boolean expressions. The logical operators used by Pascal are **AND, OR,** and **NOT. AND** and **OR** are used to connect two Boolean expressions. **NOT** is used to negate the Boolean value of an expression; hence, it is sometimes referred to as *negation.* When these connectives or negation are used to generate Boolean values, the complete expression is referred to as a *compound Boolean expression.*

If **AND** is used to join two simple Boolean expressions, the resulting compound expression is **true** only when both simple expressions are **true.** If **OR** is used, the result is **true** if either or both of the expressions are **true.** This is summarized as follows:

Expression 1 (E1)	Expression 2 (E2)	E1 AND E2	E1 OR E2
true	true	true	true
true	false	false	true
false	true	false	true
false	false	false	false

As previously indicated, **NOT** merely produces the logical complement of an expression as follows:

Expression (E)	NOT E
true	false
false	true

When using these operators with relational expressions, parentheses are required because logical operators are evaluated before relational operators. Illustrations of the Boolean values generated using logical operators are given in Table 5.3.

TABLE 5.3
Values of compound
Boolean expressions

Expression	Boolean Value
(4.2 >= 5.0) **AND** (8 = (3 + 5))	**false**
(4.2 >= 5.0) **OR** (8 = (3 + 5))	**true**
(−2 < 0) **AND** (18 >= 10)	**true**
(−2 < 0) **OR** (18 >= 10)	**true**
(3 > 5) **AND** (14.1 = 0.0)	**false**
(3 > 5) **OR** (14.1 = 0.0)	**false**
NOT (18 = (10 + 8))	**false**
NOT (−4 > 0)	**true**

Complex Boolean expressions can be generated by using several logical operators in an expression. The priority for evaluating these operators is

---

George Boole

George Boole was born in 1815 in Lincoln, England. Boole was the son of a small shopkeeper and his family belonged to the lowest social class. In an attempt to rise above his station, Boole spent his early years teaching himself Latin and Greek. During this period, he also received elementary instruction in mathematics from his father.

At the age of 16, Boole worked as a teacher in an elementary school. He used most of his wages to help support his parents. At the age of 20 (after a brief, unsuccessful attempt to study for the clergy), he opened his own school. As part of his preparation for running his school, he had to learn more mathematics. This activity led to the development of some of the most significant mathematics of the nineteenth century.

Boole's major contributions were in the field of logic. An indication of his genius is given by the fact that his early work included the discovery of invariants. The mathematical significance of this is perhaps best explained by noting that the theory of relativity developed by Albert Einstein would not have been possible without the previous work on invariants.

Boole's first published contribution was *The Mathematical Analysis of Logic,* which appeared in 1848 while he was still working as an elementary teacher and the sole support for his parents. In 1849, he was appointed Professor of Mathematics at Queen's College in Cork, Ireland. The relative freedom from financial worry and time constraints the college appointment provided allowed him to pursue his work in mathematics. His masterpiece, *An Investigation of the Laws of Thought, on which Are Founded the Mathematical Theories of Logic and Probabilities,* was published in 1854. Boole was then 39, relatively old for such original work. According to Bertrand Russell, pure mathematics was discovered by Boole in this work.

The brilliance of Boole's work laid the foundation for what is currently studied as formal logic. The data type, Boolean, is named in honor of Boole because of his contribution to the development of logic as part of mathematics. Boole died in 1864. His early death resulted from pneumonia contracted by keeping a lecture engagement when he was soaked to the skin.

Operator	Priority
NOT	1
AND	2
OR	3

When complex expressions are being evaluated, the logical operators, arithmetic expressions, and relational operators are evaluated during successive passes through the expression. The priority list is now as follows:

Expression or Operation	Priority
( )	1. Evaluate from inside out
NOT	2. Evaluate from left to right
*, /, **MOD, DIV, AND**	3. Evaluate from left to right
+, −, **OR**	4. Evaluate from left to right
<, <=, >, >=, =, <>	5. Evaluate from left to right

Thus, an expression like

```
0 < X AND X < 2
```

produces an error. It must be written as

```
(0 < X) AND (X < 2)
```

The following examples illustrate evaluation of some complex Boolean expressions.

■ EXAMPLE 5.3

```
(3 < 5)  OR  (21 <>18)  AND  (-81 > 0)  ⎫
   ↓                                     ⎪
  true   OR   (21 <>18)  AND  (-81 > 0)  ⎬ first pass
                 ↓                       ⎪ (parentheses first)
  true   OR     true     AND  (-81 > 0)  ⎭
                                 ↓        ⎫
  true   OR     true     AND    false     ⎬ second pass
                          ↓               ⎭
  true   OR            false     ⎫
             ↓                    ⎬ third pass
           true                  ⎭
```

■ EXAMPLE 5.4

```
NOT ((-5.0 >= -6.2)  OR  ((7 <> 3)  AND  (6 = (3 + 3))))
         ↓                    ↓                  ↓
NOT (     true       OR  (  true    AND  (6 =      6   )))
                                              ↓
NOT (     true       OR  (  true    AND      true      ))
                                     ↓
NOT (     true       OR             true               )
                     ↓
NOT                true
         ↓
       false
```

■ EXAMPLE 5.5

Assume X and Y are real variables, Flag is a Boolean variable, and the assignment statements

```
X := 12.5;
Y := -100;
Flag := true;
```

have been made. (X <> 7 / 3) **OR NOT** ((X > = 4) **AND (NOT** Flag)) can be evaluated as:

```
(X <> 7/3) OR NOT ((X >= 4) AND (NOT Flag))
    ↓
   true     OR NOT ((X >= 4) AND (NOT Flag))
                        ↓
   true     OR NOT (  true   AND (NOT Flag))
                                    ↓
   true     OR NOT (  true   AND   false   )
                             ↓
   true     OR NOT          false
                 ↓
   true     OR            true
            ↓
          true
```

Extra care should be taken with the syntax of Boolean expressions. For example, the expression

```
3 < 4 AND 100 > 80
```

in a program produces an error. Since relational expressions are evaluated last, the first pass through this expression would attempt to evaluate

```
4 AND 100
```

This is not valid because logical operators can only operate on Boolean values **true** and **false.**

If an expression produces a Boolean value and is evaluated before a connective, then that expression would not have to be in parentheses. For example,

```
(3 < 5) AND NOT (0 >= -2)
```

is a valid expression, evaluated as follows:

```
(3 < 5   AND   NOT (0 >= -2)
   ↓
 true    AND   NOT (0 >= -2)
                        ↓
 true    AND   NOT true
                  ↓
 true    AND       false
          ↓
        false
```

Exercises 5.1

1. Assume the variable declaration section of a program is

   ```
   VAR
      Flag1, Flag2 : boolean;
   ```

   What output is produced by the following segment of code?

   ```
   Flag1 := true;
   Flag2 := false;
   writeln (Flag1, true:6, Flag2:8);
   Flag1 := Flag2;
   writeln (Flag2:20);
   ```

2. Write a test program that illustrates what happens when Boolean expressions are not enclosed in parentheses. For example,

   ```
   3 < 5 AND 8.0 <> 4 * 3
   ```

3. Assume the variable declaration section of a program is

   ```
   VAR
      Ch : char;
      Flag : boolean;
   ```

   Indicate if the following assignment statements are valid or invalid.

   a. `Flag := 'true';`   d. `Ch := Flag;`
   b. `Flag := T;`   e. `Ch := true;`
   c. `Flag := true;`   f. `Ch := 'T';`

4. Can **eoln** and **eof** be **true** at the same time? Explain.

5. Indicate for each of the following simple Boolean expressions whether it is **true, false,** or invalid.

   a. `-3.01 <= -3.001`
   b. `-3.0 = -3`

```
c. 25 - 10 <> 3 * 5
d. 42 MOD 5 < 42 DIV 5
e. -5 * (3 + 2) > 2 * (-10)
f. 10 / 5 < 1 + 1
g. 3 + 8 MOD 5 >= 6 - 12 MOD 2
```

6. Evaluate each of the following expressions:

    a. `(3 > 7) AND (2 < 0) OR (6 = 3 + 3)`

    b. `((3 > 7) AND (2 < 0)) OR (6 = 3 + 3)`

    c. `(3 > 7) AND ((2 < 0) OR (6 = 3 + 3))`

    d. `NOT ((-4.2 <> 3.0) AND (10 < 20))`

    e. `(NOT (-4.2 <> 3.0)) OR (NOT (10 < 20))`

7. Assume the variable declaration section of a program is

    ```
    VAR
        Int1, Int2 : integer;
        Rl1, Rl2 : real;
        Flag1, Flag2 : boolean;
    ```

    and the values of the variables are

0	8	-15.2	-20.0	**false**	**true**
Int1	Int2	Rl1	Rl2	Flag1	Flag2

    Evaluate each of the following expressions:

    a. `(Int1 <= Int2) OR NOT (Rl2 = Rl1)`

    b. `NOT (Flag1) OR NOT (Flag2)`

    c. `NOT (Flag1 AND Flag2)`

    d. `((Rl1 - Rl2) < 100/Int2) AND ((Int1 < 1) AND NOT (Flag2))`

    e. `NOT ((Int2 - 16 DIV 2) = Int1) AND Flag1`

8. Indicate for each of the following expressions whether it is valid or invalid. Evaluate those that are valid.

    a. `3 < 4 OR 5 <> 6`   e. `NOT true OR NOT false`

    b. `NOT 3.0 = 6 / 2`   f. `NOT (18 < 25) AND OR (-3 < 0)`

    c. `NOT (true OR false)`   g. `8 * 3 < 20 + 10`

    d. `NOT true OR false`

9. DeMorgan's Laws state the following:

    a. `NOT (A OR B)` is equivalent to `(NOT A) AND (NOT B)`

    b. `NOT (A AND B)` is equivalent to `(NOT A) OR (NOT B)`

    Write a test program that demonstrates the validity of each of these equivalent statements.

■ ■ ■ ■

■ 5.2
IF . . . THEN Statements

OBJECTIVES

- to learn the form and syntax required for using an **IF . . . THEN** statement
- to understand the flow of control when using an **IF . . . THEN** statement
- to be able to use an **IF . . . THEN** statement in a program

The first decision-making statement we will examine is the **IF . . . THEN** statement. **IF . . . THEN** is used to make a program do something only when certain conditions are used. The form and syntax for an **IF . . . THEN** statement are

> **IF** ⟨Boolean expression⟩ **THEN**
>   ⟨statement⟩;

where ⟨statement⟩ represents any Pascal statement.

The Boolean expression can be any valid expression that is either **true** or **false** at the time of evaluation. If it is **true,** the statement following the

- to understand why compound statements are needed
- to understand how **BEGIN . . . END** are used to write compound statements
- to be able to use correct syntax in writing a compound statement
- to be able to design programs using **IF . . . THEN** statements

reserved word **THEN** is executed. If it is **false,** control is transferred to the first program statement following the complete **IF . . . THEN** statement. In general, code would have the form

⟨statement 1⟩;
IF ⟨Boolean expression⟩ **THEN**
⟨statement 2⟩;
⟨statement 3⟩;

as illustrated in Figure 5.1.

FIGURE 5.1
IF . . . THEN flow diagram

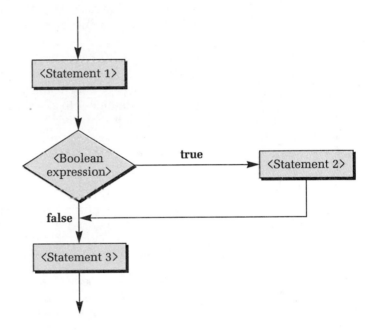

As a further illustration of how an **IF . . . THEN** statement works, consider the program fragment

```
Sum := 0.0;
read (Num);
IF Num > 0.0 THEN
   Sum := Sum + Num;
writeln (Sum:10:2);
```

If the value read is 75.85, prior to execution of the **IF . . . THEN** statement, the contents of Num and Sum are

| 75.85 | 0.0 |
| Num | Sum |

The Boolean expression Num > 0.0 is now evaluated and, since it is **true,** the statement

```
Sum := Sum + Num;
```

is executed and we have

| 75.85 | 75.85 |
| Num | Sum |

The next program statement is executed and produces the output

```
75.85
```

However, if the value read is -25.5, the variable values are

Num   Sum

The Boolean expression Num > 0.0 is **false** and control is transferred to the line

```
writeln (Sum);
```

Thus, the output is

```
0.00
```

Now, let's suppose you want a program in which one objective is to count the number of zeroes in the input. Assuming suitable initialization and declaration, a program fragment for this task could be

```
readln (Num);
IF Num = 0 THEN
   ZeroCount := ZeroCount + 1;
```

One writing style for using an **IF . . . THEN** statement calls for indenting the program statement to be executed if the Boolean expression is **true.** This, of course, is not required.

```
IF Num = 0 THEN
   ZeroCount := Zero Count + 1;
```

could be written

```
IF Num = 0 THEN ZeroCount := Zerocount + 1;
```

However, the indenting style for simple **IF . . . THEN** statements is consistent with the style used with more elaborate conditional statements.

Compound Statements

The last concept needed before looking further at selection in Pascal is a *compound statement.* Simple statements conform to the syntax diagram for statements shown in Appendix 3. In a Pascal program, simple statements are separated by semicolons. Thus,

```
readln (A, B);
A := 3 * B;
writeln (A);
```

are three simple statements.

In some instances, it is necessary to perform several simple statements when some condition is true. For example, you may want the program to do certain things if a condition is true. In this situation, several simple statements that can be written as a single compound statement would be helpful. In general, there are several Pascal constructs that require compound statements. A compound statement is created by using the reserved words **BEGIN** and **END** at the beginning and end of a sequence of simple statements. Correct syntax for a compound statement is

```
BEGIN
   ⟨statement 1⟩;
   ⟨statement 2⟩;
         .
         .
         .
   ⟨statement n⟩
END;
```

Statements within a compound statement are separated by semicolons. The last statement before **END** does not require a semicolon, but if a semicolon is used here, it will not affect the program.

When a compound statement is executed within a program, the entire segment of code between **BEGIN** and **END** is treated as a single action. This is referred to as a *BEGIN . . . END block.* It is important that you develop a consistent, acceptable writing style for writing compound statements. What you use will vary according to your instructor's wishes and your personal preferences. Examples in this text will indent each simple statement within a compound statement two spaces. Thus,

```
BEGIN
  read (A, B);
  A := 3 * B;
  writeln (A)
END;
```

is a compound statement in a program; what it does is easily identified.

Some examples of compound statements follow. Although the concept, syntax, and writing style do not appear to be difficult at this point, one of the most frequent errors for beginning programmers is incorrect use of compound statements.

■ EXAMPLE 5.6

Let's write a compound statement that allows you to read a real, print the real, and add it to a total. Assuming variables have been suitably declared and initialized, a compound statement to do this is

```
BEGIN
  writeln ('Enter a real number and press <RETURN>.');
  readln (Num);
  writeln (Num:8:2);
  Total := Total + Num
END;
```

■ EXAMPLE 5.7

Suppose you are writing a program to enable your instructor to compute grades for your class. For each student you need to read three scores, add the scores, compute the average score, print the scores, and print the test average. Again, assuming variables have been suitably declared, a compound statement for this could be

```
BEGIN
  writeln ('Enter three scores and press <RETURN>.');
  readln (Score1, Score2, Score3);
  Total := Score1 + Score2 + Score3;
  Average := Total / 3.0;
  write (Score1:6, Score2:6, Score3:6);
  writeln (Average:12:2)
END;
```

Using Compound Statements

As you might expect, compound statements can be (and frequently are) used as part of an **IF . . . THEN** statement. The form and syntax for this are

```
IF ⟨Boolean expression⟩ THEN
   BEGIN
      ⟨statement 1⟩;
      ⟨statement 2⟩;
            .
            .
            .
      ⟨statement n⟩
   END;
```

Program control is exactly as before depending on the value of the Boolean expression. For example, suppose you want to determine how many positive numbers are in a data file and also compute their sum. This can be partially accomplished by the program fragment

```
Sum := 0.0;
Count := 0;
read (Num);
IF Num > 0.0 THEN
   BEGIN
     Sum := Sum + Num;
     Count := Count + 1
   End;   {  of IF...THEN  }
```

The next example designs a program to solve a problem using an **IF . . . THEN** statement.

■ EXAMPLE 5.8

Let's write a program that reads two integers and prints them in the order larger first, smaller second. The first-level pseudocode solution is

1. Read numbers
2. Determine larger
3. Print a heading
4. Print results

Step 1 is a single line of code, and steps 3 and 4 will be some **writeln** statements. However, step 2 requires some refinement. A second-level solution could be

1. Read numbers
2. Determine larger
   2.1 **IF** Num 1 < Num 2 **THEN** exchange numbers
3. Print a heading
4. Print results
   4.1 print Num1 (larger)
   4.2 print Num2 (smaller)

Step 2.1 is further refined to produce

   2.1 **IF** Num1 < Num2 **THEN** exchange numbers
        2.1.1   Temp gets Num1
        2.1.2   Num1 gets Num2
        2.1.3   Num2 gets Temp

We can now write code for the program to solve this problem.

```
writeln ('Enter two integers and press <RETURN>.');
readln (Num1, Num2);
IF Num1 < Num2 THEN
   BEGIN
      Temp := Num1;
      Num1 := Num2;
      Num2 := Temp
   END;  {  of IF...THEN  }
writeln (Num1:15, Num2:15);
```

A complete program for this example follows.

```
PROGRAM UseIFTHEN (input, output);

{    This program illustrates using an IF ... THEN statement.     }
{    Two numbers are read and then printed in order, larger       }
{    first.                                                       }

CONST
  Skip = ' ';

VAR
  Num1,                                 {    First number          }
  Num2,                                 {    Second number         }
  Temp : integer;                       {    Temporary variable    }

{  Now start the program  }

BEGIN  {  Program  }

  writeln ('Enter two integers and press <RETURN>.');
  readln (Num1, Num2);

  {  Print a heading  }

  writeln;
  writeln ('Larger number', Skip:10, 'Smaller number');
  writeln ('-------------', Skip:10, '--------------');
  writeln;

  {  Exchange numbers  }

  IF Num1 < Num2 THEN
    BEGIN
      Temp := Num1;
      Num1 := Num2;
      Num2 := Temp
    END;
  writeln (Num1:7, Num2:23);
  writeln

END.  {  of main program }
```

A sample run of this program produces

```
Enter two integers and press <RETURN>.
?18 30

Larger number        Smaller number
-------------        --------------
     30                    18
```

Exercises 5.2

1. What is the output from each of the following program fragments? Assume the following assignment statements precede each fragment:

   ```
   := 10;
   := 5;
   ```

   a.
   ```
   IF A <= B THEN
       B := A;
   writeln (A, B);
   ```

   b.
   ```
   IF A <= B THEN
       BEGIN
           B := A;
           writeln (A,B)
       END;
   ```

   c.
   ```
   IF A < B THEN
       Temp := A;
   A := B;
   B := Temp;
   writeln (A, B);
   ```

   d.
   ```
   IF A < B THEN
       BEGIN
           Temp := A;
           A := B;
           B := Temp
       END;
   writeln (A, B);
   ```

   e.
   ```
   IF (A < B) OR (B - A < 0) THEN
       BEGIN
           A := A + B;
           B := B - 1;
           writeln (A, B)
       END;
   writeln (A, B);
   ```

   f.
   ```
   IF (A < B) AND (B - A < 0) THEN
       BEGIN
           A := A + B;
           B := B - 1;
           writeln (A, B)
       END;
   writeln (A, B);
   ```

2. Write a test program to illustrate what happens when a semicolon is inadvertently inserted after **THEN** in an **IF . . . THEN** statement. For example,

   ```
   IF A > 0 THEN;
       Sum := Sum + A;
   ```

3. Find and explain the errors in each of the following program fragments. You may assume all variables have been suitably declared.

   a.
   ```
   IF A := 10 THEN
       writeln (A);
   ```

   b.
   ```
   X := 7;
   IF 3 < X < 10 THEN
       BEGIN
           X := X + 1;
           writeln (X)
       END;
   ```

   c.
   ```
   Count := 0;
   Sum := 0;
   A := 50;
   IF A > 0 THEN
       Count := Count + 1;
       Sum := Sum + A;
   ```

   d.
   ```
   read (Ch);
   IF Ch = 'A' OR 'B' THEN
       writeln (Ch:10);
   ```

4. What is the output from each of the following program fragments? Assume variables have been suitably declared.

   a.
   ```
   J := 18;
   IF J MOD 5 = 0 THEN
       writeln (J);
   ```

   b.
   ```
   A := 5;
   B := 90;
   B := B DIV A - 5;
   IF B > A THEN
       B := A * 30;
   writeln (A, B);
   ```

5. Can a simple statement be written using a **BEGIN . . . END** block? Write a short program that allows you to verify your answer.

6. Discuss the differences in the following programs. Predict the output for each program using sample values for Num.

    a.
```
PROGRAM Exercise6a (input, output);

   VAR
     Num : integer;

   BEGIN
     writeln ('Enter an integer and press <RETURN>.');
     readln (Num);
     IF Num > 0 THEN
       writeln;
       writeln ('The number is':22, Num:6);
       writeln;
       writeln ('The number squared is':30, Num * Num:6);
       writeln ('The number cubed is':28, Num * Num * Num:6);
       writeln
   END.
```

    b.
```
PROGRAM Exercise6b (input, output);

   VAR
     Num : integer;

   BEGIN  {  Main program  }
     writeln ('Enter an integer and press <RETURN>.');
     readln (Num);
     IF Num > 0 THEN
       BEGIN  {  Start output  }
         writeln;
         writeln ('The number is ':22, Num:6);
         writeln;
         writeln ('The number squared is':30, Num * Num:6);
         writeln ('The number cubed is':28, Num * Num *
                     Num:6);
         writeln
       END  {  output for one number  }
   END.
```

7. Discuss writing style and readability of compound statements.

8. Find all errors in the following compound statements.

    a.
```
BEGIN
   read (A)
   writeln (A)
END;
```

    b.
```
BEGIN
   Sum := Sum + Num
END;
```

    c.
```
BEGIN
   read (Size1, Size2);
   writeln (Size1:8, Size2:8)
END.
```

    d.
```
BEGIN
   readln (Age, Weight);
   TotalAge := TotalAge + Age;
   TotalWeight := TotalWeight + Weight;
   writeln (Age:8, Weight:8)
```

9. Write a single compound statement that will:
   a. Read three integers from a data file.
   b. Add them to a previous total.
   c. Print the numbers on one line.
   d. Skip a line (output).
   e. Print the new total.

10. Write a program fragment that reads three reals from a data file, counts the number of positive reals, and accumulates the sum of positive reals.

11. Write a program fragment that reads three characters from a data file and then prints them only if they have been read in alphabetical order (for example, print "boy" but do not print "dog").

12. Given two integers, A and B, A is a divisor of B if B **MOD** A = 0. Write a complete program that reads two positive integers A and B and then, if A is a divisor of B,
    a. Print A.
    b. Print B.
    c. Print the result of B divided by A.

    For example, the output could be

    ```
    A is 14
    B is 42
    B divided by A is 3
    ```

■ ■ ■ ■

■ 5.3
IF . . . THEN . . . ELSE Statements

OBJECTIVES

- to learn the form and syntax required for using an **IF . . . THEN. . . ELSE** statement
- to understand the flow of control when using an **IF . . . THEN . . . ELSE** statement
- to be able to use an **IF . . . THEN. . . ELSE** statement in a program
- to be able to design programs using **IF . . . THEN . . . ELSE** statements

Form and Syntax

The previous section discussed the one-way selection statement **IF . . . THEN.** The second selection statement we will examine is the two-way selection statement **IF . . . THEN . . . ELSE.** Correct form and syntax for **IF . . . THEN . . . ELSE** are

```
IF ⟨Boolean expression⟩ THEN
    ⟨statement⟩
ELSE
    ⟨statement⟩;
```

Flow of control when using an **IF . . . THEN . . . ELSE** statement is as follows:

1. The Boolean expression is evaluated.
2. If the Boolean expression is **true,** the statement following **THEN** is executed and control is transferred to the first program statement following the complete **IF . . . THEN . . ELSE** statement.
3. If the Boolean expression is **false,** the statement following **ELSE** is executed and control is transferred to the first program statement following the **IF . . . THEN . . . ELSE** statement.

A flow diagram is given in Figure 5.2.

To illustrate this flow of control, let us consider the problem of printing the larger of two numbers using an **IF . . . THEN . . . ELSE** statement in the following code.

FIGURE 5.2
IF . . . THEN . . . ELSE flow
diagram

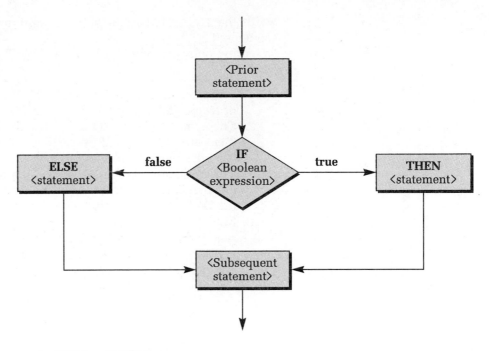

```
read (Num1, Num2);
IF Num1 > Num2 THEN
    writeln (Num1)
  ELSE
    writeln (Num2);
  writeln ('All done');
```

If the values read are

80		15
Num1		Num2

the Boolean expression Num1 > Num2 is **true** and the statement

```
    writeln (Num1)
```

is executed to produce

```
    80
```

Control is then transferred to the next program statement,

```
    writeln ('All done');
```

and the output is

```
    80
    All done
```

However, if the values read are

10		75
Num1		Num2

the Boolean expression Num1 > Num2 is **false,** control is transferred to

```
    writeln (Num2);
```

and the output is

```
    75
    All done
```

with the 75 printed from the **ELSE** option of the **IF** . . . **THEN** . . . **ELSE** statement.

A few points to remember concerning **IF** . . . **THEN** . . . **ELSE** statements are:

1. The Boolean expression can be any valid expression having a value of **true** or **false** at the time it is evaluated.
2. The complete **IF** . . . **THEN** . . . **ELSE** statement is one program statement and is separated from other complete statements by a semicolon whenever appropriate.
3. There is no semicolon preceding the reserved word **ELSE**. A semicolon preceding the reserved word **ELSE** causes the compiler to treat the **IF** . . . **THEN** portion as a complete program statement and the **ELSE** portion as a separate statement. This produces an error message indicating that **ELSE** is being used without an **IF** . . . **THEN**.
4. Writing style should include indenting within the **ELSE** option in a manner consistent with indenting in the **IF** . . . **THEN** option.

■ EXAMPLE 5.9

Let's write a program fragment to keep separate counts of the negative and nonnegative numbers entered as data. Assuming all variables have been suitably declared and initialized, an **IF** . . . **THEN** . . . **ELSE** statement could be used as follows:

```
writeln ('Please enter a number and press <RETURN>.');
readln (Num);
IF Num < 0 THEN
  NegCount := NegCount + 1
ELSE
  NonNegCount := NonNegCount + 1;
```

■

Using Compound Statements

Program statements in both the **IF** . . . **THEN** option and the **ELSE** option can be compound statements. When using compound statements in these options, you should use a consistent, readable indenting style; remember to use **BEGIN** . . . **END** for each compound statement; and do not put a semicolon before **ELSE**.

■ EXAMPLE 5.10

Suppose you want a program to read a number, count it as negative or nonnegative, and print it in either a column of nonnegative numbers or a column of negative numbers. Assuming all variables have been suitably declared and initialized, the fragment might be

```
writeln ('Please enter a number and press <RETURN>.');
readln (Num);
IF Num < 0 THEN
  BEGIN
    NegCount := NegCount + 1;
    writeln (Num:15)
  END   {  of IF...THEN option  }
ELSE
```

```
BEGIN
  NonNegCount := NonNegCount + 1;
  writeln (Num:30)
END;  {  of ELSE option  }
```

We next consider an example of a program fragment that requires the use of compound statements within an **IF . . . THEN . . . ELSE** statement.

■ **EXAMPLE 5.11**

Let's write a program fragment that computes gross wages for an employee of the Florida OJ Canning Company. A data line consists of three initials, the total hours worked, and the hourly rate. Thus a typical data line is

JHΛ 44.5 12.75

Overtime (more than 40 hours) is computed as time-and-a-half. The output should include all input data and the gross wages. A first-level pseudocode for this problem could be

1. Get the data
2. Perform computation
3. Print results

Step 1 can be accomplished by a **single readln** statement. Step 2 can be refined to

2. Perform computation
   2.1 **IF** Hours <= 40.0 **THEN**
            compute regular time
        ELSE
            compute time-and-a-half

Step 2.1 can be written as

```
IF Hours <= 40.0 THEN
  TotalWage := Hours * PayRate
ELSE
  BEGIN
    Overtime := 1.5 * (Hours - 40.0) * PayRate;
    TotalWage := 40 * PayRate + Overtime
  END;
```

Step 3 could be refined to

3. Print results
   3.1 print initials
   3.2 print Hours and PayRate
   3.3 print TotalWage

The program fragment for this problem is

```
readln (Init1, Init2, Init3, Hours, PayRate);
IF Hours <= 40.0 THEN
  TotalWage := Hours * PayRate
ELSE
  BEGIN
    Overtime := 1.5 * (Hours - 40.0) * PayRate;
    TotalWage := 40 * PayRate + Overtime
  END;
write (Init1:5, Init2, Init3);
write (Hours:10:2, PayRate:10:2);
writeln ('$':10, TotalWage:7:2);
```

If this fragment is run on the data line given at the beginning of this example, we get

```
JHA        44.50       12.75            $ 596.06
```

Robust Programs

If a program is completely protected against all possible crashes from bad data and unexpected values, it is said to be *robust*. The preceding examples have all assumed that desired data would be accurately entered from the keyboard. In actual practice, this is seldom the case. **IF . . . THEN . . . ELSE** statements can be used to guard against bad data entries. For example, if a program is designed to use positive numbers, you could guard against negatives and zero by

```
writeln ('Enter a positive number and press <RETURN>.')
readln (Number);
IF Number <= 0 THEN
  writeln ('You entered a nonpositive number.');
ELSE
  .
  .   (code for expected action here)
  .
```

This program protection can be used anywhere in a program. For example, if you are finding square roots of numbers, you could avoid a program crash by

```
IF Num < 0 THEN
  writeln ('The number ', Num, ' is negative.')
ELSE
  .
  .   (rest of action here)
  .
```

Artificial Intelligence

Artificial intelligence (AI) research seeks to understand the principles of human intelligence and apply those principles to the creation of smarter computer programs. The original goal of AI research was to create programs with humanlike intelligence and capabilities, yet after many years of research, little progress has been made toward this goal.

In recent years, however, AI researchers have pursued much more modest goals with much greater success. Programs based on AI techniques are playing increasingly important roles in such down-to-earth areas as medicine, education, recreation, business, and industry. Such programs come nowhere near to achieving human levels of intelligence, but they often have capabilities that are not easily achieved with non-AI programs.

The main principles of AI can be summarized as follows:

Search: a method whereby the computer solves a problem by searching through all logically possible solutions.

Rules: knowledge about what actions to take in particular circumstances is stored as rules; each rule has the form

IF ⟨situation⟩ **THEN** ⟨action or conclusion⟩

Reasoning: programs can use reasoning to draw conclusions from the facts and rules available to the program.

Planning: the control program plans the actions that must be taken to accomplish a particular goal, then modifies the plan if unexpected obstacles are encountered; this is most widely used in robot control.

Pattern recognition: important for rule-based systems, the **IF** part of a rule specifies a particular pattern of facts; the rule is to be applied when that pattern is recognized in the facts known to the program.

Knowledge bases: storage of the facts and rules that govern the operation of an AI program.

In actual practice, students need to balance robustness against amount of code and efficiency. An overemphasis on making a program robust can detract from time spent learning new programming concepts. You should discuss this with your instructor and decide what is best for your situation. Generally, there should be an agreement between the programmer and the customer regarding the level of robustness required. For most programs and examples in this text, it is assumed that valid data are entered when requested.

Exercises 5.3

1. What output is produced from each of the following program fragments? Assume all variables have been suitably declared.

a.
```
A := -14;
B := 0;
IF A < B THEN
   writeln (A, abs(A))
ELSE
   writeln (A * B);
```

b.
```
A := 50;
B := 25;
Count :- 0;
Sum := 0;
IF A = B THEN
   writeln (A, B)
ELSE
   BEGIN
      Count := Count + 1;
      Sum := Sum + A + B;
      writeln (A, B)
   END;
writeln (Count, Sum);
```

c.
```
Temp := 0;
A := 10;
B := 5;
IF A > B THEN
   writeln (A, B)
ELSE
   Temp := A;
   A := B;
   B := Temp;
writeln (A, B);
```

2. Write a test program that illustrates what error message occurs when a semicolon precedes **ELSE** in an **IF . . . THEN . . . ELSE** statement. For example,

```
PROGRAM SyntaxError (output);

VAR
   A, B : integer;

BEGIN
   A := 10;
   B := 5;
   IF A < B THEN
      writeln (A);
   ELSE
      writeln (B)
END.
```

3. Find all errors in the following program fragments.

a.
```
IF Ch <> '.' THEN
   CharCount := CharCount + 1;
   writeln (Ch)
ELSE
   PeriodCount := PeriodCount + 1;
```

```
b. IF Age < 20 THEN
     BEGIN
       YoungCount := YoungCount + 1;
       YoungAge := YoungAge + Age
     END;
   ELSE
     BEGIN
       OldCount := OldCount + 1;
       OldAge := OldAge + Age
     END;
c. IF Age < 20 THEN
     BEGIN
       YoungCount := YoungCount + 1;
       YoungAge := YoungAge + Age
     END
   ELSE
     OldCount := OldCount + 1;
     OldAge := OldAge + Age;
```

4. Write a program to balance your checkbook. Your program should read an entry from the data file, keep track of the number of deposits and checks, and keep a running balance. Each data file entry consists of a character, D (deposit) or C (check), followed by an amount.

■ ■ ■ ■

■ 5.4
Nested and Extended IF Statements

OBJECTIVES

- to learn the form and syntax required for using nested **IF** statements
- to know when to use nested **IF** statements
- to be able to use extended **IF** statements
- to be able to trace the logic when using nested **IF** statements
- to develop a consistent writing style when using nested **IF** statements

Multiway Selection

Sections 5.2 and 5.3 examined one-way (**IF . . . THEN**) and two-way (**IF . . . THEN . . . ELSE**) selection. Since each of these is a single Pascal statement, either can be used as part of a selection statement to achieve multiple selection. In this case, the multiple selection statement is referred to as a *nested IF statement.* These nested statements can be any combination of **IF . . . THEN** or **IF . . . THEN . . . ELSE** statements.

To illustrate, let's write a program fragment to issue interim progress reports for students in a class. If a student's score is below 50, the student is failing. If the score is between 50 and 69 inclusive, the progress is unsatisfactory. If the score is 70 or above, the progress is satisfactory. The first decision to be made is based on whether the score is below 50 or not; the design is

```
IF Score >= 50 THEN
   .
   .   (progress report here)
   .
ELSE
   writeln ('You are currently failing.':34);
```

We now use a nested **IF . . . THEN . . . ELSE** statement for the progress report for students who are not failing. The complete fragment is

```
IF Score >= 50 THEN
   IF Score > 69 THEN
     writeln ('Your progress is satisfactory.':38)
   ELSE
     writeln ('Your progress is unsatisfactory.':40)
ELSE
   writeln ('You are currently failing.':34);
```

One particular instance of nesting selection statements requires special development. When additional **IF ... THEN ... ELSE** statements are used in the **ELSE** option, we call this an *extended IF statement* and use the following form:

```
IF ⟨condition 1⟩ THEN
    .
    .  (action 1 here)
    .
ELSE IF ⟨condition 2⟩ THEN
    .
    .  (action 2 here)
    .
ELSE IF ⟨condition 3⟩ THEN
    .
    .  (action 3 here)
    .
ELSE
    .
    .  (action 4 here)
    .
```

Using this form, we could redesign the previous fragment that printed progress reports as follows:

```
IF Score > 69 THEN
  writeln ('Your progress is satisfactory.':38)
ELSE IF Score > 50 THEN
  writeln ('Your progress is unsatisfactory.':40)
ELSE
  writeln ('You are currently failing.':34);
```

If you trace through both fragments with scores of 40, 60, and 80, you will see they produce identical output.

Another method of writing the nested fragment is to use sequential selection statements as follows:

```
IF Score > 69 THEN
  writeln ('Your progress is satisfactory.':38);
IF (Score <= 69) AND (Score >= 50) THEN
  writeln ('Your progress is unsatisfactory.':40);
IF Score < 50 THEN
  writeln ('You are currently failing.':34);
```

However, this is less efficient because each **IF ... THEN** statement is executed each time through the program. You should generally avoid using sequential **IF ... THEN** statements if a nested statement can be used; this reduces execution time for a program.

Tracing the flow of logic through nested or extended **IF** statements can be tedious. However, it is essential that you develop this ability. For practice, let's trace through the following example.

■ **EXAMPLE 5.12**

Consider the nested statement

```
IF A > 0 THEN
  IF A MOD 2 = 0 THEN
    Sum1 := Sum1 + A
  ELSE
    Sum2 := Sum2 + A
ELSE IF A = 0 THEN
  writeln ('A is zero':18)
```

```
ELSE
   NegSum := NegSum + A;
writeln ('All done':17);
```

We will trace through this statement and discover what action is taken when A is assigned 20, 15, 0, and −30, respectively. For A := 20, the statement A > 0 is **true**, hence

```
A MOD 2 = 0
```

is evaluated. This is **true**, so

```
Sum1 := Sum1 + A
```

is executed and control is transferred to

```
writeln ('All done':17);
```

For A := 15, A > 0 is **true** and

```
A MOD 2 = 0
```

is evaluated. This is **false**, so

```
Sum2 := Sum2 + A
```

is executed and control is again transferred out of the nested statement to

```
writeln ('All done':17);
```

For A := 0, A > 0 is **false**, thus

```
A = 0
```

is evaluated. Since this is **true**, the statement

```
writeln ('A is zero':18)
```

is executed and control is transferred to

```
writeln ('All done':17);
```

Finally, for A := −30, A > 0 is **false**, thus

```
A = 0
```

is evaluated. This is **false**, so

```
NegSum := NegSum + A
```

is executed and then control is transferred to

```
writeln ('All done':17);
```

Note that this example traces through all possibilities involved in the nested statement. This is essential to guarantee your statement is properly constructed.

Designing solutions to problems that require multiway selection can be difficult. A few guidelines can help. If a decision has two courses of action and one is complex and the other is fairly simple, nest the complex part in the **IF . . . THEN** option and the simple part in the **ELSE** option. This method is frequently used to check for bad data. An example of the program design for this could be:

```
         .
         .   (get the data)
         .
IF DataOK THEN
         .
         .   (complex action here)
         .
ELSE
   (message about bad data)
```

This method could also be used to guard against dividing by zero in computation. For instance, we could have

```
Divisor := ⟨value⟩;
IF Divisor <> 0 THEN
     .
     .    (proceed with action)
     .
ELSE
   writeln ('Division by zero');
```

When there are several courses of action that can be considered sequentially, an extended **IF ... THEN ... ELSE** should be used. To illustrate, consider the program fragment of Example 5.13.

Let's write a program fragment that allows you to assign letter grades based on students' semester averages. Grades are to be assigned according to the scale

```
100 >= X >= 90        A
 90 > X >= 80         B
 80 > X >= 70         C
 70 > X >= 55         D
 55 > X               E
```

Extended **IF**s can be used to accomplish this as follows:

```
IF Average >= 90 THEN
   Grade := 'A'
ELSE IF Average >= 80 THEN
   Grade := 'B'
ELSE IF Average >= 70 THEN
   Grade := 'C'
ELSE IF Average >= 55 THEN
   Grade := 'D'
ELSE
   Grade := 'E';
```

Since any Average over 100 or less than zero would be a sign of some data or program error, this example could be protected with a statement as follows:

```
IF (Average <= 100) AND (Average >= 0) THEN
     .
     .   (compute letter grade)
     .
ELSE
   writeln ('There is an error. Average is':38, Average:8:2):
```
■   ■

Protecting parts of a program in this manner will help you avoid unexpected results or program crashes. It also allows you to identify the source of an error.

Form and Syntax

The rule for matching **ELSE**s in nested selection statements is

> When an **ELSE** is encountered, it is matched with the most recent **THEN** that has not yet been matched.

Matching **IF . . . THEN**s with **ELSE**s is a common source of errors. When designing programs, you should be very careful to match them correctly.

A situation that can lead to an error is an **IF . . . THEN . . . ELSE** statement such as

```
IF <condition 1> THEN
     .
     . (action 1)
     .
ELSE
     .
     . (action 2)
     .
```

where action 1 consists of an **IF . . . THEN** statement. Specifically, suppose you want a fragment of code to read a list of positive integers and print those that are perfect squares. A method of protecting against negative integers and zero could be:

```
readln (Num);
IF Num > 0 THEN
     .
     . (action 1 here)
     .
ELSE
   writeln (Num, '  is not positive.');
```

If we now develop action 1 so that it prints only those positive integers that are perfect squares, it is

```
IF sqrt(Num) = trunc(sqrt(Num)) THEN
   writeln (Num)
```

Nesting this selection statement in our design, we have

```
readln (Num);
IF Num > 0 THEN
   IF sqrt(Num) = trunc(sqrt(Num)) THEN
      writeln (Num)
ELSE
   writeln (Num, '  is not positive.');
```

If you now use this segment with input of 20 for Num, the output is

```
20  is not positive.
```

Thus, this fragment is not correct to solve the problem. The indenting is consistent with our intent, but the actual execution of the fragment treated the code as

```
readln (Num);
IF Num > 0 THEN
   IF sqrt(Num) = trunc(sqrt(Num)) THEN
      writeln (Num)
   ELSE
      writeln (Num, '  is not positive.');
```

because the **ELSE** is matched with the most recent **THEN.** This problem can be resolved two ways. First, you could use an **ELSE** option with an *empty (null) statement.* Thus, you would have

```
readln (Num);
IF Num > 0 THEN
   IF sqrt(Num) = trunc(sqrt(Num)) THEN
      writeln (Num)
   ELSE  {  Do nothing  }
ELSE
   writeln (Num, '  is not positive.');
```

Or you could redesign the fragment as follows:

```
readln (Num);
IF Num <= 0 THEN
  writeln (Num, '  is not positive.');
ELSE IF sqrt(Num) = trunc(sqrt(Num)) THEN
  writeln (Num);
```

Let's look at another example to review the importance of proper indenting.

■ EXAMPLE 5.14

What output will be produced when the following fragment of code is executed?

```
A := 15;
IF A > 0 THEN
  IF A MOD 2 = 0 THEN
    writeln (A + 100)
ELSE
  writeln (A - 100);
```

This fragment results in the output

```
-85
```

The indenting of this fragment is misleading. Since an **ELSE** is matched with the last **IF . . . THEN**, it should be written as

```
A := 15;
IF A > 0 THEN
  IF A MOD 2 = 0 THEN
    writeln (A + 100)
  ELSE
    writeln (A - 100);
```

If you want the design to be consistent with the originally written form, you could rewrite the fragment as

```
A := 15;
IF A <= 0 THEN
  writeln (A - 100)
ELSE IF A MOD 2 = 0 THEN
  writeln (A + 100);
```

STYLE TIP
■ ■ ■ ■ ■ ■ ■ ■ ■ ■ ■ ■

It is very important to use a consistent, readable writing style when using nested or extended **IF** statements. The style used here for nested **IF** statements is to indent each nested statement two spaces. Also, each **ELSE** of an **IF . . . THEN . . . ELSE** statement is in the same column as the **IF** of that statement. This allows you to see at a glance where the **ELSE**s match with the **IF . . . THEN**s. For example,

```
IF...THEN
  IF...THEN
  ELSE
ELSE
```

An extended **IF** statement has all the **ELSE**s on the same indenting level as the first **IF**. This reinforces the concept of extended **IF**. For example,

```
IF...THEN
ELSE IF...THEN
ELSE IF...THEN
ELSE
```

Using semicolons before **ELSE**s becomes more of a problem as you nest to several layers and use compound statements within the nesting. In some cases, it may be wise to redesign a complex, deeply nested fragment to enhance readability.

We conclude this section with an example that uses a complete program with nested **IF** statements.

■ **EXAMPLE 5.15**

Write a program that computes the gross pay for an employee of the Clean Products Corporation of America. The corporation produces three products: A, B, and C. Supervisors earn a commission of 7 percent of sales and representatives earn 5 percent. Bonuses of $100 are paid to supervisors whose commission exceeds $300 and to representatives whose commission exceeds $200. Each line of data is in the form

```
S 18 15 20
```

where the first position contains an 'S' or 'R' for supervisor or representative, respectively. The next three integers include the number of units of each of the products sold. Since product prices may vary over time, the constant definition section will be used to indicate the current prices. The section for this problem will be

```
CONST
   SuperRate = 0.07;
   RepRate = 0.05;
   APrice = 13.95;
   BPrice = 17.95;
   CPrice = 29.95;
```

A first-level pseudocode development for this problem might be

1. Get a line of data
2. Process the data
3. Print a heading
4. Print a summary

A structure chart for this is shown in Figure 5.3.

FIGURE 5.3
Structure chart for the Clean Products Corporation of America problem

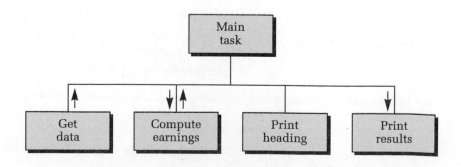

Step 1 will be a single **readln** statement. Step 2 is further developed as

2. Process the data
    2.1 **IF** employee is supervisor **THEN**
        compute supervisor's earnings
      ELSE
        compute representative's earnings

where "compute supervisor's earnings" is refined to

    2.1.1 compute commission from sales of A
    2.1.2 compute commission from sales of B
    2.1.3 compute commission from sales of C
    2.1.4 compute total commission
    2.1.5 compute supervisor's bonus
        2.1.5.1 **IF** total commission > 300 **THEN**
            bonus is 100.00
          ELSE
            bonus is 0.00

A similar development follows for computing a representative's earnings. Step 3 will be an appropriate heading. Step 4 will contain whatever you feel is appropriate for output. It should include at least the number of sales, amount of sales, commissions, bonuses, and total compensation.

A complete pseudocode solution to this problem is

1. Get a line of data
2. Process the data
    2.1 **IF** employee is a supervisor **THEN**
      2.1.1   compute commission from sales of A
      2.1.2   compute commission from sales of B
      2.1.3   compute commission from sales of C
      2.1.4   compute total commission
      2.1.5   compute supervisor's bonus
          2.1.5.1 **IF** total commission > 300 **THEN**
              bonus is 100.00
            ELSE
              bonus is 0.00
      ELSE
      2.1.6   compute commission from sales of A
      2.1.7   compute commission from sales of B
      2.1.8   compute commission from sales of C
      2.1.9   compute total commission
      2.1.10   compute representative's bonus
          2.1.10.1 **IF** total commission > 200 **THEN**
              bonus is 100.00
            ELSE
              bonus is 0.00
3. Print a heading
4. Print a summary
    4.1 print input data
    4.2 print sales data
    4.3 print commission
    4.4 print bonus
    4.5 print total earnings

A complete program to solve this problem follows.

```
PROGRAM ComputeWage (input, output);

{   This  program  uses  nested selection to  determine  total  }
{   compensation for an employee of Clean Products Corporation  }
{   of America.                                                 }

CONST
  CompanyName = 'Clean Products Corporation of America';
  Line = '----------------------------------------';
  SuperRate = 0.07;
  RepRate = 0.05;
  APrice = 13.95;
  BPrice = 17.95;
  CPrice = 29.95;
  Month = 'June';
  Skip = ' ';

VAR
  ASales,                    { Sales count for product A            }
  BSales,                    { Sales count for product B            }
  CSales : integer;          { Sales count for product C            }
  AComm,                     { Commission for sales of product A    }
  BComm,                     { Commission for sales of product B    }
  CComm,                     { Commission for sales of product C    }
  TotalComm,                 { Commission total for all sales       }
  Bonus : real;              { Bonus pay for sales level            }
  Classification : char;     { Employee classification (S or R)     }

BEGIN  {  Program  }

  {  Get the data  }

  writeln ('Enter S or R for classification, ASales, BSales, CSales.');
  writeln ('Press <RETURN> when finished.');
  readln (Classification, ASales, BSales, CSales);

  {  Now compute compensation due  }

  IF Classification = 'S' THEN                    { Supervisor }
    BEGIN
      AComm := ASales * APrice * SuperRate;
      BComm := BSales * BPrice * SuperRate;
      CComm := CSales * CPrice * SuperRate;
      TotalComm := AComm + BComm + CComm;
      IF TotalComm > 300.0 THEN
        Bonus := 100.0
      ELSE
        Bonus := 0.0
    END {  of IF...THEN statement  }
  ELSE
    BEGIN                                         { Representative }
      AComm := ASales * APrice * RepRate;
      BComm := BSales * BPrice * RepRate;
      CComm := CSales * CPrice * RepRate;
      TotalComm := AComm + BComm + CComm;
      IF TotalComm > 200.0 THEN
        Bonus := 100.0
      ELSE
        Bonus := 0.0
    END; {  of ELSE option  }
```

```
{  Print a heading  }

writeln;
writeln (Skip:10, CompanyName);
writeln (Skip:10, Line);
writeln;
writeln (Skip:10, 'Sales Report for', Month:10);
writeln;

{  Now print the results  }

write (Skip:10, 'Classification');
IF Classification = 'S' THEN
   writeln (Skip:12, 'Supervisor')
ELSE
   writeln (Skip:12, 'Representative');
writeln;
writeln (Skip:12, 'Product     Sales     Commission');
writeln (Skip:12, '-------     -----     ----------');
writeln;
writeln (Skip:15, 'A', ASales:11, AComm:16:2);
writeln (Skip:15, 'B', BSales:11, BComm:16:2);
writeln (Skip:15, 'C', CSales:11, CComm:16:2);
writeln;
writeln ('Subtotal':31, '$':3, TotalComm:9:2);
writeln ('Your bonus is:':31, '$':3, Bonus:9:2);
writeln ('------':43);
writeln;
writeln ('Total Due':31, '$':3, (TotalComm + Bonus):9:2);
writeln

END.  {  of program  }
```

If this is run with the data line

```
S 18 15 20
```

the output is

```
Enter S or R for classification, ASales, BSales, CSales.
Press <RETURN> when finished.
?S 18 15 20

            Clean Products Corporation of America
            ---------------------------------------

            Sales Report for        June

            Classification          Supervisor

                Product     Sales     Commission
                -------     -----     ----------
                   A         18          17.58
                   B         15          18.85
                   C         20          41.93

                       Subtotal  $      78.35
                  Your bonus is:  $       0.00
                                         ------
                       Total Due  $      78.35
```

Program Testing

In actual practice, a great deal of time is spent testing programs in an attempt to make them run properly when they are installed for some specific purpose. Formal program verification is discussed in Section 4.6 and is developed more fully in subsequent course work. However, examining the issue of which data are minimally necessary for program testing is appropriate when working with selection statements.

As you might expect, test data should include information that tests every logical branch in a program. Whenever a program contains an **IF . . . THEN . . . ELSE** statement of the form

```
IF ⟨condition⟩ THEN
      (action 1 here)
ELSE
      (action 2 here)
```

the test data should guarantee that both the **IF . . . THEN** and the **ELSE** option are executed.

Nesting and use of extended **IF** statements require a bit more care when selecting test data. In general, a single **IF . . . THEN . . . ELSE** statement requires at least two data items for testing. If an **IF . . . THEN . . . ELSE** statement is nested within the **IF . . . THEN** option, at least two more data items are required to test the nested selection statement.

For purposes of illustration, let's reexamine the program in Example 5.15. This program contains the logic

```
IF Classification = 'S' THEN
   .
   .
   .
   IF TotalComm > 300.00 THEN
      .
      .
      .
   ELSE
      .
      .
      .
ELSE
   .
   .
   .
   IF TotalComm > 200.00 THEN
      .
      .
      .
   ELSE
      .
      .
      .
```

To see what data should minimally be used to test all logic paths, consider the following table:

Classification	Total Commission
'S'	400.00
'S'	250.00
'R'	250.00
'R'	150.00

It is a good idea to also include boundary conditions in the test data. Thus, the previous table could also have listed 300.00 as the total commission for 'S', and 200.00 as the total commission for 'R'.

In summary, you should always make sure every logical branch is executed when running the program with test data.

Exercises 5.4

1. Consider the program fragment

```
IF X >= 0.0 THEN
   IF X < 1000.00 THEN
      BEGIN
         Y := 2 * X;
         IF X <= 500 THEN
            X := X / 10
      END
   ELSE
      Y := 3 * X
ELSE
   Y := abs(X);
```

Indicate the values of X and Y after this fragment is executed for each of the following initial values of X.

a. X := 381.5;

b. X := -21.0;

c. X := 600.0;

d. X := 3000.0;

2. Write a test program that illustrates the checking of all branches of nested **IF ... THEN ... ELSE** statements.

3. Rewrite each of the following fragments using nested or extended **IFs** without compound conditions.

```
a. IF (Ch = 'M') AND (Sum > 1000) THEN
      X := X + 1;
   IF (Ch = 'M') AND (Sum <= 1000) THEN
      X := X + 2;
   IF (Ch = 'F') AND (Sum > 1000) THEN
      X := X + 3;
   IF (Ch = 'F') AND (Sum <= 1000) THEN
      X := X + 4;
b. read (Num);
   If (Num > 0) AND (Num <= 10000) THEN
      BEGIN
         Count := Count + 1;
         Sum := Sum + Num
      END
   ELSE
      writeln ('Value out of range':27);
c. IF (A > 0) AND (B > 0) THEN
      writeln ('Both positive':22)
   ELSE
      writeln ('Some negative':22)
d. IF ((A > 0) AND (B > 0)) OR (C > 0) THEN
      writeln ('Option one':19)
   ELSE
      writeln ('Option two':19);
```

4. Consider each of the following program fragments.

```
a. IF A < 0 THEN
       IF B < 0 THEN
           A := B
   ELSE
       A := B + 10;
   writeln (A, B);

b. IF A < 0 THEN
       BEGIN
           IF B < 0 THEN
               A := B
       END
   ELSE
       A := B + 10;
   writeln (A, B);

c. IF A >= 0 THEN
       A := B + 10
   ELSE IF B < 0 THEN
       A := B;
   writeln (A, B);

d. IF A >= 0 THEN
       A := B + 10;
   IF B < 0 THEN
       A := B;
   writeln (A, B);
```

Indicate the output of each fragment for each of the following assignment statements.

```
i.  A := -5;          iii A := 10;
    B := 5;               B := 8;

ii. A := -5;          iv. A := 10;
    B := -3;              B := -4;
```

5. Look back to Example 5.13, in which we assigned grades to students, and rewrite the grade assignment fragment using a different nesting. Could you rewrite it without using any nesting? Should you?

6. Many nationally based tests report scores and indicate in which quartile the score lies. Assuming the following quartile designation,

Score	Quartile
100–75	1
74–50	2
49–25	3
24–0	4

write a program fragment to read a score from a data file and report in which quartile the score lies.

7. What are the values of A, B, and C after the following program fragment is executed?

```
A := -8;
B := 21;
C := A + B;
IF A > B THEN
    BEGIN
        A := B;
        C := A * B
    END
ELSE IF A < 0 THEN
    BEGIN
        A := abs(A);
        B := B - A;
        C := A * B
    END
ELSE
    C := 0;
```

8. Create minimal sets of test data for each part of Exercise 4 and for Exercise 7. Explain why each data item has been included.

9. Discuss a technique that could be used as a debugging aid to guarantee that all possible logical paths of a program have been used.

■ ■ ■ ■

■ 5.5
CASE Statements

OBJECTIVES

- to know the form and syntax required for using **CASE** statements
- to understand how **CASE** statements can be used as an alternate method for multiway selection
- to be able to use **CASE** statements in designing programs to solve problems

Thus far, this chapter has examined one-way selection, two-way selection, and multiway selection. Section 5.4 illustrated how multiple selection can be achieved using nested and extended **IF** statements. Since multiple selection can sometimes be difficult to follow, Pascal provides an alternative method of handling this concept, the **CASE** statement.

Form and Syntax

CASE statements can often be used when there are several options that depend on the value of a single variable or expression. The general structure for a **CASE** statement is

```
CASE ⟨selector⟩ OF
    ⟨label list 1⟩ : ⟨statement 1⟩;
    ⟨label list 2⟩ : ⟨statement 2⟩;
            .                .
            .                .
            .                .
    ⟨label list n⟩ : ⟨statement n⟩
END;
```

and is shown graphically in Figure 5.4.

FIGURE 5.4
CASE flow diagram

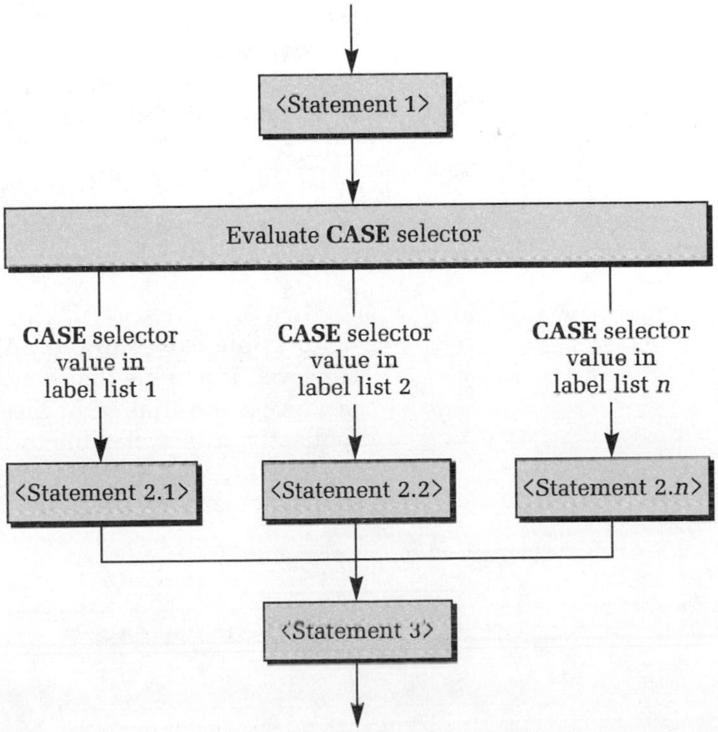

The selector can be any variable or expression whose value is any data type we have studied previously except for **real** (only ordinal data types can be used). Values of the selector constitute the label list. Thus, if Age is an integer variable whose values are restricted to 18, 19, and 20, we could have

```
CASE Age OF
  18 : ⟨statement 1⟩;
  19 : ⟨statement 2⟩;
  20 : ⟨statement 3⟩
END;
```

When this program statement is executed, the value of Age will determine to which statement control is transferred. More specifically, the program fragment

```
Age := 19;
CASE Age OF
  18 : writeln ('I just became a legal voter.');
  19 : writeln ('This is my second year to vote.');
  20 : writeln ('I am almost twenty-one.')
END;
```

produces the output

```
This is my second year to vote.
```

Before considering more examples, several comments are in order.

1. The flow of logic within a **CASE** statement is as follows:
   a. The value of the selector is determined
   b. The value is found in the label list
   c. The statement following the value in the list is executed
   d. Control is transferred to the first program statement following the **CASE** statement **END**
2. The selector can have a value of any type previously studied except **real.** Only ordinal data types may be used.
3. Several values, separated by commas, may appear on one line. For example, if Age could have any integer value from 15 to 25 inclusive, the **CASE** statement could appear as

```
CASE Age OF
  15, 16, 17   : ⟨statement 1⟩;
  18, 19, 20, 21 : ⟨statement 2⟩;
  22, 23, 24   : ⟨statement 3⟩;
  25           : ⟨statement 4⟩
END;
```

4. All possible values of the **CASE** selector do not have to be listed. However, if a value that is not listed is used, most versions of Pascal produce a run-time error message and execution is terminated. Consequently, it is preferable to list all values of the **CASE** selector. If certain values require no action, list them on the same option with a null statement; for example,

```
CASE Age OF
  18 : ⟨statement 1⟩;
  19 : ; {  Do nothing  }
  20 : ⟨statement 2⟩
END;
```

5. Values for the selector can appear only once in the list. Thus,

```
CASE Age OF
   18    : <statement 1>;
   18, 19 : <statement 2>;  { error }
   20    : <statement 3>
END;
```

produces an error since it is not clear which statement should be executed when the value of Age is 18.

6. Proper syntax for using **CASE** statements includes
   a. a colon separates each label from its respective statement;
   b. a semicolon follows each statement option except the statement preceding **END;**
   c. commas are placed between labels on the same option.

7. **END** is used without a **BEGIN.** This is our first instance of this happening. An appropriate program comment should indicate the end of a **CASE** statement. Therefore, our examples will include

```
END; { of CASE }
```

8. Statements for each option can be compound; if they are, they must be in a **BEGIN . . . END** block.

At this stage, let's consider several examples that illustrate various uses of **CASE** statements. Since our purpose is for illustration, the examples will be somewhat contrived. Later examples will serve to illustrate how these statements are used in solving problems.

EXAMPLE 5.16

The selector can have a value of type **char,** and the ordinal of the character determines the option. Thus, the label list must contain the appropriate characters in single quotation marks. If Grade has values 'A', 'B', 'C', 'D', or 'E,' a **CASE** statement could be

```
CASE Grade OF
   'A' : Points := 4.0;
   'B' : Points := 3.0;
   'C' : Points := 2.0;
   'D' : Points := 1.0;
   'E' : Points := 0.0
END; { of CASE Grade }
```

STYLE TIP

Writing style for a **CASE** statement should be consistent with your previously developed style. The lines containing options should be indented, the colons should be lined up, and **END** should start in the same column as **CASE.** Thus, a typical **CASE** statement is

```
CASE Score OF
   10,9,8   : writeln ('Excellent');
   7,6,5    : writeln ('Fair');
   4,3,2,1,0 : writeln ('Failing')
END; { of CASE Score }
```

■ **EXAMPLE 5.17**

To avoid inappropriate values for the **CASE** selector, the entire **CASE** statement may be protected by using an **IF . . . THEN . . . ELSE** statement. For example, suppose you are using a **CASE** statement for number of days worked. You expect the values to be 1, 2, 3, 4, or 5, so you could protect the statement by

```
IF (NumDays > 0) AND (NumDays < 6) THEN
   CASE NumDays OF
      1 : ⟨statement 1⟩;
      2 : ⟨statement 2⟩;
      3 : ⟨statement 3⟩;
      4 : ⟨statement 4⟩;
      5 : ⟨statement 5⟩
   END { of CASE NumDays }
ELSE
   writeln ('Value of NumDays', NumDays, 'is out of range.');
```

A good debugging technique is to print the value of the selector in your **ELSE** statement.

■

■ **EXAMPLE 5.18**

Compound statements can be used with any or all of the options in the following form.

```
CASE Age OF
   18 : BEGIN
           .
           .
           .
        END;
   19 : BEGIN
           .
           .
           .
        END;
   20 : BEGIN
           .
           .
           .
        END
END; { of CASE Age }
```

■

OTHERWISE Option

T   Some versions of Pascal provide an additional reserved word and option, **OTHERWISE,** which can be used with **CASE** statements. The general structure for this option is

```
CASE ⟨selector⟩ OF
   ⟨label 1⟩ : ⟨statement 1⟩;
           .
           .
           .
   ⟨label n⟩ : ⟨statement n⟩
OTHERWISE
   ⟨statement 1⟩;
   ⟨statement 2⟩;
           .
           .
           .
   ⟨statement n⟩
END;    {    of CASE    }
```

This option can be used if the same action is to be taken for several values of the **CASE** selector. It can also be used to protect against a **CASE** selector that is out of range. Note that the statements following **OTHERWISE** are executed sequentially and do not have to be in a **BEGIN . . . END** block. You should check your version of Pascal to see if this option is available to you.

Equivalent of Extended IFs

As previously indicated, **CASE** statements can sometimes (ordinal data types) be used instead of extended **IF**s when multiple selection is required for solving a problem. The following example illustrates this use.

■ EXAMPLE 5.19

Let us rewrite the following program fragment using a **CASE** statement.

```
IF (Score = 10) OR (Score = 9) THEN
   Grade := 'A'
ELSE IF (Score = 8) OR (Score = 7) THEN
   Grade := 'B'
ELSE IF (Score = 6) OR (Score = 5) THEN
   Grade := 'C'
ELSE
   Grade := 'E';
```

If we assume Score is an integer variable with values 0, 1, 2, . . . , 10, we could use a **CASE** statement as follows:

```
CASE Score OF
   10, 9        : Grade := 'A';
   8, 7         : Grade := 'B';
   6, 5         : Grade := 'C';
   4, 3, 2, 1, 0 : Grade := 'E'
END; {  of CASE Score  }
```

Use in Problems

CASE statements should not be used for relational tests involving large ranges of values. For example, if one wanted to examine a range from 0 to 100 to determine test scores, nested selection would be better than a **CASE** statement. We close this section with some examples that illustrate how **CASE** statements can be used in solving problems.

■ **EXAMPLE 5.20**

Suppose you are writing a program for a gasoline station owner who sells four grades of gasoline: regular, premium, unleaded, and super unleaded. Your program reads a character (R, P, U, S) that designates which kind of gasoline was purchased and then takes subsequent action. The outline for this fragment is

```
readln (GasType);
CASE GasType OF
  'R' : action for regular;
  'P' : action for premium;
  'U' : action for unleaded;
  'S' : action for super unleaded
END;  {  of CASE GasType  }
```

■

■ **EXAMPLE 5.21**

An alternative method of assigning letter grades based on integer scores between 0 and 100 inclusive is to divide the score by 10 and assign grades according to some scale. This idea could be used in conjunction with a **CASE** statement as follows:

```
NewScore := Score DIV 10;
CASE NewScore OF
  10, 9          : Grade := 'A';
  8              : Grade := 'B';
  7              : Grade := 'C';
  6, 5           : Grade := 'D';
  4, 3, 2, 1, 0 : Grade := 'E'
END;  {  of CASE NewScore  }
```

■

Exercises 5.5

1. Discuss the need for program protection when using a **CASE** statement.

2. Write a test program to see whether or not the **OTHERWISE** option is available on your system.

3. Show how the following **CASE** statement could be protected against unexpected values.

```
CASE Age DIV 10 OF
  10,9,8,7 : writeln ('These are retirement years':40);
    6,5,4 : writeln ('These are middle age years':40);
      3,2 : writeln ('These are mobile years':40);
        1 : writeln ('These are school years':40)
END;  {  of CASE Age  }
```

4. Find all errors in the following statements.

```
a. CASE A OF
   1        :  ;
   2        : A := 2 * A
   3        ; A := 3 * A;
   4; 5; 6 : A := 4 * A
   END;  {  of CASE A  }
```

```
b. CASE Num OF
     5            : Num := Num + 5;
     6, 7        ; Num := Num + 6;
     7, 8, 9, 10 : Num := Num + 10
   END;  {  of CASE Num  }

c. CASE Age OF
     15, 16, 17 : YCount := YCount + 1;
                  writeln (Age, YCount);
     18, 19, 20 : MCount := MCount + 1;
     21         : writeln (Age)
   END;  { of CASE Age  }

d. CASE Ch OF
     A : Points := 4.0;
     B : Points := 3.0;
     C : Points := 2.0;
     D : Points := 1.0;
     E : Points := 0.0
   END;  {  of CASE Ch  }

e. CASE Score OF
     5       : Grade := 'A';
     4       : Grade := 'B';
     3       : Grade := 'C';
     2, 1, 0 : Grade := 'E';

f. CASE Num / 10 of
     1 : Num := Num + 1;
     2 : Num := Num + 2;
     3 : Num := Num + 3
   END;  {  of CASE Num  }
```

5. What is the output from each of the following program fragments?

```
a. A := 5;
   Power := 3;
   CASE Power OF
     0 : B := 1;
     1 : B := A;
     2 : B := A * A;
     3 : B := A * A * A
   END;  {  of CASE Power  }
   writeln (A, Power, B);

b. GasType := 'S';
   write ('You have purchased  ');
   CASE GasType OF
     'R' : write ('Regular');
     'P' : write ('Premium');
     'U' : write ('Unleaded');
     'S' : write ('Super Unleaded')
   END;  {  of CASE GasType  }
   writeln (' gasoline');

c. A := 6;
   B := -3;
   CASE A OF
     10, 9, 8 : CASE B OF
                  -3, -4, -5 : A := A * B;
                   0, -1, -2 : A := A + B
                END;
```

```
             7, 6, 5 : CASE B OF
                         -5, -4 : A := A * B;
                         -3, -2 : A := A + B;
                         -1,  0 : A := A - B
                      END
        END;  {  of CASE A  }
        writeln (A, B);
   d. Symbol := '-';
      A := 5;
      B := 10;
      CASE Symbol OF
        '+' : Num := A + B;
        '-' : Num := A - B;
        '*' : Num := A * B
      END;  {  of CASE Symbol  }
      writeln (A, B, Num);
```

6. Rewrite each of the following program fragments using a **CASE** statement.

   a.
   ```
   IF Power = 1 THEN
      Num := A;
   IF Power = 2 THEN
      Num := A * A;
   IF Power = 3 THEN
      Num := A * A * A;
   ```

   b. Assume Score is an integer between 0 and 10.
   ```
   IF Score > 9 THEN
      Grade := 'A'
   ELSE IF Score > 8 THEN
      Grade := 'B'
   ELSE IF Score > 7 THEN
      Grade := 'C'
   ELSE IF Score > 5 THEN
      Grade := 'D'
   ELSE
      Grade := 'E';
   ```

   c. Assume Measurement is either M or N.
   ```
   IF Measurement = 'M' THEN
      BEGIN
        writeln ('This is a metric measurement.':37);
        writeln ('It will be converted to nonmetric.':42);
        Length := Num * CMToInches
      END
   ELSE
      BEGIN
        writeln ('This is a nonmetric measurement.':40);
        writeln ('It will be converted to metric.':39);
        Length := Num * InchesToCM
      END;
   ```

7. Show how a **CASE** statement could be used in a program to compute college tuition fees. Assume there are different fee rates for each of undergraduates (U), graduates (G), foreign students (F), and special students (S).

8. Use nested **CASE** statements to design a program fragment to compute postage for domestic (nonforeign) mail. The design should provide for four weight cate-

gories only for both letters and packages. Each can be sent first, second, third, or fourth class.

■ ■ ■ ■

An *assertion* is a program comment in the form of a statement about what we expect to be true at the point in the program where the assertion is placed. For example, if you wish to compute a test average by dividing the SumOfScores by NumberOfStudents, you could use an assertion in the following manner:

```
{ Assertion: NumberofStudents <> 0 }
ClassAverage := SumOfScores / NumberOfStudents;
```

Assertions are usually **boolean**-valued expressions and typically concern program action. Assertions frequently come in pairs: one preceding program action and one following the action. In this format, the first assertion is a *precondition* and the second is a *postcondition*.

To illustrate preconditions and postconditions, consider the following segment of code:

```
IF Num1 < Num2 THEN
   BEGIN
      Temp := Num1;
      Num1 := Num2;
      Num2 := Temp
   END;
```

The intent of this code is to have Num1 be greater than or equal to Num2. If we intend for both Num1 and Num2 to be positive, we can write

```
{ Assertion: Num1 >= 0 AND Num2 >= 0 }          ← Precondition

IF Num1 < Num2 THEN
   BEGIN
      Temp := Num 1;
      Num1 := Num2;
      Num2 := Temp
   END;

{ Assertion: Num1 >= Num2 >= 0 }          ← Postcondition
```

In practice, you may choose to label preconditions and postconditions as the following comments illustrate.

```
{ Precondition: Num1 >= 0 and Num2 >= 0 }

IF Num1 < Num2 THEN
   BEGIN
      Temp := Num1;
      Num1 := Num2;
      Num2 := Temp
   END;

{ Postcondition: Num1 >= Num2 >= 0 }
```

As a second example, consider a **CASE** statement used to assign grades based on quiz scores.

```
CASE Score OF
   10      : Grade := 'A';
   9,8     : Grade := 'B';
```

```
    7,6     : Grade := 'C';
    5,4     : Grade := 'D';
    3,2,1,0 : Grade := 'E'
END;  {  of CASE Score  }
```

Assertions can be used as preconditions and postconditions in the following manner.

```
{  Precondition:  Score is an integer between 0 and 10
                  inclusive  }

CASE Score OF
  10      : Grade := 'A';
  9,8     : Grade := 'B';
  7,6     : Grade := 'C';
  5,4     : Grade := 'D';
  3,2,1,0 : Grade := 'E'
END;  {  of CASE Score  }

{  Postcondition:  Grade has been assigned a letter grade
                   according to the scale

            10        → A
            8,9       → B
            6,7       → C
            4,5       → D
            0,1,2,3 → E  }
```

Assertions can be used in *program proofs*. Simply put, a program proof is an analysis of a program that attempts to verify the correctness of program results. A detailed study of program proofs is beyond the scope of this text. If, however, you use assertions as preconditions and postconditions now, you will better understand them in subsequent courses. If you do choose to use assertions in this manner, be aware that the postcondition of one action is the precondition of the next action.

**FOCUS ON
PROGRAM DESIGN**

The Gas-N-Clean Service Station sells gasoline and has a car wash. Fees for the car wash are $1.25 with a gasoline purchase of $10.00 or more and $3.00 otherwise. Three kinds of gasoline are available: regular at $0.959, unleaded at $0.979, and super unleaded at $1.099 per gallon. Write a program that prints a statement for a customer. Input consists of number of gallons purchased, kind of gasoline purchased (R, U, S, or, for no purchase, N), and car wash desired (Y or N). Use the constant definition section for gasoline prices. Your output should include appropriate messages. Sample output for this data is

```
Enter gallons
?9.7
Enter gas type <R>, <U>, <S>, or <N>
?U
Enter wash option <Y> or <N>
?Y

        ******************************************
        *                                        *
        *      Gas-N-Clean Service Station        *
        *                                        *
        *           July 25, 1992                 *
        *                                        *
        ******************************************
```

```
Amount of gasoline purchased              9.700 Gallons
Price per gallon                     $    0.979
Total gasoline cost                  $    9.50
Car wash cost                        $    3.00
                                          ------
              Total due              $   12.50
```

Thank you for stopping

Please come again

Remember to buckle up and drive safely

A first-level pseudocode development is

1. Get data
2. Compute charges
3. Print results

A structure chart for this problem is given in Figure 5.5.

FIGURE 5.5
Structure chart for the
Gas-N-Clean Service
Station problem

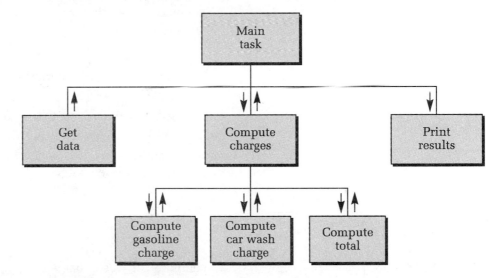

Module specifications for the main modules are

1. <u>Get Data Module</u>
    Data received: None
    Information returned: Number of gallons purchased
                         Type of gasoline
                         A choice as to whether or not a car wash is
                             desired
    Logic: Get information interactively from the keyboard.

2. <u>Compute Charges Module</u>
    Data received: NumGallons
                   GasType
                   WashOption
    Information returned: GasCost
                         WashCost
                         TotalCost
    Logic: Use a **CASE** statement to compute the GasCost.
           Use nested selection to determine the WashCost.
           Sum GasCost and WashCost to get TotalCost.

3. Print Results Module
    Data received: NumGallons
                       GasType
                       WashOption
                       GasCost
                       WashCost
                       TotalCost
  Information returned: None
  Logic: Use several **writeln** statements.

Further refinement of these modules produces

1. Get data
    1.1   read number of gallons
    1.2   read kind of gas purchased
    1.3   read car wash option
2. Compute charges
    2.1   compute gasoline charge
    2.2   compute car wash charge
    2.3   compute total
3. Print results
    3.1   print heading
    3.2   print information in transaction
    3.3   print closing message

Module 2, Compute Charges, consists of three subtasks. A refined pseudocode development of this module is

2. Compute charges
    2.1   compute gasoline charge
          2.1.1 **CASE** GasType **OF**
                'R'
                'U'
                'S'
                'N'
    2.2   compute car wash charge
          2.2.1 **IF** WashOption is yes **THEN**
                compute charge
             ELSE
                charge is 0.0
    2.3   compute total
          2.3.1 Total is GasCost plus WashCost

A Pascal program for this problem follows.

```
PROGRAM GasNClean (input, output);

{    This  program  prints  a  statement  for  customers   of   }
{    Gas-N-Clean Service Station.  It computes the amount due    }
{    for gasoline and car wash.  Features used include:         }
{                                                                }
{       1.  Defined constants                                    }
{       2.  CASE statements                                      }
{       3.  Nested selection (IF...THEN...ELSE)                  }
```

```
CONST
   Skip = ' ';
   Date = 'July 25, 1992';
   RegularPrice = 0.959;
   UnleadedPrice = 0.979;
   SuperUnleadedPrice = 1.099;

VAR
   GasType,              { Type of gasoline purchased (R-U-S-N)    }
   WashOption : char;    { Character designating wash option (Y-N) }
   NumGallons,           { Number of gallons purchased             }
   GasCost,              { Computed cost for gasoline              }
   WashCost,             { Cost of car wash                        }
   Total : real;         { Total amount due                        }

BEGIN  {  Program  }

   {  Get the data  }

   writeln ('Enter gallons');
   readln (NumGallons);
   writeln ('Enter gas type <R>, <U>, <S>, or <N>');
   readln (GasType);
   writeln ('Enter wash option <Y> or <N>');
   readln (WashOption);

   {  Compute gas cost  }

   CASE GasType OF
      'R'  :  GasCost := NumGallons * RegularPrice;
      'U'  :  GasCost := NumGallons * UnleadedPrice;
      'S'  :  GasCost := NumGallons * SuperUnleadedPrice;
      'N'  :  GasCost := 0.0
   END;  {  of CASE GasType  }

   {  Compute car wash costs  }

   IF WashOption = 'Y' THEN
     IF GasCost >= 10.0 THEN
       WashCost := 1.25
     ELSE
       WashCost := 3.0
   ELSE
       WashCost := 0.0;

   Total := GasCost + WashCost;

   {  Print a heading for the customer ticket  }

   writeln;
   writeln (Skip:20, '*****************************************');
   writeln (Skip:20, '*                                       *');
   writeln (Skip:20, '*       Gas-N-Clean Service Station      *');
   writeln (Skip:20, '*                                       *');
   writeln (Skip:20, '*', Skip:12, Date, Skip:12,             '*');
   writeln (Skip:20, '*                                       *');
   writeln (Skip:20, '*****************************************');
   writeln;

   {  Now print the results  }
```

```
           writeln (Skip:10, 'Amount of gasoline purchased', Skip:12,
                    NumGallons:6:3, ' Gallons');
           write (Skip:10, 'Price per gallon', Skip:22, '$');
           CASE GasType OF
             'R'  :   writeln (RegularPrice:7:3);
             'U'  :   writeln (UnleadedPrice:7:3);
             'S'  :   writeln (SuperUnleadedPrice:7:3);
             'N'  :   writeln (0.0:7:3)
           END;  {  of CASE GasType  }
           writeln (Skip:10, 'Total gasoline cost', Skip:19, '$', GasCost:6:2);
           writeln (Skip:10, 'Car wash cost', Skip:25, '$', WashCost:6:2);
           writeln (Skip:50, '-------');
           writeln (Skip:25, 'Total due', Skip:14, '$', Total:6:2);

           {  Print a closing message  }

           writeln;
           writeln (Skip:28, 'Thank you for stopping');
           writeln;
           writeln (Skip:30, 'Please come again');
           writeln;
           writeln (Skip: 20, 'Remember to buckle up and drive safely');
           writeln

     END.  {  of program  }
```

Output for a customer who purchased 9.7 gallons of unleaded gasoline and wanted a car wash is

```
           Enter gallons
           ?9.7
           Enter gas type <R>, <U>, <S>, or <N>
           ?U
           Enter wash option <Y> or <N>
           ?Y


              ****************************************
              *                                      *
              *      Gas-N-Clean Service Station      *
              *                                      *
              *            July 25, 1992             *
              *                                      *
              ****************************************


           Amount of gasoline purchased        9.700 Gallons
           Price per gallon                 $  0.979
           Total gasoline cost              $  9.50
           Car wash cost                    $  3.00
                                               ------
                        Total due           $ 12.50

                        Thank you for stopping

                          Please come again

                  Remember to buckle up and drive safely
```

RUNNING AND DEBUGGING TIPS

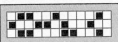

1. **IF** . . . **THEN** . . . **ELSE** is a single statement in Pascal. Thus, a semicolon before the **ELSE** creates an **IF** . . . **THEN** statement and **ELSE** appears incorrectly as a reserved word.

2. A misplaced semicolon used with an **IF** . . . **THEN** statement can also be a problem. For example,

Incorrect
```
IF A > 0 THEN;
   writeln (A);
```

Correct
```
IF A > 0 THEN
   writeln (A);
```

3. Be careful with compound statements as options in an **IF** . . . **THEN** . . . **ELSE** statement. They must be in a **BEGIN** . . . **END** block.

Incorrect
```
IF A >= 0 THEN
   writeln (A);
   A := A + 10
ELSE
   writeln ('A is negative');
```

Correct
```
IF A >= 0 THEN
   BEGIN
      writeln (A);
      A := A + 10
   END
ELSE
   writeln ('A is negative');
```

4. Your test data should include values that will check both options of an **IF** . . . **THEN** . . . **ELSE** statement.

5. **IF** . . . **THEN** . . . **ELSE** can be used to check for other program errors. In particular,
   a. Check for bad data by
```
      read (⟨data⟩);
      IF ⟨bad data⟩ THEN
         .
         .   (error message)
         .
      ELSE
         .
         .   (proceed with program)
         .
```

   b. Check for reasonable computed values by
```
      IF ⟨unreasonable values⟩ THEN
         .
         .   (error message)
         .
      ELSE
         .
         .   (proceed with program)
         .
```

   For example, if you were computing a student's test average, you could have
```
      IF (TestAverage > 100) OR (TestAverage < 0) THEN
         .
         .   (error message)
         .
      ELSE
         .
         .   (proceed with program)
         .
```

6. Be careful with Boolean expressions. You should always keep expressions reasonably simple, use parentheses, and minimize use of **NOT**.

7. Be careful to properly match **ELSE**s with **IF**s in nested **IF . . . THEN . . . ELSE** statements. Indenting levels for writing code are very helpful.

```
IF ⟨condition 1⟩THEN
    IF ⟨condition 2⟩THEN
        .
        .  (action here)
        .
    ELSE
        .
        .  (action here)
        .
ELSE
    .
    .  (action here)
    .
```

8. The form for using extended **IF** statements is

```
IF ⟨condition 1⟩THEN
    .
    .  (action 1 here)
    .
ELSE IF ⟨condition 2⟩THEN
    .
    .  (action 2 here)
    .
ELSE
    .
    .  (final option here)
```

9. Be sure to include the **END** of a **CASE** statement.

■ Summary

Key Terms

BEGIN . . . END block	extended **IF** statement	robust
compound Boolean expression	logical operators: **AND, OR, NOT**	selection statement simple Boolean expression
compound statement	negation	
control structure	nested **IF** statement	
empty (null) statement	relational operator	

Key Terms (optional)

assertion postcondition	program proof	precondition

Keywords

AND	**false**	**OR**
boolean	**IF**	**OTHERWISE (non-standard)**
CASE	**NOT**	**THEN**
ELSE	**OF**	**true**

Key Concepts

- Relational operators are $=, >, <, >=, <=, <>$.
- Priority for evaluating relational operators is last.

- Logical operators **AND**, **OR**, and **NOT** are used as operators on Boolean expressions.
- Variables of type **boolean** may only have values **true** or **false.**
- A complete priority listing of arithmetic operators, relational operators, and logical operators is

Expression or Operation	Priority
( )	1. Evaluate from inside out
NOT	2. Evaluate from left to right
*, /, **MOD, DIV, AND**	3. Evaluate from left to right
+, −, **OR**	4. Evaluate from left to right
<, <=, >, >=, =, <>	5. Evaluate from left to right

- A selection statement is a program statement that transfers control to various branches of the program.
- A compound statement is sometimes referred to as a **BEGIN . . . END** block; when it is executed, the entire segment of code between the **BEGIN** and **END** is treated like a single statement.
- **IF . . . THEN . . . ELSE** is a two-way selection statement.
- A semicolon should not precede the **ELSE** portion of an **IF . . . THEN . . . ELSE** statement.
- If the Boolean expression in an **IF . . . THEN . . . ELSE** statement is **true,** the command following **THEN** is executed; if the expression is **false,** the command following **ELSE** is executed.
- Multiple selections can be achieved by using decision statements within decision statements; this is termed multiway selection.
- An extended **IF** statement is a statement of the form

```
IF...THEN
ELSE IF...THEN
ELSE IF...THEN
ELSE
```

- Program protection can be achieved by using selection statements to guard against unexpected results.
- **CASE** statements sometimes can be used as alternatives to multiple selection.
- **CASE** statements use an **END** without any **BEGIN.**
- **OTHERWISE,** a reserved word in some versions of Pascal, can be used to handle values not listed in the **CASE** statement.

■ Programming Problems and Projects

The first 13 problems listed here are relatively short, but to complete them you must use concepts presented in this chapter.

1. A three-minute telephone call to Scio, N.Y., costs $1.15. Each additional minute costs $0.26. Given the total length of a call in minutes, print the cost.

2. When you first learned to divide, you expressed answers using a quotient and a remainder rather than a fraction or decimal quotient. For example, if you divided 7 by 2, your answers would have been given as 3 r. 1. Given two integers, divide the larger by the smaller and print the answer in this form. Do not assume that the numbers are entered in any order.

3. Revise Problem 2 so that, if there is no remainder, you print only the quotient without a remainder or the letter r.

4. Given the coordinates of two points on a graph, find and print the slope of a line passing through them. Remember that the slope of a line can be undefined.

■ 5. Dr. Lae Z. Programmer (Section 4.4, Chapter 4) wishes to change his grading system. He gives five tests, then averages only the four highest scores. An average of 90 or better earns a grade of A, 80–89 a grade of B, and so on. Write a program that accepts five test scores and prints the average and grade according to this method.

6. Given the lengths of three sides of a triangle, print whether the triangle is scalene, isosceles, or equilateral.

7. Given the lengths of three sides of a triangle, determine whether or not the triangle is a right triangle using the Pythagorean theorem. Do not assume that the sides are entered in any order.

8. Given three integers, print only the largest.

9. The island nation of Babbage charges its citizens an income tax each year. The tax rate is based upon the following table:

Income	Tax Rate
$ 0 - 5,000	0
5,000 - 10,000	3%
10,001 - 20,000	5.5%
20,001 - 40,000	10.8%
over $40,000	23.7%

Write a program that, when given a person's income, prints the tax owed rounded to the nearest dollar.

10. Many states base the cost of car registration on the weight of the vehicle. Suppose the fees are as follows:

Weight	Cost
up to 1,500 pounds	$23.75
1,500 to 2,500 pounds	27.95
2,500 to 3,000 pounds	30.25
over 3,000 pounds	37.00

Given the weight of a car, find and print the cost of registration.

11. The Mapes Railroad Corporation pays an annual bonus as a part of its profit sharing plan. This year all employees who have been with the company for ten years or more receive a bonus of 12 percent of their annual salary, and those who have worked at Mapes between five and nine years receive a bonus of 5.75 percent. Those who have been with the company less than five years receive no bonus.

Given the initials of an employee, the employee's annual salary, and the number of year employed with the company, find and print the bonus. All bonuses are rounded to the nearest dollar. Output should be in the following form.

```
      MAPES RAILROAD CORP.

Employee xxx        Years of service nn
      Bonus earned: $ yyyy
```

12. A substance floats in water if its density (mass/volume) is less than 1 g/cc. It sinks if it is 1 or more. Given the mass and volume of an object, print whether it will sink or float.

13. Mr. Arthur Einstein, your high school physics teacher, wants a program for English-to-metric conversions. You are given a letter indicating whether the measurement is in pounds (P), feet (F), or miles (M). Such measures are to be converted to newtons, meters, and kilometers respectively. (There are 4.9 newtons in a pound, 3.28 feet in a meter, and 1.61 kilometers in a mile.)

    Given an appropriate identifying letter and the size of the measurement, convert it to metric units. Print the answer in the following form.

    ```
    3.0 miles = 4.83 kilometers.
    ```

■ 14. The Caswell Catering and Convention Service has decided to revise its billing practices and is in need of a new program to prepare bills. The changes Caswell wishes to make follow.
    a. For adults, the deluxe meals will cost $15.80 per person and the standard meals will cost $11.75 per person, dessert included. Children's meals will cost 60 percent of adult meals. Everyone within a given party must be served the same meal type.
    b. There are five banquet halls. Room A rents for $55.00, room B rents for $75.00, room C rents for $85.00, room D rents for $100.00, and room E rents for $130.00. The Caswells are considering increasing the room fees in about six months and this should be taken into account.
    c. A surcharge, currently 7 percent, is added to the total bill if the catering is to be done on the weekend (Friday, Saturday, or Sunday).
    d. All customers will be charged the same rate for tip and tax, currently 18 percent. It is applied only to the cost of food.
    e. To induce customers to pay promptly, a discount is offered if payment is made within ten days. This discount depends on the amount of the total bill. If the bill is less than $100.00, the discount is .5 percent; if the bill is at least $100.00 but less than $200.00, the discount is 1.5 percent; if the bill is at least $200.00 but less than $400.00, the discount is 3 percent; if the bill is at least $400.00 but less than $800.00, the discount is 4 percent; and, if the bill is at least $800.00, the discount is 5 percent.

    Test your program on each of the following three customers.
    Customer A: this customer is using room C on Tuesday night. The party includes 80 adults and 6 children. The standard meal is being served. The customer paid a $60.00 deposit.
    Customer B: this customer is using room A on Saturday night. Deluxe meals are being served to 15 adults. A deposit of $50.00 was paid.
    Customer C: this customer is using room D on Sunday afternoon. The party includes 30 children and 2 adults, all of whom are served the standard meal.

    Output should be in the same form as that for Problem 7, Chapter 4.

■ **15.** State University charges $90.00 for each semester hour of credit, $200.00 per semester for a regular room, $250.00 per semester for an air-conditioned room, and $400.00 per semester for food. All students are charged a $30.00 matriculation fee. Graduation students must also pay a $35.00 diploma fee. Write a program to compute the fees that must be paid by a student. Your program should include an appropriate warning message if a student in taking more than 21 credit hours or fewer than 12 credit hours. A typical line of data for one student would include room type (R or A), student number (in four digits), credit hours, and graduating (T or F).

16. Write a program to determine the day of the week a person was born given his or her birth date. Following are the steps you should use to find the day of the week corresponding to any date in this century.
   a. Divide the last two digits of the birth year by 4. Put the quotient (ignoring the remainder) in Total. For example, if the person was born in 1983, divide 83 by 4 and store 20 in Total.
   b. Add the last two digits of the birth year to Total.
   c. Add the last two digits of the birth date to Total.
   d. Using the following table, find the "month number" and add it to Total

January = 1	July = 0
February = 4	August = 3
March = 4	September = 6
April = 0	October = 1
May = 2	November = 4
June = 5	December = 6

   e. If the year is a leap year and, if the month you are working with is either January or February, then subtract 1 from the Total.
   f. Find the remainder when Total is divided by 7. Look up the remainder in the following table to determine the day of the week the person was born. Note that you should not use this procedure if the person's year of birth is earlier than 1900.

1 = Sunday	5 = Thursday
2 = Monday	6 = Friday
3 = Tuesday	0 = Saturday
4 = Wednesday	

A typical line of data is

```
5 – 15 78
```

where the first entry (5–15) represents the birthdate (May 15) and the second entry (78) represents the birth year. An appropriate error message should be printed if a person's year of birth is before 1900.

■ **17.** Community Hospital needs a program to compute and print a statement for each patient. Charges for each day are as follows:
   a. room charges
      i. private room—$125.00
      ii. semiprivate room—$95.00
      iii. ward—$75.00
   b. telephone charge—$1.75
   c. television charge—$3.50

Write a program to get a line of data from a data file, compute the patient's bill, and print an appropriate statement. A typical line of data is

```
5PNY
```

where "5" indicates the number of days spent in the hospital, "P" represents the room type (P, S, or W), "N" represents the telephone option (Y or N), and "Y" represents the television option (Y or N). A statement for the data given follows.

```
           Community Hospital

       Patient Billing Statement

Number of days in hospital:      5
Type of room:                Private


Room charge               $625.00
Telephone charge          $  0.00
Television charge          $ 17.50
                          -------

   TOTAL DUE              $642.50
```

18. Write a program that converts degrees Fahrenheit to degrees Celsius and degrees Celsius to degrees Fahrenheit. In a typical data line, the temperature is followed by a designator (F or C) indicating whether the given temperature is Fahrenheit or Celsius.

19. The city of Mt. Pleasant bills its residents for sewage, water, and sanitation every three months. The sewer and water charge is figured according to how much water is used by the resident. The scale is

Amount (gallons)	Rate (per gallon)
Less than 1,000	$0.03
1,000 to 2,000	$30 + $0.02 for each gallon over 1,000
Greater than 2,000	$50 + $0.015 for each gallon over 2,000

The sanitation charge is $7.50 per month.

Write a program to read the number of months for which a resident is being billed (1, 2, or 3), and how much water was used, and then print a statement with appropriate charges and messages. Use the constant definition section for all rates and include an error check for incorrect number of months. A typical line of data is

```
3 2175
```

20. Al Derrick, owner of the Lucky Wildcat Well Corporation, wants a program to help him decide whether or not a well is making money. Data for a well are on one or two lines in the data file. The first line contains a single character (D for a dry well, O for oil found, and G for gas found) followed by a real number for the cost of the well. If an "O" or "G" is detected, the cost will be followed by an integer indicating the volume of oil or gas found. In this case, there will also be a second line containing an "N" or "S" indicating whether or not sulfur

is present. If there is sulfur, the "S" will be followed by the percentage of sulfur present in the oil or gas.

Unit prices are $5.50 for oil and $2.20 for gas. These should be defined as constants. Your program should compute the total revenue for a well (reduce output for sulfur present) and print out all pertinent information with an appropriate message to Mr. Derrick. A gusher is defined as a well with profit in excess of $50,000. A typical input file is

G 8000.00 20000 ▮

S 0.15 ▮

21. The Mathematical Association of America hosts an annual summer meeting. Each state sends one official delegate to the section officer's meeting at this summer session. The national organization reimburses the official state delegates according to the following scale:

Round-trip Mileage	Rate
Up to 500 miles	15 cents per mile
500 to 1,000 miles	$75.00 plus 12 cents for each mile over 500
1,000 to 1,500 miles	$135.00 plus 10 cents for each mile over 1,000
1,500 to 2,000 miles	$185.00 plus 8 cents for each mile over 1,500
2,000 to 3,000 miles	$225.00 plus 6 cents for each mile over 2,000
Over 3,000 miles	$285.00 plus 5 cents for each mile over 3,000

Write a program that will accept as input the number of round-trip miles for a delegate and compute the amount of reimbursement.

■ 22. Dr. Lae Z. Programmer (Problem 5) wants you to write a program to compute and print out the grade for a student in his class. The grade is based on three examinations (worth a possible 100 points each), five quizzes (10 points each), and a 200-point final examination. Your output should include all scores, the percentage grade, and the letter grade. The grading scale is

```
90 <= average <= 100     A
80 <= average  < 90      B
70 <= average  < 80      C
60 <= average  < 70      D
 0 <= average  < 60      E
```

A typical input file is

80 93 85 ▮   (examination scores)

9 10 8 7 10 ▮   (quiz scores)

175 ▮   (final examination)

■ 23. Dr. Lae Z. Programmer now wants you to modify Problem 22 by adding a check for bad data. Any time an unexpected score occurs, you are to print an appropriate error message and terminate the program.

24. A quadratic equation is one of the form

$$ax^2 + bx + c = 0$$

where $a \neq 0$. Solutions to this equation are given by

$$x = \frac{-b \pm \sqrt{b^2 - 4ac}}{2a}$$

where the quantity $(b^2 - 4ac)$ is referred to as the discriminant of the equation. Write a program to read three integers as the respective coefficients (a, b, and c), compute the discriminant, and print out the solutions. Use the following rules:

a. discriminant $= 0 \rightarrow$ single root.
b. discriminant $< 0 \rightarrow$ no real number solution.
c. discriminant $> 0 \rightarrow$ two distinct real solutions.

25. Write an interactive program that gets as input the lengths of three sides of a triangle. Output should first identify the triangle as scalene, isosceles, or equilateral. The program should use the Pythagorean theorem to determine whether or not scalene or isoceles triangles are right triangles. An appropriate message should be part of the output.

■ 26. The sign on the attendant's booth at the Pentagon parking lot is

PENTAGON VISITOR PARKING

Cars:

First 2 hours	Free
Next 3 hours	0.50/hour
Next 10 hours	0.25/hour

Trucks:

First 1 hour	Free
Next 2 hours	1.00/hour
Next 12 hours	0.75/hour

Senior Citizens: no charge

Write a program that will accept as input a one-character designator (C, T, or S) followed by the number of minutes a vehicle has been in the lot. The program should then compute the appropriate charge and print a ticket for the customer. Any part of an hour is to be counted as a full hour.

27. Milt Walker, the chief of advertising for the Isabella Potato Industry, wants you to write a program to compute an itemized bill and total cost of his "This Spud's for You!" ad campaign. The standard black and white full-page ads have base prices as follows:

Drillers' News (code N)	$ 400
Playperson (code P)	$2,000
Outdoors (code O)	$ 900
Independent News (code I)	$1,200

Each ad is allowed 15 lines of print with a rate of $20.00 for each line in excess of 15 lines. Each ad is either black and white (code B) and subject to the base prices, or is in color (code C) and subject to the following rates:

Three color (code T)	40 percent increase over base
Full color (code F)	60 percent increase over base

Write a program to input Milt's choice of magazine (N, P, O, or I), the number of lines of print (integer), and either black and white (B) or color (C) with a choice of three colors (T) or full color (F). Output should include an appropriate title, all the information and costs used to compute the price of an ad, the total price of the ad, and finally the total price of all ads.

28. Write a program that will add, subtract, multiply, and divide fractions. Input will consist of a single line representing a fraction arithmetic problem as follows:

integer/integer operation integer/integer

For example, a line of input might be

2/3 + 1/2

Your program should
a. check for division by zero.
b. check for proper operation symbols.
c. print the problem in its original form.
d. print the answer.
e. print all fractions in vertical form.

Your answer need not be in lowest terms. For the sample input

2/3 + 1/2

sample output is

$$\frac{2}{3} + \frac{1}{2} = \frac{7}{6}$$

■ 29. In Problem 12, Chapter 4, you were asked to write a program to solve a system of equations using Cramer's Rule. Rewrite that program using an **IF . . . THEN . . . ELSE** statement to protect against division by zero when you divide by the determinant of the coefficient matrix.

30. The force of gravity is different for each of the nine planets in our solar system. For example, on Mercury it is only 0.38 times as strong as on Earth. Thus, if you weigh 100 pounds (on Earth), you would weigh only 38 pounds on Mercury. Write an interactive program that allows you to enter your (Earth) weight and your choice of planet to which you would like your weight converted. Output should be your weight on the desired planet together with the planet name. Use a **CASE** statement in the program for computation and output. The relative forces of gravity are

Earth	1.00
Jupiter	2.65
Mars	0.39
Mercury	0.38
Neptune	1.23
Pluto	0.05
Saturn	1.17
Uranus	1.05
Venus	0.78

31. Contact a programmer and discuss the concept of robustness in a program. Prepare a report of your conversation for class. Your report should include a list of specific instances of how programmers make programs robust.

32. Conduct an unscientific survey of at least two people from each of the following groups: students in upper-level computer science courses, instructors of computer science, and programmers working in industry. Your survey should attempt to ascertain the importance of and use of robustness at each level. Discuss the similarities and differences of your findings with those of other class members.

33. Selecting appropriate test data for a program that uses nested selection is a nontrivial task. Create diagrams that allow you to trace the flow of logic when nested selection is used. Use your diagrams to draw conclusions about minimal test data required to test all branches of a program that uses nested selection to various levels.

Repetition Statements

The previous chapter on selection introduced you to a programming concept that takes advantage of a computer's ability to select. A second major concept utilizing the speed of a computer is repetition. Many problems require a process to be repeated. When this is the case, some form of controlled repetition is needed.

This chapter examines the different methods Pascal permits for performing some process repeatedly. For example, as yet we cannot conveniently write a program that solves the simple problem of adding the integers from 1 to 100 or processing the grades of 30 students in a class. By the end of this chapter, you will be able to solve these problems three different ways. The three forms of repetition (loops) are

1. FOR . . . TO . . . DO
2. WHILE . . . DO
3. REPEAT . . . UNTIL

Each of these three loops contains the basic constructs necessary for repetition: a variable is assigned some value, the variable value changes at some point in the loop, and repetition continues until the value reaches some predetermined value. When the predetermined value (or **boolean** condition) is reached, repetition is terminated and program control moves to the next executable statement.

Pretest and Posttest Loops

A loop that uses a condition to control whether or not the body of the loop is executed before going through the loop is a *pretest* or *entrance controlled loop*. The testing condition is the *pretest condition*. If the condition is **true**, the body of the loop is executed. If the condition is **false,** the program skips to the first line of code following the loop. The **FOR** loops and the **WHILE . . . DO** loop are pretest loops.

■ 6.1
Classifying Loops

A loop that examines a **boolean** expression after the loop body is executed is a *posttest* or *exit controlled loop*. This is the **REPEAT . . . UNTIL** loop.

Fixed Repetition versus Variable Condition Loops

Fixed repetition (*iterated*) *loops* are used when it can be determined in advance how often a segment of code needs to be repeated. For instance, you might have a predetermined number of repetitions of a segment of code for: (1) a program to add the integers from 1 to 100; (2) programs using a fixed number of data lines, for example, game statistics for a team of 12 basketball players; or (3) designing attractive output, such as a diamond of asterisks.

The number of repetitions need not be constant. For example, a user might enter information during execution of an interactive program that would determine how often a segment should be repeated. **FOR** loops are fixed repetition loops.

Variable condition loops are needed to solve problems where conditions change within the body of the loop. These conditions involve end-of-line markers, end-of-file markers, sentinel values, Boolean flags, or arithmetic expressions with changing values. A variable condition loop uses a control feature that provides more power than what is available in many old languages such as BASIC and FORTRAN. **WHILE . . . DO** and **REPEAT . . . UNTIL** are variable condition loops.

There are two kinds of **FOR** loops: the **FOR . . . TO . . . DO** loop and the **FOR . . . DOWNTO . . . DO** loop. These loops are pretest and fixed repetition loops.

FOR . . . TO . . . DO . . . Loops

The form necessary for using a **FOR . . . TO . . . DO** loop is

```
FOR ⟨index⟩ := ⟨initial value⟩ TO ⟨final value⟩ DO
    ⟨statement⟩;
```
or
```
FOR ⟨index⟩ := ⟨initial value⟩ TO ⟨final value⟩ DO
    BEGIN
        ⟨statement 1⟩;
        ⟨statement 2⟩;
            .
            .
            .
        ⟨statement n⟩
    END;
```

A **FOR . . . TO . . . DO** loop is considered to be a single executable statement. The actions performed in the loop are referred to as the body of the loop. The internal logic of a **FOR . . . TO . . . DO** loop is

1. The *index* is assigned the initial value.
2. The index value is compared to the final value.
3. If the index value is less than or equal to the final value
   a. the body of the loop is executed,
   b. the index value is incremented by one, and
   c. another check with the final value is made.
4. If the index value exceeds the final value
   a. the index may revert to an unassigned status, and
   b. control of the program is transferred to the first statement following the loop.

A flow diagram is given in Figure 6.1.

FIGURE 6.1
FOR . . . TO . . . DO
flow diagram

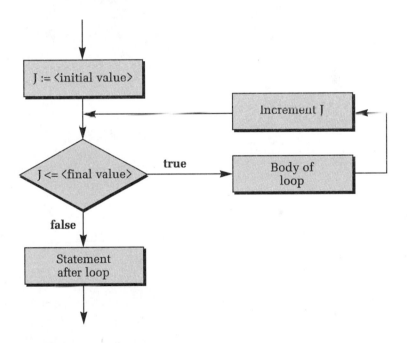

Accumulators

The problem of adding the integers from 1 to 100 needs only one statement in the body of the loop. This problem can be solved by code that constructs an *accumulator*. An accumulator merely sums values of some variable. In the following code, the index variable, LCV (loop control variable), successively assumes the values 1, 2, 3, . . . , 100.

```
Sum := 0;
FOR LCV := 1 TO 100 DO
    Sum := Sum + LCV;
```

LCV	Sum	
1	0	← Initial value
2	1	← Values on successive
3	3	passes through loop
4	6	
5	10	
.	.	
.	.	
.	.	

This program segment contains an example of graphic documentation. Throughout the text, these insets will be used to help illustrate what the code is actually doing. The insets are not part of the program; they merely show what some specific code is trying to accomplish.

To see how Sum accumulates these values, let's trace through the code for several values of LCV. Initially, Sum is set to zero by

```
Sum := 0;
```

When LCV is assigned the value 1,

```
Sum := Sum + LCV;
```

produces

1	0̸ 1
LCV	Sum

For LCV = 2, we get

2	1̸ 3
LCV	Sum

LCV = 3 yields

3	3̸ 6
LCV	Sum

Note that Sum has been assigned a value equal to 1 + 2 + 3. The final value for LCV is 100. Once this value has been assigned to Sum, the value of Sum will be 5050, which is the sum 1 + 2 + 3 + ... + 100.

Accumulators are frequently used in loops. The general form for this use is

```
Accumulator := 0;          {  before loop  }
FOR LCV := ⟨initial value⟩ TO ⟨final value⟩ DO
   BEGIN
      .
      .          (loop body here)
      .
      Accumulator := Accumulator + ⟨new value⟩
   END;  {  of FOR loop  }
```

For another example using this type of loop, assume you are writing a program that requires 30 test scores to be read from an input file where each score is on a separate line. Furthermore, each score is to be printed and added to Total. The code for this is

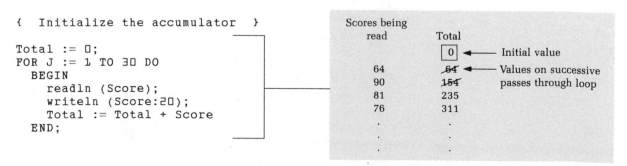

```
{  Initialize the accumulator  }

Total := 0;
FOR J := 1 TO 30 DO
   BEGIN
      readln (Score);
      writeln (Score:20);
      Total := Total + Score
   END;
```

Scores being read	Total	
	0	←— Initial value
64	6̸4̸	←— Values on successive
90	1̸5̸4̸	passes through loop
81	235	
76	311	
.	.	
.	.	
.	.	

In this fragment, Total is the accumulator.

Some comments concerning the syntax and form of **FOR . . . TO . . . DO** loops are now necessary.

1. The words **FOR, TO,** and **DO** are reserved and must be used only in the order **FOR . . . TO . . . DO**.
2. The index must be declared as a variable. Although it can be any ordinal data type, we will use mostly integer examples.
3. The index variable can be any valid identifier.
4. The index can be used within the loop just as any other variable except that the value of the index variable cannot be changed by the statements in the body of the loop.
5. The initial and final values may be constants or variable expressions with appropriate values.
6. The loop will be repeated for each value of the index in the range indicated by the initial and final values.
7. The index may not retain the last value it had during the last time through the loop. When the loop is finished, the index variable may revert to a state of having no assigned value.

At this point you might try writing some test programs to see what happens if you don't follow these rules. Then consider the following examples, which illustrate the features of **FOR . . . TO . . . DO** loops.

■ **EXAMPLE 6.1**

Write a segment of code to list the integers from 1 to 10 together with their squares and cubes. This can be done by

```
FOR J := 1 TO 10 DO
   writeln (J, J * J, J * J * J);
```

This segment produces

```
 1      1        1
 2      4        8
 3      9       27
 4     16       64
 5     25      125
 6     36      216
 7     49      343
 8     64      512
 9     81      729
10    100     1000
```

■ **EXAMPLE 6.2**

Write a segment of code that allows you to examine the value of the index variable before a loop, during each execution of the loop, and after the loop. Assume the index variable is J and that no value has been previously assigned to it. The following segment of code

```
writeln ('Before the loop, J = ', J);
writeln;
FOR J := 5 TO 10 DO
   writeln ('The value of J is', J:4);
```

```
writeln;
writeln ('After the loop, J =    ', J);
```

will, on certain machines, produce the output

```
Before the loop J =   -2882303761180260b3

The value of J is   5
The value of J is   b
The value of J is   7
The value of J is   8
The value of J is   9
The value of J is   10

After the loop J =   -576460752303423487
```

■

■   ■

■ EXAMPLE 6.3

Construct a **FOR . . . TO . . . DO** loop that shows what happens when the initial value is greater than the final value.

```
writeln ('This is before the loop.');
writeln;
FOR J := 10 TO 1 DO
  writeln (J);
writeln ('This is after the loop.');
```

This segment of code produces the output

```
This is before the loop.

This is after the loop.
```

Because the initial value of the index exceeded the ending value originally, control of the program was transferred to the first executable statement following the loop.

■

■   ■

■ EXAMPLE 6.4

Use **FOR . . . TO . . . DO** loops to produce the following design.

```
*****************************
*                           *
*                           *
*                           *
*                           *
*                           *
*****************************
```

This problem requires a bit of development. A first-level pseudocode development could be

1. Produce the top line
2. Produce the center lines
3. Produce the bottom line

and second-level development

2.   Produce the center lines
   2.1   **FOR** J := 1 **TO** 5 **DO**
              produce a middle line

We could now code the algorithm as follows:

```
PROGRAM DesignBox (output);

CONST
  Splats = '*******************************';
  Edge =   '*                             *';
  Skip = ' ';

VAR
  J : integer;

BEGIN
  writeln (Skip:10, Splats);
  FOR J := 1 TO 5 DO
    writeln (Skip:10, Edge);
  writeln (Skip:10, Splats)
END.
```

The index of a loop can also be used for formatting. This is particularly useful when the output is in the form of a design. The next example illustrates this.

EXAMPLE 6.5

Write a **FOR** . . . **TO** . . . **DO** loop to produce the following design.

```
      **
     *  *
    *    *
   *      *
  *        *
```

Assuming the first asterisk is in column 20, the following loop will produce the desired result. Note carefully how the output is formatted.

```
FOR J := 1 TO 5 DO
  writeln ('*':21-J, '*':2*J-1);
```

EXAMPLE 6.6

Use a **FOR** . . . **TO** . . . **DO** loop to print the letters of the alphabet on a diagonal. Since **char** is an ordinal data type, this can be accomplished by

```
Indent := 1;
FOR Ch := 'A' to 'Z' DO
  BEGIN
    writeln (Ch:Indent);
    Indent := Indent + 1
  END;
```

which produces

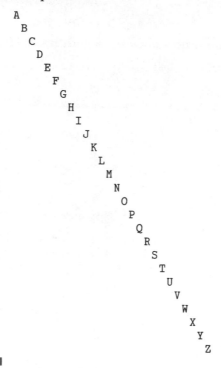

```
A
 B
  C
   D
    E
     F
      G
       H
        I
         J
          K
           L
            M
             N
              O
               P
                Q
                 R
                  S
                   T
                    U
                     V
                      W
                       X
                        Y
                         Z
```

■

■ **EXAMPLE 6.7**

When computing compound interest, it is necessary to evaluate the quantity $(1 + R)^N$ where R is the interest rate for one time period and N is the number of time periods. A **FOR . . . TO . . . DO** loop can be used to perform this computation. If we declare a variable Base, this can be solved by

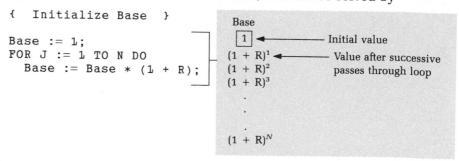

```
{  Initialize Base  }

Base := 1;
FOR J := 1 TO N DO
  Base := Base * (1 + R);
```

Base

$\boxed{1}$ ◄——————— Initial value
$(1 + R)^1$ ◄——————— Value after successive
$(1 + R)^2$ passes through loop
$(1 + R)^3$
.
.
.
$(1 + R)^N$

■   ■

FOR . . . DOWNTO . . . DO Loops

A second pretest, fixed repetition loop is the **FOR . . . DOWNTO . . . DO** loop. This loop does exactly what you expect; it is identical to a **FOR . . . TO . . . DO** loop except the index variable is decreased by one instead of increased by one each time through the loop. This is referred to as a *decrement*. The test is index value $>=$ final value. The loop terminates when the index value is less than the final value. Proper form and syntax for a loop of this type are

```
        FOR ⟨index⟩ := ⟨initial value⟩ DOWNTO ⟨final value⟩ DO
          ⟨statement⟩;

or

        FOR ⟨index⟩ := ⟨initial value⟩ DOWNTO ⟨final value⟩ DO
          BEGIN
            ⟨statement 1⟩;
            ⟨statement 2⟩;
                    .
                    .
                    .
            ⟨statement n⟩
          END;
```

The conditions for **FOR . . . DOWNTO . . . DO** loops are the same as **FOR . . . TO . . . DO** loops. We will now consider some examples of **FOR . . . DOWNTO . . . DO** loops.

EXAMPLE 6.8

Illustrate the index values of a **FOR . . . DOWNTO . . . DO** loop by writing the index value during each pass through the loop. The segment of code for this could be

```
FOR K := 20 DOWNTO 15 DO
   writeln ('K =', K:4);
```

and the output is

```
K =   20
K =   19
K =   18
K =   17
K =   16
K =   15
```

EXAMPLE 6.9

Use a **FOR . . . DOWNTO . . . DO** loop to produce the design

```
    ***
   ***
  ***
 ***
***
```

If we assume the first line of output ends in column 20, the code for this is

```
FOR J := 20 DOWNTO 16 DO
   writeln ('***':J);
```

■ **EXAMPLE 6.10**

Determine the output from the following fragment of code.

```
Sum := 0;
FOR J := 3 DOWNTO -2 DO
  BEGIN
    Sum := Sum + J;
    writeln ('*':10+abs(J))
  END;
writeln (Sum:15);
```

Before printing the output, let's trace through the variable values.

J	Sum	10+abs(J)
Unassigned	0	Undefined
3	3	13
2	5	12
1	6	11
0	6	10
−1	5	11
−2	3	12

The output is

```
        *  ←———— column 13
       *
      *
     *
      *
       *
          3
```

From this point on, both **FOR . . . TO . . . DO** and **FOR . . . DOWNTO . . . DO** loops will be referred to as **FOR** loops. The form intended should be clear from the context.

Writing Style for Loops

As you can see, writing style is an important consideration when writing code using loops. There are three features to consider. First, the body of the loop should be indented. Compare the following:

```
FOR J := 1 TO 10 DO
  BEGIN
    read (Num, Amt);
    Total1 := Total1 + Amt;
    Total2 := Total2 + Num;
    writeln ('The number is', Num:6)
  END;
writeln ('The total amount is', Total1:8:2);
Average := Total2 / 10;

FOR J := 1 TO 10 DO
BEGIN
read (Num, Amt);
Total1 := Total1 + Amt;
Total2 := Total2 + Num;
writeln ('The number is', Num:6)
END;
```

```
writeln ('The total amount is', Total1:8:2);
Average := Total2 / 10;
```

The indenting in the first segment makes it easier to determine what is contained in the body of the loop than it is in the second segment, without any indenting.

Second, blank lines can be used before and after a loop for better readability. Compare the following:

```
readln (X, Y);
writeln (X:6:2, Y:6:2);
writeln;

FOR J := -3 TO 5 DO
  writeln (J:3, '*':5);

Sum := Sum + X;
writeln (Sum:10:2);
```


```
readln (X, Y);
writeln (X:6:2, Y:6:2);
writeln;
FOR J := -3 TO 5 DO
  writeln (J:3, '*':5);
Sum := Sum + X;
writeln (Sum:10:2);
```

Again, the first segment is a bit more clear because it emphasizes that the entire loop is a single executable statement and makes it easy to locate the loop.

STYLE TIP

There are three features you may wish to incorporate as you work with **FOR** loops. First, loop limits can be defined as constants or declared as variables and then have assigned values. Thus, you could have

```
CONST
  LoopLimit = 50;
```

Second, the loop control variable could be declared as

```
VAR
  LCV : integer;
```

The loop could then be written as

```
FOR LCV := 1 TO LoopLimit DO
    .
    . (body of the loop here)
    .
```

Third, a loop limit could be declared as a variable and then have the user enter a value during execution.

```
VAR
  LoopLimit : integer;
  .
  .
  .
  write ('How many entries?  ');
  readln (LoopLimit);
  FOR LCV := 1 TO LoopLimit DO
    .
    .
    .
```

Third, comments within loops make them more readable. In particular, a comment should always accompany the **END** of a compound statement that is the body of a loop. The general form for this is

```
{  Get a test score  }
FOR J := 1 TO 50 DO
  BEGIN
      .
      .  (body of the loop)
      .
  END;  {  of FOR loop  }
```

We close this section with an example that uses a **FOR** loop to solve a problem.

■ EXAMPLE 6.11

Suppose you have been asked to write a segment of code to compute the test average for each of 30 students in a class and the overall class average. Sample data for one student are

```
THS
87 94 85 93
```

and a first-level pseudocode development is

1. Print a heading
2. Initialize Total
3. Process data for each of 30 students
4. Compute class average
5. Print a summary

A **FOR** loop could be used to implement step 3. The step could first be refined to

3. Process data for each of 30 students
   3.1 get data for a student
   3.2 compute average
   3.3 add to Total
   3.4 print student data

The code for this step is

```
FOR LCV := 1 TO ClassSize DO
  BEGIN
    writeln ('Enter three initials and press <RETURN>.');
    readln (Init1, Init2, Init3);
    writeln ('Enter four test scores and press <RETURN>.');
    readln (Score1, Score2, Score3, Score4);
    Average := (Score1 + Score2 + Score3 + Score4) / 4;
    Total := Total + Average;
    writeln;
    write (Init1:4; Init2, Init3);
    write (Score1:6, Score2:6, Score3:6, Score4:6);
    writeln (Average:10:2)
  END;
```

Exercises 6.2

1. What is the output from each of the following segments of code?

a. FOR K := 3 TO 8 DO
    writeln ('*':K);

Charles Babbage

The first person to propose the concept of the modern computer was Charles Babbage (1791–1871), a man truly ahead of his time. Babbage was a professor of mathematics at Cambridge University, as well as an inventor. As a mathematician, he realized the time-consuming and boring nature of constructing mathematical tables (squares, logarithms, sines, cosines, and so on). Since the calculators developed by Pascal and Leibniz could not provide the calculations required for these more complex tables, Babbage proposed the idea of building a machine that could compute the various properties of numbers, accurate to twenty digits.

With a grant from the British government, he designed and partially built a simple model of the difference engine. However, the lack of technology in the 1800s prevented him from making a working model. Discouraged by his inability to materialize his ideas, Babbage imagined a better version, which would be a general-purpose, problem-solving machine—the analytical engine.

The similarities between the analytical engine and the modern computer are amazing. Babbage's analytical engine, which was intended to be a steam-powered device, had four components:

1. a "mill" that manipulated and computed the data;
2. a "store" that held the data;
3. an "operator" of the system that carried out instructions; and
4. a separate device that entered data and received processed information via punched cards.

After spending many years sketching variations and improvements for this new model, Babbage received some assistance in 1842 from Ada Augusta Byron (see the next Note of Interest).

```
b. FOR J := 1 TO 10 DO
     writeln (J:4, ' :', (10-J):5);
c. A := 2;
   FOR J := (3 * 2 - 4) TO 10 * A DO
     writeln ('**', J:4);
d. FOR J := 50 DOWNTO 30 DO
     writeln (51 - J:5);
```

2. Write a test program for each of the following:
   a. Illustrate what happens when the loop control variable is assigned a value inside the loop.
   b. Demonstrate how an accumulator works. For this test program, sum the integers from 1 to 10. Your output should show each partial sum as it is assigned to the accumulator.

3. Write segments of code using **FOR . . . TO . . . DO** or **FOR . . . DOWNTO . . . DO** loops to produce the following designs.

```
a.  *              c.        *
    *                       *  *
    *                      *    *
    *                     *      *
b. ***                   **** ****
    ***                     *  *
     ***                    *  *
      ***                   ***
       ***           d. *********
        ***               *******
         ***               *****
          ***               ***
                             *
```

4. Which of the following segments of code do you think accomplish their intended task? For those that do not, what changes would you suggest?

   a. ```
      FOR K := 1 TO 5 DO;
         writeln (K);
      ```

   b. ```
      Sum := 0;
      FOR J := 1 TO 10 DO
        read (A);
        Sum := Sum + A;
      writeln (Sum:15);
      ```

   c. ```
      Sum := 0;
      FOR J = -3 TO 3 DO
        Sum := Sum + J;
      ```

   d. ```
      A := 0;
      FOR K := 1 TO 10 DO
        BEGIN
          A := A + K;
          writeln (K:5, A:5, A + K:5)
        END;
      writeln (K:5, A:5, A + K:5);
      ```

5. Produce each of the following outputs using both a **FOR . . . TO . . . DO** loop and a **FOR . . . DOWNTO . . . DO** loop.

   ```
   a. 1   2   3   4   5
   b. *
       *
        *
         *
          *
   ```

6. Rewrite the following segment of code using a **FOR . . . DOWNTO . . . DO** loop to produce the same result.

   ```
   Sum := 0;
   FOR K := 1 TO 4 DO
     BEGIN
       writeln ('*':21+K);
       Sum := Sum + K
     END;
   ```

7. Rewrite the following segment of code using a **FOR . . . TO . . . DO** loop to produce the same result.

   ```
   FOR J := 10 DOWNTO 2 DO
     writeln (J:J);
   ```

8. Write a complete program that produces a table showing the temperature equivalents in degrees Fahrenheit and degrees Celsius. If you write this as an interactive program, let the user enter the starting and ending values. Otherwise, list values between 0° C and 100° C. (In either case, use the formula CelsTemp = 5/9 * (FarenTemp − 32.)

9. Write a complete program that produces a chart consisting of the multiples of 5 from −50 to 50 together with the squares and cubes of these numbers.

10. The formula $A = P(1 + R)^N$ can be used to compute the amount due (A) when a principal (P) has been borrowed at a monthly rate (R) for a period of N months. Write a complete program that will read in the principal, annual interest rate (divide by 12 for monthly rate), and number of months and then produce a chart that shows how much will be due at the end of each month.

■ ■ ■ ■

■ 6.3
WHILE . . . DO Loops

OBJECTIVES

- to understand when variable repetition should be used in a program
- to understand why **WHILE . . . DO** is a variable repetition loop
- to understand the flow of control when using a **WHILE . . . DO** loop
- to be able to use a counter in a **WHILE . . . DO** loop
- to be able to use a **WHILE . . . DO** loop in a program

FOR loops, loops in which the body of the loop is repeated a fixed number of times, were presented in Section 6.2. There are problems in which this loop is inappropriate, since a segment of code may need to be repeated an unknown number of times. For example, if you have an input file with an unknown number of items, you will need to continue reading data until you reach the end-of-file marker. In this instance, the condition controlling the loop must be a variable rather than a constant. Recall, Pascal provides two repetition statements with variable control conditions, one with a pretest condition and one with a posttest condition.

The pretest loop with variable conditions in Pascal is the **WHILE . . . DO** loop. The condition controlling the loop is a Boolean expression written between the reserved words **WHILE** and **DO**. Correct form and syntax for such a loop are

```
      WHILE ⟨Boolean expression⟩ DO
          ⟨statement⟩;
or
      WHILE ⟨Boolean expression⟩ DO
          BEGIN
              ⟨statement 1⟩;
              ⟨statement 2⟩;
                   .
                   .
                   .
              ⟨statement n⟩
          END;
```

The flow diagram for a **WHILE . . . DO** loop is given in Figure 6.2.

Program control when using a **WHILE . . . DO** loop is in order as follows:

1. The loop condition is examined.
2. If the loop condition is **true**, the entire body of the loop is executed before another check is made.

FIGURE 6.2
WHILE . . . DO flow diagram

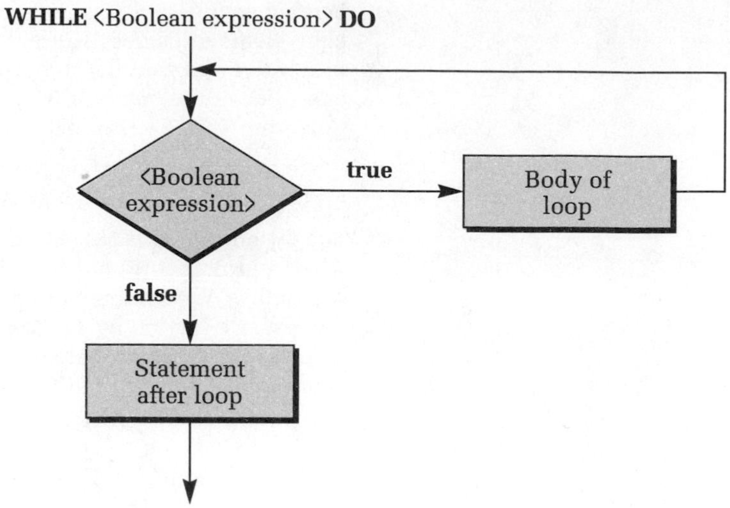

WHILE ⟨Boolean expression⟩ **DO**

3. If the loop condition is **false,** control is transferred to the first line following the loop. For example,

```
A := 1;
WHILE A < 0 DO
   BEGIN
     Num := 5;
     writeln (Num);
     A := A + 10
   END;
writeln (A);
```

produces the single line of output

```
1
```

Before analyzing the components of the **WHILE . . . DO** statement, let's consider two short examples.

■ **EXAMPLE 6.12**

This example allows you to print values from an input file as long as the values are positive (assuming there is a nonpositive value in the file).

```
read (A);
WHILE A > 0 DO
   BEGIN
     writeln (A);
     read (A)
   END;
```

■ **EXAMPLE 6.13**

This example prints some powers of two.

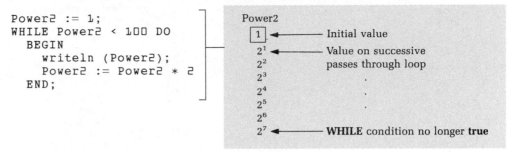

```
Power2 := 1;
WHILE Power2 < 100 DO
   BEGIN
      writeln (Power2);
      Power2 := Power2 * 2
   END;
```

The output from this segment of code is

```
 1
 2
 4
 8
16
32
64
```

■

With these examples in mind, let's examine the general form for using a **WHILE . . . DO** loop.

1. The Boolean expression can be any expression that has Boolean values. Standard examples include relational operators and Boolean variables; thus, each of the following would be appropriate.

```
WHILE J < 10 DO
WHILE A <> B DO
WHILE Flag = true DO
WHILE Flag DO
WHILE NOT eoln DO
WHILE NOT eof DO
```

2. The Boolean expression must have a value prior to entering the loop.
3. The body of the loop can be a single statement or a compound statement.
4. Provision must be made for appropriately changing the loop control condition in the body of the loop. If no such changes are made, the following could happen.
   a. If the loop condition is **true** and no changes are made, a condition called an *infinite loop* is caused. For example,

```
A := 1;
WHILE A > 0 DO
   BEGIN
      Num := 5;
      writeln (Num)
   END;
writeln (A);
```

The condition A > 0 is **true,** the body is executed, and the condition is retested. However, since the condition is not changed within the loop body, it will always be **true** and will cause an infinite loop. It will not produce a compilation error, but when you run the program, the output will be a list of 5s.

b. If the loop condition is **true** and changes are made, but the condition never becomes **false,** you again have an infinite loop. An example of this is

```
Power3 := 1;
WHILE Power3 <> 100 DO
  BEGIN
    writeln (Power3);
    Power3 := Power3 * 3
  END;
```

Since the variable Power3 never is assigned the value 100, the condition Power3 <> 100 is always **true** and you never get out of the loop.

If you are already familiar with other computer languages, you may have a tendency to overuse the **FOR** loop. You should consider a **WHILE** loop when deciding which structure to use.

Sentinel Values

The Boolean expression of a variable control loop is frequently controlled by a *sentinel value*. For example, an interactive program might want the user to enter numeric data. When there are no more data, the user will be instructed to enter a special (sentinel) value. This then signifies the end of the process. Example 6.14 illustrates the use of such a sentinel.

■ EXAMPLE 6.14

Let's write a segment of code that could be used interactively to allow the user to enter a set of test scores and then print the average score.

```
NumScores := 0;
Sum := 0;
writeln ('Enter a score and press <RETURN>, -999 to quit.');
readln (Score);
WHILE Score <> -999 DO
  BEGIN
    NumScores := NumScores + 1;
    Sum := Sum + Score;
    writeln ('Enter a score and press <RETURN>, -999 to quit.');
    readln (Score)
  END;
IF NumScores > 0 THEN
  Average := Sum / NumScores;
  writeln;
  writeln ('The average of ', NumScores:4, ' scores is ', Average:6:2);
```
■   ■

Writing Style

Writing style for **WHILE . . . DO** loops should be similar to that adopted for **FOR** loops; that is, indenting, skipping lines, and comments should all be used to enhance readability.

Using Counters

Since **WHILE . . . DO** loops may be repeated a variable number of times, it is a common practice to count the number of times the loop body is executed. This is accomplished by declaring an appropriately named integer variable, initializing it to zero before the loop, and then incrementing it by one each time through the loop. For example, if you use Count for your variable name, Example 6.13 (in which we printed some powers of two) could be modified to

```
Count := 0;
Power2 := 1;

WHILE Power2 < 100 DO
  BEGIN
    writeln (Power2);
    Power2 := Power2 * 2;
    Count := Count + 1
  END; {  of WHILE...DO  }

writeln ('There are', Count:4, ' powers of 2 less than 100.');
```

The output from this segment of code is

```
          1
          2
          4
          8
         16
         32
         64
There are    7 powers of 2 less than 100.
```

Although the process is tedious, it is instructive to trace the values of variables through a loop where a *counter* is used. Therefore, let us consider the segment of code we have just seen. Before the loop is entered, we have

0		1
Count		Power2

The loop control is Power2 < 100 (1 < 100). Since this is **true,** the loop body is executed and the new values become

1		2
Count		Power2

Prior to each successive time through the loop, the condition Power2 < 100 is checked. Thus, the loop produces the sequence of values

Count	Power2
1	2
2	4
3	8
4	16
5	32
6	64
7	128

Although Power2 is 128, the remainder of the loop is executed before checking the loop condition. Once a loop is entered, it is executed completely before the loop control condition is reexamined. Since 128 < 100 is **false,** control is transferred to the statement following the loop.

WHILE NOT eoln

A standard problem encountered when getting data from an input file is reading the data until an end-of-line marker is encountered. Since **eoln** is a Boolean function that returns the value **true** only when the data pointer is positioned at the end-of-line or end-of-file marker, a **WHILE . . . DO** loop can be used with **eoln** to solve such problems. To illustrate this use of **eoln** with **WHILE . . . DO,** consider the problem of reading and printing a line of data, character by character.

A first-level pseudocode development for solving this problem is

1.   Set left margin
2.   Get a line of data

A second-level development is

1.   Start in column 10
2.   Get a line of data
     WHILE NOT eoln DO
     2.1   get a character
     2.2   print a character

This is sufficient development from which to write code. Some implementations require a file name as an argument when using **eoln** and **eof.** Thus, you would have to write **eoln (input)** or some equivalent statement.

A segment of code to solve this problem is

```
write (' ':9);

{  Now get a data line  }

WHILE NOT eoln DO
   BEGIN
      read (Ch);
      write (Ch)
   END;
```

If this segment is executed for the data file and the pointer is as indicated,

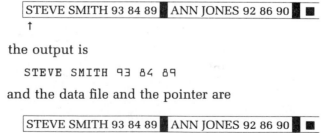

the output is

```
STEVE SMITH 93 84 89
```

and the data file and the pointer are

Now **eoln** is **true;** thus, **NOT eoln** is **false** and the loop is finished. As our next example, let's use a version of the same problem but count the number of characters (including blanks) in the line.

■ **EXAMPLE 6.15**

Write a segment of code to allow you to examine a data line. Your output should include the data line and the number of positions in the line. A first-level pseudocode development is

1. Initialize counter
2. Set left margin
3. Get a line of data
4. Print the message

A second-level development is

1. Initialize counter
2. Set left margin
3. Get a line of data
   WHILE NOT eoln DO
   3.1 get a character
   3.2 print the character
   3.3 increment counter
4. Print the message

We can now write the code.

```
Count := 0; { Initialize counter  }
write (' ':9); { Set margin  }

{  Now get a data line  }

WHILE NOT eoln DO
   BEGIN
     read (Ch);
     write (Ch);
     Count := Count + 1
   END;  {  of WHILE...DO  }

{  Now print a message  }

writeln;
writeln('There are', Count:4, ' positions in the line.');
```

■

■ **EXAMPLE 6.16**

Suppose you are asked to write a program to find the average of some numbers that are on one line of data. As a first-level pseudocode we have

1. Initialize variables
2. Get numbers from the data line
3. Compute average
4. Print the results

A refinement of this is

1. Initialize variables
   1.1 Count
   1.2 Sum

2. Get numbers from the data line
   WHILE NOT eoln DO
   2.1 get a number
   2.2 add to Sum
   2.3 increment counter
3. Compute average
4. Print the results
   4.1 print how many numbers
   4.2 print the average

We can now write the following code.

```
{  Initialize  }

Count := 0;
Sum := 0;

{  Get one line of data  }

WHILE NOT eoln DO
  BEGIN
    read (Num);
    Sum := Sum + Num;   {  accumulator  }
    Count := Count + 1  {  counter  }
  END;  {  of WHILE...DO  }

{  Now compute average  }

Average := Sum / Count;

{  Now print results  }

writeln;
writeln ('There were':19, Count:4, ' numbers in the line.');
writeln;
writeln ('Their average is':25, Average:8:2);
```

Note that this example does not work for implementations that add blanks to the end of data lines because the data pointer may not be at the end-of-line marker after the last number is read.

WHILE NOT eof

Another problem encountered in getting information from an input file is that of knowing when the end-of-file marker has been encountered. Since **eof** is a Boolean function, it can be used with a **WHILE . . . DO** loop in a manner similar to using **eoln.** For example, suppose a data file had one real number per line and you wanted to examine the file. The segment of code is then

```
WHILE NOT eof DO
  BEGIN
    readln (X);
    writeln (X:10:2)
  END;
```

Some implementations require a file variable for **eof.** In that case, the form would be

```
WHILE NOT eof(⟨file variable⟩) DO
```

If the data file is

the output from this segment is

```
   14.73
  121.45
    0.02
 -141.10
```

Many programming problems require the same manipulations and output for each line of data. In these situations, a programmer develops code for operating on one line of data and then uses that code until the end-of-file is encountered. Problems of this type require careful attention, especially with respect to two items.

1. The data lines must be correctly formatted.
2. A **readln** should be used to advance the pointer. There are methods to avoid using **readln** for this purpose, but this is the easiest way to advance the pointer to the beginning of the next data line. If the pointer is not advanced, the **eof** condition will not be recognized appropriately.

The next example illustrates the use of **WHILE . . . DO** with the **eof** condition.

■ **EXAMPLE 6.17**

Write a segment of code to compute the wages for several employees. Assume each line of data consists of information about one employee. It will contain three initials, the hourly rate (real), and the number of hours worked (integer). There are blanks before each number; thus, the data file could be

| MTM 14.60 40 | BRL 13.95 42 | HMN 10.50 20 | MJB 21.0 35 | ■ |
↑

To get the data from one line of the file, the code could be

```
read (Init1, Init2, Init3);
read (HourRate);
readln (Hours);
```

or

```
readln (Init1, Init2, Init3, HourRate, Hours);
```

or other equivalent forms. Gross wages can be computed by

```
GrossWage := HourRate * Hours;
```

If output is to be in the form of a chart, a line of output could be generated by

```
writeln (Init1:5, Init2, Init3, HourRate:15:2,
         Hours:15, GrossWage:15:2);
```

The segment of code that produces the information desired for each employee is

```
WHILE NOT eof DO
  BEGIN
    readln (Init1, Init2, Init3, HourRate, Hours);
    GrossWage := HourRate * Hours;
    writeln (Init1:5, Init2, Init3, HourRate:15:2,
             Hours:15, GrossWage:15:2)
  END;  {  of WHILE...DO  }
```

Let us now consider the design and implementation of a complete program to solve the problem of computing wages for employees. We will assume the input file has the same format and the output consists of a reasonably formatted chart. A first-level pseudocode development for the problem is

1. Print a chart heading
2. Process each data line

A second-level development is

1. Print a chart heading
2. Process each data line
   WHILE NOT eof DO
   2.1 get a line of data
   2.2 compute the wage
   2.3 print the information

We are now ready to write code for this problem. The complete program is

```
PROGRAM ComputeWages (input, output);

{    This program computes wages for several employees of a    }
{    company. The significant new feature is the use of a      }
{    WHILE...DO loop with eof as a Boolean loop control.       }
```

```
CONST
  Marks = '/////////////////////////////';
  Edge =  '/                           /';
  Skip = ' ';

VAR
  GrossWage,                        {  Wages before deductions  }
  HourRate : real;                  {  Hourly rate of pay       }
  Hours : integer;                  {  Number of hours worked   }
  Init1, Init2, Init3 : char;       {  Initials for employee    }

BEGIN  {  Program  }

{  Print a heading  }

  writeln;
  writeln (Skip:16, Marks);
  writeln (Skip:16, Edge);
  writeln (Skip:16, '/  Hi-Speed Bicycle Company  /');
  writeln (Skip:16, Edge);
  writeln (Skip:16, '/        Payroll Report        /');
  writeln (Skip:16, Edge);
  writeln (Skip:16, Marks);
  writeln;
  writeln (Skip:9, 'Employee', 'Pay Rate':14, 'Hours Worked':20, 'Gross':8);
  writeln (Skip:9, '---------------------------------------------------------');
  writeln;

  {  Now start the loop to process a line of data  }

  WHILE NOT eof DO
    BEGIN
      readln (Init1, Init2, Init3, HourRate, Hours);
      GrossWage := HourRate * Hours;
      write (Skip:11, Init1, Init2, Init3);
      writeln (HourRate:16:2, Hours:15, GrossWage:14:2)
    END;  {  of WHILE...DO loop  }

  writeln
END.  {  of program  }
```

If the data file is as indicated in Example 6.17, the output is

```
/////////////////////////////
/                           /
/   Hi-Speed Bicycle Company  /
/                           /
/        Payroll Report       /
/                           /
/////////////////////////////


    Employee      Pay Rate      Hours Worked    Gross
    --------    ----------------------------------------

      MTM         14.60            40          584.00
      BRL         13.95            42          585.90
      HMN         10.50            20          210.00
      MJB         21.00            35          735.00
```

Compound Conditions

All previous examples and illustrations of **WHILE . . . DO** loops have used simple Boolean expressions. However, since any Boolean expression can be used as a loop control condition, compound Boolean expressions can also be used. For example,

```
read (A, B);
WHILE (A > 0) AND (B > 0) DO
  BEGIN
    writeln (A, B);
    A := A - 5;
    B := B - 3
  END;
```

will go through the body of the loop only when the Boolean expression (A > 0) **AND** (B > 0) is **true.** Thus, if the values of A and B are obtained from the data file

```
17 8 ■
```

the output from this segment of code is

```
17       8
12       5
 7       2
```

Compound Boolean expressions can be as complex as you wish to make them. However, if several conditions are involved, the program can become difficult to read and debug; therefore, you may wish to redesign your solution to avoid this problem.

Exercises 6.3

1. Compare and contrast **FOR** loops with **WHILE . . . DO** loops.

2. Write a test program that illustrates what happens when you have an infinite loop.

3. What is the output from each of the following segments of code?

   a.
   ```
   K := 1;
   WHILE K <= 10 DO
     BEGIN
       writeln (K);
       K := K + 1
     END;
   ```

   b.
   ```
   A := 1;
   WHILE 17 MOD A <> 5 DO
     BEGIN
       writeln (A, 17 MOD A);
       A := A + 1
     END;
   ```

   c.
   ```
   A := 2;
   B := 50;
   WHILE A < B DO
     A := A * 3;
   writeln (A, B);
   ```

   d.
   ```
   Count := 0;
   Sum := 0;
   WHILE Count < 5 DO
     BEGIN
       Count := Count + 1;
       Sum := Sum + Count;
       writeln ('The partial sum is', Sum:4)
     END;
   writeln ('The count is', Count:4);
   ```

```
e. X := 3.0;
   Y := 2.0;
   WHILE X * Y < 100 DO
     X := X * Y;
   writeln (X:10:2, Y:10:2);
```

4. Indicate which of the following are infinite loops and explain why they are infinite.

```
a. J := 1;
   WHILE J < 10 DO
     writeln (J);
     J := J + 1;
```

```
b. A := 2;
   WHILE A < 20 DO
     BEGIN
       writeln (A);
       A := A * 2
     END;
```

```
c. A := 2;
   WHILE A <> 20 DO
     BEGIN
       writeln (A);
       A := A * 2
     END;
```

```
d. B := 15;
   WHILE B DIV 3 = 5 DO
     BEGIN
       writeln (B, B DIV 5);
       B := B - 1
     END;
```

5. Assume the variable declaration section of a program is

```
VAR
   Ch1, Ch2 : char;
   Age : integer;
   Num : real;
```

the data file is

| A 18 −14.3B | C 21 10.0D | E 19 −11.5F | ■ |

↑

and the pointer is positioned at the beginning of the file for each segment. What is the output for each of the following segments of code?

```
a. WHILE NOT eoln DO
     BEGIN
       read (Ch1);
       write (Ch1)
     END;
   writeln;
```

```
b. WHILE NOT eof DO
     BEGIN
       read (Ch1);
       write (Ch1)
     END;
   writeln;
```

```
c. WHILE NOT eoln AND NOT eof DO
     BEGIN
       read (Ch1);
       write (Ch1)
     END;
   writeln;
d. WHILE NOT eoln OR NOT eof DO
     BEGIN
       read (Ch1);
       write (Ch1)
     END;
   writeln;
e. WHILE NOT eof DO
     BEGIN
       readln (Ch1, Age, Num, Ch2);
       writeln (Ch1:3, Age:3, Num:6:2, Ch2:3)
     END;
```

6. Assume the data file and variables are as stated in Exercise 5. Is there anything wrong with the following **WHILE . . . DO** loop?

```
WHILE NOT eoln DO
  BEGIN
    readln (Ch1, Age, Num, Ch2);
    writeln (Ch1:3, Age:3, Num:6:2, Ch2:3)
  END;
```

7. Assume Ch is a character variable and a data file is

| XYZ 13 | ABC 21 | MNO 25 | ■ |
↑

What is the output from the following **WHILE . . . DO** loop?

```
WHILE NOT eof DO
  BEGIN
    read (Ch);
    write ('Ch is':10, Ch:3);
    write ('eoln is':10, eoln:7);
    writeln ('eof is':10, eof:7)
  END;
```

8. Write a segment of code that allows you to find how many lines are in a data file.

9. Write a **WHILE . . . DO** loop which accomplishes each of the following tasks.

   a. Print a positive real number, Num, and then print successive values where each value is 0.5 less than the previous value. The list should continue as long as values to be printed are positive.

   b. Print a list of squares of positive integers as long as the difference between consecutive squares is less than 50.

10. Write a segment of code that reads a positive integer and prints a list of powers of the integer that are less than 10,000.

11. Modify the program to compute employee wages (**PROGRAM** ComputeWages) by incorporating the following:

    a. a counter to count the number of employees

    b. a computation for the total hours worked by all employees

    c. a computation for the total wages paid to all employees

d. a computation for the average wage of all employees

e. a printed summary of the extra information

■ ■ ■ ■

■ 6.4
REPEAT . . . UNTIL Loops

OBJECTIVES

- to understand that a **REPEAT . . . UNTIL** loop is a posttest loop
- to understand the flow of control using a **REPEAT . . . UNTIL** loop
- to be able to use a **REPEAT . . . UNTIL** loop in a program
- to be able to use **REPEAT . . . UNTIL** loops with multiple conditions

The previous two sections discussed two kinds of repetition. We looked at fixed repetition using **FOR** loops and variable repetition using **WHILE . . . DO** loops. Pascal provides a second form of variable repetition, a **REPEAT . . . UNTIL** loop, which is a posttest or exit controlled loop.

The basic form and syntax for a **REPEAT . . . UNTIL** loop is

```
REPEAT
   ⟨statement 1⟩;
   ⟨statement 2⟩;
        .
        .
        .
   ⟨statement n⟩
UNTIL ⟨Boolean expression⟩;
```

A flow diagram for a **REPEAT . . . UNTIL** loop is given in Figure 6.3.

FIGURE 6.3
REPEAT . . . UNTIL flow diagram

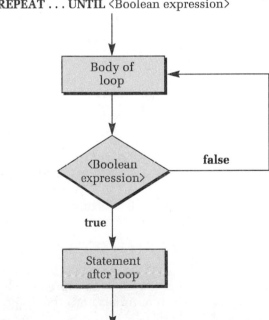

Prior to examining this form, let us consider the fragment of code

```
Count := 0;
REPEAT
  Count := Count + 1;
  writeln (Count)
UNTIL Count = 5;
writeln ('All done':10);
```

The output for this fragment is

```
1
2
3
4
5
All done
```

With this example in mind, the following comments concerning the use of a **REPEAT . . . UNTIL** loop are in order.

1. The program statements between **REPEAT** and **UNTIL** are executed in order as they appear. Thus, a **BEGIN . . . END** block is not necessary.
2. A semicolon is not required between the last statement in the body of the loop and the reserved word **UNTIL.**
3. The Boolean expression must have a value before it is used at the end of the loop.
4. The loop must be entered at least once because the Boolean expression is not evaluated until after the loop body has been executed.
5. When the Boolean expression is evaluated, if it is **false,** control is transferred back to the top of the loop; if it is **true,** control is transferred to the next program statement.
6. Provision must be made for changing values inside the loop so that the Boolean expression used to control the loop will eventually be **true.** If this is not done, you will have an infinite loop, as shown.

```
J := 0;
REPEAT
  J := J + 2;
  writeln (J)
UNTIL J = 5;
```

7. Writing style for using **REPEAT . . . UNTIL** loops should be consistent with your style for using other loop structures.

There are two important differences between **WHILE . . . DO** and **REPEAT . . . UNTIL** loops. First, a **REPEAT . . . UNTIL** loop must be executed at least once, but a **WHILE . . . DO** loop can be skipped if the initial value of the Boolean expression is **false.** Because of this, **REPEAT . . . UNTIL** loops are generally used less frequently than **WHILE . . . DO** loops. For example, if you use a **REPEAT . . . UNTIL** loop to attempt to read an empty file, a run-time error will occur.

The second difference is that a **REPEAT . . . UNTIL** loop is repeated until the Boolean expression becomes **true;** in a **WHILE . . . DO** loop, repetition continues until the Boolean expression becomes **false.**

■ **EXAMPLE 6.18**

An early method of approximating square roots was the Newton-Raphson method. This method consisted of starting with an approximation and then getting successively better approximations until the desired degree of accuracy was achieved.

Writing code for this method, each NewGuess is defined to be

```
NewGuess := 1/2 * (OldGuess + Number / OldGuess)
```

Thus, if the number entered was 34 and the first approximation was 5, the second approximation would be

```
1/2 * (5 + 34 / 5)        (5.9)
```

and the third approximation would be

```
1/2 * (5.9 + 34 / 5.9)        (5.83135593)
```

Let's see how a **REPEAT . . . UNTIL** loop can be used to obtain successively better approximations until a desired degree of accuracy is reached.

Assume Number contains the number whose square root we wish to approximate, OldGuess contains a first approximation, and DesiredAccuracy is a defined constant. A loop used in the solution of this problem is

```
writeln (NewGuess:12:8);
REPEAT
  OldGuess := NewGuess;
  NewGuess := 1/2 * (OldGuess + Number / OldGuess);
  writeln (NewGuess:12:8)
UNTIL abs(NewGuess - OldGuess) < DesiredAccuracy;
```

If DesiredAccuracy is 0.0001, Number is 34, and NewGuess is originally 5, the output from this segment is

```
5.00000000
5.90000000
5.83135593
5.83095191
5.83095189
```

Compound Conditions

The Boolean expression used with a **REPEAT . . . UNTIL** loop can be as complex as you choose to make it. However, as with **WHILE . . . DO** loops, if the expression gets too complicated, you might enhance program readability and design by redesigning the algorithm to use simpler expressions.

Suppose a data file consists of one real number per line and you want to print the numbers until either a negative number is encountered or the end-of-file condition is **true.** A loop for this is

```
REPEAT  {  Start loop  }
  readln (Num);
  writeln (Num:20:2)
UNTIL (Num < 0) OR eof;
```

The data file

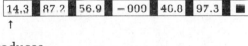
↑

produces

```
 14.30
 87.20
 56.90
-999.00
```

Data Validation

Variable condition loops can be used to make programs more robust. In particular, suppose you are writing an interactive program that expects positive integers to be entered from the keyboard, with a sentinel value of -999 to be entered when you wish to quit. You can guard against bad data by using the following:

```
REPEAT
  writeln ('Enter a positive integer, <-999> to quit.');
  readln (Num)
UNTIL (Num > 0) OR (Num = -999);
```

This process of examining data prior to its use in a program is referred to as *data validation*, and loops are useful for such validation. A second example of using a loop for this purpose follows.

■ **EXAMPLE 6.19**

One problem associated with interactive programs is guarding against typing errors. This example illustrates how a **REPEAT . . . UNTIL** loop can be used to avoid having something entered other than the anticipated responses. Specifically, suppose users of an interactive program are asked to indicate whether or not they wish to continue by entering either a 'Y' or 'N'. The screen message could be

```
Do you wish to continue?   <Y or N>
?
```

You wish to allow any of 'Y', 'y', 'N', or 'n' to be used as an appropriate response. Any other entry is considered an error. This can be accomplished by the following:

```
REPEAT
  writeln ('Do you wish to continue?   <Y or N>');
  readln (Response);
  GoodResponse := (Response = 'Y') OR (Response = 'y') OR
                  (Response = 'N') OR (Response = 'n')
UNTIL GoodResponse;
```

Any response other than those permitted as good data (Y, y, N, n) results in GoodResponse being **false** and the loop being executed again.

■   ■

Exercises 6.4

1. Discuss whether or not a priming read is needed before a **REPEAT . . . UNTI** loop used to get data.

2. Write a test program that illustrates what happens when the initial condition for a **REPEAT . . . UNTIL** loop is **false.** Compare this with a similar condition for a **WHILE . . . DO** loop.

3. Indicate what the output will be from each of the following.

   a.
   ```
   A := 0;
   B := 10;
   REPEAT
     A := A + 1;
     B := B - 1;
     writeln (A, B)
   UNTIL A > B;
   ```

   b.
   ```
   Power := 1;
   REPEAT
     Power := Power * 2;
     writeln (Power)
   UNTIL Power > 100;
   ```

   c.
   ```
   J := 1;
   REPEAT
     writeln (J);
     J := J + 1
   UNTIL J > 10;
   ```

   d.
   ```
   A := 1;
   REPEAT
     writeln (A, 17 MOD A);
     A := A + 1
   UNTIL 17 MOD A = 5;
   ```

4. Indicate which of the following are infinite loops and explain why.

```
a. J := 1;              c. A := 2;
   REPEAT                  REPEAT
     writeln (J)            writeln (A);
   UNTIL J > 10;            A := A * 2
   J := J + 1;           UNTIL A = 20;

b. A := 2;              d. B := 15;
   REPEAT                  REPEAT
     writeln (A);           writeln (B, B DIV 5);
     A := A * 2             B := B - 1
   UNTIL A > 20;          UNTIL B DIV 3 <> 5;
```

5. Assume the variable declaration section of a program is

```
VAR
   Ch1, Ch2 : char;
   Age : integer;
   Num : real;
```

the data file is

```
A 18 −1.3B   C 21 10.0D   3 19 −11.5F    ▪
↑
```

and the pointer is positioned at the beginning of the file. What is the output for each of the following segments of code?

```
a. REPEAT
     read (Ch1);
     write (Ch1)
   UNTIL eoln;
   writeln;

b. REPEAT
     read (Ch1);
     write (Ch1)
   UNTIL eof;
   writeln;

c. REPEAT
     read (Ch1);
     write (Ch1)
   UNTIL eoln OR eof;
   writeln;

d. REPEAT
     read (Ch1);
     write (Ch1)
   UNTIL eoln AND eof;
   writeln;

e. REPEAT
     readln (Ch1, Age, Num, Ch2);
     writeln (Ch1:3, Age:3, Num:6:2, Ch2:3)
   UNTIL eof;
```

6. Give an example of a situation that would require a predetermined number of repetitions.

7. Write a segment of code that will read an integer (you may assume greater than 1) and then use a **REPEAT . . . UNTIL** loop to print a list of powers of the integer that are less than 10,000.

8. Write a **REPEAT...UNTIL** loop which accomplishes each of the following tasks.

   a. Print a positive real number, Num, and then print successive values where each value is 0.5 less than the previous value. The list should continue as long as values to be printed are positive.

   b. Print a list of squares of positive integers as long as the difference between consecutive squares is less than 50.

9. In mathematics and science, many applications require a certain level or degree of accuracy obtained by successive approximations. Explain how the process of reaching the desired level of accuracy would relate to loops in Pascal.

10. Write an interactive program that utilizes the algorithm for approximating a square root as shown in Example 6.18. Let the defined accuracy be 0.0001. Input should consist of a number whose square root is desired. Your program should guard against bad data entries (negatives and zero). Output should include a list of approximations and a check of your final approximation.

■ ■ ■ ■

■ 6.5
Comparison of Loops

OBJECTIVES

- to understand the similarities and differences between any two types of loops
- to understand why variable loops cannot, in general, be converted to fixed loops
- to be able to convert (when possible) from one type of loop to another

The last three sections have presented three types of loops used in Pascal, one fixed loop (**FOR . . . TO . . . DO**), and two variable loops (**WHILE . . . DO** and **REPEAT . . . UNTIL**). It is natural to wonder if any of these can replace any other. As you will see in this section, we could get by with only one type of loop. However, program design and personal preference make it convenient to have all three loops available. This section will examine the similarities and differences among loops and show how some of the loops can be rewritten as another type of loop.

Similarities and Differences

You probably have noticed by now that the three types of loops have some similarities and differences; for easy reference, these are summarized in Table 6.1.

Conversion of Loops

It is an interesting exercise to rewrite a loop using a different type of loop. In some cases, this can always be done; in others, it can only be accomplished when certain conditions are present. There are six possibilities for such rewriting; we will examine four and leave two for the Exercises at the end of this section.

TABLE 6.1
Comparing and contrasting loops

Traits of Loops	FOR . . . TO . . . DO Loop	WHILE . . . DO Loop	REPEAT . . . UNTIL Loop
Pretest loop	yes	yes	no
Posttest loop	no	no	yes
BEGIN . . . END for compound statements	required	required	not required
Repetition	fixed	variable	variable
Loop index	yes	no	no
Index automatically incremented	yes	no	no
Boolean expression used	no	yes	yes

Let us first rewrite a **FOR** loop as a **WHILE . . . DO** loop. Both are pretest loops, but the **WHILE . . . DO** structure is a form of variable repetition. To accomplish our objective, we must use a counter in the **WHILE . . . DO** loop in a manner similar to the index in a **FOR** loop. Thus, we will initialize the counter outside the loop and change it accordingly inside the loop. The Boolean expression in the **WHILE . . . DO** loop will be written so that the last index value produces the final time through the loop.

■ **EXAMPLE 6.20**

Rewrite the following **FOR** loop using a **WHILE . . . DO** loop.

```
Sum := 0;
FOR K := 5 TO 10 DO
  BEGIN
    Sum := Sum + K;
    writeln (K)
  END;
writeln (Sum);
```

The initialization must correspond to K := 5 and the Boolean expression that causes the loop to be exited must correspond to K > 10. With these requirements in mind, the revision becomes

```
K := 5;
Sum := 0;
WHILE K < 11 DO
  BEGIN
    Sum := Sum + K;
    writeln (K);
    K := K + 1
  END;
writeln (Sum);
```

■   ■

The changes illustrated in this example can always be made; any **FOR** loop can be rewritten as a **WHILE . . . DO** loop. The only other type of loop that can always be rewritten as another type is a **REPEAT . . . UNTIL** loop; it can always be converted to a **WHILE . . . DO** loop. In this revision, the Boolean expression of the **WHILE . . . DO** loop will be the logical complement (opposite) of that used in the **REPEAT . . . UNTIL** loop. A revision of this type is illustrated in the following example.

■ **EXAMPLE 6.21**

Rewrite the **REPEAT . . . UNTIL** loop using a **WHILE . . . DO** loop.

```
read (A);
REPEAT
  writeln (A);
  A := A * A
UNTIL A > 100;
```

The Boolean expression A > 100 will be replaced by A <= 100 in the new loop.

```
read (A);
writeln (A);
A := A * A;
WHILE A <= 100 DO
   BEGIN
      writeln (A);
      A := A * A
   END;
```

As demonstrated by the last two examples, Pascal programmers could use only the **WHILE . . . DO** loop structure. However, since there are cases in which one of the other two may be preferred, beginning courses in Pascal typically present and use all three types of loops.

Some conversions require special circumstances to be true before the conversions can be made. Let us consider the problem of rewriting a **WHILE . . . DO** loop as a **FOR** loop. Since a **WHILE . . . DO** loop is a variable repetition loop and uses a Boolean expression for loop control, both of these must be suitable for conversion before the loop can be rewritten as an index loop. For example,

```
K := 1;
WHILE K < 10 DO
   BEGIN
      writeln (K);
      K := K + 1
   END;
```

can be rewritten as

```
FOR K := 1 TO 9 DO
   writeln (K);
```

This form requires less code and is certainly preferable. On the other hand, consider the loop

```
WHILE NOT eoln DO
   BEGIN
      read (Ch);
      write (Ch)
   END;
```

Since the number of characters in the data line is unknown, this cannot be conveniently rewritten as a **FOR** loop.

Let us now consider the problem of rewriting a **WHILE . . . DO** loop as a **REPEAT . . . UNTIL** loop. Since both loops use Boolean expressions for loop control, logical complements can be used for the transition. However, **WHILE . . . DO** is a pretest loop and **REPEAT . . . UNTIL** is a posttest loop. Since a posttest loop must be executed at least once before the exit condition is checked, a pretest loop that is not entered cannot be written as a posttest loop. Thus,

```
A := 10;
WHILE A < 5 DO
   BEGIN
      writeln (A);
      A := A * 2
   END;
```

cannot be rewritten as a **REPEAT . . . UNTIL** loop. However, if the **WHILE . . . DO** loop is executed at least once, it can be revised into a **REPEAT . . . UNTIL** loop. The next example illustrates this.

■ **EXAMPLE 6.22**

Rewrite the following using a **REPEAT . . . UNTIL** loop.

```
A := 1;
Power := 3;
WHILE A < 100 DO
  BEGIN
    writeln (A);
    A := A * Power
  END;
```

The Boolean expression for a **REPEAT . . . UNTIL** loop becomes A >= 100 and the revision is

```
A := 1;
Power := 3;
REPEAT
  writeln (A);
  A := A * Power
UNTIL A >= 100;
```

When considering the remaining loop conversions in the Exercises, carefully note fixed repetition versus variable repetition and pretest versus posttest conditions.

Which Loop to Use?

Which loop should you choose when repetition is needed in a program? There is no quick, easy answer to this question. We can offer some general guidelines, but even these guidelines leave the question fairly open.

First, if a process is to be repeated a predetermined number of times, a **FOR** loop is appropriate. The key to choosing this loop statement is that a variable condition is not needed to determine how often the loop is repeated.

A second, more difficult, question is whether to use a **REPEAT . . . UNTIL** or **WHILE . . . DO** loop when a variable control is necessary. As just discussed, **REPEAT** loops can always be written as **WHILE** loops and often **WHILE** loops can be written as **REPEAT** loops. How then do you decide which to use?

If you know the statements within a loop will always be executed at least once, you can use a **REPEAT . . . UNTIL** loop. When designing a solution to a problem, if you decide to repeat some process until a condition changes, using a **REPEAT . . . UNTIL** loop with an appropriate **boolean** variable allows the code to be written in a manner consistent with how you think about the solution. For example, suppose you wish to have test scores entered interactively for the purpose of computing an average. You know there will always be scores to enter, so your loop design could be:

```
REPEAT
  .
  .      (action here)
  .
UNTIL NoMoreScores;
```

Not all loops will be automatically entered. For example, loops that include reading data from a data file may need to check the **boolean** functions **eoln** or **eof** before attempting to read data. Otherwise, a program crash may occur if you attempt to read past the end-of-file marker (or to read from an empty file). This can be prevented by using a **WHILE . . . DO** loop such as

```
WHILE NOT eof DO
   BEGIN
      .
      .          (action here)
      .
   END;
```

Occasionally, the logical conditions used to decide whether or not the loop should be repeated will read in a more natural fashion in one of the repetition statements. To illustrate, suppose two **boolean** conditions need to be **true** for a loop to be repeated. A **REPEAT . . . UNTIL** loop such as

```
REPEAT
   .
   .
   .
UNTIL NOT ⟨condition 1⟩ OR NOT ⟨condition 2⟩;
```

might be rewritten as the **WHILE . . . DO** loop

```
WHILE ⟨condition 1⟩ AND ⟨condition 2⟩ DO
   BEGIN
      .
      .          (action here)
      .
   END;
```

This version appears easier to read and would be preferred by many programmers.

In summary, the issue of which loop to use is still open. You should discuss this with your instructor and be able to use any of the three loops when designing your solution to a problem.

Exercises 6.5

1. Compare and contrast the three looping structures discussed in this section.

2. Indicate whether or not each of the following can be converted as indicated.
   a.
   ```
   Sum := 0;
   FOR K := 1 TO 100 DO
      Sum := Sum + K;
   ```
   convert to **REPEAT . . . UNTIL**?

   convert to **WHILE . . . DO**?

   b.
   ```
   Count := 0;
   Sum := 0;
   WHILE NOT eof DO
      BEGIN
         readln (A);
         Sum := Sum + A;
         Count := Count + 1
      END;
   Average := Sum / Count;
   ```
   i. convert to **REPEAT . . . UNTIL**?

   ii. convert to **FOR . . . TO**?

   iii. convert to **FOR . . . DOWNTO**?

```
c. X := 0.0;
   REPEAT
      writeln (X:20:2);
      X := X + 0.5
   UNTIL X = 4.0;
```
   i. convert to **WHILE . . . DO**?
   ii. convert to **FOR . . . TO**?
   iii. convert to **FOR . . . DOWNTO**?

3. For each of the conversions you indicated were possible in Exercise 2, write the revised loop.

4. Explain completely the problems encountered when trying to make the following loop conversions.
   a. **FOR** to **REPEAT . . . UNTIL**
   b. **REPEAT . . . UNTIL** to **FOR**

5. Explain why the following cannot be rewritten as a **REPEAT . . . UNTIL** loop.

```
WHILE 6 < 5 DO
   BEGIN
      .
      .   (loop body)
      .
   END;
```

■ ■ ■ ■

■ 6.6
Loop Verification (Optional)

OBJECTIVES
- to understand how input assertions and output assertions can be used to verify loops
- to understand how loop invariants and loop variants can be used to verify loops

Loop verification is the process of guaranteeing that a loop performs its intended task. Such verification is part of program testing and correctness to which we referred in Chapter 4.

Some work has been done on constructing formal proofs that loops are "correct." We now examine a modified version of loop verification; a complete treatment of the issue will be the topic of subsequent course work.

Preconditions and Postconditions with Loops

Preconditions and postconditions can be used with loops. Loop preconditions are referred to as *input assertions*. They are comments that indicate what can be expected to be true before the loop is entered. Loop postconditions are referred to as *output assertions*. They are comments that indicate what can be expected to be true when the loop is exited.

To illustrate input and output assertions, let's consider the mathematical problem of summing the proper divisors of a positive integer. For example, we have

Integer	Proper Divisors	Sum
6	1, 2, 3	6
9	1, 3	4
12	1, 2, 3, 4, 6	16

As part of a program that will have a positive integer as input and as output will have a determination of whether the integer is perfect (Sum = integer), abundant (Sum > integer), or deficient (Sum < integer), it is necessary to sum the divisors. A loop to perform this task is

```
            DivisorSum := 0;
            FOR TrialDivisor := 1 To Num DIV 2 DO
              IF Num MOD TrialDivisor = 0 THEN
                 DivisorSum := DivisorSum + TrialDivisor;
```

An input assertion for this loop is

```
        {  Precondition: 1. Num is a positive integer.        }
        {                2. DivisorSum = 0.                    }
```

An output assertion is

```
        {  Postcondition: DivisorSum is the sum of all proper  }
        {                 divisors of Num.                     }
```

When these are placed with the previous code, we have

```
        DivisorSum := 0;

        {  Precondition: 1. Num is a positive integer.        }
        {                2. DivisorSum = 0.                    }

        FOR TrialDivisor := 1 TO Num DIV 2 DO
          IF Num MOD TrialDivisor = 0 THEN
             DivisorSum := DivisorSum + TrialDivisor;

        {  Postcondition: DivisorSum is the sum of all proper  }
        {                 divisors of Num.                     }
```

Invariant and Variant Assertions

A *loop invariant* is an assertion that expresses a relationship between variables that remains constant throughout all iterations of the loop. In other words, it is a statement that is true both before the loop is entered and after each pass through the loop. An invariant assertion for the preceding code segment would be

```
        {  DivisorSum is the sum of proper divisors of Num that  }
        {  are less than or equal to TrialDivisor.              }
```

A *loop variant* is an assertion whose truth changes between the first and final execution of the loop. The loop variant expression should be stated in such a way that it guarantees the loop is exited. Thus, it contains some statement about the loop variable being incremented (or decremented) during execution of the loop. In the preceding code, we could have

```
        {  TrialDivisor is incremented by 1 each time through   }
        {  the loop.  It eventually exceeds the value Num DIV 2, }
        {  at which point the loop is exited.                   }
```

Variant and invariant assertions usually occur in pairs.

We now use four kinds of assertions—input, output, variant, and invariant—to produce the formally verified loop.

```
DivisorSum := 0;

{  Precondition:  1.  Num is a positive integer.  }        (input
{                 2.  DivisorSum = 0.             }        assertion)

FOR TrialDivisor := 1 TO Num DIV 2 DO

{  TrialDivisor is incremented by 1 each time     }        (variant
{  through the loop. It eventually exceeds the    }        assertion)
{  value Num DIV 2, at which point the loop is    }
{  exited.                                        }
```

```
IF Num MOD TrialDivisor = 0 THEN
   DivisorSum := DivisorSum + TrialDivisor;
```

```
{  DivisorSum is the sum of proper divisors of    }      (invariant
{  Num that are less than or equal to             }      assertion)
{  TrialDivisor.                                  }

{  Postcondition: DivisorSum is the sum of        }      (output
{  all proper divisors of Num.                    }      assertion)
```

In general, code that is presented in this text does not include formal verification of the loops. This issue is similar to that of robustness. In an introductory course, a decision must be made on the trade-off between learning new concepts and writing robust programs with formal verification of loops. We encourage the practice, but space and time considerations make it inconvenient to include such documentation at this level. We close this discussion with another example illustrating loop verification.

■ **EXAMPLE 6.23**

Consider the problem of finding the greatest common divisor (GCD) of two positive integers. To illustrate, we have

Num1	Num2	GCD (Num1, Num2)
8	12	4
20	10	10
15	32	1
70	40	10

A segment of code to produce the GCD of two positive integers after they have been ordered as Small, Large, is

```
TrialGCD := Small;
GCDFound := false;
WHILE NOT GCDFound DO
  IF (Large MOD TrialGCD = 0) AND
     (Small MOD TrialGCD = 0) THEN
    BEGIN
      GCD := TrialGCD:
      GCDFound := true
    END
  ELSE
    TrialGCD := TrialGCD - 1;
```

Using assertions as previously indicated, this code would appear as

```
TrialGCD := Small;
GCDFound := false;
```

```
{  Precondition:  1.  Small <= Large                    }
{                 2.  TrialGCD (Small) is the first     }
{                     candidate for GCD                 }
{                 3.  GCDFound is false                 }
```

```
WHILE NOT GCDFound DO
```

```
{  TrialGCD assumes integer values ranging from Small  }
{  to 1. It is decremented by 1 each time through the   }
```

```
{ loop. When TrialGCD divides both Small and Large,   }
{ the loop is exited. Exit is guaranteed since 1      }
{ divides both Small and Large.                       }

  IF (Large MOD TrialGCD = 0) AND
     (Small MOD TrialGCD = 0) THEN
    BEGIN

    { When TrialGCD divides both Large and Small,   }
    { then GCD is assigned that value.              }

      GCD := TrialGCD:
      GCDFound := true
    END
  ELSE
    TrialGCD := TrialGCD - 1;

{ Postcondition:   GCD is the greatest common divisor }
{                  of Small and Large.                }
```

Exercises 6.6 (Optional)

1. Write appropriate input assertions and output assertions for each of the following loops.

   a.
   ```
   readln (Score);
   WHILE Score <> 999 DO
     BEGIN
       NumScores := NumScores + 1;
       Sum := Sum + Score;
       writeln ('Enter a score; -999 to quit.');
       readln (Score)
     END;
   ```

   b.
   ```
   Count := 0;
   Power2 := 1;
   WHILE Power2 < 100 DO
     BEGIN
       writeln (Power2);
       Power2 := Power2 * 2;
       Count := Count + 1
     END;
   ```

   c. (From Example 6.18)

   ```
   REPEAT
     OldGuess := NewGuess;
     NewGuess := 1/2 * (OldGuess + Number / OldGuess);
     writeln (NewGuess:12:8)
   UNTIL abs(NewGuess - OldGuess) < DesiredAccuracy;
   ```

2. Write appropriate loop invariant and loop variant assertions for each of the loops in Exercise 1.

3. The following loop comes from a program called HiLo. The user enters a number, Guess, and the computer then displays a message indicating whether the guess is correct, too high, or too low. Add appropriate input assertions, output assertions, loop invariant assertions, and loop variant assertions to the following code.

```
Correct := false;
Count := 0;
WHILE (Count < MaxTries) AND (NOT Correct) DO
  BEGIN
    Count := Count + 1;
    writeln ('Enter choice number ', Count);
    readln (Guess);
    IF Guess = Choice THEN
      BEGIN
        Correct := true;
        writeln ('Congratulations!')
      END
    ELSE IF Guess < Choice THEN
      writeln ('Your guess is too low')
    ELSE
      writeln ('Your guess is too high')
  END;
```

■ 6.7
Nested Loops

OBJECTIVES

■ to be able to use nested loops
■ to understand the flow of control when using nested loops
■ to be able to use a consistent writing style when using nested loops

In this chapter, we have examined three loop structures. Each of them has been discussed with respect to syntax, semantics, form, writing style, and use in programs. But remember that each loop is treated as a single Pascal statement. In this sense, it is possible to have a loop as one of the statements in the body of another loop. When this happens, the loops are said to be *nested*.

Loops can be nested to any depth; that is, a loop can be within a loop within a loop, and so on. Also, any of the three types of loops can be nested within any loop. However, a programmer should be careful not to design a program with nesting that is too complex. If program logic becomes too difficult to follow, you might better redesign the program.

Flow of Control

As a first example of using a loop within a loop, consider

```
FOR K := 1 TO 5 DO
  FOR J := 1 TO 3 DO
    writeln (K + J);
```

When this fragment is executed, the following happens:

1. K is assigned a value.
2. For each value of K, the following loop is executed.

```
FOR J := 1 TO 3 DO
  writeln (K + J);
```

Thus, for K := 1, the "inside" or nested loop produces the output

```
2
3
4
```

At this point, K := 2 and the next portion of the output produced by the nested loop is

```
3
4
5
```

The complete output from these nested loops is

```
2 ⎫
3 ⎬ from K := 1
4 ⎭
3 ⎫
4 ⎬ from K := 2
5 ⎭
4 ⎫
5 ⎬ from K := 3
6 ⎭
5 ⎫
6 ⎬ from K := 4
7 ⎭
6 ⎫
7 ⎬ from K := 5
8 ⎭
```

As you can see, for each value assigned to the index of the outside loop, the inside loop is executed completely. Suppose you want the output to be printed in the form of a chart as follows:

```
2    3    4
3    4    5
4    5    6
5    6    7
6    7    8
```

The pseudocode design to produce this output is

1. **FOR** K := 1 **TO** 5 **DO**
   produce a line

A refinement of this is

1. **FOR** K := 1 **TO** 5 **DO**
   1.1 print on one line
   1.2 advance the printer

The Pascal code for this development becomes

```
FOR K := 1 TO 5 DO
  BEGIN
    FOR J := 1 TO 3 DO
      write ((K + J):4);
    writeln
  END;
```

Our next example shows how nested loops can be used to produce a design.

■ EXAMPLE 6.24

Use nested **FOR** loops to produce the output

```
*
**
***
****
*****
```

where the left asterisks are in column 10.

The first-level pseudocode to solve this problem could be

1. **FOR** K := 1 **TO** 5 **DO**
    produce a line

A refinement of this could be

1. **FOR** K := 1 **TO** 5 **DO**
    1.1   print on one line
    1.2   advance the printer

Step 1.1 is not yet sufficiently refined, so our next level could be

1. **FOR** K := 1 **TO** 5 **DO**
    1.1   print on one line
          1.1.1   put a blank in column 9
          1.1.2   print K asterisks
    1.2   advance the printer

We can now write a program fragment to produce the desired output as follows:

```
FOR K := 1 TO 5 DO
  BEGIN
    write (' ':9);
    FOR J := 1 TO K DO
      write ('*');
    writeln
  END;  {  of outer loop  }
```

A significant feature has been added to this program fragment. Note that the loop control for the inner loop is the index of the outer loop.

■   ▨

Thus far, nested loops have been used only with **FOR** loops, but any of the loop structures may be used in nesting. Our next example illustrates a **REPEAT . . . UNTIL** loop nested within a **WHILE . . . DO** loop.

■ **EXAMPLE 6.25**

Trace the flow of control and indicate the output for the following program fragment.

```
A := 10;
B := 0;
WHILE A > B DO
  BEGIN
    writeln (A:5);
    REPEAT
      writeln (A:5, B:5, (A + B):5);
      A := A - 2
    UNTIL A <= 6;
    B := B + 2
  END;  {  of WHILE...DO  }
writeln;
writeln ('All done':20);
```

The assignment statements produce

10	0
A	B

and A > B is **true;** thus, the **WHILE . . . DO** loop is entered. The first time through this loop the **REPEAT . . . UNTIL** loop is used. Output for the first pass is

```
10
10      0   10
```

and the values for A and B are

```
┌──────┐   ┌──────┐
│   8  │   │   0  │
└──────┘   └──────┘
    A          B
```

The Boolean expression A < = 6 is **false** and the **REPEAT . . . UNTIL** loop is executed again to produce the next line of output

```
8      0    8
```

and the values for A and B become

```
┌──────┐   ┌──────┐
│   6  │   │   0  │
└──────┘   └──────┘
    A          B
```

At this point, A < = 6 is **true** and control transfers to the line of code

```
B := B + 2;
```

Thus, the variable values are

```
┌──────┐   ┌──────┐
│   6  │   │   2  │
└──────┘   └──────┘
    A          B
```

and the Boolean expression A > B is **true.** This means the **WHILE . . . DO** loop will be repeated. The output for the second time through this loop is

```
6
6      2    8
```

The inner loop is exited and the values for the variables become

```
┌──────┐   ┌──────┐
│   4  │   │   4  │
└──────┘   └──────┘
    A          B
```

Now A > B is **false** and control is transferred to the line following the **WHILE . . . DO** loop. Output for the complete fragment is

```
10
10      0   10
 8      0    8
 6
 6      2    8

         All done
```

STYLE TIP
■ ■ ■ ■ ■ ■ ■ ■ ■ ■ ■ ■

When working with nested loops, use line comments to indicate the effect of each loop control variable. For example,

```
FOR K := 1 TO 5 DO  {  Each value produces a line  }
  BEGIN
    write (' ':9);
    FOR J := 1 TO K DO  {  This moves across one line  }
      write ('*');
    writeln
  END;  {  of outer loop  }
```

Example 6.25 is a bit contrived and tracing the flow of control somewhat tedious. However, it is important for you to be able to follow the logic involved in using nested loops.

Our next example is much more standard. Be sure you understand it thoroughly, for you will need to be able to use it as part of subsequent programs.

■ **EXAMPLE 6.26**

Use nested loops to reproduce an unknown data file. The first-level pseudocode design for the solution to this problem could be

1. **WHILE NOT eof DO**
   reproduce a line of data

A second-level development could be

1. **WHILE NOT eof DO**
   1.1 set a left margin
   1.2 reproduce a data line
   1.3 advance the input data pointer
   1.4 advance the output pointer

Step 1.2 could then be refined to

   1.2 reproduce a data line
        1.2.1 **WHILE NOT eoln DO**
               1.2.1.1 read a character
               1.2.1.2 write a character

The complete algorithm for this fragment is now

1. **WHILE NOT eof DO**
   1.1 set a left margin
   1.2 reproduce a data line
        1.2.1 **WHILE NOT eoln DO**
               1.2.1.1 read a character
               1.2.1.2 write a character
   1.3 advance the input data pointer
   1.4 advance the output pointer

We can now write code for this algorithm as follows:

```
WHILE NOT eof DO  {  Process one line  }
  BEGIN
    write (' ':10);
    WHILE NOT eoln DO  {  Process one character  }
      BEGIN
        read (Ch);
        write (Ch)
      END;
    readln;
    writeln
  END;
```

If this program fragment is run using the data file

| BRL 268-36-0729 M 38 | HBT 231-48-2136 F 18 | LMN 133-24-0966 F 21 | ■ |

↑

the output is

```
BRL 268-36-0729 M 38
HBT 231-48-2136 F 18
LMN 133-24-0966 F 21
```

Being able to examine a data file is essential for beginning programmers. Consequently, in the Exercises for this section, you will be asked to write a complete program to examine a data file. You should use Example 6.26 for the basis of your program and then keep your program and run it to examine data files for subsequent programs.

Writing Style

As usual, you should be aware of the significance of using a consistent, readable style of writing when using nested loops. There are at least three features you should consider.

1. **Indenting.** Each loop should have its own level of indenting. This makes it easier to identify the body of the loop. If the loop body consists of a compound statement, the **BEGIN** and **END** should start in the same column. Using our previous indenting style, a typical nesting might be

```
FOR K := 1 TO 10 DO
  BEGIN
    WHILE A > 0 DO
      BEGIN
        REPEAT
            .
            .
            .
        UNTIL ⟨condition⟩;  {  end of REPEAT loop  }
        ⟨statement⟩
      END;  {  of WHILE...DO loop  }
    ⟨statement⟩
  END;  {  of FOR loop  }
```

If the body of a loop becomes very long, it is sometimes difficult to match the **BEGIN**s with the proper **END**s. In this case, you should either redesign the program or be especially careful.

2. **Using comments.** Comments can precede a loop and explain what the loop will do, or they can be used with statements inside the loop to explain what the statement does. They should be used to indicate the end of a loop where the loop body is a compound statement.

3. **Skipping lines.** This is an effective way of isolating loops within a program and making nested loops easier to identify.

A note of caution is in order with respect to writing style. Program documentation is important; however, excessive use of comments and skipped lines can detract from readability. You should develop a happy medium.

Statement Execution in Nested Loops

Using nested loops can significantly increase the number of times statements get executed in a program. To illustrate, suppose a program contains a **REPEAT . . . UNTIL** loop that gets executed six times before it is exited. This is illustrated by

```
         ⎡  REPEAT
         ⎢      .
6 times  ⎢      .              (action here)
         ⎢      .
         ⎣  UNTIL ⟨condition 1⟩;
```

If one of the statements inside this loop is another loop, the inner loop will be executed six times. Suppose this inner loop is repeated five times whenever it is entered. This means each statement within the inner loop will be executed 6 x 5 = 30 times when the program is run. This is illustrated by

```
         REPEAT
            .
            .         (action here)
            .
         WHILE ⟨condition 2⟩ DO
6 times     BEGIN
              ⟨statement⟩                    ┐ 30 times  │ 5 times
            END;  {  of WHILE...DO  }
            .
            .
            .
         UNTIL ⟨condition 1⟩;
```

When a third level of nesting is used, the number of times a statement is executed can be determined by the product of three factors, $n_1 \times n_2 \times n_3$, where n_1 represents the number of repetitions of the outside loop, n_2 represents the number of repetitions for the first level of nesting, and n_3 represents the number of repetitions for the innermost loop.

We close this section with two more examples of nested loops. The first one analyzes a program fragment with nested loops, and the second asks you to write a program to produce a certain output.

■ EXAMPLE 6.27

Let's find the output produced by the following program fragment of nested loops. Assume A and B have been declared as integer variables and the data file is

↑

The fragment

```
read (A, B);
REPEAT  { Produce one block of output }
  FOR K := A TO B DO
    BEGIN
      Num := A;

    {  Print one line }
      WHILE Num <= B DO
        BEGIN
          write (Num:4);
          Num := Num + 1
        END;  { of WHILE...DO loop }
      writeln

    END; { of FOR loop }
  A := A + 1;
  writeln
UNTIL A = B; { end of REPEAT...UNTIL loop }
```

produces the output

```
4    5    6    7
4    5    6    7
4    5    6    7
4    5    6    7

     5    6    7
     5    6    7
     5    6    7
          6    7
          6    7
```

∎   ∎

■ **EXAMPLE 6.28**

Write a complete program whose output is the multiplication table from 1 x 1 to 10 x 10. A suitable heading should be part of the output. A program to do this is as follows:

```
PROGRAM MultTable (output);

CONST
  Indent = ' ';

VAR
  J, K : integer;

BEGIN  {  Program  }

  {  Print a heading  }

  writeln;
  writeln (Indent:17, 'Multiplication Table');
  writeln (Indent:17, '--------------------');
  writeln (Indent:10, '( Generated by nested FOR loops )');
  writeln;
  writeln (Indent:11, '   1   2   3   4   5   6   7   8   9  10');
  writeln (Indent:8, '---!------------------------------------');

  {  Now start the loop  }

  FOR K := 1 TO 10 DO
    BEGIN                                    {  Print one row  }
      write (K:10, ' !');
      FOR J := 1 TO 10 DO
        write (K * J:4);
      writeln;
      writeln (Indent:11, '!')
    END;  {  of each row  }
  writeln
END.  {  of program  }
```

The output from this program is

```
               Multiplication Table
               --------------------
         ( Generated by nested FOR loops )

            1   2   3   4   5   6   7   8   9  10
   ---!------------------------------------------
    1 !   1   2   3   4   5   6   7   8   9  10
      !
    2 !   2   4   6   8  10  12  14  16  18  20
      !
    3 !   3   6   9  12  15  18  21  24  27  30
      !
    4 !   4   8  12  16  20  24  28  32  36  40
      !
    5 !   5  10  15  20  25  30  35  40  45  50
      !
    6 !   6  12  18  24  30  36  42  48  54  60
      !
    7 !   7  14  21  28  35  42  49  56  63  70
      !
    8 !   8  16  24  32  40  48  56  64  72  80
      !
    9 !   9  18  27  36  45  54  63  72  81  90
      !
   10 !  10  20  30  40  50  60  70  80  90 100
      !
```

Exercises 6.7

1. Write a complete program that allows you to examine a data file (see Example 6.26). Run your program using each of the following data files.

   a. | This is a one liner. | ■
   b. | bb | ■
   c. | * | ** | *** | **** | ***** | ■
   d. | 87 | 93 | 76 | 92 | 80 | −999 | ■

2. What is the output from each of the following fragments?

   ```
   a. FOR K := 2 TO 6 DO
        BEGIN
          FOR J := 5 TO 10 DO
            write (K + J);
          writeln
        END;
   ```

   ```
   b. FOR K := 2 TO 6 DO
        BEGIN
          FOR J := 5 TO 10 DO
            write (K * J);
          writeln
        END;
   ```

   ```
   c. Sum := 0;
      A := 7;
      WHILE A < 10 DO
        BEGIN
          FOR K := A TO 10 DO
            Sum := Sum + K;
          A := A + 1
        END;
      writeln (Sum);
   ```

```
d. Sum := 0;
   FOR K := 1 TO 10 DO
     FOR J := (10*K-9) TO (10*K) DO
       Sum := Sum + J;
   writeln (Sum);
```

e. Assume the data file is

```
12 3   10 3   8 3   ■
↑
```

```
HILE NOT eof DO
  BEGIN
    readln (Length, Width);
    LineCount := 1;
    REPEAT
      write (' ':9, Length);
      FOR K := 1 TO Length DO
        write ('*');
      writeln;
      LineCount := LineCount + 1
    UNTIL LineCount = Width;
    writeln
  END;  {  of WHILE NOT eof  }
```

3. Write a program fragment that uses nested loops to produce each of the following designs.

```
a. *****        b.     *         c. ***
    ****             ***            ***
     ***            *****           ***
      **           *******          ***
       *            *****          ******
                     ***           ******
                      *            ******
```

4. Write a program fragment that uses nested loops to produce the output

```
2      4      6      8     10
3      6      9     12     15
4      8     12     16     20
5     10     15     20     25
```

5. What output is produced from the following segment of code?

```
A := 4;
B := 7;
REPEAT
  Num := A;
  WHILE Num <= B DO
    BEGIN
      FOR K := A TO B DO
        write (Num:4);
      writeln;
      Num := Num + 1
    END;  {  of WHILE...DO  }
  writeln;
  A := A + 1
UNTIL A = B;  {  end of REPEAT...UNTIL loop  }
```

■ ■ ■ ■

■ 6.8
Loops and Selection

OBJECTIVES

- to be able to use a selection statement within the body of a loop
- to be able to use a loop within an option of a selection statement

Selection within Loops

In Chapter 5 we discussed the use of selection statements. In this chapter we have discussed the use of three different types of loops. It is now time to see how they are used together. We will first examine selection statements contained within the body of a loop.

■ EXAMPLE 6.29

Write a program fragment that counts all the blanks in a line of data. The loop control for this problem will be the end-of-line function. A first-level pseudocode solution is

1. Initialize variables
2. **WHILE NOT eoln DO**
   2.1   process a character

This can be refined to

1. Initialize variables
2. **WHILE NOT eoln DO**
   2.1   process a character
      2.1.1   read a character
      2.1.2   **IF** Character is a blank **THEN**
         2.1.2.1   add 1 to BlankCount

The code for this fragment is

```
BlankCount := 0;
WHILE NOT eoln DO
  BEGIN
    read (Ch);
    IF Ch = ' ' THEN
      BlankCount := BlankCount + 1
  END;  {  of WHILE...DO  }
```

Just as **IF . . . THEN** statements can be used with loops, **IF . . . THEN . . . ELSE** statements can be similarly used. The next example illustrates such a use.

■ EXAMPLE 6.30

Write a program fragment that computes gross wages for employees of the Florida OJ Canning Company. A data line consists of three initials, the total hours worked, and the hourly rate. Thus, a typical data line is

Overtime (more than 40 hours) is computed as time-and-a-half. The output should include all input data and a column of gross wages.

A first-level pseudocode development for this program is

   1. **WHILE NOT eof DO**
      1.1 process a line of data
      1.2 print results

This could be refined to

   1. **WHILE NOT eof DO**
      1.1 process a line of data
         1.1.1 get data
         1.1.2 compute wage
      1.2 print results

Step 1.1.2 can be refined to

         1.1.2 compute wage
             1.1.2.1 **IF** Hours $<=$ 40.0 **THEN**
                      compute regular time
                ELSE
                    compute time-and-a-half

and the final algorithm for the fragment is

   1. **WHILE NOT eof DO**
      1.1 process a line of data
         1.1.1 get data
         1.1.2 compute wage
             1.1.2.1 **IF** Hours $<=$ 40.0 **THEN**
                      compute regular time
                  ELSE
                    compute time-and-a-half
      1.2 print results

The code for this fragment is

```
WHILE NOT eof DO
   BEGIN
     read (Init1, Init2, Init3);
     readln (Hours, PayRate);

     IF Hours <= 40.0 THEN
        TotalWage := Hours * PayRate
     ELSE
        BEGIN
           Overtime := 1.5 * (Hours - 40.0) * PayRate;
           TotalWage := 40 * Payrate + Overtime
        END; {  of ELSE option  }
     write (Init1:5, Init2, Init3);
     write (Hours:10:2, PayRate:10:2);
     writeln ('$':10, TotalWage:7:2)

   END;  {  of WHILE...DO loop  }
```

If the data file is

| JHA 44.5 12.75 | RBT 40.0 9.8 | SML 37.5 11.50 | ■ |

†

A Digital Matter of Life and Death

The radiation-therapy machine, a Therac 25 linear accelerator, was designed to send a penetrating X-ray or electron beam deep into a cancer patient's body to destroy embedded tumors without injuring skin tissue. But in three separate instances in 1985 and 1986, the machine failed. Instead of delivering a safe level of radiation, the Therac 25 administered a dose that was more than 100 times larger than the typical treatment dose. Two patients died and a third was severely burned.

The malfunction was caused by an error in the computer program controlling the machine. It was a subtle error that no one had picked up during the extensive testing the machine had undergone. The error surfaced only when a technician happened to use a specific, unusual combination of keystrokes to instruct the machine.

The Therac incidents and other cases of medical device failures caused by computer errors have focused attention on the increasingly important role played by computers in medical applications. Computers or machines with built-in microprocessors perform functions that range from keeping track of patients to diagnosing ailments and providing treatments.

"The impact of computers on medical care and the medical community is the most significant factor that we have to face," says Frank E. Samuel Jr., president of the Health Industry Manufacturers Association (HIMA), based in Washington, D.C. "Health care will change more dramatically in the next 10 years because of software-driven products than for any other single cause." Samuel made his remarks at a recent HIMA-sponsored conference on the regulation of medical software.

At the same time, reports of medical devices with computer-related problems are appearing more and more frequently. In 1985, the Food and Drug Administration (FDA) reported that recalls of medical devices because of computer faults had roughly doubled over the previous five years. Since then, the number of such complaints has risen further.

The FDA, in its mandated role as guardian of public health and safety, is now preparing to regulate the software component of medical devices. The agency's effort has already raised questions about what kinds of products, software and information systems should be regulated.

the output from this fragment is

```
JHA      44.50       12.75         $ 596.06
RBT      40.00        9.80         $ 392.00
SML      37.50       11.50         $ 431.25
```

Loops within Selection

The next example illustrates the use of a loop within an **IF . . . THEN** statement.

■ EXAMPLE 6.31

Write a program fragment that allows you to read an integer from the data file. If the integer is between 0 and 50, you are to print a chart containing all positive integers less than the integer, their squares and cubes. Thus, if 4 is read, the chart is

```
1       1       1
2       4       8
3       9      27
```

The design for this problem has a first-level pseudocode development of

1. **read** Num
2. **IF** (Num > 0) **AND** (Num < 50) **THEN**
   2.1 print the chart

Step 2.1 can be refined to
> 2.1 print the chart
>> 2.1.1 **FOR** K := 1 **TO** Num − 1 **DO**
>>> 2.1.1.1 print each line

We can now write the code for this fragment as follows:

```
read (Num);
IF (Num > 0) AND (Num < 50) THEN
  FOR K := 1 TO Num - 1 DO
    writeln (K, K * K, K * K * K);
```

To close this section, let's consider the design of a slightly more complex problem.

■ EXAMPLE 6.32

Design a solution and write a program fragment that will do the following:
1. Check the first character of each line of a data file.
2. If the character read is a "Y," process the line. (Processing a line consists of counting the number of occurrences of the letter A contained in the line.)
3. If the character read is not a "Y," skip the line.
4. Count the total number of lines.
5. Count the number of lines processed.
6. Assume there are an unknown number of data lines.
7. Print the total number of lines, the number of lines processed, and the number of occurrences of the letter A in the lines processed.

A first-level pseudocode development for this problem is

1. Initialize counter
2. **WHILE NOT eof DO**
   check each line of data
3. Print results

A second-level development is

1. Initialize counter
   1.1 initialize TotalLines
   1.2 initialize ProcessedLines
   1.3 initialize ACount
2. **WHILE NOT eof DO**
   2.1 **read** Ch
   2.2 **IF** Ch = 'Y' **THEN**
       process the line
   2.3 increment TotalLines
3. Print results
   3.1 print TotalLines
   3.2 print ProcessedLines
   3.3 print ACount

Step 2.2 could be developed to

> 2.2 **IF** Ch = 'Y' **THEN**
>> 2.2.1   increment ProcessedLines
>> 2.2.2   **WHILE NOT eoln DO**
>>> count the A's
>> 2.2.3   advance pointer

and finally, 2.2.2 becomes

>> 2.2.2   **WHILE NOT eoln DO**
>>> 2.2.2.1   **read** Ch
>>> 2.2.2.2   **IF** Ch = 'A' **THEN**
>>>> increment ACount

A complete development of step 2 is thus

> 2. **WHILE NOT eof DO**
> 2.1 **read** Ch
> 2.2 **IF** Ch = 'Y' **THEN**
>> 2.2.1   increment ProcessedLines
>> 2.2.2   **WHILE NOT eoln DO**
>>> 2.2.2.1   **read** Ch
>>> 2.2.2.2   **IF** Ch = 'A' **THEN**
>>>> increment ACount
>> 2.2.3   advance pointer
> 2.3   increment TotalLines

The code for this part of the program is

```
WHILE NOT eof DO
  BEGIN
    read (Ch);
    IF Ch = 'Y' THEN
      BEGIN
        ProcessedLines := ProcessedLines + 1;
        WHILE NOT eoln DO
          BEGIN
            read (Ch);
            IF Ch = 'A' THEN
              ACount := ACount + 1
          END;  {  of WHILE NOT eoln  }
        readln  {  Advance pointer  }
      END;  {  of processing one line  }
    TotalLines := TotalLines + 1
  END;  {  of WHILE NOT eof  }
```

Exercises 6.8

1. Find and explain the errors in each of the following program fragments. You may assume all variables have been suitably declared.

```
a. A := 25;
   Flag := true;
   WHILE Flag = true DO
     IF A >= 100 THEN
       BEGIN
         writeln (A);
         Flag := false
       END;
```

b.
```
FOR K := 1 TO 10 DO
   writeln (K, K * K);
   IF K MOD 3 = 0 THEN
      BEGIN
         write (K);
         writeln (' is a multiple of three')
      END;
```

2. What is the output from each of the following program fragments? Assume variables have been suitably declared.

a.
```
FOR K := 1 TO 100 DO
   IF K MOD 5 = 0 THEN
      writeln (K);
```

b.
```
J := 20;
IF J MOD 5 = 0 THEN
   FOR K := 1 TO 100 DO
      writeln (K);
```

c.
```
A := 5;
B := 90;
REPEAT
   B := B DIV A - 5;
   IF B > A THEN
      B := A + 30
UNTIL B < 0;
writeln (A, B);
```

d.
```
Count := 0;
FOR K := -5 to 5 DO
   IF K MOD 3 = 0 THEN
      BEGIN
         write ('K = ', K:4, ' output ');
         WHILE Count < 10 DO
            BEGIN
               Count := Count + 1;
               writeln (Count:4)
            END;
         Count := 0;
         writeln
      END;
```

e.
```
A := 5;
B := 2;
IF A < B THEN
   FOR K := A TO B DO
      writeln (K)
ELSE
   FOR K := A DOWNTO B DO
      writeln (K);
```

f.
```
FOR K := -5 TO 5 DO
   BEGIN
      write ('K = ', K:4, ' output ');
      A := K;
      IF K < 0 THEN             { K = -5, -4, -3, -2, -1  }
         REPEAT
            writeln (-2 * A:5);
            A := A + 1
         UNTIL A > 0
```

```
              ELSE                    {  K = 0, 1, 2, 3, 4, 5  }
                WHILE (A MOD 2 = 0) DO
                  BEGIN
                    writeln (A);
                    A := A + 1
                  END;  {  of IF...THEN...ELSE  }
              writeln
          END;  {  of FOR loop  }
```

3. Write a program fragment that reads reals from a data file, counts the number of positive reals, and accumulates their sum.

4. Write a program that counts all the periods in a data file.

5. Write a program that reproduces a data file omitting all blanks.

6. Given two integers, A and B, A is a divisor of B if B **MOD** $A = 0$. Write a complete program that reads a positive integer B from a data file and then prints all the positive divisors of B.

■ ■ ■ ■

FOCUS ON	
PROGRAM DESIGN	

This problem illustrates the combined use of repetition and selection. Specifically, the problem is to write a program that accepts a positive integer as input and then prints all primes less than or equal to the integer read. Thus, if the number read is 17, typical output would be

```
-----------------------------------------------------

        The number is   17.  The prime numbers
        less than or equal to   17 are:

                       2
                       3
                       5
                       7
                      11
                      13
                      17
```

Input is from a data file, so a **WHILE NOT eof DO** loop is used as the main loop for the body of the program.

You should note the mathematical property that a number K is prime if it has no divisors (other than 1) less than its square root. Thus, when we check for divisors, it is only necessary to check up to **sqrt**(K). Also note that, by definition, 1 is not prime.

A first-level pseudocode development of this problem is

WHILE NOT eof DO
1. Get a number
2. **IF** Number is 1 **THEN**
    2.1 print message for 1
    ELSE
    2.2 process the number

A structure chart for this problem is given in Figure 6.4.

FIGURE 6.4
Structure chart for **PROGRAM**
ListPrimes

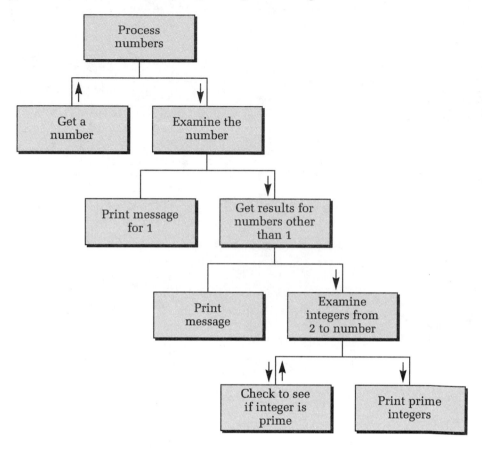

Module specifications for the main modules are

1. Get Data Module
   Data received: None
   Information returned: A positive integer
   Logic: Read an integer from the data file.

2. Examine the Number Module
   Data received: The integer read
   Information returned: None
   Logic: **IF** the number is 1 then print a message.
       ELSE
         Print a message
         FOR K := 2 **TO** Number **DO**
           Check K for a prime number.
           IF K is prime, **THEN** print it.

Further pseudocode development of this problem produces

  WHILE NOT eof DO
1. Get a number
2. **IF** Number is 1 **THEN**
     2.1 print a message for 1
     ELSE
     2.2 process the number

Step 2.2 can be refined to

> 2.2   process the number
>   2.2.1   print message
>   2.2.2   check for primes less than or equal to number

Step 2.2.2 is then refined to

> 2.2.2   **FOR** K := 2 **TO** Number **DO**
>   2.2.2.1   check to see if K is prime
>   2.2.2.2   **IF** K is prime **THEN**
>   print K in list of primes

A complete pseudocode solution for this problem is

> **WHILE NOT eof DO**
> 1.   Get a number
> 2.   **IF** Number is 1 **THEN**
>   2.1   print a message for 1
>   **ELSE**
>   2.2   process the number
>   2.2.1   print message
>   2.2.2   **FOR** K := 2 **TO** Number **DO**
>   2.2.2.1   check to see if K is prime
>   2.2.2.2   **IF** K is prime **THEN**
>   print K in list of primes

A complete program for this problem follows. This has been run on the input file

10	17	1	25	2	■

```
PROGRAM ListPrimes (input, output);

{    This program reads positive integers from an input file    }
{    and then lists prime numbers less than or equal to each     }
{    number read. Note how loops are featured.                   }

CONST
   Skip = ' ';
   Dashes = '-----------------------------------------------------';

VAR
   Candidate,              {  Loop index variable                  }
   Divisor,                {  Possible divisors of a number         }
   Number : integer;       {  Integer read from input               }
   Prime : boolean;        {  Boolean variable used in prime check  }
   LimitForCheck : real;{  Holds final value in FOR loop         }

BEGIN  {  Program  }
   WHILE NOT eof DO
     BEGIN
       readln (Number);
       IF Number = 1 THEN

     {  Print a message for #1  }

         BEGIN
           writeln;
           writeln (Skip:10, Dashes);
```

1

```
                    writeln;
                    writeln (Skip:20, '1 is not prime by definition.')
                END

            ELSE
              BEGIN
                writeln;
                writeln (Skip:10, Dashes);
                writeln;
                writeln (Skip:20, 'The number is', Number:5,
                        '. The prime numbers');
                writeln (Skip:20, 'less than or equal to', Number:5, ' are:');
                writeln;

            { Check each positive integer less than or equal to number  }

                FOR Candidate := 2 TO Number DO
                  BEGIN
                    Prime := true;
                    Divisor := 2;
                    LimitForCheck := sqrt(Candidate);
                    WHILE (Divisor <= LimitForCheck) AND Prime DO
                      IF Candidate MOD Divisor = 0 THEN
                        Prime := false              {  Candidate has a divisor  }
                      ELSE
                        Divisor := Divisor + 1;
                    IF Prime THEN           {   Print in list of primes  }
                        writeln (Candidate:35)
                  END { of FOR loop  }
              END { of ELSE option  }
          END { of WHILE NOT eof loop  }
    END. { of program  }
```

The output for this program is as follows:

```
      --------------------------------------------------

                The number is   10.  The prime numbers
                less than or equal to   10 are:

                                    2
                                    3
                                    5
                                    7

      --------------------------------------------------

                The number is   17.  The prime numbers
                less than or equal to   17 are:

                                    2
                                    3
                                    5
                                    7
                                   11
                                   13
                                   17

      --------------------------------------------------

           1 is not prime by definition.
```

```
------------------------------------------------------

        The number is   25.  The prime numbers
        less than or equal to   25 are:

                           2
                           3
                           5
                           7
                          11
                          13
                          17
                          19
                          23


------------------------------------------------------

        The number is    2.  The prime numbers
        less than or equal to    2 are:

                           2
```

More efficient algorithms than what we used here do exist. However, the purpose of this program was to see how loops can be used to solve a problem.

RUNNING AND DEBUGGING TIPS

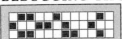

1. Most errors involving loops are not compilation errors. Thus, not until you try to run the program will you be able to detect most errors.

2. A syntax error that will not be detected by the compiler is a semicolon after a **WHILE . . . DO.** The fragment

```
WHILE NOT eof DO;
  BEGIN
    readln (A);
    writeln (A)
  END;
```

is incorrect and will not get past

```
WHILE NOT eof DO;
```

Note that this is an infinite loop.

3. Carefully check your data file when using loops to input data. Be sure that your lines are carefully formatted, you have been careful with blanks at the end of a line, and you have used **eof** and **readln** whenever possible.

4. Carefully check entry conditions for each loop.

5. Carefully check exit conditions for each loop. Make sure the loop is exited (not infinite) and that you have the correct number of repetitions.

6. Loop entry, execution, and exit can be checked by
   a. pencil and paper check on initial and final values
   b. count of the number of repetitions
   c. use of debugging **writelns** for
      i. Boolean condition prior to loop
      ii. variables inside loop
      iii. values of the counter in loop
      iv. Boolean values inside the loop
      v. values after loop is exited

■ Summary

Key Terms

accumulator
counter
data validation
decrement
fixed repetition
   (iterated) loop

index
infinite loop
nested loop
posttest (exit controlled)
   loop

pretest condition
pretest (entrance
   controlled) loop
sentinel value
variable condition loop

Key Terms (optional)

input assertion
loop invariant
loop variant

loop verification
output assertion

Keywords

DO
DOWNTO
FOR

TO
REPEAT

UNTIL
WHILE

Key Concepts

■ The following table provides a comparison summary of the three repetition
structures discussed in this chapter.

Traits of Loops	FOR . . . TO . . . DO Loop	WHILE . . . DO Loop	REPEAT . . . UNTIL Loop
Pretest loop	yes	yes	no
Posttest loop	no	no	yes
BEGIN . . . END for compound statements	required	required	not required
Repetition	fixed	variable	variable
Loop index	yes	no	no
Index automatically incremented	yes	no	no
Boolean expression used	no	yes	yes

■ A fixed repetition loop (**FOR . . . TO . . . DO**) is to be used when you know exactly how many times something is to be repeated. The basic form for a **FOR . . .
TO . . . DO** loop is

```
FOR J := 1 to 5 DO
   ⟨program statement⟩;
```
or
```
FOR J := 1 TO 5 DO
   BEGIN
      ⟨statement 1⟩;
      ⟨statement 2⟩;
         .
         .
         .
      ⟨statement n⟩
   END;
```

After the loop is finished, the value of the index variable may become unassigned and program control is transferred to the first executable statement following the loop.

- A **WHILE . . . DO** loop is a pretest loop that can have a variable loop control; a typical loop is

```
WHILE NOT eof DO
  BEGIN
    readln (Score);
    Sum := Sum + Score;
    Count := Count + 1
  END;
```

- A counter is a variable whose purpose is to indicate how often the body of a loop is executed.
- An accumulator is a variable whose purpose is to sum values.
- An infinite **WHILE . . . DO** loop is caused by having a **true** loop control condition that is never changed to **false**.
- **WHILE NOT eoln DO** is a typical Boolean condition used to detect when the end of a data line is encountered.
- **WHILE NOT eof DO** is a typical Boolean condition used to detect when the end of a data file is encountered.
- A posttest loop has a Boolean condition checked after the loop body has been completed.
- A **REPEAT . . . UNTIL** loop is a posttest loop; a typical loop is

```
REPEAT
  readln (Num);
  Sum := Sum + Num;
  Count := Count + 1
UNTIL eof;
```

- **FOR** loops can always be rewritten as equivalent **REPEAT . . . UNTIL** or **WHILE . . . DO** loops.
- **REPEAT . . . UNTIL** loops can always be rewritten as **WHILE . . . DO** loops.
- **REPEAT . . . UNTIL** and **WHILE . . . DO** are variable control loops; **FOR** is a fixed control loop.
- **WHILE . . . DO** and **FOR** are pretest loops; **REPEAT . . . UNTIL** is a posttest loop.
- Any one of these loops can be nested within any other of the loops.
- Indenting each loop is important for program readability.
- Several levels of nesting make the logic of a program difficult to follow.
- Loops and conditionals are frequently used together. Careful program design will facilitate writing code in which these concepts are integrated; typical forms are

```
WHILE ⟨condition1⟩ DO
  BEGIN
    .
    .
    .
    IF ⟨condition2⟩ THEN
      .
      .
      .
    ELSE
      .
      .
      .
      .
  END;  {  of WHILE...DO  }
and
```

```
IF ⟨conditional⟩ THEN
  BEGIN
    .
    .
    .
    FOR J := ⟨value1⟩ TO ⟨valueN⟩ DO
      BEGIN
        .
        .
        .
      END;   {  of FOR loop  }
    .
    .
    .
  END   {  of IF...THEN  }
ELSE
  .
  .
  .
```

■ Programming Problems and Projects

■ 1. The Caswell Catering and Convention Service (Problem 7, Chapter 4 and Problem 14, Chapter 5) wants you to upgrade their program so they can use it for all of their customers. Modify it to run using a data file with an unknown number of customers.

2. Modify your program for a service station owner (Focus on Program-Design, Chapter 5) so that it can be used for an unknown number of customers. Your output should include the number of customers and all other pertinent items in a daily summary.

■ 3. Modify the Community Hospital program (Problem 17, Chapter 5) so that it can be run with a data file containing information for all patients leaving the hospital in one day. Include appropriate bad data checks and daily summary items.

4. The greatest common divisor (GCD) of two integers a and b is a positive integer c such that c divides a, c divides b, and for any other common divisor d of a and b, d is less than or equal to c. (For example, the GCD of 18 and 45 is 9.) One method of finding the GCD of two positive integers (a, b) is to begin with the smaller (a) and see if it is a divisor of the larger (b). If it is, then the smaller is the GCD. If not, find the next largest divisor of a and see if it is a divisor of b. Continue this process until you find a divisor of both a and b. This is the GCD of a and b.

Write an interactive program that will accept two positive integers as input and then print out their GCD. Enhance your output by printing all divisors of a that do not divide b. A sample run could produce

```
Enter two positive integers.
?42, 72

The divisors of 42 that do not divide 72 are:

        42
        21
        14
         7

The GCD of 42 and 72 is 6.
```

5. The least common multiple (LCM) of two positive integers a and b is a positive integer c such that c is a multiple of both a and b and for any other multiple m of a and b, c is a divisor of m. (For example, the LCM of 12 and 8 is 24.)

   Write an interactive program that allows the user to enter two positive integers and then print the LCM. The program should guard against bad data and should allow the user the option of "trying another pair" or quitting.

6. A perfect number is a positive integer such that the sum of the proper divisors equals the number. Thus, $28 = 1 + 2 + 4 + 7 + 14$ is a perfect number. If the sum of the divisors is less than the number, it is deficient. If the sum exceeds the number, it is abundant. Your programs should guard against bad data and should allow the user the option of entering another interger or quitting.
   a. Write an interactive program that allows the user to enter a positive integer and then displays the result indicating whether the number entered is perfect, deficient, or abundant.
   b. Write another interactive program that allows the user to enter a positive integer N and then displays all perfect numbers less than or equal to N.

7. In these days of increased awareness of automobile mileage, more motorists are computing their miles per gallon (mpg) than ever before. Write a program that will perform these computations for a traveler. Data for the program will be entered on lines indicated by the following table.

Odometer Reading	Gallons of Fuel Purchased
18828(start)	—
19240	9.7
19616	10.2
19944	8.8
20329	10.1
20769(finish)	10.3

The program should compute the mpg for each tank and the cumulative mpg each time the tank is filled up. Your output should produce a chart with the following headings:

Odometer (begin)	Odometer (end)	Fuel (tank)	Miles (tank)	Fuel (trip)	Miles (trip)	Mpg (tank)	Mpg (trip)

8. Parkside's Other Triangle is generated from two positive integers, one for the size and one for the seed. For example,

Size 6, Seed 1
```
1 2 4 7 2 7
  3 5 8 3 8
    6 9 4 9
      1 5 1
        6 2
          3
```

Size 5, Seed 3
```
3 4 6 9 4
  5 7 1 5
    8 2 6
      3 7
        8
```

The size gives the number of columns. Seed specifies the starting value for column 1. Column *n* contains *n* values. The successive values are obtained by adding 1 to the previous value. When 9 is reached, the next value becomes 1.

Write a program that reads pairs of positive integers from a data file and produces Parkside's Other Triangle for each pair. The check for bad data should include checking for seeds between 1 and 9 inclusive.

9. Modify the sewage, water, and sanitation problem (Problem 19, Chapter 5) so that it can be used with a data file containing appropriate information for all residents of the community.

■ 10. Modify the program for the Lucky Wildcat Well Corporation (Problem 20, Chapter 5) so that it can be run on a data file containing information about all of Al Derrick's wells. The first line of the data file consists of a positive integer that represents the total number of wells drilled.

11. Modify the program concerning the Mathematical Association of America (Problem 21, Chapter 5). There will be 50 official state delegates attending the next summer national meeting. The new data file will contain the two-letter state abbreviation for each delegate. Output should include one column with the state abbreviation and another with the amount reimbursed.

12. In Fibonacci's sequence,

   0, 1, 1, 2, 3, 5, 8, 13, . . .

the first two terms are 0 and 1 and each successive term is formed by adding the previous two terms. Write a program that will read positive integers from a data file and then print the number of terms indicated by each integer read. Be sure to test your program with a data file that includes the integers 1 and 2.

■ 13. Dr. Lae Z. Programmer is at it again. Now that you have written a program to compute the grade for one student in his class (Problems 5, 22, & 23, Chapter 5), he wants you to modify this program so it can be used for the entire class. He will help you by making the first line of data be a positive integer representing the number of students in the class. Your new version should compute an overall class average and the number of students receiving each letter grade.

■ 14. Modify the Pentagon Parking Lot problem (Problem 26, Chapter 5) so that it can be used for all customers in one day. In the new data file, time should be entered in military style as a four-digit integer. The lot opens at 0600 (6:00 A.M.) and closes at 2200 (10:00 P.M.). Your program should include appropriate summary information.

■ 15. The Natural Pine Furniture Company (Problem 2, Chapter 4) now wants you to refine your program so that it will print a one-week pay report for each employee. You do not know how many employees there are, but you do know that all information for each employee is on a separate line. Each line of input will contain the employee's initials, the number of hours worked, and the hourly rate. You are to use the constant definition section for the following:

federal withholding tax rate	18%
state withholding tax rate	4.5%
hospitalization	$25.65
union dues	$ 7.85

Your output should include a report for each employee and a summary report for the company files.

16. Orlando Tree Service, Incorporated, offers the following services and rates to its customers:

a. tree removal $500 per tree

b. tree trimming $80 per hour

c. stump grinding $25 plus $2 per inch for each stump whose diameter exceeds ten inches. The $2 charge is only for the diameter inches in excess of ten.

Write a complete program to allow the manager, Mr. Sorwind, to provide an estimate when he bids on a job. Your output should include a listing of each separate charge and a total. A 10 percent discount is given for any job whose total exceeds $1000. A typical input file is

```
R 7  T 6.5  G 8   8 10 12 14 15 15 20 25
```

where "R," "T," and "G" are codes for removal, trimming, and grinding, respectively. The integer following "G" represents the number of stumps to be ground. The next line of integers represents the diameters of stumps to be ground.

17. A standard science experiment is to drop a ball and see how high it bounces. Once the "bounciness" of the ball has been determined, the ratio gives a bounciness index. For example, if a ball dropped from a height of ten feet bounces six feet high, the index is 0.6 and the total distance traveled by the ball is 16 feet after one bounce. If the ball were to continue bouncing, the distance after two bounces would be 10 ft. + 6 ft. + 6 ft. + 3.6 ft. = 25.6 ft. Note that distance traveled for each successive bounce is the distance to the floor plus 0.6 of that distance as the ball comes back up.

Write an interactive program that lets the user enter the initial height of the ball and the number of times the ball is allowed to continue bouncing. Output should be the total distance traveled by the ball. At some point in this process, the distance traveled by the ball becomes negligible. Use the **CONST** section to define a "negligible" distance (for example, 0.00001 inches). Terminate the computing when the distance becomes negligible. When this stage is reached, include the number of bounces as part of the output.

18. Write a program that prints a calendar for one month. Input consists of an integer specifying the first day of the month (1 = Sunday) and an integer specifying how many days are in a month.

19. An amortization table shows the rate at which a loan is paid off. It contains monthly entries showing the interest paid that month, the principal paid, and the remaining balance. Given the amount of money borrowed (the principal), the annual interest rate, and the

amount the person wishes to repay each month, print an amortization table. (Be certain that the payment desired is larger than the first month's interest.) Your table should stop when the loan is paid off, and should be printed with the following heads.

```
MONTH NUMBER    INTEREST PAID    PRINCIPAL PAID    BALANCE
```

20. Computers work in the binary system, which is based upon powers of 2. Write a program that prints out the first 15 powers of 2 beginning with 2 to the zero power. Print your output in headed columns.

21. Print a list of the positive integers less than 500 that are divisible by either 5 or 7. When the list is complete, print a count of the number of integers that were found.

22. Write a program that reads in 20 real numbers, then prints the average of the positive numbers and the average of the negative numbers.

■ 23. In 1626, the Dutch settlers purchased Manhattan Island from the Indians. According to legend, the purchase price was $24. Suppose that the Indians had invested this amount at 3 percent annual interest compounded quarterly. If the money had earned interest from the start of 1626 to the end of last year, how much money would the Indians have in the bank today? (*Hint:* use nested loops for the compounding.)

24. Write a program to print the sum of the odd integers from 1 to 99.

25. The theory of relativity holds that as an object moves, it gets smaller. The new length of the object can be determined from the formula:

New Length = Original Length $* \sqrt{1 - B^2}$

B^2 is the percentage of the speed of light at which the object is moving, entered in decimal form. Given the length of an object, print its new length for speeds ranging from 0 to 99 percent of the speed of light. Print the output in the following columns:

```
Percent of Light Speed      Length
------- -- ----- -----      ------
```

■ 26. Mr. Christian uses a 90 percent, 80 percent, 70 percent, 60 percent grading scale on his tests. Given a list of test scores, print out the number of As, Bs, Cs, Ds, and Fs on the test. Terminate the list of scores with a sentinel value.

27. The mathematician Gottfried Leibniz determined a formula for estimating the value of pi.

```
pi         1   1   1   1    1
-- = 1  -  -  +  -  -  -  +  -  -  -  +  . . .
4          3   5   7   9   11
```

Evaluate the first 200 terms of this formula and print its approximation of pi.

28. In a biology experiment, Carey finds that a sample of an organism doubles in population every 12 hours. If she starts with one thousand organisms, in how many hours will she have one million?

29. Pascal does not have a mathematical operator that permits raising a number to a power. We can easily write a program to perform this function, however. Given an integer to represent the base number and a positive integer to represent the power desired, write a program that prints the number raised to that power.

30. Mr. Thomas has negotiated a salary schedule for his new job. He will be paid one cent the first day, with the daily rate doubling each day. Write a program that will find his total earnings for 30 days. Print your results in a table set up as follows:

```
Day Number     Daily Salary     Total Earned
     1              .01              .01
     2              .02              .03
     3               .                .
     .               .                .
     .               .                .
     .
    30
```

31. Write a program to print the perimeter and area of rectangles using all combinations of lengths and widths running from 1 foot to 10 feet in increments of 1 foot. Print the output in headed columns.

32. Teachers in most school districts are paid on a salary schedule that provides a salary based on their number of years of teaching experience. Suppose that a beginning teacher in the Babbage School District is paid $19,000 the first year. For each year of experience after this up to 12 years, a 4 percent increase over the preceding value is received. Write a program that prints a salary schedule for teachers in this district. The output should appear as follows:

```
Years Experience              Salary
----------------              ------
       0                     $19,000
       1                     $19,760
       2                     $20,550
       3                     $21,372
       .                        .
       .                        .
       .                        .
      12
```

(Actually, most teacher's salary schedules are more complex than this. As an additional problem, you might like to find out how the salary schedule is determined in your local school district and write a program to print the salary schedule.)

33. The Euclidean Algorithm can be used to find the greatest common divisor of two positive integers (n_1, n_2). For example, suppose $n_1 = 72$ and $n_2 = 42$; you can use this algorithm in the following manner:

    1. Divide the larger by the smaller as

    $$72 = 42 * 1 + 30$$

    2. Divide the divisor (42) by the remainder (30)

    $$42 = 30 * 1 + 12$$

    3. Repeat this process until you get a remainder of zero

    $$30 = 12 * 2 + 6$$
    $$12 = 6 * 2 + 0$$

The last nonzero remainder is the GCD of n_1 and n_2.

Write an interactive program that lets the user enter two integers and then prints out each step in the process of using the Euclidean Algorithm to find their GCD.

34. Cramer's Rule for solving a system of equations was given in Problem 12, Chapter 4. It was enhanced in Problem 29, Chapter 5 by guarding against division by zero. Add a further enhancement to your program by using a loop to guarantee that the coefficients and constants entered by the user are precisely those that were intended.

35. Gaussian Elimination is another method used to solve systems of equations. To illustrate, if the system is

$$x - 2y = 1$$
$$2x + y = 7$$

Gaussian Elimination would start with the augmented matrix

$$\begin{bmatrix} 1 & -2 & | & 1 \\ 2 & 1 & | & 7 \end{bmatrix}$$

and proceed to produce the identity matrix on the left side

$$\begin{bmatrix} 1 & 0 & | & 3 \\ 0 & 1 & | & 1 \end{bmatrix}$$

At this stage, the solution to the system is seen to be $x = 3$ and $y = 1$.

Write an interactive program in which the user enters coefficients for a system of two equations containing two variables. The program should then solve the system and display the answer. Your program should include the following:

a. a check for bad data.
b. a solvable system check.
c. a display of partial results as the matrix operations are performed.

36. As you might expect, instructors of computer science do not agree on whether a **REPEAT . . . UNTIL** loop or a **WHILE . . . DO** loop is the preferred variable control loop in Pascal. Interview several computer science instructors at your institution to determine what preference (if any) they have regarding these two forms of repetition. Prepare a class report based on your interviews. Include advantages and disadvantages of each form of repetition.

37. Examine the repetition constructs of at least five other programming languages. Prepare a report that compares and contrasts repetition in each of the languages. Be sure to include information such as which languages provide for both fixed and variable repetition and which languages have more than one kind of variable repetition. Which language appears to have the most desirable form of repetition? Include your rationale for this decision in your report.

38. Examine some old computer science texts and talk to some computer science instructors who worked with the early languages to see how repetition was achieved in the "early days." Prepare a brief chronological chart for class display that depicts the various stages in developing repetition.

CHAPTER

Subprograms: Writing Procedures and Functions

Recall from Section 2.1 the process of solving a problem by stepwise refinement of tasks into subtasks. This top-down design method is especially suitable for writing Pascal programs to solve problems using *subprograms*.

The concept of a subprogram is not difficult to understand. It is a program within a program and is provided by most programming languages. Each subprogram should complete some task, the nature of which can range from simple to complex. You could have a subprogram that prints only a line of data, or you could rewrite an entire program as a subprogram. The main idea is to use a subprogram to perform some specific task.

OBJECTIVES
- to understand the concepts of modularity and bottom-up testing
- to be aware of the use of structured programming

Modularity

We have previously discussed and illustrated the process of solving a problem by top-down design. Using this method, we divide the main task into major subtasks, and then continue to divide the subtasks (stepwise refinement) into smaller subtasks until all subtasks can be easily performed. Once an algorithm for solving a problem has been developed using top-down design, the programmer then writes code to translate the general solution into a Pascal program.

As you have seen, code written to perform one well-defined subtask is referred to as a module. One should be able to design, code, and test each module in a program independently from the rest of the program. In this sense, a module is a subprogram containing all definitions and declarations needed to perform the indicated subtask. Everything required for the subtask (but not needed in other parts of the program) can be created in the subprogram. Consequently, the definitions and declarations have meaning only when the module is being used.

A program that has been created using modules to perform various tasks is said to possess *modularity*. In general, modular programs are easier to test, debug, and correct than programs that are not modular because each independent module can be tested by running it from a test driver. Then, once the modules are running correctly, they can become part of a longer program. This independent testing of modules is referred to as *bottom-up testing*.

Structured Programming

Structured programming is the process of developing a program where emphasis is placed on the communication between independent modules. Connections between these modules are specified in parameter lists and are usually controlled by the main program. Structured programming is especially suitable to large programs being worked on by teams. By carefully designing the modules and specifying what information is to be received by and returned from the module, a team of programmers can independently develop their module and then have it connect to the complete program.

The remainder of this chapter is devoted to seeing how subprograms can be written to accomplish specific tasks. There are two types of subprograms in standard Pascal: *procedures* and *functions*. We first examine the writing of procedures.

■ 7.2
Procedures without Parameters

OBJECTIVES

- to be aware of some uses for procedures
- to be aware of differences in procedures
- to understand the form for a procedure
- to be able to use a procedure in a program

A procedure can be used as a subprogram for many purposes. Two significant uses are to facilitate the top-down design philosophy of problem solving and to avoid having to write repeated segments of code.

Procedures facilitate problem solving. For instance, if the pseudocode solution to a problem is

1. Get the data
2. Process the data
3. Print the results

a procedure can be written for each of these tasks and the program can then call each procedure as needed. The idea of using a procedure to implement a line of pseudocode is very important and, as you develop more programming skills, will become an integral part of how you write a program.

Another use of procedures is for the repetition of several lines of code throughout a program. A procedure can be written using those several lines of code, and whenever that task is needed, a single call to the procedure suffices.

Form for a Procedure

Let's now see how a procedure is written. Basically, a procedure is a program and, as such, it has the same divisions as a complete program.

Procedure heading → [

Declaration section → [
(optional)

Executable section → [

Structured Programming

From 1950 to the early 1970s programs were designed and written on a linear basis. A program written and designed on such a basis can be called an unstructured program. Structured programming, on the other hand, organizes a program around separate semi-independent modules that are linked together by a single sequence of simple commands.

In 1964, mathematicians Corrado Bohm and Guiseppe Jacopini proved that any program logic, regardless of complexity, can be expressed by using sequence, selection, and iteration. This result is termed the structure theorem. This result, combined with the efforts of Edger W. Dijkstra, led to a significant move toward structured programming and away from the use of GOTO statements. In fact, in a letter to the editor of *Communications of the ACM,* Volume 11, March 1968, Dijkstra stated that the **GOTO** statement "should be abolished from all 'higher level' programming languages. . . . [The **GOTO** statement] is just too primitive; it is too much an invitation to make a mess of one's program."

The first time structured programming concepts were applied to a large-scale data processing application was the IBM Corporation's "New York Times Project" from 1969 to 1971. Using these techniques, programmers posted productivity figures from four to six times higher than those of the average programmer. In addition, the error rate was a phenomenally low 0.0004 per line of coding.

The procedure heading must contain the reserved word **PROCEDURE** followed by the procedure name, which can be any valid identifier. Since no parameters are used at this point, the form for a procedure heading is

PROCEDURE ⟨procedure name⟩;

It is important to develop the habit of using descriptive names for procedures. For example, if you are going to write a procedure to print a heading for the output, PrintHeader might be a good choice. This allows you to recognize the task the procedure is supposed to accomplish and makes the program more readable. Each of the following would be a reasonable, descriptive procedure heading.

```
PROCEDURE PrintHeader;
PROCEDURE GetData;
PROCEDURE ComputeTax;
PROCEDURE ComputeTotalPoints;
PROCEDURE PrintScores;
PROCEDURE PrintCourseInfo;
```

The declaration section of a procedure is identical to the declaration section of a program containing **CONST** and **VAR** subsections.

The executable section of a procedure resembles the executable section of a program in that it must start with the reserved word **BEGIN,** but it differs in a significant way: the **END** of a procedure is followed by a semicolon instead of a period. Thus, a procedure will have the following basic form:

```
PROCEDURE ⟨procedure name⟩;

  CONST
    (list of constants)

  VAR
    (list of variables)

  BEGIN
    .
    .  (body of procedure)
    .
  END;
```

The syntax diagram for this is

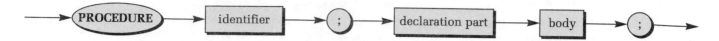

Constants and variables declared in a procedure can only be used within that procedure and are said to be local to that procedure (see Chapter 8).

Let's look at one quick procedure before our example. What will the following procedure do?

```
PROCEDURE Skip3;

  BEGIN
    writeln; writeln; writeln
  END;
```

The procedure skips three lines in the output.

■ EXAMPLE 7.1

Suppose you are writing a program for Our Lady of Mercy Hospital. The program is to print a billing statement for each patient as the patient leaves the hospital. Let's write a procedure that prints a heading for each statement as follows:

```
/////////////////////////////////////////////
/                                           /
/          Our Lady of Mercy Hospital       /
/          --------------------------       /
/                                           /
/             1306 Central City             /
/             Phone (416) 333-5555          /
/                                           /
/////////////////////////////////////////////
```

The procedure that will do this is

```
{************************************************************}

PROCEDURE DisplayStatementHeading;

  CONST
    Marks = '/////////////////////////////////////////////';
    Edge = '/                                           /';
    Skip = ' ';

  BEGIN
    writeln;
    writeln (Skip:10, Marks);
    writeln (Skip:10, Edge);
    writeln (Skip:10, '/', Skip:7, 'Our Lady of Mercy Hospital', Skip:6, '/');
    writeln (Skip:10, '/', Skip:7, '--------------------------', Skip:6, '/');
    writeln (Skip:10, Edge);
    writeln (Skip:10, '/', Skip:11, '1306 Central City', Skip:11, '/');
    writeln (Skip:10, '/', Skip:10, 'Phone (416) 333-5555', Skip: 9, '/');
    writeln (Skip:10, Edge);
    writeln (Skip:10, Marks);
    writeln
  END; {  of PROCEDURE DisplayStatementHeading  }
{************************************************************}
```

■

Placement in a Program

Procedures are an extension of the declaration section of the program; they are placed in the declaration section after the variable declaration subsection in a program. Thus, a full program with a procedure would have the following form:

```
PROGRAM ⟨program name⟩ (output);

CONST

VAR

PROCEDURE ⟨procedure name⟩;

   CONST

   VAR

   BEGIN  {  PROCEDURE  }
      .
      .  (body of procedure)
      .
   END;  {  of PROCEDURE  }

BEGIN  {  Main program  }
   .
   .  (body of program)
   .
END.  {  of main program  }
```

Using procedures in a program can make a program harder to read unless you enhance the readability by using comments, blank lines, and indenting. You should develop a style with which you are comfortable. Most examples in this text will use the following style:

1. Procedures will be preceded and followed by a row of asterisks.
2. A comment section separated by blank lines will follow the procedure heading.
3. Except for the procedure heading, the procedure code will be indented.

Therefore, our general form for putting a procedure in a program will be

```
PROGRAM ⟨program name⟩ (output);

CONST

VAR

{********************************************************************}

PROCEDURE ⟨procedure name⟩;

   {  A brief description of the procedure  }

   CONST

   VAR
```

```
    BEGIN
      .
      .  (body of procedure)
      .
    END;  {  of PROCEDURE ⟨procedure name⟩  }

{*****************************************************************}

{  Now start the main program  }

BEGIN  {  Main program  }
   .
   .  (body of main program)
   .
END.  {  of main program  }
```

Calling a Procedure

Now that you know how to write a procedure and where it belongs in a program, you need to know how to call the procedure from the main program. Since no parameters will be used in procedures at this point, a procedure name as a statement in the main program will cause the procedure to be executed by the computer. For example, if PrintHeader is the name of a procedure,

```
    BEGIN  {  Main program  }
      PrintHeader;
          .
          .  (remainder of program)
          .
    END.  {  of main program  }
```

will cause the procedure PrintHeader to be executed first in the main program.

When a procedure name is encountered as a program statement, control of execution is transferred to the procedure. At that time, the procedure is run as a separate program and when the procedure is complete, control returns to the next statement in the main program following the call to the procedure. The following short program to call a procedure illustrates this control.

```
PROGRAM FirstProcedure (output);

{*****************************************************************}

PROCEDURE PrintMessage;

  BEGIN
    writeln ('This is written from the procedure.':43)
  END;  {  of PROCEDURE PrintMessage  }

{*****************************************************************}

BEGIN  {  Main program  }
  writeln;
  writeln ('This is written from the main program.':46);
  writeln;
  PrintMessage;
  writeln
END.  {  of main program  }
```

The output from this program is

```
    This is written from the main program.

    This is written from the procedure.
```

■ **EXAMPLE 7.2**

As another example, let's construct a short program that calls a procedure several times and have the procedure print the message

```
This is written by a procedure.
Now return to the main program.
```

Furthermore, let us have the main program print a message that includes a count of how often the procedure is called. A pseudocode design could be

1. Initialize counter
2. Print message
3. Call procedure
4. Increment counter
5. Print message
6. Call procedure
7. Increment counter
8. Print message
9. Call procedure

The program for this design is

```
PROGRAM ProcedurePractice (output);

{     This program illustrates multiple calls to a procedure    }
{     for printing a message.                                   }

CONST
  Indent = ' ';

VAR
  Count : integer;


{***************************************************************** }


PROCEDURE PrintMessage;

  {  This procedure prints a two-line message every time it    }
  {  is called.                                                }

  BEGIN
    writeln;
    writeln (Indent:20, 'This is written by a procedure.');
    writeln (Indent:20, 'Now return to the main program.');
    writeln
  END;  {  of PROCEDURE PrintMessage  }


{***************************************************************** }


{  Now start the main program  }

BEGIN  {  Main program  }

  Count := 1;
  writeln (Indent:10, 'This is written from the main program.');
  writeln (Indent:10, 'It is call #', Count:3, ' to the procedure.');
  PrintMessage;

  Count := Count + 1;
  writeln (Indent:10, 'This is written from the main program.');
  writeln (Indent:10, 'It is call #', Count:3, ' to the procedure.');
  PrintMessage;
```

```
      Count := Count + 1;
      writeln (Indent:10, 'This is written from the main program.');
      writeln (Indent:10, 'It is call #', Count:3, ' to the procedure.');
      PrintMessage

END.  {  of main program  }
```

The output from this program is

```
    This is written from the main program.
    It is call #  1 to the procedure.

                This is written by a procedure.
                Now return to the main program.

    This is written from the main program.
    It is call #  2 to the procedure.

                This is written by a procedure.
                Now return to the main program.

    This is written from the main program.
    It is call #  3 to the procedure.

                This is written by a procedure.
                Now return to the main program.
```

If a constant is going to be used in several procedures, it could be declared in the constant definition section of the main program and then used by each subprogram. For example,

```
CONST
  Indent = ' ';
```

Multiple Procedures

You should now be able to write a procedure with no parameters, know where it belongs in a program, and be able to call it from the main body of the program. The next step is to use more than one procedure in a program. Each procedure is developed separately and listed sequentially after the variable declaration subsection of the main program. Thus, the basic program with multiple procedures appears as follows:

```
PROGRAM ⟨program name⟩ (output);

CONST

VAR

PROCEDURE ⟨procedure name 1⟩;

PROCEDURE ⟨procedure name 2⟩;
            .
            .
            .
PROCEDURE ⟨procedure name n⟩;
```

```
        BEGIN  {  Main program  }
                          .
                          .
                          .
        END.  {  of main program  }
```

These procedures can be called in any order and as often as needed. Just remember that when a procedure is called from the main program, control is transferred to the procedure, the procedure is executed, and control then returns to the next program statement. If one procedure contains a call to another procedure, the procedure being called must appear before the procedure from which it is called.

The following program illustrates the use of multiple procedures.

```
PROGRAM MultipleProcedures (output);

CONST
  Indent = ' ';

{*****************************************************************}

PROCEDURE Message1;

  {  This is procedure one  }

  BEGIN
    writeln;
    writeln (Indent:10, 'This is from Procedure #1')
  END;  {  of PROCEDURE Message1  }

{*****************************************************************}

PROCEDURE Message2;

  {  This is procedure two  }

  BEGIN
    writeln;
    writeln (Indent:10, 'This is from Procedure #2')
  END;  {  of PROCEDURE Message2  }

{*****************************************************************}

PROCEDURE Message3;

  {  This is procedure three  }

  BEGIN
    writeln;
    writeln (Indent:10, 'This is from Procedure #3')
  END;  {  of PROCEDURE Message3  }

{*****************************************************************}

{  Now begin the main program  }

BEGIN  {  Main program  }
  Message1;
  Message2;
  Message3;
  Message2;
  Message1;
  writeln
END.  {  of main program  }
```

The output from this program is

```
This is from Procedure #1

This is from Procedure #2

This is from Procedure #3

This is from Procedure #2

This is from Procedure #1
```

Examples of Using Procedures for Output

We close this section with some examples using procedures to produce output. By learning how to write and use procedures in this very limited fashion, you should be better able to work with them when they become more complicated.

EXAMPLE 7.3

Your computer science instructor wants course and program information included as part of the output of a program. Consequently, you are to write a procedure that can be used to print this information. Sample output is

```
**************************************
*                                    *
*    Author:        Mary Smith       *
*    Course:        CPS-150          *
*    Assignment:    Program #3       *
*    Due Date:      September 18      *
*    Instructor:    Dr. Samson       *
*                                    *
**************************************
```

The procedure to do this is

```
PROCEDURE PrintInfo;

  CONST
    Indent = ' ';

  BEGIN
    writeln (Indent:30, '**************************************');
    writeln (Indent:30, '*                                    *');
    writeln (Indent:30, '*    Author:        Mary Smith       *');
    writeln (Indent:30, '*    Course:        CPS-150          *');
    writeln (Indent:30, '*    Assignment:    Program #3       *');
    writeln (Indent:30, '*    Due Date:      September 18      *');
    writeln (Indent:30, '*    Instructor:    Dr. Samson       *');
    writeln (Indent:30, '*                                    *');
    writeln (Indent:30, '**************************************')
  END; { of PROCEDURE PrintInfo }
```

EXAMPLE 7.4

As part of a program that computes and prints grades for each student in your class, you have been asked to write a procedure that produces a heading for each student report. Assuming the columns in which the various headings should be are as follows:

- the border for the class name starts in column 30
- Student Name starts in column 20
- Test Average starts in column 40
- Grade starts in column 55

the heading should appear as

```
             *************************
             *                       *
             *   CPS 150    Pascal   *
             *                       *
             *************************

Student Name           Test Average   Grade
------------           ------------   -----
```

A descriptive name for this procedure could be PrintHeader. With this information, the procedure could be written as follows:

```
PROCEDURE PrintHeader;

  CONST
    Skip = ' ';

  BEGIN
    writeln;
    writeln (Skip:29, '*************************');
    writeln (Skip:29, '*                       *');
    writeln (Skip:29, '*   CPS 150    Pascal   *');
    writeln (Skip:29, '*                       *');
    writeln (Skip:29, '*************************');
    writeln;
    write (Skip:19, 'Student Name');
    writeln (Skip:8, 'Test Average', Skip:3, 'Grade');
    write (Skip:19, '------------');
    writeln (Skip:8, '------------', Skip:3, '-----');
    writeln
  END;  {  of PROCEDURE PrintHeader  }
```

■ EXAMPLE 7.5

The Greater Metro Airport has hired you to write a program that will print a ticket for each parking lot customer. The parking lot authorities want each ticket to contain a suitable message and the amount to be paid upon leaving the parking lot. A pseudocode design for this problem is

1. For each customer
   1.1 assign amount due
   1.2 print heading
   1.3 print amount due
   1.4 print closing message

We will write procedures for steps 1.2 and 1.4 of this design.
    Each ticket will have the following heading.

```
Greater Metro Airport

      Parking Lot
        April 15
```

Each ticket will contain the following message concerning the charge for parking:

```
Your charge is $XX.XX
```

Each ticket will contain the following closing message.

```
              Thank you for using the
                Greater Metro Airport

              Please drive carefully
--------------------------------
```

A procedure to print the heading is

```
PROCEDURE PrintHeader;

  {  This procedure prints a ticket heading  }

    CONST
      Date = 'April 15';

    BEGIN
      writeln;
      writeln (Indent:20, 'Greater Metro Airport');
      writeln;
      writeln (Indent:25, 'Parking Lot');
      writeln (Indent:27, Date);
      writeln
    END;  {  of PROCEDURE PrintHeader  }
```

A procedure to print the closing message is

```
PROCEDURE PrintMessage;

  {  This procedure prints a closing message  }

    BEGIN
      writeln;
      writeln (Indent:20, 'Thank you for using the');
      writeln (Indent:21, 'Greater Metro Airport');
      writeln;
      writeln (Indent:20, 'Please drive carefully');
      writeln (Indent:15, '--------------------------------');
      writeln
    END;  {  of PROCEDURE PrintMessage  }
```

A complete interactive program for two customers follows. This can be modified to accomodate several customers.

```
PROGRAM ParkingLot (input, output);

CONST
  Indent = ' ';

VAR
  Fee : real;

{****************************************************************************}

PROCEDURE PrintHeader;

  {  This procedure prints a ticket heading  }

    CONST
      Date = 'April 15';

    BEGIN
      writeln;
      writeln (Indent:20, 'Greater Metro Airport');
```

```
      writeln;
      writeln (Indent:25, 'Parking Lot');
      writeln (Indent:27, Date);
      writeln
   END;  {  of PROCEDURE PrintHeader  }


{***********************************************************************}

PROCEDURE PrintMessage;

   {  This procedure prints a closing message  }

   BEGIN
      writeln;
      writeln (Indent:20, 'Thank you for using the');
      writeln (Indent:21, 'Greater Metro Airport');
      writeln;
      writeln (Indent:20, 'Please drive carefully');
      writeln (Indent:15, '------------------------------------');
      writeln
   END;  {  of PROCEDURE PrintMessage  }


{***********************************************************************}

{  Now begin the main program  }

BEGIN  {  Main program  }

   {  Process customer one  }

   writeln ('Enter amount due and press <RETURN>.');
   readln (Fee);
   PrintHeader;
   writeln (Indent:20, 'Your charge is $', Fee:6:2);
   PrintMessage;

   {  Process customer two  }

   writeln ('Enter amount due and press <RETURN>.');
   readln (Fee);
   PrintHeader;
   writeln (Indent:20, 'Your charge is $', Fee:6:2);
   PrintMessage

END.  {  of main program  }
```

The output from this program for each of two customers is

```
Enter amount due and press <RETURN>.
?5.75

                    Greater Metro Airport

                        Parking Lot
                        April 15

             Your charge is $  5.75

             Thank you for using the
              Greater Metro Airport

             Please drive carefully
    -----------------------------------
```

```
Enter amount due and press <RETURN>.
?8.00

                    Greater Metro Airport

                        Parking Lot
                        April 15

                    Your charge is $  8.00

                    Thank you for using the
                    Greater Metro Airport

                    Please drive carefully
            -----------------------------------
```

Procedures without parameters can be used for more than just prin
headings and closing messages. To illustrate, consider the follow
example.

Interactive programming frequently requires the use of a menu to give the
user a choice of options. For example, suppose you want a menu to be

```
Which of the following recipes do you wish to see?

    (T)acos
    (J)ambalaya
    (G)umbo
    (Q)uit

Enter the first letter and press <RETURN>.
```

This screen message could then be written as a procedure menu and the
main program could use a REPEAT . . . UNTIL loop a follows:

```
REPEAT
  Menu;
  readln (Selection);
  CASE Selection OF
    'T' : Tacos;
    'J' : Jambalaya;
    'G' : Gumbo;
    'Q' : GoodbyeMessage
  END  {  of CASE Selection  }
UNTIL Selection = 'Q';
```

where Tacos, Jambalaya, Gumbo, and GoodbyeMessage are each separate
procedures with appropriate messages.

Exercises 7.2

1. Explain the difference between a procedure and a program.

2. What output will be produced when the following procedure is called from
   the main program?

```
PROCEDURE ExerciseTwo;
  CONST
    Splats = '*****************************';
    Line = '--------------';
    Skip = ' ';
  BEGIN
    writeln (Skip: 24, Splats);
    writeln (Skip:9, '*', Skip:19' '*');
    write (Skip:9, '*', '  Sample Output');
    writeln ('*':5);
    writeln (Skip:9, '*', Line:15, '*':5);
    writeln (Skip:9, '*', Skip:19, '*');
    writeln (Skip: 24, Splats)
  END;
```

3. Write a procedure that will produce the following:

```
*****************************
*                           *
*      your name here       *
*      today's date here    *
*                           *
*****************************
```

4. Write a program that calls the procedure in Exercise 3 five times.

5. Several commercial establishments use computers to print bills for their customers. For each of the following businesses, create a suitable message for the heading of the billing statements and write a procedure that will print the heading when called from the main program.

   a. R & R Produce Company

   b. Atlas Athletic Equipment

   c. Sleep E-Z-E Motel

   d. Pump-Your-Own Service Station

6. Consider the output

```
///////////////////////////
/                         /
/      Special Olympics   /
/      ------- --------    /
///////////////////////////

///////////////////////////
/                         /
/      Special Olympics   /
/      ------- --------    /
///////////////////////////

///////////////////////////
/                         /
/      Special Olympics   /
/      ------- --------    /
///////////////////////////
```

   a. Write a program that produces this output without using procedures.

   b. Write a program that produces this output using a procedure.

7. Consider the following program:

```
PROGRAM ExerciseSeven (output);

CONST
  Splats = '**************************';
  Edge = '*                        *';
  Skip = ' ';
```

```
            VAR
              Interest : real;

            BEGIN {  Main program  }
              writeln;
              writeln (Skip:15, Splats);
              writeln (Skip:15, Edge);
              writeln (Skip:15, '*     Federal Savings     *');
              writeln (Skip:15, '*     Monthly Report      *');
              writeln (Skip:15, Edge);
              writeln (Skip:15, Splats);
              writeln;
              Interest := 114.53;
              writeln (Skip:10, 'Thank you for banking with Federal Savings.');
              writeln (Skip:10, 'Your current interest payment is below.');
              writeln ('$':20, Interest:8:2);
              writeln;
              Interest := 87.93;
              writeln (Skip:10, 'Thank you for banking with Federal Savings.');
              writeln (Skip:10, 'Your current interest payment is below.');
              writeln ('$':20, Interest:8:2);
              writeln
            END.  {  of main program  }
```

and its output.

```
                ************************
                *                      *
                *     Federal Savings  *
                *     Monthly Report   *
                *                      *
                ************************

      Thank you for banking with Federal Savings.
      Your current interest payment is below.
               $   114.53

      Thank you for banking with Federal Savings.
      Your current interest payment is below.
               $    87.93
```

Rewrite this program using

a. a procedure for the heading.

b. a procedure for the customer message.

8. What is the output from the following program?

```
PROGRAM ExerciseEight (output);

CONST
  Skip = ' ';

PROCEDURE Number1;
  BEGIN
    writeln (Skip:10, 'She loves me.')
  END;  {  of PROCEDURE Number1  }

PROCEDURE Number2;
  BEGIN
    writeln (Skip:10, 'She loves me not.')
  END;  {  of PROCEDURE Number2  }

BEGIN  {  Main program  }
  Number1;
  Number2;
```

```
       Number1;
       Number2;
       Number1
END.  {  of main program  }
```

9. Rewrite the following program using indenting, blank lines, comments, and comment sections to enhance readability.

```
PROGRAM Plain (output);
VAR
Score1, Score2 : integer;
Average : real;
PROCEDURE PrintHeader;
BEGIN
writeln;
writeln ('Your test results are below.':36);
writeln;
writeln ('Keep up the good work!':30);
writeln
END;
BEGIN
PrintHeader;
Score1 := 89;
Score2 := 95;
Average := (Score1 + Score2) / 2.0;
writeln ('Score1':20, Score1:6);
writeln ('Score2':20, Score2:6);
writeln;
writeln ('Your average is':23, Average:8:2)
END.
```

10. Write a complete Pascal program that will display any of the numbers 9, 8, 7, 6, 5, 4, 3, 2, 1, or 0 on the screen using the numbers shown as follows:

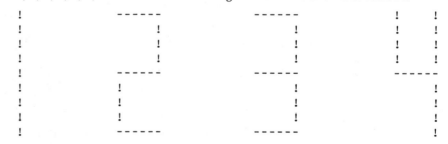

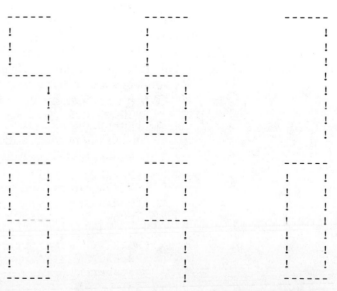

Use a procedure for each number. Allow the user the option of repeating the program.

■ ■ ■ ■

Procedures with Parameters

OBJECTIVES

- to be able to use correct form and syntax for writing a procedure
- to understand the difference between variable and value parameters
- to understand the difference between formal and actual parameters
- to be able to use a procedure in a program

Form and Syntax

Procedures for headings are written in the following form.

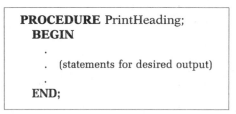

```
PROCEDURE PrintHeading;
  BEGIN
    .
    .   (statements for desired output)
    .
  END;
```

Procedures of this type are very limited in that there is no data transmission or changing of variables between the procedure and the main program. The general form for a procedure with parameters is

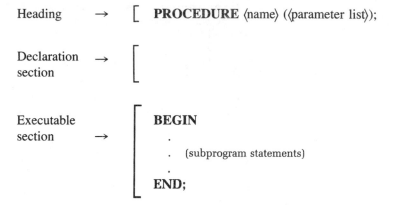

Heading   →   [**PROCEDURE** ⟨name⟩ (⟨parameter list⟩);

Declaration   →   [
section

Executable   →   [**BEGIN**
section   .
                           .   (subprogram statements)
                           .
                        END;

Parameters

The significant change between this form and our previous use of procedures for headings is the use of parameters. Parameters are used so that values of variables may be transmitted, or passed, from the main program to the procedure and from the procedure to the main program. If values are to be passed only from the main program to the procedure, the parameters are called *value parameters*. If values are to be changed in the main program, the parameters are called *variable parameters*.

When using parameters with procedures, the following should be noted:

1. The number and order of parameters in the parameter list must match the number and order of variables or values used when calling the procedure from the main program.
2. The type of parameters must match the corresponding type of variables or values used when calling the procedure.
3. The parameter types are declared in the procedure heading.

Parameters contained in the procedure are *formal parameters*. Parameters contained in the procedure call from the main program are *actual parameters*. Formal parameters can be thought of as blanks in the heading of the procedure waiting to receive values from actual parameters in a calling program. Actual parameters are also referred to as arguments. To illustrate formal and actual parameters used with procedures, consider the following complete program.

```
PROGRAM ProcDemo1 (output);

VAR
  Num1, Num2 : integer;
  Num3 : real;

{*******************************************************************}

PROCEDURE PrintNum (N1, N2 : integer;
                    N3 : real);

  BEGIN
    writeln;
    writeln ('Number 1 = ', N1:3);
    writeln ('Number 2 = ', N2:3);
    writeln ('Number 3 = ', N3:6:2)
  END;  {  of PROCEDURE PrintNum  }

{*******************************************************************}

BEGIN  {  Main program  }
  Num1 := 5;
  Num2 := 8;
  Num3 := Num2 / Num1;
  PrintNum (Num1, Num2, Num3)
END.  {  of main program  }
```

When this program is run, the output is

```
Number 1 =    5
Number 2 =    8
Number 3 =    1.60
```

In this program, N1, N2, and N3 are formal parameters; Num1, Num2, and Num3 are actual parameters. Let us now examine the relationship between the parameter list in the procedure

```
PROCEDURE PrintNum (N1, N2 : integer; N3 : real);
```

and the procedure call in the main program.

```
PrintNum (Num1, Num2, Num3);
```

In this case, Num1 corresponds to N1, Num2 corresponds to N2, and Num3 corresponds to N3. Notice that both the number and type of variables in the parameter list correspond with the number and type of variables listed in the procedure call.

Value Parameters

The preceding procedure demonstrates the use of value parameters or of one-way transmission of values. Different memory areas have been set aside for the variables Num1, Num2, and Num3 and for N1, N2, and N3. Thus, initially we have

Main Program   Procedure

```
[        ]            [        ]
  Num1                   N1

[        ]            [        ]
  Num2                   N2

[        ]            [        ]
  Num3                   N3
```

The assignment statements

```
Num1 := 5;
Num2 := 8;
Num3 := Num2 / Num1;
```

produce

Main Program   Procedure

```
[   5    ]            [        ]
  Num1                   N1

[   8    ]            [        ]
  Num2                   N2

[  1.6   ]            [        ]
  Num3                   N3
```

When the procedure PrintNum is called from the main program by

```
PrintNum (Num1, Num2, Num3)
```

the values are transmitted to N1, N2, and N3, respectively, as follows:

Main Program   Procedure

```
[   5    ]            [   5    ]
  Num1                   N1

[   8    ]            [   8    ]
  Num2                   N2

[  1.6   ]            [  1.6   ]
  Num3                   N3
```

At this stage, the procedure PrintNum can use N1, N2, and N3 in any appropriate manner.

These are value parameters because values are passed from the main program to the procedure only. If the procedure changes the value of N1, N2, or N3, the values of Num1, Num2, and Num3 will not be changed. For example, suppose the procedure is changed to

```
PROCEDURE PrintNum (N1, N2 : integer;
                    N3 : real);

    BEGIN
      writeln;
      writeln (N1:10, N2:10, N3:10:2);
```

```
N1 := 2 * N1;
N2 := 2 * N2;
N3 := 2 * N3;
writeln (N1:10, N2:10, N3:10:2);
writeln
END;  {  of PROCEDURE PrintNum  }
```

Furthermore, suppose the main program is changed to

```
BEGIN  {  Main program  }
  Num1 := 5;
  Num2 := 8;
  Num3 := Num2 / Num1;
  writeln;
  writeln (Num1:10, Num2:10, Num3:10:2);
  PrintNum (Num1, Num2, Num3);
  writeln (Num1:10, Num2:10, Num3:10:2);
  writeln
END.  {  of main program  }
```

When this program is run, the output is

```
  5         8        1.60        (from main program)
  5         8        1.60        (from procedure)
 10        16        3.20        (from procedure)
  5         8        1.60        (from main program)
```

The first line of this output is produced by the first

```
writeln (Num1:10, Num2:10, Num3:10:2);
```

of the main program. The next two lines of output come from the procedure. The last line of output is produced by the second

```
writeln (Num1:10, Num2:10, Num3:10:2);
```

of the main program. You should carefully note that, although the procedure changes the values of N1, N2, and N3, the values of Num1, Num2, and Num3 have not been changed. Thus, we have

Main Program	Procedure
5	10
Num1	N1
8	16
Num2	N2
1.6	3.2
Num3	N3

Variable Parameters

You will frequently want a procedure to change several values in the main program. This can be accomplished by using variable parameters in the parameter list. Variable parameters are declared by using the reserved word **VAR** to precede appropriate formal parameters in the procedure heading. This causes all of the formal parameters listed between **VAR** and the subsequent data type to be variable parameters. If value parameters of the same type are needed, they must be listed elsewhere. A separate **VAR** declaration is needed for each data type used when listing variable parameters. The use of **VAR** in a parameter list is a slightly different use than in the declaration of variables, yet it is the same reserved word.

When variable parameters are declared, transmission of values appears to be two-way rather than one-way. That is, values are sent from the main program to the procedure and from the procedure to the main program. Actually, when variable parameters are used, values are not transmitted at all. Variable parameters in the procedure heading are merely aliases for actual variables used in the main program. Thus, variables are said to be *passed by reference* rather than by value. When variable parameters are used, any change of values in the procedure produces a corresponding change of values in the main program.

To illustrate the declaration of variable parameters, consider the procedure heading

```
PROCEDURE PrintNum (VAR N1, N2 : integer; N3 : real);
```

In this case, N1 and N2 are variable parameters corresponding to integer variables in the main program. N3 is a value parameter corresponding to a real variable. This procedure can be called from the main program by

```
PrintNum (Num1, Num2, Num3);
```

To illustrate the passing of values, assume the procedure is

```
PROCEDURE PrintNum (VAR N1, N2 : integer; N3 : real);
  BEGIN
    writeln (N1, N2, N3:10:2);
    N1 := 2 * N1;
    N2 := 2 * N2;
    N3 := 2 * N3;
    writeln (N1, N2, N3:10:2)
  END;  {  of PROCEDURE PrintNum  }
```

If the corresponding variables in the main program are Num1, Num2, and Num3, respectively, initially we have

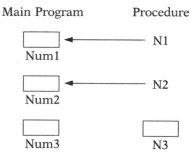

Technically, N1 and N2 do not exist. There are no separate memory locations for them. They are merely aliases for Num1 and Num2. They access the same memory locations as Num1 and Num2 respectively. Thus, a statement in the procedure such as

```
N1 := 5;
```

really causes the memory location reserved for Num1 to receive the value 5. That is, it causes the net action

```
Num1 := 5;
```

Thus, constants cannot be used when calling a procedure with variable parameters. For example,

```
PrintNum (3, 4, 5);
```

produces an error because 3 and 4 correspond to variable parameters.

If the main program makes the assignment statements

```
Num1 := 5;
Num2 := 8;
Num3 := Num2 / Num1;
```

we have

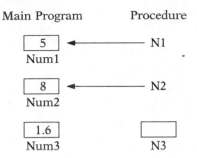

When the procedure is called and the following statements from the procedure

```
N1 := 2 * N1;
N2 := 2 * N2;
N3 := 2 * N3;
```

are executed, we have

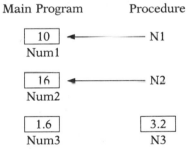

Notice that the variable parameters N1 and N2 produce changes in the corresponding variables in the main program, but the value parameter N3 does not.

Let us now consider a short, complete program that illustrates the difference between variable and value parameters. In this program (and throughout the text), the graphic documentation that accompanies the program highlights the way in which parameters are passed between the main program and the procedure.

```
PROGRAM ProcDemo2 (output);

VAR
  X, Y : real;
  Ch : char;

{*********************************************************************}

PROCEDURE DemonstrateVAR (VAR X1 : real;
                              Y1 : real;
                          VAR Ch1 : char);

BEGIN
  writeln (X1:10:2, Y1:10:2, Ch1:5);
  X1 := 2 * X1;
  Y1 := 2 * Y1;
  Ch1 := '*';
  writeln (X1:10:2, Y1:10:2, Ch1:5)
END; { of PROCEDURE DemonstrateVAR }

{*********************************************************************}
```

```
BEGIN  {  Main program  }
  X := 3.6;
  Y := 5.2;
  Ch := 'A';
  writeln (X:10:2, Y:10:2, Ch:5);
  DemonstrateVAR (X, Y, Ch);
  writeln (X:10:2, Y:10:2, Ch:5);
END.  {  of main program  }
```

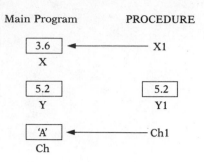

The output from the program is

3.60	5.20	A	(from main program)
3.60	5.20	A	(from procedure)
7.20	10.40	*	(from procedure)
7.20	5.20	*	(from main program)

The variables can be depicted as

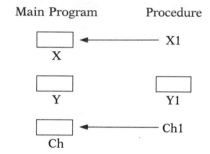

The assignment statements

```
X  := 3.6;
Y  := 5.2;
Ch := 'A';
```

produce

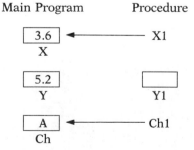

When the procedure is called by

```
DemonstrateVAR (X, Y, Ch);
```

the contents can be envisioned as

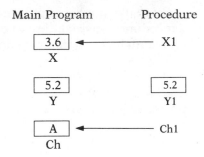

When the procedure assignment statements

```
X1 := 2 * X1;
Y1 := 2 * Y1;
Ch1 := '*';
```

are executed, the variables become

Main Program   Procedure

| 7.2 | ◄——————— X1
  X

| 5.2 | | 10.4 |
  Y   Y1

| * | ◄——————— Ch1
 Ch

Notice that changes in the variable parameters X1 and Ch1 produce corresponding changes in X and Ch, but a change in the value parameter Y1 does not produce a change in Y.

Side Effects

A *side effect* is an unintentional change in a variable that is the result of some action taken in a program. A side effect is frequently caused by the misuse of variable parameters. Since any change in a variable parameter causes a change in the corresponding actual parameter in the calling program or procedure, you should use variable parameters only when your intent is to produce such changes. In all other cases, use value parameters.

Writing Style

As previously discussed, procedures are located in the declaration section of a program.

Program heading   → [

Declaration   → [**CONST**
section   **VAR**
                      (procedures here)

                      [**BEGIN**
Executable   →
section
                      [**END.**

There is no limit to the number of procedures that can be used in a program. Within the procedure, consistent use of comments, blank lines, and indenting should be maintained. A program containing three procedures might be organized as follows:

```
PROGRAM ThreeProcs (input, output);

CONST

VAR

PROCEDURE ⟨one here⟩

PROCEDURE ⟨two here⟩

PROCEDURE ⟨three here⟩

BEGIN   {   Main program   }
  ⟨Main program here⟩
END.   {   of main program   }
```

When a program contains several procedures, they can be called from the main part of the program in any order. However, if one procedure contains a call to another procedure (or function), the subprogram being called must appear before the procedure from which it is called.

Documenting Subprograms

Each subprogram should contain documentation sufficient to allow the reader to understand what information is given to the subprogram, what task is to be performed, and what information is to be returned to the calling program. This information aids in debugging programs. In this text, the headings of subprograms in complete programs will be followed by documentation in the form

```
{  Given:   Statement of information sent to the program  }
{  Task:    Statement of task(s) to be performed          }
{  Return:  Statement of value(s) to be returned          }
```

When subprograms are separately developed and illustrated, this documentation will not be included; instead, text development immediately preceding the subprogram will serve the same purpose.

We close this section with a sample program using four procedures. The program reads three reals from one line of a data file, computes their average, and then prints the results. A first-level pseudocode development for this program is

1. Get data
2. Process data
3. Print header
4. Print results

We can write a procedure for each of the pseudocode steps.

1. Get data

becomes

```
PROCEDURE GetData (VAR S1, S2, S3 : real);
  BEGIN
    readln (S1, S2, S3)
  END;  {  of PROCEDURE GetData  }
```

Note that this procedure uses variable parameters so that values from the procedure are transmitted back to the program.

2. Process data

becomes

```
PROCEDURE FindAverage (S1, S2, S3 : real;
                          VAR Aver : real);
  BEGIN
    Aver := (S1 + S2 + S3) / 3
  END;  {  of PROCEDURE FindAverage  }
```

Note that S1, S2, and S3 are value parameters and Aver is a variable parameter. When this procedure is called from the main program, it returns the computed average.

3. Print header

becomes

```
PROCEDURE PrintHeader;
  CONST
    Indent = ' ';
  BEGIN
    writeln;
    writeln (Indent:30, 'Scores');
    writeln (Indent:30, '------');
    writeln
  END;  {  of PROCEDURE PrintHeader  }
```

4. Print results

becomes

```
PROCEDURE PrintResults (S1, S2, S3, Av : real);
  BEGIN
    writeln (S1:36:2);
    writeln (S2:36:2);
    writeln (S3:36:2);
    writeln ('------':36);
    writeln;
    writeln (Av:36:2)
  END;  {  of PROCEDURE PrintResults  }
```

The main part of the program is

```
BEGIN  { Main program  }
  GetData (Score1, Score2, Score3);
  FindAverage (Score1, Score2, Score3, Average);
  PrintHeader;
  PrintResults (Score1, Score2, Score3, Average)
END.  {  of main program  }
```

The complete program is

```
PROGRAM ProcDemo (input, output);

{    This program demonstrates  the use of procedures.  Both     }
{    value and variable parameters are featured.  Notice how     }
{    the main program  consists only of calling  appropriate     }
{    procedures.                                                  }

VAR
  Average : real;                    {  The average of three reals  }
  Score1, Score2,                    {  Three scores to be read     }
  Score3 : real;

{*********************************************************************}

PROCEDURE GetData (VAR S1, S2, S3 : real);

  {  Given:    Nothing                                            }
  {  Task:     Read three scores                                  }
  {  Return:   Scores read                                        }

  BEGIN
    readln (S1, S2, S3)
  END;  {  of PROCEDURE GetData }

{*********************************************************************}

PROCEDURE FindAverage (S1, S2, S3 : real;
                       VAR Aver : real);

  {  Given:    Three scores                                       }
  {  Task:     Find their average                                 }
  {  Return:   The average score                                  }

  BEGIN
    Aver := (S1 + S2 + S3) / 3
  END;  {  of PROCEDURE FindAverage  }

{*********************************************************************}

PROCEDURE PrintHeader;

  {  Given:    Nothing                                            }
  {  Task:     Print a heading                                    }
  {  Return:   Nothing                                            }

  CONST
    Indent = '';

  BEGIN
    writeln;
    writeln (Indent:30, 'Scores');
    writeln (Indent:30, '------');
    writeln
  END;  {  of PROCEDURE PrintHeader  }

{*********************************************************************}

PROCEDURE PrintResults (S1, S2, S3, Av : real);

  {  Given:    Three scores and their average                     }
  {  Task:     Print the scores and their average                 }
  {  Return:   Nothing                                            }
```

```
    BEGIN
      writeln (S1:36:2);
      writeln (S2:36:2);
      writeln (S3:36:2);
      writeln ('------':36);
      writeln;
      writeln (Av:36:2)
    END:  {  of PROCEDURE PrintResults  }
```

`{***************************************************************}`

```
BEGIN  {  Main program  }
  GetData (Score1, Score2, Score3);
  FindAverage (Score1, Score2, Score3, Average);
  PrintHeader;
  PrintResults (Score1, Score2, Score3, Average)
END.  {  of main program  }
```

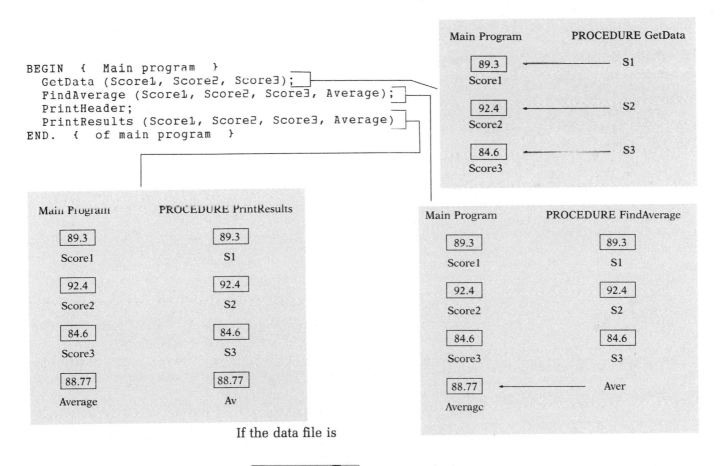

If the data file is

```
89.3 92.4 84.6
```

the output from the program will be

```
                              Scores
                              ------

                              89.30
                              92.40
                              84.60
                              -------

                              88.77
```

Computer Ethics: Hacking and Other Intrusions

A famous sequence of computer intrusions was originally detailed by Clifford Stoll. The prime intruder came to Stoll's attention in August 1986, when he attempted to penetrate a computer at Lawrence Berkeley Laboratory (LBL). Management at LBL went along with Stoll's recommendation that they attempt to unmask the intruder, even though the risk was substantial because the intruder had gained system-manager privileges.

Markus H., a member of a small group of West Germans, was an unusually persistent intruder, but no computer wizard. He made use of known deficiencies in the half-dozen or so operating systems with which he was familiar, but he did not invent any new modes of entry. He penetrated 30 of the 450 computers then on the network system at LBL.

After Markus H. was successfully traced, efforts were instituted to make LBL's computers less vulnerable. To insure security, it would have been necessary, for instance, to change all passwords overnight and recertify each user. This and other demanding measures were deemed impractical. Instead, deletion of all expired passwords was instituted; shared accounts were eliminated; monitoring of incoming traffic was extended, with alarms set in key places; and education of users was attempted.

The episode was summed up by Stoll as a powerful learning experience for all those concerned about computer security. That the intruder was caught at all is a testimony to the ability of a large number of concerned professionals to keep the tracing effort secret.

In a later incident, an intruder left the following embarrassing message in the computer file assigned to Clifford Stoll: "The cuckoo has egg on his face." The reference is to Stoll's book, *The Cuckoo's Egg*, which tracks the intrusions of the West German hacker just described. The embarrassment was heightened by the fact that the computer, owned by Harvard University, with which astronomer Stoll is now associated, is on the Internet network. The intruder, or intruders, who goes by the name of Dave, also attempted to break into dozens of other computers on the same network—and succeeded.

The name, Dave, was used by one or more of three Australians recently arrested by the federal police down under. The three, who, at the time of their arrest were, respectively 18, 20, and 21 years of age, successfully penetrated computers in both Australia and the United States.

The three Australians went beyond browsing to damage data in computers in their own nation and the United States. At the time they began their intrusions in 1988 (when the youngest was only 16), there was no law in Australia under which they could be prosecuted. It was not until legislation making such intrusions prosecutable was passed that the police began to take action.

Exercises 7.3

1. Explain the difference between value parameters and variable parameters. Also explain the difference between actual parameters and formal parameters.

2. Write a test program to find what happens if the parameter lists do not match when a procedure is called from the main program. Investigate each of the following:

   a. correct number of parameters, wrong order

   b. incorrect number of parameters

3. Indicate which of the following parameters are value parameters and which are variable parameters.

   a. `PROCEDURE Demo1 (VAR A, B : integer;`
   `                X : real);`

   b. `PROCEDURE Demo2 (VAR A : integer;`
   `                B : integer;`
   `                VAR X : real;`
   `                Ch : char);`

   c. `PROCEDURE Demo3 (A, B : integer;`
   `                VAR X, Y, Z : real;`
   `                Ch : char);`

4. Indicate which of the following are appropriate procedure headings. Explain the problem with those that are inappropriate.

   a. `PROCEDURE Prac1 (A : integer : Y : real);`

   b. `PROCEDURE Error? (Ch1, Ch2 : char);`

   c. `PROCEDURE Prac2 (A, VAR B : integer);`

d. PROCEDURE Prac3 (A, B, C : integer

        VAR X, Y : real

        Ch : char

        Flag : boolean);

e. PROCEDURE Prac4 (VAR A : integer,

        X : real);

5. Indicate how each of the following procedures would be called from the main program.

a. PROCEDURE Prob5 (A, B : integer;

        Ch : char);

b. PROCEDURE PrintHeader;

c. PROCEDURE FindMax (N1, N2 : integer;

        VAR NewMax : integer);

d. PROCEDURE Switch (VAR X, Y : real;

e. PROCEDURE SwitchAndTest (VAR X, Y : real;

        VAR F1 : boolean);

6. Suppose a program contains the following procedure:

```
PROCEDURE Switch (VAR A, B : integer);

  VAR
    Temp : integer;

  BEGIN
    Temp := A;
    A := B;
    B := Temp
  END; { of PROCEDURE Switch }
```

Indicate the output from each of the following fragments of code in the main program.

a.
```
Num1 := 5;
Num2 := 10;
writeln (Num1, Num2);
Switch (Num1, Num2);
writeln (Num1, Num2);
Switch (Num1, Num2);
writeln (Num1, Num2);
```

b.
```
Num1 := -3;
Num2 := 2;
IF Num1 > Num2 THEN
   Switch (Num1, Num2)
ELSE
   Switch (Num2, Num1);
writeln (Num2, Num1);
```

c.
```
N := 3;
M := 20;
Switch (M, N);
writeln (M, N);
Switch (N, M);
writeln (N, M);
```

d.
```
Count := 0;
Max := 10;
WHILE Count < Max DO
   BEGIN
      Switch (Count, Max);
      writeln (Count, Max);
      Count := Count + 1
   END; { of WHILE...DO }
```

7. Write a procedure for each of the following and indicate how it would be called from the main program.

a. Print the heading for the output.

```
Acme National Electronics
    Board of Directors
      Annual Meeting
```

b. Find the maximum and average of three reals. Both values are to be returned to the main program.

c. Count the number of occurrences of the letter A in a line of character data. The count should be returned to the main program and the line of data should be printed.

    d. Convert Fahrenheit temperature to Celsius.

    e. Find and print all divisors of a positive integer.

8. Assume a program contains the variable declaration section

```
VAR
  Num1, Num2 : integer;
  X, Y : real;
  Ch1, Ch2 : char;
```

Furthermore, suppose the same program contains a procedure whose heading is

```
PROCEDURE Demo (VAR N1, N2 : integer;
                    X1 : real;
                    Ch : char);
```

Indicate which of the following are appropriate calls to the procedure Demo. Explain those that are inappropriate.

    a. `Demo (Num1, Num2);`

    b. `Demo (Num1, Num2, X);`

    c. `Demo (Num1, Num2, X, Ch1);`

    d. `Demo (X, Y, Num1, Ch2);`

    e. `Demo (Num2, X, Y, Ch1);`

    f. `Demo (Num1, Num2, Ch2);`

    g. `Demo;`

    h. `Demo (Num2, Num1, Y, Ch1);`

■ ■ ■ ■

■ 7.4
User-Defined Functions

OBJECTIVES
- to be able to use the correct form and syntax for writing a function
- to be able to call a function from the main program
- to be able to write a function to perform a specific task

The standard functions **sqr, sqrt, abs, round,** and **trunc** were introduced in Section 3.5. To briefly review, some concepts to note when using these functions are

1. An argument is required for each; thus, **sqrt**(Y) and **abs**(-21) are appropriate.
2. Standard functions can be used in expressions; for example,

```
X := sqrt(Y) + sqrt(Z);
```

3. Standard functions can be used in output statements; for example,

```
writeln (sqr(3):8);
```

Need for User-Defined Functions

It is relatively easy to envision the need for functions that are not on the list of standard functions available in Pascal. For example, if you must frequently cube numbers, it would be convenient to have a function Cube so you could make an assignment such as

```
X := Cube(Y);
```

Other examples from mathematics include an exponential function (x^Y), computing a factorial ($n!$), computing a discriminant ($b^2 - 4ac$), and finding roots of a quadratic equation

$$\left(\frac{-b \pm \sqrt{b^2 - 4ac}}{2a} \right)$$

In business, a motel might like to have available a function to determine a customer's bill given the number in the party, the length of stay, and any telephone charges. Similarly, a hospital might like a function to compute the room charge for a patient given the type of room (private, ward, and so on) and various other options, including telephone (yes or no) and television (yes or no). Functions such as these are not standard functions. However, in Pascal, we can create *user-defined functions* to perform these tasks.

Form for User-Defined Functions

A user-defined function is a subprogram and has the components

Heading   →   [

Declaration
section   →   [

Executable
section   →   [

The general form for a function heading is

> **FUNCTION** ⟨function name⟩ (⟨parameter list⟩) : ⟨return type⟩;

A syntax diagram for this is

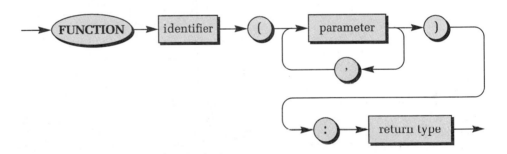

A function to compute the cube of an integer could therefore use the following as a heading:

```
FUNCTION Cube (X : integer) : integer;
```

As with procedures, the formal parameter list (variables in the function heading) must match the number and corresponding types of actual parameters (variables in the function call) used when the function is called from the main program. Thus, if you are writing a function to compute the area of a rectangle and you want to call the function from the main program by

```
RectArea := Area(Width, Length);
```

the function Area might have

```
FUNCTION Area (W, L : integer) : integer;
```

as a heading. The two formal parameters, W and L, correspond to the actual parameters, Width and Length, assuming that Width and Length are of type **integer.** In general, you should make sure the formal parameter list and actual parameter list match up as indicated.

```
(W, L : integer)
(Width, Length)
```

An exception to this is that an actual parameter of **integer** type may be associated with a formal parameter of **real** type.

Several additional comments on the general form for a function heading are now in order.

1. **FUNCTION** is a reserved word and must be used only as indicated.
2. The term "function name" is any valid identifier.
   a. The function name should be descriptive.
   b. Some value must be assigned to the function name in the executable section of the function. The last assigned value will be the value returned to the main program; for example, in the function Cube, we have

   ```
   Cube := X * X * X;
   ```

   c. The function name can only be used on the left side of an assignment statement within the function. For example,

   ```
   Cube := Cube + 1;
   ```

   and

   ```
   writeln (Cube);
   ```

   produce errors. (An exception to this rule involves recursion and will be discussed in Chapter 8.)
3. The term "return type" declares the data type for the function name. This indicates what type will be returned to the main program.

As in the main program, there does not have to be a declaration section for a function, but when there is one, only variables needed in the function are declared. Further, the section is usually not very elaborate because the purpose of a function is normally a small, single task.

Finally, the executable section for a function must perform the desired task, assign a value to the function name, terminate with a semicolon rather than a period, and have the general form

```
BEGIN
  .
  . (work of function here)
  .
END;
```

We will now illustrate user-defined functions with several examples.

■ **EXAMPLE 7.7**

Write a function to compute the cube of an integer. Since the actual parameter from the main program will be of **integer** type, we have

```
FUNCTION Cube (X : integer) : integer;
  BEGIN
    Cube := X * X * X
  END;
```

A typical call to this function from the main program is

```
A := Cube(5);
```

EXAMPLE 7.8

Write a function to compute the average of three reals. We know the actual parameters will be three reals, so our function could be written as

```
FUNCTION Average (N1, N2, N3 : real) : real;
  BEGIN
    Average := (N1 + N2 + N3) / 3
  END;
```

and called from the main program by

```
X := Average(Num1, Num2, Num3);
```

EXAMPLE 7.9

Given two positive integers, *m* and *n*, write a function to compute m^n (*m* to the power of *n*). Since there will be two actual parameters, the formal parameter list will require two variables of type **integer**. The function will return an integer, so the return type will be **integer**. The desired function is

```
FUNCTION Power (Base, Exponent : integer) : integer;

  VAR
    Temp, K : integer;

  BEGIN
    Temp := Base;
    For K := 2 TO Exponent DO
      Temp := Temp * Base;
    Power := Temp
  END; {  of FUNCTION Power  }
```

This could be called from the main program by

```
A := Power(3, 5);
```

Since the function given in Example 7.9 is more elaborate than those we have seen previously, we should examine it more closely. First, note that we need additional variables, Temp and K. Next, let's trace what happens to the various values and variables.

When Power (3,5) is encountered in the main program, control is transferred to **FUNCTION** Power, and Base and Exponent receive their respective values. At this stage, the variables could be depicted as

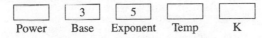

	3	5		
Power	Base	Exponent	Temp	K

The first executable statement in the function causes

	3	5	3	
Power	Base	Exponent	Temp	K

The first pass through the loop produces

	3	5	9	2
Power	Base	Exponent	Temp	K

At the completion of the loop, K becomes unassigned and Power is assigned the final value of Temp to produce

243	3	5	243	
Power	Base	Exponent	Temp	K

Each iteration multiplies Temp by an additional factor of Base. After the final iteration, control is transferred back to the main program and the value in Power is assigned accordingly. Thus

```
A := Power (3, 5)
```

yields

243
A

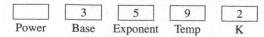

EXAMPLE 7.10

Let's now write a function to compute the total charge for a hospital room. Actual parameters will be the number of days (**integer**) and room type (**char**). We may assume rates for private (P), semiprivate (S), and ward (W) have been defined in the **CONST** definition section of the main program. A typical function is

```
FUNCTION RoomCharge (NDays : integer;
                     RmType : char) : real;

  BEGIN
    CASE RmType OF
      'P' : RoomCharge := NDays * PrivateRate;
      'S' : RoomCharge := NDays * SemiprivateRate;
      'W' : RoomCharge := NDays * WardRate
    END {  of CASE RmType  }
  END; {  of FUNCTION RoomCharge  }
```

This function could be called from the main program by

```
RoomAmount := RoomCharge (NumDays, RoomType);
```

Use in a Program

Now that you have seen several examples of user-defined functions, let's consider their use in a program. Once they are written, they can be used in the same manner as standard functions. This usually means in one of the following forms.

1. Assignment statements

```
A := 5;
B := Cube(A);
```

2. Arithmetic expressions

```
A := 5;
B := 3 * Cube(A) + 2;
```

3. Output statements

```
A := 5;
writeln (Cube(A):17);
```

4. Boolean expressions

```
IF Cube(A) < B THEN
              .
              .
              .
```

In general, a function (rather than a procedure) should be used when a single value is to be returned from a subprogram.

Position in a Program

All procedures and functions (subprograms) are placed after the variable declaration section for the main program. Program execution begins with the first statement of the main program. Execution of the function occurs only when it is called from the main program or from some other subprogram. Writing style for functions will be consistent with that used for procedures. We now illustrate this with a complete program that prints a chart of the integers 1 to 10 together with their squares and cubes. The function Cube will be used as previously written.

```
PROGRAM Table (output);

VAR
  J : integer;

{*****************************************************************}

PROCEDURE PrintHeading;

  {  Given:    Nothing                                           }
  {  Task:     Print a heading for the table                     }
  {  Return:   Nothing                                           }

  BEGIN
    writeln;
    writeln ('Number':28, 'Number Squared':18, 'Number Cubed':16);
    writeln ('------':28, '--------------':18, '------------':16);
    writeln
  END;  {  of PROCEDURE PrintHeading  }

{*****************************************************************}

FUNCTION Cube (X : integer) : integer;

  {  Given:    An integer                                        }
  {  Task:     Cube the integer                                  }
  {  Return:   The cube of the integer                           }

  BEGIN
    Cube := X * X * X
  END;  {  of FUNCTION Cube  }

{*****************************************************************}
```

```
BEGIN  {  Main program  }
  PrintHeading;
  FOR J := 1 TO 10 DO
    writeln (J:25, sqr(J):14, Cube(J):17);
  writeln
END.  {  of main program  }
```

The output from this program is

Number	Number Squared	Number Cubed
1	1	1
2	4	8
3	9	27
4	16	64
5	25	125
6	36	216
7	49	343
8	64	512
9	81	729
10	100	1000

A Power Function

Example 7.9 illustrated how an integer could be raised to a positive integer power, but it would not allow you to compute $3^{2.5}$. Now that you know how to write a function, you can use the built-in functions **ln** and **exp** to write a power function. Before writing this, however, let's consider how these functions can be used to produce the desired result.

First, **exp** and **ln** are inverse functions in the sense that **exp** $(\mathbf{ln}(X)) = X$ for all positive X. Thus, we have $3^{2.5} = \mathbf{exp}(\mathbf{ln}(3^{2.5}))$. Using properties of logarithms,

$$\mathbf{ln}(a^b) = b * \mathbf{ln}(a)$$

Hence, $\mathbf{exp}(\mathbf{ln}(3^{2.5}))$ $\mathbf{exp}(2.5 * \mathbf{ln}(3))$. Since each of these operations can be performed in standard Pascal, we can compute $3^{2.5}$ by

$$3^{2.5} = \mathbf{exp}(2.5 * \mathbf{ln}(3))$$

or more generally,

$$A^x = \mathbf{exp}(X * \mathbf{ln}(A))$$

If we let Base denote the base A and Exponent denote the exponent X, we can now write a function Power as

```
FUNCTION Power (Base, Exponent : real) : real;
  BEGIN
    Power := exp(Exponent * ln(Base))
  END;  {  of FUNCTION Power  }
```

This can be called from the main program by

```
Base := 3;
Exponent := 2.5;
Num := Power(Base, Exponent);
```

Guarding against Overflow

As we discussed in Chapter 3, integer overflow occurs when the absolute value of an integer exceeds **maxint** and real overflow occurs when a value is obtained that is too large to be stored in a memory location. Both of these values vary according to the compiler being used. The maximum value of an integer is stored in **maxint**. Unfortunately, there is no convenient analogue for reals. You will need to check your system manual to determine how large a real can be. Typically, this limit will be given in the form $9999 * 10^x$. Both the number of nines and the integer x will vary.

One method that is used to guard against integer overflow is based on the principle of checking a number against some function of **maxint**. Thus, if you want to multiply a number by 10, you would first compare it to **maxint DIV** 10. A typical segment of code could be

```
IF Num > maxint DIV 10 THEN
    .
    .   (overflow message)
    .
ELSE
  BEGIN
    Num := Num * 10;
      .
      .   (rest of action)
      .
  END;
```

We can now use this same idea with a **boolean** valued function. For example, consider the function

```
FUNCTION NearOverflow (Num : integer) : boolean;
  BEGIN
    NearOverflow := (Num > maxint DIV 10)
  END;
```

This could be used in the following manner:

```
IF NearOverflow (Num) THEN
    .
    .   (overflow message)
    .
ELSE
  BEGIN
    Num := Num * 10;
      .
      .   (rest of action)
      .
  END;
```

This same idea could be incorporated into a variable control loop. A typical **WHILE** loop could be

```
WHILE <condition> AND NOT NearOverflow(Num) DO
  BEGIN
      .
      .   (action here)
      .
  END;
```

In this case, as soon as Num gets relatively close to **maxint**, the loop would be terminated.

Multiple Functions

Programs can contain more than one function. When several user-defined functions are needed in a program, each one should be developed and positioned in the program as previously indicated. For readability, be sure to use blank lines and comment sections to separate each function.

When a program contains several functions, they can be called from the main part of the program in any order. However, if one function contains a call to another function, the function being called must appear before the function from which it is called. (We will examine an exception to this when we consider forward reference in Section 8.3.)

Exercises 7.4

1. Explain the difference between procedures and functions.

2. Write a test program to see what happens when the function name is used on the right side of an assignment statement. For example,

```
FUNCTION Total (OldSum, NewNum : integer) : integer;
  BEGIN
    Total := OldSum;
    Total := Total + NewNum
  END;
```

3. Indicate which of the following are valid function headings. Explain what is wrong with those that are invalid.

   a. `FUNCTION RoundTenth (X : real);`

   b. `FUNCTION MakeChange (X, Y) : real;`

   c. `FUNCTION Max (M1, M2, M3 : integer) : integer;`

   d. `FUNCTION Sign (Num : real) : char;`

   e. `FUNCTION Truth (Ch : char, Num : real) : boolean;`

4. Find all errors in each of the following functions.

   a.
   ```
   FUNCTION MaxOf2 (N1, N2 : integer) : integer;
     BEGIN
       IF N1 > N2 THEN
         MaxOf2 := N1
     END;
   ```

   b.
   ```
   FUNCTION AvOf2 (N1, N2 : integer) : integer;
     BEGIN
       AvOf2 := (N1 + N2) / 2
     END;
   ```

   c.
   ```
   FUNCTION Total (L : integer) : integer;
     VAR
       J : integer;
     BEGIN
       Total := 0;
       FOR J := 1 TO L DO
         Total := Total + J
     END;
   ```

5. Write a function for each of the following:

   a. Find the maximum of two reals.

   b. Find the maximum of three reals.

   c. Round a real to the nearest tenth.

   d. Convert degrees Fahrenheit to degrees Celsius.

   e. Determine the sign of a real number.

   f. Examine an integer to see if it is a multiple of five; if so, return the **boolean** value **true**; if not, return the **boolean** value **false**.

   g. Compute the charge for cars at a parking lot; the rate is 75 cents per hour or fraction thereof.

6. Write a program that uses the function you wrote for Exercise 5g to print a ticket for a customer who parks in the parking lot. Assume the input is in minutes.

7. The factorial of a positive integer n is defined as

$$n! = n * (n - 1) * \ldots * 2 * 1$$

for $n > 1$. Write a function (Factorial) that will compute and return $n!$.

8. Write a complete program using Cube and Factorial that will produce a table of the integers 1 to 10 together with their squares, cubes, and factorials.

9. Write a function (Arithmetic) that will receive a sign (+ or *) and two integers (N1, N2) and then compute and return either N1 + N2 or N1 * N2 depending on the sign received.

10. Write an interactive program that allows the user to enter a Base (a) and Exponent (x) and then have the program print the value of a^x.

11. Algebra teachers often have students play "guess the rule." This consists of having the first person write down a rule (function) such as $y = x^2 + 1$. A second person then gives a value for x. The first person indicates the function value associated with the input. Thus, for x = 3, y would be 10 if $y = x^2 + 1$. The game continues until the second person "guesses the rule." Write a program which allows you to play this game with another student. Write it in such a way that it can be easily modified to use different functions.

■ ■ ■ ■

FOCUS ON PROGRAM DESIGN

The summary program for this chapter is one that illustrates using procedures as part of a modular development. More specifically, consider the problem of finding the least common multiple (LCM) of integers A and B. The LCM of two positive integers A and B is the smallest positive integer that is a multiple of both A and B. For example, the LCM of 12 and 15 is 60.

Our program is an interactive program that gets two positive integers as input. Output consists of the numbers given as input and their least common multiple. A sample run of this program produces

```
This program allows you to find the
LEAST COMMON MULTIPLE of two positive integers.

Please enter the first integer
?12
Please enter the second integer
?15

The LCM of 12 and 15 is 60

In this case we have          12 *    5 = 60
                              15 *    4 = 60
```

Features of this program include a check for bad data and a special message if the numbers entered are relatively prime. A reasonable first-level pseudocode design for this program is

1. Get the data
2. Put the numbers in order Small, Large
3. Find the least common multiple
4. Print the results

A structure chart for this pseudocode is given in Figure 7.1.

FIGURE 7.1
Structure chart for **PROGRAM** LeastCommonMultiple

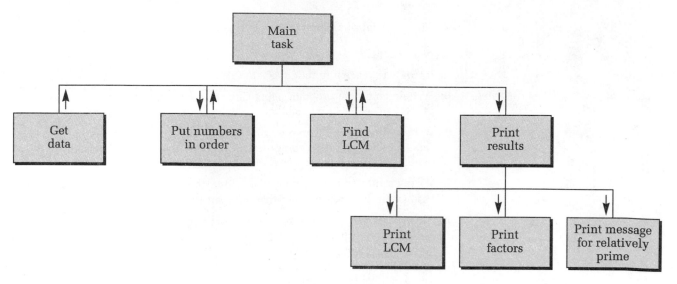

Module specifications for this problem are

1. GetNumbers Module
    Data received: None
    Information returned: Two positive integers
    Logic: Have the user enter two positive integers.

2. Order Module
    Data received: Two positive integers
    Information returned: The integers in order Small, Large
    Logic: IF Num2 is less than Num1 **THEN** switch them.

3. FindLCM Module
    Data received: Two positive integers in order Small, Large
    Information returned: The LCM of Num1, Num2
    Logic: Increase multiples of the larger number until a multiple of the
           smaller number is found.

4. PrintResults Module
    Data received: Num1, Num2, and their LCM
    Information returned: None
    Logic: Print the LCM.
           Print the products that show how Num1, Num2 are factors of
             LCM.
           Print a special message if the LCM is Num1 * Num2.

The GetNumbers module has the user enter two positive integers as input.
There is a bad data check to assure that each integer is positive. The Order
module guarantees that Num1 <= Num2.

The FindLCM module can be further developed as

3. Find the least common multiple
    3.1   initialize Factor to 1
    3.2   initialize LCMFound to false
          WHILE NOT LCMFound **DO**

3.3   IF Num1 divides Num2 * Factor **THEN**
    3.3.1   LCM is Num2 * Factor
    3.3.2   LCMFound is **true**
    ELSE
    3.3.3   increment Factor by 1

The PrintResults module can be as simple as printing the LCM but we will display slightly more descriptive information. Thus, PrintResults module is developed as

4.   Print the results
    4.1   display the LCM
    4.2   display how Num1 divides LCM
    4.3   display how Num2 divides LCM
    4.4   display a special message if Num1 * Num2 equals LCM

A complete program to solve this problem is

```
PROGRAM LeastCommonMultiple (input, output);

{  This program finds and displays the least common multiple (LCM) }
{  of two positive integers.  The procedure for input  illustrates }
{  the  robust  property  of  guaranteeing  that  each  integer is  }
{  positive.  After the numbers are put in order Num1 <= Num2, the  }
{  algorithm for finding the LCM is to consider multiples of  Num2  }
{  until Num1 divides some multiple.  At that point, the  multiple  }
{  of  Num2 is the LCM.  Note that a special message is  displayed  }
{  when Num1 and Num2 are relatively prime (no factors in common).  }

CONST
  Skip = ' ';

VAR
  Small, Large, LCM : integer;

{*********************************************************************}

PROCEDURE GetNumbers (VAR Num1, Num2 : integer);

  {  Given:    Nothing                                              }
  {  Task:     Get two positive integers as input                  }
  {  Return:   Two positive integers: Num1, Num2                   }

  BEGIN
    writeln ('This program allows you to find the');
    writeln ('LEAST COMMON MULTIPLE of two positive integers.');
    writeln;
    REPEAT
      writeln ('Please enter the first integer.');
      readln (Num1)
    UNTIL Num1 > 0;
    REPEAT
      writeln ('Please enter the second integer.');
      readln (Num2)
    UNTIL Num2 > 0
  END;  {  of PROCEDURE GetNumbers  }

{*********************************************************************}
```

```
PROCEDURE Order (VAR Num1, Num2 : integer);

  {  Given:    Two positive integers                                         }
  {  Task:     Put them in order so that Num1 <= Num2                        }
  {  Return:   Two positive integers: Num1 <= Num2                          }

  VAR
    Temp : integer;

  BEGIN
    IF Num2 < Num1 THEN
      BEGIN
        Temp := Num1;
        Num1 := Num2;
        Num2 := Temp
      END  {  of IF . . . THEN  }
  END;  {  of PROCEDURE Order  }


{***********************************************************************}

PROCEDURE FindLCM (Small, Large : integer;
                   VAR LCM : integer);

  {  Given:    Two positive integers (Num1, Num2) with Num1 <= Num2  }
  {  Task:     Find their LCM by considering multiples of Num2        }
  {  Return:   The LCM of Num1, Num2                                  }

  VAR
    Factor : integer;
    LCMFound : boolean;

  BEGIN
    Factor := 1;
    LCMFound := false;
    WHILE NOT LCMFound DO
      IF (Large * Factor MOD Small = 0) THEN
        BEGIN
          LCM := Large * Factor;
          LCMFound := true
        END  {  of IF...THEN option  }
      ELSE
        Factor := Factor + 1
  END;  {  of PROCEDURE FindLCM  }


{***********************************************************************}

PROCEDURE PrintResults (Num1, Num2, LCM : integer);

  {  Given:    Num1, Num2, LCM of Num1 and Num2                    }
  {  Task:     Display the LCM, products that show that Num1 and   }
  {            Num2 divide LCM, and a special message if           }
  {            Num1 * Num2 = LCM                                   }
  {  Return:   Nothing                                            }

  VAR
    OtherFactor : integer;

  BEGIN
    writeln;
    writeln ('The LCM of ', Num1, ' and ', Num2, ' is ', LCM);
    writeln;
    write ('In this case we have ');
    OtherFactor := LCM DIV Num1;
```

```
      writeln (Skip:9, Num1:4, ' *', OtherFactor:4, ' = ', LCM);
      OtherFactor := LCM DIV Num2;
      writeln (Skip:30, Num2:4, ' *', OtherFactor:4, ' = ', LCM);
      IF LCM = Num1 * Num2 THEN
         BEGIN
            writeln;
            writeln ('Notice that these numbers are relatively prime.')
         END  {  of IF...THEN  }
   END;  {  of PROCEDURE PrintResults  }

{*******************************************************************}

BEGIN  {  Main program  }
   GetNumbers (Small, Large);
   Order (Small, Large);
   FindLCM (Small, Large, LCM);
   PrintResults (Small, Large, LCM)
END.  {  of main program  }
```

Sample runs of this program produce the following:

```
            This program allows you to find the
            LEAST COMMON MULTIPLE of two positive integers.

            Please enter the first integer.
            ?12
            Please enter the second integer.
            ?15

            The LCM of 12 and 15 is 60

            In this case we have            12 *    5 = 60
                                            15 *    4 = 60


            This program allows you to find the
            LEAST COMMON MULTIPLE of two positive integers.

            Please enter the first integer.
            ?18
            Please enter the second integer.
            ?25

            The LCM of 18 and 25 is 450

            In this case we have            18 *   25 = 450
                                            25 *   18 = 450

            Notice that these numbers are relatively prime.

            This program allows you to find the
            LEAST COMMON MULTIPLE of two positive integers.

            Please enter the first integer.
            ?10
            Please enter the second integer.
            ?20

            The LCM of 10 and 20 is 20

            In this case we have            10 *    2 = 20
                                            20 *    1 = 20


            This program allows you to find the
            LEAST COMMON MULTIPLE of two positive integers.
```

```
Please enter the first integer.
?-4
Please enter the first integer.
?4
Please enter the second integer.
?6

The LCM of 4 and 6 is 12

In this case we have              4 *      3 = 12
                                  6 *      2 = 12
```

RUNNING AND DEBUGGING TIPS

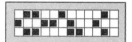

1. Each subprogram can be tested separately to see if it is producing the desired result. This is accomplished by a main program that calls and tests only the subprogram in question.

2. Be sure the type and order of actual parameters and formal parameters agree. You can see this by listing them one below the other. For example,

```
PROCEDURE GetData (VAR Init1, Init2:char; Sc:integer);
       {  GetData (Initial1, Initial2, Score);  }
```

3. Carefully distinguish between value parameters and variable parameters. If a value is to be returned to the main program, it must be passed through a variable parameter. This means it must be declared with **VAR** in the procedure heading.

■ Summary

Key Terms

actual parameter	passed by reference	subprogram
bottom-up testing	procedure	user-defined function
formal parameter	side effect	value parameter
function	structured programming	variable parameter
modularity		

Keywords

FUNCTION	ln	**PROCEDURE**
exp		

Key Concepts

- A subprogram is a program within a program; procedures and functions are subprograms.
- Subprograms can be utilized to perform specific tasks in a program. Procedures are often used to initialize variables (variable parameters), get data (variable parameters), print headings (no variables needed), perform computations (value and/or variable parameters), and print data (value parameters).
- The general form for a procedure heading is

PROCEDURE ⟨name⟩ (⟨parameter list⟩);

- A typical procedure heading that could be used when writing a procedure to produce the heading for the output is

```
PROCEDURE PrintHeader;
```

- A procedure is called, or invoked, from the main program by a reference to the procedure name.

```
BEGIN  {  Main program  }
  PrintHeader
END.  {  of main program  }
```

- Procedures are placed in a program after the variable declaration section and before the start of the main program.

```
PROGRAM Practice (input, output);

VAR

PROCEDURE PrintTitle;
  BEGIN
     .
     .
     .
   END;  {  of PROCEDURE PrintTitle  }

BEGIN  {  Main program  }
   .
   .
   .
END.  {  of main program  }
```

placement of procedure

- Value parameters are used when values are passed only from the main program to the procedure; a typical parameter list is

```
PROCEDURE PrintData (N1, N2 : integer;
                     X, Y : real);
```

- Variable parameters are used when values are to be returned to the main program; a typical parameter list is

```
PROCEDURE GetData (VAR Init1, Init2 : char;
                   VAR N1 : integer);
```

- A formal parameter is one listed in a subprogram heading; it is like a blank waiting to receive a value from the calling program.

formal parameters

```
PROCEDURE PrintNum (N1, N2 : integer; N3 : real);
```

- An actual parameter is a variable listed in a subprogram call in the calling program.

actual parameters

```
PrintNum (Num1, Num2, Num3);
```

- The formal parameter list in the subprogram heading must match the number and types of actual parameters used in the main program when the function is called.

```
PROCEDURE PrintNum (N1, N2 : integer; N3 : real);
PrintNum (Num1, Num2, Num3);
```

- A user-defined function is a subprogram that performs a specific task.
- The form for a user-defined function is

```
FUNCTION ⟨function name⟩ (⟨parameter list⟩) : ⟨return type⟩,
   VAR
   BEGIN
      .
      . (work of function here)
      .
END;
```

- An assignment must be made to the function name in the body of the function.
- Within the function, the function name can only be used on the left of an assignment statement.

■ Programming Problems and Projects

In order to facilitate the use of subprograms in writing programs to solve problems, the programming problems for this chapter consist of redesigning previous programs.

■ 1. In Chapter 6 (Problem 1), you modified the program for the Caswell Catering and Convention Service (Problem 7, Chapter 4 and Problem 14, Chapter 5) so that they could use it for all of their customers. Now, revise the program so that you use a separate procedure for each of the following:
   a. compute meal cost.
   b. compute room rate.
   c. compute surcharge.
   d. compute discount.
   e. print a statement.

   Use functions to compute the tax and tip.

2. A prime number is a positive integer that can be divided evenly only by 1 and the number itself (for example, 17). Write a program that will determine whether or not a given positive integer is prime. (*Hint:* you only have to check for divisors less than or equal to the square root of the number being tested. Thus, if 79 is the positive integer being examined, the check of divisors would be 2, 3, . . . , 9.) Write a function that returns a **boolean** value of **true** for a prime number or **false** otherwise (a composite number). Make use of the fact that if 2 is not a divisor, then no other even integer will be a divisor.

3. The Fairfield College faculty recently signed a three-year contract that included salary increments of 7 percent, 6 percent, and 5 percent respectively for the next three years. Write a program that allows a user to enter the current salary and then prints out the compounded salary for each of the next three years.

4. In Chapter 5 (Problem 17) and Chapter 6 (Problem 3) you wrote and revised a program for the Community Hospital. Now, write functions for each of the following:
   a. compute room charge.
   b. compute telephone charge.
   c. compute television charge.

5. In Chapter 6 (Problem 7) you wrote a program to compute the miles per gallon for each tank of gas used by a traveler and the cumulative miles per gallon each time the tank was filled. Revise that program by writing procedures to get a line of data and print a line of output. Write functions to compute the mileage per tank and the total mileage.

6. In Chapter 6 (Problem 8), you wrote a program that read pairs of positive integers and produced Parkside's Other Triangle for each pair. Write procedures for each of the following:
   a. get the data.
   b. check for bad data.
   c. print the triangle.

■ **7.** Back in Chapter 5 you wrote a program for Dr. Lae Z. Programmer (Problems 5, 22, and 23). You revised that program in Chapter 6 (Problem 13). Now it's time to revise it yet again. Write procedures to get the data Dr. Lae Z. Programmer has requested (the overall class average and the number of students receiving each letter grade) and to print the results. Use a function to compute the grade.

■ **8.** Problem 14 in Chapter 6 asked that you revise the Pentagon Parking Lot problem you worked on in Chapter 5 (Problem 26). Using that program, write procedures to get the data and print results. Develop one function to compute the number of hours in the parking lot and another to compute the parking fee.

■ **9.** Write a program to get the coefficients of a quadratic equation

$$ax^2 + bx + c = 0$$

from the keyboard and then print the value of the discriminant $b^2 - 4ac$

A sample display for getting input is

```
Enter coefficients a, b, and c for the quadratic
    equation ax² + bx + c = 0
a = ?
b = ?
c = ?
```

Run this program at least three times usng test data that result in $b^2 - 4ac = 0$, $b^2 - 4ac > 0$, and $b^2 - 4ac < 0$.

10. The program written in the Focus on Program Design segment of this chapter allows the user to enter two positive integers and then have the least common multiple displayed. Enhance this program by including a procedure that allows the user to decide whether or not to continue. The new main program should be

```
BEGIN  {  Main program  }
  MoreTrials := true;
  WHILE MoreTrials DO
    BEGIN
      GetNumbers (Num1, Num2);
      Order (Num1, Num2);          {  Num1 <= Num2  }
      FindLCM (Num1, Num2, LCM);
      PrintResults (Num1, Num2, LCM);
      CheckForRepetition (MoreTrials)
    END  {  of WHILE...DO  }
END.  {  of main program  }
```

11. Reconsider Problem 9 in which you were asked to write a program to display the value of the discriminant of a quadratic equation. Solutions to the quadratic equation depend on the value of the discriminant as follows:
a. $b^2 - 4ac = 0$ ---exactly one solution
b. $b^2 - 4ac > 0$ --- two distinct solutions
c. $b^2 - 4ac < 0$ --- no real solutions

Create a modular development for a program that will evaluate the discriminant, indicate how many real solutions there are, and display any real solutions that exist. Write module specifications for each module in your design. Assuming a subprogram is used for each module, give a complete description of all parameters used in your design.

12. Discuss the issue of documenting subprograms with instructors of computer science, upper-level students majoring in computer science, and some of your classmates. Prepare a report for the class on this issue. Your report should contain information about different forms of documentation, the perceived need for documentation by various groups, significance of documenting data transmission, and so forth. If possible, use specific examples to illustrate good documentation of subprograms versus poor documentation of subprograms.

Subprograms: Using Procedures and Functions

Being able to write procedures and functions represents a major step in learning to use Pascal to solve problems. Now that you have some familiarity with subprograms, we look at some aspects of their use in the design of solutions to programming problems.

■ 8.1
Scope of Identifiers

OBJECTIVES

- to understand what is meant by local identifiers
- to understand what is meant by global identifiers
- to understand the scope of an identifier
- to recognize appropriate and inappropriate uses for global identifiers
- to be able to use appropriate names for local and global identifiers

Global and Local Identifiers

Identifiers used to declare variables in the declaration section of a program can be used throughout the entire program. For purposes of this section, we will think of the program as a *block* and envision it as in Figure 8.1. Furthermore, if X1 is a variable in ShowScope, we will indicate this as shown in Figure 8.2, where an area in memory has been set aside for X1. When a program contains a subprogram, a separate memory area within the memory area for the program is set aside for the subprogram. This is sometimes referred to as a *subblock* or block for the subprogram. Thus, if ShowScope

FIGURE 8.1
Program heading and main block

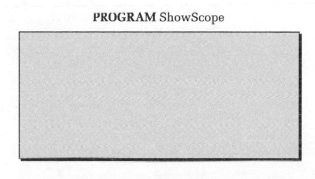

PROGRAM ShowScope

contains a procedure named Subprog1, we can envision this as shown in Figure 8.3. If Subprog1 contains the variable X2, we have the program shown in Figure 8.4.

FIGURE 8.2
Variable location in main block

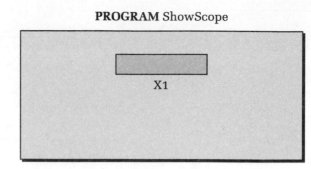

FIGURE 8.3
Illustration of a subblock

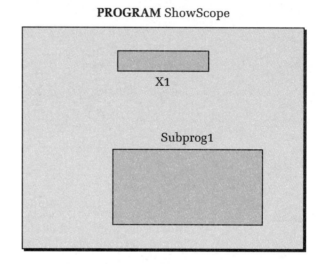

FIGURE 8.4
Variable location within a subblock

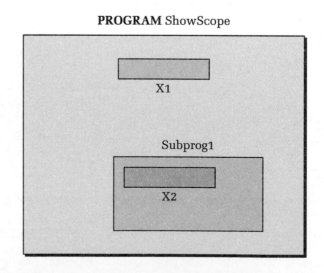

This could be indicated in the program by

```
PROGRAM ShowScope (input, output);

VAR
  X1 : real;

PROCEDURE Subprog1 (X2 : real);
```

We now must consider which identifiers are available to the various parts of the program. When subprograms are used, each identifier is available to the block in which it is declared; this includes all subprograms contained within its block. Identifiers are not available outside their blocks.

Identifiers that can be used by all subprograms in a program are called *global identifiers* (or *global variables*); identifiers that are restricted to use within a subblock are called *local identifiers* (or *local variables*). Variable X1 in the previous illustration can be used in the main program and in the procedure Subprog1; therefore it is a global identifier. On the other hand, X2 can only be used within the procedure where it is declared; it is a local identifier. Any attempt to reference X2 outside the procedure will result in an error.

As you can see, global and local are relative terms. If a subprogram contains a subprogram (see Section 8.3), as in Figure 8.5, with variables X1, X2, and X3 as indicated, X2 is local with respect to the procedure Outer but global with respect to the procedure Inner. There are, however, two nonrelative uses of these terms: identifiers used in the main program are always global and identifiers used in the innermost subprogram are always local.

FIGURE 8.5
Local and global identifiers

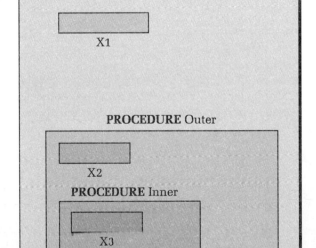

PROGRAM ShowScope

The *scope of an identifier* refers to the largest block in which the variable is available. Hence, in the previous illustration, the scope of X3 is the procedure Inner, the scope of X2 is the procedure Outer, and the scope of X1 is the program ShowScope.

Let us now examine an illustration of local and global identifiers. Consider the program and procedure declaration

```
PROGRAM ScopePrac (output);

VAR
  A, B : integer;

PROCEDURE Subprog (A1 : integer);

  VAR
    X : real;
```

Memory area for this program could then be envisioned as shown in Figure 8.6.

FIGURE 8.6
Relation of variables for **PRO-GRAM** ScopePrac

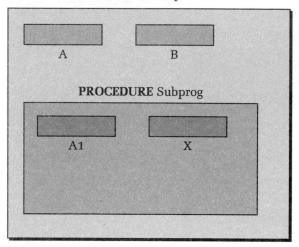

Since A and B are global, the statement

```
writeln (A, B, A1, X:10:2);
```

could be used in the procedure Subprog although A and B have not been specifically declared there. However,

```
writeln (A, B, A1, X:10:2);
```

could not be used in the main program because A1 and X are local to the procedure Subprog.

Using Global Variables and Constants

In general, it is not good practice to refer to global variables within procedures. Using locally defined variables helps to avoid unexpected side effects and protects your programs. In addition, locally defined variables facilitate debugging and top-down design and also enhance the portability of procedures. This is especially important if a team is developing a program by having different people work on different procedures.

Using global constants is different. Since the values cannot be changed by a procedure, it is preferred that constants be defined in the **CONST** section of the main program and then be used whenever needed by any subprogram. This is especially important if the constant is subject to change over time, for example, StateTaxRate. When a change is necessary, one change in the main program is all that is needed to make all subprograms current. If a constant is used in only one procedure (or function), some programmers prefer to have it defined near the point of use. Thus, they would define it in the subprogram in which it is used.

Name of Identifiers

Since separate areas in memory are set aside when subprograms are used, it is possible to have identifiers with the same name in both the main program and a subprogram. Thus

```
PROGRAM Demo (input, output);

VAR
  Age : integer;

PROCEDURE Subprog (Age : integer);
```

can be envisioned as shown in Figure 8.7.

FIGURE 8.7
Using identifiers in subprograms

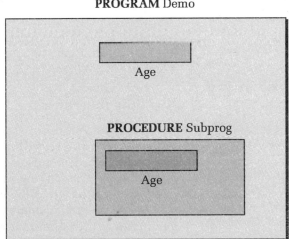

When the same name is used in this manner, any reference to this name will result in action being taken as locally as possible. Thus, the assignment statement

```
AGE := 20;
```

made in the procedure Subprog assigns 20 to Age in the procedure but not in the main program (see Figure 8.8).

Now that you know you can use the same name for an identifier in a subprogram and the main program, the question is, "Should you?" There are two schools of thought regarding this issue. If you use the same name in the procedures, it facilitates matching parameter lists and independent development of procedures. However, this practice can be confusing when you first start working with subprograms. Thus, some instructors prefer using different, but related, identifiers. For example,

```
GetData (Score1, Score2);
```

FIGURE 8.8
Assigning values in subprograms

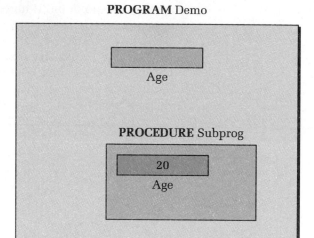

in the main program could have a procedure heading of

```
PROCEDURE GetData (VAR Sc1, Sc2 : integer);
```

In this case, the use of Sc1 and Sc2 is obvious. Although this may facilitate better understanding in early work with subprograms, it is less conducive to portability and independent development of procedures. Both styles are used in this text.

Multiple Procedures

More than one procedure can be used in a program. When this occurs, all the previous uses and restrictions of identifiers apply to each procedure. Blocks for multiple procedures can be depicted as shown in Figure 8.9. Identifiers in the main program can be accessed by each procedure. However, local identifiers in the procedures cannot be accessed outside their blocks.

When a program contains several procedures, they can be called from the main part of the program in any order. However, if one procedure contains a call to another procedure (or function), the subprogram being called must appear before the procedure from which it is called.

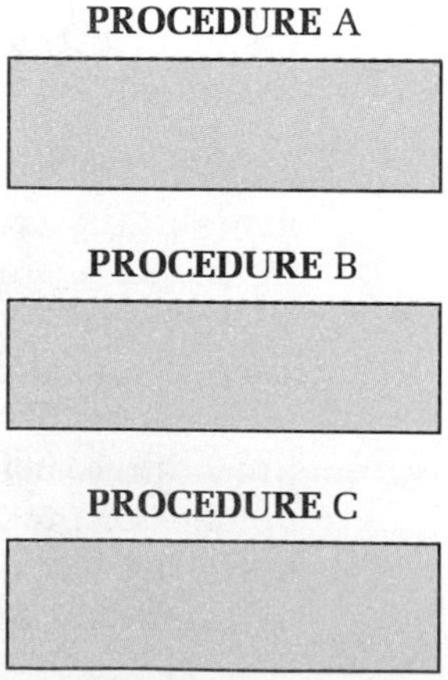

FIGURE 8.9
Blocks for multiple subprograms

PROCEDURE A

PROCEDURE B

PROCEDURE C

The same names for identifiers can be used in different procedures. Thus, if the main program uses variables Wage and Hours, and both of these are used as arguments in calls to different procedures, you have the situation shown in Figure 8.10. Using the same names for identifiers in different procedures makes it easier to keep track of the relationship between variables in the main program and their associated parameters in each subprogram. For example, if Wage and Hours are used in the main program, W and H can be used as corresponding parameters in all procedures.

FIGURE 8.10
Identifiers in multiple subprograms

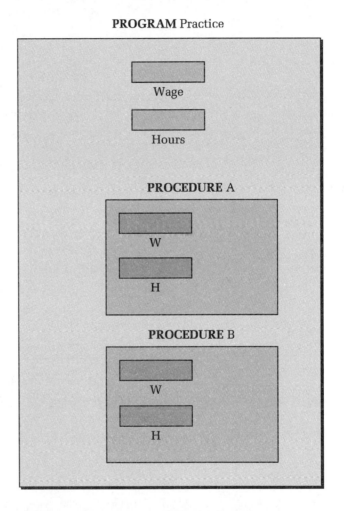

Exercises 8.1

1. Explain the difference between local and global identifiers.

2. State the advantages of using local identifiers.

3. Discuss some appropriate uses for global identifiers. List several constants that would be appropriate global definitions.

4. What is meant by the scope of an identifier?

5. Write a test program that will enable you to see
   a. what happens when an attempt is made to access an identifier outside of its scope; and
   b. how the values change as a result of assignments in the subprogram and the main program when the same identifier is used in the main program and a procedure.

6. Review the following program:

```
PROGRAM Practice (input, output);

VAR
  A, B : integer;
  X : real;
  Ch : char;

PROCEDURE Sub1 (A1 : integer);
  VAR
    B1 : integer;
  BEGIN
    .
    .
    .
  END;  {  of PROCEDURE Sub1  }

PROCEDURE Sub2 (A1 : integer;
                   VAR B1 : integer);
  VAR

    X1 : real;
    Ch1 : char;
  BEGIN
    .
    .
    .
  END;  {  of PROCEDURE Sub2  }
```

a. List all global variables.

b. List all local variables.

c. Indicate the scope of each identifier.

7. Provide a schematic representation of the program and all subprograms and variables in Exercise 6.

8. Using the program with variables and subprograms as depicted in Figure 8.11, state the scope of each identifier.

9. What is the output from the following program?

```
PROGRAM Exercise9 (output);

VAR
  A : integer;

PROCEDURE Sub1 (A : integer);
  BEGIN
    A := 20;
    writeln (A)
  END;  {  of PROCEDURE Sub1  }

PROCEDURE Sub2 (VAR A : integer);
  BEGIN
    A := 30;
    writeln (A)
  END;  {  of PROCEDURE Sub2  }

BEGIN  {  Main program  }
  A := 10;
  writeln (A);
  Sub1 (A);
  writeln (A);
  Sub2 (A);
  writeln (A)
END.  {  of main program  }
```

FIGURE 8.11

PROGRAM Exercise8

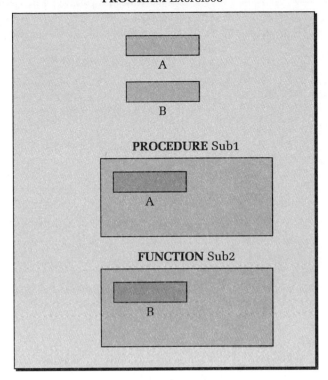

10. Review the following program.

```
PROGRAM ExerciseTen (output);

VAR
  Num1, Num2, : integer;
PROCEDURE Change (X : integer;
                    VAR Y : integer);

  VAR
    Num2 : integer;

  BEGIN
    Num2 := X;
    Y := Y + Num2;
    X := Y
  END;

BEGIN
  Num1 := 10;
  Num2 := 7;
  Change (Num1, Num2);
  writeln (Num1, Num2)
END.
```

a. What is the output of the program as written? Determine the output of the program if the following procedure headings are substituted

b. `PROCEDURE Change (VAR X : integer; Y : integer);`

c. `PROCEDURE Change (X, Y : integer);`

d. `PROCEDURE Change (VAR X, Y : integer);`

11. Assume the variable declaration section of a program is

```
VAR
  Age, Hours : integer;
  Average : real;
  Initial : char;
```

Furthermore, assume that procedure headings and declaration sections for procedures in this program are as follows. Find all errors in each.

a. `PROCEDURE Average (Age1, Hrs : integer;`
   `                   VAR Aver : real);`

b. `PROCEDURE Sub1 (Hours : integer;`
   `                VAR Average : real);`

```
  VAR
    Age : integer;
    Init : char;
```

c. `PROCEDURE Compute (Hrs : integer;`
   `                   VAR Aver : real);`

```
  VAR
    Age : real;
```

12. Write appropriate headings and declaration sections for the program and subprograms illustrated in Figure 8.12.

FIGURE 8.12

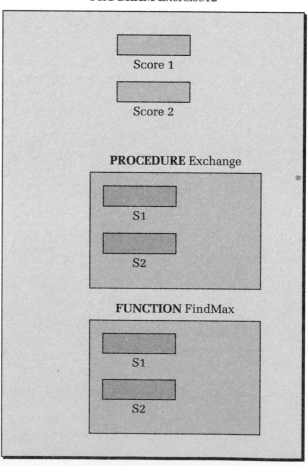

PROGRAM Exercise12

13. Find all errors in the following program.

```
PROGRAM Exercise13 (output);

VAR
  X, Y : real;

PROCEDURE Sub1 (VAR X1 : real);
  BEGIN
    writeln (X1:20:2);
    writeln (X:20:2);
    writeln (Y:20:2)
  END;  { of PROCEDURE Sub1 }

BEGIN { Main program }
  X := 10.0;
  Y := 2 * X;
  writeln (X:20:2, Y:20:2);
  Sub1 (X);
  writeln (X1:20:2);
  writeln (X:20:2);
  writeln (Y:20:2)
END. { of main program }
```

14. Discuss the advantages and disadvantages of using the same names for identifiers in a subprogram and the main program.

■ ■ ■ ■

■ 8.2
Using Subprograms

OBJECTIVE

- to understand how subprograms can be used in designing programs
- to be able to use procedures to get data for programs
- to be able to use subprograms to perform tasks required in programs
- to be able to use procedures for output

Throughout this text you have seen examples of problems solved by the development of a sequence of tasks. Tasks are stated in the order in which they are to be performed and then each task is refined according to its level of complexity. Now that you are capable of using procedures and functions in a program, you should see how they can be used to design a program for solving a problem. After the algorithm for solving the problem has been developed in pseudocode, subprograms can be written for the various tasks and then called from the main program as needed.

To illustrate, let us consider how a program could be designed using subprograms. We will not write the subprograms at this point; we will only indicate how they would be used in designing the program. Our problem is to compute grades for a class. A first-level pseudocode development could be

1. Initialize variables
2. Print a heading
3. Process grades for each student
4. Print a summary

This could be refined to

1. Initialize variables
2. Print a heading
3. Process grades for each student
   WHILE NOT eof DO
   3.1 get a line of data
   3.2 compute average
   3.3 compute letter grade
   3.4 print data
   3.5 compute totals

4. Print a summary
    4.1   print class average
    4.2   Print number receiving each grade

Subprograms can be used to design a program consistent with this algorithm as illustrated in Table 8.1. Note that this particular choice of procedures and functions is not the only solution available to us; there are many other ways to use subprograms in a program to solve our problem.

TABLE 8.1
Subprograms from pseudocode

Pseudocode Statement	Subprogram
1. Initialize variables	**PROCEDURE** Initialize
2. Print a heading	**PROCEDURE** PrintHeading
3. Process grades for each student	
WHILE NOT eof DO	
3.1 get a line of data	**PROCEDURE** GetData
3.2 compute average	**FUNCTION** Average
3.3 compute letter grade	**FUNCTION** LetterGrade
3.4 print data	**PROCEDURE** PrintData
3.5 compute totals	**PROCEDURE** ComputeTotals
4. Print a summary	
4.1 print class average	**PROCEDURE** PrintAverage
4.2 print number receiving each grade	**PROCEDURE** PrintNumGrades

Now that we have identified procedures and functions for various tasks in this problem, we can write the program design. Since we are relatively early in the design state, we will not include parameters for the subprograms, but as we develop each subprogram, we will indicate appropriate value and variable parameters.

The main program could be

```
BEGIN  {  Main program  }
  Initialize (            );
  PrintHeader;
  WHILE NOT eof DO
    BEGIN
      GetData (        );
      Aver := Average (        );
      LetGrade := LetterGrade (          );
      PrintData (        );
      ComputeTotals (          )
    END;
  PrintAverage (          );
  PrintNumGrades (        )
END.  {  of main program  }
```

Procedures for Initializing Variables

Programs may require variables to be initialized at the beginning of the program. This initialization can be done in the main program or in a procedure; it is generally the first step in developing an algorithm. Thus,

1. Initialize variables

will frequently be listed as a line of pseudocode and, when a procedure is written to implement this task, the program design becomes

```
BEGIN   {  main program  }
  Initialize (          );
```

Procedures for initializing require variable parameters because variables in the main program will subsequently be used with the initial values assigned in **PROCEDURE** Initialize.

The program for our grading problem will require initialization of variables Count, ClassTotal, NumA, NumB, NumC, NumD, and NumE. Appropriate initialization can be accomplished by the following procedure.

```
PROCEDURE Initialize (VAR Count : integer;
                      VAR ClassTotal : real;
                      VAR NumA, NumB, NumC, NumD, NumE : integer);
  BEGIN
    Count := 0;
    ClassTotal := 0.0;
    NumA := 0;
    NumB := 0;
    NumC := 0;
    NumD :– 0;
    NumE := 0
  END;  { of PROCEDURE Initialize  }
```

This procedure can be called from the main program by

```
Initialize (Count, ClassTotal, NumA, NumB,
            NumC, NumD, NumE);
```

Procedures for Headers

Procedures for headers facilitate program design. Unless you are using page numbers, inputting dates, or some other heading change, no parameters are needed for this kind of procedure. You should include such a procedure in all programs you write.

Procedures for Input

As noted earlier, a simplified pseudocode version of most programs is

1. Get the data
2. Process the data
3. Print results

Let's now take a closer look at procedures for input. Since the data obtained will be used in the program as well as the procedure, you will need variable parameters declared in the procedure heading. Thus, if each line of data contains three integer test scores, a reasonable procedure heading is

```
PROCEDURE GetData (VAR Score1, Score2, Score3 : integer);
```

The procedure could be called from the main program by

```
GetData (Score1, Score2, Score3);
```

Note that the identifiers are selected so the program will be easier to read and debug.

The following example demonstrates a procedure to get data for a program.

Niklaus Wirth

Niklaus Wirth began his work in the computing field by taking a course in numerical analysis at Laval University in Quebec, Canada. However, the computer (Alvac III E) was frequently out of order and the hexadecimal code programming exercises went untested. He received his doctorate from the University of California, Berkeley, in 1963.

After other early experiences in programming, it became apparent to Wirth that computers of the future had to be more effectively programmable. Consequently, he joined a research group that worked on developing a compiler for an IBM 704. This language was NELIAC, a dialect of ALGOL 58. In rapid succession, he developed or contributed to the development of Euler,

ALGOL W, and PL360. In 1967, he returned to Switzerland and established a team of three assistants with whom he developed and implemented the language Pascal.

Pascal was the first major programming language to implement the ideas and methodology of structured programming and was initially developed to teach programming concepts. It is particularly successful as a teaching language because it allows the teacher to focus on structures and concepts rather than features and peculiarities. However, it has rapidly expanded beyond its initial purpose and has found increasing acceptance in business and scientific applications.

EXAMPLE 8.1

Write a procedure to get data for a program to print payroll checks for a company. Each line of data contains one employee's initials, the hours worked (integer), and the hourly rate (real). Thus, the data file could be depicted as

RJS 38 11.50   TRM 42 9.85   JAH 40 10.0   ■

A complete procedure for getting a line of data is

```
PROCEDURE GetData (VAR Initial1, Initial2, Initial3 : char;
                   VAR Hours : integer;
                   VAR HourlyRate : real);
   BEGIN
      readln (Init1, Init2, Init3, Hours, HourlyRate)
   END;  { of PROCEDURE GetData  }
```

This procedure could be called from the main program by

```
   GetData (Initial1, Initial2, Initial3, Hours, HourlyRate);
```

Subprograms for Tasks

The second step in the problem solution

2. Process the data

can be quite complex. When an algorithm is developed to solve a problem, this step usually requires several levels of refinement. When these levels have been sufficiently refined, subprograms can be developed to implement each level. Then the main program can call a major subprogram; this subprogram in turn calls the appropriate subprograms as needed.

When writing procedures for various tasks, you need to be careful with the use of value and variable parameters. If the main program needs a different value of the variable for later use in the program, you must then use a variable parameter. For instance, you would need a variable parameter if a count is being made in a procedure or if a running total is being kept. However, if the procedure merely performs some computation with the values received, then the values may be passed with value parameters.

To illustrate, let's consider some of the tasks from our earlier problem of computing grades for a class. One task was to print the data for one student. The initials, three test scores, test average, and letter grade are available for each student. Since the procedure only prints the data, all values can be passed by value parameters. If typical output for one student is the line

```
BRL            89   93   95      92.33      A
```

the procedure could be as follows:

```
PROCEDURE PrintData (Initial1, Initial2, Initial3 : char;
                     Score1, Score2, Score3 : integer;
                     Aver : real;
                     LetGrade : char);
   BEGIN
     write (Initial1:20, Initial2, Initial3);
     write (Score1:10, Score2:5, Score3:5);
     writeln (Aver:10:2, LetGrade:5)
   END;  {  of PROCEDURE PrintData  }
```

Another task from the same problem was to compute running totals for the class. Therefore, we need to count the number of students, accumulate averages so we can compute a class average, and count the number of students receiving each letter grade. In this case, both value and variable parameters will be needed. Formal variable parameters will be used for the actual parameters

```
Count
ClassTotal
NumA, NumB, NumC, NumD, NumE
```

and formal value parameters will be used for the actual parameters

```
Aver
LetGrade
```

With the variables thus identified, the procedure could be

```
PROCEDURE ComputeTotals (Aver : real;
                         LetGrade : char;
                         VAR Count : integer;
                         VAR ClassTotal : real;
                         VAR NumA, NumB, NumC, NumD, NumE : integer);
   BEGIN
     Count := Count + 1;
     ClassTotal := ClassTotal + Aver;
     CASE LetGrade OF
       'A' : NumA := NumA + 1;
       'B' : NumB := NumB + 1;
       'C' : NumC := NumC + 1;
       'D' : NumD := NumD + 1;
       'E' : NumE := NumE + 1
     END {  of CASE LetGrade  }
   END; {  of PROCEDURE ComputeTotals  }
```

This procedure could be called from the main program by

```
ComputeTotals (Aver, LetGrade, Count, ClassTotal,
               NumA, NumB, NumC, NumD, NumE);
```

Finally, let us consider the function Average. This function receives three integer test scores, computes their average, and returns a real to the main program. The function could be

```
FUNCTION Average (Score1, Score2, Score3 : integer) : real;
  BEGIN
    Average := (Score1 + Score2 + Score3) / 3
  END;  {  of FUNCTION Average  }
```

This could be called from the main program by

```
Aver := Average(Score1, Score2, Score3);
```

Procedures for Output

A standard part of every program is to generate some output. Thus, when designing a program, the general task

3. Print results

can either have a single procedure written for it or it can be refined into subtasks and have a procedure written for each subtask. When writing procedures for output, only value parameters are needed. Since you are only printing results, it is not necessary to pass values back to the main program.

Writing procedures for output can be tedious because of the need for neat, attractive output. Be careful to use columns when appropriate, the center of the page, underlining, blank lines, spacing within a line (formatting), and appropriate messages.

Functions Versus Procedures

When should you use a function rather than a procedure in a program? A general rule is to think of a function as a construct that returns only one value; thus, a function would be used when a single value is required in the main program. Variable parameters can be used with function, but this is discouraged in good programming practices.

Using Stubs

As programs get longer and incorporate more subprograms, a technique frequently used to get the program running is *stub programming*. A stub program is a no-frills, simple version of what will be a final program. It does not contain details of output and full algorithm development. It does contain a rough version of each subprogram and all parameter lists. When the stub version runs, you know your logic is correct and values are appropriately being passed to and from subprograms. Then you can fill in necessary details to get a complete program.

Using Drivers

The main program is sometimes referred to as the *main driver*. When subprograms are used in a program, this driver can be modified to check subprograms in a sequential fashion. For example, suppose a main driver is

```
BEGIN  {  Main driver  }
  Initialize (Count, Sum);
  WHILE NOT eof DO
    BEGIN
      GetData (Num);
      ProcessData (Sum, Num, Count)
    END;
  PrintResults (Sum, Count)
END.
```

The first procedure could be checked by putting comment indicators around the rest of the program and temporarily adding a statement to print values of variables. Thus, you could run the following version:

```
BEGIN  {  Main driver  }
  Initialize (Count Sum);
  writeln ('Count is ', Count, '; Sum is ', Sum);
{ WHILE NOT eof DO
    BEGIN
      GetData (Num);
      ProcessData (Sum, Num, Count)
    END;
  PrintResults (Sum, Count)  }
END.
```

Once you are sure the first subprogram is running, you can remove the comment indicators and continue through the main driver to check successive programs.

Cohesive Subprograms

The cohesion of a subprogram is the degree to which the subprogram performs a single task. A subprogram that is developed in such a way is called a *cohesive subprogram*. As you use subprograms to implement a design based on modular development, you should always try to write cohesive subprograms.

The property of cohesion is not well defined. Subtask complexity varies in the minds of different programmers. In general, if the task is unclear, the corresponding subprogram will not be cohesive. When this happens, you should subdivide the task until a subsequent development allows cohesive subprograms.

To briefly illustrate the concept of cohesion, reconsider the first-level design of a problem at the beginning of this section. Step 3 of this design is

   3. Process grades for each student.

Clearly, this is not a well-defined task. Thus, if you were to write a subprogram for this task, the subprogram would not be cohesive. When we look at the subsequent development

   3. Process grades for each student
         WHILE NOT eof DO
        3.1 get a line of data
        3.2 compute average
        3.3 compute letter grade
        3.4 print data
        3.5 compute totals

we see that procedures to accomplish subtasks 3.1, 3.2, 3.3, and 3.4 would be cohesive because each subtask consists of a single task. The final subtask, compute totals, may or may not result in a cohesive subprogram. More information is needed before you can decide what is to be done at this step.

Procedural Abstraction

The purpose of using procedures is to simplify reasoning. During the design stage, as a problem is subdivided into tasks, the problem solver (you) should have to consider only what a procedure is to do and not be concerned about details of the procedure. Instead, the procedure name and comments at the beginning of the procedure should be sufficient to inform the user as to what the procedure does. Developing procedures in this manner is referred to as *procedural abstraction*.

Procedural abstraction is the first step in designing and writing a procedure. The list of parameters and comments about the action of the procedure should precede writing the procedure body. This forces clarity of thought and aids design. Using this method might perhaps cause you to discover that your design is not sufficient to solve the task and that redesigning is necessary. Therefore, you could reduce design errors and save time when writing code.

Procedural abstraction becomes especially important when teams work on a project. Each member of the writing team should be able to understand the purpose and use of procedures written by other team members without having to analyze the body of each procedure. This is analogous to the situation in which you use a predefined function without really understanding how the function works.

Procedural abstraction is perhaps best formalized in terms of preconditions and postconditions. Recall from Sections 5.6 and 6.6, a precondition is a comment which states precisely what is true before a certain action is taken and a postcondition states what is true after the action has been taken. Carefully written preconditions and postconditions used with procedures enhance the concept of procedural abstraction.

In summary, procedural abstraction means that, when writing or using procedures, you should think of them as single, clearly understood units that each accomplishes a specific task.

Encapsulation

Encapsulation can be thought of as the process of hiding the implementation details of a subprogram. This is what we do when we use a top-down design to solve a problem; we decide which tasks and subtasks are necessary to solve a problem without worrying about how the specific subtasks will be accomplished. In the sense of software engineering, encapsulation is what allows teams to work on a large system; it is only necessary to know what another team is doing, not how they are doing it.

Interface

Independent subprograms need to communicate with the main program and other subprograms. A formal statement of how such communication occurs is called the *interface* of the subprogram. This usually consists of comments at the beginning of a subprogram and includes all the information a programmer needs to use the subprogram. This information typically consists of

1. what is received by the subprogram when called
2. what task the subprogram performs
3. what is returned after the subprogram performs its task
4. how the subprogram is called

In this text, as explained in Section 7.3, our interface consists of the three-part documentation section

```
{  Given:    Statement of information sent to the program  }
{  Task:     Statement of task(s) to be performed           }
{  Return:   Statement of value(s) to be returned           }
```

How a subprogram is called is usually apparent from the identifiers listed in the subprogram heading.

Software Engineering

Perhaps the greatest difference between beginning students in computer science and "real world" programmers is how they perceive the need for documentation. Typically, beginning students want to make a program run; they view anything that delays this process as an impediment. Thus, some students consider using descriptive identifiers, writing variable dictionaries, describing a problem as part of program documentation, and using appropriate comments throughout a program as a nuisance.

In contrast, system designers and programmers who write code for a living often spend up to 50 percent of their time and effort on documentation. There are at least three reasons for this difference in perspective.

First, real programmers work on large, complex systems with highly developed logical paths. Without proper documentation, even the person who developed an algorithm will have difficulty following the logic six months later. Second, communication between and among teams is required as systems are developed. Complete, clear statements about what problems are and how they are being solved is essential. And third, programmers know they can develop algorithms and write subsequent code. They are trained so that problems of searching, sorting, and file manipulation are routine. Knowing that they can solve a problem thus allows them to devote more time and energy to documenting how the solution has been achieved.

To conclude this section, let's consider the following example.

■ EXAMPLE 8.2

Positive integers are considered to be perfect if the sum of the proper divisors equals the number. For example, 6, with proper divisors of 1, 2, and 3 is a perfect number. If the sum is greater than the number, the positive integer is abundant. If the sum is less than the number, the integer is deficient. Given these descriptions, let's consider the development of an interactive program that will get a positive integer as input, determine whether it is deficient, perfect, or abundant, and print an appropriate message.

A first-level pseudocode development for this is

1. Get the number
2. Sum the divisors
3. Print the results

A structure chart for this problem is given in Figure 8.13.

Module specifications for the main modules follow. Here, and in the remainder of the text, the module names are written as they would be in functions and procedures in code.

FIGURE 8.13
Structure chart for **PROGRAM**
PerfectNumbers

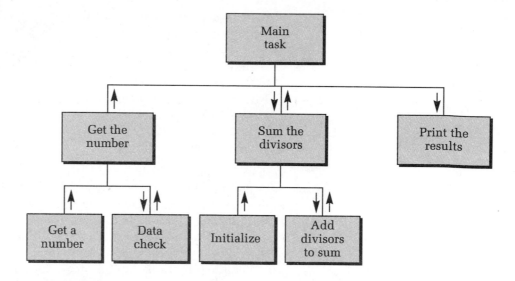

1. <u>GetNumber Module</u>
   Data received: None
   Information returned: Positive integer
   Logic: Get a number interactively.
          Use a **REPEAT . . . UNTIL** loop to guarantee good data.

2. <u>SumDivisors Module</u>
   Data received: Number
   Information returned: SumOfDivisors
   Logic: Initialize SumOfDivisors to zero.
          Use a **FOR** loop to check for divisors.
          In each case, add each divisor to SumOfDivisors.

3. <u>PrintResults Module</u>
   Data received: Number
                   SumOfDivisors
   Information returned: None
   Logic: Use nested **IF . . . THEN . . . ELSE** to print appropriate
          message.

A second-level pseudocode development is

1. Get the number
    1.1   get a number
    1.2   check for good data
2. Sum the divisors
    2.1   initialize sum of divisors to zero
    2.2 **FOR** each divisor less than the number, add divisor to sum of
         divisor
3. Print the results
    3.1 **IF** SumOfDivisors is less than Number **THEN**
         deficient message
        ELSE IF SumOfDivisor equals Number **THEN**
         perfect message
        ELSE
         abundant message

The main program for this would be

```
GetNumber (Number);
SumDivisors (Number, SumOfDivisors);
PrintResults (Number, SumOfDivisors);
```

The complete program for this is

```
PROGRAM PerfectNumbers (input, output);

VAR
  Number,                              {  Number to be examined       }
  SumOfDivisors : integer;             {  Sum of divisors of number   }

{******************************************************************* }

PROCEDURE GetNumber (VAR Number : integer);

  {  Given:    Nothing                                               }
  {  Task:     Read a positive integer entered from the keyboard }
  {  Return:   The number read                                       }

  BEGIN
    REPEAT
      writeln ('Enter a positive integer and press <RETURN>.');
      readln (Number)
    UNTIL Number > 0
  END;  {  of PROCEDURE GetNumber  }

{******************************************************************* }

PROCEDURE SumDivisors (Number : integer;
                       VAR SumOfDivisors : integer);

  {  Given:    A positive integer, Number                            }
  {  Task:     Sum the divisors of Number                            }
  {  Return:   SumOfDivisors of Number                               }

  VAR
    TrialDivisor : integer;

  BEGIN
    SumOfDivisors := 0;
    FOR TrialDivisor := 1 TO Number DIV 2 DO
      IF Number MOD TrialDivisor = 0 THEN
        SumOfDivisors := SumOfDivisors + TrialDivisor
  END;  {  of PROCEDURE SumDivisors  }

{******************************************************************* }

PROCEDURE PrintResults (Number, SumOfDivisors : integer);

  {  Given:    Number and SumOfDivisors                              }
  {  Task:     Print a message that indicates whether the integer}
  {            read was deficient, perfect, or abundant             }
  {  Return:   Nothing                                               }

  BEGIN
    writeln;
    write ('The number ', Number, ' is ');
    IF SumOfDivisors < Number THEN
      writeln ('deficient.')
    ELSE IF SumOfDivisors = Number THEN
      writeln ('perfect.')
```

```
        ELSE
          writeln ('abundant.');
        writeln; writeln
      END;  {  of PROCEDURE PrintResults  }


{**************************************************************** }

BEGIN  {  Main program  }
  GetNumber (Number);
  SumDivisors (Number, SumOfDivisors);
  PrintResults (Number, SumOfDivisors)
END.  {  of main program  }
```

Sample runs of this program produce

```
    Enter a positive integer and press <RETURN>.
    ?-9
    Enter a positive integer and press <RETURN>.
    ?6

    The number 6 is perfect.


    Enter a positive integer and press <RETURN>.
    ?100

    The number 100 is abundant.


    Enter a positive integer and press <RETURN>.
    ?28

    The number 28 is perfect.


    Enter a positive integer and press <RETURN>.
    ?50

    The number 50 is deficient.


    Enter a positive integer and press <RETURN>.
    ?35

    The number 35 is deficient.
```

Exercises 8.2

1. Discuss whether value parameters or variable parameters should be used in a procedure to

   a. initialize variables.

   b. get data.

   c. print results.

2. Write a test program that utilizes subprograms for solving the problem of reading integers from a data file, computing their sum and average, and printing results. The main program should be along the lines of

```
BEGIN
   Initialize (Count, Total);
   WHILE NOT eof DO
      GetData (Count, Total);
```

```
Average := FindAverage (Count, Total);
PrintHeading;
PrintResults (Count, Total, Average)
END.
```

3. Suppose the pseudocode for solving a problem is

   1. Initialize variables
   2. Print a heading
   3. **WHILE** Flag = **true DO**
      3.1 get new data
      3.2 perform computations
      3.3 increment counter
      3.4 check Flag condition
   4. Print results

   Show how subprograms could be used to design a program to implement this algorithm.

4. Write a function for each of the following tasks.

   a. Given positive integer a and any integer b (positive, negative, or zero), compute a^b.

   b. Given real numbers a, b, and c, compute the discriminant ($b^2 - 4ac$).

5. You have been asked to write a program for the Sleep Cheap motel chain. Each line of the data file contains information for one customer. This information consists of number of nights occupancy (integer), room rate (real), and telephone charges (real). Your program should print a statement for each customer and keep totals for the number of customers served, total room charges, and total telephone charges.

   Assume the pseudocode for solving this problem is

   1. Initialize variables
   2. **WHILE NOT eof DO**
      2.1 get customer data
      2.2 perform computations
      2.3 print statement
      2.4 add totals
   3. Print summary

   a. Design a program to implement this algorithm.

   b. Write a procedure or function for each statement of the algorithm.

6. Write a complete program to solve the grading problem posed at the beginning of this section.

7. Modify the program of Example 8.2 to allow the user to check several numbers without having to rerun the program each time.

■ ■ ■ ■

■ 8.3
Forward Reference and Nesting

OBJECTIVES
- to be able to use forward reference for multiple subprograms
- to be able to use multiple subprograms in a program
- to be able to use nested subprograms in a program
- to understand the scope of identifiers when using multiple and nested subprograms

By now you should be familiar with the important concepts of procedures and functions and relatively comfortable with using them for the modular design of a program. As you examined material in Chapter 7 and in the first two sections of this chapter, you may have noticed that use of subprograms was restricted to the main program calling procedures or functions and procedures or functions calling previously declared subprograms. In this section we will examine more sophisticated uses of subprograms, specifically, forward reference and nesting.

Subprograms That Call Other Subprograms

Sections 7.2, 7.3, and 7.4 included brief discussions concerning the use of multiple procedures and functions. In review, suppose a program has two functions (**FUNCTION** A and **FUNCTION** B) and a procedure (**PROCEDURE** C). Schematically, this could be envisioned as shown in Figure 8.14.

FIGURE 8.14
Multiple subprograms

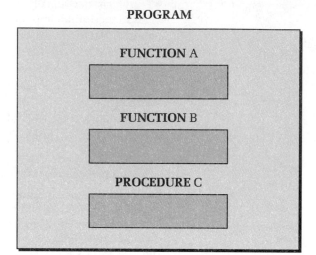

Thus far we have been able to have a subprogram call only subprograms that have been previously declared. For example, in the schematic, **FUNCTION** B could call **FUNCTION** A and **PROCEDURE** C could call either **FUNCTION** A or **FUNCTION** B. Any other calls would result in errors.

Forward Reference

These restrictions on function and procedure calls impose limitations on program development. There may be times when it is either desirable or necessary for a subprogram to call another subprogram that appears later in the declaration section. This can be accomplished by a *forward reference.*

A forward reference is achieved by listing the function or procedure heading with all parameters followed by the reserved word **FORWARD**. If a function is to be forward referenced, the function type should be included as part of the heading listed; for example,

```
FUNCTION B (X : real) : real; FORWARD;
```

When the function or procedure is declared later in the program, the parameter list and function type are omitted. To illustrate, consider

```
FUNCTION B (X : real) : real; FORWARD;

FUNCTION A (Ch : char) : char;
  BEGIN
     .
     .
     .
  END;  {  of FUNCTION A  }
```

```
FUNCTION B;
  BEGIN
        .
        .
        .
  END;  {  of FUNCTION B  }
```

In this case, **FUNCTION** A can call **FUNCTION** B because **FUNCTION** B has been forward referenced. **FUNCTION** B can call **FUNCTION** A because **FUNCTION** A is declared before **FUNCTION** B.

Forward reference is necessary to list subprograms in a particular order to make a program more readable. A programmer may, for instance, choose to list functions in order of complexity from least complex to most complex or from most complex to least complex. Either listing might necessitate a forward reference. Also, a program design may require a forward reference for some subprograms. If **FUNCTION** A has an option that calls **FUNCTION** B and **FUNCTION** B has an option that calls **FUNCTION** A, one of them must have a forward reference.

In summary, when using forward reference, you should

1. List all parameters and function types when the forward reference is made.
2. Use the reserved word **FORWARD** as a statement when the forward reference is made.
3. Omit the parameter list when the forward-referenced subprogram is written.
4. Use a comment to indicate what the parameter list is for the forward-referenced subprogram.

STYLE TIP
■ ■ ■ ■ ■ ■ ■ ■ ■ ■ ■ ■ ■

When using a forward reference, use a line comment to indicate parameters when the subprogram is developed.

```
FUNCTION First (S1,S2,S3:integer):integer;  FORWARD;
        .
        .
        .

FUNCTION Second (<parameter list>):<return type>;
  BEGIN
        .
        .
        .
  END;  {  of FUNCTION Second  }

FUNCTION First;  {  (S1,S2,S3:integer):integer  }
                 └─────────────────────────────┘
                           comment here
```

Nesting

Since a subprogram can contain the same sections as the main program, the declaration section of a function or procedure can contain functions or procedures. When this occurs, the subprograms are said to be nested. Subprograms can be nested to any level desired by the programmer. However, as we've seen, several levels of nesting tend to make programs difficult to follow and debug. If the nesting is too complicated, you should redesign the program.

Nested subprograms may be represented as shown in Figure 8.15.

FIGURE 8.15
Nested subprograms

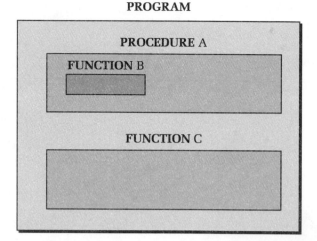

This schematic representation of nesting assists us in understanding the scope of various identifiers. Recall, identifiers are restricted to the block (and all subblocks) in which they are declared. To illustrate, suppose variables are declared in a program as shown in Figure 8.16. X, which is declared in the main program, can be accessed by any subprogram in this program. In particular, even the nested function, **FUNCTION** B, could use values in X from

FIGURE 8.16
Variables in nested subprograms

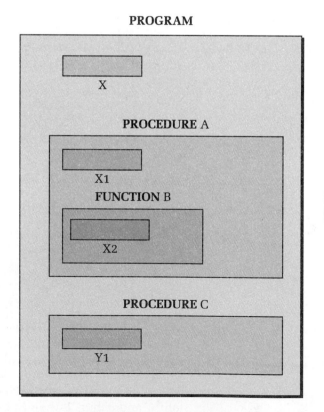

the main program. However, X1 can only be used by **PROCEDURE** A and **FUNCTION** B. The variables used in this illustration and their scope are shown in Table 8.2.

TABLE 8.2
Scope of variables for nested subprograms

Variable	Scope (can be accessed by)
X	Main Program **PROCEDURE** A **FUNCTION** B **PROCEDURE** C
X1	**PROCEDURE** A **FUNCTION** B
X2	**FUNCTION** B
Y1	**PROCEDURE** C

We conclude the discussion on nesting subprograms with an example that illustrates nested functions. The principles behind it apply to any combination of nested subprograms and to any level of nesting.

■ **EXAMPLE 8.3**

Write a function TotalCharge to compute the total charge for guests of a motel chain. You may assume that RoomRate and TaxRate have been defined in a **CONST** section of the main program and that NumNights has been assigned an appropriate value. The function will be called by

```
AmountDue := TotalCharge(NumNights);
```

For purposes of this example, the tax will be computed by a nested function Tax. Thus, we have

```
FUNCTION TotalCharge (NumNights : integer) : real;

  VAR
    RoomCharge, RoomTax : real;

  FUNCTION Tax (RoomCharge : real) : real;
    BEGIN
      TAX := RoomCharge * TaxRate
    END; {  of FUNCTION Tax  }

  BEGIN  {  TotalCharge  }
    RoomCharge := NumNights * RoomRate;
    RoomTax := Tax(RoomCharge);
    TotalCharge := RoomCharge + RoomTax
  END;  {  of FUNCTION TotalCharge  }
```

■   ■

Figure 8.17 is a schematic representation of the constants, variables, and functions used in Example 8.3.

FIGURE 8.17
Schematic for Example 8.3

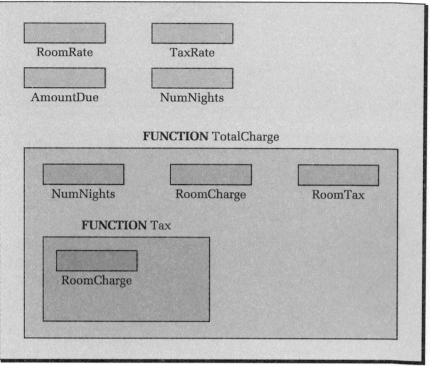

Exercises 8.3

1. Explain why forward reference could be necessary in a program.

2. Write a test program to illustrate what happens when one subprogram calls another subprogram that is listed later and a forward reference is not made.

3. Discuss the scope of identifiers in nested subprograms.

4. Find and correct all errors in each of the following program segments.

```
a. FUNCTION AddOne (A : integer) : integer;
   BEGIN
     AddOne := A + 1
   END;  {  of FUNCTION AddOne  }
   PROCEDURE AddTwo (VAR B : integer);
   BEGIN
     B := AddOne(B);
     B := AddOne(B)
   END;  {  of PROCEDURE AddTwo  }
b. PROCEDURE AddTwo (VAR B : integer);
   BEGIN
     B := AddOne(B);
     B := AddOne(B)
   END;  {  of PROCEDURE AddTwo  }
   FUNCTION AddOne (A : integer) : integer;
   BEGIN
     AddOne := A + 1
   END;  {  of FUNCTION AddOne  }
```

```
  c. FUNCTION AddOne (A : integer) : integer; FORWARD;
     PROCEDURE AddTwo (VAR B : integer);
        BEGIN
          B := AddOne(B);
          B := AddOne(B)
        END;  {  of PROCEDURE AddTwo  }
     FUNCTION AddTwo (A : integer) : integer;
        BEGIN
          AddOne := A + 1
        END; {  of FUNCTION AddOne  }
  d. FUNCTION AddOne (A : integer) : integer; FORWARD;
     PROCEDURE AddTwo (VAR B : integer);
        BEGIN
          B := AddOne(B);
          B := AddOne(B)
        END;  {  of PROCEDURE AddTwo  }
     FUNCTION AddOne;
        BEGIN
          AddOne := A + 1
        END;  {  of FUNCTION AddOne  }
  e. FUNCTION AddOne (A : integer) : integer; FORWARD;
     PROCEDURE AddTwo (Var B : integer);
        BEGIN
          B := AddOne(B);
          B := AddOne(B)
        END;   {  of PROCEDURE AddTwo  }
     FUNCTION AddOne;  {  (A : integer) : integer  }
        BEGIN
          AddOne := A + 1
        END;  {  of FUNCTION AddOne  }
```

5. Give a schematic representation and indicate the scope of identifiers for the following subprograms contained in **PROGRAM** ExerciseFive.

```
PROGRAM ExerciseFive (input, output);

VAR
  X, Y : real;
  Ch : char;

PROCEDURE A (VAR X1 : real;
             Ch1 : char);
  VAR
    J : integer;
  FUNCTION Inner (M : integer;
                  Y1 : real) : real;
     BEGIN
       .
       .
     END;  {  of FUNCTION Inner  }
   BEGIN  {  PROCEDURE A  }
     .
     .
   END;  {  of PROCEDURE A  }

PROCEDURE B (X1 : real;
             VAR Ch2 : char);
  BEGIN  {  PROCEDURE B  }
    .
    .
  END;  {  of PROCEDURE B  }
```

6. Consider the block structure shown in Figure 8.18 for **PROGRAM** ExerciseSix.

   a. Indicate which subprograms can be called from the main program.

   b. Indicate all appropriate calls from one subprogram to another subprogram.

   c. List three inappropriate calls and explain why they cannot be made.

FIGURE 8.18

PROGRAM ExerciseSix

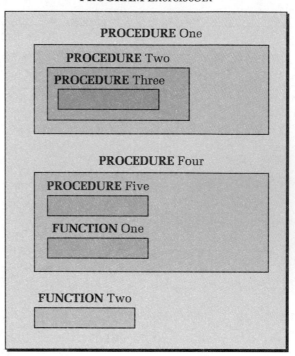

7. Consider the following program.

```
PROGRAM ExerciseSeven (input, output);

VAR
  A, B, Num : integer;

FUNCTION MaxPower (A1, B1 : integer) : integer;
  VAR
    Prod, K : integer;

  PROCEDURE Sort (VAR A2, B2 : integer);
    VAR
      Temp : integer;
    BEGIN  {  PROCEDURE Sort  }
      IF B2 < A2 THEN
        BEGIN
          Temp := A2;
          A2 := B2;
          B2 := Temp
        END  {  of IF...THEN  }
    END;  {  of PROCEDURE Sort  }
  BEGIN  {  FUNCTION MaxPower  }
    Sort (A1, B1);
    Prod := A1;
    FOR K := 1 to B1 - 1 DO
      Prod := Prod * A1;
    MaxPower := Prod
  END;  {  of FUNCTION MaxPower  }
```

```
BEGIN  {  Main program  }
  read (A, B);
  Num := MaxPower (A, B);
  writeln (Num)
END.  {  of main program  }
```

a. Give a schematic representation and indicate the scope of identifiers.

b. What is the output if the numbers read for A and B are 5 and 3, respectively?

c. Explain what this program does for positive integers A and B.

■ ■ ■ ■

■ 8.4 Recursion

OBJECTIVES

■ to understand how recursion can be used to solve a problem
■ to be able to use recursion to solve a problem
■ to understand what happens in memory when recursion is used

In your previous work with subprograms, you have seen instances in which one subprogram calls another subprogram. Let's now consider the situation in which a subprogram calls itself.

Recursive Processes

Many problems can be solved by having a subtask call itself as part of the solution. This process is called *recursion;* subprograms that call themselves are *recursive subprograms.* Recursion is frequently used in mathematics. Consider, for example, the definition of $n!$ (n factorial) for a nonnegative integer n. This is defined by

$$0! = 1$$
$$1! = 1$$
for $n > 1$, $n! = n * (n - 1)!$
Thus, $6! = 6 * 5!$
$$= 6 * 5 * 4!$$
$$= 6 * 5 * 4 * 3!$$
$$= 6 * 5 * 4 * 3 * 2!$$
$$= 6 * 5 * 4 * 3 * 2 * 1$$

Another well-known mathematical example is the Fibonacci sequence. In this sequence, the first term is 1, the second term is 1, and each successive term is defined to be the sum of the previous two. More precisely, the Fibonacci sequence

$$a_1, a_2, a_3, \ldots, a_n$$

is defined by

$$a_1 = 1$$
$$a_2 = 1$$
$$a_n = a_{n-1} + a_{n-2} \text{ for } n > 2$$

This generates the sequence

$$1, 1, 2, 3, 5, 8, 13, 21, \ldots$$

In both examples, note that the general term was defined by using the previous term or terms.

What applications does recursion have for computing? In many instances, a procedure or function can be written to accomplish a recursive task. If the language allows a subprogram to call itself (Pascal does, FORTRAN does not), it is sometimes easier to solve a problem by this process.

■ EXAMPLE 8.4

As an example of a recursive function, consider the sigma function—denoted by $\sum_{i=1}^{n} i$ —which is used to compute the sum of integers from 1 to n.

```
FUNCTION Sigma (N : integer) : integer;
   BEGIN
      IF N <= 1 THEN
         Sigma := N
      ELSE
         Sigma := N + Sigma(N-1)
      END;  {  of FUNCTION Sigma  }
```

To illustrate how this recursive function works, suppose it is called from the main program by a statement such as

```
Sum := Sigma(5);
```

In the **ELSE** portion of the function, we first have

```
Sigma := 5 + Sigma(4)
```

At this stage, note that Sigma(4) must be computed. This call produces

```
Sigma := 4 + Sigma(3)
```

If we envision these recursive calls as occurring on levels, we have

```
1. Sigma := 5 + Sigma(4)
   2. Sigma := 4 + Sigma(3)
      3. Sigma := 3 + Sigma(2)
         4. Sigma := 2 + Sigma(1)
            5. Sigma := 1
```

Now the end of the recursion has been reached and the steps are reversed for assigning values. Thus, we have

```
            5. Sigma := 1
         4. Sigma := 2 + 1
      3. Sigma := 3 + 3
   2. Sigma := 4 + 6
1. Sigma := 5 + 10
```

Thus, Sigma is assigned the value 15.

■   ■

Before analyzing what happens in memory when recursive subprograms are used, some comments about recursion are in order.

1. The recursive process must have a well-defined termination. This termination is referred to as a *stopping state*. In Example 8.4, the stopping state was

```
IF N <= 1 THEN
   Sigma := N
```

2. The recursive process must have well-defined steps that lead to the stopping state. These steps are usually called *recursive steps*. In Example 8.4, these steps were

```
Sigma := N + Sigma(N-1)
```

Note that, in the recursive call, the parameter is simplified toward the stopping state.

What Really Happens?

What really happens when a subprogram calls itself? First, we need to examine the idea of a *stack*. Imagine a stack as a pile of cafeteria trays: the last one put on the stack is the first one taken off the stack. This is what occurs in memory when a recursive subprogram is used. Each call to the subprogram can be thought of as adding a tray to the stack. In the previous function, the first call creates a level of recursion that contains the partially complete assignment statement

```
Sigma := 5 + Sigma(4)
```

This corresponds to the first tray in the stack. In reality, this is an area in memory waiting to receive a value for 5 + Sigma(4). At this level, operation is temporarily suspended until a value is returned for Sigma(4). However, the call Sigma(4) produces

```
Sigma := 4 + Sigma(3)
```

This corresponds to the second tray on the stack. As before, operation is temporarily suspended until Sigma(3) is computed. This process is repeated until finally the last call, Sigma(1), returns a value.

At this stage, the stack may be envisioned as illustrated in Figure 8.19. Since different areas of memory are used for each successive call to Sigma, each variable Sigma represents a different memory location.

FIGURE 8.19
Stack for **FUNCTION** Sigma

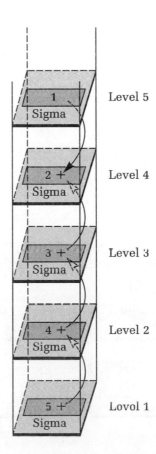

Level 5

Level 4

Level 3

Level 2

Lovol 1

The levels of recursion that have been temporarily suspended can now be completed in reverse order. Thus, since the assignment

```
Sigma(1) := 1
```

has been made, then

```
Sigma(2) := 2 + Sigma(1)
```

becomes

```
Sigma(2) := 2 + 1
```

This then permits

```
Sigma(3) := 3 + Sigma(2)
```

to become

```
Sigma(3) := 3 + 3
```

Continuing until the first level of recursion has been reached, we obtain

```
Sigma := 5 + 10
```

This "unstacking" is illustrated in Figure 8.20.

FIGURE 8.20
"Unstacking" **FUNCTION** Sigma

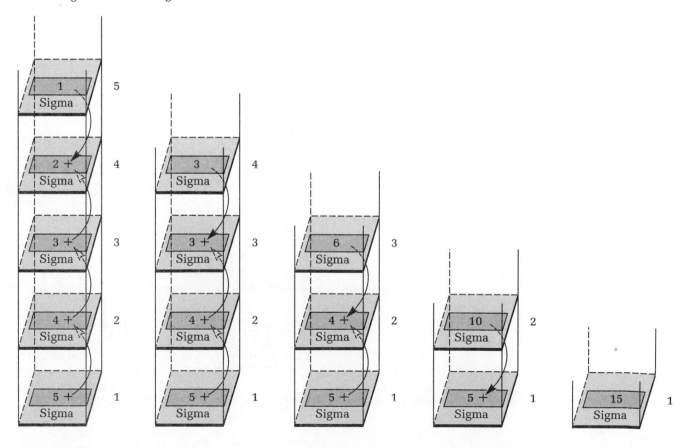

■ **EXAMPLE 8.5**

Let's now consider a second example of recursion. In this example, a procedure is used recursively to print a line of text in reverse order. Assume the line of text has only one period (and this is at the end of the line); the stopping state is when the character read is a period. Using the data line

This is a short sentence.

a complete program is

```
PROGRAM LineInReverse (input, output);

{    This program uses a procedure recursively to print a line   }
{    of text in reverse.                                         }

{*****************************************************************}

PROCEDURE StackItUp;

{  Given:    Nothing                                              }
{  Task:     Read one character; if a period, print it;  if not, }
{                 call this same procedure                        }
{  Return:   Nothing                                             }

VAR
  OneChar : char;

BEGIN
  read (OneChar);
  IF OneChar <> '.' THEN
    StackItUp;
  write (OneChar)
END;  {  of PROCEDURE StackItUp  }

{*****************************************************************}

BEGIN  {  Main program  }
  StackItUp;
  writeln
END.  {  of main program  }
```

Output from this program is

    .ecnetnes trohs a si sihT

■   ■

In Example 8.5, as each character is read, it is placed on a stack until the period is encountered. At that time, the period is printed and then, as each level in the stack is passed through in reverse order, the character on that level is printed. The stack created while this program is running is illustrated in Figure 8.21.

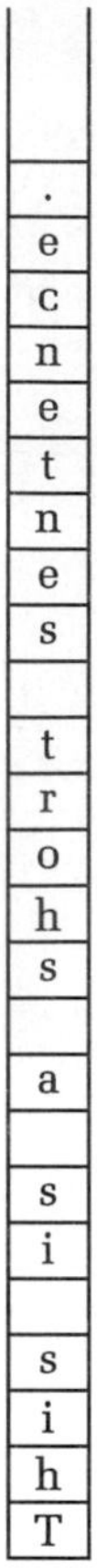

FIGURE 8.21
Stack created by **PROCEDURE**
StackItUp

```
.
e
c
n
e
t
n
e
s

t
r
o
h
s

a

s
i

s
i
h
T
```

■ EXAMPLE 8.6

Let's now consider another example of a recursive function. Recall, the factorial of a nonnegative integer, n, is defined to be

$$1 * 2 * 3 * \ldots * (n - 1) * n$$

and is denoted by $n!$. Thus,

$$4! = 1 * 2 * 3 * 4$$

For the sake of completing this definition, $1! = 1$ and $0! = 1$. A recursive function to compute $n!$ is

```
FUNCTION Factorial (N : integer) : integer;
  BEGIN
    IF N = 0 THEN
      Factorial := 1
    ELSE
      Factorial := N * Factorial(N-1)
  END;  {  of FUNCTION Factorial  }
```

If this function is called from the main program by a statement such as

```
Product := Factorial(4);
```

we envision the levels of recursion as

```
1.  Factorial := 4 * Factorial(3)
  2.  Factorial := 3 * Factorial(2)
    3.  Factorial := 2 * Factorial(1)
```

```
    4.  Factorial := 1 * Factorial(0)
    5.  Factorial(0) := 1
```

Successive values would then be assigned in reverse order to produce

```
    5.  Factorial(0) := 1
    4.  Factorial := 1 * 1
  3.  Factorial := 2 * 1
 2.  Factorial := 3 * 2
1.  Factorial := 4 * 6
```

■   ■

Why Use Recursion?

You may have noticed that the previous recursive functions Sigma and Factorial could have been written using iteration rather than recursion. For example, we could write

```
FUNCTION SigmaByIteration (N : integer) : integer;

  VAR
    J, Sum : integer;

  BEGIN
    Sum := 0;
    FOR J := 1 TO N DO
      Sum := Sum + J;
    SigmaByIteration := Sum
  END;  {  of FUNCTION SigmaByIteration  }
```

It is not coincidental that the recursive function Sigma can be rewritten using the iterative function SigmaByIteration. In fact, any recursive subprogram can be rewritten in a nonrecursive manner. Furthermore, recursion generally requires more memory than equivalent iteration and is usually difficult for beginning programmers to comprehend. Why then do we use recursion? There are several reasons. First, a recursive thought process may be the best way to think about solving the problem. If so, it naturally leads to using recursion in a program. A classical example of this is the Towers of Hanoi problem, which requires a sequence of moving disks on pegs. This problem is fully developed as our next example.

Second, some recursive solutions can be very short compared to iterative solutions. Iterative versions of recursive procedures may require an explicit stack and unusual coding. In some instances, use of a recursive algorithm can be very simple, and some programmers consider recursive solutions elegant because of this simplicity.

Third and finally, subsequent work in Pascal can be aided by recursion. For example, one of the fastest sorting algorithms available, the quick sort, uses recursion (see Chapter 14). Also, recursion is a valuable tool when working with dynamic data structures (Chapter 16).

Having now seen several reasons why recursion should be used, let's consider when recursion should not be used. If a solution to a problem is easier to obtain using iteration rather than recursion, it is usually preferable to use the iterative solution. A nonrecursive solution may require less execution time and use memory more efficiently. Using the previous examples, the recursive function Factorial should probably be written using iteration, but the nth term of the Fibonacci sequence would typically be found using recursion because a nonrecursive solution is difficult to write.

In summary, recursion is a powerful and necessary programming technique. You should therefore become familiar with using recursive subprograms, be able to recognize when a recursive algorithm is appropriate, and be able to implement a recursive subprogram.

■ **EXAMPLE 8.7**

A classic problem called the Towers of Hanoi problem involves three pegs and disks as depicted in Figure 8.22.

FIGURE 8.22
Towers of Hanoi problem

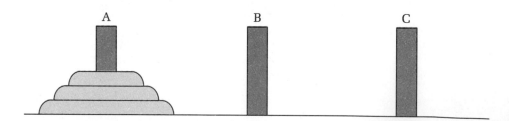

The object is to move the disks from peg A to peg C. The rules are that only one disk may be moved at a time and a larger disk can never be placed on a smaller disk. (Legend has it that this problem—but with 64 disks—was given to monks in an ancient monastery. The world was to come to an end when all 64 disks were in order on peg C.)

To see how this problem can be solved, let's start with a one-disk problem. In this case, merely move the disk from peg A to peg C. The two-disk problem is almost as easy. Move disk 1 to peg B, disk 2 to peg C, and use the solution to the one-disk problem to move disk 1 to peg C. (Note the reference to the previous solution.)

Things get a little more interesting with a three-disk problem. First, use the two-disk solution to get the top two disks in order on peg B. Then move disk 3 to peg C. Finally, use a two-disk solution to move the two disks from peg B to peg C. Again, notice how a reference was made to the previous solution. By now you should begin to see the pattern for solving the problem. However, before generalizing, let's first look at the four-disk problem. As expected, the solution is to

1. use the three-disk solution to move three disks to peg B.
2. move disk four to peg C.
3. use the three-disk solution to move the three disks from peg B to peg C.

This process can be generalized as a solution to the problem for n disks.

1. use the $(n - 1)$-disk solution to move $(n - 1)$ disks to peg B.
2. move disk n to peg C.
3. use the $(n - 1)$-disk solution to move $(n - 1)$ disks from peg B to peg C.

This general solution is recursive in nature because each particular solution depends on a solution for the previous number of disks. This process continues until there is only one disk to move. This corresponds to the stopping state when a recursive program is written to solve the problem. A complete interactive program that prints out each step in the solution to this problem is

```
PROGRAM TowersOfHanoi (input, output);

{   This program uses recursion to solve the classic  Towers     }
{   of Hanoi problem.                                            }

VAR
  NumDisks : integer;

{*********************************************************************** }

PROCEDURE ListTheMoves (NumDisks : integer;
                        StartPeg, LastPeg, SparePeg : char);

  {  Given:    The number of disks to move, the initial peg       }
  {                 StartPeg, the working peg SparePeg, and       }
  {                 the destination peg LastPeg                    }
  {  Task:     Move NumDisks from StartPeg to LastPeg using       }
  {                 SparePeg; involves recursive calls            }
  {  Return:   Nothing                                           }

  BEGIN
    IF NumDisks = 1 THEN
      writeln ('Move a disk from ', StartPeg, ' to ', LastPeg)
    ELSE
      BEGIN
        ListTheMoves (NumDisks-1, StartPeg, SparePeg, LastPeg);
        writeln ('Move a disk from ', StartPeg, ' to ', LastPeg);
        ListTheMoves (NumDisks-1, SparePeg, LastPeg, StartPeg)
      END { of ELSE option  }
  END; { of PROCEDURE ListTheMove  }

{*********************************************************************** }

BEGIN { Main program  }
  write ('How many disks in this game?  ');
  readln (NumDisks);
  writeln;
  writeln ('Start with ', NumDisks, ' disks on Peg A');
  writeln;
  writeln ('Then proceed as follows:');
  writeln;
  ListTheMoves (NumDisks, 'A', 'C', 'B')
END. { of main program  }
```

Sample runs for three-disk and four-disk problems produce the following:

```
How many disks in this game?  3

Start with 3 disks on Peg A

Then proceed as follows:

Move a disk from A to C
Move a disk from A to B
Move a disk from C to B
Move a disk from A to C
Move a disk from B to A
Move a disk from B to C
Move a disk from A to C
```

```
How many disks in this game?   4

Start with 4 disks on Peg A

Then proceed as follows:

Move a disk from A to B
Move a disk form A to C
Move a disk from B to C
Move a disk from A to B
Move a disk from C to A
Move a disk from C to B
Move a disk from A to B
Move a disk from A to C
Move a disk from B to C
Move a disk from B to A
Move a disk from C to A
Move a disk from B to C
Move a disk from A to B
Move a disk from A to C
Move a disk from B to C
```

Exercises 8.4

1. Explain what is wrong with the following recursive function:

```
FUNCTION Recur (X : real) : real;
  BEGIN
    Recur := Recur(X / 2)
  END;
```

2. Write a recursive function that reverses the digits of a positive integer. If the integer used as input is 1234, output should be 4321.

3. Consider the following recursive function:

```
FUNCTION A (X : real;
            N : integer) : real;
  BEGIN
    IF N = 0 THEN
      A := 1.0
    ELSE
      A := X * A(X, N-1)
  END; {  of FUNCTION A  }
```

   a. What would the value of Y be for each of
      i. Y := A(3.0, 2);
      ii. Y := A(2.0, 3);
      iii. Y := A(4.0, 4);
      iv. Y := A(1.0, 6);
   b. Explain what standard computation is performed by **FUNCTION** A.
   c. Rewrite **FUNCTION** A using iteration rather than recursion.

4. Recall the Fibonacci sequence
   1, 1, 2, 3, 5, 8, 13, 21, . . .
   where for $n > 2$ the nth term is the sum of the previous two. Write a recursive function to compute the nth term in the Fibonacci sequence.

5. Write a function that uses iteration to compute $n!$.

This chapter ending program is an updated version of the program from Chapter 6. This version is interactive and includes

- a bad data check
- a sentinel value for input
- procedures and functions to accomplish subtasks

Typical output for the integer 17 is

```
Enter a positive integer, <-999> to quit.
?17


-------------------------------------------------

               The number is 17.  The prime numbers
               less than or equal to 17 are:

                            2
                            3
                            5
                            7
                           11
                           13
                           17
Enter a positive integer, <-999> to quit.
?-999
```

A first-level pseudocode development for this problem is

1. Get a number
   WHILE MoreData **DO**
2. Examine the number
3. Get a number

A second-level development is

1. Get a number
   1.1 Get entry from the keyboard
   1.2 Check for valid entry
   WHILE MoreData **DO**
2. Examine the number
   IF Number is 1 **THEN**
   2.1 print a message for one
   ELSE
   2.2 print primes less than Number
3. Get a number
   3.1 Get entry from keyboard
   3.2 Check for valid entry

Step 2.2 can be refined to

2.2 print primes less than Number
   2.2.1 print a message
   2.2.2 check for primes less than or equal to Number

Step 2.2.2 can be further developed to

2.2.2 check for primes less than or equal to Number
   FOR K := 2 **TO** Number **DO**
   2.2.2.1 check to see if K is prime
   2.2.2.2 If K is prime **THEN** print K in list of primes

Thus, the complete pseudocode development is

1. Get a number
    1.1   Get entry from the keyboard
    1.2   Check for valid entry
    WHILE MoreData **DO**
2. Examine the number
    IF Number is 1 **THEN**
    2.1   print a message for one
    ELSE
    2.2   print primes less than Number
          2.2.1   print a message
          2.2.2   check for primes less than or equal to Number
                  FOR K := 2 **TO** Number **DO**
                  2.2.2.1   check to see if K is prime
                  2.2.2.2   **IF** K is prime **THEN** print K in list of primes
3. Get a number
    3.1   Get entry from the keyboard
    3.2   Check for valid entry

With this pseudocode development, the main program would be

```
BEGIN  {  Main program  }
  GetANumber (Num, MoreData);
  WHILE MoreData DO
    BEGIN
      IF Num = 1 THEN
        PrintOneMessage
      ELSE
        BEGIN
          PrintMessage (Num);
          ListAllPrimes (Num)
        END;  {  of ELSE option  }
      GetANumber (Num, MoreData)
    END {  of WHILE loop  }
END;  {  of main program  }
```

Procedures would be written for each of the following modules:

    GetANumber
    PrintOneMessage
    PrintMessage
    ListAllPrimes

Module specifications for these modules are

1. GetANumber Module
    Data received: None
    Information returned: Number
                         Boolean flag MoreData
    Logic: Get an entry from the keyboard.
           Make sure the entry is valid or the sentinel value for terminat-
           ing the process.
           If the entry is the sentinel value, set the **boolean** variable More-
           Data to false.
2. PrintOneMessage Module
    Data received: None
    Information returned: None
    Logic: Print a message about one.

3. PrintMessage Module
   Data received: Number
   Information returned: None
   Logic: Print a heading for the list of primes.

4. ListAllPrimes Module
   Data received: Number
   Information returned: None
   Logic: For each integer less than or equal to Number, check to see if it
          is prime.
          If it is prime, print it in a list of primes.

A complete program for this problem is

```
PROGRAM ListPrimes (input, output);

{  This program is an enhancement of the program in Chapter 6.   }
{  This version features:                                        }
{     a. a bad data check                                        }
{     b. a sentinel value for input                             }
{     c. procedures and functions to accomplish tasks           }

CONST
  Skip = ' ';
  Dashes = '---------------------------------------------------';

VAR
  Num : integer;
  MoreData : boolean;

{*****************************************************************}

PROCEDURE GetANumber (VAR Num : integer;
                      VAR MoreData : boolean);

  {  Given:   Nothing                                            }
  {  Task:    Read an integer entered from the keyboard          }
  {  Return:  The integer read                                   }

  BEGIN
    REPEAT
      writeln ('Enter a positive integer, <-999> to quit.');
      readln (Num);
      MoreData := Num <> -999
    UNTIL (Num > 0) OR (Num = -999)
  END;  {  of PROCEDURE GetANumber  }

{*****************************************************************}

PROCEDURE PrintOneMessage;

  {  Given:   Nothing                                            }
  {  Task:    Print a message for 1                              }
  {  Return:  Nothing                                            }

  BEGIN
    writeln;
    writeln (Skip:10, Dashes);
    writeln;
    writeln (Skip:20, '1 is not prime by definition ');
    writeln
  END;  {  of PROCEDURE PrintOneMessage  }

{*****************************************************************}
```

```
PROCEDURE PrintMessage (Num : integer);

  {  Given:    The integer read                                    }
  {  Task:     Print a heading for the output                      }
  {  Return:   Nothing                                             }

  BEGIN
    writeln;
    writeln (Skip:10, Dashes);
    writeln;
    writeln (Skip:20, 'The number is ', Num,'.  The prime numbers')
    writeln (Skip:20, 'less than or equal to ', Num, ' are:');
    writeln
  END;  {  of PROCEDURE PrintMessage  }
```

```
{************************************************************** }
```

```
FUNCTION StillChecking (Candidate, Divisor : integer): boolean;

{  Given:    Candidate, Divisor                                 }
{  Task:     See if divisor needs to be checked                 }
{  Return:   A boolean flag to terminate divisor checks         }

  BEGIN
    StillChecking := Divisor <= sqrt(Candidate)
  End;  {  of FUNCTION StillChecking  }
```

```
{************************************************************** }
```

```
PROCEDURE ListAllPrimes (Num : integer);

  {  Given:    The integer read                                    }
  {  Task:     List all primes less than or equal to the integer   }
  {            read                                                }
  {  Return:   Nothing                                             }

  VAR
    Prime : boolean;
    Divisor, Candidate : integer;
  BEGIN
    PrintMessage (Num);      {  call another procedure  }
    FOR Candidate := 2 TO Num DO
      BEGIN
        Prime := true;
        Divisor := 2;
        WHILE StillChecking (Candidate, Divisor) AND Prime DO
          IF Candidate MOD Divisor = 0 THEN
            Prime := false              {  Candidate has a divisor }
          ELSE
            Divisor := Divisor + 1                                }
        IF Prime THEN
          writeln (Candidate:35)        {  print each prime        }
      END;  {  of FOR loop  }
    writeln
  END;  {  of PROCEDURE ListAllPrimes  }
```

```
{************************************************************** }
```

```
BEGIN  {  Main program  }
  GetANumber (Num, MoreData);
  WHILE MoreData DO
    BEGIN
      IF Num = 1 THEN
        PrintOneMessage
```

```
        ELSE
          ListAllPrimes (Num);
        GetANumber (Num, MoreData)
      END  {  of WHILE loop  }
END.  {  of main program  }
```

Sample output for this program is

```
Enter a positive integer, <-999> to quit.
?10


----------------------------------------------------

                        The number is 10.  The prime numbers
                        less than or equal to 10 are:

                                        2
                                        3
                                        5
                                        7


Enter a positive integer, <-999> to quit.
?17


----------------------------------------------------

                        The number is 17.  The prime numbers
                        less than or equal to 17 are:

                                        2
                                        3
                                        5
                                        7
                                        11
                                        13
                                        17


Enter a positive integer, <-999> to quit.
?1


----------------------------------------------------

                        1 is not prime by definition.

Enter a positive integer, <-999> to quit.
?25


----------------------------------------------------

                        The number is 25.  The prime numbers
                        less than or equal to 25 are:

                                        2
                                        3
                                        5
                                        7
                                        11
                                        13
                                        17
                                        19
                                        23
```

```
Enter a positive integer, <-999> to quit.
?-3
Enter a positive integer, <-999> to quit.
?2

------------------------------------------------------

                The number is 2.  The prime numbers
                less than or equal to 2 are:

                                2

Enter a positive integer, <-999> to quit.
?-999
```

RUNNING AND DEBUGGING TIPS

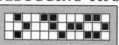

1. You can use related or identical variable names in the parameter lists. For example,

```
PROCEDURE Compute (N1, N2 : integer;
                   VAR Av : real);
```

or

```
PROCEDURE Compute (Number1, Number2 : integer;
                   VAR Average : real);
```

could be called by

```
Compute (Number1, Number2, Average);
```

2. When using recursion, make sure the recursive process will reach the stopping state.

■ Summary

Key Terms

block	interface	recursive subprogram
cohesive subprogram	local identifier (variable)	scope of an identifier
encapsulation	main driver	stack
forward reference	procedural abstraction	stopping state
global identifier	recursion	stub programming
(variable)	recursive step	subblock

Keyword

FORWARD

Key Concepts

- Global identifiers can be used by the main program and all subprograms.
- Local identifiers are available only to the subprogram in which they are declared.
- Each identifier is available to the block in which it is declared; this includes all subprograms contained within the block.
- Identifiers are not available outside their blocks.
- The scope of an identifier refers to the blocks in which the identifier is available.
- Understanding scope of identifiers is aided by graphic illustration of blocks in a program; thus,

```
PROGRAM Practice (input, output);
VAR
  X, Y, Z : real;
PROCEDURE Sub1 (X1 : real);
  VAR
    X2 : real;
  BEGIN
    .
    .
    .
  END;  {  of PROCEDURE Sub1  }

PROCEDURE Sub2 (X1 : real);
  VAR
    Z2 : real;
```

can be visualized as shown in Figure 8.23.

FIGURE 8.23

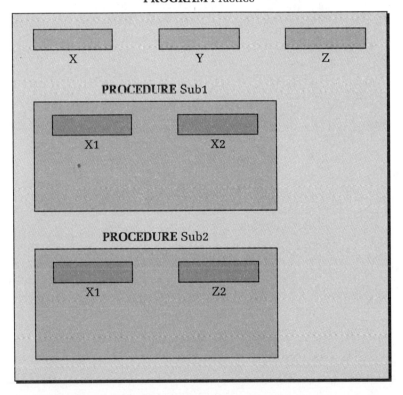

PROGRAM Practice

- Forward reference of a subprogram can be achieved by listing the function or procedure heading with all parameters and following that with the reserved word **FORWARD**, as

```
FUNCTION B (X : real) : real; FORWARD;
```

- Recursion is a process whereby a subprogram calls itself.
- A recursive subprogram must have a well-defined stopping state.
- Recursive solutions are usually elegant and short, but generally require more memory than iterative solutions.

■ Programming Problems and Projects

In order to facilitate the use of subprograms in writing programs to solve problems, some programming problems for this chapter consist of redesigning previous programs.

1. Several instructors use various weights (percentage of the final grade) for test scores. Write a program that allows the user to enter three test scores. Output should consist of the input data, the weighted score for each test and the total score (sum of the weighted scores).

2. The Natural Pine Furniture Company (Problem 2, Chapter 4 and Problem 15, Chapter 6) has recently hired you to help them convert their antiquated payroll system to a computer-based model. They know you are still learning, so all they want right now is a program that will print a one-week pay report for three employees. You should use the constant definition section for the following:
   a. federal withholding tax rate   18%
   b. state withholding tax rate   4.5%
   c. hospitalization $25.65
   d. union dues $7.85

The input will contain the employee's initials, the number of hours worked, and the employee's hourly rate. Your output should include a report for each employee and a summary report for the company files. A sample employee form follows:

```
Employee:      JIM
Hours Worked:  40.00
Hourly Rate:    9.75

     Total Wages:

     Deductions:
          Federal Withholding
          State Withholding
          Hospitalization
          Union Dues
               Total Deductions

     Net Pay
```

Output for a summary report could be

```
          Natural Pine Furniture Company
                    Weekly Summary

Gross Wages:

Deductions:
     Federal Withholding
     State Withholding
     Hospitalization
     Union Dues
          Total Deductions

Net Wages
```

3. The Child-Growth Encyclopedia Company (Problem 3, Chapter 4) wants a computer program that will print a monthly sales chart. Products produced by the company, prices, and sales commissions for each are

a. Basic encyclopedia $325.00   22%
b. Child educational supplement $127.50   15%
c. Annual update book $ 18.95   20%

Write a program that will get the monthly sales data for two sales regions and produce the desired company chart. Monthly sales data for one region consist of a two-letter region identifier (such as MI) and three integers, representing the number of units sold for each product listed above. A typical input screen would be:

```
What is your sales region?
?MI

How many Basic Encyclopedia were sold?
?150

How many Child Supplements were sold?
?120

How many Annual Updates were sold?
?105
```

The prices may vary from month to month and should be defined in the constant definition section. The commissions are not subject to change. Sample input is

```
MI  150  120  105
TX  225  200  150
```

Typical output could be

```
                    Monthly Sales Chart

                            Basic        Child        Annual
                Region   Encyclopedia  Supplement     Update

Units sold       MI          150          120          105
(by region)      TX          225          200          150

Total units sold:           375          320          255

      Price/unit          $325.00      $127.50       $18.95

Gross Sales:            $121,875.00   $40,800.00    $4,832.25

   Commission rate         22%          15%          20%

Commissions paid:        $26,812.50    $6,120.00     $966.45
```

4. As a part-time job this semester, you are working for the Family Budget Assistance Center (Problem 6, Chapter 4). Your boss has asked you to write and execute a program that will analyze data for a family. Input for each family will consist of

Family ID number   **(integer)**
Number in family   **(integer)**
Income   **(real)**
Total debts   **(real)**

Your program should output the following:

a. An appropriate header.

b. The family's identification number, number in family, income, and total debts.

c. Predicted family living expenses ($3000 times the size of the family).

d. The monthly payment necessary to pay off the debt in one year.

e. The amount the family should save (the family size times 2 percent of the income minus debt—FamilySize * 0.02 (income − debt)).

f. Your service fee (.5 percent of the income).

Run your program for the following two families:

Indentification Number	Size	Income	Debt
51	4	18000.00	2000.00
72	7	26000.00	4800.00

Output for the first family could be

```
        Family Budget Assistance Center
                  March 1992
            Telephone: (800) 555-1234

Identification number              51
Family size                         4
Annual income              $ 18000.00
Total debt                 $  2000.00
Expected living expenses   $ 12000.00
Monthly payment            $    166.67
Savings                    $   1280.00
Service fee                $     90.00
```

5. A Pythagorean triple consists of three integers A, B, and C such that $A^2 + B^2 = C^2$. For example, 3, 4, 5 is such a triple because $3^2 + 4^2 = 5^2$. These triples can be generated by positive integers m, n, $(m > n)$ where $a = m^1 - n^2$, $b = 2mn$, and $c = m^2 + n^2$. These triples will be primitive (no common factors) if m and n have no common factors and are not both odd. Write a program that allows the user to enter a value for m and then prints out all possible primitive Pythagorean triples such that $m > n$. Use one function to find the greatest common factor of m and n, another to see if m and n are both odd, and another to guard against overflow. For the input value of $m = 5$, typical output would be

m	n	a	b	c	a²	b²	c²
2	1	3	4	5	9	16	25
3	2	5	12	13	25	144	169
4	1	15	8	17	225	64	289
4	3	7	24	25	49	576	625
5	2	21	20	29	441	400	841
5	4	9	40	41	81	1600	1681

6. This chapter's Focus on Program Design problem determined whether or not an integer was prime by checking for divisors less than or equal to the square root of the number. The check started with 2 and incremented trial divisors by 1 each time as seen by the code

```
Prime := true;
Divisor := 2;
WHILE (Divisor <= sqrt(Candidate)) AND Prime DO
  IF Candidate MOD Divisor = 0 THEN
    Prime := false
  ELSE
    Divisor := Divisor + 1;
```

Other methods can be used to determine whether or not an integer N is prime. For example, you may

a. check divisors from 2 to $N - 1$ incrementing by 1.
b. check divisors from 2 to $(N - 1)/2$ incrementing by 1.
c. check divisor 2, 3, 5, . . . $(N - 1)/2$ incrementing by 2.
d. check divisor 2, 3, 5, . . . sqrt(N) incrementing by 2.

Write an interactive program that allows the user to choose between these options in order to compare relative efficiency of different algorithms. Use a function for each option.

7. The prime factorization of a positive integer is the positive integer written as the product of primes. For example, the prime factorization of 72 is

$$72 = 2 * 3 * 3 * 4$$

Write an interactive program that allows the user to enter a positive integer and then displays the prime factorization of the integer. A minimal main program could be

```
BEGIN  {  Main program  }
  GetANumber (Num);
  NumberIsPrime := PrimeCheck(Num);
  IF NumberIsPrime THEN
    writeln (Num, ' is prime.')
  ELSE
    PrintFactorization(Num)
END.  { of main program  }
```

Enhancements to this program could include an error trap for bad data and a loop for repeated trials.

8. The greatest common divisor of two positive integers a and b, GCD (a,b), is the largest positive integer that divides both a and b. Thus, GCD(102, 30) = 6. This can be found using the division algorithm as follows:

$$102 = 30 * 3 + 12$$
$$30 = 12 * 2 + 6$$
$$12 = 6 * 2 + 0$$

Note that

$$GCD(102,30) = GCD(30, 12)$$
$$= GCD(12, 6)$$
$$= 6$$

In each case, the remainder is used for the next step. The process terminates when a remainder of zero is obtained. Write a recursive function that returns the GCD of two positive integers.

9. A palindrome is a number or word that is the same when read either forwards or backwards. For example, 12321 and mom are palindromes. Write a recursive function that can be used to determine whether or not an integer is a palindrome. Use this function in a complete program that reads a list of integers and then displays the list with an asterisk following each palindrome.

10. Recall the Fibonacci sequence discussed at the beginning of this chapter. Write a recursive function that returns the nth Fibonacci number. Input for a call to the function will be a positive integer.

11. Probability courses often contain problems which require students to compute the number of ways r items can be chosen from a set of n objects. It is shown that there are

$$C\,(n,\,r)\ =\ \frac{n!}{r!\,(n\ -\ r)!}$$

such choices. This is sometimes referred to as "n choose r". To illustrate, if you wish to select three items from a total of five possible objects, there are

$$C(5,\,3)\ =\ \frac{5!}{3!\,(5\ -\ 3)!}\ =\ \frac{5\,*\,4\,*\,3\,*\,2\,*\,1}{(3\,*\,2\,*\,1)\,(2\,*\,1)}\ =\ 10$$

such possibilities.

   In mathematics, the number of $C(n,r)$ is a binomial coefficient because, for appropriate values of n and r, it produces coefficients in the expansion of $(x\ +\ y)^n$. Thus,
$(x\ +\ y)^4\ =\ C(4,0)x^4\ +\ C(4,1)x^3y\ +\ C(4,2)xy^2\ +\ C(4,3)xy^3\ +\ C(4,4)y^4$
   a. Write a function that returns the value $C(n,r)$. Arguments for a function call will be integers n,r such that $n > r \geqslant 0$. (*Hint:* Simplify the expression $\dfrac{n!}{r!\,(n\ -\ r)!}$ before computing.)
   b. Write an interactive program that receives as input the power to which a binomial is to be raised. Output should be the expanded binomial.

12. Reread the material in Section 8.2 concerning procedural abstraction. Then, from Problems 1, 2, 3, and 4, select one that you have not yet worked. Develop a structure chart and write module specifications for each module required for the problem you have chosen. Also, write a main driver for your program and write complete documentation for each subprogram including comments about all parameters.

13. Return to Problem 7 and solve it as a team project for a four-member team and one project director. The project director is responsible for the final design of the main program and must ensure that adequate communication exists among team members. Each of the four team members should develop complete documentation for one of the following four tasks:
   a. a loop for repeated trials
   b. data input with a bad data check
   c. a function to determine whether or not the number is prime
   d. a procedure that lists the prime factors of the composite numbers
      The final team project should be a report that includes a complete main driver, a description of the tasks for each team member, complete documentation for each subtask, and a summary of the communication required for the team to work together.

Text Files and Enumerated Data Types

Having now completed eight chapters, you've made a significant step in the process of learning to use a programming language for the purpose of solving problems. We have covered the essential elements of arithmetic, variables, input/output, selection, repetition, and subprograms and are now ready to look at a somewhat different area of Pascal.

Thus far, you have been unable to work with large amounts of data. In order to write programs that solve problems using large data bases, it is necessary to be able to store, retrieve, and manage the data. In this chapter, we first look at storage and retrieval of data (text files) and then study a feature of Pascal (enumerated data types) that facilitates handling the data.

These topics are not closely related but, since both are essential for working with data structures which are presented in Chapter 10, we present them together. As you study this material, remember that we are "setting the stage" for working with large amounts of data.

■ 9.1
Text Files

OBJECTIVES

- to understand how data can be stored in text files
- to be able to **read** from a text file
- to be able to **write** to a text file
- to understand the difference between internal and external files

The implementation of concepts presented in this section depends on the computer you are using; it is very system dependent. It will probably be necessary for your instructor to supplement this material with examples and explanations suitable for your particular environment. At the very least, you should be able to use the manual for your system for reference.

Consider the relatively simple problem of using a computer to compute and print water bills for a community of 30,000 customers. If the data needed consist of a customer name, address, and amount of water used, you can imagine that entering this information interactively every billing period would involve an enormous amount of time. In addition to saving that time, it is often desirable to save information between runs of a program for later use.

To avoid these problems, we can store data in some secondary storage device, usually magnetic tapes or disks. Data can be created separately from a program, stored on these devices, and then accessed by programs when necessary. It is also possible to modify and save this information for other runs of the same program or for running another program using this same data. For now we will store all data in *text files* (other kinds of files are examined in Chapter 13).

Text files can be created by a text editor or by a program. Often the editor you use to create your program can be used to create a text file. The use of text editors varies significantly and you should consult your instructor and/ or manual to use this method. This, however, is how your instructor may create data files for you to use with subsequent programming problems.

Data in a text file can be thought of as a sequence of characters stored in a sequence of lines. As you've already seen, each line has an end-of-line (**eoln**) marker (▌) after it; each file has an end-of-file (**eof**) marker (■) after the last end-of-line marker. For example, suppose a text file is used to store data for students in a class. If each line consists of an identification number for each student followed by three scores, a typical file can be envisioned as

00723 85 93 100 ▌

00131 78 91 85 ▌

00458 82 75 86 ▌ ■

Technically these lines are stored as one continuous stream with end-of-line markers used to differentiate between lines and the end-of-file marker to signify the end of one file.

00723 85 93 100 ▌ 00131 78 91 85 ▌ 00458 82 75 86 ▌ ■

However, we frequently use separate lines to illustrate lines in a text file. Both end-of-line and end-of-file markers are appropriately placed by the computer at the time a file is created. When characters are read, **eoln** markers are read as blanks.

When a text file in secondary storage is to be used by a program, a file variable (or symbolic file name) must be included in the file list along with the standard files **input** and **output** as part of the program heading. Thus, if ClassList is the file variable, a heading might be

```
PROGRAM ClassRecordBook (input, output, ClassList);
```

This file variable must be declared in the variable declaration section and is of type **text.** Thus, the declaration section would be

```
VAR
   ClassList : text;
```

The file variable ClassList must be associated with the text file, which is stored externally. This may be done with a procedure file prior to compiling and running the program. It may also be accomplished within the program; for example, in Turbo Pascal, an **assign** statement is used for this purpose. Thus, if the data needed in a program are stored on a disk under the name Data1, the statement

```
assign (ClassList, 'Data1');
```

establishes the desired relationship between the file variable ClassList and the data stored externally in the text file, Data1.

Reading from a Text File

Before data can be read from a file, the file must be *opened for reading.* This is done by the statement

```
reset (⟨file variable⟩);
```

This statement moves a data pointer to the first position of the first line of the data file to be read. Thus,

```
reset (ClassList);
```

positions the pointer as follows:

```
00723 85 93 100 ┃ 00131 78 91 85 ┃ 00458 82 75 86 ┃ ■
↑
pointer here
```

Reading from a text file is very similar to getting input interactively or reading from a standard input file. Standard procedures **read** and **readln** are used with appropriate variables as arguments in either format as shown.

> **read** (⟨file variable⟩, ⟨input list⟩);
> or
> **readln** (⟨file variable⟩, ⟨input list⟩);

If the file variable is not specified, the standard file **input** is assumed. Thus, data from one line of the file of student test scores, ClassList, can be obtained by

```
readln (ClassList, IDNumber, Score1, Score2, Score3);
```

As data items are read using **readln,** values are stored in the designated variables and the pointer is moved to the first position past the end-of-line marker. Thus,

```
reset (ClassList);
readln (ClassList, IDNumber, Score1, Score2, Score3);
```

results in

```
 00723      85       93      100
IDNumber  Score1   Score2   Score3
```

```
00723 85 93 100 ┃ 00131 78 91 85 ┃ 00458 82 75 86 ┃ ■
                  ↑
                pointer
```

It is not necessary to read all values in a line of data. If only some values are read, a **readln** statement still causes the pointer to move to the first position past the end-of-line marker. Thus,

```
reset (ClassList);
readln (ClassList, IDNumber, Score1);
```

results in

```
 00723      85       ?        ?
IDNumber  Score1   Score2   Score3
```

```
┌─────────────────┬──────────────┬──────────────┬───┐
│ 00723 85 93 100 │ 00131 78 91 85│ 00458 82 75 86│ ■ │
└─────────────────┴──────────────┴──────────────┴───┘
         ↑
      pointer
```

However, when data items are read using **read,** the pointer moves to the first position past the last data item read. Thus, the statement

```
read (ClassList, IDNumber, Score1);
```

results in the following:

```
┌────────┐   ┌──────┐
│ 00723  │   │  85  │
└────────┘   └──────┘
IDNumber    Score1
```

```
┌─────────────────┬──────────────┬──────────────┬───┐
│ 00723 85 93 100 │ 00131 78 91 85│ 00458 82 75 86│ ■ │
└─────────────────┴──────────────┴──────────────┴───┘
         ↑
      pointer
```

Variables in the variable list of **read** and **readln** can be listed one at a time or in any combination that does not result in a type conflict. For example,

```
readln (ClassList, IDNumber, Score1);
```

can be replaced by

```
read (ClassList, IDNumber);
readln (ClassList, Score1);
```

Pascal has two Boolean-valued functions that may be used when working with text files: **eoln** (for end-of-line) and **eof** (for end-of-file). Only if the data pointer is at an end-of-line or end-of-file marker is the Boolean function **eoln** (⟨file variable⟩) true. Similarly, **eof** (⟨file variable⟩) is true only when the data pointer is positioned at the end-of-file marker. This allows both **eoln** (⟨file variable⟩) and **eof** (⟨file variable⟩) to be used as Boolean conditions when designing problem solutions. Thus, part of a solution might be

```
WHILE NOT eof(⟨file variable⟩) DO
    process a line of data
```

In this loop, data from one line of the text file would typically be read by a **readln** statement. This allows the end-of-file condition to become **true** after the last data line has been read.

Text files can contain any character available in the character set being used. When numeric data are stored, the system converts a number to an appropriate character representation. When this number is retrieved from the file, another conversion takes place to change the character representation to a number.

■ **EXAMPLE 9.1**

Let's now write a short program that uses the text file ClassList and the end-of-file (**eof**) condition. If the problem is to print a listing of student identification numbers, test scores, and test averages, a first-level pseudocode development is

1. Open the file
2. Print a heading
3. **WHILE NOT eof** (⟨file variable⟩) **DO**
   3.1 process a line of data

Step 3.1 can be refined to

    3.1   process a line of data
        3.1.1   get the data
        3.1.2   compute test average
        3.1.3   print the data

A short program to accomplish this task is

```pascal
PROGRAM ClassRecordBook (input, output, ClassList);

{   This program uses data from a text file.  Data for each     }
{   student are on a separate line in the file.  Lines  are     }
{   processed until there are no more lines.                    }

VAR
  Score1, Score2, Score3,            {  Test scores              }
  IDNumber : integer;                {  Student number           }
  TestAverage : real;                {  Average of three tests   }
  ClassList : text;                  {  Text file                }

{**************************************************************** }

FUNCTION Average (Score1, Score2, Score3 : integer) : real;

  {  Given:   Three integers                                     }
  {  Task:    Compute their average                              }
  {  Return:  The average of three integers                      }

  BEGIN
    Average := (Score1 + Score2 + Score3) / 3
  END;  {  of FUNCTION Average  }

{**************************************************************** }

PROCEDURE PrintHeading;

  {  Given:   Nothing                                            }
  {  Task:    Print the heading                                  }
  {  Return:  Nothing                                            }

  CONST
    Skip = ' ';

  BEGIN
    writeln;
    writeln ('Identification Number', Skip:5, 'Test Scores',
             Skip:5, 'Average');
    writeln ('---------------------', Skip:5, '-----------',
             Skip:5, '-------');
    writeln
  END;   {  of PROCEDURE PrintHeading  }

{**************************************************************** }

BEGIN { Main Program }
  reset (ClassList);
  PrintHeading;
  WHILE NOT eof(ClassList) DO
    BEGIN
      readln (ClassList, IDNumber, Score1, Score2, Score3);
      TestAverage := Average(Score1, Score2, Score3);
      writeln (IDNumber:10, Score1:19, Score2:4, Score3:4,
               TestAverage:11:2)
```

```
        END  {  of WHILE NOT eof DO loop  }
    END.  {  of main program  }
```

When this program is run using the text file ClassList with values

```
00123 85 93 100 ▊ 00131 78 91 85 ▊ 00458 82 75 86 ▊ ■
```

the output produced is

```
    Identification Number          Test Scores        Average
    ---------------------          -----------        -------

                  123              85  93 100          92.67
                  131              78  91  85          84.67
                  458              82  75  86          81.00
```

A note of caution is in order. Any attempt to **read** beyond the end of a file results in an error. To illustrate, if

```
    read (ClassList, IDNumber, Score1, Score2, Score3);
```

had been used in the previous example instead of

```
    readln (ClassList, IDNumber, Score1, Score2, Score3);
```

an error would have occurred because, when **read** is used with the last line of data, the data pointer is positioned as

```
00458 82 75 86 ▊ ■
              ↑
           pointer
```

At this point, even though **eoln** (ClassList) is **true, eof** (ClassList) is still **false** and the loop for processing a line of data would be entered one more time. Using **readln,** however, positions the data pointer as

```
00458 82 75 86 ▊ ■
              ↑
           pointer
```

and this causes the end-of-file condition to be **true** when expected.

Writing to a Text File

It is also possible to write to a text file. If you want the file saved for later use, a file variable must be included in the file list as part of the program heading just as is done when reading from files. The file variable must also be declared to be of type **text.** Before writing a file, it must be *opened for writing* by

```
    rewrite (⟨file variable⟩);
```

This standard procedure creates an empty file with the specified name. If there were any values previously in the file, they are erased by this statement. Data are then written to the file by using standard procedures **write** and **writeln.** The general form is

---

      write (⟨file variable⟩, ⟨list of values⟩);

or

      writeln (⟨file variable⟩, ⟨list of values⟩);

These both cause the list of values to be written on one line in the file. The difference is that **writeln** causes an end-of-line marker to be placed after the last data item. Using **write** allows you to continue entering data items on the same line with subsequent **write** or **writeln** statements. If you wish,

```
writeln (⟨file variable⟩);
```

can be used to place an end-of-line marker at the end of a data line.

Formatting can be used to control spacing of data items in a line of text. For example, since numeric items must be separated, you might choose to put test scores in a file by

```
writeln (ClassList, Score1:4, Score2:4, Score3:4);
```

If the scores are 85, 72, and 95, the line of data created is

```
 85  72  95
```

and each integer is allotted four columns. Let's now illustrate writing to a file with an example.

■ **EXAMPLE 9.2**

Let's write a program that allows you to create a text file containing data for students in a class. Each line in the file is to contain a student identification number followed by three test scores. A first-level pseudocode development is

1. Open the file
2. **WHILE** more data **DO**
   2.1 process a line

Step 2.1 can be refined to

   2.1 process a line
       2.1.1 get data from keyboard
       2.1.2 write data to text file

A complete program for this is

```
PROGRAM CreateFile (input, output, ClassList);

{    This program creates a text file.  Each line of the file    }
{    contains data for one student.  Data are entered inter-     }
{    actively from the keyboard and then written to the file.    }

VAR
   Score1, Score2, Score3,        {  Scores for three tests         }
   IDNumber : integer;            {  Student number                 }
   Response : char;               {  Indicator for continuation     }
   MoreData : boolean;            {  Loop control variable          }
   ClassList : text;              {  External text file             }


{***************************************************************}


PROCEDURE GetStudentData (VAR IDNumber, Score1, Score2,
                          Score3 : integer);

{  Given:    Nothing                                            }
{  Task:     Get IDNumber and three test scores from the        }
{            keyboard                                            }
{  Return:   IDNumber, Score1, Score2, and Score3               }
```

```
      BEGIN
        write ('Please enter a student ID number');
        writeln (' and three test scores.');
        writeln ('Separate entries by a space.');
        writeln;
        readln (IDNumber, Score1, Score2, Score3)
      END;  { of PROCEDURE GetStudentData  }


{****************************************************************** }

BEGIN  {  Main program  }
  rewrite (ClassList);                       {  Open for writing  }
  MoreData := true;
  WHILE MoreData DO
    BEGIN
      GetStudentData (IDNumber, Score1, Score2, Score3);
      writeln (ClassList, IDNumber, Score1:4, Score2:4, Score3:4);

      {  Check for more data  }

      writeln;
      writeln ('Any more students? Y or N');
      readln (Response);
      IF (Response = 'N') OR (Response = 'n') THEN
        MoreData := false
    END  {  of WHILE...DO loop  }
END.  {  of main program  }
```

External and Internal Files

Files used thus far have been *external files,* files that are stored in secondary memory and are external to main memory. If a program is to use an external file, a file variable must be included in the file list portion of the program heading. The file variable must then be declared in the variable declaration section as type **text.**

On some occasions, it is desirable to use a file only while the program is running and it is not necessary to save the contents for later use. In this case, an *internal file* (also called a *temporary* or *scratch file*) can be created by declaring a file variable of type **text** in the variable declaration section, but it should not be included in the file list of the program heading. Internal files are normally used during file processing when it is desirable to temporarily save the contents of a file that is being altered. Our next example illustrates use of an internal file.

■ **EXAMPLE 9.3**

Let's write a program that allows you to update the text file ClassList by adding one more test score to each line of data. We need two text files in this program: ClassList (external) and TempFile (internal). With these two files, we can create new lines in TempFile by reading a line from ClassList and getting a score from the keyboard. When all lines have been updated, we copy TempFile to ClassList.

A first-level pseudocode solution for this problem is

1. Open files (**reset** ClassList, **rewrite** TempFile)
2. **WHILE NOT eof** (ClassList) **DO**
   2.1   read one line

2.2 get new score
2.3 write one line to TempFile
3. Open files (**reset** TempFile, **rewrite** ClassList)
4. Update file
WHILE NOT eof (TempFile) **DO**
4.1 read one line from TempFile
4.2 write one line to ClassList

A complete program for its problem is

```
PROGRAM UpdateClassList (input, output, ClassList);

{   This program updates an existing text  file.  The  process  }
{   requires a second file.  Contents of the external file are  }
{   copied to a temporary internal file and the external  file  }
{   is then updated one line at a time.                         }

VAR
  Score1, Score2,                     {  Scores for four tests  }
  Score3, Score4,
  IDNumber : integer;                 {  Student number         }
  ClassList, TempFile : text;         {  Text files             }

BEGIN  {  Main program  }
  reset (ClassList);                                {  Open files  }
  rewrite (TempFile);
  WHILE NOT eof(ClassList) DO             {  Copy to TempFile    }
    BEGIN
      readln (ClassList, IDNumber, Score1, Score2, Score3);
      writeln ('Enter a new test score for student ', IDNumber);
      readln (Score4);
      writeln (TempFile, IDNumber, Score1:4, Score2:4,
               Score3:4, Score4:4)
    END;  { of lines in ClassList  }
  reset (TempFile);                                {  Open files  }
  rewrite (ClassList); { Note: contents of old ClassList erased }
  WHILE NOT eof(TempFile) DO              {  Copy to ClassList   }
    BEGIN
      readln (TempFile, IDNumber, Score1, Score2, Score3, Score4);
      writeln (ClassList, IDNumber, Score1:4, Score2:4, Score3:4,
               Score4:4)
    END  {  of copying TempFile to ClassList  }
END.  {  of main program  }
```

■ **EXAMPLE 9.4**

As an illustration of using **eoln,** let's write a program that replaces all blanks in a text file with asterisks. Output is directed to the monitor and a new text file is created for the purpose of saving the altered form of the original text file. Note that reading a character advances the data pointer only one character position unless **readln** is used.

A first-level pseudocode development is

1. Open the files
WHILE NOT eof (FileWithBlanks) **DO**
2. Process one line
3. Prepare for the next line

A second-level pseudocode development is

1. Open the files
   1.1 Open FileWithBlanks
   1.2 Open FileWithoutBlanks
   WHILE NOT eof (FileWithBlanks) **DO**
2. Process one line
   2.1 Read a character
   2.2 **IF** character is a blank **THEN**
        2.2.1   replace with an asterisk
   2.3 Write character to FileWithoutBlanks
   2.4 Write character to the screen
3. Prepare for the next line
   3.1 Insert end-of-line in FileWithoutBlanks
   3.2 End-of-line to screen
   3.3 Advance pointer in FileWithBlanks

A complete program for this is

```
PROGRAM DeleteBlanks (input, output, FileWithBlanks,
                      FileWithoutBlanks);

{  This  program illustrates  using eof  and eoln  with a text  }
{  file.  It replaces blanks with asterisks.                    }

VAR
  FileWithBlanks,                    {  Existing text file       }
  FileWithoutBlanks : text;          {  Altered text file        }
  Ch : char;                         {  Used for reading characters }

BEGIN
  reset (FileWithBlanks);                        {  Open the files  }
  rewrite (FileWithoutBlanks);
  WHILE NOT eof(FileWithBlanks) DO
    BEGIN                                         {  Process one line  }
      WHILE NOT eoln(FileWithBlanks) DO
        BEGIN
          read (FileWithBlanks, Ch);
          IF Ch = ' ' THEN
            Ch := '*';
          write (FileWithoutBlanks, Ch);
          write (Ch)                       {  Write to the screen  }
        END;   {  of reading one line  }
      writeln (FileWithoutBlanks);         {  Insert end-of-line  }
      writeln;
      readln (FileWithBlanks)              {  Advance the pointer  }
    END {  of lines in text file  }
END. {  of main program  }
```

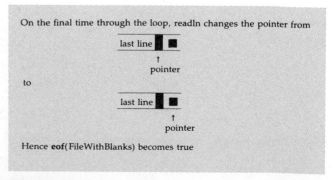

On the final time through the loop, readln changes the pointer from

last line   ■
↑
pointer

to

last line   ■
↑
pointer

Hence **eof**(FileWithBlanks) becomes true

When this is run using the text file

```
This is a text file with normal blanks.
After it has been processed by
PROGRAM DeleteBlanks, every blank will
be replaced with an asterisk "*".
```

the output to the screen is

```
This*is*a*text*file*with*normal*blanks.
After*it*has*been*processed*by
PROGRAM*DeleteBlanks,*every*blank*will
be*replaced*with*an*asterisk*"*".
```

The external text file FileWithoutBlanks also contains the version shown as output.

■   ■

The material in this section allows us to make a substantial change in our approach to writing programs. We can now proceed assuming data files exist for a program. This somewhat simplifies program design and also allows us to design programs for large sets of data. Consequently, most programs developed in the remainder of this text use text files for input. If you wish to continue with interactive programs, you should be able to make appropriate modifications.

Exercises 9.1

1. Explain the difference between an external file and an internal file. Give appropriate uses for each.

2. Write a test program that allows you to print a line of text from a file to the output file.

3. Explain what is wrong with using

   ```
   writeln (ClassList, Score1, Score2, Score3);
   ```

   if you want to write three scores to the text file ClassList.

4. Write a program that allows you to display a text file line by line.

5. Assume that a text file, InFile, is as illustrated.

   | 18 | 19M | −14.3 | JO | 142.1F | ■ |

   For each question, the pointer is positioned at the beginning of the file and the variable declaration section of a program is

   ```
   VAR
     A, B : integer;
     X, Y : real;
     Ch : char;
     InFile : text;
   ```

   What output is produced from each segment of code?

   a. ```
   read (InFile, A);
   read (Infile, B, Ch);
   writeln (A:5, B:5, Ch:5);
   ```

   b. ```
   read (Infile, Ch);
   write (Ch:10);
   readln (InFile, Ch);
   writeln (Ch);
   read (InFile, Ch);
   writeln (Ch:10);
   ```

```
c. read (InFile, A, B, Ch, X);
   writeln (A, B, Ch, X);
   writeln (A:5, B:5, Ch:5, X:10:2);
   read (InFile, Ch);
   writeln (Ch:5);
d. readln (InFile);
   read (InFile, Ch, Ch);
   readln (InFile, Y);
   writeln (Ch:5, Y:10:2);
```

6. Using the same text file and variable declaration section in Exercise 5, indicate the contents of each variable location and the position of the pointer after the segment of code is executed. Assume the pointer is positioned at the beginning for each problem.

    a. `read (InFile, Ch, A);`

    b. `readln (InFile, Ch, A);`

    c. `readln (InFile);`

    d. `readln (InFile);`
       `readln (InFile);`

    e. `readln (InFile, A, B, Ch, X);`

    f. `read (InFile, A, B, Ch, Y);`

    g. `readln (InFile, A, Ch);`
       `readln (Infile, Ch, Ch, B);`

    h. `read (InFile, A, B, Ch, X, Ch);`

7. Again use the text file and variable declaration section as in Exercise 5. For each of the following segments of code, indicate if the exercise produces an error and, if so, explain why an error occurs.

    a. `read (InFile, X, Y);`

    b. `readln (InFile, A);`
       `read (InFile, B);`

    c. `readln (InFile, Ch);`
       `readln (InFile, Ch);`
       `readln (InFile, Ch);`

    d. `read (InFile, X , A, Ch, B, Ch);`

    e. `readln (InFile);`
       `read (InFile, Ch, Ch, A, Ch, B);`

8. Write a complete Pascal program that reads your (three) initials and five test scores from a text file. Your program should then compute your test average and print out all information in a reasonable form with suitable messages.

9. Write a program that allows you to create a text file that contains your name, address, social security number, and age. **Reset** the file and have the information printed as output. Save the file in secondary storage for later use.

10. Show what output is produced from the following program. Also indicate the contents of each file after the program is run.

```
PROGRAM Exercise10 (input, output, F2);
VAR
   Ch : char;
   F1, F2 : text;
BEGIN
   rewrite (F1);
   rewrite (F2);
   writeln (F1, 'This is a test.');
```

```
           writeln (Fl, 'This is another line.');
           reset (Fl);
           WHILE NOT eof(Fl) DO
             BEGIN
               WHILE NOT eoln(Fl) DO
                 BEGIN
                   read (Fl, Ch);
                   IF Ch = ' ' THEN
                     writeln ('*')
                   ELSE
                     write (F2, Ch)
                 END;
               readln (Fl)
             END
    END.
```

11. Write a program that deletes all blanks from a text file. Your program should save the revised file for later use.

12. Write a program using a **CASE** statement to scramble a text file by replacing all blanks with an asterisk (*), and interchanging all A's and U's and E's with I's. Your program should print out the scrambled file and save it for subsequent use.

13. Write a program to update a text file by numbering the lines consecutively as 1, 2, 3, ...

14. Write a program to count the number of words in a text file. Assume that each word is followed by a blank or a period.

15. Write a program to find the longest word in a text file. Output should include the word and its length.

16. Write a program to compute the average length of words in a text file.

■ ■ ■ ■

■ 9.2
TYPE Definitions in Pascal

OBJECTIVES

- to understand what is meant by ordinal data type
- to be able to declare enumerated data types
- to be able to use enumerated data types in a program
- to understand why enumerated data types are of value in writing programs

Ordinal Data Types

Of the data types we have previously used, **integer, char,** and **boolean** are called ordinal data types. A data type is ordinal if values of that type have an immediate predecessor and an immediate successor. The exception is that the first listed element has only a successor and the last listed element has only a predecessor. Data of type **integer** are ordinal and can be listed as $-\textbf{maxint}, \ldots, -1, 0, 1, 2, \ldots, +\textbf{maxint}$. Boolean values **false** and **true,** and data of type **char** are listed according to the collating sequence shown in Appendix 4. Data of type **real** are not ordinal because a given real has neither an immediate predecessor nor an immediate successor. Permissible values for data of these three ordinal data types are summarized as follows:

Data Type	Values
integer	−**maxint** to **maxint**
char	Character set in a collating sequence
boolean	true, false

The four data types **integer, char, boolean,** and **real** used thus far are standard data types. We are now ready to see how Pascal allows us to define other data types called *enumerated data types.*

Simple Enumerated Data Types

The declaration section of a program may contain a **TYPE** definition section that can be used to define a data type. For example,

```
TYPE
   Weekday = (Mon, Tues, Wed, Thur, Fri);
```

After such a definition has been made, the variable declaration section can contain identifiers of the type Weekday. Thus, we could have

```
VAR
   Day : Weekday;
```

Values in an enumerated data type can be any legal identifier. Several comments are now in order concerning the **TYPE** definition.

1. Simple enumerated data types are also referred to as *user-defined data types*. (Other user-defined data types include subranges and structured data types, which will be studied later.)

2. This defined type will be an ordinal data type with the first defined constant having ordinal zero. Ordinal values increased by one in order from left to right. Every constant except the first has a predecessor and every constant except the last has a successor. Every constant except the first has a predecessor and every constant except the last has a successor. Using the previously defined **TYPE** Weekday, we have

```
Mon        Tues       Wed        Thurs      Fri
 ↕          ↕          ↕          ↕          ↕
 0          1          2          3          4
```

3. Variables can be declared to be of the new type.

4. The values defined in the **TYPE** definition section are constants that can be used in the program. These values must be valid identifiers.

5. No identifier can belong to more than one enumerated data type.

6. Identifiers that are defined values cannot be used as operands in arithmetic expressions.

7. Enumerated data types are for internal use only; you cannot **read** or **write** values of these variables.

Thus, given the previous **TYPE** definition of Weekday and the variable declaration of Day, each of the following would be an appropriate program statement.

```
a. Day := Tues;
b. Day := pred(Day);
c. IF Day = Mon THEN
      .
      .
      .
   ELSE
      .
      .
      .
```

d. `FOR Day := Mon TO Fri DO`
`    BEGIN`
`         .`
`         .`
`         .`
`    END;`

Having seen an example of an enumerated data type and some typical related program statements, let us look at a more formal method of definition. In general, we have

```
TYPE
   ⟨type identifier⟩ = (⟨constant1⟩, ⟨constant2⟩, . . . ⟨constantn⟩);
VAR
   ⟨identifier⟩ : ⟨type identifier⟩;
```

The **TYPE** definition section is part of the declaration section of a program. It follows the constant definition section (**CONST**) and precedes the variable declaration section (**VAR**) as shown in Figure 9.1.

FIGURE 9.1
Placement of **TYPE** definition section

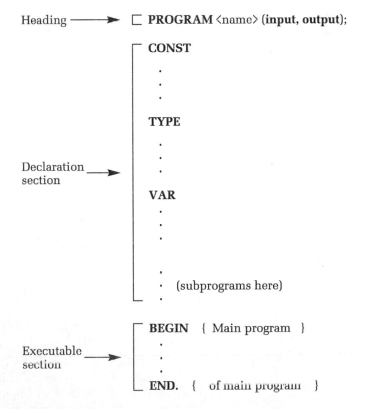

The following short program illustrates the placement and use of enumerated data types.

```
PROGRAM TypePrac (output);

CONST
   Skip = ' ',
```

```
TYPE
  Weekday = (Mon, Tues, Wed, Thur, Fri);

VAR
  Day : Weekday;

BEGIN
  Day := Wed;
  IF Day < Fri THEN
    writeln (Skip:20, 'Not near the weekend.')
  ELSE
    writeln (Skip:20, 'The weekend starts tomorrow.')
END.
```

The output from this program is

```
Not near the weekend.
```

Reasons for Using Enumerated Data Types

At first it may seem like a lot of trouble to define new types for use in a Pascal program, but there are several reasons for using them. In fact, being able to create enumerated data types is one of the advantages of using Pascal as a programming language. Why? With enumerated data types, you can express clearly the logical structure of data, enhance the readability of your program, provide program protection against bad data values, and declare parameters in subprograms.

Suppose you are working on a program to count the number of days in the month of a certain year. Enumerated data types allow you to use the following definition and subsequent declaration.

```
TYPE
  AllMonths = (Jan, Feb, March, April, May, June, July,
               Aug, Sept, Oct, Nov, Dec);
VAR
  Month : AllMonths;
```

With this definition it is easier to understand what the code does. It could contain statements such as

```
FOR Month := Jan TO April DO
    .
    .
    .
```

or

```
IF (Month = Feb) AND (Year MOD 4 = 0) THEN
  NumDays := 29;
```

This second segment of code clearly indicates that you are counting the extra day in February for a leap year. (This is an over-simplification of checking for a leap year. See Exercise 7 at the end of this section.)

Enumerated data types may be used in **CASE** statements. For example, movie ticket prices are frequently broken into three categories: youth, adult, and senior citizen. If the following definition and declaration were made,

```
TYPE
  Categories = (Youth, Adult, Senior);
VAR
  Patron : Categories;
```

a program statement could be something like

```
CASE Patron OF
   Youth  : Price := YouthPrice;
   Adult  : Price := AdultPrice;
   Senior : Price := Senior Price
END;  {  of CASE Patron  }
```

Once an enumerated data type has been defined at the global level, it is available to all subprograms. Thus, if you have a function for counting the days, a typical function heading might be

```
FUNCTION NumDays (Month : AllMonths;
                  Year : integer) : integer;
```

This aspect of user-defined data types will become more significant when we examine structured data types, including arrays and records.

Recall the limitation imposed on variables that are of a user-defined type: they are for internal use only; you cannot **read** or **write** values of these variables. Thus, in the earlier example using months of the year, you could have the following statement:

```
Month := June;
```

but not

```
writeln (Month);
```

However, (as we'll see in Section 9.4), use of a **CASE** statement allows translation procedures to be written with relative ease.

We close this section with some typical definitions for enumerated data types. These are intended to improve program readability. You are encouraged to incorporate enumerated data types in your subsequent programs. In general, you are limited only by your imagination.

```
TYPE
   SoftDrinks = (Pepsi, Coke, SevenUp, Orange, RootBeer);
   Seasons = (Winter, Spring, Summer, Fall);
   Colors = (Red, Orange, Yellow, Green, Blue, Indigo, Violet);
   ClassStanding = (Freshman, Sophomore, Junior, Senior);
   Fruits = (Apple, Orange, Banana);
   Vegetables = (Corn, Peas, Broccoli, Spinach);
```

With these type definitions, each of the following would be a reasonable variable declaration:

```
VAR
   Pop, Soda : SoftDrinks;
   Season : Seasons;
   Hue : Colors;
   Class : ClassStanding;
   Appetizer : Fruits;
   SideDish : Vegetables;
```

Career Opportunities in Computer Science

In May 1990, the Bureau of Labor Statistics projected that two of the occupations with the largest job growth between 1988 and 2000 would be computer programmers and computer system analysts.

From 1976 to 1988, the total number of computer specialists increased 357% (from 125,900 to 575,800); the number of women increased 605% (from 24,300 to

	1988	2000	Increase	Percent
Computer Programmer	519,000	769,000	250,000	48.1%
Computer System Analyst	403,000	617,000	214,000	53.3%

The average starting salary for undergraduate computer science majors, who graduated between September 1, 1989, and August 31, 1990, was $29,804 (College Placement Council, October 1990). The previous year, the averge starting salary was $28,659. Unemployment among computer specialists is traditionally exceptionally low and almost all who enter the work force find jobs.

171,200), blacks increased 739% (2,300 to 19,300), and Asians increased 830% (4,000 to 37,200). The future is bright! All able students, particularly women and minorities who have traditionally been under-represented in the sciences, are encouraged to consider computer science as a career.

Exercises 9.2

1. Explain what is meant by ordinal data type.

2. Write a test program to see what happens in each of the following instances.

   a. Try to **write** the value of a variable that is an enumerated data type.

   b. Try to find the predecessor (**pred**) of a defined constant whose ordinal is zero in an enumerated type.

3. Find all errors in the following definitions.

   a.
   ```
   TYPE
      Names = (John, Joe, Mary, Jane);
      People = (Henry, Sue, Jane, Bill);
   ```

   b.
   ```
   TYPE
      Colors = (Red, Blue, Red, Orange);
   ```

   c.
   ```
   TYPE
      Letters = A, C, E;
   ```

4. Assume the **TYPE** definition

   ```
   TYPE
      Colors = (Red, Orange, Yellow, Blue, Green);
   ```

   has been given. Indicate whether each of the following is **true** or **false**.

   a. `Orange < Blue`

   b. `(Green <> Red) AND (Blue >Green)`

   c. `(Yellow < Orange) OR (Blue >= Red)`

5. Assume the **TYPE** definition and variable declaration

   ```
   TYPE
      AllDays = (Sun, Mon, Tues, Wed, Thur, Fri, Sat);
   VAR
      Day, Weekday, Weekend : AllDays;
   ```

   have been given. Indicate which of the following are valid program statements.

For those that are not, given an explanation.

a. `Day := Tues;`

b. `Day := Tues + Wed;`

c. `Weekday := Sun;`

d. `IF Day = Sat THEN`
`   writeln ('Clean the garage.':30);`

e. `IF (Day < Sat) AND (Day > Sun) THEN`
`   writeln ('It is a workday.':30)`
`ELSE`
`   writeln ('It is the weekend.':30);`

f. `FOR Day := Mon TO Fri DO`
`   writeln (Day);`

g. `read (Day);`
`IF Day < Sat THEN`
`   Weekday := Day;`

h. `Wed := Tues + 1;`

6. Assume the following definitions and declarations have been made in a program.

```
TYPE
   Cloth = (Flannel, Cotton, Rayon, Orlon);
VAR
   Material : Cloth;
   NumberOfYards, Price : real;
```

What would be the output from the following segment of code?

```
Material := Cotton;
NumberOfYards := 3.5;
IF (Material = Rayon) OR (Material = Orlon) THEN
   Price := NumberOfYards * 4.5
ELSE IF Material = Cotton THEN
   Price := NumberOfYards * 2.75
ELSE
   Price := NumberOfYards * 2.5;
writeln (Price:30:2);
```

7. Find the complete definition of a leap year in the Gregorian calendar. Define appropriate data types and write a segment of code that would indicate whether or not a given year was a leap year.

■ ■ ■ ■

■ 9.3
Subrange as a Data Type

OBJECTIVES

- to be able to define a subrange as a data type
- to be able to use subrange data types in a program
- to understand compatibility of data types
- to understand why subrange data types are used in a program

Defining Subranges

In the previous section, we learned how to define new data types using the **TYPE** definition section. Now we will investigate another way to define new data types.

A *subrange* of an existing ordinal data type may be defined as a data type by

```
TYPE
   ⟨identifier⟩ = ⟨initial value⟩. .⟨final value⟩;
```

where the initial value and final value are separated by two periods. For example, we could have a subrange of the integers defined by

```
TYPE
    USYears = 1776..1992;
```

When defining a subrange, the following items should be noted.

1. The original data type must be an ordinal type.
2. Any valid identifier may be used for the name of the type.
3. The initial and final values must be of the original data type.
4. Since the underlying data type is ordinal, it is ordered. In this ordering, the initial value of a defined subrange must occur before the final value.
5. Only values in the indicated subrange (endpoints included) may be assigned to a variable of the type defined by the subrange.
6. The same value may appear in different subranges.

We illustrate some of these points in the following example.

■ **EXAMPLE 9.5**

Consider the subranges Weekdays and Midweek of the enumerated ordinal Days.

```
TYPE
    Days = (Sun, Mon, Tues, Wed, Thur, Fri, Sat);    {  Enumerated  }
    Weekdays = Mon..Fri;                             {  Subrange    }
    Midweek = Tues..Thur;                            {  Subrange    }
VAR
    SchoolDay : Weekdays;
    Workday : Midweek;
```

In this case, Days is defined first and we can then define appropriate subranges. With the variable SchoolDay declared as of type Weekdays, you can use any of the values Mon, Tues, Wed, Thur, or Fri with SchoolDay. However, you cannot assign either Sat or Sun to SchoolDay.

Notice that Tues, Wed, and Thur are values that appear in different type definitions. However, since they appear in subranges, this will not produce an error. Furthermore,

```
    Workday := Tues;
    SchoolDay := Workday;
```

are both acceptable statements.

■

Some other subrange definitions are

```
TYPE
    Grades = 'A'..'E';
    Alphabet = 'A'..'Z';
    ScoreRange = 0..100;
    Months = (Jan, Feb, Mar, Apr, May, June, July, Aug, Sept,
              Oct, Nov, Dec);
    Year = Jan..Dec;
    Summer = June..Aug;
```

Months is not a subrange here. However, once defined, an appropriate subrange such as Summer may be defined. With these subranges defined, each of the following declarations would be appropriate.

```
VAR
    FinalGrade : Grades;
    Letter : Alphabet;
    TestScore : ScoreRange;
    SumMonth : Summer;
```

Compatible and Identical Types

Now that we know how to define subranges of existing ordinal data types, we need to look carefully at compatibility of variables. Variables are of *compatible type* if they have the same base type. Thus, in

```
TYPE
   AgeRange = 0..110;
VAR
   Age : AgeRange;
   Year : integer;
```

the variables Age and Year are compatible because they both have **integer** as the base type (AgeRange is a subrange of integers). If variables are compatible, assignments may be made between them or they may be manipulated in any manner that variables of that base type may be manipulated.

Even when variables are compatible, you should exercise caution when making assignment statements. To illustrate, using Age and Year as previously declared, consider the statements

```
Age := Year;
Year := Age;
```

Since Age is of type AgeRange and AgeRange is a subrange of **integer**, any value in Age is acceptable as a value that can be assigned to Year. Thus,

```
Year := Age;
```

is permissible. However, since values for Age are restricted to the defined subrange, it is possible that

```
Age := Year;
```

will produce a run-time error. Since they are compatible, there will not be a compilation error, but consider

```
Year := 150;
Age := Year;
```

Since 150 is not in the subrange for Age, execution would be halted and an error message printed.

Two variables are said to be of *identical type* if—and only if—they are declared with the same type identifier. It is important to distinguish between compatible and identical types for variables when using subprograms. A value parameter and its argument must be of compatible type; a variable parameter and its argument must be of identical type. A type compatibility error will be generated if these rules are not followed. To illustrate, consider

```
TYPE
   GoodScore = 60..100;
VAR
   Score1, Score2 : GoodScore;
PROCEDURE Compute (HS1 : integer;
                   VAR HS2 : GoodScore);
```

This procedure may be called by

```
Compute (Score1, Score2);
```

Note that HS1 is a value parameter and need only be compatible with Score1. HS2 is a variable parameter and must be identical in type to Score2.

When used as data types for parameters, **TYPE** definitions must be defined in the main program since they cannot be defined in a subprogram heading. You may, however, define **TYPE**s internally for subprograms.

Using Subranges

There are several good reasons for using subranges, in particular, for batch programs. Although they require extra time and thought when you are writing a program, the long-range benefits far outweigh these minor inconveniences. One of the more obvious benefits is program protection. By carefully defining subranges, you avoid the possibility of working with bad data or data out of the expected range. Although such data will not be detected during compilation, an inappropriate assignment will halt execution in most versions of Pascal. This makes it easier to locate the source of an error. It also avoids the possibility of producing incorrect results. If, for example, a data entry operator inadvertently types in 400 rather than 40 for the hours worked by an employee, a definition and declaration such as

```
TYPE
  TotalHours = 0..60;
VAR
  Hours : TotalHours;
```

would cause execution to be stopped with the statement

```
read (Hours);
```

since 400 is not in the defined subrange. This is not necessarily the best way to avoid bad data with an interactive program, but it is better than allowing bad data to go undetected.

Another alternative for interactive programs is to use a conditional **IF . . . THEN . . . ELSE** or a **REPEAT . . . UNTIL** loop to guarantee that the data are in the appropriate range. This approach prevents program crashes and makes a program more user-friendly. For example, if you wanted to guarantee the number of hours entered is between 0 and 60, you could use a validation loop as follows:

```
REPEAT
  writeln ('Enter hours worked <0..60> or <-999 to quit>.');
  readln (Hours)
UNTIL (Hours >= 0) AND (Hours <= 60) OR (Hours = -999);
```

If you had a longer interactive example where the user could choose whether or not to repeat some process you could use

```
REPEAT
  .
  .  (    action here    )
  .
  writeln ('Do you wish to continue? <Y> or <N>');
  readln (Ch);
  Continue := (Ch = 'Y') OR (Ch = 'y')
UNTIL NOT Continue;
```

STYLE TIP
■ ■ ■ ■ ■ ■ ■ ■ ■ ■ ■

The **CONST** and **TYPE** definition sections can be used together to enhance readability and facilitate program design. For example, rather than use the subrange

```
TYPE
  USYears = 1776..1992;
```

you could define an ending constant and then use it as indicated.

```
CONST
  CurrentYear = 1992;
TYPE
  USYears = 1776..CurrentYear;
```

Software Engineering

Enumerated types and subranges are features of Pascal that are consistent with principles of software engineering. As has been previously stated, communication, readability, and maintenance are essential in developing large systems. Use of enumerated types and subranges is important for all of these areas. To illustrate, suppose a program includes working with a chemical reaction that normally occurs around 180 degrees Fahrenheit. If the definition section includes

```
TYPE
   ReactionRange = 150..210;
```

subsequent modules could use a variable such as

```
VAR
   ReactionTemp : ReactionRange;
```

As we progress into the next chapter, you will see how use of enumerated or user-defined data types becomes even more essential to maintaining principles of software engineering. Specifically, defining data structures becomes an important design consideration.

Exercises 9.3

1. Indicate whether the following **TYPE** definitions, subsequent declarations, and uses are valid or invalid. Explain what is wrong with those that are invalid.

   a. ```
   TYPE
      Reverse = 10..1;
   ```

   b. ```
   TYPE
      Bases = (Home, First, Second, Third);
      Double = Home..Second;
      Score = Second..Home;
   ```

   c. ```
   TYPE
      Colors = (Red, White, Blue);
      Stripes = Red..White;
   VAR
      Hue : Stripes;
   BEGIN
      Hue := Blue;
   ```

   d. ```
   TYPE
      Weekdays = Mon..Fri;
      Days = (Sun, Mon, Tues, Wed, Thur, Fri, Sat);
   ```

   e. ```
   TYPE
      ScoreRange = 0..100;
      HighScores = 70..100;
      Midscores = 50..70;
      LowScores = 20..60;
   VAR
      Score1 : Midscores;
      Score2 : HighScores;
   BEGIN
      Score1 := 60;
      Score2 := Score1 + 5;
   ```

2. Write a test program to see what happens when you try to use (assign, read, and so on) a value for a variable that is not in the defined subrange.
   ```

3. Explain why each of the following subrange definitions might be used in a program.
   a. `Dependents = 0..20;`   c. `QuizScores = 0..10;`
   b. `HoursWorked = 0..60;`   d. `TotalPoints = 0..700;`

4. Indicate reasonable subranges for each of the following. Explain your answers.
   a. `TwentiethCentury =`
   b. `Digits =`
   c. `JuneTemp =`
   d. `WinterRange =`
   e. `Colors = (Black, Brown, Red, Pink, Yellow, White);`
      `LightColors =`

5. Assume the declaration section of a program contains

```
TYPE
  ChessPieces = (Pawn, Knight, Bishop, Rook, King, Queen);.
  Expendable = Pawn..Rook;
  Valuable = King..Queen;
  LowRange = 0..20;
  Midrange = 40..80;
VAR
  Piece1 : Valuable;
  Piece2 : Expendable;
  Piece3 : ChessPieces;
  Score1 : LowRange;
  Score2 : Midrange;
  Score3 : integer;
```

   Indicate which of the following pairs of variables are of compatible type.
   a. `Piece1 and Piece2`
   b. `Piece2 and Piece3`
   c. `Piece3 and Score1`
   d. `Score1 and Score2`
   e. `Score1 and Score3`
   f. `Piece2 and Score3`

6. Assume the declaration section of a program contains the following:

```
TYPE
  PointRange = 400..700;
  FlowerList = (Rose, Iris, Tulip, Begonia);
  Sublist = Rose..Tulip;
VAR
  TotalPts : PointRange;
  Total : integer;
  Flower : Sublist;
  OldFlower : FlowerList;
```

   The procedure heading is

```
PROCEDURE TypePrac (A : PointRange;
                    VAR B : integer;
                    Fl : Sublist);
```

   Indicate which of the following are valid calls to this procedure.
   a. `TypePrac (TotalPts, Total, Flower);`
   b. `TypePrac (Total, TotalPts, Flower);`
   c. `TypePrac (TotalPts, Total, OldFlower);`

d. TypePrac (Total, Total, Flower);

e. TypePrac (Total, Total, OldFlower);

■ ■ ■ ■

■ 9.4
Operations on Ordinal Data Types

OBJECTIVES

- to be able to use functions **ord,** **pred,** and **succ** with enumerated data types
- to be able to use ordinal data types in Boolean expressions
- to be able to use ordinal data types in **CASE** statements
- to be able to use ordinal data types as loop indices

Functions for Ordinal Data Types

Earlier we characterized ordinal data types as those in which there was a first and last listed element and each element other than the first and last had an immediate predecessor and an immediate successor. Of the standard data types, only **real** is not ordinal. Since the enumerated data types are all ordinal, the functions **ord, pred,** and **succ** may be used on them. Thus, if we have the definition

```
TYPE
    Days = (Sun, Mon, Tues, Wed, Thur, Fri, Sat);
    Weekdays = Mon..Fri;
```

the following function calls have the indicated values.

Function Call	Value
ord(Sun)	0
ord(Wed)	3
pred(Thur)	Wed
succ(Fri)	Sat
ord(**pred**(Fri))	4

When using functions on enumerated ordinals, the following should be noted.

1. The first-listed identifier has ordinal zero.
2. Successive ordinals are determined by the order in which identifiers are listed.
3. You cannot use **pred** on the first identifier or **succ** on the final identifier.
4. If a subrange data type is defined, the functions return values consistent with the underlying base type; for example, **ord**(Wed) = 3.

Using Ordinal Values of Enumerated Data Types

Now that you have some familiarity with ordinal data types and functions that use them as arguments, let us consider some ways they could be incorporated into programs. One typical use is in Boolean expressions. Suppose you are writing a program to compute the payroll for a company that pays time-and-a-half for working on Saturday. Assume the definition and declaration

```
TYPE
    Workdays = (Mon, Tues, Wed, Thur, Fri, Sat);
VAR
    Day : Workdays;
```

have been made. A typical segment of code is

```
Day := ⟨some value⟩;
IF Day = Sat THEN
   ComputeOvertime(⟨calculation⟩)
ELSE
   ComputeRegularPay(⟨calculation⟩)
```

A second use is with **CASE** statements. As previously explained, one limitation of enumerated data types is that they have no external representation (that is, you cannot **read** or **write** their values). However, you can circumvent this limitation by appropriate use of a **CASE** statement. For example, suppose we have the definition and declaration

```
TYPE
   Colors = (Red, White, Blue);
VAR
   Hue : Colors;
```

If you wish to print the value of Hue, you could do so by

```
CASE Hue OF
   Red   : writeln ('Red':20);
   White : writeln ('White':20);
   Blue  : writeln ('Blue':20)
END;  {  of CASE Hue  }
```

since most versions of Pascal do not permit

```
writeln (Hue:20);
```

A third use is as a loop index. For example, consider

```
TYPE
   AllDays = (Sun, Mon, Tues, Wed, Thur, Fri, Sat);
VAR
   Day : AllDays;
```

Each of the following would be an appropriate loop.

```
1. FOR Day := Mon TO Fri DO
     BEGIN
        .
        .
        .
     END;
2. Day := Mon;
   WHILE Day < Sat DO
     BEGIN
        Day := succ(Day);
        .
        .
        .
     END;
3. Day := Sun;
   REPEAT
     Day := succ(Day);
        .
        .
        .
   UNTIL Day = Fri;
```

The loop control in a **FOR** loop is based on the ordinals of the values of the loop index. Thus, the statement

```
FOR Day := Mon TO Fri DO
```

is treated like the statement

```
FOR J := 1 TO 5 DO
```

because **ord**(Mon) is 1 and **ord**(Fri) is 5.

In the **WHILE . . . DO** and **REPEAT . . . UNTIL** loops, you must be sure to increment—increase the ordinal of—the variable. One method of doing this is to use the function **succ**.

Exercises 9.4

1. Suppose the following **TYPE** definition is given.

```
TYPE
  Trees = (Oak, Ash, Maple, Pine);
  SlackType = (Denim, Cotton, Polyester);
```

   Give the value of each of the following expressions. Indicate any expression that is invalid.

   a. **pred** (Ash)   e. **ord** (**succ** (Maple))

   b. **succ** (Denim)   f. **succ** (Polyester)

   c. **ord** (Polyester)   g. **ord** (**pred** (**succ** (Oak)))

   d. **ord** (**pred** (Oak))

2. Write a test program that lists the ordinals of values in a subrange of an enumerated data type.

3. The character set for some computers is such that **ord**('A') = 1 and **ord**('Z') = 26. Assuming such a sequence, what is the value of each of the following? Indicate any expressions that are invalid.

   a. **chr**(**ord**('D'))   d. **ord**(**chr**(10 **MOD** 3) + **chr**(20))

   b. **ord**(**chr**(10))   e. **ord**(**pred**('K') + 3)

   c. **chr**(3 * **ord**('E'))   f. **succ**(**chr**(**ord**('Z') − 1))

4. Write a program that will list the letters of the alphabet and their respective ordinals for the character set used with your machine.

5. Assume the **TYPE** definition and variable declaration

```
TYPE
  AllDays = (Sun, Mon, Tues, Wed, Thur, Fri, Sat);
VAR
  Day : AllDays;
```

   are made.

   a. What would be the output from the following **REPEAT . . . UNTIL** loop?

```
Day := Sun;
REPEAT
  CASE Day OF
    Sat, Sun                   : writeln ('Weekend':20);
    Mon, Tues, Wed, Thur, Fri : writeln ('Weekday':20)
  END;  {  of CASE Day  }
  Day := succ(Day)
UNTIL Day = Sat;
```

   b. Rewrite the previous loop as both a **WHILE . . . DO** loop and a **FOR** loop.

   c. Find another method to control the loop variable (for example, replace

```
Day := succ(Day)
```

   and make any other necessary changes).

   d. Revise the loop so that all seven days are considered.

Computer Ethics: Viruses

Tiny programs that deliberately cause mischief are epidemic among computers and are causing nervousness among those who monitor them. Written by malicious programmers, the "computer viruses" are sneaked into computer systems by piggybacking them on legitimate programs and messages. There, they may be passed along or instructed to wait until a prearranged moment to burst forth and destroy data.

At NASA headquarters in Washington, several hundred computers had to be resuscitated after being infected. NASA officials have taken extra precautions and reminded their machines' users to follow routine computer hygiene: Don't trust foreign data or strange machines.

Viruses have the eerie ability to perch disguised among legitimate data just as biological viruses hide among genes in human cells, then spring out unexpectedly, multiplying and causing damage. Experts say that even when they try to study viruses in controlled conditions, the programs can get out of control and erase everything in a computer. The viruses can be virtually impossible to stop if their creators are determined enough.

"The only way to protect every body against them is to do something much worse than the viruses: Stop talking to one another with computers," say William H. Murray, an information-security specialist at Ernst and Whinney financial consultants in Hartford, Conn.

Hundreds of programs and files have been destroyed by the viruses, and thousands of hours of repair or prevention time have been logged. Programmers have quickly produced antidote programs with such titles as "Vaccine," "Flu Shot," "Data Physician" and "Syringe."

Experts say known damage is minimal compared with the huge, destructive potential. They express the hope that the attacks will persuade computer users to minimize access to programming and data.

Viruses are the newest of evolving methods of computer mayhem. One type of virus is the "Trojan horse": it looks and acts like a normal program but contains hidden commands that eventually take effect, ordering mischief. The "time bomb" explodes at a set time; the "logic bomb" goes off when the computer arrives at a certain result during normal computation. The "salami attack" executes barely noticeable small acts, such as shaving a penny from thousands of accounts.

A virus typically is written as perhaps only a few hundred characters in a program containing tens of thousands of characters. When the computer reads legitimate instructions, it encounters the virus, which instructs the computer to suspend normal operations for a fraction of a second.

During that time, the virus instructs the computer to check for other copies of itself and, if none is found, to make and hide copies. Instruction to commit damage may be included.

Is Your Machine at Risk?

1. Computer viruses are actually miniature computer programs. Most were written by malicious programmers intent on destroying information in computers for fun.
2. Those who write virus programs often conceal them on floppy disks that are inserted in the computer.
3. A malicious programmer makes the disk available to others, saying it contains a useful program or game. These programs can be lent to others or put onto computerized "bulletin boards" where anyone can copy them for personal use.
4. A computer receiving the programs will "read" the disk and the tiny virus program at the same time. The virus may then order the computer to do a number of things:

- Tell it to read the virus and follow instructions.
- Tell it to make a copy of the virus and place it on any disk inserted in the machine today.
- Tell it to check the computer's clock, and on a certain date destroy all information that tells where data is stored on any disk: if an operator has no way of retrieving information, it is destroyed.
- Tell it not to list the virus programs when the computer is asked for an index of programs.

5. In this way, the computer will copy the virus onto many disks—perhaps all or nearly all the disks used in the infected machine. The virus may also be passed over the telephone, when one computer sends or receives data from another.
6. Ultimately hundreds or thousands of people may have infected disks and potential time bombs in their systems.

6. A standard programming problem is to convert an integer character to its corresponding numerical value, for example, the character '2' to the number 2. Since the digits are listed sequentially in every character set, this could be accomplished by

```
ord('2') - ord('0');
```

   a. Write a function to convert a single character digit ('0', '1', . . ., '9') to its corresponding numerical value.

   b. Write a function to convert a two-digit number read as consecutive characters into the corresponding numerical value.

7. Suppose you are working with a program that reads an integer representing a month of the year (Jan = 1). Write a function to convert the integer into the appropriate month.

■ ■ ■ ■

**FOCUS ON
PROGRAM DESIGN**

The summary program for this chapter computes the number of days in your birth year from your birthday to the end of the year. Sample input (if you were born on March 16, 1971) would be

```
3 16 71
```

We want the output to be

```
During your birth year,  1971,
you were alive  291 days.
```

Features of this program include enumerated data types and subranges. In particular, note the data type

```
AllMonths = (Jan, Feb, March, April, May, June,
             July, Aug, Sept, Oct, Nov, Dec);
```

A reasonable first-level pseudocode design for this program is

1. Get data
2. Assign month
3. Compute days
4. Print results

A structure chart for this is given in Figure 9.2.

FIGURE 9.2
Structure chart for **PROGRAM** Birthday

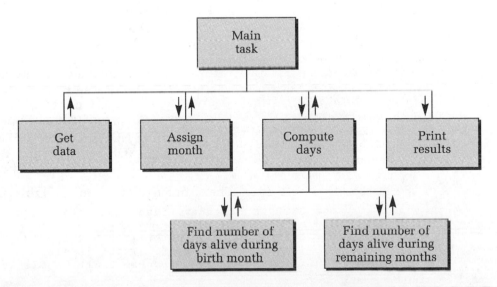

Module specifications for this problem are

1. GetData Module
   Data received: None
   Information returned: Day
                                 Month
                                 Year of birth
   Logic: Have the user enter his/her birth date.

2. AssignMonth Module
   Data received: A numerical equivalent of the birth month
   Information returned: The name of the birth month
   Logic: A **CASE** statement assigns the name of the birth month to
               BirthMonth, which is an enumerated data type.

3. ComputeDays Module
   Data received: Month
                       Day
                       Year of birth
   Information returned: The number of days alive during the year of
                                      birth
   Logic: Compute the number of days alive during the month of birth.
               Compute the number of days in the remaining months.

4. PrintResults Module
   Data received: Number of days alive during the year of birth
   Information returned: None
   Logic: Use **write(ln)** statements to print the results in a readable
               form.

GetData merely consists of a **readln** statement; AssignMonth is a procedure using a **CASE** statement (a function could be used here instead), and Print-Results prints the information in a readable form. A function for computing the number of days is further developed as

    3.   Compute days
        3.1   compute days alive during birth month
        3.2   compute total of days in remaining months

This could be refined to

    3.   Compute days
        3.1   compute days alive during birth month
            3.1.1   compute for months with 31 days
            3.1.2   compute for months with 30 days
            3.1.3   compute for February
                     IF leap year **THEN** use 29 days
                     ELSE use 28 days
        3.2   compute total of days in remaining months
              IF NOT December **THEN**
                  FOR rest of months **DO**
                     add number of days in month

The complete program to solve this problem is

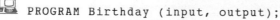

```
PROGRAM Birthday (input, output);

{ This program determines how many days you were alive during }
{ your  birth year.  Input is your  birth date.  Later,  you  }
{ can use this  program as the basis for a biorhythm program.  }
```

```
{   Pay special attention to the use of enumerated data types    }
{   and subranges.                                               }


TYPE
   AllMonths = (Jan, Feb, March, April, May, June,
                July, Aug, Sept, Oct, Nov, Dec);
   DayRange = 1..31;
   MonthRange = 1..12;
   YearRange = 0..99;


VAR
   BirthMonth : AllMonths;      {   Literal form of birth month   }
   DayNum : DayRange;           {   The day you were born          }
   Month : MonthRange;          {   Birth month                    }
   TotalDays : integer;         {   Days alive in birth year       }
   Year : YearRange;            {   Representation of birth year    }

{*************************************************************** }

PROCEDURE GetData (VAR Month : MonthRange;
                   VAR Day : DayRange;
                   VAR Year : YearRange);


   {   Given:    Nothing                                       }
   {   Task:     Enter your birthdate in the form 3 16 71      }
   {   Return:   Month, day, and year of birth                 }


   BEGIN
      writeln ('Please enter your birth date in the form 3 16 71.');
      writeln ('Press <RETURN> when finished.');
      readln (Month, Day, Year)
   END;  {  of PROCEDURE GetData  }

{*************************************************************** }

PROCEDURE AssignMonth (Month : MonthRange;
                       VAR BirthMonth : AllMonths);
   {   Given:    A numerical equivalent of the birth month     }
   {   Task:     Convert to literal BirthMonth                 }
   {   Return:   Literal BirthMonth                            }


   BEGIN
      CASE Month OF
          1 : BirthMonth := Jan;
          2 : BirthMonth := Feb;
          3 : BirthMonth := March;
          4 : BirthMonth := April;
          5 : BirthMonth := May;
          6 : BirthMonth := June;
          7 : BirthMonth := July;
          8 : BirthMonth := Aug;
          9 : BirthMonth := Sept;
         10 : BirthMonth := Oct;
         11 : BirthMonth := Nov;
         12 : BirthMonth := Dec
      END  {  of CASE Month  }
   END;  {  of PROCEDURE AssignMonth  }

{*************************************************************** }
```

```
            FUNCTION ComputeDays (BirthMonth : AllMonths;
                                  DayNum : DayRange;
                                  Year : YearRange) : integer;

               {  Given:    The month, day, and year of birth          }
               {  Task:     Compute the days alive during the year of birth  }
               {  Return:   Number of days alive during the year of birth    }

               VAR
                 Days : integer;
                 Mon : AllMonths;

            BEGIN

               {  Compute days alive in birth month  }

               CASE BirthMonth OF
                 Jan, March, May, July, Aug, Oct, Dec : Days := 31-DayNum+1;
                 April, June, Sept, Nov               : Days := 30-DayNum+1;
                 Feb                                  : IF Year MOD 4 = 0 THEN
                                                           Days := 29-DayNum+1
                                                        ELSE
                                                           Days := 28-DayNum+1
               END;  {  of CASE BirthMonth  }

               {  Now compute days in remaining months  }

               IF BirthMonth <> Dec THEN
                 FOR Mon := succ(BirthMonth) TO Dec DO
                   CASE Mon OF
                     Jan, March, May, July, Aug, Oct, Dec : Days := Days+31;
                     April, June, Sept, Nov               : Days := Days+30;
                     Feb                                  : IF Year MOD 4 = 0 THEN
                                                              Days := Days+29
                                                           ELSE
                                                              Days := Days+28

                   END;  {  of CASE Mon  }

               {  Assign total days to functions name  }

               ComputeDays := Days

            END;    {  of FUNCTION ComputeDays  }

{******************************************************************** }

PROCEDURE PrintResults (TotalDays : integer;
                        Year : YearRange);

   {  Given:    Birth year and total days alive during that year  }
   {  Task:     Print a message indicating the year of birth and  }
   {            number of days alive during that year             }
   {  Return:   Nothing                                           }

   BEGIN
     writeln;
     writeln ('During your birth year,', (Year+1900):6, ',');
     writeln ('you were alive', TotalDays:5, ' days.');
     writeln
   END; {  of PROCEDURE PrintResults  }


{******************************************************************** }
```

```
BEGIN  {  Main program  }
  GetData (Month, DayNum, Year);
  AssignMonth (Month, BirthMonth);
  TotalDays := ComputeDays (BirthMonth, DayNum, Year);
  PrintResults (TotalDays, Year)
END.  {  of main program  }
```

A sample run of this program produces

```
Please enter your birthdate in the form 3 16 71.
Press <RETURN> when finished.
3 16 71
During your birth year, 1971,
you were alive  291 days.
```

RUNNING AND DEBUGGING TIPS

1. An end-of-line marker is read as a blank. When reading numeric data, this is not a problem. However, when reading data of type **char,** you may forget to advance the pointer to the next line.

2. Permanent text files must be listed in the program heading file list as well as in the variable declaration section.

3. Be aware of the possibility of extra blanks at the beginning or end of lines in a text file. Some implementations cause these to be inserted when creating a text file.

4. The end-of-line marker is read as a blank. Thus, when working with character data in a text file, it may appear that extra blanks are in the file. However, the **eoln** function still returns **true** when the pointer is positioned at an end-of-line marker.

5. Subranges should be used if the bounds of a variable are known.

6. Enumerated data types should be used to enhance readability.

7. Be careful not to use **pred** on the first element in a list or **succ** on the last element.

8. Make sure variable parameters passed to subprograms are of identical type. For example, using the following declaration

```
TYPE
  Weekdays = (Mon, Tues, Wed, Thur, Fri);
VAR
  Day : Weekdays;
```

if a procedure call was

```
PrintChart (Day);
```

a procedure heading could be

```
PROCEDURE PrintChart (VAR Wkday : Weekdays);
```

9. A value parameter and its argument must be of compatible type.

■ Summary

Key Terms

compatible type	internal file	subrange
enumerated data type	opened for reading	temporary file
external file	opened for writing	text file
identical type	scratch file	user-defined data type

Keywords

assign	**text**
reset	**TYPE**
rewrite	

Key Concepts

- Text files can be used to store data between runs of a program.
- A text file can be declared by

```
VAR
   <file name> : text;
```

- An external file exists outside the program block in secondary storage. When used, it must be included in the file list as part of the program heading.
- An internal file exists within the program block. Values stored there will be lost when the program is no longer running.
- Text files must be opened before they can be written to or read from. Before reading from a file, it can be opened by

  reset (⟨file variable⟩);

  Before writing to a file, it can be opened by

  rewrite (⟨file variable⟩);

- Reading from a text file can be accomplished by

  read (⟨file variable⟩, ⟨list of variables⟩);
  or
  readln (⟨file variable⟩, ⟨list of variables⟩);

  If no file variable is given, the procedures apply to the standard file **input**.

- Writing to a text file can be accomplished by

  write (⟨file variable⟩, ⟨list of values⟩);
  or
  writeln (⟨file variable⟩, ⟨list of values⟩);

  If no file variable is given, the procedures apply to the standard file (**output**).

- A data type is ordinal if data of that type have a first and last listed element and each element other than the first and last has an immediate predecessor and an immediate successor.
- Enumerated data types can be defined by using the **TYPE** definition section; typical syntax and form are

```
TYPE
   Weekdays = (Mon, Tue, Wed, Thur, Fri);
```

- When a simple enumerated data type has been defined,
  1. The newly defined type will be an ordinal data type.
  2. Variables can be declared to be of the new type.
  3. The identifiers declared in the **TYPE** definition section are constants that can be used in the program.
  4. No identifier can belong to more than one data type.
  5. Identifiers that are defined values cannot be used as operands in expressions.
- You cannot **read** or **write** values of an enumerated data type.
- A subrange of an existing ordinal data type can be defined by

  TYPE
  　　⟨identifier⟩ = ⟨initial value⟩..⟨final value⟩;

  For example:

```
TYPE
   ScoreRange = 0..100;
   Alphabet = 'A'..'Z';
```

- Type compatible variables must have the same base type.
- Type identical variables must have the same type identifier.
- Two significant reasons for using subranges are program protection and program readability.
- The functions **pred, succ,** and **ord** can be used on enumerated data types and subranges of existing ordinal data types.
- When one of the functions **pred, succ,** or **ord** is used with an argument whose value is in a subrange, reference is to the base data type, not the subrange; thus, in

```
TYPE
  Letters = 'J'..'O';
```

ord('J') does not have the value 0. Rather, it yields the appropriate ordinal for the collating sequence being used. In the ASCII collating sequence, **ord**('J') yields 74 and in EBCDIC it yields 209.

■ Programming Problems and Projects

1. Write a program to compute the payroll for a company. Data for each employee will be on two lines. Line 1 contains an employee number followed by the hourly wage rate. Line 2 contains seven integer entries indicating the hours worked each day. Wages are to be computed at time-and-a-half for anything over eight hours on a weekday and double time for any weekend work. Deductions should be withheld as follows:
   - **a.** state income tax   4.6%
   - **b.** federal income tax   21.0%
   - **c.** social security (FICA)   6.2%
   - **d.** Medicare tax   1.45%

   Employee numbers are the subrange 0001..9999. You should define and use a data type for the days of the week.

2. The Caswell Catering and Convention Service (Problem 7, Chapter 4; Problem 14, Chapter 5; Problem 1, Chapter 6; and Problem 1, Chapter 7) wants to upgrade their existing computer program. Use the **TYPE** definition section for each of the following and revise the program you developed previously as appropriate.
   - **a.** The room names have been changed to a color-coded scheme as follows:

Room A	RedRoom
Room B	BlueRoom
Room C	YellowRoom
Room D	GreenRoom
Room E	BrownRoom

   - **b.** Use a subrange for the room rents.
   - **c.** Use defined constants for the low value and high value of the room rents.

■ 3. State University (Problem 15, Chapter 5) wants you to upgrade their computer program by using the **TYPE** definition section for each of the following:
   - **a.** The room types will be Regular or AirConditioned.
   - **b.** Students' numbers will be between 0001 and 9999 (use **CONST** for end values).
   - **c.** Credit hours taken must be between 1 and 25.
   - **d.** The GoodRange for credit hours is 12 to 21.

Your new version should be able to be used on a data file with several students' information.

4. Al Derrick (Problem 20, Chapter 5, and Problem 10, Chapter 6) wants you to revise his program by using the **TYPE** definition section to enhance readability and ensure protection against bad data. Your new version should run for several wells and include: types of wells (Dry, Oil, and Gas), volume for gas (between 10,000 and 100,000), and volume for oil (between 2,000 and 50,000).

■ 5. Dr. Lae Z. Programmer is relentless. He wants you to modify your latest version of the grading program (Problems 5, 22, and 23, Chapter 5; Problem 13, Chapter 6; or Problem 7, Chapter 7) by using the **TYPE** definition section. Your new version should include a range for test scores (from 0 to 100), a range for quiz scores (from 0 to 10), and a range for the final examination (from 0 to 200).

6. Upgrade your most recent version of the Pentagon Parking Lot program (Problem 26, Chapter 5; Problem 14, Chapter 6; or Problem 8, Chapter 7) by using the **TYPE** definition section. Time in and time out will be between 0600 and 2200 (6:00 A.M. and 10:00 P.M.). Vehicle type should be denoted by Car, Truck, or Senior.

7. Read a text file containing a paragraph of text. Count the number of words in the paragraph. Assume that consecutive words are separated by at least one blank.

8. Write a program to print the contents of a text file omitting any occurrences of the letter "e" from the output.

9. A text file contains a list of integers in order from lowest to highest. Write a program to read and print the text file with all duplications eliminated.

10. Mr. John Napier, Professor at Lancaster Community College, wants a program to compute grade point averages. Each line of a text file contains three initials followed by an unknown number of letter grades. These grades are A, B, C, D, or E. Write a program that reads the file and prints a list of the students' initials and their grade point averages. (Assume an A is 4 points, a B is 3 points, and so on.) Print an asterisk next to any grade point average that is greater than 3.75.

11. An amortization table (Problem 19, Chapter 6) shows the rate at which a loan is paid off. It contains monthly entries showing the interest paid that month, the principal paid, and the remaining balance. Given the amount of money borrowed (the principal), the annual interest rate, and the amount the person wishes to repay each month, print an amortization table. (The payment desired must be larger than the first month's interest.) Your table should stop when the loan is paid off, and should be printed with the following heads:

```
MONTH NUMBER   INTEREST PAID   PRINCIPAL PAID   BALANCE
```

Create an enumerated data type for the month number. Limit this to require that the loan be paid back within 60 months.

12. In 1626, the Dutch settlers purchased Manhattan Island from the Indians (Problem 23, Chapter 6). According to legend, the purchase price was $24. Suppose the Indians had invested this amount at 3 percent annual interest compounded quarterly. If the money had earned inter-

est from the start of 1626 to the end of last year, how much money would the Indians have in the bank today? (*Hint:* Use nested loops for the compounding.) Create an enumerated data type for the range of years (1626 to last year) that will be used.

13. Mr. Christian (Problem 26, Chapter 6) uses a 90 percent, 80 percent, 70 percent, 60 percent grading scale on his tests. Given a list of test scores, print the number of A's, B's, C's, D's, and E's on the test. Terminate the list of scores with a sentinel value. Use a subrange of the integers for the input grades.

14. Write a program to print the perimeter and area of rectangles using all combinations of lengths and widths running from 1 foot to 10 feet in increments of 1 foot. Print the output in headed columns. Use a subrange to restrict the lengths and widths from 1 to 10.

15. Contact a programmer, graduate student, or upper-division major in computer sciences and discuss the issue of using enumerated and other user-defined data types. Among other things, find how often (or even if) that person uses such data types, how important he or she considers such data types as part of a programming language, and some specific examples of how he or she uses enumerated data types. Give an oral report of your findings to your class.

16. It was reported in this chapter that enumerated and other user-defined data types are one of the advantages of Pascal as a programming language. Examine several other programming languages to see if they include a comparable feature. Prepare a chart that summarizes your findings.

17. Using a team of three or four students, contact businesses and offices that use computers for data storage. Find exactly how they enter, store, and retrieve data. Discuss with them methods by which they use their databases and how large the databases are. Discuss what they like and dislike about data entry and retrieval. Ask if they have suggestions for modifying any aspect of working with their databases. Prepare a report for class that summarizes your team's findings.

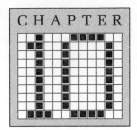

One-Dimensional Arrays

This chapter begins a significant new stage of programming. Prior to now, we have been unable to manipulate and store large amounts of data in a convenient way. For example, if we wanted to work with a long list of numbers or names, we had to declare a separate variable for each number or name. Fortunately, Pascal (and all other programming languages) provides several structured variables to facilitate solving problems that require working with large amounts of data. Simply put, a structured variable uses one identifier to reserve a large amount of memory. This memory is capable of holding several individual values. Structured variables included in this text are arrays, records, files, and sets.

Arrays, the topic of this chapter, are designed to handle large amounts of data of the same type in an organized manner. They are used whenever there is a need to store data for subsequent use in a program. Using arrays permits us to set aside a group of memory locations that we can then manipulate as a single entity or have direct access to any component. Some very standard applications for array variables include creating tabular output (tables), alphabetizing a list of names, analyzing a list of test scores, manipulating character data, and keeping an inventory.

■ 10.1
Arrays

OBJECTIVES

- to understand the basic concept of an array
- to use correct notation for arrays
- to be able to declare arrays with both variable declarations and type definitions
Objectives continued.

Basic Idea and Notation

As previously mentioned, there are many instances in which several variables of the same data type are required. Let us at this point work with a list of five integers: 18, 17, 21, 18, and 19. Prior to this chapter, we would have declared five variables—A, B, C, D, and E—and assigned them appropriate values, or read them from an input file. This would have produced five values in memory each accessed by a separate identifier.

18	17	21	18	19
A	B	C	D	E

■ to be able to use array components with appropriate arithmetic operations
■ to be able to use array components with appropriate **read** and **write** statements

If the list was very long, this would be an inefficient way to work with these data; an alternative is to use an array. In Pascal, we declare a variable as an array variable using either of the following methods:

1. VAR
      List : ARRAY [1..5] OF integer;
2. TYPE
      Numbers = ARRAY [1..5] OF integer;
   VAR
      List : Numbers;

With either of these declarations, we now have five integer variables with which to work. They are denoted by

   List[1]   List[2]   List[3]   List[4]   List[5]

and each is referred to as a *component* or (*element*) *of the array*. A good method of visualizing these variables is to assume that memory locations are aligned in a column on top of each other and the name of the column is List. If we then assign the five values of our list to these five variables, we have the following in memory.

List

18	List[1]
17	List[2]
21	List[3]
18	List[4]
19	List[5]

The components of an array are referred to by their relative position in the array. This relative position is called the *index* or *subscript* of the component. In the array of our five values, the component List[3] has an index of 3 and value of 21.

For the sake of convenience, you may choose to depict an array by listing only the index beside its appropriate component. Thus, List could be shown as

List

	1
	2
	3
	4
	5

If you choose this method, remember that the array elements are referenced by the array name and the index; for example, List[3] for the third component. Whichever method you use, it is important to remember that each array component is a variable and can be treated exactly as any other declared variable of that base type in the program.

Declaring an Array

An array type can be defined as a user-defined type and then an appropriate variable can be declared to be of this type. An earlier declaration was

```
TYPE
   Numbers = ARRAY [1..5] OF integer;
VAR
   List : Numbers;
```

Let us now examine this declaration more closely. Several comments are in order.

1. "Numbers" is a user-defined data type.
2. "**ARRAY**" is a reserved word and is used to indicate that an array type is being defined.
3. "[1 . . 5]" is the syntax that indicates the array consists of five memory locations accessed by specifying each of the numbers, 1, 2, 3, 4, and 5. We frequently say the array is of length five. The information inside the brackets is the *index type* and is used to refer to components of an array. This index type can be any ordinal data type that specifies a beginning value and an ending value. However, subranges of integer data type are the most easily read and frequently used index types.
4. The reserved word **OF** refers to the data type for the components of the array.
5. The key word **integer** indicates the data type for the components. This can, of course, be any valid data type.
6. "List" can be any valid identifier. As always, it is good practice to use descriptive names to enhance readability.

The general form for defining an array type is

TYPE
   ⟨name⟩ = **ARRAY** [⟨index type⟩] **OF** ⟨component type⟩;

---

where "name" is any valid identifier, "index type" is any ordinal data type that specifies both an initial value and a final value, and "component type" is any predefined or user-defined data type (except files). The syntax diagram for this is

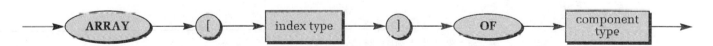

The following example illustrates another declaration of an array variable.

■ **EXAMPLE 10.1**

Suppose you want to create a list of ten integer variables for the hours worked by ten employees as follows:

Employee Number	Hours Worked
1	35
2	40
3	20
4	38
5	25
6	40
7	25
8	40
9	20
10	45

Declare an array that has ten components of type **integer** and show how it can be visualized. A descriptive name could be Hours. There are ten items, so we will use **ARRAY** [1 .. 10] in the definition. Since the data consist of integers, the component type will be **integer**. An appropriate definition and subsequent declaration could be

```
TYPE
   HourList = ARRAY [1..10] OF integer;
VAR
   Hours : HourList;
```

At this stage, the components can be visualized as

Hours

	Hours[1]
	Hours[2]
	Hours[3]
	Hours[4]
	Hours[5]
	Hours[6]
	Hours[7]
	Hours[8]
	Hours[9]
	Hours[10]

After making appropriate assignment statements, Hours can be visualized as

Hours

35	Hours[1]
40	Hours[2]
20	Hours[3]
38	Hours[4]
25	Hours[5]
40	Hours[6]
25	Hours[7]
40	Hours[8]
20	Hours[9]
45	Hours[10]

Other Indices and Data Types

The previous two arrays used index types that were subranges of the **integer** data type. Although this is a common method of specifying the index to an array, one could use subranges of any ordinal type for this definition. The following examples illustrate some array definitions with other indices and data types.

■ **EXAMPLE 10.2**

Declare an array to allow you to store the hourly price for a share of IBM stock. A descriptive name could be StockPrice. A price is quoted at each hour from 9:00 A.M. to 3:00 P.M., so we will use **ARRAY** [9 . . 15] in the declaration section. Since the data consist of reals, the data type must be **real**. A possible declaration could be

```
TYPE
   StockPriceList = ARRAY [9..15] OF real;
VAR
   StockPrice : StockPriceList;
```

This would then allow us to store the 9:00 A.M. price in StockPrice[9], the 1:00 P.M. price in StockPrice[13], and so on.

■

■ **EXAMPLE 10.3**

The declaration

```
TYPE
   AlphaList = ARRAY [-2..3] OF char;
VAR
   Alpha : AlphaList;
```

will reserve components, which can be depicted as

Alpha

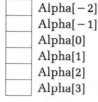

Alpha[−2]
Alpha[−1]
Alpha[0]
Alpha[1]
Alpha[2]
Alpha[3]

Each component is a character variable.

■

■ **EXAMPLE 10.4**

The declaration

```
TYPE
   TotalHoursList = ARRAY ['A'..'E'] OF integer;
VAR
   TotalHours : TotalHoursList;
```

will reserve components which can be depicted as

TotalHours

	'A'
	'B'
	'C'
	'D'
	'E'

Components of this array are integer variables.

■   ■

■ EXAMPLE 10.5

The declaration

```
TYPE
  FlagValues = ARRAY [1..4] OF boolean;
VAR
  Flag : FlagValues;
```

will produce an array whose components are **boolean** variables.

■   ■

It is important to note that in each example, the array components will have no values assigned until the program specifically makes some kind of assignment. Declaring an array does not assign values to any of the components.

Two additional array definitions and subsequent declarations follow.

1. ```
   TYPE
     Days = (Mon, Tues, Wed, Thur, Fri, Sat, Sun);
     Workdays = ARRAY [Mon..Fri] OF real;
   VAR
     HoursWorked : Workdays;
   ```
2. ```
   TYPE
     List50 = ARRAY [1..50] OF real;
     List25 = ARRAY [1..25] OF integer;
     String20 = ARRAY [1..20] OF char;
   VAR
     PhoneCharge : List50;
     Score : List25;
     Word : String20;
     A, B, C, D : List50;
   ```

A more efficient method of manipulating character data than the strings just used will be presented in Section 10.5 when we discuss packed arrays.

STYLE TIP
■ ■ ■ ■ ■ ■ ■ ■ ■ ■ ■

Descriptive constants and type identifiers should be utilized when working with arrays. For example, if you are working with an array of test scores for a class of 35 students, you could have

```
CONST
  ClassSize = 35;
TYPE
  TestScores = 0..100;
  ScoreList = ARRAY [1..ClassSize] OF TestScores;
VAR
  Score : ScoreList;
```

Assignment Statements

Suppose we have declared an array

```
A : ARRAY [1..5] OF integer;
```

and we want to put the values 1, 4, 9, 16, and 25 into the respective components. We can accomplish this with the assignment statements

```
A[1] := 1;
A[2] := 4;
A[3] := 9;
A[4] := 16;
A[5] := 25;
```

If variables B and C of type **integer** are declared in the program, then the following are also appropriate assignment statements.

```
A[3] := B;
C := A[2];
A[2] := A[5];
```

If you want to interchange values of two components (for example, exchange A[2] with A[3]), you could use a third integer variable.

```
B := A[2];
A[2] := A[3];
A[3] := B;
```

This exchange is frequently used in sorting algorithms, so let us examine it more closely. Assume B contains no previously assigned value, and A[2] and A[3] contain 4 and 9, respectively.

The assignment statement

```
B := A[2];
```

produces

The assignment statement

```
A[2] := A[3];
```

produces

and finally the assignment statement

```
A[3] := B;
```

produces

in which the original values of A[2] and A[3] have been interchanged.

The next example illustrates the use of a **TYPE** definition and a subsequent assignment statement.

Given the following definitions,

```
TYPE
   Seasons = (Fall, Winter, Spring, Summer);
   TemperatureList = ARRAY [Seasons] OF real;
VAR
   AvTemp : TemperatureList;
```

an assignment statement such as

```
AvTemp[Fall] := 53.2;
```

would be appropriate. The array would then be

AvTemp

53.2	Fall
	Winter
	Spring
	Summer

■

Arithmetic

Components of an array can also be used in any appropriate arithmetic operation. For example, suppose A is the array of integers

A

1	A[1]
4	A[2]
9	A[3]
16	A[4]
25	A[5]

and the values of the components of the array are to be added. This could be accomplished by the statement

```
Sum := A[1] + A[2] + A[3] + A[4] + A[5];
```

Each of the following would also be a valid use of an array component.

```
B := 3 * A[2];
C := A[4] MOD 3;
D := A[2] * A[5];
```

For the array A given, these assignment statements produce

55	12	1	100
Sum	B	C	D

Some invalid assignment statements and the reasons they are invalid follow.

```
A[0] := 7;          (0 is not a valid subscript.)
A[2] := 3.5;        (Component A[2] is not of type real.)
A[2.0] := 3;        (A subscript of type real is not allowed.)
```

Reading and Writing

Since array components are names for variables, they can be used with **read, readln, write,** and **writeln**. For example, if Score is an array of five integers and you want to input the scores 65, 43, 98, 75, and 83 from a data file, you could use the code

```
readln (Score[1], Score[2], Score[3], Score[4], Score[5]);
```

This would produce the array

Score

65	Score[1]
43	Score[2]
98	Score[3]
75	Score[4]
83	Score[5]

If you want to print the scores above 80, you could use the code

```
writeln (Score[3]:10, Score[5]:10);
```

to produce

```
        98          83
```

It is important to note that you cannot **read** or **write** values into or from an entire array by a reference to the array name (an exception will be explained in Section 10.5). Statements such as

```
read(A), writeln(A)
```

are invalid if A is an array.

Be careful to avoid out-of-range array references. For example, if the array A has index values 1 . . 5, a reference to A[6] or A[0] would then produce an error. This becomes more of a problem when you start processing arrays with loops in the next section.

Monolithic Idea: Invention of the Integrated Circuit

One of the most significant breakthroughs in the history of technology occurred in the late 1950s. Prior to 1958, computer circuitry was limited because transistors, diodes, resistors and capacitors were separate units that had to be wired together and soldered by hand. Although designers could design intricate computer supercircuits using 500,000 transistors, they were almost impossible to build because of the extensive handwork involved. For example, a circuit with 100,000 components could require over 1,000,000 soldered connections. It was virtually impossible to assemble that many components without human error. Thus, the electronics industry was faced with an apparently insurmountable limit.

About this time, Jack St. Clair Kilby developed what has come to be known as the Monolithic Idea. He decided you could put the components of an entire circuit in a monolithic block of silicon. The idea, together with Robert Noyce's work on interconnecting circuits, allowed electronics engineers to overcome the obstacle presented by separate components. Kilby and Noyce's work resulted in the integrated circuit, the most important new product in the history of electronics. For their efforts, both men were awarded the National Medal of Science.

Exercises 10.1

1. Using descriptive names, define an array type and declare subsequent variables for each of the following:

   a. A list of 35 test scores

   b. The prices of 20 automobiles

   c. The answers to 50 true or false questions

   d. A list of letter grades for the classes you are taking this semester

2. Write a test program in which you declare an array of three components, read values into each component, sum the components, and print out the sum and value of each component.

3. Find all errors in the following definitions of array types.

   a. ```
TYPE
    Time = ARRAY [1..12] OF Hours;
```

   b. ```
TYPE
    Scores = ARRAY [1..30] OF integer;
```

   c. ```
TYPE
    Alphabet = ARRAY OF char;
```

   d. ```
TYPE
    List = ARRAY [1 TO 10] OF real;
```

   e. ```
TYPE
    Answers = ARRAY [OF boolean];
```

   f. ```
TYPE
    X = ARRAY [1...5] OF real;
```

4. Assume the array List is declared as

   ```
TYPE
    Scores = ARRAY [1..100] OF integer;
VAR
    List : Scores;
```

   and that all other variables have been appropriately declared. Label the following as valid or invalid. Include an explanation for any that are invalid.

   a. `read (List[3]);`

   b. `A := List[3] + List[4];`

   c. `writeln (List);`

   d. `List[10] := 3.2;`

   e. `Max := List[50];`

   f. `Average := (List[1] + List[8]) / 2;`

   g. `write (List[25, 50, 75, 100]);`

   h. `write ((List[10] + List[90]):25);`

   i. ```
FOR J := 1 TO 100 DO
    read (List);
```

   j. `List[36] := List[102];`

   k. `Scores[47] := 92;`

   l. `List[40] := List[41] / 2;`

5. Change each of the following so that the **TYPE** definition section is used to define the array type.

   a. ```
VAR
    LetterList : ARRAY [1..100] OF 'A'..'Z';
```

b. VAR
```
CompanyName : ARRAY [1..30] OF char;
```
c. VAR
```
ScoreList : ARRAY [30..59] OF real;
```

6. Consider the array declared by

```
TYPE
   ListOfSizes = ARRAY [1..5] OF integer;
VAR
   WaistSize : ListOfSizes;
```

a. Sketch how the array should be envisioned in memory.

b. After assignments

```
WaistSize[1] := 34;
WaistSize[3] := 36;
WaistSize[5] := 32;
WaistSize[2] := 2 * 15;
WaistSize[4] := (WaistSize[1] + WaistSize[3]) DIV 2;
```

have been made, sketch the array and indicate the contents of each component.

7. Let the array Money be declared by

```
TYPE
   List3 = ARRAY [1..3] OF real;
VAR
   Money : List3;
```

Let Temp, X, and Y be real variables and assume Money has the indicated values

Money

19.26	Money[1]
10.04	Money[2]
17.32	Money[3]

Assuming Money contains the values indicated before each segment is executed, indicate what the array would contain after each section of code.

a.
```
Temp := 173.21;
X := Temp + Money[2];
Money[1] := X;
```

b.
```
IF Money[2] < Money[1] THEN
   BEGIN
      Temp := Money[2];
      Money[2] := Money[1];
      Money[1] := Temp
   END;
```

c.
```
Money[3] := 20 - Money[3];
```

8. Let the array List be declared by

```
TYPE
   Scores = ARRAY [1..5] OF real;
VAR
   List : Scores;
```

Write a program segment to initialize all components of List to 0.0.

■ 10.2
Using Arrays

OBJECTIVES

■ to be able to use loops to read data into an array from an input file
■ to be able to use loops to write data from an array
■ to be able to assign array values by aggregate assignment and by component assignment
■ to be able to use loops with arrays to solve programming problems

Loops for Input and Output

One advantage of using arrays is the small amount of code needed when loops are used to manipulate array components. For example, suppose a list of 100 scores stored in a data file is to be used in a program. If an array is declared by

```
TYPE
   List100 = ARRAY [1..100] OF integer;
VAR
   Score : List100;
   J : integer;
```

the data file can be read into the array using a **FOR** loop as follows:

```
FOR J := 1 TO 100 DO
   read (Score[J]);
```

Remember, a statement such as **read** (Score) is invalid. You may only read data into individual components of the array.

Loops can be similarly used to produce output of array components. For example, if the array of test scores just given is to be printed in a column,

```
FOR J := 1 TO 100 DO
   writeln (Score[J]);
```

will accomplish this. If the components of Score contain the values

Score

78	Score[1]
93	Score[2]
.	.
.	.
.	.
82	Score[100]

the loop for writing produces

```
78
93
 .
 .
82
```

Note that you cannot cause the array components to be printed by a statement such as **write** (Score) or **writeln** (Score). These are invalid. You must refer to the individual components.

Loops for output are seldom this simple. Usually we are required to format the output in some manner. For example, suppose the array Score is as declared and we wish to print these scores ten to a line, each with a field width of five spaces. The following segment of code would accomplish this.

```
FOR J := 1 TO 100 DO
  BEGIN
    write (Score[J]:5);
    IF J MOD 10 = 0 THEN
      writeln
  END;
```

Loops for Assigning

Loops can also be used to assign values to array components. In certain instances, you might wish to have an array contain values that are not read from an input file. The following examples show how loops can be used to solve such instances.

■ **EXAMPLE 10.7**

Recall the array A in Section 10.1 in which we made the following assignments.

```
A[1] := 1;
A[2] := 4;
A[3] := 9;
A[4] := 16;
A[5] := 25;
```

These assignments could have been made with the loop

```
FOR J := 1 TO 5 DO
   A[J] := J * J;
```

■

■ **EXAMPLE 10.8**

Suppose an array is needed whose components contain the letters of the alphabet in order from A to Z. Assuming you are using the ASCII character set, the desired array could be declared by

```
TYPE
   Letters = ARRAY [1..26] OF char;
VAR
   Alphabet : Letters;
```

The array Alphabet could then be assigned the desired characters by the statement

```
FOR J := 1 TO 26 DO
   Alphabet[J] := chr(J-1 + ord('A'));
```

If

```
J := 1;
```

we have

```
Alphabet[1] := chr(ord('A'));
```

Thus,

```
Alphabet[1] := 'A';
```

Similarly, for

```
J := 2;
```

we have

```
Alphabet[2] := chr(1 + ord('A'));
```

Eventually we obtain

Alphabet

'A'	Alphabet[1]
'B'	Alphabet[2]
'C'	Alphabet[3]
.	.
.	.
.	.
'Z'	Alphabet[26]

Assignment of values from components of one array to corresponding components of another array is a frequently encountered problem. For example, suppose the arrays A and B are declared as

```
TYPE
  List50 = ARRAY [1..50] OF real;
VAR
  A, B : List50;
```

If B has been assigned values and you want to put the contents of B into A component by component, you could use the loop

```
FOR J := 1 TO 50 DO
  A[J] := B[J];
```

However, for problems of this type, Pascal allows the entire array to be assigned by

```
A := B;
```

This aggregate assignment actually causes 50 assignments to be made at the component level. The arrays must be of the same type to do this.

Processing with Loops

Loops are especially suitable for reading, writing, and assigning array components, and can be used in conjunction with arrays to process data. For example, suppose A and B are declared as

```
TYPE
  List100 = ARRAY [1..100] OF real;
VAR
  A, B : List100;
```

and you want to add the values of components of B to the respective values of components of A. You could use the loop

```
FOR J := 1 TO 100 DO
  A[J] := A[J] + B[J];
```

It would appear that since

```
A := B;
```

is valid,

```
A := A + B;
```

would accomplish this. Not true. Pascal does not allow the aggregate addition of A + B where A and B are arrays.

The following examples illustrate additional uses of loops for processing data contained in array variables.

■ **EXAMPLE 10.9**

Recall the problem earlier in this section in which we read 100 test scores into an array. Assume the scores have been read and you now wish to find the average score and the largest score. Assume variables Sum, Max, and Average have been appropriately declared. The following segment will compute the average.

```
Sum := 0;
FOR J := 1 TO 100 DO
   Sum := Sum + Score[J];
Average := Sum / 100;
```

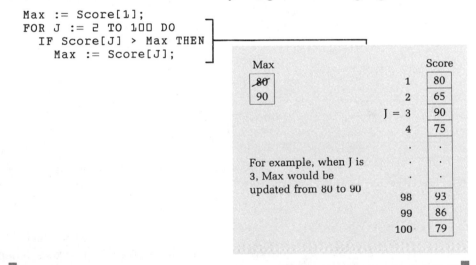

The maximum score can be found by using the following segment of code.

```
Max := Score[1];
FOR J := 2 TO 100 DO
   IF Score[J] > Max THEN
      Max := Score[J];
```

■ **EXAMPLE 10.10**

Write a segment of code to find the smallest value of array A and the index of the smallest value. Assume the variables have been declared as

```
TYPE
   Column100 = ARRAY [1..100] OF real;
VAR
   A : Column100;
   Min : real;
   Index : integer;
```

and the values have been read into components of A. The following algorithm will solve the problem.

1. Assign 1 to Index
2. **FOR** J := 2 **TO** 100 **DO**
   IF A[J] < A[Index] **THEN** assign J to Index
3. Assign A[Index] to Min

The segment of code is

```
Index := 1;
FOR J := 2 TO 100 DO
  IF A[J] < A[Index] THEN
    Index := J;
Min := A[Index];
```

Index		A
2 / 4	1	80
	2	65
	3	90
	J = 4	62
	.	.
	98	93
	99	86
	100	79

For this data, when J is 4, Index would be updated from 2 to 4

EXAMPLE 10.11

Suppose arrays A, B, and C have been declared as

```
TYPE
  List100 = ARRAY [1..100] OF real;
  List50 = ARRAY [1..50] OF real;
VAR
  A : List100;
  B, C : List50;
```

and we want to assign B to the top half of A, and C to the bottom half. The loop

```
FOR J := 1 TO 50 DO
  A[J] := B[J];
```

will accomplish the first part of the task. To assign C to the bottom half of A we could use these 50 assignment statements:

```
A[51] := C[1];
A[52] := C[2];
    .       .
    .       .
    .       .
A[100] := C[50];
```

However, by examining the indices, we see this can be done more efficiently by

```
FOR J := 1 TO 50 DO
  A[50+J] := C[J];
```

These two assignment loops can be visualized as

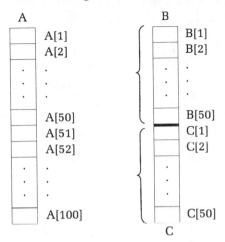

A very standard problem encountered when working with arrays is, what do you do when you don't know exactly how many components of an array will be needed? You must decide some upper limit for the length of the array. A standard procedure is to declare a reasonable limit, keeping two points in mind.

1. The length must be sufficient to store all the data.
2. The amount of storage space must not be excessive; do not set aside excessive amounts of space that will not be used.

To guard against the possibility of not reading all the data into array elements, an **IF . . . THEN** statement, such as

```
IF NOT eof THEN
    writeln ('There are more data.');
```

could be included in the procedure used to get data from the data file. These points are illustrated in Example 10.12. The array will be partially filled when the number of checks is less than the array length. This information can be retained by including a program statement such as

```
NumberOfChecks := J;
```

after the loop is exited.

■ **EXAMPLE 10.12**

Suppose an input file contains an unknown number of dollar amounts from personal checks. Write a segment of code to read them into an array and output the number of checks. Since the data are in dollars, we use real components and the identifier Check.

```
TYPE
    List = ARRAY [1..?] OF real;
VAR
    Check : List;
```

If we think there are fewer than 50 checks, we could define a constant by

```
CONST
  MaxChecks = 50;
```

and then define List by

```
List = ARRAY [1..MaxChecks] OF real;
```

The data could then be accessed using a **WHILE . . . DO** loop.

```
J := 0;
WHILE NOT eof AND (J < MaxChecks) DO
  BEGIN
    J := J + 1;
    readln (Check[J])
  END;
IF NOT eof THEN
  writeln ('There are more data.');
NumberOfChecks := J;
```

Now we have the data in the array, we know the number of data items, and NumberOfChecks can be used as a loop limit. Then the loop

```
FOR J := 1 TO NumberOfChecks DO
  BEGIN
    writeln;
    writeln ('Check number':20, J:4, '$':5, Checks[J]:7:2)
  END;
```

will print the checks on every other line.

We close this section with a final example using more elaborate **TYPE** definitions, loops, and arrays.

EXAMPLE 10.13

```
PROGRAM Economy (input, output);

{   This program illustrates the use of TYPE definitions, loops, and   }
{   arrays. Values are read into an array and the maximum and average  }
{   are found. The array contents, maximum, and average are printed.   }

CONST
  StartYear = 1982;
  LastYear = 1990;

TYPE
  RecentYears = StartYear..LastYear;
  EconIndicator = ARRAY [RecentYears] OF real;

VAR
  GrossNatlProd : EconIndicator;  { Array of gross national product }
  Max : real;                     { Maximum value in the array      }
  Sum : real;                     { Total of values in the array    }
  Average : real;                 { Average of values in the array  }
  NumYears : integer;             { Number of years used            }
  Year : RecentYears;             { Years from StartYear to LastYear }
```

```
BEGIN  {  Main program  }

  {  Get the data  }

  Sum := 0;
  FOR Year := StartYear TO LastYear DO
    BEGIN
      readln (GrossNatlProd[Year]);
      Sum := Sum + GrossNatlProd[Year]
    END;

  {  Find the maximum  }

  Max := GrossNatlProd[StartYear];              {  Get initial value        }
  FOR Year := StartYear + 1 TO LastYear DO
    IF GrossNatlProd[Year] > Max THEN           {  Check for larger value  }
      Max := GrossNatlProd[Year];

  {  Find the average  }

  NumYears := LastYear - StartYear + 1;
  Average := Sum / NumYears;

  {  Now display all data  }

  writeln ('Year', 'Gross National Product':30);
  writeln ('(in billions)':29);
  writeln ('----', '--------------------':30);
  writeln;
  FOR Year := StartYear TO LastYear DO
    writeln (Year, GrossNatlProd[Year]:20:1);

  {  Now display the maximum and average  }

  writeln;
  writeln ('The greatest GNP in recent years was',
           Max:10:2,' billion dollars.');
  writeln ('The average GNP for ', NumYears, ' years was',
           Average:10:2, ' billion dollars.');
  writeln

END.  {  of main program  }
```

The output for this program is

```
Year            Gross National Product
                      (in billions)

----            --------------------

1982                  3160.0
1983                  3405.7
1984                  3772.2
1985                  4014.9
1986                  4231.6
1987                  4524.3
1988                  4880.6
1989                  5200.8
1990                  5463.6

The greatest GNP in recent years was   5463.60 billion dollars.
The average GNP for 7 years was   4274.06 billion dollars.
```

STYLE TIP

■ ■ ■ ■ ■ ■ ■ ■ ■ ■ ■

Indices with semantic meaning can be useful when working with arrays. For example, suppose you are writing a program that includes the inventory for shoe styles in a shoe store. If the styles are loafer, wing tip, docksider, high pump, low pump, and plain tie, you would define

```
TYPE
   Style = (Docksider, HighPump, Loafer, LowPump,
            PlainTie, WingTip);
   ShoeInventory = ARRAY [Docksider..WingTip] OF integer;
VAR
   Stock : ShoeInventory;
   ShoeType : Style;
```

Typical program statements could be

```
Stock[WingTip] := 25;
Stock[Loafer] := Stock[Loafer] - 3;
FOR ShoeType := Docksider TO WingTip DO
   writeln (Stock[ShoeType]);
```

Exercises 10.2

1. Assume the following array declarations.

```
TYPE
   NumList = ARRAY [1..5] OF integer;
   AnswerList = ARRAY [1..10] OF boolean;
   NameList = ARRAY [1..20] OF char;
VAR
   List, Score : NumList;
   Answer : AnswerList;
   Name : NameList;
```

Indicate the contents of the arrays after each segment of code.

a.
```
FOR J := 1 TO 5 DO
   List[J] := J DIV 3;
```

b.
```
FOR J := 2 TO 6 DO
   BEGIN
      List[J-1] := J + 3;
      Score[J-1] := List[J-1] DIV 3
   END;
```

c.
```
FOR J := 1 TO 10 DO
   IF J MOD 2 = 0 THEN
      Answer[J] := true
   ELSE
      Answer[J] := false;
```

d.
```
FOR J := 1 TO 20 DO
   Name[J] := chr(J + 64);
```

2. Write a test program to illustrate what happens when you try to use an index that is not in the defined subrange for an array; for example, try to use the loop

```
FOR J := 1 TO 10 DO
   read (A[J]);
```

when A has been declared as

```
TYPE
   NumList = ARRAY [1..5] OF integer;
VAR
   A : NumList;
```

3. Let the array Best be declared by

```
TYPE
   List30 = ARRAY [1..30] OF integer;
VAR
   Best : List30;
```

and assume that test scores have been read into Best. What does the following section of code do?

```
Count := 0;
FOR J := 1 TO 30 DO
   IF Best[J] > 90 THEN
      Count := Count + 1;
```

4. Declare an array and write a segment of code to

   a. Read 20 integer test scores into the array.

   b. Count the number of scores greater than or equal to 55.

5. Declare an array using the **TYPE** definition section and write a section of code to read a name of 20 characters from a line of input.

6. Let the array List be declared by

```
TYPE
   Numbers = ARRAY [11..17] OF integer;
VAR
   List : Numbers;
```

and assume the components have values of

List

−2	List[11]
3	List[12]
0	List[13]
−8	List[14]
20	List[15]
14	List[16]
−121	List[17]

Show what the array components would be after the following program segment is executed.

```
FOR J := 11 TO 17 DO
   IF List[J] < 0 THEN
      List[J] := 0;
```

7. Assume the array A is declared as

```
TYPE
   List100 = ARRAY [1..100] OF real;
VAR
   A : List100;
```

Write a segment of code that uses a loop to initialize all components to zero.

8. The following can be used to input the values in Example 10.12. Discuss how it is different.

```
FOR J := 1 TO 50 DO
   IF NOT eof THEN
      readln (Check[J]);
```

9. Let the array N be declared as

```
TYPE
   String10 = ARRAY [1..10] OF char;
VAR
   N : String10;
```

and assume the array components have been assigned the values

J	O	H	N		S	M	I	T	H
N[1]	N[2]	N[3]	N[4]	N[5]	N[6]	N[7]	N[8]	N[9]	N[10]

What output is produced by the following?

a.
```
FOR J := 1 TO 10 DO
   write (N[J]);
writeln;
```

b.
```
FOR J := 1 TO 5 DO
   write (N[J+5]);
write (', ');
FOR J := 1 TO 4 DO
   write (N[J]);
writeln;
```

c.
```
FOR J := 10 DOWNTO 1 DO
   write (N[J]);
```

10. Let arrays A, B, and C be declared as

```
TYPE
   FirstList = ARRAY [21..40] OF real;
   SecondList = ARRAY [-4..15] OF real;
VAR
   A, B : FirstList;
   C : Secondlist;
```

Indicate if the following are valid or invalid. Include an explanation for those that are invalid.

a.
```
FOR J := 21 TO 40 DO
   A[J] := C[J-25];
```

b.
```
A := B;
```

c.
```
A := C;
```

d.
```
FOR J := 1 TO 10 DO
   B[J+20] := C[J+10];
```

e.
```
FOR J := 11 TO 20 DO
   B[J+20] := A[J+20];
```

11. Assume an array has been declared as

```
TYPE
   List50 = ARRAY [1..50] OF integer;
VAR
   TestScore : List50;
```

Write a segment of code to print a suitable heading (assume this is a list of test scores) and then output a numbered list of the array components.

12. Write a program segment to read 100 real numbers from a data file, compute the average, and find both the largest and smallest values.

■ ■ ■ ■

■ 10.3
Selection Sort

■ to be able to sort an array using the selection sort

A common problem involving arrays is sorting the components of the array in either ascending or descending order. Several sorting algorithms are given in Chapter 14, but let us now consider one of the easier methods, the *selection sort*.

Suppose we have an array A of five integers that we wish to sort from smallest to largest. The values currently in A are as depicted on the left; we wish to end up with values as on the right.

A	
6	A[1]
4	A[2]
8	A[3]
10	A[4]
1	A[5]

A	
1	A[1]
4	A[2]
6	A[3]
8	A[4]
10	A[5]

The basic idea of a selection sort is

1. Find the smallest number in the array and exchange it with A[1].
2. Find the smallest number among A[2] through A[5] and exchange it with A[2].
3. Continue this process until the array is sorted.

The first step produces

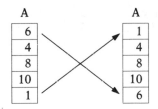

The second step produces

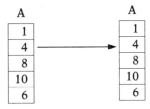

Notice that since the second smallest number was already in place, we need not exchange anything. The third step produces

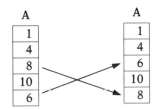

The fourth and final step yields the sorted list.

A
| 1 |
| 4 |
| 6 |
| 10 |
| 8 |

A
| 1 |
| 4 |
| 6 |
| 8 |
| 10 |

Before writing the algorithm for this sorting procedure, note the following:

1. If the array is of length n, we need $n - 1$ steps.
2. We must be able to find the smallest number.
3. We need to exchange appropriate array components.

Too Few Women in the Computer Science Pipeline?

Studies show that women in computer science programs in U.S. universities terminate their training earlier than men do. Between 1983 and 1986 (the latest year for which we have such figures) the percentage of bachelor's degrees in computer science awarded to women was in the range 36–37 percent and the percentage of master's degrees was in the range of 28–30 percent. During the same time span, the percentage of doctoral degrees awarded to women was in the range of only 10–12 percent, and it has remained at that level, with the exception of a slight increase in 1989.

If we look at the people who are training the future computer scientists, we may find a clue as to why this discrepancy exists. Women currently hold only 6.5 percent of the faculty positions in the computer science and computer engineering departments in the 158 Ph.D-granting institutions included in the 1988–1989 Taulbee Survey. In fact, a third of these departments have no female faculty members at all. This pattern of decreasing representation is often described as pipeline shrinkage: as women move along the academic pipeline, their percentages continue to shrink.

The ACM Committee on the Status of Women has made a number of recommendations to promote change. These recommendations include:

Ensure equal access to computers for young girls and boys and develop educational software appealing to both.

Establish programs (such as science fairs, scouting programs, and conferences in which women speak about their careers in science and engineering) to encourage high school girls to continue with math and science.

Develop programs to pair undergraduate women with women graduate students or faculty members who serve as role models, providing encouragement and advice.

Provide women with opportunities for successful professional experiences (such as involvement in research projects) beginning as early as the undergraduate years.

Establish programs that make women computer scientists visible to undergraduates and graduate students. Women can be invited to campuses to give talks or to serve as visiting faculty members (as, for example, in the National Science Foundation's Visiting Professorships for Women).

Encourage men and women to serve as mentors for young women in the field.

Maintain lists of qualified women computer scientists to increase the participation of women in influential positions such as program committees, editorial boards, and policy boards.

Establish more reentry programs that enable women who have stopped their scientific training prematurely to retrain as computer scientists.

Increase awareness of, and sensitivity to, subtle discrimination and its effects.

Develop and enforce safety procedures on campus. Provide safe access at all hours to public terminal areas, well-lit routes from offices to parking lots, and services to escort those walking on campus after dark.

Provide affordable, quality childcare.

If two or more values in the list are equal, an exchange would not be made when finding the smallest number. Thus, rather than find the smallest numbers, we must be able to find one of the remaining smallest numbers.

When the code is written for this sort, note that strict inequality ($<$) rather than weak inequality ($<=$) is used when looking for the smallest remaining value. The algorithm to sort by selection is

1. **FOR** J := 1 **TO** N − 1
    1.1 find the smallest value among A[J], A[J + 1], . . . A[N] and store the index of the smallest value in Index
    1.2 exchange the values of A[J] and A[Index], if necessary

In Section 10.2 (Example 10.10) we saw a segment of code required to find the smallest value of array A. With suitable changes, we will incorporate this in the segment of code for a selection sort.

```
Index := 1;
FOR J := 2 TO ArrayLength DO
  IF A[J] < A[Index] THEN
    Index := J;
```

Let A be an array of length *n* and assume all variables have been appropriately declared. Then the following will sort A from low to high.

```
FOR J := 1 TO N-1 DO       {  Find the minimum N-1 times  }
  BEGIN
    Index := J;
    FOR K := J + 1 TO N DO
      IF A[K] < A[Index] THEN
        Index := K;   {  Find index of smallest number  }
    IF Index <> J THEN
      BEGIN
        Temp := A[Index];
        A[Index] := A[J];
        A[J] := Temp
      END  {  of exchange  }
END;  {  of FOR J loop  }
```

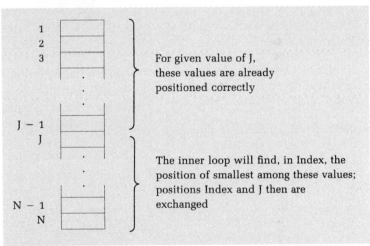

For given value of J, these values are already positioned correctly

The inner loop will find, in Index, the position of smallest among these values; positions Index and J then are exchanged

Let us now trace this sort for the five integers in the array we sorted in the beginning of this section.

A

6	A[1]
4	A[2]
8	A[3]
10	A[4]
1	A[5]

For J := 1, Index := 1, and this produces

1

Index

For the loop **FOR** K := 2 **TO** 5, we get successive assignments

K	Index
2	2
3	2
4	2
5	5

The statements

```
Temp := A[Index];
A[Index] := A[J];
A[J] := Temp;
```

produce the partially sorted array

A

1	A[1]
4	A[2]
8	A[3]
10	A[4]
6	A[5]

Each successive J value continues to partially sort the array until J := 4. This pass produces a completely sorted array.

■ **EXAMPLE 10.14**

Our concluding example

1. Inputs real numbers from an input file.
2. Echo prints the numbers in a column of width six with two places to the right of the decimal (:6:2).
3. Sorts the array from low to high.
4. Prints the sorted array using the same output format.

An expanded pseudocode development for this is

1. Print header—prints a suitable explanation of the program and includes a heading for the unsorted list
2. Get data (echo print)—uses a **WHILE** loop to read the data and print it in the same order in which it is read
3. Sort list—uses the selection sort to sort the array from low to high
4. Output sorted list—uses a **FOR** loop to output the sorted list

```
PROGRAM ArraySample (input, output);

{    This program illustrates the use of a sorting algorithm      }
{    with an array of reals.  Output includes data in both an     }
{    unsorted and a sorted list.  The data are formatted  and     }
{    numbered to enhance readability.                             }

CONST
  Skip = ' ';
  ListMax = 20;

TYPE
  NumList = ARRAY [1..ListMax] OF real;

VAR
  Index : integer;       {  Stores position of an element         }
  J, K : integer;        {  Indices                               }
  NumReals : integer;    {  Size of the list                      }
  Temp : real;           {  Temporary storage for array elements  }
  List : NumList;        {  Array of reals                        }

{*************************************************************************}
```

```
PROCEDURE PrintHeading;

  {  Given:    Nothing                                           }
  {  Task:     Print a heading for the output  }                 }
  {  Return:   Nothing                                           }

  BEGIN
    writeln;
    writeln (Skip:10, 'This sample program does the following:');
    writeln;
    writeln (Skip:12, '<1> Gets reals from a data file.');
    writeln (Skip:12, '<2> Echo prints the data.');
    writeln (Skip:12, '<3> Sorts the data from low to high.');
    writeln (Skip:12, '<4> Prints a sorted list of the data.');
    writeln
  END;  {  of PROCEDURE PrintHeading  }


{**************************************************************}

BEGIN {  Main program  }

  {  Print the heading  }

  PrintHeading;

  {  Get the data and echo print it  }

  writeln (Skip:10, 'The original data are as follows:');
  writeln;
  NumReals := 0;
  WHILE NOT eof AND (NumReals < ListMax) DO
    BEGIN
      NumReals := NumReals + 1;
      readln (List[NumReals]);
      writeln (Skip:12, '<', NumReals:2, '>', List[NumReals]:6:2)
    END;  {  of WHILE NOT loop  }
  IF NOT eof THEN
    writeln ('There are more data.');

  {  Now sort the list  }

  FOR J := 1 TO NumReals - 1 DO
    BEGIN
      Index := J;
      FOR K := J + 1 TO NumReals DO
        IF List[K] < List[Index] THEN
          Index := K;
        IF Index <> J THEN
          BEGIN
            Temp := List[Index];
            List[Index] := List[J];
            List[J] := Temp
          END  {  of exchange  }
    END;  {  of FOR loop (selection sort)  }

  {  Now print the sorted list  }

  writeln;
  writeln (Skip:10, 'The sorted list is as follows:');
  writeln;
  FOR J := 1 TO NumReals DO
    writeln (Skip:12, '<' J:2, '>', List[J]:6:2)

END.  {  of main program  }
```

The output for this program is

```
This sample program does the following:

    <1> Gets reals from a data file.
    <2> Echo prints the data.
    <3> Sorts the data from low to high.
    <4> Prints a sorted list of the data.

The original data are as follows:

    < 1> 34.56
    < 2> 78.21
    < 3> 23.30
    < 4> 89.90
    < 5> 45.00
    < 6> 56.80
    < 7> 39.01
    < 8> 45.56
    < 9> 34.40
    <10> 45.10
    <11> 98.20
    <12>  5.60
    <13>  8.00
    <14> 45.00
    <15> 99.00
    <16> 56.78
    <17> 56.78
    <18> 45.00

The sorted list is as follows:

    < 1>  5.60
    < 2>  8.00
    < 3> 23.30
    < 4> 34.40
    < 5> 34.56
    < 6> 39.01
    < 7> 45.00
    < 8> 45.00
    < 9> 45.00
    <10> 45.10
    <11> 45.56
    <12> 56.78
    <13> 56.78
    <14> 56.80
    <15> 78.21
    <16> 89.90
    <17> 98.20
    <18> 99.00
```

■   ■

Exercises 10.3

1. Assume the array Column is to be sorted from low to high using the selection sort.

Column

−20
10
0
10
8
30
−2

a. Sketch the contents of the array after each of the first two passes.

b. How many exchanges are made during the sort?

2. Write a test program that prints the partially sorted arrays after each pass during a selection sort.

3. Change the code for the selection sort so it sorts an array from high to low.

4. Write a complete program to

a. Read ten reals into an array from an input file.

b. If the first real is positive, sort the array from high to low; if it is negative, sort the array from low to high.

c. Print a numbered column containing the sorted reals with the format :10:2.

5. Modify the selection sort by including a counter that counts the number of assignments of array elements made during a sort.

6. Using the modification in Exercise 5, sort lists of differing lengths that contain randomly generated numbers. Display the results of how many assignments were made for each sort on a graph similar to that shown here. Use lists whose lengths are multiples of ten.

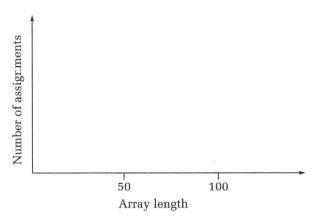

■ 10.4
Arrays and Subprograms

OBJECTIVES

■ to be able to use arrays correctly with subprograms

Procedures and functions should be used with arrays to maintain the structured design philosophy. Before we look at specific examples, let us examine the method and syntax necessary for passing an array to a procedure. Recall that to pass either a value or variable parameter to a procedure, we must declare an actual parameter of exactly the same type as the formal parameter in the procedure heading. In addition, if more than one parameter is passed, there must be a one-for-one ordered matching of the actual parameters with the formal parameters in the heading of the procedure. Consider, for example, the following program that reads two integer test scores, computes their average in a procedure called CalcMean, and outputs the results.

■ **EXAMPLE 10.15**

```
PROGRAM AverageOfTwo (input, output);

VAR
   Num1, Num2 : integer;
   Ave : real;
```

```
{*******************************************************************}
PROCEDURE CalcMean (Num1, Num2 : integer;
                    VAR Ave : real);

  {  Given:    Two integers                                     }
  {  Task:     Compute their average                            }
  {  Return:   Average of the two integers                      }

  VAR
    Sum : integer;

  BEGIN
    Sum := Num1 + Num2;
    Ave := Sum / 2.0
  END; {  of PROCEDURE CalcMean  }

{*******************************************************************}
BEGIN {  Main program  }
  readln (Num1, Num2);
  CalcMean (Num1, Num2, Ave);
  writeln ('The average of ', Num1:5, ' and ', Num2:5, ' is ',
          Ave:6:2)
END.  {  of main program  }
```

The procedure call

```
     CalcMean (Num1, Num2, Ave);
```

and the procedure heading

```
     PROCEDURE CalcMean (Num1, Num2 : integer;
                         VAR Ave : real);
```

have the desired matching of variables.

■   ■

Let us now modify the program so it will determine the average of 100 test
scores in the array Scores. The procedure call in the program will be

```
     CalcMean (Scores, Ave);
```

and the procedure heading will have to match these variables. If Scores also
is the variable name to be used in the procedure heading, we have

```
     PROCEDURE CalcMean (Scores : ???;
                         VAR Ave : real);
```

Pascal requires that a **TYPE** definition be given. For example, if we have

```
     CONST
       MaxLength = 100;
     TYPE
       List = ARRAY [1..MaxLength] OF integer;
     VAR
       Scores : List;
```

the procedure heading could be

```
     PROCEDURE CalcMean (Scores : List;
                         VAR Ave : real);
```

This is consistent with allowing only identifiers of identical or compatible
types to be associated. A common mistake is to attempt to build a data type
inside the procedure heading. This will not work. The statement

```
PROCEDURE CalcMean (Scores : ARRAY [1..MaxLength] OF integer;
                    VAR Ave : real);
```

produces an error message because Pascal compilers check for name equivalence rather than structure equivalence. To illustrate, you could have two arrays

```
Position  : ARRAY [1..3] OF real;
Nutrition : ARRAY [1..3] OF real;
```

where Position is used to represent coordinates of a point in space and Nutrition is used to represent the volume, weight, and caloric content of a serving of food. Although Position and Nutrition have the same structure, they have significantly different meanings. Thus, by insisting on name equivalence, the chances of inadvertent or meaningless uses of structured variables are decreased. Also, compiler implementation of name equivalence is easier than compiler implementation of structure equivalence.

We can now write a revised version of the program in Example 10.15 to find the average and include a procedure that requires passing an array variable.

■ **EXAMPLE 10.16**

```
PROGRAM Average (input, output);

CONST
  MaxLength = 100;

TYPE
  List = ARRAY [1..MaxLength] OF integer;

VAR
  Scores : List;
  Ave : real;
  J, Length : integer;

{******************************************************************* }

PROCEDURE CalcMean (Scores : List;
                    VAR Ave : real;
                    Length : integer);

  {  Given:   An array of scores and number of scores in the      }
  {                array                                           }
  {  Task:    Compute the average of scores in the array          }
  {  Return:  The average score                                   }

  VAR
    J, Sum : integer;

  BEGIN
    Sum := 0;
    FOR J := 1 TO Length DO
      Sum := Sum + Scores[J];
    Ave := Sum / Length
  END;   { of PROCEDURE CalcMean  }

{******************************************************************* }
```

```
BEGIN  {  Main program  }
  Length := 0;
  WHILE NOT eof AND (Length < MaxLength) DO
    BEGIN
      Length := Length + 1;
      readln (Scores[Length])
    END;  {  of WHILE NOT eof  }
  CalcMean (Scores, Ave, Length);
  writeln ('The average of ':20);
  writeln;
  FOR J := 1 TO Length DO
    writeln (Scores[J]:12);
  writeln;
  writeln ('is':10, Ave:8:2)
END.  {  of main program  }
```

Before we consider more procedures with arrays, we restate a rule: To pass an array to a procedure or function, the array must be declared with an identifier that uses a **TYPE** identifier; the matching variable in the procedure must use the same **TYPE** identifier.

Now that we know how to pass an array, let's rewrite our last example using a completely modular development. In this version, CalcMean is a function instead of a procedure. The first-level pseudocode development is

1. Get the scores (**PROCEDURE** GetData)
2. Compute the average (**FUNCTION** CalcMean)
3. Print a header (**PROCEDURE** PrintHeader)
4. Print the results (**PROCEDURE** PrintResults)

The procedure to get the scores requires a **VAR** declaration in the procedure heading for the array. If List is defined as a data type, we have

```
PROCEDURE GetData (VAR Scores : List;
                   VAR Length : integer);
  BEGIN
    Length := 0;
    WHILE NOT eof AND (Length < MaxLength) DO
      BEGIN
        Length := Length + 1;
        readln (Scores[Length])
      END
  END;  {  of PROCEDURE GetData  }
```

The average score could be computed by the function CalcMean.

```
FUNCTION CalcMean (Scores : List;
                   Length : integer) : real;
  VAR
    J, Sum : integer;
  BEGIN
    Sum := 0;
    FOR J := 1 TO Length DO
      Sum := Sum + Scores[J];
    CalcMean := Sum / Length
  END;  {  of FUNCTION CalcMean  }
```

A procedure to print a heading would be written in a manner similar to that we have used previously. If we want the output to be

```
              Test Scores
              ---- ------

                  99
                  98
                  97
                  96
                  95
```

The average score on this test was 97.00.

the procedure for the heading could be

```
PROCEDURE PrintHeader;
  BEGIN
    writeln;
    writeln ('Test Scores');
    writeln ('---- ------');
    writeln
  END;  {  of PROCEDURE PrintHeader  }
```

A procedure to print the results could be

```
PROCEDURE PrintResults (Scores : List;
                        Ave : real;
                        Length : integer);

  VAR
    J : integer;
  BEGIN
    FOR J := 1 TO Length DO
      writeln (Scores[J]:5);
    writeln;
    writeln ('The average score on this test was',
             Ave:6:2, '.')
  END;  {  of PROCEDURE PrintResults  }
```

This procedure could be called by

```
PrintResults (Scores, Ave, Length);
```

where Ave is found by

```
Ave := CalcMean(Scores, Length);
```

The following example is a complete program for this development.

■ EXAMPLE 10.17

```
PROGRAM TestScores (input, output);

CONST
  MaxLength = 100;

TYPE
  List = ARRAY [1..MaxLength] OF integer;

VAR
  Scores : List;
  Ave : real;
  Length : integer;

{ ************************************************************** }
```

```
FUNCTION CalcMean (Scores : List;
                   Length : integer) : real;

  {  Given:    A list of scores                                          }
  {  Task:     Compute the average score                                 }
  {  Return:   The average score                                         }

  VAR
    J, Sum : integer;

  BEGIN
    Sum := 0;
    FOR J := 1 TO Length DO
      Sum := Sum + Scores[J];
    CalcMean := Sum / Length
  END;  {  of FUNCTION CalcMean  }


{******************************************************************** }


PROCEDURE GetData (VAR Scores : List;
                   VAR Length : integer);

  {  Given:    Nothing                                                   }
  {  Task:     Read scores from a data file into an array               }
  {  Return:   Array of scores (with length)                            }

  BEGIN
    Length := 0;
    WHILE NOT eof AND (Length < MaxLength) DO
      BEGIN
        Length := Length + 1;
        readln (Scores[Length])
      END
  END;  {  of PROCEDURE GetData  }


{******************************************************************** }


PROCEDURE PrintHeader;

  {  Given:    Nothing                                                   }
  {  Task:     Print a heading for the output                           }
  {  Return:   Nothing                                                   }

  BEGIN
    writeln;
    writeln ('Test Scores');
    writeln ('---- ------');
    writeln
  END;  {  of PROCEDURE PrintHeader  }


{******************************************************************** }


PROCEDURE PrintResults    (Scores : List;
                           Ave : real;
                           Length : integer);

  {  Given:    Array of scores and average score                        }
  {  Task:     Print the scores in a list and print the average         }
  {                    score                                             }
  {  Return:   Nothing                                                   }

  VAR
    J : integer;
```

```
    BEGIN
      FOR J := 1 TO Length DO
        writeln (Scores[J]:5);
      writeln;
      writeln ('The average score on this test was', Ave:6:2, '.')
    END;  {  of PROCEDURE PrintResults  }

{********************************************************************* }

BEGIN  {  Main program  }
  GetData (Scores, Length);
  Ave := CalcMean(Scores, Length);
  PrintHeader;
  PrintResults (Scores, Ave, Length)
END.  {  of main program  }
```

As previously mentioned, sorting arrays is a standard problem for programmers. Now that we can pass arrays to procedures and functions, let us consider a problem in which an unknown number of reals are to be read from an input file and a sorted list (high to low) is to be printed as output. A first-level pseudocode design is

1. Get data (**PROCEDURE** GetData)
2. Sort list (**PROCEDURE** Sort)
3. Print header (**PROCEDURE** PrintHeader)
4. Print sorted list (**PROCEDURE** PrintData)

Since the number of data items is unknown, we will have to declare an array that is of sufficient length to store all the data but that does not use an unreasonable amount of memory. The nature of the problem will provide sufficient information for this declaration. For now, assume we know there are at most 50 data items. Then the following declaration will be sufficient.

```
CONST
  MaxLength = 50;
TYPE
  NumList = ARRAY [1..MaxLength] OF real;
VAR
  List : NumList;
  Length : integer;
```

The procedure to sort the array uses a version of the selection sort from Section 10.3. Both the array and the number of data items need to be passed to the procedure. An appropriate procedure is

```
PROCEDURE Sort (VAR List : NumList;
                    Length : integer);
  VAR
    J, K, Index : integer;
    Temp : real;
  BEGIN
    FOR J := 1 TO Length - 1 DO
      BEGIN
        Index := J;
        FOR K := J + 1 TO Length DO
          IF List[K] > List[Index] THEN
            Index := K;
        IF Index <> J THEN
```

```
        BEGIN
          Temp := List[Index];
          List[Index] := List[J];
          List[J] := Temp
        END  {  of exchange  }
    END  {  of FOR J loop  }
  END;  {  of PROCEDURE Sort  }
```

This procedure could be called by the statement

```
Sort (List, Length);
```

After suitable procedures are written for getting the data, printing a header and printing the data, the main body of the program could be

```
BEGIN  {  Main Program  }
  GetData (List, Length);
  Sort (List, Length);
  PrintHeader;
  PrintData (List, Length)
END.  {  of main program  }
```

Arrays and Variable Parameters

Let's now reconsider the issue of value parameters and variable parameters used with arrays. Because value parameters require separate memory of approximately the same size as that used by actual parameters in the main program, value parameters that are array types can require a great deal of memory. Thus, many programmers use only variable parameters when they work with arrays. This saves memory and speeds execution. Since most of your programs are relatively short and process small data files, this will not be a major problem. However, as data bases become larger and you use more elaborate structures, you may wish to consider using variable parameters even when changes are not made in the variables.

Software Engineering

Passing arrays is a software engineering concern. Passing arrays by reference results in a significant savings of memory. The problem this creates when several modules (teams) use the same array is that inadvertent changes made in an array within a specific module now become changes in the array used by other modules. These side effects would not occur if the array was passed as a value parameter.

How do designers solve this problem? There is no clear solution. If the arrays are fairly small and memory allocation is not a problem, arrays should be passed as value parameters when possible. When conditions require arrays to be passed by reference, it is extremely important to guarantee that no unwanted changes are made. This necessity increases the need for careful and thorough documentation.

Data Abstraction

Now that you are somewhat comfortable with the concept of an array as a data structure, it is time to take a broader look at how data relate to structures used to store and manipulate data. When designing the solution to a problem, it is not important to be initially concerned about the specifics of how data will be manipulated. These are implementation details that can (and should) be dealt with at a fairly low level in a modular development. The properties of a data structure will, however, be part of the design at a fairly high level.

The separation between the conceptual definition of a data structure and its eventual implementation is called *data abstraction*. This process of deferring details to the lowest possible level parallels the method of designing algorithms; that is, design first and do implementation details last.

Data abstraction is not a well-defined process, but we attempt to illustrate data abstraction with the following. Suppose you are designing a program that will be required to work with a list of names and an associated list of numbers (student names and test scores). Reasonable tasks would be to

```
Get the data
Sort the lists by name or number
Print the lists
```

In your design, you might have procedures such as

```
GetNames (⟨procedure here⟩);
GetScores (⟨procedure here⟩);
SortByName (⟨procedure here⟩);
PrintNamesAndScores (⟨procedure here⟩);
SortByScore (⟨procedure here⟩);
PrintNamesAndScores (⟨procedure here⟩);
```

Even though you have not yet worked with implementation details required to write the procedures, you could use data structure properties in a design. For example, at this point, you probably could design a problem solution using some of the previously mentioned procedures that work with an array of names and/or an array of associated test scores.

Abstract Data Types

Two abstraction concepts have been previously discussed: procedural abstraction and data abstraction. A third form of abstraction arises from the use of defined types. Specifically, an *abstract data type* (*ADT*) consists of a class of objects, a defined set of properties of these objects, and a set of operations for processing the objects.

Our work thus far is fairly limited in terms of what could be considered an abstract data type. However, it is possible to think of an array as a list. The class of objects would then be lists. Some properties of these lists include identical element type, order, varying lengths, and direct access of individual components. Operations for processing the lists include searching for an element, sorting in ascending or descending order, inserting an element, and deleting an element.

As before, it is not necessary that you be overly concerned about specific implementation details at this point. But your growth as a computer scientist will be enhanced if you develop a perspective of abstract data types and use this perspective in the design of problem solutions.

Much of the remainder of this book is devoted to developing properties of data structures and operations for processing the structures. As you progress through the material on higher-dimensional arrays, records, files, and sets, try to analyze each structure with related properties and operations as an abstract data type.

Exercises 10.4

1. Assume the following declarations have been made in a program.

```
TYPE
    Row = ARRAY [1..10] OF integer;
    Column = ARRAY [1..30] OF real;
    String20 = ARRAY [1..20] OF char;
    Week = (Sun, Mon, Tues, Wed, Thur, Fri, Sat);
VAR
    List1, List2 : Row;
    Aray : Column;
    Name1, Name2 : String20;
    Day : Week;
    A, B : ARRAY [1..10] OF integer;
```

Indicate which of the following are valid **PROCEDURE** declarations. Write an appropriate line of code that will call each of those that are valid. Include an explanation for those that are invalid.

a. PROCEDURE NewList (X : Row; Y : Column);

b. PROCEDURE NewList (VAR X : Row : VAR Y : Column);

c. PROCEDURE NewList (X : ARRAY [1..10] OF integer);

d. PROCEDURE NewList (VAR X, Y : Row);

e. PROCEDURE NewList (VAR Column : Column);

f. PROCEDURE WorkWeek (Days : ARRAY [Mon..Fri] OF Week);

g. PROCEDURE Surname (X : Name);

h. PROCEDURE Surnames (X, Y : String20);

i. PROCEDURE GetData (X : Week; VAR Y : Name);

j. PROCEDURE Table (VAR X : Row; VAR Y : Row);

2. Write a test program that illustrates what happens when you define an array structure in a procedure heading. For example,

```
PROCEDURE Sort (List : ARRAY [1..20] OF real);
```

3. When possible, use the **TYPE** and **VAR** declaration sections of Exercise 1 to write **PROCEDURE** declarations so that each of the following statements in the main program is an appropriate call to a procedure. Explain any inappropriate calls.

a. OldList (List1, Aray);

b. ChangeList (List1, Name1, Day);

c. Scores (A, B);

d. Surname (String20);

4. Write an appropriate **PROCEDURE** declaration and a line of code to call the procedure for each of the following.

a. A procedure to **read** 20 test scores into an array and save them for later use.

b. A procedure to count the number of occurrences of the letter A in an array of 50 characters.

c. A procedure to take two arrays of 10 integers each and produce a sorted array of 20 integers for later use.

d. A procedure to **read** integer test scores from a data file, count the number of scores, count the number of scores greater than or equal to 90, and save this information for later use.

5. Assume the following declarations have been made.

```
TYPE
    Column10 = ARRAY [1..10] OF integer;
```

```
VAR
  List1, List2 : Column10;
  K : integer;
```

Indicate the contents of each array after the call to the corresponding procedure.

a.
```
PROCEDURE Sample (VAR List1 : Column10;
                      List2 : Column10);
  VAR
    J : integer;
  BEGIN
    FOR J := 1 TO 10 DO
      BEGIN
        List1[J] := J * J;
        List2[J] := List[J] MOD 2
      END
  END;  {  of PROCEDURE Sample  }
BEGIN  {  Main program  }
  .
  .
  .
  FOR K := 1 TO 10 DO
    BEGIN
      List1[K] := 0;
      List2[K] := 0
    END;
  Sample (List1, List2);
```

b. Replace the procedure call with

```
Sample (List2, List1);
```

c. Replace the procedure call with consecutive calls

```
Sample (List1, List2);
Sample (List2, List1);
```

6. For the following, declare appropriate variables, write the indicated procedures, and call the procedures from the main program.

   a. **read** a line of text from an input file that contains 30 characters.

   b. Count the number of blanks in the line of text.

   c. Print the line of text in reverse order and print the number of blanks.

7. Write a procedure to examine an array of integers and then return the maximum value, minimum value, and number of negative values to the main program.

8. Discuss some of the implementation details you would need in order to read a list of names into an array.

9. Suppose you have an array of student names and an array of these students' test scores. How would the array of names be affected if you sorted the test scores from high to low?

■ ■ ■ ■

■ 10.5
Packed Arrays

- to be able to use correct notation for packed arrays
- to understand the advantages and disadvantages of packed arrays
- to use string variables

One weakness of standard Pascal is the absence of a *string data type*. Since this text is written assuming standard Pascal is being used, this section shows how arrays can be used to simulate a string data type. Most nonstandard versions of Pascal do, however, have such a type. If your version of Pascal has the string data type available, you may wish to skip this section.

Basic Idea and Notation

Arrays, as you recall, are useful for handling large amounts of data. One of the disadvantages of using arrays, however, is that they require large amounts of memory. In particular, arrays of character data use much more memory than is necessary. To illustrate, let us take a closer look at an array declared by

```
VAR
    Examine : ARRAY [1..5] OF char;
```

When this structured variable is declared, the following variables are reserved.

Examine

	Examine[1]
	Examine[2]
	Examine[3]
	Examine[4]
	Examine[5]

Each component of the array Examine is one *word* in memory and each word consists of several *bytes*. Let us consider the array Examine in which each word consists of four bytes. The array would be pictured as

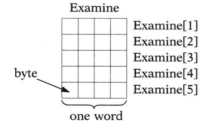

We could assign the word "HELLO" to the array Examine by either

```
Examine[1] := 'H';
Examine[2] := 'E';
Examine[3] := 'L';
Examine[4] := 'L';
Examine[5] := 'O';
```

or

```
Examine := 'HELLO'
```

depending on which version of Pascal is being used. In either case, after the assignment, the array would look like

Examine

H			Examine[1]
E			Examine[2]
L			Examine[3]
L			Examine[4]
O			Examine[5]

because a byte is the unit of storage necessary for storing a character variable.

As you can see, 20 bytes of storage have been reserved, but only 5 have been used. Pascal provides a more efficient way of defining arrays that does not use unnecessary amounts of storage space. Instead of declaring a variable as an array, we can declare a variable as a *packed array*. With this declaration, the computer then packs the data in consecutive bytes.

Packed arrays can be used with any data type (**char, real, integer, boolean,** and so on). However, it is not always wise to do so because it takes longer to access individual components of a packed array than it does to access individual components of an array that has not been declared as packed. Storage space is saved, but time is lost. For more information on using arrays that are packed and those that are not (*unpacked arrays*), see Appendix 8.

Let us now consider the declaration

```
TYPE
   String5 = PACKED ARRAY [1..5] OF char;
VAR
   Examine : String5;
```

and the assignment of the word "HELLO" as before. Using a packed array, we then have the following in memory.

Examine

| H | E | L | L | O | | | |

Notice that less than two words (5 bytes) are used to store what previously required five words (20 bytes). We can still access the individual components as before. For example,

```
writeln (Examine[2]);
```

produces

```
E
```

as a line of output.

Character Strings

Every programming language needs to be able to handle character data. Names, words, phrases, and sentences are frequently used as part of some information that must be analyzed. In standard Pascal, character strings are formed by declaring packed arrays of character variables. For example, if the first 20 spaces of an input line are reserved for a customer's name, an appropriate character string could be declared by

```
TYPE
   String20 = PACKED ARRAY [1..20] OF char;
VAR
   Name : String20;
```

If the line of input is

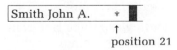

position 21

we could read the name into the packed array by the code

```
FOR J := 1 TO 20 DO
   read (Name[J]);
```

Now when we refer to the array Name, we can envision the string

```
'Smith John A.'
```

But since we declared a fixed length string, the actual string is

```
'Smith John A.
```

There are at least three important uses for string variables.

1. String variables of the same length can be compared (Boolean values); this permits alphabetizing.
2. String variables can be written using a single **write** or **writeln** statement; they cannot be read using a single **read** statement.
3. A single assignment statement can assign text to a string variable.

Let's examine each use individually.

Comparing String Variables. Strings of the same length can be compared using the standard relational operators: "=, <, >, <>, <=, and >=." For example, if 'Smith' and 'Jones' are strings, then 'Smith' < 'Jones', 'Smith' <> 'Jones', and so on are all valid Boolean expressions. The Boolean value is determined by the collating sequence. Using the collating sequence for the ASCII character set, the following comparisons yield the indicated values.

Comparison	Boolean Value
'Smith' < 'Jones'	**false**
'Jake' < 'John'	**true**
'ABC' = 'ABA'	**false**
'Smith Doug' < 'Smith John'	**true**

What would happen if you wanted to evaluate 'William Joe' < 'Williams Bo'? Since a character-by-character comparison is implemented by the computer, no decision is made until the blank following the *m* of William is compared to the *s* of Williams. Using the full ASCII character code, this Boolean expression is **true,** which is how these strings are alphabetized.

Writing String Variables. Recall the declaration

```
TYPE
   String20 = PACKED ARRAY [1..20] OF char;
VAR
   Name : String20;
```

When data are read from an input file, a loop is used to get the data one character at a time.

```
FOR J := 1 TO 20 DO
   read (Name[J]);
```

If we now wish to write the string Name, we could use a similar loop and write it one character at a time.

```
FOR J := 1 TO 20 DO
   write (Name[J]);
```

However, Pascal provides a more convenient method for writing strings. The write loop could be replaced by

```
write (Name);
```

T **Assigning Text to a String.** The third feature of string variables is that a single assignment can be used to assign text to a string. If Name is a string of length 20, then

```
Name := 'Smith John A.          ';
```

is a valid statement. Note that there must be exactly 20 characters in the text string in order for this assignment to be valid. The statements

```
Name := 'Smith John A.';
Name := 'Theodore Allen Washington';
```

are both invalid because the text strings are not exactly 20 characters long.

There are some standard problems that will be encountered when trying to read data into a packed array. First, assume we have to read a line of data that consists of a company name. Furthermore, assume we do not know the length of the name. The input line could be

```
Prudent Investors Company
```

or

```
Com Mfg. Co.
```

If we know the company name will be no more than 30 characters, we can declare a fixed length array in the following manner.

```
TYPE
   String30 = PACKED ARRAY [1..30] OF char;
VAR
   CompanyName : String30;
```

and then read the name with the segment of code

T
```
FOR J := 1 TO 30 DO
  IF NOT eoln THEN
    read (CompanyName[J])
  ELSE
    CompanyName[J] := ' ';
readln;  {  Advance the pointer  }
```

This will read the name as desired and then fill the array with blanks to the desired length. Applied to the two data lines just mentioned, this segment of code would produce the following character strings.

```
'Prudent Investors Company     '
'Com Mfg. Co.                  '
```

Second, we may want to read data from an input file in which a field of fixed length is used for some character data. For example, suppose the first 30 columns of an input line are reserved for the company name and then some other information is on the same line. We could have

Prudent Investors Company   1905 South Drive

```
                    ↑
                 column 31
```

This data could be accessed by the loop

```
FOR J := 1 TO 30 DO
  read (CompanyName[J]);
```

Although the second format for an input file is easier to use, it is sometimes difficult to obtain data in such a precise format. Hence, we must be able to read data both ways.

We are now ready to write a short program using packed arrays. Suppose the problem is to get two names from a data file, arrange them alphabetically, and then print the alphabetized list. Assume the names are in a field of fixed length 25 on two adjacent lines. A first-level pseudocode development is

1. Get the data (**PROCEDURE** GetData)
2. Arrange alphabetically (**PROCEDURE** Alphabetize)
3. Print the data (**PROCEDURE** PrintData)

A procedure to get one line of data is

```
PROCEDURE GetData (VAR Name : String25);
  VAR
    J : integer;
  BEGIN
    FOR J := 1 to 25 DO
      read (Name[J]);
    readln  {  Advance the pointer  }
  END;  {  of PROCEDURE GetData  }
```

After the two names have been read from the input file, they could be arranged alphabetically by

```
PROCEDURE Alphabetize (VAR Name1, Name2 : String25);
  VAR
    Temp : String25;
  BEGIN
    IF Name2 < Name1 THEN
      BEGIN  {  Exchange when necessary  }
        Temp := Name1;
        Name1 := Name2;
        Name2 := Temp
      END  {  of IF...THEN  }
  END;  {  of PROCEDURE Alphabetize  }
```

The procedure for printing the name should include some header and some formatting of the names. For example, suppose you want to say

```
The alphabetized list is below.
--- ------------ ---- -- -----
```

and then print the list indented ten spaces after skipping two lines. A procedure to do this is

```
PROCEDURE PrintData (Name1, Name2 : String25);
  BEGIN
    writeln;
    writeln (Skip:10, 'The alphabetized list is below.');
    writeln (Skip:10, '--- ------------ ---- -- -----');
    writeln;
    writeln (Skip:20 Name1);
    writeln (Skip:20 Name2)
  END;  {  of PROCEDURE PrintData  }
```

We can now write the complete program.

```
PROGRAM SampleNames (input, output);

CONST
  Skip = ' ';

TYPE
  String25 = PACKED ARRAY [1..25] OF char;

VAR
  Name1, Name2 : String25;

{ ****************************************************************** }
```

```
PROCEDURE GetData (VAR Name : String25);

  {  Given:    Nothing                                        }
  {  Task:     Read a name from the data file                 }
  {  Return:   One name (string of 25 characters)             }

  VAR
    J : integer;

  BEGIN
    FOR J := 1 TO 25 DO
      read (Name[J]);
    readln                              {  Advance the pointer  }
  END;  {  of PROCEDURE GetData  }


{********************************************************************}

PROCEDURE Alphabetize  (VAR Name1, Name2 : String25);

  {  Given:    Two names                                      }
  {  Task:     Sort the names alphabetically                  }
  {  Return:   The names in sorted order                      }

  VAR
    Temp : String25;

  BEGIN
    IF Name2 < Name1 THEN
      BEGIN                             {  Exchange when necessary  }
        Temp := Name1;
        Name1 := Name2;
        Name2 := Temp
      END  {  of IF...THEN  }
  END;  {  of PROCEDURE Alphabetize  }


{********************************************************************}

PROCEDURE PrintData (Name1, Name2 : String25);

  {  Given:    Names in alphabetical order              }
  {  Task:     Print the names                          }
  {  Return:   Nothing                                  }

  BEGIN
    writeln;
    writeln (Skip:10, 'The alphabetized list is below.');
    writeln (Skip:10, '--- -----------  ---            ;);
    writeln;
    writeln (Skip:20, Name1);
    writeln (Skip:20, Name2)
  END;  {  of PROCEDURE PrintData


{********************************************************************}

BEGIN  {  Main program  }
  GetData (Name1);
  GetData (Name2);
  Alphabetize (Name1, Name2);
  PrintData (Name1, Name2)
END.  {  of main program  }
```

Exercises 10.5

1. Indicate which of the following string comparisons are valid. For those that are, indicate whether they are **true** or **false** using the full ASCII character set.

   a. `'Mathematics' <> 'CompScience'`

   b. `'Jefferson' < 'Jeffersonian'`

   c. `'Smith Karen' < 'Smithsonian'`

   d. `'#45' <= '$45'`

   e. `'Hoof in mouth' = 'Foot in door'`

   f. `'453012' > '200000'`

2. Write a test program that allows you to examine the Boolean expression

   `'William Joe' < 'Williams Bo'`

3. Suppose Message is declared as

```
TYPE
  String50 = PACKED ARRAY [1..50] OF char;
VAR
  Message : String50;
```

   and the input file consists of the line

   `To err is human. Computers do not forgive.`

   What output is produced by each of the following segments?

   a.
```
FOR J := 1 TO 50 DO
   IF NOT eoln THEN
     read (Message[J])
   ELSE
     Message[J]:= ' ';
writeln (Message);
```

   b.
```
FOR J := 1 TO 50 DO
   IF NOT eoln THEN
     read (Message[J])
   ELSE
     Message[J]:= ' ';
Count := 0;
FOR J := 1 TO 50 DO
   IF Message[J]:= ' ' THEN
     Count := Count + 1;
writeln (Message);
writeln ('There are', Count:3, 'blanks.':8);
```

   c.
```
FOR J := 1 TO 20 DO
   read (Message[2+J]);
FOR J := 21 TO 40 DO
   Message[J]:= ' ';
FOR J := 41 TO 50 DO
   Message[J]:= '*';
writeln (Message);
```

   d.
```
FOR J := 1 TO 50 DO
   IF NOT eoln THEN
     read (Message[J])
   ELSE
     Message[J]:= ' ';
writeln (Message);
FOR J := 50 DOWNTO 1 DO
   write (Message[J]);
```

4. Assume the following declarations.

```
TYPE
  String10 = PACKED ARRAY [1..10] OF char;
  String20 = PACKED ARRAY [1..20] OF char;
VAR
  A, B : String10;
  C : String20;
```

a. Indicate whether the following are valid or invalid.

```
  i. A := B;

 ii. C := A + B;

iii. FOR J := 1 TO 20 DO
        C[J] := A[J] + B[J];

 iv. FOR J := 1 TO 20 DO
        IF J <= 10 THEN
          A[J]:= C[J]
        ELSE
          B[J-10]:= C[J];
```

b. Write a segment of code that will make the string C consist of the strings A and B where the lesser (alphabetically) of A and B is the first half of C.

5. Assume a packed array Message of length 100 has been declared and data have been read into it from an input file. Write a segment of the code to count the number of occurrences of the letter *M* in the string Message.

6. Write a test program to see what happens if you try to read in an entire packed array with one **read** or **readln** statement.

■ ■ ■ ■

■ 10.6
Searching Algorithms

OBJECTIVES

- to be able to use a sequential search to find the first occurrence of a value
- to be able to use a sequential search to find all occurrences of a value
- to be able to use a binary search to find a value
- to understand the relative efficiency of a binary search compared to a sequential search

The need to search an array for a value is a common problem. For example, you might wish to replace a test score for a student, delete a name from a directory or mailing list, or upgrade the pay scale for certain employees. These and other problems require you to be able to examine elements in some list until the desired value is located. When it is found, some action is taken. The lists, of course, could be either arrays or files. In this section, we assume all lists are nonempty.

Sequential Search

The first searching algorithm we will examine is the most common method, a *sequential (linear) search*. This process is accomplished by examining the first element in some list and then proceeding to examine the elements in the order they appear until a match is found. Variations of this basic process include searching a sorted list for the first occurrence of a value, searching a sorted list for all occurrences of a value, and searching an unsorted list for the first occurrence of a value.

To illustrate a sequential search, suppose you have an array A of integers and you want to find the first occurrence of some particular value (Num). As you search the array, if the desired value is located, you want to print its position. If the value is not in the array, an appropriate message should be printed. The code for such a search is

```
Index := 1;
WHILE (Num <> A[Index]) AND (Index < Length) DO
  Index := Index + 1;
```

A reasonable message for output is

```
IF Num = A[Index] THEN
  writeln (Num, ' is in position', Index:5)
ELSE
  writeln (Num, ' is not in the list.')
```

Let's now consider some variations of this problem. Our code works for both a sorted and an unsorted list. However, if we are searching a sorted list, the algorithm can be improved. For example, if the array components are sorted from low to high, we need to continue the search only until the value in an array component exceeds the value of Num. At that point, there is no need to examine the remaining components. The only change required in the loop for searching is to replace

```
Num <> A[Index]
```

with

```
Num > A[Index]
```

Thus, we have

```
Index := 1;
WHILE (Num > A[Index]) AND (Index < Length) DO
  Index := Index + 1;
```

A relatively easy modification of the sequential search is to examine a list for all occurrences of some value. If searching an array, you would generally print the positions and values when a match is found. To illustrate, if A is an array of integers and Num has an integer value, we can search A for the number of occurrences of Num by

```
Count := 0;
FOR Index := 1 TO Length DO
  IF Num = A[Index] THEN
    BEGIN
      Count := Count + 1;
      writeln (Num, ' is in position', Index:5)
    END;
```

This code works for an unsorted list. A modification of the code for working with a sorted list is included as an exercise.

Binary Search

Searching relatively small lists sequentially does not require much computer time. However, when the lists get longer (as, for example, telephone directories and lists of credit card customers), sequential searches are inefficient. In a sense, they correspond to looking up a word in the dictionary by starting at the first word and proceeding word-by-word until the desired word is found. Since extra computer time means considerably extra expense for most companies where large amounts of data must be frequently searched, a more efficient way of searching is needed.

If the list to be searched has been sorted, it can be searched for a particular value by a method referred to as a *binary search*. Essentially, a binary search consists of examining a middle value of an array to see which half contains the desired value. The middle value of this half is then examined to see which half of the half contains the value in question. This halving process is continued until the value is located or it is determined that the value is not in the list. (Remember, however, in order to use a binary search, the list must be sorted and the sorting process has its own costs which should be evaluated, but this subject is outside the scope of this text.)

The code for this process is relatively short. If A is the array to be searched for Num, and First, Mid, and Last are integer variables such that First contains the index of the first possible position to be searched and Last contains the index of the last possible position, the code for a list in ascending order is

```
Found := false;
WHILE NOT Found AND (First <= Last) DO
  BEGIN
    Mid := (First + Last) DIV 2;
    IF Num < A[Mid] THEN
      Last := Mid - 1
```

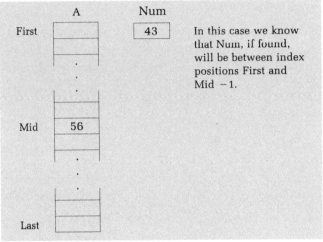

In this case we know that Num, if found, will be between index positions First and Mid −1.

```
    ELSE IF Num > A[Mid] THEN
      First := Mid + 1
    ELSE
      Found := true
END;
```

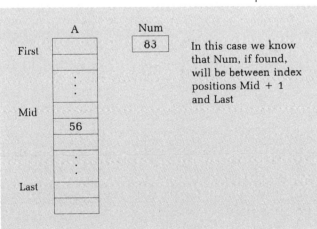

In this case we know that Num, if found, will be between index positions Mid + 1 and Last

When this loop is executed, it is exited when the value is located or it is determined that the value is not in the list. Depending on what you want done with the value being looked for, you can modify action at the bottom of the loop or use the values in Found and Mid outside the loop. For example, if you just want to know where the value is, you can change

```
Found := true
```

to

```
BEGIN
  Found := true;
  writeln (Num, ' is in position', Mid:5)
END;
```

Before continuing, let's walk through this search to better understand how it works. Assume A is the array

4	7	19	25	36	37	50	100	101	205	220	271	306	321

A[1]   A[14]

with values as indicated. Furthermore, assume Num contains the value 25. Then initially, First, Last, and Num have the values

1		14		25

First   Last   Num

A listing of values by each pass through the loop produces

	First	Last	Mid	A[Mid]	Found
Before loop	1	14	Undefined	Undefined	false
After first pass	1	6	7	50	false
After second pass	4	6	3	19	false
After third pass	4	4	5	36	false
After fourth pass	4	4	4	25	true

To illustrate what happens when the value being looked for is not in the array, suppose Num contains 210. The listing of values then produces

	First	Last	Mid	A[Mid]	Found
Before loop	1	14	Undefined	Undefined	false
After first pass	8	14	7	50	false
After second pass	8	10	11	220	false
After third pass	10	10	9	101	false
After fourth pass	11	10	10	205	false

At this stage, First > Last and the loop is exited.

Inserting and Deleting in a Sorted Array

Arrays are typically searched because you want to either insert an element into the array or delete an element from the array. To illustrate, let's consider the array A

2	5	8	10	10	12	15	18	21	30

A[1] A[2]   A[10]

If we wish to remove the element 12 from the array, we would end up with

2	5	8	10	10	15	18	21	30

A[1] A[2]   A[9]

Note that 12 has been deleted from the array and then elements listed "after" 12 in the array have been "advanced" one position.

To illustrate what happens when an element is to be inserted into an array, again consider the array A

2	5	8	10	10	12	15	18	21	30

A[1] A[2]   A[10]

If we want to insert 17 into the sorted array, we would first determine that it belongs between 15 and 18. We would then reassign elements 18, 21, and 30 to produce

2	5	8	10	10	12	15		18	21	30

A[1] A[2]   ↑   A[11]

17 goes here

17 is then assigned to the appropriate array component to produce the array

2	5	8	10	10	12	15	17	18	21	30

A[1] A[2]   A[11]

Writing the code for inserting and deleting in a sorted array is deferred to the Exercises.

Relative Efficiency of Searches

Let's now examine briefly the efficiency of a binary search compared to a sequential search. For purposes of this discussion, assume a sequential search on a list of 15 items requires at most 15 microseconds. The nature of a sequential search is such that every time you double the list length, the maximum searching time is also doubled; Figure 10.1 illustrates this increase.

Next, assume a list of 15 items requires a maximum of 60 microseconds when searched by a binary search. Since this process consists of successively halving the list, at most four passes will be required to locate the value. This means each pass uses 15 microseconds. When the list length is doubled, it requires only one more pass. Thus, a list of 30 items requires 75 microseconds and a list of 60 items requires 90 microseconds. This is shown graphically in Figure 10.2. The comparison of these two searches is shown on the same graph in Figure 10.3.

FIGURE 10.1
Sequential search

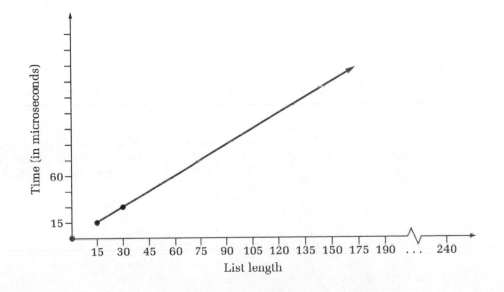

FIGURE 10.2
Binary search

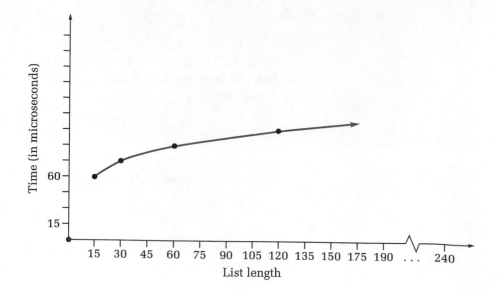

FIGURE 10.3
Sequential search versus binary search

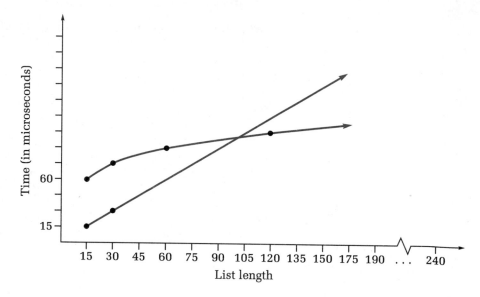

Exercises 10.6

1. Write a sequential search using a **FOR** loop to locate and print all occurrences of the same value.

2. Write a procedure for the sequential search and show how it can be called from the main program.

3. Modify the sequential search by putting a counter in the loop to count how many passes are made when searching a sorted array for a value. Write and run a program that uses this version on lists of length 15, 30, 60, 120, and 240. In each case, search for a value as follows and plot your results on a graph.

   a. In the first half
   b. In the second half
   c. That is not there

4. Repeat Exercise 3 for a binary search.

5. Suppose the array A is

18	25	37	92	104

A[1]   A[5]

Trace the values using a binary search to look for

a. 18

b. 92

c. 76

6. Write a procedure to search a sorted list and remove all duplicates.

7. Suppose a sorted list of social security numbers is in secondary storage in a file named StudentNum.

   a. Show how this file can be searched for a certain number using a sequential search.

   b. Show how this file can be searched for a certain number using a binary search.

   c. Show how a binary search can be used to indicate where a new number can be inserted in proper order.

   d. Show how a number can be deleted from the file.

8. Write a procedure to read text from an input file and determine the number of occurrences of each vowel.

9. Using a binary search on an array of length 35, what is the maximum number of passes through the loop that can be made when searching for a value?

10. Using worst-case possibilities of 3 microseconds for a sequential search of a list of ten items and 25 microseconds for a binary search of the same list, construct a graph illustrating relative efficiency for these two methods applied to lists of longer lengths.

11. Modify the sequential search that you developed in Exercise 1 to list all occurrences of a value so that it can be used on a sorted list. That is, have it stop after the desired value has been passed in the list.

12. Discuss methods that can be used to design programs to guard against searching empty lists.

13. Write a section of code for each of the following:

    a. Insert an element into a sorted array.

    b. Delete an element from a sorted array.

14. The length of a string is the number of positions from the first nonblank character to the last nonblank character. Thus, the packed array

| T | h | i | s | | i | s | | a | | s | t | r | i | n | g | . | | | | | | | | | | | | | |

would have length = 17. Write a function that receives a packed array of type [1 . . 30] of **char** and returns the length of the string.

■ ■ ■ ■

<table>
<tr><td>FOCUS ON
PROGRAM DESIGN</td><td>The sample program for this chapter features the use of arrays and subprograms. Since sorting an array is a common practice, it has been included as part of the program. Specifically, suppose the Home Sales Realty Company, Inc. wants to print a list containing the amount of all sales for a month. Each</td></tr>
</table>

sale amount is recorded on a separate line of input and the number of homes sold is less than 20. Write a program to do the following:

1. Read the data from the input file.
2. Print the data in the order in which it is read with a suitable header and format.
3. Print a sorted list (high to low) of sales with a suitable header and format.
4. Print the total number of sales for the month, the total amount of sales, the average sale price, and the company commission (7 percent).

Sample input would be

```
 85000
 76234
115100
 98200
121750
 76700
```

where each line represents the sale price of a home. Typical output would include an unsorted list of sales, a sorted list of sales, and appropriate summary data.

A first-level pseudocode development is

1. Get data (**PROCEDURE** GetData)
2. Print header (**PROCEDURE** PrintH1)
3. Print unsorted list (**PROCEDURE** PrintList)
4. Sort list (**PROCEDURE** Sort)
5. Print header (**PROCEDURE** PrintH2)
6. Print sorted list (**PROCEDURE** PrintList)
7. Compute data (**FUNCTION** Total and **PROCEDURE** Compute)
8. Print results (**PROCEDURE** PrintResults)

Notice that **PROCEDURE** PrintList is called twice and **PROCEDURE** PrintResults includes output for number of sales, total of sales, average sale price, and company commission. These are printed with suitable headings.

A structure chart for this is given in Figure 10.4.

FIGURE 10.4
Structure chart for Home Sales Realty Company, Inc. program

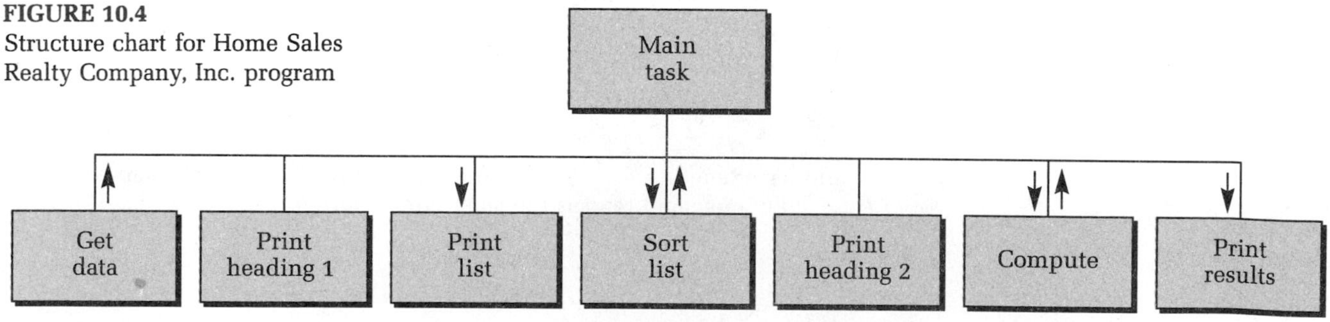

Module specifications for the main modules are

1. <u>GetData Module</u>
   Data received: None
   Information returned: Sales for a month
                        Number of sales
   Logic: Use a **WHILE** loop to read entries into an array.

2. PrintHeading1 Module
   Data received: None
   Information returned: None
   Logic: Use **writeln** statements to print a suitable heading for an un-
   sorted list.

3. PrintList Module
   Data received: Array of sales with number of sales
   Information returned: None
   Logic: Use a **FOR** loop with the array length as a loop control variable
   to print the list of sales for a month.

4. Sort Module
   Data received: Unsorted array of sales
                  Number of sales
   Information returned: Sorted array of sales
   Logic: Use a selection sort to sort the array.

5. PrintHeading2 Module
   Data received: None
   Information returned: None
   Logic: Use **writeln** statements to print a suitable heading for the sorted
   list.

6. Compute Module
   Data received: Array of sales with number of sales
   Information returned: Total sales
                        Average sale
                        Company commission
   Logic: Use a function to compute the total sales.
          Use a procedure to compute the average sale.
          Compute company commission by using a defined constant,
          CommissionRate.

7. PrintResults Module
   Data received: Number of sales
                  Total sales
                  Average sales
                  Company commission
   Information returned: None
   Logic: Use **writeln** statements to print a summary report.

The main program is

```
BEGIN  {  Main program  }
   GetData (JuneSales, Length);
   PrintHeading1;
   PrintList (JuneSales, Length);
   Sort (JuneSales, Length);
   PrintHeading2;
   PrintList (JuneSales, Length);
   Compute (TotalSales, AverageSale, CompanyCom, JuneSales, Length);
   PrintResults (TotalSales, AverageSale, CompanyCom, Length)
END.  {  of main program  }
```

The complete program for this problem is

```
PROGRAM MonthlyList (input, output);

{  This program illustrates the use of arrays with procedures   }
{  and  functions.  Note the  use of both  value and variable   }
{  parameters.  Also note  that a procedure  is  used to sort    }
{  the array.

CONST
  Skip = ' ';
  CommissionRate = 0.07;
  MaxLength = 20;

TYPE
  List = ARRAY [1..MaxLength] OF real;

VAR
  JuneSales : List;          {  Number of June sales       }
  TotalSales,                {  Total of June sales        }
  AverageSale,               {  Amount of average sale     }
  CompanyCom : real;         {  Commission for the company }
  Length : integer;          {  Array length of values     }

{*****************************************************************}


PROCEDURE GetData (VAR JuneSales : List;
                   VAR Length : integer);

  {  Given:    Nothing                                          }
  {  Task:     Read selling prices into array JuneSales         }
  {  Return:   Array of JuneSales and array length             }

  BEGIN
    Length := 0;
    WHILE NOT eof AND (Length < MaxLength) DO
      BEGIN
        Length := Length + 1;
        readln (JuneSales[Length])
      END  {  of WHILE NOT eof  }
  END;  {  of PROCEDURE GetData  }
```

1

```
{*****************************************************************}

PROCEDURE PrintHeading1;

  {  Given:    Nothing                                          }
  {  Task:     Print a heading for the unsorted list of sales   }
  {  Return:   Nothing                                          }

  BEGIN
    writeln;
    writeln (Skip:10, 'An unsorted list of sales for the');
    writeln (Skip:10, 'month of June is as follows:');
    writeln (Skip:10, '--------------------------------');
    writeln
  END;  {  of PROCEDURE PrintHeading1  }
```

2

```
{*****************************************************************}
```

```
PROCEDURE PrintList (JuneSales : List;
                     Length : integer);

  { Given:   An unsorted array (with length) of Sales for June }
  { Task:    Print the list                                    }
  { Return:  Nothing                                           }

  VAR
    J : integer;

  BEGIN
    FOR J := 1 TO Length DO
      writeln (Skip:14, '<', J:2, '>', '$':2, JuneSales[J]:11:2)
  END;  { of PROCEDURE PrintList  }
```

`{ ****************************************************************** }`

```
PROCEDURE Sort (VAR JuneSales : List;
                Length : integer);

  { Given:   An unsorted array (with length) of sales for June }
  { Task:    Use a selection sort to sort the list             }
  { Return:  A sorted list of sales for June                   }

  VAR
    J, K, Index : integer;
    Temp : real;

  BEGIN
    FOR J := 1 TO Length - 1 DO
      BEGIN
        Index := J;
        FOR K := J + 1 TO Length DO
          IF JuneSales[K] > JuneSales THEN
            Index := K;
        IF Index <> J THEN
          BEGIN
            Temp := JuneSales[Index];
            JuneSales[Index] := JuneSales[J];
            JuneSales[J] := Temp
          END { of exchange  }
      END  { of FOR J loop  }
  END;  { of PROCEDURE Sort  }
```

`{ ****************************************************************** }`

```
PROCEDURE PrintHeading2;

  { Given:   Nothing                                    }
  { Task:    Print a heading for the sorted list of sales }
  { Return:  Nothing                                    }

  BEGIN
    writeln;
    writeln (Skip:10, 'Sales for the month of June');
    writeln (Skip:10, 'sorted from high to low are:');
    writeln (Skip:10, '----------------------------');
    writeln
  END; { of PROCEDURE PrintHeading2  }
```

`{ ****************************************************************** }`

```
FUNCTION Total (JuneSales : List;
                Length : integer) : real;

   { Given:   An array (with length) of June sales     }
   { Task:    Sum the array components                  }
   { Return:  Total of sales for June                   }

     VAR
       J : integer;
       Sum : real;

   BEGIN
     Sum := 0;
     FOR J := 1 TO Length DO
       Sum := Sum + JuneSales[J];
     Total := Sum
   END;  {  of FUNCTION Total  }
```

6

```
{*******************************************************************}
```

```
PROCEDURE Compute (VAR TotalSales, AverageSale, CompanyCom : real;
                   VAR JuneSales : List;
                   Length : integer);

   { Given:   An array (with length) of June sales      }
   { Task:    Compute TotalSales, AverageSale, and CompanyCom  }
   {               for the month of June                }
   { Return:  TotalSales, AverageSale, and CompanyCom   }

   BEGIN
     TotalSales := Total(JuneSales, Length);
     AverageSale := TotalSales / Length;
     CompanyCom := TotalSales * CommissionRate
   END;  {  of PROCEDURE Compute  }
```

6

```
{*******************************************************************}
```

```
PROCEDURE PrintResults (TotalSales, AverageSale, CompanyCom : real;
                        Length : integer);

   { Given:   TotalSales, AverageSale, CompanyCom, and number  }
   {               of sales (Length) for June           }
   { Task:    Print summary information for the month   }
   { Return:  Nothing                                   }

   BEGIN
     writeln;
     writeln (Skip:10, 'There were', Length:3 ' sales during June.');
     writeln;
     writeln (Skip:10 'The total sales were', '$':2, TotalSales:12:2);
     writeln;
     writeln (Skip:10, 'The average sale was', '$':2, AverageSale:12:2);
     writeln;
     writeln(Skip:10, 'The company commission was', '$':2,
             CompanyCom:11:2);
     writeln
   END;  {  of PROCEDURE PrintResults  }
```

7

```
{*******************************************************************}
```

```
BEGIN  {  Main program  }
   GetData (JuneSales, Length);
   PrintHeading1;
   PrintList (JuneSales, Length);
   Sort (JuneSales, Length);
   PrintHeading2;
   PrintList (JuneSales, Length);
   Compute (TotalSales, AverageSale, CompanyCom, JuneSales, Length);
   PrintResults (TotalSales, AverageSale, CompanyCom, Length)
END.  {  of main program  }
```

The output for this program is

```
An unsorted list of sales for the
month of June is as follows:
-----------------------------

        < 1> $     85000.00
        < 2> $     78234.00
        < 3> $    115100.00
        < 4> $     98200.00
        < 5> $    121750.00
        < 6> $     76700.00


Sales for the month of June
sorted from high to low are:
-----------------------------

        < 1> $    121750.00
        < 2> $    115100.00
        < 3> $     98200.00
        < 4> $     85000.00
        < 5> $     76700.00
        < 6> $     78234.00
```

There were 6 sales during June.

The total sales were $ 572984.00

The average sale was $ 95497.33

The company commission was $ 40108.88

RUNNING AND DEBUGGING TIPS

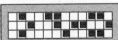

1. Be careful not to misuse type identifiers. For example, in

```
TYPE
   String = PACKED ARRAY [1..10] OF char;
VAR
   Word : String;
```

String is a data type; hence, a reference such as String := 'First name' is incorrect.

2. Do not attempt to use a subscript that is out of range. Suppose we have

```
VAR
   List : ARRAY [1..6] OF integer;
```

An inadvertent reference such as

```
FOR J := 1 TO 10 DO
   writeln (List[J]);
```

may produce an error message indicating that the subscript is out of range.

3. Counters are frequently used with loops and arrays. Be careful to make the final value the correct value. For example,

```
Count := 1;
WHILE NOT eof DO
  BEGIN
    readln (A[Count]);
    Count := Count + 1
  END;
```

used on the data file

will have a value of 4 in Count when this loop is exited. This could be corrected by rewriting the segment as

```
Count := 0;
WHILE NOT eof DO
  BEGIN
    Count := Count + 1;
    readln (A[Count])
  END;
```

4. Comparing array components to each other can lead to errors in using subscripts. Two common misuses are shown.
   a. Attempting to compare A[J] to A[J + 1]. If this does not stop at array length − 1, then J + 1 will be out of range.
   b. Attempting to compare A[J − 1] to A[J]. This presents the same problem at the beginning of an array. Remember, J − 1 cannot have a value less than the initial index value.

5. Make sure the array index is correctly initialized. For example,

```
J := 0;
WHILE NOT eof DO
  BEGIN
    J := J + 1;
    readln (A[J])
  END;
```

Note that the first value is then read into A[1].

6. After using a sequential search, make sure you check to see if the value has been found. For example, if Num contains the value 3 and A is the array

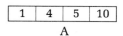

A

the search

```
Index := 1;
WHILE (Num <> A[Index]) AND (Index < Length) DO
  Index := Index + 1;
```

yields values

Num   Index   A[Index]

Depending on program use, you should check for Num = A[Index] or use a Boolean flag to indicate if a match has been found.

■ Summary

Key Terms

abstract data type (ADT)	data abstraction	selection sort
array	index (subscript)	sequential (linear)
binary search	index type	search
byte	packed array	string data type
component (element) of		unpacked array
an array		word

Keywords

ARRAY	**PACKED**	**string**

Key Concepts

- An array is a structured variable; a single declaration can reserve several variables.
- It is good practice to define array types in the **TYPE** declaration section and then declare a variable of that type; for example,

```
TYPE
   List10 = ARRAY [1..10] OF real;
VAR
   X : List10;
```

- Arrays can be visualized as lists; thus, the previous array could be envisioned as

```
X
 ┌───┐
 │   │ 1
 ├───┤
 │   │ 2
 ├───┤
 │   │ 3
 ├───┤
 │   │ 4
 ├───┤
 │   │ 5
 ├───┤
 │   │ 6
 ├───┤
 │   │ 7
 ├───┤
 │   │ 8
 ├───┤
 │   │ 9
 ├───┤
 │   │ 10
 └───┘
```

- Each component of an array is a variable of the declared type and can be used the same as any other variable of that type.
- Loops can be used to read data into arrays; for example,

```
J := 0;
WHILE NOT eof AND (J < MaxLength) DO
   BEGIN
      J := J + 1;
      readln (List[J])
   END;
```

- Loops can be used to print data from arrays; for example, if Score is an array of 20 test scores, they can be printed by

```
FOR J := 1 TO 20 DO
   writeln (Score[J]);
```

- Manipulating components of an array is generally accomplished by using the index as a loop variable; for example, assuming the previous Score, to find the smallest value in the array we can use

```
Small := Score[1];
FOR J := 2 TO 20 DO
   IF Score[J] < Small THEN
      Small := Score[J];
```

- A selection sort is one method of sorting elements in an array from high to low or low to high; for example, if A is an array of length n, a low-to-high sort is

```
FOR J := 1 TO N - 1 DO
  BEGIN
    Index := J;
    FOR K := J + 1 TO N DO
      IF A[K] < A[Index] THEN
        Index := K;
    IF Index <> J THEN
      BEGIN
        Temp := A[Index];
        A[Index]:= A[J];
        A[J]:= Temp
      END {  of exchange  }
  END; {  of selection sort  }
```

- When arrays are to be passed to subprograms, the type should be defined in the **TYPE** section; thus, we could have

```
TYPE
  List200 = ARRAY [1..200] OF real;

PROCEDURE Practice (X : List200);
```

- If the array being passed is a variable parameter, it should be declared accordingly; for example,

```
PROCEDURE GetData (VAR X : List200);
```

- Sorting arrays is conveniently done using procedures; such procedures facilitate program design.
- Data abstraction is the process of separating a conceptual definition of a data structure from its implementation details.
- An abstract data type (ADT) consists of a class of objects, a defined set of properties for these objects, and a set of operations for processing the objects.
- Packed arrays are used for character strings to reduce memory required for string storage and manipulation; a typical packed array declaration is

```
TYPE
  String20 = PACKED ARRAY [1..20] OF char;
VAR
  Name : String20;
```

- Character strings (packed arrays of characters) can be compared; this facilitates alphabetizing a list of names.
- Character strings can be printed using a single **write** or **writeln** statement; thus, if Name is a packed array of characters, it can be printed by

```
writeln (Name:30);
```

- Packed arrays of characters must still be read one character at a time.
- A single assignment statement can be used to assign a string to a packed array of the same length; for example,

```
Name := 'Smith John';
```

- A sequential search of a list consists of examining the first item in a list and then proceeding through the list in sequence until the desired value is found or the end of the list is reached; code for this search is

```
Index := 1;
WHILE (Num <> A[Index] AND (Index < Length) DO
  Index := Index + 1;
```

- A binary search of a list consists of deciding which half of the list contains the value in question and then which half of that half, and so on; code for this search is

```
Found := false;
WHILE NOT Found AND (First <= Last) DO
  BEGIN
    Mid := (First + Last) DIV 2;
    IF Num < A[Mid] THEN
      Last := Mid - 1
    ELSE IF Num > A[Mid] THEN
      First := Mid + 1
    ELSE
      Found := true
  END;
```

■ Programming Problems and Projects

1. Write a program to read an unknown number of integer test scores from an input file (assume at most 150 scores). Print out the original list of scores, the scores sorted from low to high, the scores sorted from high to low, the highest score, the lowest score, and the average score.

2. Write a program to help you balance your checkbook. The input consists of the beginning balance and then a sequence of transactions, each followed by a transaction code. Deposits are followed by a "D" and withdrawals are followed by a "W." The output should consist of a list of transactions, a running balance, an ending balance, the number of withdrawals, and the number of deposits. Include an appropriate message for overdrawn accounts.

3. Write a program to read a line of text as input. Print out the original line of text, the line of text in reverse order, and the number of vowels contained in the line.

4. Write a program that sorts data of type **real** as it is read from the input file. Do this by putting the first data item in the first component of an array and then inserting each subsequent number in the array in order from high to low. Print out the sorted array. Assume there are at most 25 numbers.

5. A palindrome is a word (or number) that is the same forwards and backwards. Write a program to read several lines of text as input. Inspect each word to see if it is a palindrome. The output should list all palindromes and a count of the number of palindromes in the message.

6. One of the problems faced by designers of word processors is that of printing text without separating a word at the end of a line. Write a program to read several lines of text as input. Then print the message with each line starting in column 10 and no line exceeding column 70. No word should be separated at the end of a line.

7. Your local state university has to raise funds for an art center. As a first step, they are going to approach 20 previously identified donors and ask for additional donations. Because the donors wish to remain anonymous, only the respective totals of their previous donations are listed in a data file. After they are contacted, the additional donations are listed at the end of the data file in the same order as the first 20 entries. Write a computer program to read the first 20 entries into one array and the second 20 entries into a second array. Compute the previous total donations and the new donations for the art center. Print the following:

  a. The list of previous donations
  b. The list of new donations
  c. An unsorted list of total donations
  d. A sorted list of total donations
  e. Total donations before the fund drive
  f. Total donations for the art center
  g. The maximum donation for the art center

8. Write a program that can be used as a text analyzer. Your program should be capable of reading an input file and keeping track of the frequency of occurrence of each letter of the alphabet. There should also be a count of all characters (including blanks) encountered that are not in the alphabet. Your output should be the data file printed line-by-line followed by a histogram reflecting the frequency of occurrence of each letter in the alphabet. For example, the following histogram indicates five occurrences of a, two of b, and three of c.

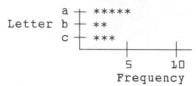

9. The Third Interdenominational Church has on file a list of all of its benefactors (a maximum of 20 names, each up to 30 characters) along with an unknown number of amounts that each has donated to the church. You have been asked to write a program that does the following:
   a. Print the name of each donor and the amount (in descending order) of any donations given by each.
   b. Print the total amounts in ascending order.
   c. Print the grand total of all donations.
   d. Print the largest single amount donated and the name of the benefactor who made this donation.

10. Read in a list of 50 integers from the data file NumberList. Place the even numbers into an array called Even, the odd numbers into an array called Odd, and the negatives into an array called Negative. Print all three arrays after all numbers have been read.

11. Read in 300 real numbers. Print the average of the numbers followed by all the numbers that are greater than the average.

12. Read in the names of five candidates in a class election and the number of votes received by each. Print the list of candidates, the number of votes they received, and the percentage of the total vote they received sorted into order from the winner to the person with the fewest votes. You may assume that all names are 20 characters in length.

13. In many sports events, contestants are rated by judges with an average score being determined by discarding the highest and lowest scores and averaging the remaining scores. Write a program in which eight scores are entered, computing the average score for the contestant.

14. Given a list of 20 test scores (integers), print the score that is nearest to the average.

15. The Game of Nim is played with three piles of stones. There are three stones in the first pile, five stones in the second, and eight stones in

the third. Two players alternate taking as many stones as they like from any one pile. Play continues until someone is forced to take the last stone. The person taking the last stone loses. Write a program which permits two people to play the game of Nim using an array to keep track of the number of stones in each pile.

16. There is an effective strategy that can virtually guarantee victory in the game of Nim. Devise a strategy and modify the program in Problem 15 so that the computer plays against a person. Your program should be virtually unbeatable if the proper strategy is developed.

17. The median of a set of numbers is the value in the middle of the set if the set is arranged in order. The mode is the number listed most often. Given a list of 21 numbers, print the median and mode of the list.

18. Rewrite Problem 17 to permit the use of any length list of numbers.

19. The standard deviation is a statistic frequently used in education measurement. Write a program that, given a list of test scores, will find and print the standard deviation of the numbers. The standard deviation formula can be found in most statistics books.

20. Revise Problem 19 so that after the standard deviation is printed, you can print a list of test scores that are more than one standard deviation below the average and a list of the scores more than one standard deviation above the average.

21. The z-score is defined as the score earned on a test divided by the standard deviation. Given a data file containing an unknown number of test scores (maximum of 100), print a list showing each test score (from highest to lowest) and the corresponding z-score.

■ 22. Salespeople for the Wellsville Wholesale Company earn a commission based on their sales. The commission rates are as follows:

Sales	Commission
$0–1000	3%
1001–5000	4.5%
5001–10000	5.25%
over 10000	6%

In addition, any salesperson who sells above the average of all salespeople receive a $50 bonus, and the top salesperson receives an additional $75 bonus.

Given the names and amounts sold by each of 20 salespeople, write a program that prints a table showing the salesperson's name, the amount sold, the commission rate, and the total amount earned. The average sales should also be printed.

23. Ms. Alicia Citizen, your school's Student Government advisor, has come to you for help. She wants a program to total votes for the next Student Government election. Fifteen candidates will be in the election with five positions to be filled. Each person can vote for up to five candidates. The five highest vote getters will be the winners.

A data file called VoteList contains a list of candidates (by candidate number) voted for by each student. Any line of the file may contain up to five numbers, but if it contains more than five numbers, it is discarded as a void ballot. Write a program to read the file and print a list of the total votes received by each candidate. Also, print the five highest vote getters in order from highest to lowest vote totals.

24. The data file InstructorList contains a list of the instructors in your school along with the room number to which each is assigned. Write a program that, given the name of the instructor, does a linear search to find and print the room to which the instructor is assigned.

25. Rewrite Problem 24 so that when given a room number, the name of the instructor assigned to that room is found using a binary search. Assume the file is arranged in order of room numbers.

26. Write a language translation program that permits the entry of a word in English, with the corresponding word of another language being printed. The dictionary words can be stored in parallel arrays, with the English array being sorted into alphabetical order prior to the first entry of a word. Your program should first sort the dictionary words.

27. Elementary and middle school students are often given the task of converting numbers from one base to another. For example, 19 in base 10 is 103 in base 4 ($1 \times 4^2 + 0 \times 4^1 + 3 \times 4^0$). Conversely, 123 in base 4 is 27 in base 10. Write an interactive program that allows the user to choose from the following:

```
<1>   Convert from base 10 to base A
<2>   Convert from base A to base 10
<3>   Quit
```

If options 1 or 2 are chosen, the user should then enter the intended base and the number to be converted. A sample run of the program would produce the output:

```
This program allows you to convert between bases. Which
of the following would you like?

    <1>   Convert from base 10 to base A
    <2>   Convert from base A to base 10
    <3>   Quit

Enter your choice and press <RETURN>.
?1

Enter the number in base 10 and press <RETURN>.
?237

Enter the new base and press <RETURN>.
?4

The number 237 in base 4 is:   3231

Press <RETURN> to continue

This program allows you to convert between bases. Which
of the following would you like?

    <1>   Convert from base 10 to base A
    <2>   Convert from base A to Base 10
    <3>   Quit

Enter your choice and press <RETURN>.
?2

What number would you like to have converted?
?2332
```

```
Converting to base 10, we get:

        2 *     1 =           2
        3 *     4 =          12
        3 *    16 =          48
        2 *    64 =         128
                          -----
The base 10 value is       190

Press <RETURN> to continue

This program allows you to convert between bases. Which
of the following would you like?

        <1>   Convert from base 10 to base A
        <2>   Convert from base A to base 10
        <3>   Quit

Enter your choice and press <RETURN>.
?3
```

28. One of the principles underlying the concept of data abstraction is that implementation details of data structures should be deferred to the lowest possible level. To illustrate, consider the high-level design to which we referred in our previous discussion of data abstraction. Our program required you to work with a list of names and an associated list of numbers (student names and test scores). The following first-level design was suggested:

```
GetNames (⟨procedure here⟩);
GetScores (⟨procedure here⟩);
SortByName (⟨procedure here⟩);
PrintNamesAndScores (⟨procedure here⟩);
SortByScore (⟨procedure here⟩);
PrintNamesAndScores (⟨procedure here⟩);
```

Write complete documentation for each of these modules, including a description of all parameters and data structures required. Present your documentation to the class. Ask if your classmates have questions about the number or type of parameters, the data structures required, and/or the main tasks to be performed by each module.

29. Contact programmers at your university and/or some businesses and discuss with them the use of lists as a data type. Ask what kinds of programming problems require the use of a list, how the programmers handle data entry (list length), and what operations they perform on the list (search, sort, and so on).

    Give an oral report of your findings to the class.

30. Select a programming problem from this chapter that you have not yet worked. Construct a structure chart and write all documentary information necessary for the problem you have chosen. Do not write code. When you are finished, have a classmate read your documentation to see if what is to be done is clear.

Arrays of More Than One Dimension

Chapter 10 illustrated the significance and uses of one-dimensional arrays. There are, however, several kinds of problems that require arrays of more than one dimension. For example, if you want to work with a table that has both rows and columns, a one-dimensional array will not suffice. Other programming problems require the use of a list of names; these are not conveniently written as one-dimensional arrays. Such problems can be solved using arrays of more than one dimension.

■ 11.1 Two-Dimensional Arrays

OBJECTIVES

- to be able to declare two-dimensional arrays
- to be able to use correct notation for two-dimensional arrays
- to be able to create tabular output using two-dimensional arrays
- to be able to **read** and **write** with two-dimensional arrays
- to be able to manipulate components of two-dimensional arrays
- to be able to use two-dimensional arrays with procedures

Basic Idea and Notation

One-dimensional arrays are very useful when working with a row or column of numbers. However, suppose we want to work with data that are best represented in tabular form. For example, box scores in baseball are reported with one player name listed for each row and one statistic listed for each column. Another example is an instructor's grade book in which a student name is listed for each row and test and/or quiz scores are listed for each column. In both cases, a multiple reference is needed for a single data item.

Pascal accomplishes multiple reference by using *two-dimensional arrays*. In these arrays, the row subrange always precedes the column subrange and they are separated by commas. To illustrate, suppose we want to print the table

1	2	3	4
2	4	6	8
3	6	9	12

where we need to access both the row and column for a single data entry. This table could be produced by either of the following declarations.

```
1. VAR
     Table : ARRAY [1..3, 1..4] OF integer;
2. TYPE
     Matrix = ARRAY [1..3, 1..4] OF integer;
   VAR
     Table : Matrix;
```

It is the index—[1 .. 3, 1 .. 4]—of each of these declarations that differs from one-dimensional arrays. These declarations reserve memory that can be visualized as three rows, each of which holds four variables. Thus, 12 variable locations have been reserved as shown.

Table

As a second illustration of the use of two-dimensional arrays, suppose we want to print the batting statistics for a softball team of 15 players. If the statistics consist of at bats (AB), hits (H), runs (R), and runs batted in (RBI) for each player, we naturally choose to work with a 15 × 4 table. Hence, a reasonable variable declaration is

```
TYPE
   Table15X4 = ARRAY [1..15, 1..4] OF integer;
VAR
   Stats : Table15X4;
```

The reserved memory area can be visualized as

Stats

with 60 variable locations reserved.

Before proceeding further, let's examine another method of declaring two-dimensional arrays. Our 3 × 4 table could be thought of as three arrays each of length four, as follows:

Hence, we have a list of arrays and we could have declared the table by

```
TYPE
   Row = ARRAY [1..4] OF integer;
   Matrix = ARRAY [1..3] OF Row;
VAR
   Table : Matrix;
```

The softball statistics could be declared by

```
CONST
   NumberOfStats = 4;
   RosterSize = 15;
TYPE
   PlayerStats = ARRAY [1..NumberOfStats] OF integer;
   TeamTable = ARRAY [1..RosterSize] OF PlayerStats;
VAR
   Stats : TeamTable;
```

Semantic indices could be utilized by

```
TYPE
   Stat = (AtBat, Hits, Runs, RBI);
   StatChart = ARRAY [1..RosterSize, Stat] OF integer;
VAR
   Player : StatChart;
```

In this case, a typical entry is

```
Player[5, Hits] := 2;
```

In general, a two-dimensional array can be defined by

ARRAY [⟨row index⟩, ⟨column index⟩] **OF** ⟨element type⟩;

or

TYPE
   RowType = **ARRAY** [⟨column index⟩] **OF** ⟨element type⟩;
   Matrix = **ARRAY** [⟨row index⟩] **OF** RowType;

Whichever method of declaration is used, the problem now becomes one of accessing individual components of the two-dimensional array. For example, in the table

1	2	3	4
2	4	6	8
3	6	9	12

the "8" is in row two and column four. Note that both the row and column position of an element must be indicated. Therefore, in order to put an "8" in this position, we can use an assignment statement such as

```
Table[2,4] := 8;
```

This assignment statement would be used for either of the declaration forms mentioned earlier.

Next let's assign the values just given to the appropriate variables in Table by 12 assignment statements as follows:

```
Table[1,1] := 1;
Table[1,2] := 2;
Table[1,3] := 3;
```

STYLE TIP

■ ■ ■ ■ ■ ■ ■ ■ ■ ■ ■ ■

When working with charts or tables of a fixed grid size (say 15 × 4), descriptive identifiers could be

```
Chart15X4
```

or

```
Table15X4
```

If the number of rows and columns vary for different runs of the program (for example, the number of players on a team could vary from year to year), you could define a type by

```
CONST
  NumRows = 15;
  NumColumns = 4;
TYPE
  RowRange = 1..NumRows;
  ColumnRange = 1..NumColumns;
  Table = ARRAY [RowRange, ColumnRange] OF integer;
VAR
  Stats : Table;
```

```
Table[1,4] := 4;
Table[2,1] := 2;
Table[2,2] := 4;
Table[2,3] := 6;
Table[2,4] := 8;
Table[3,1] := 3;
Table[3,2] := 6;
Table[3,3] := 9;
Table[3,4] := 12;
```

As you can see, this is extremely tedious. Instead, we can note the relationship between the indices and the assigned values and make the row index Row and the column index Column. The values to be assigned are then Row * Column and we can use nested loops to perform these assignments as follows:

```
FOR Row := 1 TO 3 DO
  FOR Column := 1 TO 4 DO
    Table[Row, Column] := Row * Column;
```

Since two-dimensional arrays frequently require working with nested loops, let us examine more closely what this segment of code does. When Row := 1, the loop

```
FOR Column := 1 TO 4 DO
  Table[1, Column] := 1 * Column;
```

is executed. This performs the four assignments

```
Table[1,1] := 1 * 1;
Table[1,2] := 1 * 2;
Table[1,3] := 1 * 3;
Table[1,4] := 1 * 4;
```

and we have the memory area

Table

1	2	3	4

Similar results hold for Row := 2 and Row := 3 and we produce a two-dimensional array that can be visualized as

Table

1	2	3	4
2	4	6	8
3	6	9	12

The following examples will help you learn to work with and understand the notation for two-dimensional arrays.

■ EXAMPLE 11.1

Assume the declaration

```
TYPE
   Table5X4 = ARRAY [1..5, 1..4] OF integer;
VAR
   Table : Table5X4;
```

has been made and consider the segment of code

```
FOR Row := 1 TO 5 DO
   FOR Column := 1 TO 4 DO
      Table[Row, Column] := Row DIV Column;
```

When Row := 1, the loop

```
FOR Column := 1 TO 4 DO
   Table[1, Column] := 1 DIV Column;
```

is executed. This causes the assignment statements

```
Table[1,1] := 1 DIV 1;
Table[1,2] := 1 DIV 2;
Table[1,3] := 1 DIV 3;
Table[1,4] := 1 DIV 4;
```

The contents of the memory area after that first pass through the loop are

Table

1	0	0	0

When Row := 2, the assignments are

```
Table[2,1] := 2 DIV 1;
Table[2,2] := 2 DIV 2;
Table[2,3] := 2 DIV 3;
Table[2,4] := 2 DIV 4;
```

Table now has values as follows:

Table

1	0	0	0
2	1	0	0

The contents of Table after the entire outside loop has been executed are

Table

1	0	0	0
2	1	0	0
3	1	1	0
4	2	1	1
5	2	1	1

■ **EXAMPLE 11.2**

Declare a two-dimensional array and write a segment of code to produce the memory area and contents depicted as follows:

2	3	4	5	6	7	8
3	4	5	6	7	8	9
4	5	6	7	8	9	10
5	6	7	8	9	10	11

An appropriate definition is

```
TYPE
   Table4X7 = ARRAY [1..4, 1..7] OF integer;
```

or

```
TYPE
   Table4X7 = ARRAY [1..4] OF
              ARRAY [1..7] OF integer;
VAR
   Table : Table4X7;
```

and a segment of code to produce the desired contents is

```
FOR Row := 1 TO 4 DO
  FOR Column := 1 TO 7 DO
    Table[Row, Column] := Row + Column;
```

Reading and Writing

Most problems using two-dimensional arrays require reading data from an input file into the array and writing values from the array to create some tabular form of output. For example, suppose we have our two-dimensional array for softball statistics.

```
TYPE
   Table15X4 = ARRAY [1..15, 1..4] OF integer;
VAR
   Stats : Table15X4;
```

If the data file consists of 15 lines and each line contains statistics for one player as follows,

```
AB  H   R   RBI
4   2   1   1      (player #1)

3   1   0   1      (player #2)
       .       .
       .       .
       .       .
0   0   0   0      (player #15)
```

we can get the data from the file by reading it one line at a time for 15 lines. This is done using nested loops as follows:

```
FOR Row := 1 TO 15 DO
  BEGIN
    FOR Column := 1 TO 4 DO
      read (Stats[Row, Column]);
    readln
  END;
```

When Row := 1, the loop

```
FOR Column := 1 TO 4 DO
  read (Stats[Row, Column]);
```

reads the first line of data. In a similar manner, as Row assumes the values 2 through 15, the lines 2 through 15 would be read. After reading the data into an array, some operations and/or updating will be performed and we will output the data in tabular form. For example, suppose we want to print the softball statistics in the 15 × 4 table using only three spaces for each column. We note the following:

1. Three spaces per column can be controlled by formatting the output.
2. One line of output can be generated by a **FOR** loop containing a **write** statement; for example,

```
FOR Column := 1 TO 4 DO
  write (Stats[Row, Column]:3);
```

3. The output buffer will be dumped to the printer after each **write** loop by using **writeln**.
4. We do this for 15 lines by another loop

```
FOR Row := 1 TO 15 DO
  BEGIN
    FOR Column := 1 TO 4 DO
      write (Stats[Row, Column]:3);
    writeln
  END;
```

This last segment of code produces the desired output.

In actual practice, we will also be concerned with headings for our tables and controlling where the data occur on the page. For example, suppose we want to identify the columns of softball statistics as AB, H, R, and RBI; underline the headings; and start the output (AB) in column 25. The following segment of code accomplishes our objectives.

```
writeln (Skip:24,'AB H  R RBI');
writeln (Skip:24,'-----------');
writeln;
FOR Row := 1 TO 15 DO
  BEGIN
    write (Skip:22);  {  Set the left margin  }
    FOR Column := 1 TO 4 DO
      write (Stats[Row, Column]:3);
    writeln  {  Advance to next line  }
  END;
```

The data file used earlier for our ballplayers causes an output of

```
AB H  R RBI
-----------

4  2  1  1
3  1  0  0
      .
      .
      .
0  0  0  0
```

Manipulating Two-Dimensional Array Components

Often we want to work with some but not all of the components of an array. For example, suppose we have a two-dimensional array of test scores for students in a class. If there are 20 students with five scores each, an appropriate two-dimensional array could be declared as

```
TYPE
  Table20X5 = ARRAY [1..20, 1..5] OF integer;
VAR
  Score : Table20X5;
```

After scores have been read into the array Score, we can envision the memory area as follows:

Score

98	86	100	76	95	(student #1)
72	68	65	74	81	(student #2)
85	81	91	84	83	(student #3)
					.
					.
					.
					.
					.
					.
					.
					.
					.
					.
					.
					.
					.
76	81	72	87	80	(student #20)

When printing a table with test scores, one would normally compute several items, including total points for each student, percentage grade for each student, and average score for each test. Let's examine what is required for each of these computations. First, to get the total points for each student, we declare a one-dimensional array to store these values, so assume the declaration

```
TYPE
   List20 = ARRAY [1..20] OF integer;
VAR
   TotalPoints : List20;
```

Since the first student's test scores are in the first row, we could write

```
TotalPoints[1] := Score[1,1] + Score[1,2] +
                  Score[1,3] + Score[1,4] +
                  Score[1,5];
```

To compute this total for each student, we could use the loop

```
FOR Student := 1 TO 20 DO
   TotalPoints[Student] := Score[Student, 1] +
                           Score[Student, 2] +
                           Score[Student, 3] +
                           Score[Student, 4] +
                           Score[Student, 5];
```

and this would produce the array of totals

TotalPoints

455	TotalPoints[1]
360	TotalPoints[2]
424	TotalPoints[3]
.	.
.	.
.	.
396	TotalPoints[20]

If the two-dimensional array has several columns, we can use a loop to sum an array of numbers. We can, for instance, write a loop to sum the five test scores for the first student in our table.

```
TotalPoints[1] := 0;
FOR Test := 1 TO 5 DO
   TotalPoints[1] := TotalPoints[1] + Score[1, Test];
```

To do this for each student, we use a second loop.

```
FOR Student := 1 TO 20 DO
   BEGIN
      TotalPoints[Student] := 0;
      FOR Test := 1 TO 5 DO
         TotalPoints[Student] := TotalPoints[Student] +
                                 Score[Student, Test]
   END;
```

The second task in our problem is to compute the percentage grade for each student. If we want to save these percentages, we can declare an array as follows:

```
TYPE
   Column20 = ARRAY [1..20] OF real;
VAR
   Percent : Column20;
```

and include a segment of code

```
FOR Student := 1 TO 20 DO
  Percent[Student] := TotalPoints[Student] / 5;
```

The third task is to find the average score for each test. To find these numbers, we need to add all 20 scores for each test and divide the respective total by 20. We first have to find the sum of each column and we need to declare an array in which to store the averages. The declaration could be

```
TYPE
  List5 = Array [1..5] OF real;
VAR
  TestAv: List5;
```

We now need a loop to find the total of each column. Assuming we have an integer variable Sum declared, we can sum column one by

```
Sum := 0;
FOR Student := 1 TO 20 DO
  Sum := Sum + Score[Student, 1];
```

TestAv[1] can now be found by

```
TestAv[1] := Sum / 20;
```

To do this for each column, we use a second loop as follows:

```
FOR Test := 1 TO 5 DO              {  Test is the column subscript  }
  BEGIN
    Sum := 0;
    FOR Student := 1 TO 20 DO    {   Student is the row subscript   }
      Sum := Sum + Score[Student, Test];
    TestAv[Test] := Sum / 20
  END;
```

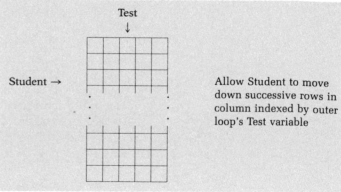

Test
↓

Student →

Allow Student to move down successive rows in column indexed by outer loop's Test variable

As a concluding example of manipulating elements of two-dimensional arrays, consider the following.

■ EXAMPLE 11.3

Assume we have the declarations

```
CONST
  NumRows = 20;
  NumColumns = 50;
TYPE
  TableSize = ARRAY [1..NumRows,
                     1..NumColumns] OF integer;
  List = ARRAY [1..NumRows] OF integer;
VAR
  Table : TableSize;
  Max : List;
```

and values have been read into the two-dimensional array from an input file. Let's write a segment of code to find the maximum value in each row and then store this value in the array Max. To find the maximum of row one, we can write

```
Max[1] := Table[1,1];
FOR Column := 2 TO NumColumns DO
  IF Table[1, Column] > Max[1] THEN
    Max[1] := Table[1, Column];
```

To do this for each of the rows, we use a second loop as follows:

```
FOR Row := 1 TO NumRows DO
  BEGIN
    Max[Row] := Table[Row, 1];
    FOR Column := 2 TO NumColumns DO
      IF Table[Row, Column] > Max[Row] THEN
        Max[Row] := Table[Row, Column]
  END;
```

Procedures and Two-Dimensional Arrays

When we start writing programs with two-dimensional arrays, we will use procedures as before to maintain the top-down design philosophy. As with one-dimensional arrays, there are three relatively standard uses of procedures in most problems: to get the data, to manipulate the data, and to display the data.

When using procedures with data that require an array as a data structure, the array type must be defined in the **TYPE** section. The actual parameters and formal parameters can then be of the defined array type. As with one-dimensional arrays, we pass two-dimensional arrays by reference to conserve memory allocation.

■ **EXAMPLE 11.4**

Western Jeans, Inc. wants a program to help them keep track of their inventory of jeans. The jeans are coded by waist size and inseam. The waist sizes are the integer values from 24 to 46 and the inseams are the integer values from 26 to 40. Thus, there are 23 waist sizes and 15 inseams for each waist size. The first 23 lines of the data file contain the starting inventory. Each line corresponds to a waist size and contains 15 integers, one for each inseam. The next 23 lines of the data file contain the sales information for a day. Let's write a program to find and print the closing inventory.

A first-level pseudocode development for this program is

1. Get starting inventory
2. Get new sales
3. Update inventory
4. Print heading
5. Print closing inventory

Each of these steps uses a procedure.

Since there are 23 waist sizes and 15 inseams, we use definitions as follows:

```
CONST
  FirstWaist = 24;
  LastWaist = 46;
  FirstInseam = 26;
  LastInseam = 40;
TYPE
  WaistSizes = FirstWaist..LastWaist;
  InseamSizes = FirstInseam..LastInseam;
  Table = ARRAY [WaistSizes, InseamSizes] OF integer;
```

We use variables declared as follows:

```
VAR
  Inventory : Table;
  Sales : Table;
```

Assuming variables have been declared as needed, let's now write a procedure to get the starting inventory.

```
PROCEDURE GetData (VAR Matrix : Table);
  VAR
    Row, Column : integer;
  BEGIN
    FOR Row := FirstWaist TO LastWaist DO
      BEGIN
        FOR Column := FirstInseam TO LastInseam DO
          read (Matrix[Row, Column]);
        readln
      END
  END;
```

Note that **VAR** is used because the new data will be needed later in the program. This procedure will be called from the main program by

```
GetData (Inventory);
```

The next task is to get the sales for a day. Since this merely requires reading the next 23 lines from the data file, we do not need to write a new procedure. We call GetData again by

```
GetData (Sales);
```

We now need a procedure to update the starting inventory. This updating can be accomplished by sending both two-dimensional arrays to a procedure and then finding the respective differences of components.

```
PROCEDURE Update (VAR Inventory : Table;
                  VAR Sales : Table);
  VAR
    Row, Column : integer;
  BEGIN
    FOR Row := FirstWaist TO LastWaist DO
      FOR Column := FirstInseam TO LastInseam DO
        Inventory[Row, Column] := Inventory[Row, Column] -
                                  Sales[Row, Column]
  END;
```

This is called by the statement

```
Update (Inventory, Sales);
```

The procedure for the heading is as before, so we need not write it here. Let's assume the arrays have been assigned the necessary values. The output procedure will be

```
PROCEDURE PrintData (VAR Inventory : Table);
  CONST
    Mark = ' !';
```

```
VAR
  Row, Column : integer;
BEGIN
  FOR Row := FirstWaist TO LastWaist DO
    BEGIN
      write (Row:6, Mark);
      FOR Column := FirstInseam TO LastInseam DO
        write (Inventory[Row, Column]:4);
      writeln;
      writeln (Mark:6)
    END  {  of printing one row  }
END;
```

This procedure could be called from the main program by

```
PrintData (Inventory);
```

Once these procedures have been written, the main program becomes

```
BEGIN
  GetData (Inventory);
  GetData (Sales);
  Update (Inventory, Sales);
  PrintHeading;
  PrintData (Inventory)
END.  {  of main program  }
```

Exercise 11.1

1. Define a two-dimensional array type for each of the following using both the **ARRAY** [. . , . .] and **ARRAY** [. .] **OF ARRAY** [. .]forms.

   a. A table with real number entries that shows the prices for four different drugs charged by five drug stores.

   b. A table with character entries that shows the grades earned by 20 students in six courses.

   c. A table with integer entries that shows the 12 quiz scores earned by 30 students in a class.

2. Write a test program to read integers into a 3 × 5 array and then print out the array components together with each row sum and each column sum.

3. For each of the following declarations, sketch what is reserved in memory. In each case, state how many variables are available to the programmer.

   a. ```
TYPE
    ShippingCostTable = ARRAY [1..10] OF
                                ARRAY [1..4] OF real;
    GradeBookTable = ARRAY [1..35, 1..6] OF integer;
VAR
    ShippingCost : ShippingCostTable;
    GradeBook : GradeBookTable;
```

   b. ```
TYPE
    Matrix = ARRAY [1..3, 2..6] OF integer;
VAR
    A : Matrix;
```

   c. ```
TYPE
    Weekdays = (Mon, Tues, Wed, Thur, Fri);
    Chores = (Wash, Iron, Clean, Mow, Sweep);
    ScheduleTable = ARRAY [Weekdays, Chores] OF boolean;
VAR
    Schedule : ScheduleTable;
```

   d. ```
TYPE
    Questions = 1..50;
    Answers = 1..5;
    Table = ARRAY [Questions, Answers] OF char;
VAR
    AnswerSheet : Table;
```

4. Assume the array A has been declared as

   ```
TYPE
    Table3X5 = ARRAY [1..3, 1..5] OF integer;
VAR
    A : Table3X5;
```

   Indicate the array contents produced by each of the following:

   a. ```
FOR J := 1 TO 3 DO
    FOR K := 1 TO 5 DO
        A[J,K] := J - K;
```

   b. ```
FOR J := 1 TO 3 DO
    FOR K := 1 TO 5 DO
        A[J,K] := J;
```

   c. ```
FOR K := 1 TO 5 DO
    FOR J := 1 TO 3 DO
        A[J,K] := J;
```

   d. ```
FOR J := 3 DOWNTO 1 DO
    FOR K := 1 TO 5 DO
        A[J,K] := J MOD K;
```

5. Let the two-dimensional array A be declared by

   ```
TYPE
    Table3X6 = ARRAY [1..3, 1..6] OF integer;
VAR
    A : Table3X6;
```

Write nested loops that causes the following values to be stored in A:

a.

A

3	4	5	6	7	8
5	6	7	8	9	10
7	8	9	10	11	12

b.

A

0	0	0	0	0	0
0	0	0	0	0	0
0	0	0	0	0	0

c.

A

2	2	2	2	2	2
4	4	4	4	4	4
6	6	6	6	6	6

6. Declare a two-dimensional array and write a segment of code that reads the following input file into the array.

```
13.2 15.1 10.3 8.2 43.6
```

```
37.2 25.6 34.1 17.0 15.2
```

7. Suppose an input file contains 50 lines of data and the first 20 spaces of each line are reserved for a customer's name. The rest of the line contains other information. Declare a two dimensional array to hold the names and write a segment of code to read the names into the array. A sample line of input is

```
Smith John O          268-14-1801
```
```
                      ↑
                   position 21
```

8. Assume the declaration

```
TYPE
   Table4X5 = ARRAY [1..4, 1..5] OF real;
VAR
   Table : Table4X5;
```

has been made and values have been read into Table as follows:

Table

-2.0	3.0	0.0	8.0	10.0
0.0	-4.0	3.0	1.0	2.0
1.0	2.0	3.0	8.0	-6.0
-4.0	1.0	4.0	6.0	82.0

Indicate what the components of Table would be after each of the following segments of code is executed.

```
a. FOR J := 1 TO 4 DO
      FOR K := 1 TO 5 DO
         IF J MOD K = 0 THEN
            A[J,K] := 0.0
         ELSE
            A[J,K] := -1.0;
b. FOR J := 1 TO 4 DO
      IF A[J,1] <> 0.0 THEN
         FOR K := 1 TO 5 DO
            A[J,K] := A[J,K] / A[J,1];
```

```
c. FOR K := 1 TO 5 DO
      IF A[1,K] = 0.0 THEN
         FOR J := 1 TO 4 DO
            A[J,K] := 0.0;
```

9. Let the two-dimensional array Table be declared as in Exercise 8. Declare additional arrays as needed and write segments of code for each of the following:

   a. Find and save the minimum of each row.

   b. Find and save the maximum of each column.

   c. Find the total of all the components.

10. Example 11.4 illustrates the use of procedures with two-dimensional arrays. For actual use, you would also need a list indicating what to order to maintain the inventory. Write a procedure (assuming all declarations have been made) to print a table indicating which sizes of jeans have a supply fewer than four. Do this by putting an '*' in the cell if the supply is low or a ' ' if the supply is adequate.

11. Suppose you want to work with a table that has three rows and eight columns of integers.

    a. Declare an appropriate two-dimensional array that can be used with procedures.

    b. Write a procedure to replace all negative numbers with zero.

    c. Show what is needed to call this procedure from the main program.

12. If A and B are matrices of size $m \times n$, their sum $A + B$ is defined by $A + B = [a + b]_{ij}$, where a and b are corresponding components in A and B. Write a program to

    a. Read values into two matrices of size $m \times n$.

    b. Compute the sum.

    c. Print out the matrices together with the sum.

13. If A and B are matrices of sizes $m \times n$ and $n \times p$, their product is defined to be the $m \times p$ matrix AB where

$$AB = [c_{ik}], \; c_{ik} = \sum_{j=1}^{n} a_{ij}b_{jk}$$

Write a program that will

    a. Read values into two matrices whose product is defined.

    b. Compute their product.

    c. Print out the matrices together with their product.

■ ■ ■ ■

■ 11.2
Arrays of String Variables

OBJECTIVES

- to understand that an array of string variables is a two-dimensional array
- to be able to declare an array of string variables

Basic Idea and Notation

T Recall from Section 10.5 that we defined string variables as packed arrays of characters. At that time, we learned that strings of the same length can be compared and strings can be printed using a single **write** or **writeln** command. A typical declaration for a name 20 characters in length is

```
TYPE
   String20 = PACKED ARRAY [1..20] OF char;
VAR
   Name : String20;
```

- to be able to read data into an array of string variables
- to be able to alphabetize a list of names

Thus, Name could be envisioned as

Name

It is a natural extension to next consider the problem of working with an array of strings. For example, if we need a data structure for 50 names, this can be declared by

```
TYPE
   String20 = PACKED ARRAY [1..20] OF char;
   NameList = ARRAY [1..50] OF String20;
VAR
   Name : NameList;
```

Name can then be envisioned as

Name

	Name[1]
	Name[2]
	Name[3]
. . .	. . .
	Name[50]

where each component of Name is a packed array.

Alphabetizing a List of Names

One standard problem faced by programmers is that of alphabetizing a list of names. For example, programs that work with class lists, bank statements, magazine subscriptions, names in a telephone book, credit card customers, and so on require alphabetizing. As indicated, Pascal provides the facility for using an array of packed arrays as a data structure for such lists.

Problems that require alphabetizing names contain at least three main tasks: get the data, alphabetize the list, and print the list. Prior to writing procedures for each of these tasks, let's consider some associated problems. When getting the data, you will usually encounter one of two formats. First, data may be entered with a constant field width for each name. Each name would typically be followed by some additional data item. Thus, if each name uses 20 character positions and position 21 contains the start of numeric data, the input file might be

Smith John	18	Jones Harriet	19
↑		↑	
position 21		position 21	

In this case, the name can be read into the appropriate component by a fixed loop. The first name can be accessed by

```
FOR K := 1 TO 20 DO
   read (Name[1,K]);
```

and the second name by

```
FOR K := 1 TO 20 DO
   read (Name[2,K]);
```

A second form for entering data is to use some symbol to indicate the end of a name. When the data are in this form, you must be able to recognize the symbol and fill the remaining positions with blanks. Thus, the data file could be

| Smith John*18 | Jones Harriet*19 |

In this case, the first name can be obtained by

```
K := 0;
read (Ch);
WHILE (Ch <> '*') AND (K < 20) DO
  BEGIN
    K := K + 1;
    Name[1,K] := Ch;
    read (Ch)
  END;
FOR J := K + 1 TO 20 DO
  Name[1,J] := ' ';
```

This process will fill the remaining positions in the name with blanks. Thus, Name[1] would be

| S | m | i | t | h | | J | o | h | n | | | | | | | | | | |

Name [1]

The second name in the data file would be similarly read. The only change is from Name[1,K] to Name[2,K].

The next problem in getting data is determining how many lines are available. If the number of lines is known, you can use a **FOR** loop. More realistically, however, there will be an unknown number of lines and you will need the **eof** condition in a variable control loop and a counter to determine the number of names. To illustrate, assume there are an unknown number of data lines where each line contains a name in the first 20 positions. If the declaration section of a program is

```
TYPE
  String20 = PACKED ARRAY [1..20] OF char;
  NameList = ARRAY [1..50] OF String20;
VAR
  Name: NameList;
  Length : integer;
```

a procedure to get the data is

```
PROCEDURE GetData (VAR Name : NameList;
                   VAR Length : integer);
  VAR
    K : integer;
  BEGIN
    Length := 0;
    WHILE NOT eof AND (Length < 50) DO
      BEGIN
        Length := Length + 1           {  Increment counter     }
        FOR K := 1 TO 20 DO
          read (Name[Length, K]);      {  Get a name            }
        readln                         {  Advance the pointer   }
      END;
    IF NOT eof THEN
      writeln ('There are more data.')
  END;  {  of PROCEDURE GetData  }
```

This procedure is called from the main program by

```
GetData (Name, Length);
```

Let's now consider the problem of alphabetizing a list of names. If we assume the same data structure we've just seen and let Length represent the number of names, a procedure to sort the list alphabetically (using the selection sort discussed in Section 10.3) is

```
PROCEDURE SelectionSort (VAR Name : NameList;
                             Length : integer);
  VAR
    J, K, Index : integer;
    Temp : String20;
  BEGIN
    FOR J := 1 TO Length - 1 DO
      BEGIN
        Index := J;
        FOR K := J + 1 TO Length DO
          IF Name[K] < Name[Index] THEN
            Index := K;
        IF Index <> J THEN
          BEGIN
            Temp := Name[Index];
            Name[Index] := Name[J];
            Name[J] := Temp
          END  {  of exchange  }
      END  {  of sort  }
  END;  {  of PROCEDURE SelectionSort  }
```

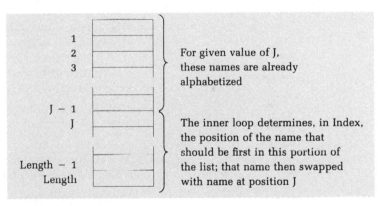

This procedure could be called from the main program by

```
SelectionSort (Name, Length);
```

Once the list of names has been sorted, you usually want to print the sorted list. A procedure to do this is

```
PROCEDURE PrintData (VAR Name : NameList;
                         Length : integer);
  VAR
    J : integer;
  BEGIN
    FOR J := 1 TO Length DO
      writeln (Name[J]:50)
  END;  {  of PROCEDURE PrintData  }
```

This could be called from the main program by

```
PrintData (Name, Length);
```

We can now use the procedures in a simple program that gets the names, sorts them, and prints them as follows:

```
BEGIN  {  Main program  }
  GetData (Name, Length);
  SelectionSort (Name, Length);
  PrintData (Name, Length)
END.  {  of main program  }
```

Exercises 11.2

1. Assume the declarations and definitions

```
TYPE
  String20 = PACKED ARRAY [1..20] OF char;
  StateList = ARRAY [1..50] OF String20;
VAR
  State : StateList;
```

have been made and an alphabetical listing of the 50 states of the United States of America is contained in the data structure State. Furthermore, assume that each state name begins in position one of each component. Indicate the output for each of the following:

a.
```
FOR J := 1 TO 50 DO
  IF State[J,1] = 'O' THEN
    writeln (State[J]:35);
```

b.
```
FOR J := 50 DOWNTO 1 DO
  IF J MOD 5 = 0 THEN
    writeln (State[J]:35);
```

c.
```
FOR J := 1 TO 50 DO
  writeln (State[J,1]:10, State[J,2]);
```

d.
```
CountA := 0;
FOR J := 1 TO 50 DO
  FOR K := 1 TO 20 DO
    IF State[J,K] = 'A' THEN
      CountA := CountA + 1;
writeln (CountA:20);
```

2. Assume you have a sorted list of names. Write a fragment of code to inspect the list of names and print the full name of each Smith on the list.

3. The procedure in this section to get names from a data file assumed the names in the data file were of fixed length and that there were an unknown number of data lines. Modify the procedure for each of the following situations.

   a. Variable length names followed by an '*' and a known number of data lines
   b. Variable length names followed by an '*' and an unknown number of data lines
   c. Fixed length names (20 characters) and a known number of data lines
   d. Names are entered in the form first name, space, last name and you want to sort by last name.

4. If each line of a data file contains a name followed by an age, for example,

position 21

the data will be put into two arrays, one for the names and one for the ages. Show how the sorting procedure can be modified so that the array of ages will keep the same order as the array of names.

5. Write a complete program to read ten names from an input file (where each line contains one name of 20 characters), sort the names in reverse alphabetical order, and print the sorted list.

■ 11.3
Parallel Arrays

- to understand when parallel arrays should be used to solve a problem
- to be able to use parallel arrays to solve a problem

There are many practical situations in which more than one type of array is required to handle the data. For example, you may wish to keep a record of names of people and their donations to a charitable organization. You could accomplish this by using a packed array of names and an equal length array of donations—of **real** or **integer**. Programs for these situations can use *parallel arrays,* a term used for arrays of the same length, where elements in each array must be in the same relative positions. These arrays have the same index type. However, most uses of parallel arrays have the added condition of different data types for the array components. Otherwise, a two-dimensional array would suffice. Generally, situations that call for two or more arrays of the same length but of different data types are situations in which parallel arrays can be used. Later we will see that this situation can also be handled as a single array of records.

Using Parallel Arrays

Let's look at a typical problem that requires working with both a list of names and a list of numbers. Suppose the input file consists of 30 lines and each line contains a name in the first 20 spaces and an integer starting in space 21 that is the amount of a donation. We are to read all data into appropriate arrays, alphabetize the names, print the alphabetized list with the amount of each donation, and find the total of all donations.

This problem can be solved using parallel arrays for the list of names and the list of donations. Appropriate declarations are

```
CONST
  NumberOfDonors = 30;
TYPE
  String20 = PACKED ARRAY [1..20] OF char;
  IndexType = 1..NumberOfDonors;
  NameList = ARRAY [IndexType] OF String20;
  AmountList = ARRAY [IndexType] OF integer;
VAR
  Donor : NameList;
  Amount : AmountList;
```

A procedure to read the data from an input file is

```
PROCEDURE GetData (VAR Donor : NameList;
                   VAR Amount : AmountList);
  VAR
    J, K : integer;
  BEGIN
    FOR J := 1 TO NumberOfDonors DO
      BEGIN
        FOR K := 1 TO 20 DO
          read (Donor[J,K]);
        readln (Amount[J])
      END
  END; { of PROCEDURE GetData }
```

STYLE TIP

■ ■ ■ ■ ■ ■ ■ ■ ■ ■

Since parallel arrays use the same index type, definitions could have the form

```
CONST
  NumberOfDonors = 30;
TYPE
  String20 = PACKED ARRAY [1..20] OF char;
  IndexType = 1..NumberOfDonors;
  NameList    ARRAY [IndexType] OF String20;
  AmountList = ARRAY [IndexType] OF integer;
```

This procedure could be called by

```
GetData (Donor, Amount);
```

After this procedure has been called from the main program, the parallel arrays could be envisioned as

	Donor		Amount	
Donor[1]	Smith John		100	Amount[1]
Donor[2]	Jones Jerry		250	Amount[2]
.	.		.	.
.	.		.	.
.	.		.	.
Donor[30]	Generous George		525	Amount[30]

The next task is to alphabetize the names. However, we must be careful to keep the amount donated with the name of the donor. This can be accomplished by passing both the list of names and the list of donations to the sorting procedure and modifying the code to include exchanging the amount of donation whenever the names are exchanged. Since NumberOfDonors is defined in the constant section, a Length argument is not needed. Using the procedure heading

```
PROCEDURE Sort (VAR Donor : NameList;
                VAR Amount : AmountList);
```

the code for sorting would be changed in order to interchange both a name and an amount. Thus,

```
Temp := Donor[Index];
Donor[Index] := Donor[J];
Donor[J] := Temp;
```

would become

```
Temp := Donor[Index];
TempAmount := Amount[Index];
Donor[Index] := Donor[J];
Amount[Index] := Amount[J];
Donor[J] := Temp;
Amount[J] := TempAmount;
```

The procedure for sorting the list of names and rearranging the list of donations accordingly is called by

```
Sort (Donor, Amount);
```

Our next task is to print the alphabetized list together with the donations. If Donor and Amount have been sorted appropriately, we can use the following procedure to produce the desired output.

```
PROCEDURE PrintData (VAR Donor : NameList;
                     VAR Amount : AmountList);
  VAR
    J : integer;
  BEGIN
    FOR J := 1 TO NumberOfDonors DO
      BEGIN
        write (Donor[J]:40);
        writeln ('$':3, Amount[J]:5)
      END
  END; {  of PROCEDURE PrintData  }
```

Computer Ethics: Worms

In *The Shockwave Rider* (1975), J. Brunner developed the notion of an omnipotent "tapeworm" program running loose through a network of computers—an idea that then seemed rather disturbing, but which was then well beyond our capabilities. The basic model, however, was a very provocative one: a program or a computation that can move from machine to machine, harnessing resources as needed, and replicating itself when necessary.

On November 2, 1988, Cornell computer science graduate student Robert Morris released a worm program into the ARPANET. Over an eight-hour period it invaded between 2,500 and 3,000 VAX and Sun computers running the Berkeley UNIX operating system. The worm program disabled virtually all of the computers by replicating rampantly and clogging them with many copies. Many of the computers had to be disconnected from the network until all copies of the worm could be expurgated and until the security loopholes that the worm used to gain entry could be plugged. Most computers were fully operational within two or three days. No files were damaged on any of the computers invaded by the worm.

This incident gained much public attention and produced a widespread outcry in the computing community, perhaps because so many people saw that they had been within a hair's breadth of losing valuable files. After an investigation, Cornell suspended Morris and decried his action as irresponsible. In July 1989, a grand jury brought an indictment against Morris for violation of the Federal Computer Privacy Act of 1986. He was tried and convicted in January 1990.

This would be called by

```
PrintData (Donor, Amount);
```

The last task this program requires is to find the total of all donations. The following function could perform this task.

```
FUNCTION Total (Amount : AmountList) : integer;
  VAR
    Sum, J : integer;
  BEGIN
    Sum := 0;
    FOR J := 1 TO NumberOfDonors DO
      Sum := Sum + Amount[J];
    Total := Sum
  END;  {  of FUNCTION Total  }
```

This function could be called by

```
TotalDonations := Total(Amount);
```

where TotalDonations has been declared as an **integer** variable. A complete program for this problem could be written as follows:

```
PROGRAM Donations (input, output);

{   This program reads data from an input file where each line   }
{   consists of a donor name followed by the  amount  donated.   }
{   Output consists of an alphabetically sorted list  together   }
{   with the amount of each donation.  This is accomplished by    }
{   using parallel arrays.  The  total amount  donated is also    }
{   listed.                                                       }

CONST
  NumberOfDonors = 30;
```

```
TYPE
  String20 = PACKED ARRAY [1..20] OF char;
  IndexType = 1..NumberOfDonors;
  NameList = ARRAY [IndexType] OF String20;
  AmountList = ARRAY [IndexType] OF integer;

VAR
  Amount : AmountList;          {   An array for amounts donated }
  Donor : NameList;            {   An array for donor names     }
  TotalDonations : integer;     {   Total amount donated         }

{************************************************************** }

PROCEDURE GetData (VAR Donor : NameList;
                   VAR Amount : AmountList);

  { Given:    Nothing                                          }
  { Task:     Read names and donations into respective arrays  }
  { Return:   Parallel arrays of names and donations           }

  VAR
    J, K : integer;

  BEGIN
    FOR J := 1 TO NumberOFDonors DO
      BEGIN
        FOR K := 1 TO 20 DO
          read (Donor[J,K]);
        readln (Amount[J])
      END
  END;  {  of PROCEDURE GetData  }

{************************************************************** }

PROCEDURE SelectionSort (VAR Donor : NameList;
                         VAR Amount : AmountList);

  { Given:    Unsorted parallel arrays of names and donations  }
  { Task:     Sort alphabetically                              }
  { Return:   An alphabetically sorted list of names with      }
  {                     respective donations                   }

  VAR
    TempDonor : String20;
    TempAmount : integer;
    J, K, Index : integer;

  BEGIN
    FOR J := 1 TO NumberOfDonors - 1 DO
      BEGIN
        Index := J;
        FOR K := J + 1 TO NumberOfDonors DO
          IF Donor[K] < Donor[Index] THEN
            Index := K;
        IF Index <> J THEN      {  Exchange if necessary  }
          BEGIN
            TempDonor := Donor[Index];
            TempAmount := Amount[Index];
            Donor[Index] := Donor[J];
            Amount[Index] := Amount[J];
            Donor[J] := TempDonor;
            Amount[J] := TempAmount
          END {  of exchange  }
      END {  of one pass  }
  END;  {  of PROCEDURE SelectionSort  }
```

```
{********************************************************************* }

FUNCTION Total (Amount : AmountList) : integer;

  { Given:    An array of amounts                                      }
  { Task:     Sum the components of the array                          }
  { Return:   The total of array components                            }

  VAR
    Sum, J : integer;

  BEGIN
    SUM := 0;
    FOR J := 1 TO NumberOfDonors DO
      Sum := Sum + Amount[J];
    Total := Sum
  END;  {  of FUNCTION Total  }

{********************************************************************* }

PROCEDURE PrintHeading;

  { Given:    Nothing                                       }
  { Task:     Print a heading for the output                }
  { Return:   Nothing                                       }

  BEGIN
    writeln;
    writeln ('Donor Name':33, 'Donation':17);
    writeln ('----------':33, '--------':17);
    writeln
  END;  {  of PROCEDURE PrintHeading  }

{********************************************************************* }

PROCEDURE PrintData (VAR Donor : NameList;
                     VAR Amount : AmountList;
                     TotalDonations : integer);

  { Given:    Parallel arrays of names and donations and total  }
  {                donations                                     }
  { Task:     Print a list of names and amounts donated; end    }
  {                with the total of all donations              }
  { Return:   Nothing                                           }

  VAR
    J : integer;

  BEGIN
    FOR J := 1 TO NumberOfDonors DO
      BEGIN
        write (Donor[J]:40);
        writeln ('$':3, Amount[J]:5)
      END;  {  of FOR J loop  }
    writeln ('------':49);
    writeln ('Total':40, '$':3, TotalDonations:5);
    writeln
  END;  {  of PROCEDURE PrintData  }

{********************************************************************* }

BEGIN  {  Main program  }
  GetData (Donor, Amount);
  SelectionSort (Donor, Amount);
```

```
        TotalDonations := Total(Amount);
        PrintHeading;
        PrintData (Donor, Amount, TotalDonations)
 END.  {  of main program  }
```

Output created from an input file of 30 lines is

```
        Donor Name              Donation
        ----------              --------

    Alexander Candy          $   300
    Anderson Tony            $   375
    Banks Marj               $   375
    Born Patty               $   100
    Brown Ron                $   200
    Darnell Linda            $   275
    Erickson Thomas          $   100
    Fox William              $   300
    Francis Denise           $   350
    Generous George          $   525
    Gillette Mike            $   350
    Hancock Kirk             $   500
    Higgins Sam              $   300
    Janson Kevin             $   200
    Johnson Ed               $   350
    Johnson Martha           $   400
    Jones Jerry              $   250
    Kelly Marvin             $   475
    Kneff Susan              $   300
    Lasher John              $   175
    Lyon Elizabeth           $   425
    Moore Robert             $   100
    Muller Marjorie          $   250
    Smith John               $   100
    Trost Frostie            $    50
    Trudo Rosemary           $   200
    Weber Sharon             $   150
    Williams Art             $   350
    Williams Jane            $   175
    Wilson Mary              $   275
                             ------
                 Total $ 8275
```

Exercises 11.3

1. Which of the following are appropriate declarations for parallel arrays? Explain.

   a.
   ```
   TYPE
       String15 = PACKED ARRAY [1..15] OF char;
       List15 = ARRAY [1..15] OF real;
   VAR
       Names : ARRAY [1..10] OF String15;
       Amounts : List15;
   ```

   b.
   ```
   TYPE
       Chart = ARRAY [1..12, 1..10] OF integer;
       String10 = PACKED ARRAY [1..10] OF char;
       List = ARRAY [1..12] OF String10;
   VAR
       Table : Chart;
       Names : List;
   ```

2. Write a test program to read names and amounts from a data file. Your program should print out both lists and the total of the amounts. Assume each line of data is similar to

↑
position 21

3. Parallel arrays could be used when working with a list of student names and the grades the students receive in a class.

    a. Define array types and declare subsequent arrays that could be used in such a program.

    b. Write a function that counts the number of occurrences for each letter grade A, B, C, D, and E.

4. Declare appropriate arrays and write a procedure to read data from an input file where there are an unknown number of lines (but less than 100) and each line contains a name (20 spaces), an age (integer), a marital status (character), and an income (real). A typical data line is

> Smith John   35M 28502.16 ▐

5. Modify the code of Exercise 4 to accommodate data entered in the data file in the following format:

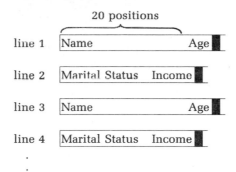

6. Write a procedure to sort the arrays of Exercise 4 according to income.

■ ■ ■ ■

■ 11.4
Higher-Dimensional Arrays

OBJECTIVES
- To understand when arrays of dimensions greater than two are needed in a program
- to be able to define and declare data structures for higher-dimensional arrays
- to be able to use higher-dimensional arrays in a program

Thus far we have worked with arrays of one and two dimensions. Arrays of three, four, or higher dimensions can also be declared and used. Pascal places no limitation on the number of dimensions of an array.

Declarations of Higher-Dimensional Arrays

Declarations of *higher-dimensional arrays* usually assume one of two basic forms. First, a three-dimensional array type can be defined using the form

> **ARRAY** [1 . . 3, 1 . . 4, 1 . . 5] **OF** ⟨data type⟩;

Each dimension can vary in any of the ways used for arrays of one or two dimensions and the data type can be any standard or user-defined ordinal data type. Second, a three-dimensional array can be defined as an array of two-dimensional arrays using the form

> **ARRAY** [1 . . 3] **OF ARRAY** [1 . . 4, 1 . . 5] **OF integer**;

Each of these declarations will reserve 60 locations in memory. This can be visualized as shown in Figure 11.1.

FIGURE 11.1
Three-dimensional array with
components A[I,J,K]

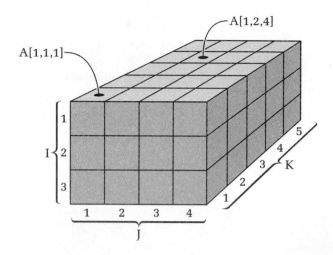

An array of dimension n can be defined by

ARRAY $[1 .. a_1, 1 .. a_2, \ldots, 1 .. a_n]$ **OF** ⟨data type⟩;

which would reserve $a_1 * a_2 * \ldots * a_n$ locations in memory. A general definition is

ARRAY $[a_1 .. b_1, a_2 .. b_2, \ldots, a_n .. b_n]$ **OF** ⟨data type⟩;

where $a_i \leq b_i$, for $1 \leq i \leq n$.

Declarations and uses of higher-dimensional arrays are usually facilitated by descriptive names and user-defined data types. For example, suppose we want to declare a three-dimensional array to hold the contents of a book of tables. If there are 50 pages and each page contains a table of 15 rows and 10 columns, a reasonable declaration is

```
TYPE
  Page = 1..50;
  Row = 1..15;
  Column = 1..10;
  Book = ARRAY [Page, Row, Column] OF integer;
VAR
  Item : Book;
```

When this declaration is compared to

```
TYPE
  Book = ARRAY [1..50, 1..15, 1..10] OF integer;
VAR
  Item : Book;
```

we realize that both arrays are identical in structure, but, in the first declaration, it is easier to see what the dimensions represent.

Accessing Components

Elements in higher-dimensional arrays are accessed and used in a manner similar to two-dimensional arrays. The difference is that in a three-dimensional array, each element needs three indices for reference. A similar result holds for other dimensions. To illustrate using this notation, recall the declaration

```
TYPE
  Page = 1..50;
  Row = 1..15;
  Column = 1..10;
  Book = ARRAY [Page, Row, Column] OF integer;
VAR
  Item : Book;
```

If you want to assign a ten to the item on page three, row five, column seven, the statement

```
Item[3,5,7] := 10;
```

accomplishes this. Similarly, this item can be printed by

```
write (Item[3,5,7]);
```

Using this same declaration, we can

1. Print the fourth row of page 21 with the following segment of code.

```
FOR K := 1 TO 10 DO
  write (Item[21,4,K]:5);
writeln;
```

2. Print the top row of every page with

```
FOR I :- 1 TO 50 DO
  BEGIN
    FOR K := 1 TO 10 DO
      write (Item[I,1,K]:5);
    writeln
  END;
```

3. Print page 35 with

```
FOR J := 1 TO 15 DO
  BEGIN
    FOR K := 1 TO 10 DO
      write (Item[35,J,K]:5);
    writeln
  END;
```

4. Print every page that does not have a zero in the first row and the first column with

```
FOR I := 1 TO 50 DO
  IF Item[I,1,1] <> 0 THEN
    FOR J :- 1 TO 15 DO
      BEGIN
        FOR K := 1 TO 10 DO
          write (Item[I,J,K]:5);
        writeln
      END;
```

As another illustration of the use of higher-dimensional arrays, consider the situation where the manager of a high-rise office complex wants a program to assist in keeping track of the tenants in each office. Suppose there are 20 floors, each with the floor plan shown in Figure 11.2. Each wing contains five rooms.

Let's first declare an appropriate array where the tenant's name can be stored (assume each name consists of 20 characters). This can be accomplished by

Figure 11.2
High-rise floor plan

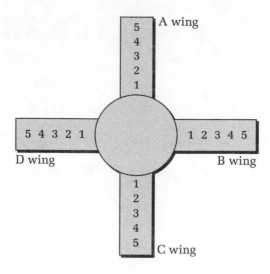

```
TYPE
  Floors = 1..20;
  Wings = 'A'..'D';
  Offices = 1..5;
  Name = PACKED ARRAY [1..20] OF char;
  Occupant = ARRAY [Floors, Wings, Offices] OF Name;
VAR
  Tenant : Occupant;
  Floor : Floors;
  Wing : Wings;
  Office : Offices;
```

Note that this is really a four-dimensional array, since the data type Name is **PACKED ARRAY.**

Now let's write a segment of code to print a list of names of all tenants on the top floor. To get the names of all tenants of the twentieth floor, we need to print the names for each office in each wing. Assuming a field width of 30 columns, the following code completes the desired task.

```
FOR Wing := 'A' TO 'D' DO
  FOR Office := 1 TO 5 DO
    writeln (Tenant[20, Wing, Office]:30);
```

How would we write a segment of code to read the name of the new tenant on the third floor, B wing, room 5 from the data file? Recall that character strings must be read one character at a time. Tenant [3,'B',5] is the variable name. Since this is a packed array, the code for reading is

```
FOR L := 1 TO 20 DO
  read (Tenant[3,'B',5,L]);
```

Assume the string 'Unoccupied   ' has been entered for each vacant office and we are to write a segment of code to list all vacant offices. This problem requires us to examine every name and print the location of the unoccupied offices.

Hence, when we encounter the name 'Unoccupied   ', we want to print the respective indices. This is accomplished by

```
FOR Floor := 1 TO 20 DO
  FOR Wing := 'A' TO 'D' DO
    FOR Office := 1 TO 5 DO
      IF Tenant[Floor, Wing, Office] = 'Unoccupied
        THEN writeln (Floor:5, Wing:5, Office:5);
```

As you can see, working with higher-dimensional arrays requires very careful handling of the indices. Nested loops are frequently used for processing array elements and proper formatting of output is critical.

Exercises 11.4

1. How many memory locations are reserved in each of the following declarations?

   a. TYPE
   ```
   Block = ARRAY [1..2, 1..3, 1..10] OF char;
   VAR
     A : Block;
   ```

   b. TYPE
   ```
   Block = ARRAY [-2..3] OF ARRAY [2..4, 3..6] OF real;
   VAR
     A : Block;
   ```

   c. TYPE
   ```
   Color = (Red, Black, White);
   Size = (Small, Large);
   Year = 1950..1960;
   Specifications - ARRAY [Color, Size, Year];
   VAR
     A : Specifications;
   ```

   d. TYPE
   ```
   String15 = PACKED ARRAY [1..15] OF char;
   List10 = ARRAY [1..10] OF String15;
   NameTable = ARRAY [1..4] OF List10;
   VAR
     A : NameTable;
   ```

2. Write a test program to read values into an array of size 3 × 4 × 5. Assuming this represents three pages, each of which contains a 4 × 5 table, print out the table for each page together with a page number.

3. Declare a three-dimensional array that a hospital could use to keep track of the types of rooms available: private (P), semiprivate (S), and ward (W). The hospital has four floors, five wings, and 20 rooms in each wing.

4. Consider the declaration
   ```
   TYPE
     Pages = 1..50;
     Rows = 1..15;
     Columns = 1..10;
     Book = ARRAY [Pages, Rows, Columns] OF integer;
   VAR
     Page : Pages;
     Row : Rows;
     Column : Columns;
     Item : Book;
   ```

   a. Write a segment of code to do each of the following:

      i. Print the fourth column of page 3.

      ii. Print the top seven rows of page 46.

      iii. Create a new page 30 by adding the corresponding elements of page 31 to page 30.

b. What is a general description of the output produced by the following segments of code?

```
i. FOR Page := 1 TO 15 DO
     BEGIN
       FOR Column := 1 TO 10 DO
         write (Item[Page, Page, Column]:4);
       writeln
     END;
```

```
ii. For Page := 1 TO 50 DO
      FOR Column := 1 TO 10 DO
        writeln (Item[Page, Column, Column]:(Column+4));
```

Use the following problem statement, definitions, and declarations for Exercises 5–8.

An athletic conference consisting of ten universities wishes to have a program to keep track of the number of athletic grants-in-aid for each team at each institution. The conference programmer has defined the following structure:

```
CONST
  MaxGrants = 90;

TYPE
  Schools = 'A'..'J';
  Sports = (Baseball, Basketball, CrossCountry,
            FieldHockey, Football, Golf, Gymnastics,
            Swimming, Tennis, Track, Volleyball, Wrestling);
  Sex = (Male, Female);
  NumberOfGrants = 0..MaxGrants;
  GrantChart = ARRAY [Schools, Sports, Sex] OF NumberOfGrants;
VAR
  NumGrants : integer;
  Grants : GrantChart;
  School : Schools;
  Sport : Sports;
  Gender : Sex;
```

5. How many memory locations are reserved in the array Grants?

6. Explain what tasks are performed by each of the following segments of code.

```
a. NumGrants := 0;
   FOR School := 'A' TO 'J' DO
     FOR Sport := Baseball TO Wrestling DO
       NumGrants := NumGrants + Grants[School, Sport, Female];
```

```
b.  Sum := 0;
    FOR School := 'A' TO 'J' DO
      FOR Sport := Baseball TO Wrestling DO
        FOR Gender := Male TO Female DO
          IF Grants[School, Sport, Gender] = 0 THEN
            Sum := Sum + 1;
```

7. Write a segment of code for each of the following tasks.

   a. Find the total number of grants for each university.

   b. Find the total number of grants for each sport.

   c. List all schools that have ten or more grants in field hockey.

8. Explain how a **CASE** statement can be used to help display all sports (indicate male or female) and the number of grants in each sport for school 'D'.

■ ■ ■ ■

This program simulates the solution to a problem that could be posed by a small airline. Mountain-Air Commuters, Inc., is a small airline commuter service. Each of their planes is a 30-passenger plane with a floor plan as follows:

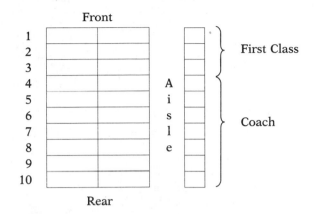

The first three rows are designated as first class because the seats are wider and there is more leg room. (In reality, most commuter planes do not have a first class section. However, rather than include the large data base needed for larger planes, we simulate the problem using a seating plan with only ten rows.)

Write a program that assigns seats to passengers on a first-come, first-served basis according to the following rules:

1. First class and coach requests must be honored; if seats in the requested sections are all full, the customer's name should go on a waiting list for the next flight.
2. Specific seat requests should be honored next; if a requested seat is occupied, the person should be placed in the same row, if possible.
3. If a requested row is filled, the passenger should be seated as far forward as possible.
4. If all seats are filled, the passenger's name is put on a waiting list for the next flight.

Output should include a seating chart with passenger names appropriately printed and a waiting list for the next flight. Each data line (input) contains the passenger's name, first class (F) or coach (C) designation, and seat request indicating the row and column desired.

A typical line of data would be

    | Smith John   C 5 2 ▮

where C represents a coach choice, 5 is a request for row five, and 2 represents the preferred seat.

A first-level pseudocode development for this problem is

1. Initialize variables
2. **WHILE NOT eof DO** process a name
3. Print a seating chart
4. **IF** there is a waiting list **THEN** print the list

A complete structure chart for this problem is given in Figure 11.3.

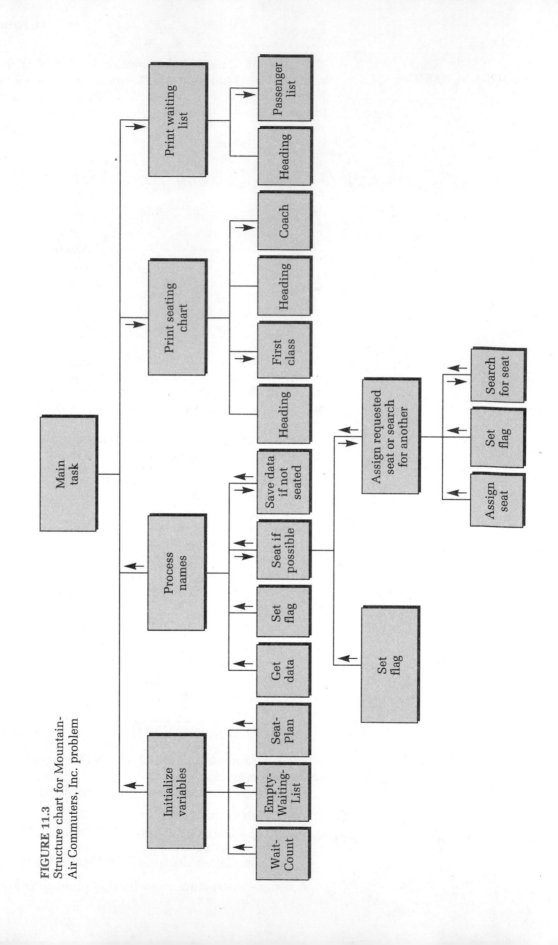

FIGURE 11.3
Structure chart for Mountain-Air Commuters, Inc. problem

Module specifications for the main modules are

1. Initialize Module
   Data received: None
   Information returned: Value for WaitCount
                                  Value for EmptyWaitingList
                                  Value for SeatPlan
   Logic: Assign beginning values to the parameters.
          Use nested loops to initialize the array SeatPlan.

2. ProcessAName Module
   Data received: None
   Information returned: A seating chart
                                  A **boolean** value for extra passengers
                                  A waiting list for the next flight
   Logic: Get a name, section preference, and seat choice.
          Search to see if a seat can be found.
          If yes, then ticket.
          If no, then save relevant information.

3. PrintSeatingChart Module
   Data received: A two-dimensional array of names of ticketed passengers.
   Information returned: None
   Logic: Print the seating plan indicating row, seat, and section choice for each passenger.

4. PrintWaitingList Module
   Data received: Parallel arrays for the passenger's name, section choice, and seat preference
   Information returned: None
   Logic: Use a loop to print an appropriately titled list of passengers for the next flight.

A further development of the pseudocode is

1. Initialize variables
   1.1 initialize WaitCount
   1.2 initialize EmptyWaitingList
   1.3 initialize SeatPlan
2. **WHILE NOT eof DO** process a name
   2.1 get passenger information
   2.2 set **boolean** flag Seated for **false**
   2.3 seat if possible
   2.4 **IF NOT** seated **THEN** save relevant information
3. Print a seating chart
   3.1 print a heading
   3.2 print the first class section
   3.3 print a heading
   3.4 print the coach section
4. **IF** there is a waiting list **THEN** print the list
   4.1 print a heading
   4.2 print passenger list with four columns

Step 2.3 needs some additional refinement. Further development yields

2.3   seat if possible
   2.3.1   set Seated to **false**
   2.3.2   **IF** requested seat is available **THEN**
      2.3.2.1   assign seat
      2.3.2.2   set Seated to **true**
     ELSE
      2.3.2.3   search for another seat

A complete program for this is

```
PROGRAM SeatingPlan (input, output);

{  This   program   prints   a   seating   plan   for   an   airline.  }
{  Passengers   are   assigned   seats   on   a   first-come,   first-  }
{  served basis.   Requests   for first class or   coach must be        }
{  honored.   If   all   seats   are   filled   in   a   section,   the }
{  passenger's name and seat preference are placed on a waiting         }
{  list for the next flight.   Features of this program include         }
{                                                                       }
{       a.   defined constants                                          }
{       b.   user-defined data types                                    }
{       c.   multidimensional arrays                                    }
{       d.   subprograms for modular development                        }

CONST
  NumRows = 10;
  NumColumns = 3;
  MaxLength = 50;
  FirstClassBegin = 1;
  FirstClassEnd = 3;
  CoachBegin = 4;
  CoachEnd = 10;
  EmptyString = '                    ';
  Skip = ' ';

TYPE
  String20 = PACKED ARRAY [1..20] OF char;
  SeatingPlan = ARRAY [1..NumRows, 1..NumColumns] OF String20;
  NotSeatedList = ARRAY [1..MaxLength] OF String20;
  SectionOptionList = ARRAY [1..MaxLength] OF char;
  SeatChoiceList = ARRAY [1..MaxLength, 1..2] OF integer;

VAR
  Seated : boolean;                        { Indicator for seat found }
  WaitingList : NotSeatedList;             { Name list for next flight}
  WaitCount : integer;                     { Counter for waiting list }
  EmptyWaitingList : boolean;              { Indicator for empty list }
  Seat : SeatingPlan;                      { 2-dim array of seats     }
  Name : String20;                         { String for names         }
  SectionChoice : char;                    { First class or coach     }
  RowChoice, ColumnChoice : integer;       { Seat preference          }
  SectionOption : SectionOptionList;       { Array of section options }
  SeatChoice : SeatChoiceList;             { Array of seat choices    }

{***************************************************************** }

PROCEDURE Initialize (VAR Seat : SeatingPlan);

  { Given:   A two-dimensional array of strings        }
  { Task:    Initialize all cells to an empty string   }
  { Return:  An initialized two-dimensional array       }
```

```
    VAR
      J, K : integer;

    BEGIN
      FOR J := 1 TO NumRows DO
        FOR K := 1 TO NumColumns DO
          Seat[J,K] := EmptyString
    END;  {  of PROCEDURE Initialize  }
```

{ *** }

```
PROCEDURE GetAName (VAR Name : String20;
                    VAR SectionChoice : char;
                    VAR RowChoice,
                    ColumnChoice : integer);

  {  Given:    Nothing                                           }
  {  Task:     Read a name, section option, and seat preference  }
  {            from the input file                               }
  {  Return:   Passenger name, section and seat preference       }

VAR
  J : integer;

BEGIN
  FOR J := 1 TO 20 DO
    read (Name[J]);
  readln (SectionChoice, RowChoice, ColumnChoice)
END;  {  of PROCEDURE GetAName  }
```

{ *** }

```
PROCEDURE SeatIfPossible (Name : String20;
                          VAR Seat : SeatingPlan;
                          RowChoice,
                          ColumnChoice : integer;
                          SectionChoice : char;
                          VAR Seated : boolean);

  {  Given:    Passenger name, section and seat preference       }
  {  Task:     If requested seat is available, assign seat       }
  {            If not available, use Search to check for an      }
  {              alternate seat                                  }
  {  Return:   Seat assignment if one has been made             }
  {            Boolean flag to indicate if seat was found       }

  PROCEDURE Search (Name : String20;
                    VAR Seat : SeatingPlan;
                    VAR Seated : boolean;
                    FirstRow,
                    LastRow : integer);

    {  Given:    Passenger name, current seating chart, row      }
    {              designators for first class and coach         }
    {              sections                                      }
    {  Task:     Search indicated rows to see if an alternate    }
    {              seat is available; if yes, assign            }
    {              passenger to it                              }
    {  Return:   Updated seating plan and Boolean flag indica-   }
    {              ting whether or not a seat was found          }
```

```
          VAR
            Row, Column : integer;

          BEGIN  {  PROCEDURE Search  }
            Seated := false;
            Row := FirstRow;
            REPEAT
              Column := 1;                        {  Start searching rows }
                REPEAT                            {  Search one row        }
                  IF Seat[Row, Column] = EmptyString THEN
                    BEGIN
                      Seat[Row, Column] := Name;
                      Seated := true
                    END
                  ELSE
                    Column := Column + 1
                UNTIL Seated OR (Column > NumColumns);
                Row := Row + 1                    {  Search next row       }
            UNTIL Seated OR (Row > LastRow)
          END;  {  of PROCEDURE Search  }

        BEGIN  {  PROCEDURE SeatIfPossible  }
          Seated := false;
          IF Seat[RowChoice, ColumnChoice] = EmptyString THEN
            BEGIN
              Seat[RowChoice, ColumnChoice] := Name;
              Seated := true
            END
          ELSE
            CASE SectionChoice OF
              'F'  :  Search (Name, Seat, Seated,
                             FirstClassBegin, FirstClassEnd);
              'C'  :  Search (Name, Seat, Seated,
                             CoachBegin, CoachEnd)
            END {  of CASE SectionChoice  }
        END;  {  of PROCEDURE SeatIfPossible  }

{******************************************************************** }

PROCEDURE PrintSeatingChart (VARSeat : SeatingPlan);

  {  Given:    The seating chart, a two-dimensional array of        }
  {                  names                                           }
  {  Task:     Print the passenger names in rows and columns        }
  {                  according to their assigned seats              }
  {  Return:   Nothing                                              }

  VAR
    J, K : integer;

  BEGIN
    writeln;
    writeln (Skip:10, 'MOUNTAIN-AIR COMMUTERS');
    writeln (Skip:15, 'Seating Chart');
    writeln;
    writeln ('First class section');
    writeln ('--------------------');
    writeln;
    FOR J := 1 TO FirstClassEnd DO
      BEGIN
        FOR K := 1 TO NumColumns DO
          write (Seat[J,K]:22);
        writeln
      END; {  of FOR J loop  }
```

3

```
      writeln;
      writeln ('Coach section');
      writeln ('-------------');
      writeln;
      FOR J := CoachBegin TO CoachEnd DO
        BEGIN
          FOR K := 1 TO NumColumns DO
            write (Seat[J,K]:22);
          writeln
        END;  {  of FOR K loop  }
      writeln
    END;  {  of PROCEDURE PrintSeatingChart  }

{***************************************************************** }

PROCEDURE PrintWaitingList  (VAR WaitingList : NotSeatedList;
                             VAR SectionOption : SectionOptionList;
                             VAR SeatChoice : SeatChoiceList;
                             WaitCount : integer);

  {  Given:    An array of names of passengers not seated, the   }
  {            section choice and seat preference for each        }
  {  Task:     Print a waiting list for the next flight           }
  {  Return:   Nothing                                            }

  VAR
    J : integer;

  BEGIN
    writeln;
    writeln (Skip:10, 'Waiting list for next flight');
    writeln;
    writeln ('NAME':10, 'SECTION CHOICE':27,
             'ROW NUMBER':15, 'COLUMN NUMBER':15);
    write ('----------------------------------');
    writeln ('-------------------------------');
    writeln;
    FOR J := 1 TO WaitCount DO
      writeln ('<', J:2, '>', WaitingList[J]:22, SectionOption[J]:4,
               SeatChoice[J,1]:15, SeatChoice[J,2]:15)
  END;  {  of PROCEDURE PrintWaitingList  }

{***************************************************************** }

BEGIN  {  Main program  }
  WaitCount := 0;
  EmptyWaitingList := true;
  Initialize (Seat);
  WHILE NOT eof DO
    BEGIN
      GetAName (Name, SectionChoice, RowChoice, ColumnChoice);
      Seated := false;
      SeatIfPossible (Name, Seat, RowChoice, ColumnChoice,
                      SectionChoice, Seated);
      IF NOT Seated THEN   {  Save information for waiting list  }
        BEGIN
          WaitCount := WaitCount + 1;
          WaitingList[WaitCount] := Name;
          SectionOption[WaitCount] := SectionChoice;
          SeatChoice[WaitCount, 1] := RowChoice;
          SeatChoice[WaitCount, 2] := ColumnChoice;
          EmptyWaitingList := false
        END  {  of IF NOT Seated  }
    END;  {  of WHILE NOT eof  }
```

```
          PrintSeatingChart (Seat);
          IF NOT EmptyWaitingList THEN
             PrintWaitingList (WaitingList, SectionOption, SeatChoice,
                              WaitCount)
      END.  { of main program  }
```

Using the data file

```
          Smith John          F  3  2
          Alexander Joe       C  9  3
          Allen Darcy         F  3  2
          Jones Mary          C  8  1
          Humphrey H          C  8  2
          Johnson M           F  3  1
          Eastman Ken         F  1  1
          Winston Sam         C  8  3
          Smythe Susan        C  9  1
          Hendricks J B       C  9  2
          Hanson Cynthia      C  9  3
          Zoranson Steve      C 10  1
          Radamacher Joe      C 10  3
          Borack Bill         C 10  2
          Seracki Don         C  9  2
          Henry John          F  1  2
          Steveson Enghart    F  1  3
          Johansen Mary       F  2  1
          Smith Martha        F  2  2
          Jones Martha        F  2  3
          Rinehart Jim        F  3  3
          Rinehart Jane       F  3  2
          Swenson Cecil       C  4  1
          Swenson Carol       C  4  2
          Byes Nikoline       C  4  3
          Byes Jennifer       C  5  3
          Harris John         C  5  2
          Harris Judy         C  5  1
          Hartman F G         C  6  1
          Hartman D T         C  6  2
          Lakes William       C  6  3
          Lampton George      C  7  1
          Hayes Woodrow       C  7  2
          Champion M G        C  7  3
          Thomas Lynda        C  8  1
          Sisler Susan        C  8  2
          Stowers Steve       C  8  3
          Banks M J           C  5  3
          Banks H W           C  5  2
          Brown Susan         C  3  1
          Wince Ann           C  8  2
          Wince Joanne        C  8  1
```

sample output is

```
          MOUNTAIN-AIR COMMUTERS
             Seating Chart


First class section
-------------------

   Allen Darcy          Eastman Ken          Henry John
   Steveson Enghart     Johansen Mary        Smith Martha
   Johnson M            Smith John           Jones Martha
```

```
Coach section
-------------

   Hanson Cynthia      Seracki Don        Swenson Cecil
   Swenson Carol       Byes Nikoline      Byes Jennifer
   Harris John         Harris Judy        Hartman F G
   Hartman D T         Lakes William      Lampton George
   Jones Mary          Humphrey H         Winston Sam
   Smythe Susan        Hendricks J B      Alexander Joe
   Zoranson Steve      Borack Bill        Radamacher Joe

        Waiting list for next flight
```

	NAME	SECTION CHOICE	ROW NUMBER	COLUMN NUMBER
< 1>	Rinehart Jim	F	3	3
< 2>	Rinehart Jane	F	3	2
< 3>	Hayes Woodrow	C	7	2
< 4>	Champion M G	C	7	3
< 5>	Thomas Lynda	C	8	1
< 6>	Sisler Susan	C	8	2
< 7>	Stowers Steve	C	8	3
< 8>	Banks M J	C	5	3
< 9>	Banks H W	C	5	2
<10>	Brown Susan	C	3	1
<11>	Wince Ann	C	8	2
<12>	Wince Joanne	C	8	1

RUNNING AND DEBUGGING TIPS

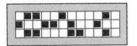

1. Use subrange types with descriptive identifiers for specifying index ranges. For example,

```
TYPE
   Page = 1..50;
   Row = 1..15;
   Column = 1..10;
   Book = ARRAY [Page, Row, Column] OF real;
```

2. Develop and maintain a systematic method of processing nested loops. For example, students with mathematical backgrounds will often use I, J, and K as index variables for three-dimensional arrays.

3. Be careful to properly subscript multidimensional array components.

4. When using an array of packed arrays as a list of strings, remember that in standard Pascal, strings must be read in one character at a time. However, strings can be written by a single **writeln** command.

5. When sorting one array in a program that uses parallel arrays, remember to make similar component exchanges in all arrays.

6. Define all·data structures in the **TYPE** definition section.

■ Summary

Key Terms

higher-dimensional array   parallel array   two-dimensional array

Key Concepts

- Two-dimensional arrays can be declared in several ways; one descriptive method is

```
TYPE
   Chart4X6 = ARRAY [1..4, 1..6] OF real;
VAR
   Table : Chart4X6;
```

- Nested loops are frequently used to **read** and **write** values in two-dimensional arrays; for example, data can be read by

```
FOR Row := 1 TO 4 DO
  FOR Column := 1 TO 6 DO
    read (Table[Row, Column]);
```

- When processing the components of a single row or single column, leave the appropriate row or column index fixed and let the other index vary as a loop index; for example, to sum row 3, use

```
Sum := 0;
FOR Column := 1 TO NumOfColumns DO
  Sum := Sum + A[3, Column];
```

To sum column 3, use

```
Sum := 0;
FOR Row := 1 TO NumOfRows DO
  Sum := Sum + A[Row, 3];
```

- An array of strings in Pascal is a special case of a two-dimensional array; the data structure is an array of packed arrays and can be declared by

```
TYPE
   String20 = PACKED ARRAY [1..20] OF char;
   NameList = ARRAY [1..50] OF String20;
VAR
   Name : NameList;
```

- Arrays of strings (packed arrays of characters) can be alphabetized by using the selection sort.
- Three standard procedures used in programs that work with arrays of strings are (1) get the data, (2) alphabetize the array, and (3) print the alphabetized list.
- Parallel arrays may be used to solve problems that require arrays of the same index type but of different data types.
- A typical problem in which one would use parallel arrays involves working with a list of names and an associated list of numbers (for example, test scores). In the next chapter, we will see that this can also be done with a single array of records.
- A typical data structure declaration for using names and scores is

```
TYPE
   String20 = PACKED ARRAY [1..20] OF char;
   NameList = ARRAY [1..30] OF String20;
   ScoreList = ARRAY [1..30] OF integer;
VAR
   Name : NameList;
   Score : ScoreList;
```

- Data structures for solving problems can require arrays of three or more dimensions.
- A typical declaration for an array of three dimensions is

```
TYPE
   Dim1 = 1..10;
   Dim2 = 1..20;
   Dim3 = 1..30;
   Block = ARRAY [Dim1, Dim2, Dim3] OF real;
```

```
VAR
  Item : Block;
```

In this array, a typical component is accessed by

```
Item[I,J,K]
```

- Nested loops are frequently used when working with higher-dimensional arrays; for example, all values on the first level of array Item as just declared can be printed by

```
FOR J := 1 TO 20 DO
  BEGIN
    FOR K := 1 TO 30 DO
      BEGIN
        write (Item[1,J,K]:5:2);
        writeln
      END;  { of 1 line  }
    writeln
  END;  { of 20 lines  }
```

- When working with subprograms, array variables are usually passed by reference.

Programming Problems and Projects

1. The local high school sports boosters are conducting a fund drive to help raise money for the athletic program. As each donation is received, the person's name and amount of donation are entered on one line in a data file. Write a program to
   a. Print an alphabetized list of all donors together with their corresponding donation.
   b. Print a list of donations from high to low together with the donors' names.
   c. Compute and print the average and total of all donations.

2. Due to not meeting the original goal, your local high school sports boosters (Problem 1) are at it again. For their second effort, each donor's name and donation are added as a separate line at the end of the previously sorted list. Write a program to produce lists, sum, and average as in Problem 1. No donor's name should appear more than once in a list.

3. Dr. Lae Z. Programmer (Problems 5, 22, and 23, Chapter 5; Problem 13, Chapter 6; Problem 7, Chapter 7; Problem 5, Chapter 9) now expects you to write a program to do all record keeping for the class. For each student, consecutive lines of the data file contain the student's name, ten quiz scores, six program scores, and three examination scores. Your output should include
   a. An alphabetized list together with
      i. quiz total
      ii. program total
      iii. examination total
      iv. total points
      v. percentage grade
      vi. letter grade
   b. The overall class average
   c. A histogram depicting the grade distribution

4. The All Metro Basketball Conference consists of ten teams. The conference commissioner has created a data file in which each line contains one school's name, location, and nickname for the school team.

You are to write a program to read this data and then produce three lists, each of which contains all information about the school. All lists are to be sorted alphabetically, the first by school name, the second by school location, and the third by nickname.

5. Upgrade the program for Mountain-Air Commuters, Inc. (Focus on Program Design) so it can be used for each of five daily flights. Passengers on a waiting list must be processed first. Print a seating chart for each flight.

6. Add yet another upgrade to the Mountain-Air Commuters, Inc. program. Write an interactive version to consider the possibility of seating passengers who wish to be seated together in the same row. If no such seating is possible, they should then be given a choice of alternate seating (if possible) or taking a later flight.

7. Salespersons at McHenry Tool Corporation are given a monthly commission check. The commission is computed by multiplying the salesperson's gross monthly sales by the person's commission rate.

    Write a program to compute a salesperson's monthly commission computed to the nearest penny. The program should prepare a list of all salespersons in descending order based on monthly commission earned (the person earning the highest commission on top). Each salesperson's commission should be printed next to his or her name. At the bottom of the list, indicate the total monthly commission (summed across all salespersons) and the average commission per salesperson. McHenry never employs more than 60 salespersons.

    Any names of persons who have invalid data should be printed out separately. Data are invalid if the commission rate is not between 0.01 and 0.50, or if the gross monthly sales figure is negative.

8. In order to reduce their costs, the McHenry Tool Corporation (Problem 7) is switching from monthly to biannual commission checks. The commission is now computed by multiplying a person's commission rate by the sum of his or her gross monthly sales for a six-month period.

    The McHenry Tool Corporation has asked that you develop the necessary computer program. The program should differ from Problem 7 in the following ways:

    a. Each name on the output should be followed by the six figures for gross monthly sales. The columns should be labeled "January" through "June." Total six-month gross sales should be given next, followed by rate of commission, and amount of six-month commission check to the nearest penny.

    b. Commission rates are based on gross six-month sales. If sales are less than $20,000, the commission rate is 3 percent. If sales are at least $20,000 but less than $40,000, the commission rate is 5 percent. If sales are at least $40,000 but less than $60,000, the commission rate is 5.5 percent. If sales are at least $60,000 but less than $80,000, the commission rate is 6 percent. If sales are at least $80,000 but less than $90,000, the commission rate is 6.5 percent. If sales are at least $90,000, the commission rate is 8 percent.

c. At the bottom of each column, the program should provide the total and the mean for that column (the column for commission rates does not require a total, only a mean).

9. The dean of a small undergraduate college (enrollment less than 2,000) has asked you to write a program to figure grade point average for an unknown number of students.

The output should be an alphabetized roster showing the sex, identification number (social security number), grade point average (rounded to three decimal places), and class status (freshman, sophomore, junior, or senior) for each student.

The data provide the name, sex (M or F), social security number (ID), and number of semesters completed. Also provided are the number of courses taken and the letter grade and number of credits for each course. The possible letter grades are A (4 points), B (3 points), C (2 points), D (1 point), and E (0 points). Class status is determined by the number of credits as follows:

1–25 credits	Freshman
26–55 credits	Sophomore
56–85 credits	Junior
86 or more credits	Senior

10. You have just started work for the Michigan Association of Automobile Manufacturers and have been asked to analyze sales data on five subcompact cars for the last six months. Your analysis should be in table form and should include the name of each make and model, a model's sales volume for each month, a model's total and average sales volume for six months, a model's total sales revenue for six months, and the total and average sales volume for each month. In addition, your output should include the total and average sales volume of all models for the entire six months and the make and model name of the car with the largest total sales revenue and the amount of that revenue.

11. You have been asked to write a program to assist with the inventory and ordering for Tite-Jeans, Inc. They manufacture three styles: straight, flair, and peg. In each style, waist sizes vary by integer values from 24 to 46 and inseams vary by integer values from 26 to 40. Write a program to :
   a. Read in the starting inventory.
   b. Read in daily sales.
   c. Print the ending inventory for each style.
   d. Print order charts for each style that is low in stock (fewer than three).
   e. Print an emergency order list for those that are out of stock.

12. You have been asked to write a program that will grade results of a True-False quiz and display the results in tabular form. The quiz consists of ten questions. The data file for this problem consists of
   a. correct responses (answer key) on line one; and
   b. a four-digit student identification number followed by that student's ten responses on each successive line.

Thus, the data file would be

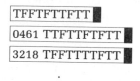

. . .

Your program should read the key and store it in an array. It should then read the remaining lines, storing the student identification numbers in one array and the number of correct responses in a parallel array. Output should consist of a table with three columns: one for the student identification number, one for the number of correct responses, and one for the quiz grade. Grades are assigned as follows:

10	A
9	B
8	} C
7	
6	} D
5	
4	
or	} E
less	

Your output should also include the quiz average for the entire class.

13. A few members (total unknown, but no more than 25) at Oakland Mountain Country Club want to computerize their golf scores. Each member plays 20 games, some 18 holes and some 9 holes. Each member's name (no more than 20 characters) is written on a data card, followed on a second card by the 20 scores. Each score is immediately followed by an 'E' or an 'N', indicating 18 or 9 holes, respectively.

    Write a program to read all the names and scores into two parallel two-dimensional arrays. Calculate everyone's 18-hole average. (Double the 9-hole scores before you store them in the array and treat as 18-hole scores.) Calculate how much each average is over or under par (par is 72 and should be declared as a constant). Output should be each name, average, difference from par, and scores.

14. Write a program to keep statistics for a basketball team consisting of 15 players. Statistics for each player should include shots attempted, shots made, and shooting percentage; free throws attempted, free throws made, and free throw percentage; offensive rebounds and defensive rebounds; assists; turnovers; and total points. Appropriate team totals should be listed as part of the output.

15. A magic square is a square array of positive integers such that the sum of each row, column, and diagonal is the same constant. For example,

16	3	2	13
5	10	11	8
9	6	7	12
4	15	14	1

is a magic square whose constant is 34.

Write a program to have as input four lines of four positive integers. The program should then determine whether or not the square is a magic square.

16. Pascal's Triangle can be used to recognize coefficients of a quantity raised to a power. The rules for forming this triangle of integers are such that each row must start and end with a 1, and each entry in a row is the sum of the two values diagonally above the new entry. Thus, four rows of Pascal's Triangle are

```
      1
    1   1
  1   2   1
1   3   3   1
```

This triangle can be used as a convenient way to get the coefficients of a quantity of two terms raised to a power (binomial coefficients). For example,

$$(a + b)^3 = 1a^3 + 3a^2b + 3ab^2 + 1b^3$$

where the coefficients 1, 3, 3, and 1 come from the fourth row of Pascal's Triangle.

Write a complete program to print out Pascal's Triangle for ten rows.

17. Your former high school principal has come to you for help. He wants you to develop a program to maintain a list of the 20 students in the school with the highest scores on the SAT test. Input is from a text file containing the name (20 characters), and the total SAT score (verbal plus mathematical). Write a program that, when all data have been read, prints out a list of the 20 highest scores from highest to lowest, and the students' names. You may assume that no two students have the same score.

18. The transpose of a matrix (table) is a new matrix with the row and column positions reversed. That is, the transpose of matrix A, an M by N matrix is an N by M matrix, with each element, $A[m,n]$ stored in $B[n,m]$. Given a 3×5 matrix of integers, create a matrix that is its transpose. Print both the original matrix and the new matrix.

■ 19. Mr. Laven, a mathematics instructor at your college, wants you to write a program to help him keep his students' grades. He wants to keep track of up to 30 grades for each of up to 35 students. Your program should read grades and names from a text file, and then print the following:

   a. A table showing the names in alphabetical order and grades received by each student.

   b. An alphabetical list of students with their total points and average score.

   c. A list of averages from highest to lowest with corresponding students' names.

20. Write a program in which a person can enter data into a 5 × 7 matrix. Print the original matrix along with the average of each row and column.

21. Matrix M is symmetric if it has the same number of rows as columns, and if each element $M[x,y]$ is equal to $M[y,x]$. Write a program to check a matrix entered by the user to see if it is symmetric or not.

■ 22. The following table shows the total sales for salespeople of the Falcon Manufacturing Company.

Salesperson	Week 1	Week 2	Week 3	Week 4
Anna, Michael	30	25	45	18
Henderson, Marge	22	30	32	35
Johnson, Fred	12	17	19	15
Striker, Nancy	32	30	33	31
Ryan, Renee	22	17	28	16

The price of the product being sold is $1,985.95. Write a program that permits the input of the previous data, and prints both a replica of the original table and a table showing the dollar value of sales for each individual during each week along with their total sales. Also, print the total sales for each week and the total sales for the company.

23. The computer science office wants a computerized system for finding telephone numbers of students. The program should read a list of up to 20 students and their telephone numbers from a text file. It should permit the entry of a student's name, and then print the name and telephone number. (A binary search could be used for this.) If the name is not found, an appropriate message should be printed.

24. Write a program to permit two people to play the game of Battleship. Your program should record the ship positions, hits, misses, and ship sinkings for each player.

25. Rewrite the Battleship program (Problem 24) to have a person play against the computer.

26. Arrange a visit with a travel agent or an airlines reservation agent. Discuss with the agent the information each requests from prospective passengers. If possible, have the agent set up a mock booking using the computerized reservation system. Examine the screen displays.

   Prepare a report of your visit for the class. Be sure to discuss how the designers of the reservation system may have used multidimensional arrays.

27. Contact someone who routinely uses a spreadsheet as part of his or her daily work. Have the person show you several usual operations with the spreadsheet. In particular, see how to adjust the size of the spread sheet, sum rows, sum columns, and use functions to define entries for specific locations.

   Give an oral report of your discussion to your class. Explain how the various spreadsheet operations relate to what you have studied about two-dimensional arrays.

28. Select an unworked problem from the previously listed programming problems for this chapter. Construct a structure chart and write all documentary information necessary for the problem you have chosen. Do not write code. When you are finished, have a classmate read your documentation to see if precisely what is to be done is clear.

Records

 The previous two chapters dealt extensively with the concept of the structured data type **ARRAY.** Recall that when you declare an array, you reserve a predetermined number of memory locations. The variables representing these memory locations are of the same base type and can be accessed by reference to the index of an array element.

All components of an array must be of the same data type; this is a serious limitation since there are many situations in which this is not possible; for example, a bank may wish to keep a record of the name, address, telephone number, marital status, social security number, annual salary, total assets, and total liabilities of each customer. Fortunately, Pascal provides another structured data type, **RECORD,** which allows heterogeneous information to be stored, accessed, and manipulated. A record contains fields, which can be of different data types. This chapter shows you how to declare records, how to access the various fields within a record, and how to work with arrays of records.

■ 12.1
Record Definitions

OBJECTIVES

- to understand the basic idea of **RECORD** as a structured data type
- to be able to declare a **RECORD**
- to be able to use fields of a **RECORD**

Record as a Structured Data Type

A *record* is a collection of *fields* that may be treated as a whole or individually. To illustrate, a record that contains fields for a customer's name, age, and annual income could be visualized as shown in Figure 12.1.

This schematic representation may help you understand why a record is considered a structured data type and familiarize you with the idea of using fields in a record.

Declaring a RECORD

Let's now consider our first example of a formally declared record. Assume we want a record to contain a customer's name, age, and annual income. The following definition and subsequent declaration can be made.

FIGURE 12.1
Fields in a record

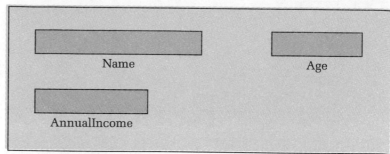

```
TYPE
   CustomerInfo = RECORD
                      Name : PACKED ARRAY [1..30] OF char;
                      Age : integer;
                      AnnualIncome : real
                  END; { of RECORD CustomerInfo }
VAR
   Customer : CustomerInfo;
```

Components of a record are called fields and each field has an associated data type. The general form for defining a record data type using the **TYPE** definition section is

TYPE
⟨type identifier⟩ = **RECORD**
                        ⟨field identifier 1⟩ : ⟨data type 1⟩;
                        ⟨field identifier 2⟩ : ⟨data type 2⟩;
                        .
                        .
                        .
                        ⟨field identifier *n*⟩ : ⟨data type *n*⟩
                    END; { of **RECORD** definition }

The syntax diagram for this is

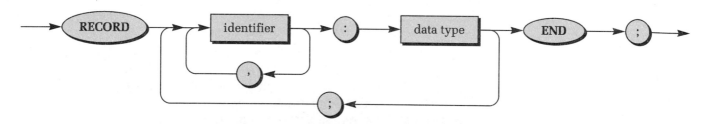

The following comments are in order concerning this form.

1. The type identifier can be any valid identifier. It should be descriptive to enhance program readability.
2. The reserved word **RECORD** must precede the field identifiers.
3. Each field identifier within a record must be unique. However, field identifiers in different records may use the same name. Thus,

```
FirstRecord = RECORD
                  Name : PACKED ARRAY [1..30] OF char;
                  Age : integer
              END; { of RECORD FirstRecord }
```

and

```
SecondRecord = RECORD
                 Name : PACKED ARRAY [1..30] OF char;
                 Age : integer;
                 IQ : integer
               END;  { of RECORD SecondRecord  }
```

can both be defined in the same program.

4. Data types for fields can be user-defined. Thus, our earlier definitions could have been

```
TYPE
   String30 = PACKED ARRAY [1..30] OF char;
   CustomerInfo = RECORD
                    Name : String30;
                    Age : integer;
                    AnnualIncome : real
                  END;  { of RECORD CustomerInfo  }
VAR
   Customer : CustomerInfo;
```

5. **END;** is required to signify the end of a **RECORD** definition. This is the second instance (remember **CASE**?) in which **END** is used without a **BEGIN**.

6. Fields of the same base type can be declared together. Thus,

```
Info = RECORD
         Name : String30;
         Age, IQ : integer
       END;  { of RECORD Info  }
```

is appropriate. However, you are encouraged to list each field separately to enhance readability and reinforce the concept of fields in a record. The following example defines another record.

■ **EXAMPLE 12.1**

Suppose you want to keep a record for a college student. The record is to contain a field for each of the following: student's name (Smith Jane), social security number (111-22-3333), class status (Fr, So, Jr, or Sr), previous credit hours earned (56), credit hours being taken (17), and grade point average (3.27). We can define a record and declare an appropriate variable as follows:

```
TYPE
   String30 = PACKED ARRAY [1..30] OF char;
   String11 = PACKED ARRAY [1..11] OF char;
   Class = (Fr, So, Jr, Sr);
   StudentInfo = RECORD
                   Name : String30;
                   SSN : String11;
                   Status : Class;
                   HoursEarned : 0..999;
                   HoursTaking : 0..30;
                   GPA : real
                 END;  { of RECORD StudentInfo  }
VAR
   Student : StudentInfo;
```

STYLE TIP
■ ■ ■ ■ ■ ■ ■ ■ ■ ■ ■

Use descriptive field names, appropriate subranges, and a descriptive variable name when defining records. For example, if you want a record with fields for a student's name, age, gender, and class status, you can use

```
TYPE
   String20 = PACKED ARRAY [1..20] OF char;
   StudentRecord = RECORD
                       Name : String20;
                       Age : 0..99;
                       Gender : (Male, Female);
                       ClassStatus : (Fr, So, Jr, Sr)
                   END;  {  of RECORD StudentRecord  }
VAR
   Student : StudentRecord;
```

The fields would then be

```
Student.Name
Student.Age
Student.Gender
Student.ClassStatus
```

and you can use program statements such as

```
IF Student.Gender = Male THEN
```

or

```
IF Student.Age < 21 THEN
```

Fields in a Record

Now that you know how to define a record, you need to examine how to access fields in a record. For our discussion, let us consider a record defined by

```
TYPE
   String30 = PACKED ARRAY [1..30] OF char;
   Employee = RECORD
                  Name : String30;
                  Age : integer;
                  MaritalStatus : char;
                  Wage : real
              END;  {  of RECORD Employee  }
VAR
   Programmer : Employee;
```

Programmer can be visualized as pictured in Figure 12.2.

FIGURE 12.2
Defined fields in Programmer

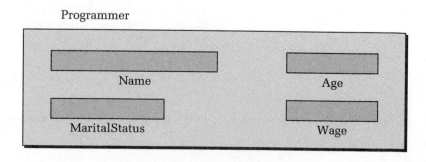

Programmer

Name   Age

MaritalStatus   Wage

Each field within a record is a variable and can be uniquely identified by

〈record name〉.〈field name〉

where a period separates the record name from the field name. Thus, the four field variables are

```
Programmer.Name
Programmer.Age
Programmer.MaritalStatus
Programmer.Wage
```

Each of these variables may be used in any manner consistent with the defined base type. To illustrate, suppose Programmer.Name and Programmer.Age have been assigned values and you wish to print the names of those employees under 30 years of age. You could have a fragment of code such as

```
IF Programmer.Age < 30 THEN
   writeln (Programmer.Name:40);
```

If you wish to compute gross salary, you might have

```
read (Hours);
Gross := Hours * Programmer.Wage;
```

Other Fields

Thus far, our fields have been declared in a relatively direct fashion. This is not always the case. Sometimes, when establishing the structure of a record, the data type of a field needs more development. For example, suppose you wish to declare a record for each student in a class and the record is to contain student name, class name, four test scores, ten quiz scores, final average, and letter grade. This can be visualized as shown in Figure 12.3.

FIGURE 12.3
Fields in Student

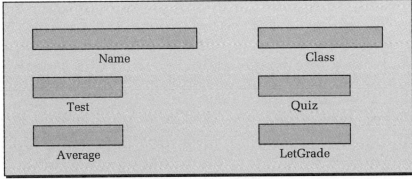

In this case, Test and Quiz are both arrays. Thus, a subsequent development is shown in Figure 12.4.

FIGURE 12.4
Arrays as fields in a record

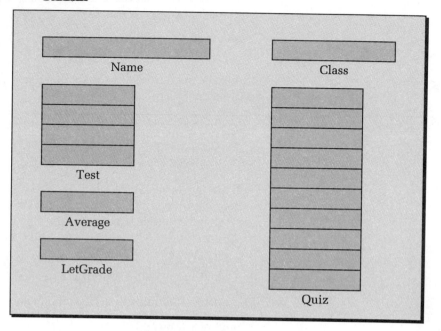

This record can now be formally defined by

```
TYPE
   String30 = PACKED ARRAY [1..30] OF char;
   String10 = PACKED ARRAY [1..10] OF char;
   TestScores = ARRAY [1..4] OF integer;
   QuizScores = ARRAY [1..10] OF integer;
   StudentInfo = RECORD
                    Name : String30;
                    Class : String10;
                    Test : TestScores;
                    Quiz : QuizScores;
                    Average : real;
                    LetGrade : char
                 END;  {  of RECORD StudentInfo  }
VAR
   Student : StudentInfo;
```

If the student associated with this record earned an 89 on the first test and a
9 (out of 10) on the first quiz, this information could be entered by reading
the values or by assigning them appropriately. Thus, either of the following
would suffice.

```
read (Student.Test[1], Student.Quiz[1]);
```

or

```
Student.Test[1] := 89;
Student.Quiz[1] := 9;
```

Exercises 12.1

1. Explain why records are structured data types.

2. Write a test program to

   a. Define a **RECORD** type in which the record contains fields for your name and
   your age.

   b. Declare a record variable to be of this type.

   c. Read in your name and age from a data file.

   d. Print out your name and age.

3. Discuss the similarities and differences between arrays and records as structured data types.

4. Use the **TYPE** definition section to define a record for each record illustrated in Figure 12.5(a), (b), and (c), respectively. In each case, also declare a record variable to be of the defined type.

FIGURE 12.5
Records with fields illustrated

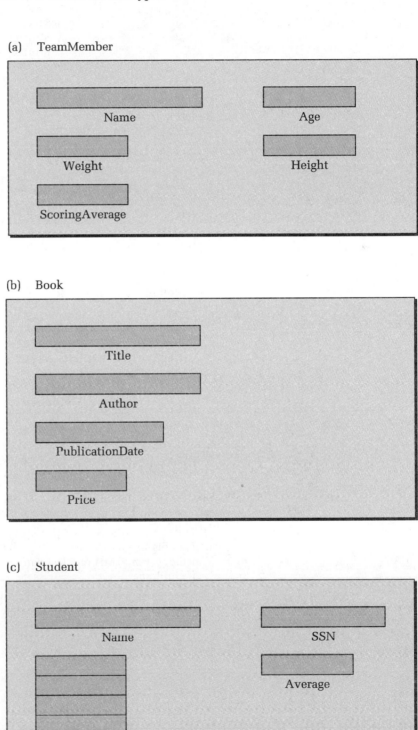

(a) TeamMember

Name

Age

Weight

Height

ScoringAverage

(b) Book

Title

Author

PublicationDate

Price

(c) Student

Name

SSN

Test

Average

5. Draw a schematic representation of each of the following record definitions.

a.
```
TYPE
   String30 = PACKED ARRAY [1..30] OF char;
   String11 = PACKED ARRAY [1..11] OF char;
   EmployeeInfo = RECORD
                     Name : String30;
                     SSN : String11;
                     NumOfDep : integer;
                     HourlyWage : real
                  END;
VAR
   Employee : EmployeeInfo;
```

b.
```
TYPE
   HouseInfo = RECORD
                  Location : PACKED ARRAY [1..20]
                                OF char;
                  Age : integer;
                  NumRooms : integer;
                  NumBaths : integer;
                  BuildingType : (Brick, Frame);
                  Taxes : real;
                  Price : real
               END;
VAR
   House : HouseInfo;
```

c.
```
TYPE
   String20 = PACKED ARRAY [1..20] OF char;
   String30 = PACKED ARRAY [1..30] OF char;
   String8 = PACKED ARRAY [1..8] OF char;
   PhoneBook = RECORD
                  Name : String30;
                  Address : ARRAY [1..4]
                               OF String20;
                  PhoneNum : String8
               END;
VAR
   PhoneListing : PhoneBook;
```

6. Use the **TYPE** definition section to define an appropriate **RECORD** type for each of the following. In each case, also declare an appropriate record variable.

a. Families in your former school district: each record should contain the last name, parents' first and last names, address, number of children, and the ages of children.

b. Students in a school system: each record should contain the student's name, identification number, classification (Fr, So, Jr, or Sr), courses being taken (at most six), and grade point average.

7. Find all errors in each of the following definitions or declarations.

a.
```
TYPE
   Info:  RECORD
             Name = PACKED ARRAY [1..30] OF char;
             Age : 0..100
          END;
```

```
b. TYPE
     Member = RECORD
                  Age : integer;
                  IQ : integer
              END;
   VAR
     Member : Member;
c. VAR
     Member = RECORD
                  Name : PACKED ARRAY [1..30] OF char;
                  Age : 0..100;
                  IQ = 50..200
              END;
```

8. Given the record defined by

```
TYPE
   String30 = PACKED ARRAY [1..30] OF char;
   Weekdays = (Mon, Tues, Wed, Thur, Fri);
   ListOfScores = ARRAY [1..5] OF integer;
   Info = RECORD
              Name : String30;
              Day : Weekdays;
              Score : ListOfScores;
              Average : real
          END;
VAR
   Contestant : Info;
   Sum : integer;
```

assume values have been assigned as indicated in Figure 12.6.

FIGURE 12.6

Contestant

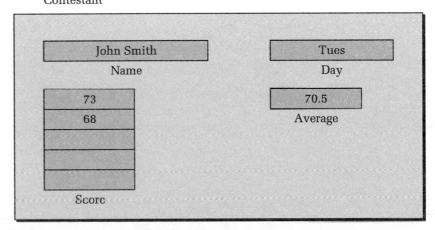

Indicate which of the following are valid and, if invalid, explain why.

a. `Day := Wed;`

b. `Contestant.Day := Wed;`

c. `Score := 70;`

d. `Score[3] := 70;`

e. `Contestant.Score[3] := 70;`

f. `Contestant[3].Score := 70;`

```
g. FOR J := 1 TO 5 DO
     Sum := Sum + Contestant.Score[J];
h. Contestant.Score[3] := Score[2];
i. Contestant.Score[3] := Contestant.Score[2] + 3;
j. Average := (Score[1] + Score[2] + Score[3]) / 3;
k. IF Contestant.Day < Wed THEN
     Contestant.Average := Contestant.Score[1] +
                                Contestant.Score[2];
l. writeln (Contestant.Name:40, Contestant.Average:10:2);
```

■ ■ ■ ■

■ 12.2
Using Records

OBJECTIVES

- to be able to use **WITH . . . DO** when using records in a program
- to be able to copy complete records
- to be able to use a procedure to read data into a record
- to be able to use a procedure to print data from a record

The previous section introduced you to the concept of **RECORD** as a structured data type. At this stage, you should be comfortable with this concept and be able to use the **TYPE** definition section to define such a data type. In this section, we will examine methods of working with records.

WITH . . . DO Using Records

Let's consider a record that contains fields for a student's name, three test scores, and test average. It could be defined by

```
TYPE
   String20 = PACKED ARRAY [1..20] OF char;
   List3 = ARRAY [1..3] OF integer;
   StudentRecord = RECORD
                      Name : String20;
                      Score : List3;
                      Average : real
                   END;  { of RECORD StudentRecord }
VAR
   Student : StudentRecord;
```

and envisioned as shown in Figure 12.7.

FIGURE 12.7
Fields in Student

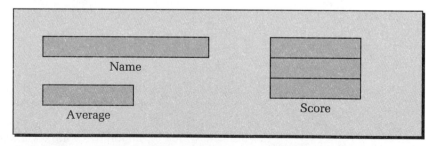

To use this record, we need to assign or read data into appropriate fields. Therefore, assume a line of data is

Washington Joe   79 83 94

This data can be read by the fragment of code

```
FOR J := 1 TO 20 DO
  read (Student.Name[J]);
```

```
FOR J := 1 TO 3 DO
  read (Student.Score[J]);
readln;
```

The average can be computed by

```
Student.Average := (Student.Score[1] +
                    Student.Score[2] +
                    Student.Score[3]) / 3;
```

Notice that each field identifier includes the record name. Fortunately, when working with fields of a record, Pascal provides a more convenient method of referring to these fields: a **WITH . . . DO** statement. Using this option, the previous fragment can be rewritten as

```
WITH Student DO
  BEGIN
    FOR J := 1 TO 20 DO
      read (Name[J]);
    FOR J := 1 TO 3 DO
      read (Score[J]);
    readln;
    Average := (Score[1] + Score[2] + Score[3]) / 3
  END;  {  of WITH...DO  }
```

Formally, a **WITH . . . DO** statement has the form

```
WITH ⟨record name⟩ DO
  BEGIN
    ⟨statement 1⟩;
    ⟨statement 2⟩;
          .
          .
          .
    ⟨statement n⟩
  END;
```

where the statements used may refer to the field identifiers but do not include the record name as part of the field identifier. This eliminates use of the period following the record name. Thus, instead of Student.Score[J], you can use Score[J].

As a second illustration, suppose you have a record defined as

```
TYPE
  String20 = PACKED ARRAY [1..20] OF char;
  PatientInfo = RECORD
                  Name : String20;
                  Age : integer;
                  Height : integer;
                  Weight : integer;
                  Gender : char
                END;  {  of RECORD PatientInfo  }
VAR
  Patient : PatientInfo;
```

Values can be assigned to the various fields specifically by

```
Patient.Name := 'Jones Connie        ';
Patient.Age := 19;
Patient.Height := 67;
Patient.Weight := 125;
Patient.Gender := 'F';
```

or by

```
WITH Patient DO
  BEGIN
    Name := 'Jones Connie       ';
    Age := 19;
    Height := 67;
    Weight := 125;
    Gender := 'F'
  END;  {  of WITH...DO  }
```

A single **WITH . . . DO** statement can be used with more than one record. For example, using the previous two record definitions, it is possible to write

```
WITH Student, Patient DO
  BEGIN
    Average := (Score[1] + Score[2] + Score[3]) / 3;
    Age := 19
  END;  {  of WITH...DO  }
```

This is equivalent to the nested use of **WITH . . . DO,** as follows:

```
WITH Student DO
  WITH Patient DO
    BEGIN
      Average := (Score[1] + Score[2] + Score[3]) / 3;
      Age := 19
    END;
```

In this nesting, the record identifier is associated with each field defined in that record. Thus,

```
Age := 19
```

can be thought of as

```
Patient.Age := 19
```

Since Average is not a field in Patient, it will not be associated with the record identifier Patient. It will, however, be associated with the record identifier Student.

When using more than one record in a single **WITH . . . DO** statement, each field identifier should have a unique reference to exactly one of the listed records. If a field identifier is used in more than one of the records, the reference may be ambiguous and a logic error may result. Thus,

```
WITH Student, Patient DO
  writeln (Name);
```

is incorrect and could produce a result different from what you expect; it is not clear whether the reference is to Student.Name or Patient.Name. In some versions of Pascal, this is a compilation error. In others, it is a logic error and does not produce either a run-time error or a compilation error. Thus, while you might want to print Student.Name, you would print Patient.Name instead. This is because successive identifiers used as we just have are treated as if they are nested.

Copying Records

How can information contained in one record be transferred to another record? For example, we need to do this when we want to sort an array of records. To illustrate how records can be copied, consider the following definitions and declarations.

```
TYPE
  InfoA = RECORD
            Field1 : integer;
            Field2 : real;
            Field3 : char
         END;  {  of RECORD InfoA  }
  InfoB = RECORD
            Field1 : integer;
            Field2 : real;
            Field3 : char
         END;  {  of RECORD InfoB  }
VAR
  Rec1, Rec2 : InfoA;
  Rec3 : InfoB;
```

The three records declared can be envisioned as shown in Figure 12.8.

FIGURE 12.8
Copying records

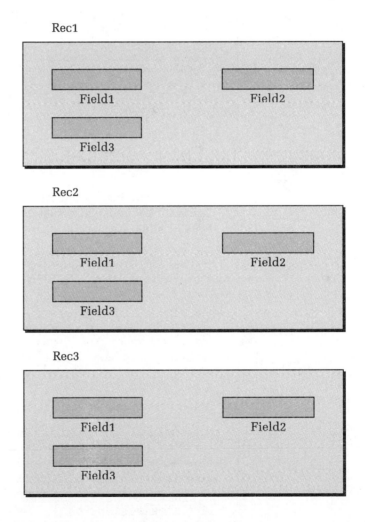

Now, suppose data have been assigned to Rec1 by

```
WITH Rec1 DO
  BEGIN
    Field1 := 25;
    Field2 := 89.5;
    Field3 := 'M'
  END;  {  of WITH...DO  }
```

These data can be copied to the corresponding fields of Rec2 by

```
Rec2 := Rec1;
```

This single assignment statement accomplishes all the following:

```
Rec2.Field1 := Rec1.Field1;
Rec2.Field2 := Rec1.Field2;
Rec2.Field3 := Rec1.Field3;
```

It is important to note that such an assignment can only be made when the records are of identical type. For example, notice that InfoA and InfoB have the same structure but have been defined as different types. In this case, if you wish to assign the values in the fields of Rec1 to the corresponding fields of Rec3, the statement

```
Rec3 := Rec1;
```

produces a compilation error. Although Rec1 and Rec3 have the same structure, they are not of identical type. In this case, the information can be transferred by

```
WITH Rec3 DO
  BEGIN
    Field1 := Rec1.Field1;
    Field2 := Rec1.Field2;
    Field3 := Rec1.Field3
  END;  {  of WITH...DO  }
```

Reading Data into a Record

Once a record has been defined for a program, one task is to get data into the record. This is usually accomplished by reading from a data file. To illustrate, assume we have a record defined by

```
TYPE
  String20 = PACKED ARRAY [1..20] OF char;
  PatientInfo = RECORD
                   Name : String20;
                   Age : integer;
                   Height : integer;
                   Weight : integer;
                   Gender : char
                END;  {  of RECORD PatientInfo  }
VAR
  Patient : PatientInfo;
```

and a line of data is

```
Smith Mary        21 67 125F
```

One method of getting the data is to use a **WITH . . . DO** statement in the main body of a program such as

```
BEGIN  {  Main program  }
  WITH Patient DO
    BEGIN
      FOR J := 1 TO 20 DO
        read (Name[J]);
      readln (Age, Height, Weight, Gender)
    END;  {  of WITH...DO  }
```

However, good program design would have us use a procedure for this task. Therefore, in order to use a procedure, we must be careful to use the user-defined data type PatientInfo and a variable parameter in the procedure heading. With these two considerations, an appropriate procedure is

```
PROCEDURE GetData (VAR Patient : PatientInfo);
  VAR
    J : integer;
  BEGIN
    WITH Patient DO
      BEGIN
        FOR J := 1 TO 20 DO
          read (Name[J]);
        readln (Age, Height, Weight, Gender)
      END  {  of WITH...DO  }
  END;  {  of PROCEDURE GetData  }
```

This is called from the main program by

```
GetData (Patient);
```

As a second example of getting data for a record, suppose you are writing a program to be used to compute grades of students in a class. As part of the program, a record type can be declared as

```
CONST
  NumQuizzes = 10;
  NumTest = 4;
TYPE
  String20 = PACKED ARRAY [1..20] OF char;
  QuizList = ARRAY [1..NumQuizzes] OF integer;
  TestList = ARRAY [1..NumTests] OF integer;
  StudentRecord = RECORD
                    Name : String20;
                    Quiz : QuizList;
                    Test : TestList;
                    QuizTotal : integer;
                    TestAverage : real;
                    LetterGrade : 'A'..'E'
                  END;  {  of RECORD StudentRecord  }
VAR
  Student : StudentRecord;
```

If each line of data contains a student's name, ten quiz scores, and four test scores and looks like

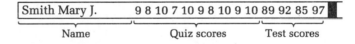

A procedure to get this data could be

```
PROCEDURE GetData (VAR Student : StudentRecord);
  VAR
    J : integer;
  BEGIN
    WITH Student DO
      BEGIN
        FOR J := 1 TO 20 DO
          read (Name[J]);
        FOR J := 1 TO NumQuizzes DO
          read (Quiz[J]);
        FOR J := 1 TO NumTests DO
          read (Test[J])
      END;  {  of WITH...DO  }
    readln
  END;  {  of PROCEDURE GetData  }
```

It would be called from the main program by

```
GetData (Student);
```

Let's now continue this example by writing a function to compute the test average for a student. Since this average is found by using the four test scores in the record, such a function could be

```
FUNCTION TestAv (Test : TestList) : real;
  VAR
    J : integer;
    Sum : integer;
  BEGIN
    Sum := 0;
    FOR J := 1 TO NumTests DO
      Sum := Sum + Test[J];
    TestAv := Sum / NumTests
  END;  {  of FUNCTION TestAv  }
```

Since the array of test scores was the only parameter sent to the function and the average would normally be stored in the field TestAverage, this function could be called by

```
Student.TestAverage := TestAv(Student.Test);
```

Printing Data from a Record

After information has been assigned or read from a data file and appropriate calculations have been made, you will want to print information from the record. Since this is frequently done in a procedure, let us assume the previous record for a student has the values illustrated in Figure 12.9.

FIGURE 12.9
Fields with values

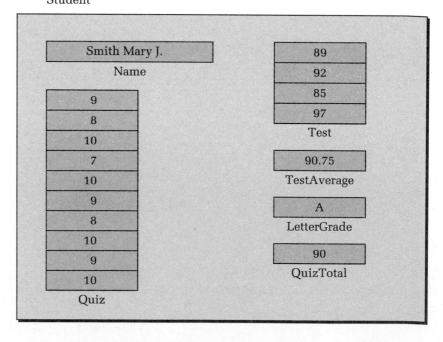

Student

Smith Mary J.
Name

| Quiz |
| 9 |
| 8 |
| 10 |
| 7 |
| 10 |
| 9 |
| 8 |
| 10 |
| 9 |
| 10 |

| Test |
| 89 |
| 92 |
| 85 |
| 97 |

90.75
TestAverage

A
LetterGrade

90
QuizTotal

If you want the output for a student to be

```
Name:            Smith Mary J.
Quiz Scores:     9 8 10 7 10 9 8 10 9 10
Quiz Total:      90
Test Scores:     89 92 85 97
Test Average: 90.75
Letter Grade: A
```

a procedure for producing this is

```
PROCEDURE PrintData (Student : StudentRecord);
  CONST
    Skip = ' ';
  VAR
    J : integer;
BEGIN
  writeln;
  WITH Student DO
    BEGIN
      writeln (Skip:10, 'Name:', Name:29);
      write (Skip:10, 'Quiz Scores:');
      FOR J := 1 TO NumQuizzes DO
        write (Quiz[J]:3);
      writeln;
      writeln (Skip:10, 'Quiz Total:', QuizTotal:5);
      write (Skip:10, 'Test Scores:');
      FOR J := 1 TO NumTests DO
        write (Test[J]:4);
      writeln;
      writeln (Skip:10, 'Test Average:', TestAverage:6:2);
      writeln, (Skip:10, 'Letter Grade:', LetterGrade:2)
    END   {  of WITH...DO  }
  END;  {  of PROCEDURE PrintData  }
```

This procedure would be called from the main program by

```
PrintData (Student);
```

■ EXAMPLE 12.2

As a concluding example, let's consider a short interactive program that uses records and procedures to perform the arithmetic operation of multiplying two fractions. The fractions should be entered in the form

```
1/2
```

The program declares a record for each fraction and uses procedures to get the data, multiply the fractions, and print the results.

Before writing this program, let's examine appropriate record definitions and a procedure for computing the product. A definition is

```
TYPE
  RationalNumber = RECORD
                     Numerator : integer;
                     Denominator : integer
                   END;  {  of RECORD RationalNumber  }
VAR
  X, Y, Product : RationalNumber;
```

A procedure for computing the product is

Using Key Fields in Records

The need to search records by certain key fields is a basic and very important process. To illustrate, consider how Ted Celentino, a former director of PARS applications for the on-line reservation system of TWA, responded to the question: "How are reservations indexed?" He said: "By the passenger's name, flight num-

ber, and departure date. All three are needed. If a passenger forgets his or her flight number, the agent can try to find a record of it by looking through all flights to the appropriate destination at that particular travel time. It's rare that a passenger doesn't know at least a couple of pieces of information that lead to his or her record."

```
PROCEDURE ComputeProduct (X, Y : RationalNumber;
                                  VAR Product : RationalNumber);
BEGIN
   WITH Product DO
     BEGIN
       Numerator := X.Numerator * Y.Numerator;
       Denominator := X.Denominator * Y.Denominator
     END {  of WITH...DO  }
END; {  of PROCEDURE ComputeProduct  }
```

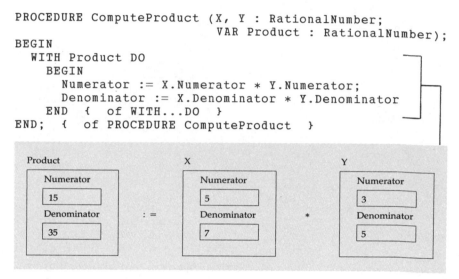

This procedure is called from the main program by

```
ComputeProduct (X, Y, Product);
```

A complete program for this problem follows.

```
PROGRAM Fractions (input, output);

{  This program illustrates the use of records with procedures. }
{  In particular, procedures are used to                         }
{                                                                }
{       1.  get the data                                         }
{       2.  perform computations                                 }
{       3.  print the results                                    }
{                                                                }
{  The specific task is to compute the product of two rational   }
{  numbers.                                                       }

TYPE
   RationalNumber = RECORD
                 Numerator : integer;
                 Denominator : integer
               END; {  of RECORD RationalNumber  }

VAR
   X, Y, Product : RationalNumber;
   MoreData : boolean;
   Response : char;

{******************************************************************* }
```

```
PROCEDURE GetData (VAR X, Y : RationalNumber);

   {  Given:    Nothing                                            }
   {  Task:     Have entered from the keyboard the numerator and   }
   {                denominator of two fractions                   }
   {  Return:   Two records, each containing a field for the       }
   {                numerator and denominator of a fraction        }

   VAR
     Slash : char;

   BEGIN
     WITH X DO
       BEGIN
         write ('Enter a fraction in the form a/b.  ');
         readln (Numerator, Slash, Denominator)
       END;  {  of WITH X DO  }
     WITH Y DO
       BEGIN
         write ('Enter a fraction in the form a/b.  ');
         readln (Numerator, Slash, Denominator)
       END  {  of WITH Y DO  }
   END;  {  of PROCEDURE GetData  }


{***************************************************************** }


PROCEDURE ComputeProduct (X, Y : RationalNumber;
                          VAR Product : RationalNumber);

   {  Given:    Records for two fractions                          }
   {  Task:     Compute the product and store result              }
   {  Return:   Product of the fraction                           }

   BEGIN
     WITH Product DO
       BEGIN
         Numerator := X.Numerator * Y.Numerator;
         Denominator := X.Denominator * Y.Denominator
       END  {  of WITH...DO  }
   END;  {  of PROCEDURE ComputeProduct  }


{***************************************************************** }


PROCEDURE PrintResults (X, Y, Product : RationalNumber);

   {  Given:    Records for each of two given fractions and their }
   {                product                                        }
   {  Task:     Print an equation stating the problem and answer; }
   {                standard fraction form should be used as       }
   {                output                                         }
   {  Return:   Nothing                                            }

   BEGIN
     writeln;
     writeln (X.Numerator:13, Y.Numerator:6, Product.Numerator:6);
     writeln ('--- * --- = ---':25);
     writeln (X.Denominator:13, Y.Denominator:6, Product.Denominator:6);
     writeln
   END;  {  of PROCEDURE PrintResults  }


{***************************************************************** }
```

```
BEGIN  {  Main program  }
  MoreData := true;
  WHILE MoreData DO
    BEGIN
      GetData (X, Y);
      ComputeProduct (X, Y, Product);
      PrintResults (X, Y, Product);
      write ('Do you wish to see another problem?  <Y> or <N>  ');
      readln (Response);
      Moredata := (Response = 'Y') OR (Response = 'y');
      writeln
    END  {  of WHILE...DO  }
END.  {  of main program  }
```

With input from the keyboard of

```
3/4 1/2
3/2 7/10
2/3 4/5
```

sample output is

```
Enter a fraction in the form a/b.  3/4
Enter a fraction in the form a/b.  1/2


          3       1       3
         --- * --- = ---
          4       2       8


Do you wish to see another problem?  <Y> or <N>   Y

Enter a fraction in the form a/b.  3/2
Enter a fraction in the form a/b.  7/10


          3       7      21
         --- * --- = ---
          2      10      20


Do you wish to see another problem?  <Y> or <N>   Y

Enter a fraction in the form a/b.  2/3
Enter a fraction in the form a/b.  4/5


          2       4       8
         --- * --- = ---
          3       5      15


Do you wish to see another problem?  <Y> or <N>   N
```

Exercises 12.2

1. Assume a program contains the following **TYPE** definition and **VAR** declaration sections.

```
TYPE
  Info1 = RECORD
              Initial : char;
              Age : integer
          END;
  Info2 = RECORD
              Initial : char;
              Age : integer
          END;
```

```
VAR
   Cust1, Cust2 : Info1;
   Cust3, Cust4 : Info2;
```

Indicate which of the following statements are valid. Give an explanation for those that are invalid.

a. `Cust1 := Cust2;`

b. `Cust2 := Cust3;`

c. `Cust3 := Cust4;`

d.
```
WITH Cust1 DO
   BEGIN
      Initial := 'W';
      Age := 21
   END;
```

e.
```
WITH Cust1, Cust2 DO
   BEGIN
      Initial :- 'W';
      Age := 21
   END;
```

2. Write a test program to see what happens when two different records with the same field name are used in a single **WITH ... DO** statement. Use the declarations and **TYPE** definitions in Exercise 1. For example,

```
WITH Student1, Student2 DO
   Age := 21;
writeln (Student1.Age);
writeln (Student2.Age);
```

3. Assume the **TYPE** and **VAR** sections of a program include

```
TYPE
   String11 = PACKED ARRAY [1..11] OF char;
   String20 = PACKED ARRAY [1..20] OF char;
   Info = RECORD
             Name : String20;
             SSN : String11;
             Age : integer;
             HourlyWage : real;
             HoursWorked : real;
             Volunteer : boolean
          END;
VAR
   Employee1, Employee2 : Info;
```

a. Show three different methods of transferring all information from the record for Employee1 to the record for Employee2.

b. Suppose you wished to transfer all information from the record for Employee1 to the record for Employee2 except HoursWorked. Discuss different methods for doing this. Which do you feel is the most efficient?

4. Assume the **TYPE** and **VAR** sections of a program are the same as in Exercise 3. Write a procedure to be used to read information into such a record from a data file. A typical line of data is

Smith Jane M.	111-22-3333 25 10.50 41.5Y

where 'Y' indicates the worker is a volunteer (**true**) and 'N' indicates the worker is not a volunteer (**false**).

5. Assume a record has been declared by

```
TYPE
   String20 = PACKED ARRAY [1..20] OF char;
   StudentInfo = RECORD
                    Name : String20;
                    TotalPts : 0..500;
                    LetterGrade : char
                 END;
VAR
   Student : StudentInfo;
```

Write a function to compute the student's letter grade based on cutoff levels of 90 percent, 80 percent, 70 percent, and 60 percent. Show how this function is used in a program to assign the appropriate letter grade to the appropriate field of a student's record.

6. Review Example 12.2, in which two fractions were multiplied. In a similar fashion, write procedures for

a. Dividing two fractions (watch out for zero).

b. Adding two fractions.

c. Subtracting two fractions.

7. Some instructors throw out the lowest test score for each student when computing the student's test average. Assume a record Student of type StudentRecord has been declared and data have been read into appropriate fields.

a. Write a function to compute the test average using the best three scores.

b. Show how a constant in the **CONST** section can be used to generalize this to finding the best $n - 1$ of n scores.

c. Rewrite the function using a sort to sort the array of scores from high to low and then add the first three from the array.

d. Must the entire array be sorted in order to find the three highest scores? Explain.

8. Show how the program Fractions in Example 12.2 can be modified to check for nonzero denominators.

■ 12.3
Data Structures with Records

OBJECTIVES

- to be able to declare a nested record
- to be able to use nested records in a program
- to be able to declare an array of records
- to be able to use an array of records in a program
- to be able to sort an array of records by a field
- to be able to use procedures for working with an array of records

Nested Records

The first concept to be examined in this section is that of *nested record*. A nested record is a record which is a field in another record. For example, suppose you are working on a program to be used by a biology department and part of your work is to declare a record for a faculty member. This record is to contain fields for the person's name, office number, telephone number, and supply order. Let us assume that the supply order information is to contain the company name, a description of the item ordered, its price, and the quantity ordered. The record for each faculty member, with SupplyOrder as a record within a record, can be visualized as shown in Figure 12.10.

Let's now look at how such a record can be declared. One possible method is

```
TYPE
   String20 = PACKED ARRAY [1..20] OF char;
   String12 = PACKED ARRAY [1..12] OF char;
   OrderInfo = RECORD
                  CompanyName : String20;
                  Item : String20;
```

FIGURE 12.10
Illustration of a nested record

Faculty

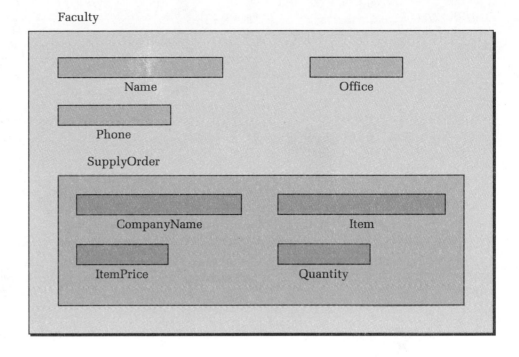

```
                        ItemPrice : real;
                        Quantity : integer
                   END;  {  of RECORD OrderInfo  }
         FacultyInfo = RECORD
                        Name : String20;
                        Office : integer;
                        Phone : String12;
                        SupplyOrder : OrderInfo
                   END;  {  of RECORD FacultyInfo  }
     VAR
       Faculty : FacultyInfo;
```

We must now consider how to access fields in the nested record. We do this by continuing our notation for field designators. Thus,

```
Faculty.Name
Faculty.Office
Faculty.Phone
```

refer to the first three fields of Faculty, and

```
Faculty.SupplyOrder.CompanyName
Faculty.SupplyOrder.Item
Faculty.SupplyOrder.ItemPrice
Faculty.SupplyOrder.Quantity
```

are used to access fields of the nested record

```
Faculty.SupplyOrder
```

Using WITH . . . DO

As expected, **WITH . . . DO** can be used with nested records. Let us consider the problem of assigning data to the various fields of Faculty as previously declared. If we wish to have values assigned as in Figure 12.11, we can use the following assignment statements.

FIGURE 12.11
Values in fields of a nested record

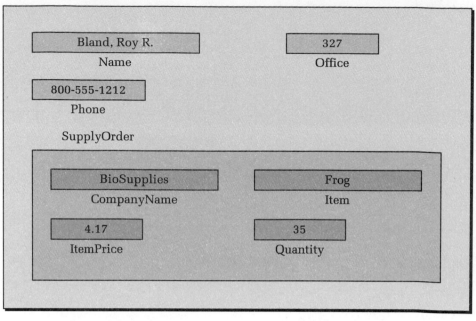

```
WITH Faculty DO
  BEGIN
    Name := 'Bland Roy R.          ';
    Office := 327;
    Phone := '800-555-1212';
    SupplyOrder.CompanyName := 'BioSupplies          ';
    SupplyOrder.Item := 'Frog                 ';
    SupplyOrder.ItemPrice := 4.17;
    SupplyOrder.Quantity := 35
  END;
```

Note that the last four assignment statements all used fields in the record SupplyOrder. Thus, a **WITH . . . DO** statement can be used there as follows:

```
WITH Faculty DO
  BEGIN
    Name := 'Bland Roy R.          ';
    Office := 327;
    Phone := '800-555-1212';
    WITH SupplyOrder DO
      BEGIN
        CompanyName := 'BioSupplies          ';
        Item := 'Frog                 ';
        ItemPrice := 4.17;
        Quantity := 35
      END  {  of WITH SupplyOrder DO  }
  END;  {  of WITH Faculty DO  }
```

There is yet a third way to accomplish our task. **WITH . . . DO** can be used with both the main record name and the nested record name as follows:

```
WITH Faculty, SupplyOrder DO
  BEGIN
    Name := 'Bland Roy R.          ';
    Office := 327;
    Phone := '800-555-1212';
    CompanyName := 'BioSupplies          ';
```

```
      Item := 'Frog              ';
      ItemPrice := 4.17;
      Quantity := 35
   END;  {  WITH...DO  }
```

Since SupplyOrder is nested within Faculty, each reference is distinctly identified and the fragment accomplishes our objective. When using nested records, you must be careful to identify fields distinctly. To illustrate, suppose Faculty1 and Faculty2 are also of type FacultyInfo. Then each of the following is valid.

```
Faculty1.Name := Faculty2.Name;
Faculty1.SupplyOrder.Item := Faculty2.SupplyOrder.Item;
Faculty1.SupplyOrder := Faculty2.SupplyOrder;
```

Note that in the third statement, you are transferring the contents of an entire record. This statement is valid because both records are of type OrderInfo.

To illustrate some attempts to use inappropriate designators, assume Faculty, Faculty1, and Faculty2 are of type FacultyInfo. Consider the following inappropriate references.

```
Faculty.Item := 'Frog                 '; { Incorrect }
```

In this designator, the intermediate descriptor is missing. Thus, something like

```
Faculty.SupplyOrder.Item
```

is needed. In

```
SupplyOrder.Quantity := 35; { Incorrect }
```

no reference is made to which record is being accessed. A record name must be stated, such as

```
Faculty1.SupplyOrder.Quantity
```

As our final example of working with nested records, let's write a procedure to get data from a data file for a record of type FacultyInfo with the following definitions and declarations.

```
TYPE
   String20 = PACKED ARRAY [1..20] OF char;
   String12 = PACKED ARRAY [1..12] OF char;
   OrderInfo = RECORD
                  CompanyName : String20;
                  Item: String20;
                  ItemPrice : real;
                  Quantity : integer
               END;  {  of RECORD OrderInfo  }
   FacultyInfo = RECORD
                    Name : String20;
                    Office : 100..399;
                    Phone : String12;
                    SupplyOrder : OrderInfo
                 END;  {  of RECORD FacultyInfo  }
VAR
   Faculty : FacultyInfo;
```

If we assume the data for a faculty member are on two lines of the data file as

| (line 1) | Bland, Roy R.   327 800-555-1212 |

| (line 2) | BioSupplies   Frog   4.17 35 |

Impact of Computers on Art

Dana J. Lamb recently discussed the impact of computers on the arts in an article appearing in *Academic Computing*. Among other things, she reported part of a conversation held with Alice Jones, a freelance graphic designer, who was a member of a summer arts program studying developments in full-color graphics on personal computers. When Jones was asked about the use of computers in her professional pursuits, she indicated her study led her to believe that the time required to produce a typical paste-up could be reduced by as much as 75 percent, depending on the proficiency of the graphic artist. She pointed out that the traditional means of production art required the teamwork of a graphic artist, typesetter, copy camera operator, photographer, and/or illustrator. The logistics of even the simplest paste-up with a few black and white photographs often required days in transit as copy was typeset at one location; photos and illustrations created, then reduced or enlarged at two other locations; and all traveling from each place of business to another while the graphic designer sits waiting. Jones observed that this dispersion of design components has been suddenly unified and put into the hands of the designer.

Later in the article, Lamb addressed the issue of how artists perceive the computer. According to Lamb, the opinions of those in the art world can be divided into three major groups:

1. those who deny that the computer has any legitimate place in the creation of art;
2. those who believe that the computer should be included in the realm of traditional and/or nontraditional tools in the creation of art; and
3. those who believe that the computer, together with its fundamental structure, is an art medium unto itself.

Lamb concluded her article with the following paragraph:

It is easy to forget that we are witnessing the infancy of this medium in relationship to the arts because of its phenomenal growth in eight years. Artists have been using computers since the 1950s but up to the last decade were viewed as oddities with few arenas to exhibit or share their work. Those days are over, and as the image of these machines becomes less a philosophical issue and simply another tool in the creative process, we can move on to develop the "clear path" between the visual concept and final product espoused.

a procedure to obtain this data is

```
PROCEDURE GetData (VAR Faculty : FacultyInfo);
  VAR
    J : integer;
    Blank : char;
  BEGIN
    WITH Faculty, SupplyOrder DO
      BEGIN
        FOR J := 1 TO 20 DO
          read (Name[J]);
        read (Office);
        read (Blank);  {  Move the pointer  }
        FOR J := 1 TO 12 DO
          read (Phone[J]);
        readln;  {  Go to beginning of the next line  }

{  Now read the second line  }

        FOR J := 1 TO 20 DO
          read (CompanyName[J]);
        FOR J := 1 TO 20 DO
          read (Item[J]);
        readln (ItemPrice, Quantity)
      END  {  of WITH Faculty, SupplyOrder DO  }
  END;  {  of PROCEDURE GetData  }
```

This procedure is called from the main program by

```
GetData (Faculty);
```

Array of Records

Next we will use structured data types to look at an *array of records*. It is easy to imagine needing to make a list of information about several people, events, or items. Furthermore, it is not unusual for the information about a particular person, event, or item to consist of several different data items. When this situation occurs, a record can be defined for each person, event, or item and an array of these records can be used to achieve the desired result. In such situations, you can frequently use an array of records rather than a parallel array.

For example, suppose the local high school sports boosters want you to write a program to enable them to keep track of the names and donations of its members. Assume there is a maximum of 50 members making a donation. This problem was solved in Chapter 10 using parallel arrays; it can now be solved by using an array of records. Each record will have two fields: the donor's name and the amount donated. The record could be visualized as shown in Figure 12.12.

FIGURE 12.12
Fields in TempDonor

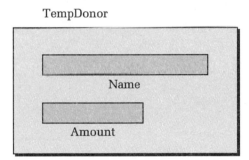

TempDonor

We will now declare an array of these records to produce the arrangement shown in Figure 12.13. The definitions and declarations needed are

```
CONST
   ClubSize = 50;
TYPE
   String20 = PACKED ARRAY [1..20] OF char;
   MemberInfo = RECORD
                   Name : String20;
                   Amount : real
                END;  { of RECORD MemberInfo }
   DonorList = ARRAY [1..ClubSize] OF MemberInfo;
VAR
   Donor : DonorList;
   TempDonor : MemberInfo;
   Count : integer;
```

Before proceeding, note the following:

1. Structures are built in the **TYPE** definition section to facilitate later work with procedures and functions.
2. Each record is now an array element and can be accessed by a reference to the index. Thus, if the third member's name is Tom Jones and he donates $100.00, you can write

```
Donor[3].Name := 'Jones Tom            ';
Donor[3].Amount := 100.0;
```

FIGURE 12.13
Illustration of an array of
records

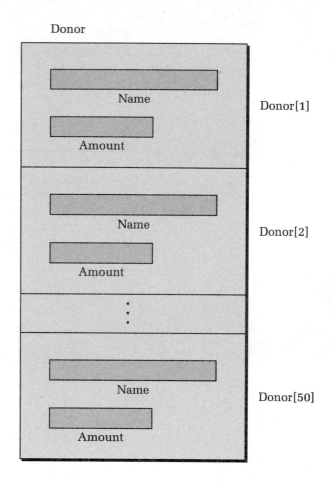

Better still, you can use **WITH . . . DO** to get

```
WITH Donor[3] DO
  BEGIN
    Name := 'Jones Tom           ';
    Amount := 100.0
  END;  {  of WITH...DO  }
```

3. Since all records in an array are of identical type, contents of two
   records can be interchanged by

```
TempDonor := Donor[J];
Donor[J] := Donor[K];
Donor[K] := TempDonor;
```

This is needed if records are to be sorted by one of their fields.

4. Be careful with syntax when using an array of records or an array as
   a field within a record. For example, if an array of five scores has
   been defined as a field in an array of records as shown in Figure
   12.14, note the following distinctions:

FIGURE 12.14
Array of records

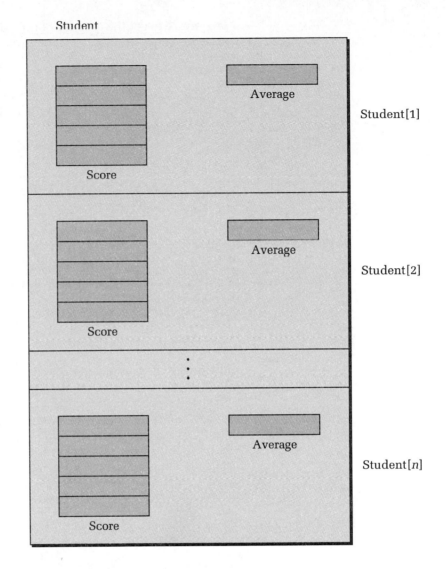

a. Student[2].Average   (Average for student 2)
b. Student[2].Score[4]   (Score on test 4 for student 2)
c. Student.Score[2]   (Not defined; student is an array)

Let's now return to the problem posed by the sports boosters. A first-level pseudocode design is

1. Get the data
2. Sort alphabetically by name
3. Print the sorted list

If we assume each line of the data file is of the form

Jones Tom   100.0

a procedure to get the data is not difficult. We have to remember, however, to count the actual number of donors read. Such a procedure is

```
PROCEDURE GetData (VAR Donor : DonorList;
                        VAR Count : integer);
   VAR
     J : integer;
   BEGIN
     Count := 0;
     WHILE NOT eof AND (Count < ClubSize) DO
       BEGIN
         Count := Count + 1;
         WITH Donor[Count] DO
           BEGIN
             FOR J := 1 TO 20 DO
               read (Name[J]);
             readln (Amount)
           END  {  of WITH Donor[Count] DO  }
       END  {  of WHILE NOT eof  }
   END;  {  of PROCEDURE GetData  }
```

This procedure is called from the main program by

```
GetData (Donor, Count);
```

and Count will contain the actual number of donors after the procedure is called.

The next procedure in this problem will require a sort. A sort which actually exchanges entire records is not very efficient. When working with an array of records, it is more efficient to use an *index sort*, which essentially uses a separate array to reorder the indices in the desired order. However, the formal development of this sorting technique is not covered here; it is deferred to a subsequent course. Therefore, for now, recall the selection sort developed in Chapter 10 as follows:

```
FOR J := 1 TO N-1 DO                  {  Find the minimum N-1 times  }
   BEGIN
     Index := J;
     FOR K := J + 1 TO N DO
       IF A[K] < A[Index] THEN        {  Find smallest number        }
         Index := K;
     IF Index <> J THEN
       BEGIN
         Temp := A[Index];
         A[Index] := A[J];
         A[J] := Temp
       END {  of exchange  }
   END; {  of one pass  }
```

With suitable changes, the array of records can be sorted alphabetically by

```
PROCEDURE Sort (VAR Donor : DonorList;
                    Count : integer);
   VAR
     J, K, Index : integer;
     Temp : MemberInfo;
```

```
BEGIN
  FOR J := 1 TO Count-1 DO
    BEGIN
      Index := J;
      FOR K := J + 1 TO Count DO
        IF Donor[K].Name < Donor[Index].Name THEN
          Index := K;
      IF Index <> J THEN
        BEGIN
          Temp := Donor[Index];
          Donor[Index] := Donor[J];
          Donor[J] := Temp
        END  {  of exchange  }
    END  {  of FOR loop  }
END;  {  of PROCEDURE Sort  }
```

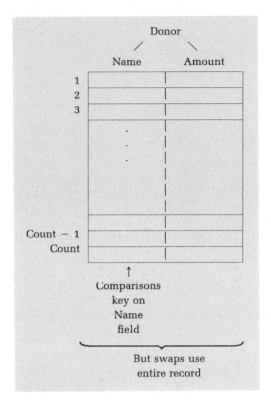

This procedure would be called from the main program by

```
Sort (Donor, Count);
```

In this procedure, note that the sort is by only one field in the record, specifically, the donor's name

```
IF Donor[K].Name < Donor[Index].Name THEN
```

However, when the names are to be exchanged, contents of the entire record are exchanged by

```
Temp := Donor[Index];
```

We conclude this example by writing a procedure to print the results. If we want the output to be

```
                      Local Sports Boosters
                         Donation List
          ----------------------------------------

              Name                        Amount
              ----                        ------

          Anerice Sue                     150.00
          Compton John                    125.00
                   .                         .
                   .                         .
                   .                         .
```

a procedure to produce this is

```
PROCEDURE PrintList (VAR Donor : DonorList;
                         Count : integer);
  CONST
    Skip = ' ' ;
  VAR
    J : integer;
  BEGIN
    writeln;
    writeln (Skip:20, 'Local Sports Boosters');
    writeln (Skip:24, 'Donation List');
    writeln (Skip:10, '----------------------------------------');
    writeln;
    writeln (Skip:13, 'Name', Skip:27, 'Amount');
    writeln (Skip:13, '----', Skip:27, '------');
    writeln;

  {  Now print the list  }

    FOR J := 1 TO Count DO
      WITH Donor[J] DO
        writeln (Skip:10, Name, Amount:20:2);
    writeln
  END;  {  of PROCEDURE PrintList  }
```

With these three procedures available, the main program is then

```
    BEGIN  {  Main program  }
      GetData (Donor, Count);
      Sort (Donor, Count);
      PrintList (Donor, Count)
    END.  { of main program  }
```

This example is less involved than many of your problems will be, but it does illustrate an array of records, appropriate notation for fields in an array of records, sorting an array of records by using one field of the records, and using procedures with an array of records.

Exercises 12.3

1. Consider the declaration

```
    TYPE
      B = RECORD
            C : real;
            D : integer
          END;
      A = RECORD
            E : boolean;
            F : B
          END;
    VAR
      G : A;
```

a. Give a schematic representation of the record G.

b. Indicate which of the following are valid references.

    i. `G.E`

    ii. `G.C`

    iii. `G.F.D`

    iv. `F.D`

    v. `G.A`

    vi. `A.F.C`

    vii. `A.E`

    viii. `WITH G DO`

    ix. `WITH G, F DO`

    x. `G.F.C`

c. Why would it be incorrect to define record A before record B?

2. Write a test program that illustrates the difference between an array of records and a record with an array component.

3. Give an appropriate definition and declaration for a record that will contain fields for a person's name, address, social security number, annual income, and family information. Address is a record with fields for street address, city, state abbreviation, and zip code. Family information is a record with fields for marital status (S, M, W, or D) and number of children.

4. Consider the following definitions and subsequent declarations.

```
TYPE
   String20 = PACKED ARRAY [1..20] OF char;
   Mood = (Quiet, Bright, Surly);
   CurrentHealth = (Poor, Average, Good);
   PatientStatus = RECORD
                      Mental : Mood;
                      Physical : CurrentHealth
                   END;   {  of RECORD PatientStatus  }
   PatientInfo = RECORD
                    Name : String20;
                    Status : PatientStatus;
                    PastDue : boolean
                 END;   { of RECORD PatientInfo }
VAR
   Patient1, Patient2 : PatientInfo;
```

a. Give a schematic representation for Patient1.

b. Show how a single letter (Q, B, or S) can be read from a data file and then have the appropriate value assigned to Patient1.Status.Mental.

c. Write a procedure to read a line of data and assign (if necessary) appropriate values to the various fields. A typical data line is

```
Smith Sue          BAF
```

and indicates that Sue Smith's mood is bright, her health is average, and her account is not past due.

5. Declare an array of records to be used for 15 players on a basketball team. The following information is needed for each player: name, age, height, weight, scoring average, and rebounding average.

6. Declare an array of records to be used for students in a classroom (at most 40 students). Each record should contain fields for a student's name, social security number, ten quiz scores, three test scores, overall average, and letter grade.

7. Consider the following declaration of an array of records.

```
CONST
  ClassSize = 35;
TYPE
  String20 = PACKED ARRAY [1..20] OF char;
  Attendance = (Excellent, Average, Poor);
  TestList = ARRAY [1..4] OF integer;
  StudentInfo = RECORD
                  Name : String20;
                  Atten : Attendance;
                  Test : TestList;
                  Aver : real
                END;
  StudentList = ARRAY [1..ClassSize] OF StudentInfo;
VAR
  Student : StudentList;
```

a. Give a schematic representation for Student.

b. Explain what the following function accomplishes.

```
FUNCTION GuessWhat (Test : TestList) : real;
  VAR
    K, Sum : integer;
  BEGIN
    Sum := 0;
    FOR K := 1 TO 4 DO
      Sum := Sum + Test[K];
    GuessWhat := Sum / 4
  END;
```

c. Write a procedure to print out the information for one student. In this procedure, the entire word describing attendance is to be printed.

8. Reconsider the problem in this section that kept a record of the name and amount donated for each member of the local high school boosters club. Expanding on that problem, write a procedure or function for each of the following.

a. Find the maximum donation and print out the amount together with the donor's name.

b. Find the sum of all donations.

c. Find the average of all donations.

d. Sort the array according to size of the donation, largest first.

■ ■ ■ ■

■ 12.4
Record Variants

OBJECTIVES

- to be able to define a record with a variant part
- to be able to use a record that contains a variant part

You should have noticed by now that when records are defined, each record has certain fixed fields. Since it is sometimes desirable to use a record structure in which the number and type of fields vary, Pascal allows records to be defined with a *variant part*. For example, a real estate company might want the records for their customers to contain different information depending on whether the property for sale is a house or a business. For houses, the number of bedrooms, bathrooms, and whether or not there is a fireplace could be indicated; for businesses, the number of offices and amount of possible rental income could be listed.

Defining a Variant Part

In order to define the variant part of a record, we use a form of the **CASE** statement to specify which fields should be included. Then, depending on the value of the identifier in the **CASE** part of the definition, the desired fields are listed. In the real estate example, we could have

```
TYPE
  PropertyType = (House, Business);
  Listing = RECORD
                CASE Kind : PropertyType OF
                  House    : (NumBedrms : integer;
                              NumBaths : integer;
                              Fireplace : boolean);
                  Business : (NumOffices : integer;
                              RentalIncome : integer)
              END;  {  of RECORD Listing  }
VAR
  Property : Listing;
```

Now Property is a record with a variant part. Kind is not a reserved word and is called the *tag field*. Depending on the value assigned to Kind, the appropriate fields are available. If the assignment

```
Property.Kind := House;
```

is made, the record can be envisioned as shown in Figure 12.15(a). If the assignment

```
Property.Kind := Business;
```

is made, we have the record illustrated in Figure 12.15(b).

FIGURE 12.15
Fields in a variant record

(a)   Property

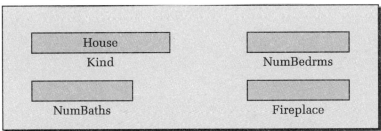

(b)   Property

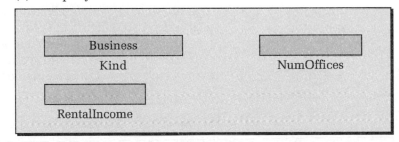

In actual practice, records with variant parts usually have fixed parts also. Suppose the address and price of each property listed for sale should be included. Since fields for these would be defined for every record, these fields would be referred to as the *fixed part*. A complete definition is as follows:

```
TYPE
  PropertyType = (House, Business);
  String30 = PACKED ARRAY [1..30] OF char;
  Listing = RECORD
                Address : String30;          }  fixed
                Price : integer;             }  part
```

```
                CASE Kind : PropertyType OF
                   House    : (NumBedrms : integer;
                               NumBaths : integer;
                               Fireplace : boolean);        variant
                   Business : (NumOffices : integer;        part
                               RentalIncome : integer)
                END;  {  of RECORD Listing  }
     VAR
       Property : Listing;
```

The following points concerning variant parts should now be made.

1. The variant part of a record must be listed after the fixed part.
2. Only one variant part can be defined in a record.
3. The data type for the tag field must be ordinal.
4. Only one **END** is used to terminate the definition. This terminates both **CASE** and **RECORD**.

Records with variant parts are defined by a form as follows:

⟨record name⟩ = **RECORD**
     ⟨field 1⟩ : ⟨type⟩;
     ⟨field 2⟩ : ⟨type⟩;
       .
       .   fixed
       .   part
     ⟨field *n*⟩ : ⟨type⟩;
     CASE ⟨tag field⟩ : ⟨tag type⟩ **OF**
       ⟨value 1⟩ : (⟨field list⟩);
       ⟨value 2⟩ : (⟨field list⟩);
        .
        .   variant
        .   part
      ⟨value *m*⟩ : (⟨field list⟩)
    END;

It is possible to completely avoid the use of variant parts of a record. One can list all possible fields in the fixed part and then use them appropriately. However, this usually means that more storage is required. To illustrate, let's consider how memory is allocated. For each field in the fixed part of the previous example, an area in memory is reserved as follows:

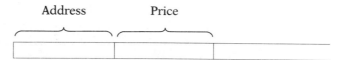

For the variant part of the record, a single area is reserved that will subsequently be utilized by whichever fields are determined by the value of the tag field. In this sense, they overlap as indicated.

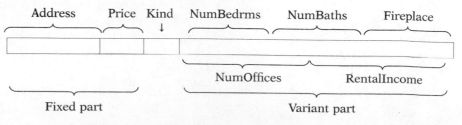

A note of caution is in order for those who include variant records as part of programs. Careful programming is needed to properly initialize the variant part or unexpected results may be obtained. For example, using the previous illustration, suppose Kind is first House with values for NumBedrms, NumBaths, and Fireplace. If a subsequent value of Kind is Business and no new data are read or assigned, the value of NumOffices may in fact be NumBedrms.

We close this section with an example that illustrates a definition and subsequent use of a record with a variant part.

■ **EXAMPLE 12.3**

Define a record to be used when working with plane geometric figures. The record should have fixed fields for the type of figure (a single character designator) and area. The variant part should have fields for information needed to compute the area. After the record is defined, write a procedure to get data from a line of the data file. Then write a function that can be used to compute the area of the plane figure.

To complete the definition of the record, let's assume we are working with at most the geometric figures circle, square, and triangle (C, S, and T, respectively). An appropriate definition is

```
TYPE
   FigureShape = (Circle, Square, Triangle);
   FigureInfo = RECORD
                   Object : char;
                   Area : real;
                   CASE Shape : FigureShape OF
                      Circle   : (Radius : real);
                      Square   : (Side : real);
                      Triangle : (Base, Height : real)
                END;  {  of RECORD FigureInfo  }
VAR
   Figure : FigureInfo;
```

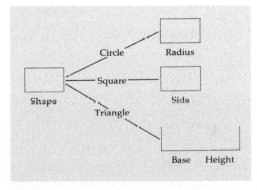

Each data line has a single character designating the kind of figure followed by appropriate information needed to compute the area. For example,

    T 6.0 8.0

represents a triangle with base 6.0 and height 8.0. A procedure to get a line of data is

```
                    PROCEDURE GetData (VAR Figure : FigureInfo);
                      BEGIN
                        WITH Figure DO
                          BEGIN
                            read (Object);
                            CASE Object OF
                              'C' : BEGIN
                                      Shape := Circle;
                                      readln (Radius)
                                    END;
                              'S' : BEGIN
                                      Shape := Square;
                                      readln (Side)
                                    END;
                              'T' : BEGIN
                                      Shape := Triangle;
                                      readln (Base, Height)
                                    END
                            END { of CASE Object }
                        END { of WITH...DO }
                    END; { of PROCEDURE GetData }
```

This is called from the main program by

```
   GetData (Figure);
```

Finally, a function to compute the area is

```
   FUNCTION ComputeArea (Figure : FigureInfo) : real;
     CONST
       Pi = 3.14159;
     BEGIN
       WITH Figure DO
         BEGIN
           CASE Shape OF
             Circle   : ComputeArea := Pi * Radius * Radius;
             Square   : ComputeArea := Side * Side;
             Triangle : ComputeArea := 0.5 * Base * Height
           END { of CASE Shape }
         END   {of WITH...DO }
     END; { of FUNCTION ComputeArea }
```

This function is called by

```
   Figure.Area := ComputeArea(Figure);
```

Exercises 12.4

1. Explain how memory may be saved when records with variant parts are declared.

2. Assume a record is defined by

```
   TYPE
     TagType = (One, Two);
     Info = RECORD
              Fixed : integer;
              CASE Tag : TagType OF
                One : (A, B : integer);
                Two : (X : real;
                       Ch : char)
            END;
```

and the variable declaration section of a program includes

```
   VAR
     RecordCheck : Info;
```

ıt is the output from the following fragment of code?

```
H RecordCheck DO
EGIN
  Fixed := 1000;
  Tag := One;
  A := 100;
  B := 500;
  writeln (Fixed:15, A:15, B:15);
  Tag := Two;
  X := 10.5;
  Ch := 'Y';
  writeln (Fixed:15, X:15.2, Ch:15);
  writeln (A:15, B:15, X:15:2, Ch:15)
END;
```

3.   nd all errors in the following definitions.

a.
```
TYPE
  Info = RECORD
            A : real;
            CASE Tag : TagType OF
              B : (X, Y : real);
              C : (Z : boolean)
          END;
```

b.
```
TYPE
  TagType = (A, B, C);
  Info = RECORD
            D : integer;
            Flag : boolean;
            CASE Tag : TagType OF
              A : (X, Y : real);
              B : (Z : real)
          END;
```

c.
```
TYPE
  TagType = (A, B, C);
  Info = RECORD
            D : integer;
            Flag : boolean
            CASE Tag OF
              A : (X : real);
              B : (Y : real);
              C : (Z : real)
          END;
```

d.
```
TYPE
  TagType = (A, B, C);
  Info = RECORD
            D : integer;
            CASE Tag1 : TagType OF
              A : (X : real);
              B : (Y : real);
              C : (Z : real)
            END; {  of CASE  }
            CASE Tag2 : TagType OF
              A : (X1 : real);
              B : (Y1 : real);
              C : (Z1 : real)
          END; {  of RECORD Info  }
```

4. Redefine the following record without using a variant part.

```
TYPE
    Shapes = (Circle, Square, Triangle);
    FigureInfo = RECORD
                    Object : char;
                    Area : real;
                    CASE Shape : Shapes OF
                      Circle   : (Radius : real);
                      Square   : (Side : real);
                      Triangle : (Base, Height : real)
                 END;
VAR
    Figure : FigureInfo;
```

5. Using the record defined in Exercise 4, indicate the names of the fields available and provide an illustration of these fields after each of the following assignments is made.

a. `Shape := Circle;`

b. `Shape := Square;`

c. `Shape := Triangle;`

6. Redefine the record defined in Exercise 4 to include rectangles and parallelograms.

7. Define a record with a variant part to be used for working with various publications. For each record, there should be fields for the author, title, and date. If the publication is a book, there should be fields for the publisher and city. If the publication is an article, there should be fields for the journal name and volume number.

■ ■ ■ ■

A NOTE OF INTEREST

Artist of Interface

Millions of people encounter the graphic art of Susan Kare every day and many more will experience her unusual work in the months ahead. Her carefully crafted images have won a place among the cultural symbols of our age, yet few people have any idea who she is or where her work can be seen.

Only a handful of industry insiders know that Kare is the artist responsible for the graphic appearance of some of the country's best-known computer software. Based in San Francisco, she designed most of the distinctive icons, typefaces and other graphic elements that gave the original Macintosh computer its characteristic—and widely emulated—appearance. Many consider her to be the mother of the famous Macintosh trash can.

Since then, Kare has parlayed her initial work for Apple Computer Inc. into a full-time business, designing graphical user interfaces, or GUIs, for computer companies and software developers. The user interface is the software that allows an operator to control a personal computer and direct its functions. A decade ago, most interfaces forced the user to type cryptic commands in a blank space on the display.

With the introduction of the Macintosh in 1984, Apple pushed the world toward the graphic interface, which provides greater ease of use. A graphic interface allows an operator to control the computer by manipulating symbols displayed on its monitor, usually with a mouse or trackball.

The growing demand for graphical user interfaces has forced Kare to turn down work. She has rejected potential clients in part because she refuses to hire people to share the work load. "I do every job myself because I think of it as an art," she said. She works almost entirely on a computer, shunning traditional artist's tools for their electronic successors. "Anything that's bound for the screen, I do on the screen," she said. If there is a secret to her work, it is simplicity, restraint and common sense.

FOCUS ON
PROGRAM DESIGN

The sample program for this chapter features working with an array of records. The array is first sorted using the field containing a name. It is then sorted using the field containing a real number.

Let's write a program to help your local high school sports boosters keep records of donors and amounts donated. The data file consists of a name (first 20 positions) and an amount donated (starting in position 21) on each line. For example,

Jones Jerry   250

Your program should get the data from the data file and read it into a record for each donor. Output should consist of two lists as follows:

1. alphabetical listing together with the amount donated.
2. a listing sorted according to the amount donated.

A first-level pseudocode development for this problem is

1.   Get the data
2.   Sort by name
3.   Print the first list
4.   Sort by amount
5.   Print the second list

Module specifications for the main modules are

1. GetData Module
   Data received: None
   Information returned: Array of records containing names, amounts,
                      and array length
   Logic: Use a **WHILE NOT eof** loop with a counter to read the data file.

2. SortByName Module
   Data received: Unsorted array of records containing names and
                      amounts with the list length
   Information returned: An alphabetized list of names with associated
                      amounts
   Logic: Use a selection sort to sort the array of records.

3. PrintList Module
   Data received: Array of records
                      Array length
   Information returned: None
   Logic: Call procedure PrintHeading.
              Use a loop to print the names and amounts.

4. SortByAmount Module
   Data received: Array of records sorted alphabetically
                      List length
   Information returned: Array of records sorted by size of donation
   Logic: Use a selection sort to sort the list of donations.

A refinement of the pseudocode yields

1.   Get the data
     WHILE NOT eof DO
     1.1   get a name
     1.2   get the amount

2. Sort by name (use selection sort)
3. Print the first list
   3.1 print a heading
   3.2 print the names and amounts
4. Sort by amount (use selection sort)
5. Print the second list
   5.1 print a heading
   5.2 print the names and amounts

A complete structure chart is given in Figure 12.16.

FIGURE 12.16
Structure chart for boosters
problem

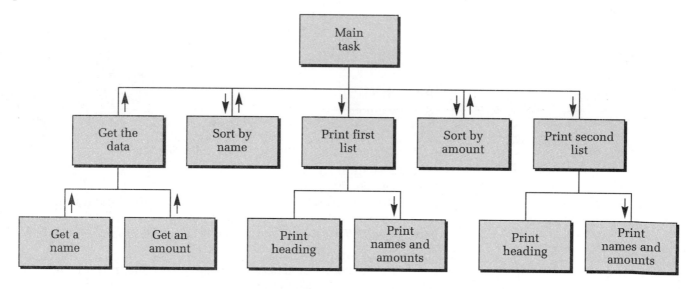

The main driver for the program is

```
BEGIN  {  Main program  }
  GetData (Donor, Count);
  SortByName (Donor, Count);
  PrintList (Donor, Count);
  SortByAmount (Donor, Count);
  PrintList (Donor, Count)
END.  {  of main program  }
```

A complete program for this problem is

```
PROGRAM Boosters (input, output, Data);

{  This program uses an array of records to process information  }
{  for donors to the local high school sports boosters.  Output  }
{  includes two lists, one  sorted by name and  one sorted  by  }
{  amount donated. Information is stored in the text file data.  }

CONST
  ClubSize = 50;

TYPE
  String20 = PACKED ARRAY [1..20] OF char;
  MemberInfo = RECORD
```

```
                        Name : String20;
                        Amount : real
                   END;  {  of RECORD MemberInfo  }
      DonorList = ARRAY [1..ClubSize] OF MemberInfo;

   VAR
     Count : integer;       {  Counter for number of donors        }
     Donor : DonorList;     {  Array of records, one for each donor }
     Data : text;           {  Data file of names and amounts       }


{********************************************************************** }

PROCEDURE GetData (VAR Donor : DonorList;
                   VAR Count : integer);

   {  Given:    Nothing                                              }
   {  Task:     Read donor names and amounts from the text file,     }
   {                 Data, into an array of records                  }
   {  Return:  An array of records and number of donors             }

   VAR
     J : integer;

   BEGIN
     Count := 0;
     WHILE NOT eof(Data) AND (Count < ClubSize) DO
       BEGIN
         Count := Count + 1;
         WITH Donor[Count] DO
           BEGIN
             FOR J := 1 TO 20 DO
               read (Data, Name[J]);
             readln (Data, Amount)
           END  {  of WITH...DO  }
       END;  {  of WHILE NOT eof  }
     IF NOT eof(Data) THEN
       writeln ('Not all data read.')
   END;  {  of PROCEDURE GetData  }


{********************************************************************** }

PROCEDURE SortByName (VAR Donor : DonorList;
                      Count : integer);

   {  Given:    An array of records and number of records           }
   {  Task:     Sort alphabetically by the field Donor[J].Name       }
   {  Return:  An alphabetized array of records                     }

   VAR
     J, K, Index : integer;
     Temp : MemberInfo;

   BEGIN
     FOR J := 1 TO Count - 1 DO
       BEGIN
         Index := J;
         FOR K := J + 1 TO Count DO
           IF Donor[K].Name < Donor[Index].Name THEN
             Index := K;
         IF Index <> J THEN
```

1

2

```
              BEGIN
                Temp := Donor[Index];
                Donor[Index] := Donor[J];
                Donor[J] := Temp
              END  {  of exchange  }
        END  {  of FOR J loop  }
   END;  {  of PROCEDURE SortByName  }


  ***********************************************************}

PROCEDURE SortByAmount (VAR Donor : DonorList;
                            Count : integer);

   {  Given:    An array of records and number of records      }
   {  Task:     Sort by amount donated, Donor[J].Amount        }
   {  Return:   An array of records sorted by amount donated   }

   VAR
     J, K, Index : integer;
     Temp : MemberInfo;

   BEGIN
     FOR J := 1 TO Count - 1 DO
       BEGIN
         Index := J;
         FOR K := J + 1 TO Count DO
           IF Donor[K].Amount > Donor[Index].Amount THEN
             Index := K;
         IF Index <> J THEN
           BEGIN
             Temp := Donor[Index];
             Donor[Index] := Donor[J];
             Donor[J] := Temp
           END  {  of exchange  }
       END  {  of FOR J loop  }
   END;  {  of PROCEDURE SortByAmount  }


{*************************************************************** }

PROCEDURE PrintHeading;

   {  Given:    Nothing                                        }
   {  Task:     Print a heading for the output                 }
   {  Return:   Nothing                                        }

   CONST
     Skip = ' ';

   BEGIN
     writeln;
     writeln (Skip:20, 'Local Sports Boosters');
     writeln (Skip:24, 'Donation List');
     writeln (Skip:10, '----------------------------------------');
     writeln;
     writeln (Skip:13, 'Name', Skip:21, 'Amount');
     writeln (Skip:13, '----', Skip:21, '------');
     writeln
   END;  {  of PROCEDURE PrintHeading  }


{*************************************************************** }

PROCEDURE PrintList (VAR Donor : DonorList;
                         Count : integer);
```

```
{  Given:    An array of records and number of records          }
{  Task:     Print a list containing one column for the name    }
{                    and one column for the amount donated       }
{  Return:   Nothing                                             }

CONST
  Skip = ' ';

VAR
  J : integer;

BEGIN
  PrintHeading;
  FOR J := 1 TO Count DO
    WITH Donor[J] DO
      writeln (Skip:10, Name, Amount:14:2);
  writeln
END;  {  of PROCEDURE PrintList  }
```

```
{*********************************************************************** }

BEGIN  {  Main program  }
  Reset (Data);
  GetData (Donor, Count);
  SortByName (Donor, Count);
  PrintList (Donor, Count);
  SortByAmount (Donor, Count);
  PrintList (Donor, Count)
END.  {  of main program  }
```

The output from this program is

```
              Local Sports Boosters
                  Donation List
    ----------------------------------------

          Name                    Amount
          ----                    ------

    Alexander Candy               300.00
    Anderson Tony                 375.00
    Banks Marj                    375.00
    Born Patty                    100.00
    Brown Ron                     200.00
    Darnell Linda                 275.00
    Erickson Thomas               100.00
    Fox William                   300.00
    Francis Denise                350.00
    Generous George               525.00
    Gillette Mike                 350.00
    Hancock Kirk                  500.00
    Higgins Sam                   300.00
    Janson Kevin                  200.00
    Johnson Ed                    350.00
    Johnson Martha                400.00
    Jones Jerry                   250.00
    Kelly Marvin                  475.00
    Kneff Susan                   300.00
    Lasher John                   175.00
    Lyon Elizabeth                425.00
    Moore Robert                  100.00
    Muller Marjorie               250.00
    Smith John                    100.00
```

(List continued on next page)

```
Trost Frostie                          50.00
Trudo Rosemary                        200.00
Weber Sharon                          150.00
Williams Art                          350.00
Williams Jane                         175.00
Wilson Mary                           275.00


                    Local Sports Boosters
                       Donation List
          ------------------------------------------

                  Name                  Amount
                  ----                  ------

          Generous George              525.00
          Hancock Kirk                 500.00
          Kelly Marvin                 475.00
          Lyon Elizabeth               425.00
          Johnson Martha               400.00
          Anderson Tony                375.00
          Banks Marj                   375.00
          Francis Denise               350.00
          Gillette Mike                350.00
          Johnson Ed                   350.00
          Williams Art                 350.00
          Higgins Sam                  300.00
          Alexander Candy              300.00
          Kneff Susan                  300.00
          Fox William                  300.00
          Darnell Linda                275.00
          Wilson Mary                  275.00
          Muller Marjorie              250.00
          Jones Jerry                  250.00
          Trudo Rosemary               200.00
          Brown Ron                    200.00
          Janson Kevin                 200.00
          Lasher John                  175.00
          Williams Jane                175.00
          Weber Sharon                 150.00
          Erickson Thomas              100.00
          Born Patty                   100.00
          Smith John                   100.00
          Moore Robert                 100.00
          Trost Frostie                 50.00
```

RUNNING AND DEBUGGING TIPS

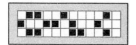

1. Be sure to use the full field name when working with fields in a record. You may only leave off the record name when using **WITH . . . DO**.

2. Terminate each record definition with an **END**. This is an instance when **END** is used without a **BEGIN**.

3. Although field names in different record types can be the same, you are encouraged to use distinct names. This enhances readability and reduces the chances of making errors.

4. Be careful with syntax when using an array of records or an array as a field within a record. For example, be able to distinguish between Student[K].Average, Student.Score[J], and Student[K].Score[J].

■ Summary

Key Terms

array of records	index sort	tag field
field	nested records	variant part
fixed part	record	

Keywords

RECORD   **WITH**

Key Concepts

- A **RECORD** is a structured data type that is a collection of fields; the fields may be treated as a whole or individually.
- Fields in a record can be of different data types.
- Records can be declared or defined by

  ⟨record name⟩ = **RECORD**

          ⟨field identifier 1⟩ : ⟨data type 1⟩;

          ⟨field identifier 2⟩ : ⟨data type 2⟩;

          .

          .

          .

          ⟨field identifier *n*⟩ : ⟨data type *n*⟩

      END;   {   of **RECORD** definition   }

- Fields can be accessed as variables by
  ⟨record name⟩.⟨field identifier⟩
- Records can be schematically represented as in Figure 12.17.

FIGURE 12.17
Fields in a record

⟨record name⟩

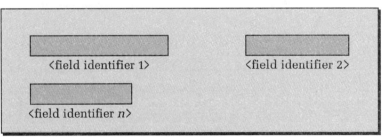

- **WITH** ⟨record name⟩ **DO** can be used instead of a specific reference to the record name with each field of a record; thus, you could have

```
WITH Student DO
  BEGIN
    Name := 'Smith John           ';
    Average := 93.4;
    Grade := 'A'
  END;
```

instead of

```
Student.Name := 'Smith John           ';
Student.Average := 93.4;
Student.Grade := 'A';
```

- If two records, A and B, are of identical type, contents of all fields of one may be assigned to corresponding fields of the other by a single assignment statement such as

```
A := B;
```

- Either entire records or fields within a record can be passed to appropriate sub-programs.
- A record may be used as a field in another record.
- A **WITH . . . DO** statement may be used to access fields of nested records.
- Records may be used as components of an array.
- An array of records may be sorted by one of the fields in each record.
- Records with variant parts list all fixed fields (if any) first and then list the variant fields using a **CASE** statement; for example,

```
TYPE
   MaritalStatus = (Married, Single, Divorced);
   String20 = PACKED ARRAY [1..20] OF char;
   Info = RECORD
               Name : String20;
               CASE Status : MaritalStatus OF
                  Married  : (SpouseName : String20;
                              NumKids : integer);
                  Single   : (Gender : char;
                              Age : integer);
                  Divorced : (NumKids : integer;
                              Age : integer;
                              Gender : char;
                              LivesAlone : boolean)
            END;  {  of RECORD Info  }
VAR
   Customer : Info;
```

- After a value has been assigned to a tag field, the remaining record fields are the ones listed in the **CASE** part of the definition; for example, if we use the previous definition and we have

```
Customer.Status := Divorced;
```

the record fields are as shown in Figure 12.18.

FIGURE 12.18
Value of a tag field

Customer

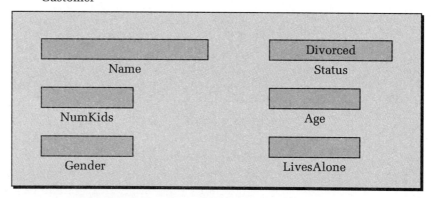

■ **Programming Problems and Projects**

1. Write a program to be used by the registrar of a university. The program should get information from a data file and the data for each student should include student name, student number, classification (1 for freshman, 2 for sophomore, 3 for junior, 4 for senior, or 7 for special student), hours completed, hours taking, and grade point average.

Output should include an alphabetical listing of all students, an alphabetical listing of students in each class, and a listing of all students ordered by grade point average.

2. Robert Day, basketball coach at Indiana College, wants you to write a program to help him analyze information about his basketball team. He wants a record for each player containing the player's name, position played, high school graduated from, height, scoring average, rebounding average, grade point average, and seasons of eligibility remaining.

   The program should read the information for each player from a data file. The output should include an alphabetized list of names together with other pertinent information, a list sorted according to scoring average, an alphabetized list of all players with a grade point average above 3.0, and an alphabetized list of high schools together with an alphabetized list of players who graduated from each school.

■ 3. Final grades in Dr. Lae Z. Programmer's (Problems 5, 22, and 23, Chapter 5; Problem 13, Chapter 6; Problem 7, Chapter 7; Problem 5, Chapter 9; and Problem 3, Chapter 11) computer science class are to be computed using the following course requirements.

Requirement	Possible Points
1. Quiz scores (ten points each and the best 10 out of 12 are counted)	100 points
2. Two hourly tests	200 points
3. Eight programming assignments (25 points each)	200 points
4. Test program assignments (two at 50 points each)	100 points
5. Final examination	100 points
Total	700 points

Cutoff percentages for the grades of A, B, C, D, and E are 90 percent, 80 percent, 70 percent, and 55 percent, respectively.

Write a program to keep a record of each student's name, social security number, quiz scores (all 12), hourly examination scores, programming assignment scores, test program scores, and final examination score.

Your program should read data from a data file, compute total points for each student, calculate the letter grade, and output results. The output should be sorted by total points from high to low and include all raw data, the ten best quiz scores, total points and percentage score, and letter grade. Use procedures and functions where appropriate.

4. Write a program to input an unknown number of pairs of fractions with an operation (either +, −, *, or /) between the fractions. The program should perform the operation on the fractions or indicate that the operation is impossible. Answers should be reduced to lowest terms.

Sample Input	Sample Output
3/4 + 5/6	$\dfrac{3}{4} + \dfrac{5}{6} = \dfrac{19}{12}$
4/9 - 1/6	$\dfrac{4}{9} - \dfrac{1}{6} = \dfrac{5}{18}$
4/5 / 0/2	$\dfrac{4}{5} / \dfrac{0}{2} = $ Impossible
4/3 + 7/0	$\dfrac{4}{3} + \dfrac{7}{0} = $ Impossible
6/5 * 20/3	$\dfrac{6}{5} * \dfrac{20}{3} = \dfrac{8}{1}$

5. Complex numbers are numbers of the form $a + bi$ where a and b are real and i represents $\sqrt{-1}$. Complex number arithmetic is defined by

Sum	$(a + bi) + (c + di) = (a + c) + (b + d)i$
Difference	$(a + bi) - (c + di) = (a - c) + (b - d)i$
Product	$(a + bi)(c + di) = (ac - bd) + (ad + bc)i$
Quotient	$(a + bi)/(c + di) = \dfrac{ac + bd}{c^2 + d^2} + \dfrac{bc - ad}{c^2 + d^2} i$

Write a program to be used to perform these calculations on two complex numbers. Each line of data consists of a single character designator (S, D, P, or Q) followed by four reals representing two complex numbers. For example, $(2 + 3i) + (5 - 2i)$ are represented by

```
S2 3 5 -2
```

A record should be used for each complex number. The output should be in the form $a + bi$.

■ 6. The Readmore Public Library wants a program to keep track of the books checked out. Information for each book should be kept in a record and the fields should include the author's name, a nonfiction designator (**boolean**), the title, the library catalog number, and the copyright date. Each customer can check out at most ten books.

Your program should read information from a data file and print two lists alphabetized by author name, one for nonfiction and the other for fiction. A typical data line is

```
Kidder Tracy    T Soul of a New Machine    81.6044 1982
                ↑                          ↑
                position 21                position 52
```

■ 7. Modify Problem 6 so that a daily printout is available that contains a summary of the day's transactions at the Readmore Public Library.

You will need a record for each customer containing the customer's name and library card number. Be sure to make provision for books that are returned.

8. Write a program to be used to keep track of bank accounts. Define a record that includes each customer's name, account number, starting balance, transaction record, and ending balance.

   The transaction record should list all deposits and withdrawals. A special message should be printed whenever there are insufficient funds for a withdrawal. When a name is read from the data file, all previous records should be searched to see if you are processing a new account. The final output for each customer should look like a typical bank statement.

9. Write a program that uses records to analyze poker hands. Each hand consists of five records (cards). Each record should have one field for the suit and one for the value. Rankings for the hands from high to low are

   straight flush
   four of a kind
   full house
   flush
   straight
   three of a kind
   two pair
   one pair
   none of the above

   Your program should read data for five cards from a data file, evaluate the hand, and print out the hand together with a message indicating its value.

10. Problem 9 can be modified several ways. A first modification is to compare two different hands using only the ranking indicated. A second (more difficult) modification is to also compare hands that have the same ranking. For example, a pair of 8s is better than a pair of 7s. Extend Problem 9 to incorporate some of these modifications.

11. Divers at the Olympics are judged by seven judges. Points for each dive are awarded according to the following procedure.
    a. Each judge assigns a score between 0.0 and 10.0 inclusive.
    b. The high score and low score are eliminated.
    c. The five remaining scores are summed and this total is multiplied by 0.6. This result is then multiplied by the degree of difficulty of the dive (0.0 to 3.0).

    The first level of competition consists of 24 divers each making ten dives. Divers with the 12 highest totals advance to the finals.

    Write a program to keep a record for each diver. Each record should contain information for all ten dives, the diver's name, and the total score. One round of competition consists of each diver making one dive. A typical line of data consists of the diver's name, degree of difficulty for the dive, and seven judges' scores. Part of your output should include a list of divers who advance to the finals.

12. The University Biology Department has a Conservation Club that works with the state Department of Natural Resources. Their project

for the semester is to help capture and tag migratory birds. You have been asked to write a computer program to help them store information. In general, the program must have information for each bird tagged entered interactively into an array of records and then stored in a text file for subsequent use. For each bird tagged, you need a field for the tag number, tagging site, sex, bird type, date, and name of the DNR officer doing the tagging. After all data have been entered, the program should print one list sorted by tag number and one sorted by bird type.

■ 13. Mrs. Crown, your computer science instructor, wishes to keep track of the maintenance record of her computers and has turned to you for help. She wants to keep track of the type of machine, its serial number (up to ten characters), the year of purchase, and a **boolean** variable indicating whether the machine is under service contract.

Write a program that permits the entry of records, then prints a list of the machines that are under warranty and a list of those not under warranty. Both lists should be arranged in order of serial number.

14. Most microcomputer owners soon develop a large, often unorganized, library of software on several floppy disks. This is your chance to help them. Define a record containing the disk number of each disk, and a list of up to 30 program titles on each disk. Write a program to read a text file containing the information for a disk and then print an alphabetized listing of the program titles on that disk.

15. Revise the program in Problem 14 to permit the user of the program to enter the program name desired, and have the program print the number of the disk(s) containing the program.

16. Write a program to read records containing the name, address, telephone number, and class of some of your friends. Print a list of the names of the students in the file who are in your class.

■ 17. The Falcon Manufacturing Company (Problem 22, Chapter 11) wishes to keep computerized records of its telephone-order customers. They want the name, street address, city, state, and zip code for each customer. They include either a "T" if the customer is a business, or an "F" if the customer is an individual. A 30-character description of each business is also included. An individual's credit limit is in the record.

Write a program to read the information for the customer from a text file and print a list of the information for businesses and a separate list of the information for individuals. There are no more than 50 records in the file.

18. Visit your local registrar and discuss how records of students are processed. Discover what data are kept in each record, how the data are entered, and what the fields of each record are. Have the registrar explain what operations are used with a student's record. Specifically, how is information added to or deleted from a record? Discuss the issue of sorting records. What kinds of lists must the registrar produce for those within the system who need information about students?

Prepare a written report of your visit for the class. Be sure to include a graphic that shows a student's record can be envisioned.

19. Select an unworked problem from the previously listed programming problems for this chapter. Construct a structure chart and write all documentary information necessary for this problem. Do not write code. When finished, have a classmate read your documentation to see if precisely what is to be done is clear.

CHAPTER

More about Files

Chapter 9 introduced the concept of text files that are used to provide data for a program and to store data between runs of a program. All data in a text file are stored as a sequence of characters of type **char.** We are now ready to examine these files in more detail.

But first, a note of caution is in order. File manipulation is extremely system dependent. This is especially true with microcomputers. Since it is likely that your system has some differences from standard Pascal, you are encouraged to consult your system manual.

T

■ 13.1
File Definition

Basic Idea and Notation

You can save information between runs of a program by using secondary storage devices such as tapes or disks (personal computers use floppy or hard disks). As a beginning programmer, you need not normally be concerned with the actual physical construct of these storage devices, but you do need to know how to work with them. To oversimplify, you need to be able to get data into a program, manipulate these data, and save the data (and results) for later use. For example, if you write a program that computes grades for students in a class, you need to periodically enter data for processing. Pascal solves this problem with a structured data type **FILE.** A *file* is a data structure that consists of a sequence of components all of the same type. A **FILE** data type is defined by

> **TYPE**
>   ⟨file identifier⟩ = **FILE OF** ⟨data type⟩;
> **VAR**
>   ⟨file name⟩ : ⟨file identifier⟩;

Thus, if you wish to work with a file of integers, you define

```
TYPE
  FileOfInt = FILE OF integer;
VAR
  File1 : FileOfInt;
```

In this case, File1 is the desired file. Several comments are now in order.

1. Data entries in a file are called *components of the file*.
2. All components of a file must be of the same data type.
3. The only data type not permitted as a component of a file is another file type. This differs from arrays in that

   ARRAY [ ] OF ARRAY [ ] OF ⟨data type⟩;

   is permitted, but

   FILE OF FILE OF ⟨data type⟩;

   is not permitted.

Each of the following is a valid definition of a file type.

```
TYPE
   Identifier1 = FILE OF real;
   Identifier2 = FILE OF ARRAY [1..20] OF integer;
   Identifier3 = FILE OF boolean;
```

Files of records are frequently used in programs. Thus, to keep a record for each student in a class, you could have the definition

```
TYPE
   String20 = PACKED ARRAY [1..20] OF char;
   ExamScores = ARRAY [1..4] OF integer;
   QuizScores = ARRAY [1..10] OF integer;
   StudentInfo = RECORD
                    Name : String20;
                    IDNumber : 0..999;
                    Exam : ExamScores;
                    Quiz : QuizScores;
                    Average : real;
                    Grade : char
                 END;  {  of RECORD StudentInfo  }
   StudentFile = FILE OF StudentInfo;
VAR
   Student : StudentFile;
```

There is a difference between a text file and a file of characters. Although a text file consists of a sequence of characters, it also has "lines" separated by end-of-line markers. A file of characters, which is of the type **FILE OF char,** does not have line separators.

Comparison to Arrays

Files and one-dimensional arrays have some similarities: both are structured data types and components must be of the same type. There are, however, some important differences.

1. Files permit you to store and retrieve information between runs of a program.
2. Only one component of a file is available at a time.
3. In standard versions of Pascal, files must be sequentially accessed; that is, when working with files, you start at the beginning and process the components in sequence. It is not possible (as with arrays) to access some component directly without first having somehow moved through the previous components.
4. Files do not have a defined length. Once a file has been defined, the number of components is limited only by the amount of storage

available. However, this is usually so large you could think of it as unbounded.

5. Files are stored in secondary storage; arrays are only stored in memory.

File Window and Buffer Variables

Before we get to specific work with files, we need to examine the concepts of a *file window* and a *buffer variable.* A file can be visualized as a sequence of components as follows:

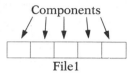

Only one of these components can be "seen" at a time. An imaginary window is associated with a file and values can be transferred to (or from) a component of the file only through this window. Thus, the window must be properly positioned before attempting to transmit data to or from a component.

This imaginary window, which is called a file window, has no name in Pascal. However, there is a related concept, called a buffer variable, that is the actual vehicle through which values are passed to or from the file component. When a file is declared in a program, a buffer variable is automatically declared and therefore available to the programmer. To illustrate, given the following declaration of FileA,

```
TYPE
  FileInfo = FILE OF integer;
VAR
  FileA : FileInfo;
```

the buffer variable (FileA^ or FileA↑) can be used in the program. The buffer variable is always the file name followed by a caret (^) or an up arrow (↑). Historically, the phrase "up arrow" has been used when referring to buffer variables. However, we will use the caret symbol when designating buffer variables because it is available on computer keyboards (above the 6).

The buffer variable is not declared in the variable declaration section. In general, we have

Declaration	Buffer Variable
VAR	
⟨file name⟩ : **FILE OF** ⟨data type⟩;	⟨file name⟩ ^

The buffer variable is of the same data type as one component of the file. It allows us to access data at the position of the file marker or pointer that was used when illustrating text files. Although its use is intended for passing values to and from a file, it can be used very much like a regularly declared variable of that type. Specifically, from FileA, FileA^ is a variable of type **integer** and statements such as

```
FileA^ := 21;
Age := FileA^;
GetData (FileA^);  (where GetData is a procedure)
```

are appropriate.

A NOTE OF INTEREST

Relational Databases

One advance in data management that has gained tremendously in popularity, and in fact is revolutionizing system development practices, is the increased use of the database management system, known as DBMS. An especially important development in database technology is the relational database.

The relational DBMS is based on the concept of multiple "flat files" that are "related" via common fields. A flat file is essentially a two-dimensional matrix of columns and rows where columns represent the fields contained in a record and rows contain different records. A simple example of the flat file concept is a spreadsheet such as Lotus 1-2-3, although the analogy is somewhat misleading since spreadsheets are most commonly used for purposes other than database management.

In a relational database there are usually several flat files, each of which is used to store information about a different "entity" in the world. The objectives of relational technology are to ensure that each file in the database contains information about only the entity with which it is associated, and to provide linkages between files that represent the relationships between those entities that exist in the real world.

Let's look at a simple example of a relational database that is used to process customer orders. Such a relational database would contain at least two files, one for customer data and one for order data. The customer file would contain information (that is, fields) such as the customer's account number, name, address, and phone number; the order file would contain fields such as product number, product name, order quantity, unit cost, and total order cost. To enable the system to match an order to the customer who placed it, the customer's account number would also be contained in the order file. Thus, when the user needs combined order and customer information (as, for example; to prepare and mail an invoice), the two files can be temporarily "joined" together based on common values in each file's respective customer account number fields.

At the mainframe level of computing, the relational DBMS is one of several types of database management systems, along with other types such as hierarchical and network. At the microcomputer level, however, DBMS software is almost exclusively relational. Common packages such as dBASE III, RBase System V, and SQLBase are all relational and provide essentially the same basic structures and capabilities, even though they require different syntax to accomplish similar activities.

Exercises 13.1

1. Discuss the similarities between arrays and files.

2. Discuss the differences between arrays and files.

3. Indicate which of the following are valid declarations of files. Give an explanation for those that are invalid. State what the component type is for those that are valid.

   a. ```
TYPE
    FileOfAges = FILE OF 0..120;
VAR
    AgeFile : FileOfAges;
```

   b. ```
TYPE
    String20 = PACKED ARRAY [1..20] OF char;
    FileOfNames = ARRAY [1..100] OF String20;
VAR
    NameFile : FileOfNames;
```

   c. ```
TYPE
    FileA = FILE OF real;
    FileB = FILE OF FileA;
VAR
    RealFile : FileB;
```

   d. ```
TYPE
    FileOfInt = FILE [1..100] OF integer;
VAR
    File1 : FileOfInt;
```

```
e. TYPE
      IntFile = FILE OF integer;
   VAR
      OldFile, NewFile, TempFile : IntFile;
```

4. Assume a program contains definition and declaration sections as listed. State which buffer variables are available and the data type of each.

```
TYPE
   FileOfAges = FILE OF 0..120;
   IntFile = FILE OF integer;
   RealFile = FILE OF real;
   TruthFile = FILE OF boolean;
   List20 = ARRAY [1..20] OF real;
   ListFile = FILE OF List20;
   StudentInfo = RECORD
                     Name : PACKED ARRAY [1..20] OF char;
                     Age : 0..120
                  END;
   StudentFile = FILE OF StudentInfo;
VAR
   File1, File2 : FileOfAges;
   OldFile : StudentFile;
   NewFile : ListFile;
   TempFile : RealFile;
   TransFile : TruthFile;
   A, B, C : IntFile;
```

5. Define a file type and then declare a file to be used with records of patients for a physician. Information should include the name, address, height, weight, age, gender, and insurance company of each patient.

■ ■ ■ ■

■ 13.2
Working with Files

OBJECTIVES

- to understand the concept of opening a file [T]
- to be able to put data into a file using **write** or **put**
- to be able to retrieve data from a file using **read** or **get**
- to understand the difference between internal and external files
- to be able to use procedures when working with files

Now that we have examined the concepts of files, file windows, and buffer variables, we need to see how values are transmitted to and from file components. Let's first examine the process of putting data into a file.

Creating a File

Once a file has been declared in a program, entering data to the file is referred to as *writing to the file*. Before writing to a file, the file window must be positioned at the beginning of the file, by using the standard procedure **rewrite.** This is referred to as *opening a file.* Thus, if FileA is declared by

```
TYPE
   IntFile = FILE OF integer;
VAR
   FileA : IntFile;
```

then

```
rewrite (FileA);
```

opens FileA for receiving values of type **integer.** At this stage, the window is positioned at the beginning of FileA; FileA is ready to have any previous information overwritten, thus any previous values in FileA are no longer available; and values may now be stored in successive components of FileA (each value transferred is appended to the previous list of values).

Most versions of Pascal allow values to be transferred (written) to a file by assigning the desired value to the buffer variable and using the standard

T

procedure **put** with the buffer variable as an argument. We can, for instance, store the values 10, 20, and 30 in FileA by

```
rewrite (FileA);  {  Open for writing  }
FileA^ := 10;
put (FileA);
FileA^ := 20;
put (FileA);
FileA^ := 30;
put (FileA);
```

The **put** procedure has the effect of transferring the value of the buffer variable to the component in the window and then advancing the window to the next component. After **put** is called, the buffer variable becomes unassigned; this sequence is illustrated in Table 13.1.

TABLE 13.1
Using **put** to write to a file

Pascal Statement	Buffer	Effect
rewrite (FileA);	FileA^	window … FileA
FileA^ := 10;	10 — FileA^	window … FileA
put (FileA);	FileA^	10 … window … FileA
FileA^ := 20;	20 — FileA^	10 … window … FileA
put (FileA);	FileA^	10 20 … window … FileA
FileA^ := 30;	30 — FileA^	10 20 … window … FileA
put (FileA);	FileA^	10 20 30 … window … FileA

Standard Pascal also allows values to be written to a file using the procedure **write**. When this is used, the arguments for **write** are the file name followed by one argument. Thus, the previous fragment could be

```
rewrite (FileA);  {  Open for writing  }
write (FileA, 10);
write (FileA, 20);
write (FileA, 30);
```

The procedure **writeln** can only be used with files of type **text**.

The Standard Function eof

The Boolean function **eof** can be used on all files much the same as it is used on text files. When a file is opened for writing, an end-of-file marker is placed at the beginning of the file. This can be thought of as the window being positioned at the end-of-file marker. When a value is transferred by **put** or **write,** the end-of-file marker is advanced to the same component position to which the window moves. The reason for this is relatively obvious. When retrieving data from a file, we need to know when we have reached the end of the file. The function **eof** is used with the file name for an argument. As expected, **eof** (⟨file name⟩) is **true** when the window is positioned at the end-of-file marker. When writing to a file, **eof** (⟨file name⟩) is always **true.**

Retrieving File Data

The process of retrieving data from a file is referred to as *reading from a file.* In order to retrieve data from a file, you must first open the file for reading. This is accomplished by using the standard procedure

> **reset** (⟨file name⟩);

This has the effect of repositioning the window at the beginning of the file. Furthermore, when a file is open for reading, the value of the file component in the window is automatically assigned to the buffer variable. The window can be advanced to the next file component by a call to the standard procedure

> **get** (⟨file name⟩);

Using the previous example of FileA with values as depicted

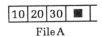

FileA

we could transfer values to the main program by

```
reset (FileA);
N1 := FileA^;
get (FileA);
N2 := FileA^;
get (FileA);
N3 := FileA^;
```

Positioning of the window and transferring of values for this segment of code is illustrated in Table 13.2.

This example of retrieving data is a bit contrived since we know there are exactly three components before the end-of-file marker. A more realistic retrieval would use the **eof** function; for example,

```
reset (FileA);
WHILE NOT eof(FileA) DO
  BEGIN
    .
    .    (process FileA^)
    .
    get (FileA)
  END;
```

The standard procedure **read** can also be used to transfer data from a file. After the file has been opened for reading, **read** can be used with the file

TABLE 13.2
Using **get** to read from a file

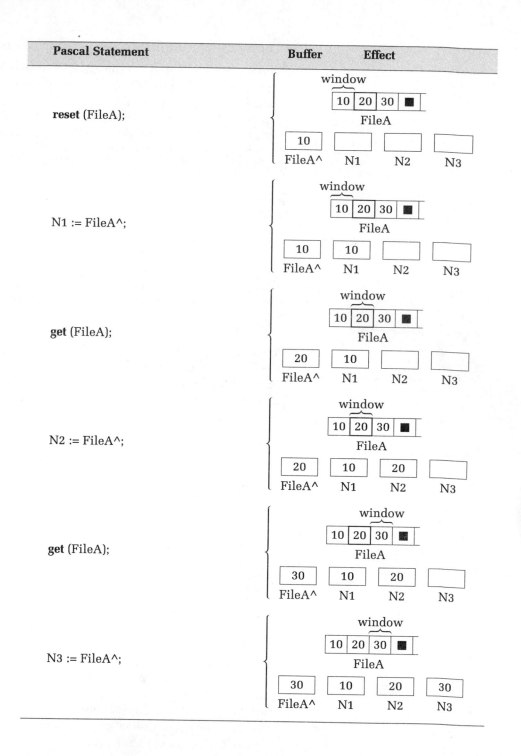

Pascal Statement	Buffer	Effect
reset (FileA);		
N1 := FileA^;		
get (FileA);		
N2 := FileA^;		
get (FileA);		
N3 := FileA^;		

name and variable names as arguments. Thus, the following could replace the previous code fragment.

```
reset (FileA);
read (FileA, N1);
read (FileA, N2);
read (FileA, N3);
```

The previous code using **get** is helpful in understanding the function of a buffer. However, many students find **read** easier to use.

Opening Files

A file cannot be opened for writing and reading at the same time. When a file is opened for writing, it remains open for receiving values that will be appended to the file until the window is repositioned by **rewrite** or **reset,** or until the program is terminated. Thus, you may create a file and then, later in the program, add to the file without reopening it. In a similar fashion, before you first read from a file, it must be opened by **reset** (⟨file name⟩). You can then transfer values from the file using either **read** or **get.**

Let's now consider a short example in which we do something with each component of a file.

■ EXAMPLE 13.1

Suppose we have a file of reals and we want to create another file by subtracting 5.0 from each component. Assume the following definitions and declarations.

```
TYPE
  RealFile = FILE OF real;
VAR
  OldFile : RealFile;
  NewFile : RealFile;
```

We can accomplish our objective by

```
reset (OldFile);  {  Open OldFile  }
rewrite (NewFile);  {  Open NewFile  }
WHILE NOT eof(OldFile) DO
  BEGIN
    NewFile^ := OldFile^ - 5.0;
    put (NewFile);
    get (OldFile)
  END;
```

■

Procedures and Files

Much of the work of processing files is accomplished by using procedures. Thus, you should continue using the **TYPE** definition section for defining file types. Files can be used as arguments in a procedure call, but in the procedure heading, files must be listed as variable parameters. This requirement is implicit in the fact that you cannot assign a file variable all at once (as you can a value parameter).

■ EXAMPLE 13.2

Let's write a procedure to accomplish the task of Example 13.1.

```
PROCEDURE Subtract5 (VAR OldFile, NewFile : RealFile);
  BEGIN
    reset (OldFile);
    rewrite (NewFile);
    WHILE NOT eof(OldFile) DO
      BEGIN
        NewFile^ := OldFile^ - 5.0;
        put (NewFile);
        get (OldFile)
      END  {  of WHILE...DO  }
  END;  {  of PROCEDURE Subtract5  }
```

This procedure is called from the main program by

```
Subtract5 (OldFile, NewFile);
```

Note that even though no changes are made in OldFile, it is passed as a variable parameter.

■   ■

Internal and External Files

Recall from Chapter 9, files used to store data in secondary storage between runs of a program are called external files, and files that are used for processing only and are not saved in secondary storage are internal files. External files must be listed in the program heading in the following form:

> **PROGRAM** ⟨name⟩ (**input, output,** ⟨external file name⟩);

They are declared in the variable declaration section. Internal files are not listed in the program heading but are declared in the variable declaration section.

Typically, a programming problem has some external file in secondary storage that is to be updated in some form. This requires some temporary internal files to be declared for use in the program. When the program is exited, all external files are saved in secondary storage while the internal files are no longer available.

Processing Files

Before looking at a specific problem for processing files, let's consider the general problem of updating an external file. Since we eventually will **re-write** the external file, we must be careful not to erase the original contents before they have been saved and/or processed in some temporary internal file. In our early work with files, we accomplish this by copying external files to temporary files and then working with the temporary files until the desired tasks are completed. At this point, we then copy the appropriate temporary file to the external file. In reality, this method may prove to be inefficient but until you become more experienced in file manipulation, it is good practice to avoid working directly with external files.

Let's now consider a relatively short example of updating a file of test scores for students in a class. In the last section of this chapter, we will see a detailed treatment of processing files.

■ **EXAMPLE 13.3**

Assume we have an external file consisting of total points for each student in a class. Furthermore, assume the data file **(input)** contains test scores that are to be added (in the same order) to the previous totals to obtain new totals. A first-level pseudocode solution to this problem is

1. Copy the totals to a temporary file from the external file
2. Process the temporary file
3. Copy the temporary file to the external file

Assume the program heading is

```
PROGRAM Grades (input, output, TotalPts);
```

and the definitions and declarations are

```
TYPE
  IntFile = FILE OF integer;
VAR
  TotalPts : IntFile;
  Temp1File : IntFile;
  Temp2File : IntFile;
```

A procedure to copy the contents from one file to another is

```
PROCEDURE Copy (VAR OldFile, NewFile : IntFile);
  BEGIN
    reset (OldFile);
    rewrite (NewFile);
    WHILE NOT eof(OldFile) DO
      BEGIN
        NewFile^ := OldFile^;
        put (NewFile);
        get (OldFile)
      END  {  of WHILE...DO  }
  END;  {  of PROCEDURE Copy  }
```

This is called from the main program by

```
Copy (TotalPts, Temp1File);
```

We can now process Temp1File by adding corresponding scores from the data file. A procedure for this is

```
PROCEDURE AddScores (VAR OldFile, NewFile : IntFile);
  VAR
    NewScore : integer;
  BEGIN
    reset (OldFile);
    rewrite (NewFile);
    WHILE NOT eof(OldFile) DO
      BEGIN
        read (NewScore);  {  Get scores from data file  }
        NewFile^ := NewScore + OldFile^;
        put (NewFile);
        get (OldFile)
      END  {  of WHILE...DO  }
  END;  {  of PROCEDURE AddScores  }
```

This procedure could be called from the main program by

```
AddScores (Temp1File, Temp2File);
```

At this stage, the updated scores are in Temp2File and they need to be stored in the external file TotalPts before the program is exited. This is done by another call to Copy in the main program. Thus,

```
Copy (Temp2File, TotalPts);
```

achieves the desired results. The main program is then

```
BEGIN  {  Main program  }
  Copy (TotalPts, Temp1File);
  AddScores (Temp1File, Temp2File);
  Copy (Temp2File, TotalPts)
END.  {  of main program  }
```

■   ■

This example obviously overlooks some significant points; for example, how do we know the scores match up, that each student's new score is added to that student's previous total? We will address these issues later in the chapter. Let's now see how one file can be appended to an existing file.

■ **EXAMPLE 13.4**

Assume the files are named OldFile and NewFile and the task is to append NewFile to OldFile. We will use a temporary file, TempFile, for completing this task. A first-level pseudocode development for this problem is

1. Reset OldFile and NewFile
2. Open TempFile for writing
3. **WHILE NOT eof** (OldFile) **DO**
   3.1 write elements to TempFile
4. **WHILE NOT eof** (NewFile) **DO**
   4.1 write elements to TempFile
5. Copy TempFile to OldFile

Step 3 can be refined to

3. **WHILE NOT eof** (OldFile) **DO**
   3.1 write elements to TempFile
       3.1.1   assign OldFile buffer value to TempFile buffer
       3.1.2   write value to TempFile
       3.1.3   advance window of OldFile

The code for this step is

```
WHILE NOT eof(OldFile) DO
  BEGIN
    TempFile^ := OldFile^;
    put (TempFile);
    get (OldFile)
  END;  {  of WHILE NOT eof  }
```

The complete code for this example is left as an exercise.

■

A NOTE OF INTEREST

Backup and Recovery of Data

The need for organizational backup and recovery procedures to prevent loss of data is due to two types of events; in particular, natural disasters and simple human errors. Natural disasters, although infrequent, are typically large-scale emergencies that can completely shut down, if not ruin, an organization's computer facilities. Examples are such potentially catastrophic events as fires, floods, and earthquakes. Human errors, on the other hand, are the most frequent cause of computer problems (has anyone NEVER erased the wrong file by mistake?), but may not be as crippling as natural disasters. Although they may not result in catastrophic loss, human errors are, at the least, a nuisance to affected individuals.

Organizations have developed a variety of backup and recovery procedures to cope with system failures and to reduce resultant losses. To reduce losses from natural disasters, some organizations have prepared contingency plans covering backup computer locations, off-site program and data storage, and emergency staffing requirements. These contingency plans can usually be put into effect quickly and with minimal disruption of computer services. To minimize human errors (accidents can never be eliminated), organizations typically try to provide sound user-training programs and user-based physical backup measures.

A more recent problem regarding backup and recovery of data has emerged. Specifically, as storage and retrieval technology changes, old data storage can become difficult to access. As an illustration, see the next Note of Interest.

Exercises 13.2

1. Review the difference between internal files and external files.

2. Write test programs that illustrate the following.
   a. What happens when you try to write to a file that has not been opened for writing.
   b. What happens when you try to get data from a file that has not been reset.
   c. What happens when a procedure uses a file as a value parameter.

3. Declare an appropriate file and store the positive multiples of 7 that are less than 100.

4. Explain how the file of Exercise 3 can be saved for another program to use.

5. Consider the file with integer components as shown.

   FivesFile

   Write a segment of code that would assign the values respectively to variables A, B, C, and D. Use both **get** and **read.**

6. Consider the following file with component values as illustrated.

   ```
   TYPE
      RealFile = FILE OF real;
   VAR
      Prices : RealFile;
   ```

   | 15.95 | 17.99 | 21.95 | 19.99 | ■ | |
   Prices

   a. Declare a new file and put values in the components that are 15 percent less than the values in components of Prices.
   b. Update the values in Prices so that each value is increased by 10 percent.

7. Discuss the difference between **reset** and **rewrite.**

8. You have been asked to write a program to examine a file of integers and replace every negative number with zero. Assume IntFile has been appropriately declared and contains five integer values. Why will the following segment of code not work?

   ```
   rewrite (IntFile);
   FOR J := 1 TO 5 DO
     BEGIN
        get (IntFile);
        IF IntFile^ < 0 THEN
          IntFile^ := 0;
        put (IntFile)
     END;
   ```

9. Consider the files declared by

   ```
   TYPE
      FileOfInt = FILE OF integer;
   VAR
      File1, File2 : FileOfInt;
   ```

   Find all errors in each of the following.

   ```
   a. reset (File1);
      FOR J := 1 TO 5 DO
        BEGIN
           File1^ := 10 * J;
           put (File1)
        END;
   ```

```
   b. rewrite (File1);
        FOR J := 1 TO 5 DO
          BEGIN
            File1^ := 10 * J;
            put (File1)
          END;
   c. rewrite (File1);
        FOR J := 1 TO 5 DO
          BEGIN
            File1 := 10 * J;
            put (File1)
          END;
   d. rewrite (File1);
        FOR J := 1 TO 5 DO
          File1^ := J * 10;
   e. reset (File2);
        WHILE NOT eof(File1) DO
          BEGIN
            File2^ := File1^;
            put (File2);
            get (File1)
          END;
   f. reset (File2);
      rewrite (File1);
      WHILE NOT eof(File2) DO
          BEGIN
            File1^ := File2^;
            put (File1);
            get (File2)
          END;
```

10. Assume the files OldFile and NewFile are declared as

```
TYPE
   IntFile = FILE OF integer;
VAR
   OldFile, NewFile : IntFile;
```

Furthermore, for each of the following, assume OldFile has component values as illustrated.

−2	−1	0	1	2	▓

OldFile

Indicate the values in components of both OldFile and NewFile after each of the following segments of code.

```
a. reset (OldFile);
   rewrite (NewFile);
   WHILE NOT eof(OldFile) DO
     BEGIN
       IF OldFile^ > 0 THEN
         BEGIN
           NewFile^ := OldFile^;
           put (NewFile)
         END;
       get (OldFile)
     END;
```

```
  b. rewrite (OldFile);
     rewrite (NewFile);
     WHILE NOT eof(OldFile) DO
       BEGIN
         IF OldFile^ > 0 THEN
           BEGIN
             NewFile^ := OldFile^;
             put (NewFile)
           END
       END;
  c. reset (OldFile);
     rewrite (NewFile);
     WHILE NOT eof(OldFile) DO
       BEGIN
         NewFile^ := abs(OldFile^);
         put (NewFile);
         get (OldFile)
       END;
     rewrite (OldFile);
     reset (NewFile);
     WHILE NOT eof(NewFile) DO
       BEGIN
         OldFile^ := NewFile^;
         put (OldFile);
         get (NewFile)
       END;
```

11. Assume OldFile and NewFile are as declared in Exercise 10. Furthermore, assume OldFile contains the values

8	-17	0	-4	21	■	

OldFile

Indicate the output from the following segment of code and the values of the components in OldFile and NewFile.

```
reset (OldFile);
rewrite (NewFile);
WHILE NOT eof(OldFile) DO
  BEGIN
    NewFile^ :- OldFile^;
    IF NewFile^ < 0 THEN
      writeln (NewFile^)
    ELSE
      put (NewFile);
      get (OldFile)
  END;
```

12. Assume you have declared three files (File1, File2, and File3) in a program such that the component type for each file is **real**. Furthermore, assume that both File1 and File2 contain an unknown number of values. Write a segment of code to transfer the corresponding sum of components from File1 and File2 into File3. Since File1 and File2 may have a different number of components, after one end-of-file is reached, you should add zeros until the next end-of-file is reached. Thus, your segment produces

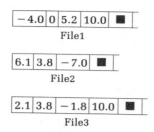

```
 -4.0  0  5.2  10.0  ■
        File1

 6.1  3.8  -7.0  ■
      File2

 2.1  3.8  -1.8  10.0  ■
        File3
```

13. Write a complete program that finishes the work started in Example 13.4. Your program should print out the contents of each file used and of the final file.

■ ■ ■ ■

■ 13.3
Files with Structured Components

OBJECTIVES

- to be able to declare files whose components are records or arrays
- to understand why files with structured components are used
- to be able to create a file of records from a text file
- to be able to manipulate files with structured components

In actual practice, components of files are frequently some structured data type. A program might use a file of arrays or a file of records and when such a file is desired, you declare it as an external file and then create components from a text file. Once the data have been thus converted, you can access an entire array or record rather than accessing individual fields or components. The data are also saved in structured form between runs of a program. When data have been stored in structured components, it is relatively easy to update and work with these files. For example, a doctor might have a file of records for patients and wish to insert or delete records of the patients, choose to examine the individual fields of each record, print an alphabetical list, or print a list of patients with unpaid bills.

Let's now examine a typical declaration. Suppose you are writing a program to use a file of records. Each record contains information about a student in a computer science class: in particular, the student's name, three test scores (in an array), identification number, and test average. A declaration for such a file could be

```
TYPE
   String20 = PACKED ARRAY [1..20] OF char;
   Scores = ARRAY [1..3] OF 0..100;
   StudentInfo = RECORD
                    Name : String20;
                    Score : Scores;
                    IDNumber : 0..999;
                    Average : real
                 END;  {  of RECORD StudentInfo  }
   StudentFile = FILE OF StudentInfo;
VAR
   Student : StudentFile;
```

Student is a file of records that can be illustrated as shown in Figure 13.1.

After Student has been properly opened for reading by **reset** (Student), the statement

```
get (Student);
```

causes the contents of a record to be transferred to Student∧. The field identifiers are

```
Student^.Name
Student^.IDNumber
Student^.Score
Student^.Average
```

FIGURE 13.1
File Student

Student

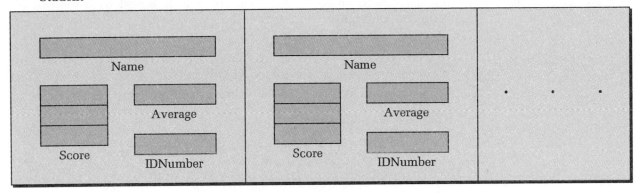

Student^.Score is an array. Components of this array are

```
Student^.Score[l]
Student^.Score[2]
Student^.Score[3]
```

If you wish to compute the average for a student whose record is in the buffer, you can write

```
Sum := 0;
WITH Student^ DO
  BEGIN
    FOR J := 1 TO 3 DO
      Sum := Sum + Score[J];
    Average := Sum / 3
  END;
```

At this stage, you may want to save this computed average for later use. Unfortunately, **put** (Student) will not work because the file is open for reading rather than writing. We will solve this and other problems in the remainder of this section as we investigate methods of manipulating files.

Creating a File of Records

One of the first problems to be solved when working with files whose components are structured variables is to transfer data from some text file (usually **input**) into the appropriate file of structured components. Once the new file with structured components has been created, it can be saved in secondary storage by declaring it as an external file. To illustrate the process of creating a file of records, let's continue the example of records for students in a computer science class. Recall the definitions and subsequent declaration

```
TYPE
  String20 = PACKED ARRAY [1..20] OF char;
  Scores = ARRAY [1..3] OF 0..100;
  StudentInfo = RECORD
                  Name : String20;
                  IDNumber : 0..999;
                  Score : Scores;
                  Average : real
                END; { of RECORD StudentInfo }
  StudentFile = FILE OF StudentInfo;
VAR
  Student : StudentFile;
```

Before we can create the file of records, we need to know how data were entered in the text file (assume **input**). For purposes of this example, assume data for each student are contained on a single line, 20 positions are used for the name, and an identification number is followed by three test scores. Thus, the data file could be

| Smith John 065 89 92 76 | Jones Mary 021 93 97 85 ■ |

T A procedure to create the file of records is

```
PROCEDURE CreateFile (VAR Student : StudentFile);
  VAR
    J : integer;
  BEGIN
    rewrite (Student);  {  Open for writing  }
    WHILE NOT eof(input) DO
      BEGIN  {  Get data for one record  }
        WITH Student^ DO
          BEGIN
            FOR J := 1 TO 20 DO
              read (Name[J]);
            read (IDNumber);
            readln (Score[1], Score[2], Score[3])
          END;
        put (Student)  {  Put buffer contents in file  }
      END
  END;  {  of PROCEDURE CreateFile  }
```

This procedure is called from the main program by

```
CreateFile (Student);
```

After it is executed, we have the records shown in Figure 13.2.

FIGURE 13.2
File Student with values

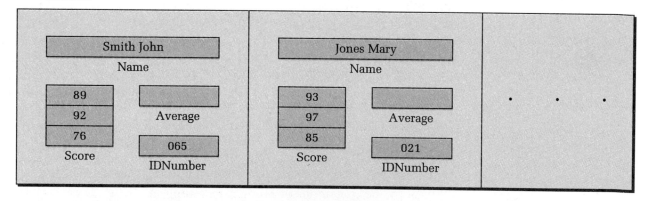

Storing Structured Files

Structured files may be stored in secondary memory for subsequent use. When files other than those of type **text** are stored, they are stored as binary files. In this form, the data may be accessed by a program. However, an attempt to "look at" such a file by using a text editor or some other system command usually results in a display of gibberish characters.

Programmers need not worry about the form of data being stored. The change in representation is performed by the operating system. Even though you cannot "see" components of a file that has been saved in secondary memory, you should use files of structured components for the following reasons:

1. Values of structured file types can be read from or written to nontext files. For example, you can read or write an entire record.
2. The information in structured file types can be transferred more rapidly than with files of type **text** since the operating system does not do as much encoding and decoding.
3. Data are usually stored more compactly when saved as part of a structured file type.

A common error for beginning programmers is to create a text file that "looks like" a structured file and then attempt to use it as a structured file. For example, a text file of data may be arranged to look like a file of records by using a text editor. However, an attempt to read a record from this file results in an error. You must first create a file of records as discussed previously.

File Manipulation

Several problems are typically involved with manipulating files and file components. Generally, a program starts with an existing file, revises it in some fashion, and then saves the revised file. Because files in standard Pascal must be accessed sequentially, this usually necessitates copying the existing external file to a temporary internal file, revising the temporary file, and copying the revised file to the external file. The existing external file is often referred to as the *master file*. The file containing changes to be made in the master file is called the *transaction file*.

To illustrate a simple update problem, let's consider again the problem using the file containing records for students in a computer science class. Assume that the external file has been named Student. Now suppose we wish to delete a record from Student (master file) because some student moved to Australia. This problem can be solved by searching Student sequentially for the record in question. As the name in each record is examined, if the record is to be kept, it is put in a temporary file. The desired record is not transferred, thus accomplishing the update. Finally, Student is rewritten by copying the contents of the temporary file to Student.

A first-level pseudocode development is

1. Get the name to be deleted
2. Search Student for a match copying each nonmatch to TempFile
3. Copy the remainder of Student to TempFile
4. Copy TempFile to Student

Using the previous declarations and assuming that the name of the student whose record is to be deleted has been read into MovedAway, step 2 can be solved by

```
reset (Student);  {  Open the files  }
rewrite (TempFile);
Found := false;
WHILE NOT eof(Student) AND NOT Found DO
```

```
BEGIN
  IF Student^.Name = MovedAway THEN
    Found := true
  ELSE
    BEGIN
      TempFile^ := Student^;
      put (TempFile)
    END;
  get (Student)
END;  {  of search for a student name  }

{  Now copy the rest of student file  }

WHILE NOT eof(Student) DO
  BEGIN
    TempFile^ := Student^;
    put (TempFile);
    get (Student)
  END;
```

We now need to copy TempFile to Student so that the revised master file is saved as an external file. A procedure for this was developed in Section 13.2; it is called from the main program by

```
Copy (TempFile, Student);
```

As a second illustration of file manipulation, let's consider the standard problem of merging two sorted files. For example, suppose the master file is a file of records and each record contains a field for the name of a customer. Furthermore, assume this file has been sorted alphabetically by name. Now suppose an alphabetical listing of new customers is to be merged with the old file to produce a current file containing records for all customers sorted alphabetically by name.

As before, we use a temporary file to hold the full sorted list and then copy the temporary file to the master file. This can be envisioned as illustrated in Figure 13.3.

FIGURE 13.3
Merging files

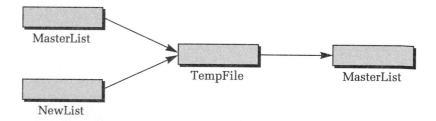

An algorithm for the merge is not too difficult. All files are first opened. Then the initial records from MasterList and NewList are compared. The record containing the name that comes first alphabetically is transferred to Temp-File and, as shown in the graphic documentation for the following program segment, the next record is obtained from the file containing the record that was transferred. This process continues until the end of one file is reached. At that time, the remainder of the other file is copied into TempFile.

Assuming that each record has a field identified by Name, which is of type String30, and that FileType has been defined as the type for files being used, a procedure for merging is

```
PROCEDURE Merge (VAR Master, NewFile : FileType);
  VAR
    TempFile : FileType;
  BEGIN
    reset (Master);
    reset (NewFile);
    rewrite (TempFile);

{  Compare top records until an eof of one of the
   input files is reached  }

    WHILE NOT eof(Master) AND NOT eof(NewFile) DO
      BEGIN
        IF Master^.Name < NewFile^.Name THEN
          BEGIN
            TempFile^ := Master^;
            get (Master)
          END
        ELSE
          BEGIN
            TempFile^ := NewFile^;
            get (NewFile)
          END;
        put (TempFile)
      END;
```

Current
Last
Record

Current
Record

Current
Record

Master   NewFile   TempFile

The smaller of
these two records
must be transferred
to the end of TempFile.
Then advance within
the file from which
that record was taken.

```
{  Now copy the remaining names  }

    WHILE NOT eof(Master) DO
      BEGIN
        TempFile^ := Master^;
        put (TempFile);
        get (Master)
      END;
```

```
WHILE NOT eof(NewFile) DO
  BEGIN
    TempFile^ := NewFile^;
    put (TempFile);
    get (NewFile)
  END;

{  Now copy back to Master  }

rewrite (Master);
reset (TempFile);
WHILE NOT eof(TempFile) DO
  BEGIN
    Master^ := TempFile^;
    put (Master);
    get (TempFile)
  END

END;  {  of PROCEDURE Merge  }
```

This procedure can be called from the main program by

```
Merge (Master, NewFile);
```

A final comment is in order. It is frequently necessary to work with files of records that have been sorted according to a field of the record. Since you might want to work with the records sorted by some other field, you must first be able to sort an unsorted file. In general, this is done by transferring the file components to array components, sorting the array, and transferring the

History Stuck on Old Computer Tapes

A slice of recent U.S. history has become as unreadable as Egyptian hieroglyphics before the discovery of the Rosetta stone. And more historic, scientific, and business data is in danger of dissolving into a meaningless jumble of letters, numbers, and computer symbols.

Paying millions to preserve the information is part of the price for the country's embrace of more and more powerful computers. Much information from the past 30 years is stranded on computer tape from primitive or discarded systems—it's unintelligible or soon to be so.

Hundreds of thousands of Americans researching family history—the largest use of the National Archives—will find records of their relatives beyond reach. Detection of diseases, environmental threats or shifts in social class could be delayed because data was lost before researchers even knew which questions to ask.

"The ability to read our nation's historical records is threatened by the complexity of modern computers," said Representative Bob Wise, chairman of a House information subcommittee that wants the government to start buying computers to preserve data for future researchers. A number of records already are lost or out of reach:

Two hundred reels of 17-year-old Public Health Service computer tapes were destroyed because no one could find out what the names and numbers on them meant.

The government's Agent Orange Task Force, asked to determine whether Vietnam soldiers were sickened by exposure to the herbicide, was unable to decode Pentagon computer tapes containing the date, site, and size of every U.S. herbicide bombing during the war.

The most extensive record of Americans who served in World War II exists only on 1,600 reels of microfilm of computer punch cards. No staff, money, or machine is available to return the data to a computer so citizens could trace the war history of their relatives.

Census data from the 1960s and NASA's early scientific observations of the earth and planets exist on thousands of reels of old tape. Some may have decomposed; others may fall apart if run through the balky equipment that survives from that era.

sorted array components back to the file. This means that you must have some idea of how many components are in the file and declare the array length accordingly. The physical setting of a problem usually provides this information. For example, physicians will have some idea of how many patients (100, 200, or 1,000) they see.

Exercises 13.3

1. Declare appropriate files for each of the following. Fields for each record are indicated.

   a. Flight information for an airplane; include flight number, airline, arrival time, arriving from, departure time, and destination.

   b. Bookstore inventory; include author, title, stock number, price, and quantity.

   c. Records for a magazine subscription agency; include name and address, indicating street number, street name, city, state, and zip code.

2. Write a test program that allows you to declare a file of records, read data into the file, and print information from selected records according to the value in some key field.

3. Suppose data in a text file contains information for students in a class. Each student's information will use three data lines as illustrated.

Name	Student Number	Ten Quiz Scores	Four Test Scores
Jones John	111		

   ↑
   position 21

   a. Declare a file of records to be used to store this data.

   b. Write a procedure to create a file of records containing appropriate information from the text file.

   c. Write a procedure to sort the file alphabetically.

4. Illustrate the values of components and fields in Student and Student^ during the first pass through the loop in **PROCEDURE** CreateFile.

5. Consider the file Student declared by

   ```
   TYPE
     String20 = PACKED ARRAY [1..20] OF char;
     Scores = ARRAY [1..3] OF 0..100;
     StudentInfo = RECORD
                     Name : String20;
                     IDNumber : 0..444;
                     Score : Scores;
                     Average : real
                   END;
     StudentFile = FILE OF StudentInfo;
   VAR
     Student : StudentInfo;
   ```

   Write a procedure for each of the following tasks. In each case, show how the procedure is called from the main program. (You may assume the file has been alphabetized.)

   a. Add one record in alphabetical order.

   b. Add one record to the bottom of the file.

   c. Update the record of 'Smith Jane   ' by changing her score on the second test from an 82 to an 89.

   d. The scores from test three have just been entered into a data file. Each line contains an identification number followed by three integer scores. Update Student to include these scores (the first two scores have already been transferred to the appropriate student records).

    e. Assume all test scores have been entered. Update Student by computing the test average for each student.

    f. Print a list containing each student's name and test average; the list should be sorted by test average from high to low.

■ ■ ■ ■

FOCUS ON
PROGRAM DESIGN

The chapter summary program for this chapter is an elementary version that could be expanded to a comprehensive programming project. Suppose the registrar at your institution wants a program to allow updating a file of student records. A master file of student records currently exists; it is sorted alphabetically. Each record contains a field for the student's name, ID number, grade point average, and total hours completed. This file is to be updated by information contained in a transaction file. Each line in the transaction file contains a student number, letter grade for a course taken, and number of credit hours for the course. A typical data line would be

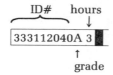

For each data line in the transaction file, your program should search the contents of the master file for a match. If a match is found, appropriate changes should be made in grade point average and total hours completed. If no match is found, the information should be printed in an Exception Report. After all transactions are completed, an alphabetized list should be printed and the master file should be updated.

A first-level pseudocode development for this is

1. Open the files
2. Copy contents of MasterFile to an array
3. Update the records
4. Print the list
5. Update MasterFile

A complete structure diagram for this program is given in Figure 13.4. Module specifications for the main modules are

1. <u>OpenFiles Module</u>
   Data received: None
   Information returned: None
   Logic: Use **reset** to prepare files for reading.

2. <u>LoadArray Module</u>
   Data received: File of records
   Information returned: Array of records
                                     Number of records
   Logic: Copy contents of each record in MasterFile to a record in Student.
              Count the number of records in the array.

FIGURE 13.4
Structure chart for the file update program

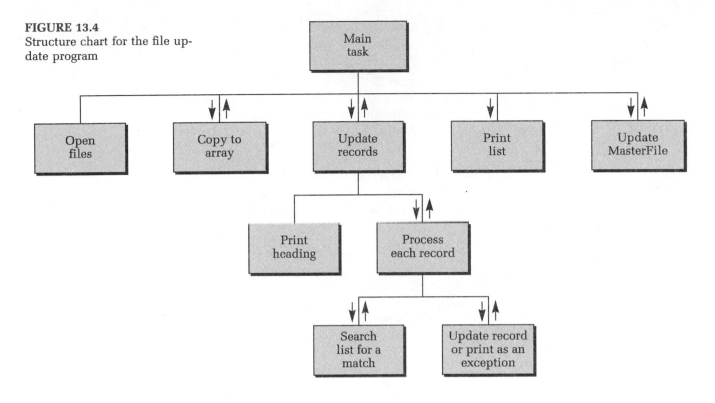

3. UnderlineUpdateRecords Module
   Data received: An array of records
                  Length of the array
                  A transaction file
   Information returned: An updated array of records
   Logic: For each data line in TransactionFile, search for a match in the array.
          IF a match is found, **THEN**
          update the record
          ELSE
          print out an Exception Report

4. PrintList Module
   Data received: A sorted array of records
                  Length of the array
   Information returned: None
   Logic: Print a heading.
          Print contents of each record.

5. UpdateMasterFile Module
   Data received: An array of records
                  Length of the array
                  MasterFile of records
   Information returned: An updated MasterFile
   Logic: For each record in Student, copy contents into a record in MasterFile

Further pseudocode development is

1. Open the files
   1.1 **reset** MasterFile
   1.2 **reset** TransactionFile
2. Copy contents of MasterFile to an array
   2.1 set counter to zero
   2.2 **REPEAT**
       2.2.1 increment counter
       2.2.2 copy contents of one record
       UNTIL eof (MasterFile)
3. Update the records
   3.1 print Exception Report heading
   3.2 **WHILE NOT eof** (TransactionFile) **DO**
       3.2.1 search for a match
       3.2.2 **IF NOT** Found **THEN**
             print as part of Exception Report
             ELSE
             update the record
4. Print the list
   4.1 print a heading
   4.2 print an alphabetized list
5. Update the MasterFile
   5.1 **rewrite** MasterFile
   5.2 **FOR** each record in the array **DO**
       copy contents to a record in MasterFile

Step 3.2.1 is a sequential search of the array. If a match is found, the array position is returned. If not, a zero is returned. The portion of step 3.2.2 designed to update the record consists of incrementing the grade point average. A **CASE** statement is used to direct action for grades of 'A', 'B', 'C', 'D', 'E', 'W', 'I'. This program assumes valid data are contained in Transaction-File. A complete program for this problem is

```
PROGRAM FileUpdate (input, output, MasterFile, TransactionFile);

{  This program updates a file of student records. Transactions }
{  are   stored in the text  file  TransactionFile.  Each  line }
{  consists of a student number, grade for a course taken,  and }
{  credit hours for the course.  The file of records is  copied }
{  to  an array  of records  for processing.  This  facilitates }
{  searching for matches of student numbers.  It is assumed the }
{  master file is alphabetized.  If it is not, one could add  a }
{  procedure to sort the array before rewriting the master file.}

CONST
  MaxLength = 200;

TYPE
  String9 = PACKED ARRAY [1..9] OF char;
  String20 = PACKED ARRAY [1..20] OF char;
  StudentRecord = RECORD
                    Name : String20;
                    IDNumber : String9;
                    GPA : real;
                    Hours : integer
                  END; { of RECORD StudentRecord }
  StudentList = ARRAY [1..MaxLength] OF StudentRecord;
  RecordsFile = FILE OF StudentRecord;
```

```
VAR
  NumberOfRecords : integer;  {  Number of records read        }
  Student : StudentList;      {  Array of student records      }
  MasterFile : RecordsFile;   {  Master file of student records }
  TransactionFile : text;     {  Transaction file for updating  }

{************************************************************** }

PROCEDURE OpenFiles (VAR MasterFile : RecordsFile;
                     VAR TransactionFile : text);

{  Given:    Nothing                                          }
{  Task:     Open the files for reading                       }
{  Return:   MasterFile and TransactionFile ready to be read  }

BEGIN
  reset (MasterFile);
  reset (TransactionFile)
END;  {  of PROCEDURE OpenFiles  }

{************************************************************** }

PROCEDURE LoadArray (VAR MasterFile : RecordsFile;
                     VAR Student : StudentList;
                     VAR NumberOfRecords : integer);

  {  Given:   Master file containing data for each student    }
  {  Task:    Create an array of student records from MasterFile }
  {  Return:  Array of student records and number of records  }

  BEGIN
    NumberOfRecords := 0;
    get (MasterFile);
    WHILE NOT eof(MasterFile) AND (NumberOfRecords < MaxLength) DO
      BEGIN
        NumberOfRecords := NumberOfRecords + 1;
        Student[NumberOfRecords] := MasterFile^;
        get (MasterFile)
      END;  {  of WHILE...DO  }
    IF NOT eof(MasterFile) THEN
      writeln ('There are more data.')
  END;  {  of PROCEDURE LoadArray  }

{************************************************************** }

FUNCTION NewGPA (Hours, CourseHours : integer;
                 GPA, HonorPoints : real) : real;

  {  Given:   Total hours accumulated, credit hours for the   }
  {                  course completed, current GPA, HonorPoints }
  {                  corresponding to the letter grade received }
  {  Task:    Compute the new grade point average             }
  {  Return:  New grade point average                         }

  VAR
    OldHours : integer;

  BEGIN
    OldHours := Hours;
    Hours := Hours + CourseHours;
    NewGPA := (OldHours * GPA + CourseHours * HonorPoints) / Hours
  END;  {  of FUNCTION NewGPA  }

{************************************************************** }
```

1

2

```
FUNCTION SeqSearch (Student : StudentList;
                    IDNumber : String9;
                    NumberOfRecords : integer) : integer;

{  Given:    An array of student records, a student ID number,   }
{                  and the number of records                     }
{  Task:     Sequentially search the array to find a match for   }
{                  the ID number                                 }
{  Return:   The index of the record where a match was found;    }
{                  return 0 if not match                         }

VAR
  Found : boolean;
  LCV : integer;

BEGIN
  SeqSearch := 0;
  Found := false;
  LCV := 0;
  WHILE (LCV < NumberOfRecords) AND (NOT Found) DO
    BEGIN
      LCV := LCV + 1;
      IF Student[LCV].IDNumber = IDNumber THEN
        BEGIN
          SeqSearch := LCV;
          Found := true
        END {  of IF...THEN  }
    END  {  of WHILE loop  }
END;  {  of FUNCTION SeqSearch  }

{************************************************************** }

PROCEDURE UpdateRecords (VAR TransactionFile : text;
                         VAR Student : StudentList;
                         NumberOfRecords : integer);

{  Given:    A transaction file for updating records, an array   }
{                  of student records, and the number of student }
{                  records                                       }
{  Task:     Read a line from the transaction file; search array }
{                  Student for a match of IDNumber; IF match THEN }
{                  update hours and GPA; ELSE print as part of    }
{                  Exception Report                               }
{  Return:   An updated array of student records                 }

CONST
  Skip = ' ';

VAR
  J, Index, CourseHours : integer;
  IDNumber : String9;
  Grade : char;
  MatchFound : boolean;

BEGIN

  {  Print heading for the Exception Report  }

  writeln ('EXCEPTION REPORT':35);
  writeln ('ID NUMBER':20, 'GRADE':12, 'HOURS':10);
  writeln (Skip:10, '-------------------------------');
  writeln;
```

3

```
      {  Now read the transaction file  }

   WHILE NOT eof(TransactionFile) DO
     BEGIN
       FOR J := 1 TO 9 DO
         read (TransactionFile, IDNumber[J]);
       readln (TransactionFile, Grade, CourseHours);
       Index := SeqSearch(Student, IDNumber, NumberOfRecords);
       MatchFound := Index <> 0;
       IF MatchFound THEN                { Update student record }
         WITH Student[Index] DO
           CASE Grade OF
             'A'  :  BEGIN
                       GPA := NewGPA(Hours, CourseHours, GPA, 4.0);
                       Hours := Hours + CourseHours
                     END;
             'B'  :  BEGIN
                       GPA := NewGPA(Hours, Coursehours, GPA, 3.0);
                       Hours := Hours + CourseHours
                     END;
             'C'  :  BEGIN
                       GPA := NewGPA(Hours, Coursehours, GPA, 2.0);
                       Hours := Hours + CourseHours
                     END;
             'D'  :  BEGIN
                       GPA := NewGPA(Hours, CourseHours, GPA, 1.0);
                       Hours := Hours + CourseHours
                     END;
             'E'  :  BEGIN
                       GPA := NewGPA(Hours, CourseHours, GPA, 0.0);
                       Hours := Hours + CourseHours
                     END;
             'W', 'I'  :                        {  do nothing  }
           END  {  of CASE Grade  }
       ELSE               {  Print as part of Exception Report  }
         writeln (IDNumber:20, Grade:10, CourseHours:10)
     END  {  of WHILE NOT eof (TransactionFile)  }
 END;  {  of PROCEDURE UpdateRecords  }

{**************************************************************** }

PROCEDURE PrintList (VAR Student : StudentList;
                     NumberOfRecords : integer);

  {  Given:   An array of student records and number of records  }
  {  Task:    Print a list of records with appropriate heading   }
  {  Return:  Nothing                                            }

  VAR
    J : integer;

  BEGIN

    {  Print a heading for the revised list  }

    writeln;
    writeln ('UPDATED REPORT':30);
    writeln ('STUDENT FILE LISTING':34);
    writeln;
    writeln ('NAME':10, 'ID NUMBER':25, 'GPA':8, 'CREDITS':10);
    writeln ('-----------------------------------------------------------');
    writeln;
```

4

```
                { Now print the list }

          FOR J := 1 TO NumberOfRecords DO
            WITH Student[J] DO
              writeln (Name:20, IDNumber:15, GPA:8:2, Hours:8)
        END; { of PROCEDURE PrintList }

{*********************************************************************** }

PROCEDURE UpdateMasterFile (VAR MasterFile : RecordsFile;
                              VAR Student : StudentList;
                              NumberOfRecords : integer);

  { Given:   An array of student records and the array length    }
  { Task:    Copy the records into MasterFile for storage         }
  { Return:  A file of student records                            }

  VAR
    J : integer;

  BEGIN
    rewrite (MasterFile);
    FOR J := 1 TO NumberOfRecords DO
      BEGIN
        MasterFile^ := Student[J];
        put (MasterFile)
      END { of FOR loop }
    END; { of PROCEDURE UpdateMasterFile }

{*********************************************************************** }

BEGIN { Main program }
  OpenFiles (MasterFile, TransactionFile);
  LoadArray (MasterFile, Student, NumberOfRecords);
  UpdateRecords (TransactionFile, Student, NumberOfRecords);
  PrintList (Student, NumberOfRecords);
  UpdateMasterFile (MasterFile, Student, NumberOfRecords)
END. { of main program }
```

5

If you use data in MasterFile as

```
BARRETT RODA        345678901 3.67 23
BORGNINE ERNIST     369325263 4.12 14
CADABRA ABRA        123450987 3.33 23
DJIKSTRA EDGAR      345998765 3.90 33
GARZELONI RANDY     444226666 2.20 18
GLUTZ AGATHA        320678230 3.00 22
HOLBRUCK HALL       321908765 3.50 29
HUNTER MICHAEL      234098112 2.50 22
JOHNSON ROSALYN     345123690 3.25 20
LOCKLEAR HEATHER    369426163 4.00 30
MCMANN ABAGAIL      333112040 3.97 41
MILDEW MORRIS       234812057 3.67 34
MORSE SAMUEL        334558778 3.00 28
NOVAK JAMES         348524598 1.50 13
OHERLAHE TERRY      333662222 2.75 21
RACKHAM HORACE      345878643 4.00 30
SNYDER JUDITH       356913580 2.75 24
VANDERSYS RALPH     367120987 3.23 22
VAUGHN SARAH        238498765 3.00 24
WIDGET WENDELL      444113333 1.25 10
WILSON PHILIP       345719642 3.00 25
WITWERTH JANUARY    367138302 2.10 20
WORDEN JACK         359241234 3.33 25
WOURTHY CONSTANCE   342092834 3.50 32
```

and data in TransactionFile as

```
333112040A 3
333112040A 4
333112040A 4
444113333A 3
444113333A 4
444113333A 3
444113333A 2
238498765A 3
238498765A 3
238498765A 4
238498766A 4
369325263A 3
369325263A 3
369325263A 4
369325263C 4
320678230A 5
320678230A 3
320678230A 3
320678230A 4
444226666A 3
444226666A 4
444226666A 3
444226667A 4
367138302A 3
367138302A 3
367130302A 3
367138302B 3
367120987A 4
367120987A 4
367120987A 3
367120987I 3
367120987A 3
369426163A 4
369426163A 3
345678901A 3
345678901A 4
345678901A 3
345678900A 4
123450987A 3
123450987A 3
123450987A 4
123450987E 3
234098112A 3
234098112A 3
444226666D 3
367138302D 3
123450987C 4
123450987D 3
123450987A 2
333112040D 4
333112040A 3
444113333D 4
444113333A 3
369235263D 4
369235263A 3
320678230D 3
320678230D 4
320678230W 3
334229023D 4
```

output for this program is

```
                    EXCEPTION REPORT
          ID NUMBER        GRADE      HOURS
          -----------------------------------

          238498766          A          4
          444226667          A          4
          345678900          A          4
          369235263          D          4
          369235263          A          3
          334229023          D          4

                    UPDATED REPORT
                 STUDENT FILE LISTING
```

NAME	ID NUMBER	GPA	CREDITS
BARRETT RODA	345678901	3.77	33
BORGNINE ERNIST	369325263	3.77	28
CADABRA ABRA	123450987	3.01	45
DJIKSTRA EDGAR	345998765	3.90	33
GARZELONI RANDY	444226666	2.66	31
GLUTZ AGATHA	320678230	3.02	44
HOLBRUCK HALL	321908765	3.50	29
HUNTER MICHAEL	234098112	2.82	28
JOHNSON ROSALYN	345123690	3.25	20
LOCKLEAR HEATHER	369426163	4.00	37
MCMANN ABAGAIL	333112040	3.78	59
MILDEW MORRIS	234812057	3.67	34
MORSE SAMUEL	334558778	3.00	28
NOVAK JAMES	348524598	1.50	13
OHERLAHE TERRY	333662222	2.75	21
RACKHAM HORACE	345878643	4.00	30
SNYDER JUDITH	356913580	2.75	24
VANDERSYS RALPH	367120987	3.53	36
VAUGHN SARAH	238498765	3.29	34
WIDGET WENDELL	444113333	2.64	29
WILSON PHILIP	345719642	3.00	25
WITWERTH JANUARY	367138302	2.53	32
WORDEN JACK	359241234	3.33	25
WOURTHY CONSTANCE	342092834	3.50	32

RUNNING AND DEBUGGING TIPS

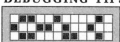

1. Be sure all files (except **input** and **output**) are properly opened for reading and writing. Remember, you must **reset** before reading from a file and **rewrite** before writing to a file.

2. Don't try to read past the end-of-file marker. This is a common error that occurs when trying to **read** without a sufficient check for **eof**.

3. Be careful to use file names as arguments correctly when using **read, readln, write, writeln, and eof.**

4. List all external files in the program heading and then be sure to declare them in the variable declaration section.

5. All files listed in a procedure heading must be variable parameters.

6. Protect against working with empty files or empty lines of a text file.

7. Remember, the file buffer is undefined when **eof** (⟨file name⟩) is **true.**

■ Summary

Key Terms

buffer variable	file window	reading from a file
component of a file	master file	transaction file
file	opening a file	writing to a file

Keywords

FILE   **put**
get

Key Concepts

- A file is a sequence of components all of the same data type; a typical declaration is

```
TYPE
   RealFile = FILE OF real;
VAR
   FileA : RealFile;
```

- In standard implementations of Pascal, files must be accessed sequentially.
- File window is a phrase commonly used to describe which component of the file is available for having data passed to or from it.
- A buffer variable is an undeclared variable that is used to transfer data to or from a file component; if the file name is FileA, then the identifier for the buffer variable is FileA^.
- Before transferring values to a file—writing to a file—the file must be opened for writing by **rewrite** (⟨file name⟩); values can then be transferred from the file buffer using **put** or **write** (⟨file name⟩, ⟨value⟩); for example,

```
rewrite (NewFile);
NewFile^ := 10;
put (NewFile);
```

or

```
rewrite (NewFile);
write (NewFile, 10);
```

- Before transferring values from a file—reading from a file—the file must be opened for reading by **reset** (⟨file name⟩); values can then be transferred from the file by assignments from the file buffer and by using **get** (⟨file name⟩) or **read** (⟨file name⟩, ⟨variable name⟩); for example,

```
reset (NewFile);
A := NewFile^;
get (NewFile);
```

or

```
reset (NewFile);
read (NewFile, A);
```

- An end-of-file marker is automatically placed at the end of the file—**eof** (⟨file name⟩)—when a file is created.
- A file cannot be opened for reading and writing at the same time.
- When a file is declared as a parameter in a procedure heading, it must be listed as a variable parameter; for example,

```
PROCEDURE Update (VAR OldFile, NewFile : ⟨file type⟩);
```

- Components of a file can be arrays; the declaration

```
VAR
   F : FILE OF ARRAY [1..10] OF real;
```

can be depicted as shown in Figure 13.5, where F^ is an array and array components are denoted by F^[J].

FIGURE 13.5
File of arrays

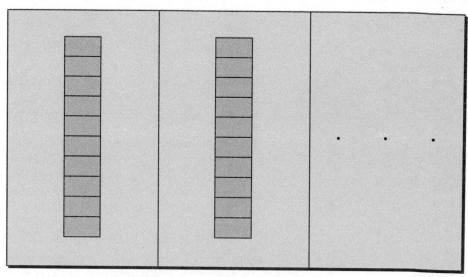

F

- File components can also be records and can be declared by

```
TYPE
  RecType = RECORD
              Name : PACKED ARRAY [1..20] OF char;
              Age : 0..120;
              Gender : char
            END;  {  of RECORD RecType  }
VAR
  F : FILE OF RecType;
```

and depicted as shown in Figure 13.6. In this case, the buffer variable F^ is a
record and fields can be denoted by

```
F^.Name
F^.Age
F^.Gender
```

FIGURE 13.6
File of records

F

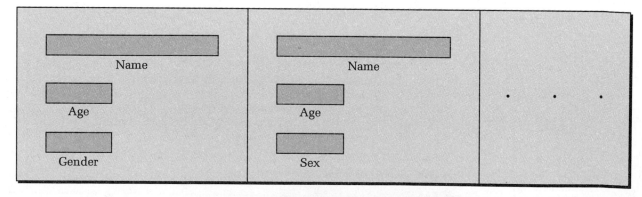

- Files with structured components frequently have to be processed and/or updated; for a file of records, you might insert or delete a record, sort the file by a

field, merge two files, update each record, or produce a printed list according to some field.
- When updating or otherwise processing a file, changes are normally made in a transaction (temporary) file and then copied back into the master (permanent) file.
- Since input data are generally in a text file, you need to create a file of structured components from the text file; you can then use **get** and **put** to transfer entire structures at one time.

■ Programming Problems and Projects

1. *The Pentagon* is a mathematics magazine published by Kappa Mu Epsilon, a mathematics honorary society. Write a program to be used by the business manager for the purpose of generating mailing labels. The subscribers' information should be read into a file of records. Each record should contain the subscriber's name; address, including street and street number, apartment number (if any), city, two-letter abbreviation for the state, and the zip code; expiration information, including month and year.

   Your program should create an alphabetically sorted master file, print an alphabetical list for the office, print a mailing list sorted by zip code for bulk mailing, and denote all last issues by a special symbol.

2. The relentless Dr. Lae Z. Programmer (Problems 5, 22, and 23; Chapter 5; Problem 13, Chapter 6; Problem 7, Chapter 7; Problem 5, Chapter 9; Problem 3, Chapter 11; Problem 3, Chapter 12) now wants you to create a file of records for students in his computer science course. You should provide fields for the student's name, ten quiz scores, six program scores, and three examination scores. Your program should
   a. Read in the names from a text file.
   b. Include procedures for updating quiz scores, program scores, and examination scores.
   c. Be able to update the file by adding or deleting a record.
   d. Print an alphabetized list of the data base at any given time.

3. Write a program to do part of the work of a word processor. Your program should read a text file and print it in paragraph form. The left margin should be in column 10 and the right margin in column 72. In the input file, periods will designate the end of sentences and the "*" symbol will denote a new paragraph. No word should be split between lines. Your program should save the edited file in a file of type **text.**

4. Slow-pitch softball is rapidly becoming a popular summer pastime. Assume your local community is to have a new women's league this year consisting of eight teams, with 15 players each. This league gets the field one night per week for four games. They will play a double round-robin (each team plays every other team twice, resulting in 14 games). Write a program to
   a. Create a file of records (one record for each team) in which the team name is included.
   b. Print a schedule.
   c. List the teams alphabetically by team name.
   d. Print a list of players for each team.

5. The registrar at State University (Problem 15, Chapter 5; Problem 3, Chapter 9) wants you to write an interactive program to assist with record keeping. Your program should create a file of records. The record for each student should contain the student's name, identification number, credit hours completed, the number of credit hours in which currently enrolled, and grade point average. Your program should also contain a procedure for each of the following updates.
   a. Semester-end data of hours completed and grade point average for the semester.
   b. Insert a record.
   c. Delete a record.
   d. Print a list sorted alphabetically.
   e. Print a list sorted by grade point average.

6. The local high school sports boosters (Problems 1 and 2, Chapter 11) need more help. They want you to write a program to create a file of records in which each record contains the parents' names, the children's first names (at most ten children), and the names of the sports in which the children participated.
   A typical record is shown in Figure 13.7. Your program should create a file from a text file and save it for later use, print an alphabetical list of parents' names, and print a list of the names of parents of football players.

FIGURE 13.7
Typical values for fields in a record

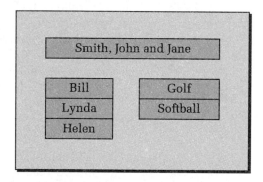

7. A popular use of text files is for teachers to create a bank of test items and then use them to generate quizzes using some form of random generation. Write a program to allow you to create files of type **text** that contain questions for each of three chapters. Second, generate two quizzes of three questions for each of the three chapters.

8. Public service departments must always be on the lookout for those who try to abuse the system by accepting assistance from similar agencies in different geographic areas. Write a program to compare names from one county with those from another county and print all names that are on both lists.

9. Write a program to be used by flight agents at an airport (see Exercise 1a, Section 13.3). Your program should use a file of records where the record for each flight contains flight number, airline, arrival time, arriving from, departure time, and destination. Your program should list incoming flights sorted by time, list departing flights sorted by time, add flights, and delete flights.

10. Congratulations! You have just been asked to write a program that will assign dates for the Valentine's Day dance. Each student record will contain the student's name, age, gender (M or F), and the names of three date preferences (ranked). Your program should
    a. Create a master file from the input file.
    b. Create and save alphabetically sorted files of males and females.
    c. Print a list of couples for the dance. The genders must be opposite and the age difference may be no more than three years. Dating preferences should be in the following form.

    CAN'T MISS!

First request	Matches	First request

    GOOD BET!

First request	Matches	Second request
Second request	Matches	First request

    GOOD LUCK!
    Any other matches
    OUT OF LUCK!
    You are not on any list

    It's obvious (isn't it?) that a person can have at most one date for the dance.

11. A data file consists of an unknown number of real numbers. Write a program to read the file and print the highest value, lowest value, and average of the numbers in the file.

■ 12. The Falcon Manufacturing Company (Problem 22, Chapter 11; Problem 17, Chapter 12) wants you to write an inventory file program. The file should contain a 30-character part name, an integer part number, the quantity on hand, and the price of an item. The program should permit the entry of new items into the file and the deletion of existing items. The items to be changed will be entered from the keyboard.

■ 13. Write a program for the Falcon Manufacturing Company (Problem 12) to allow a secretary to enter an item number and a quantity, and whether it is to be added to or deleted from the stock. The program should prepare a new data file with the updated information. If the user requests to remove more items than are on hand, an appropriate warning message should be issued.

■ 14. Write a program to read the inventory file of the Falcon Manufacturing Company (Problems 12 and 13) and then print a listing of the inventory. The program should print an asterisk (*) next to the quantity of any item of which there are fewer than 50 on hand.

■ 15. Revise the program that you wrote in answer to Problem 22 in Chapter 11 to permit the sales figures of the Falcon Manufacturing Company to be read from a file. Also revise the program so that the information on the total dollar amount of sales for each product by each salesperson is written to a file for later use.

■ 16. Write a program to read the total dollars sales file from Problem 15 for last month and the corresponding file for this month and print out a table showing the total sales by each salesperson for each product during the two-month period.

17. A data file contains an alphabetized list of the secondary students in your high school, and another contains an alphabetized list of the ele-

mentary students. Write a program to merge these two files and print an alphabetized list of all students in your former school.

18. The Andover Telephone Company (whose motto is "We send your messages of Andover.") wants a computerized directory information system. The data file should contain the customer names and telephone numbers. Your program should permit:
    a. The entry of new customers' names and telephone numbers.
    b. The deletion of existing customers' names and telephone numbers.
    c. The printing of all customers' names and their telephone numbers.
    d. The entry from the keyboard of a customer's name with the program then printing the telephone number (if found).

    Whenever customers' names and numbers are to be added or deleted, the file should be updated accordingly. You may assume there are no more than 50 customers.

19. Revise the program written to keep the grades of Mr. Laven's students (Problem 19, Chapter 11) to read the grades entered previously from a file and, when the program is complete, print the updated list of grades.

20. Recognizing your talents as a programmer, the principal of the local high school wants you to write a program to work with a data file containing the names of the students who were absent at the start of the school day. These names are kept as 30-character packed arrays. The program should permit the principal to enter the name of a student later in the day to check to see if the student was absent at the start of the day.

21. Revise Problem 13 from Chapter 12 to permit Mrs. Crown's computer maintenance records to be kept in a file. Your program should allow the data on a machine to be changed and new machines to be added.

22. Contact a programmer at your university or some company or corporation to discuss data structures. Find out how much (if any) he or she uses arrays, records, and files. If the programmer does use arrays, records, or files, what kinds of programming problems require their use? Find out what kinds of operations are used with these data structures. What limitations do these structures possess for the problems that need to be solved?

    Write a complete report summarizing your discussion.

23. Problems involving data management are routinely addressed in non-programming courses taught in schools of business. These courses may be taught in departments such as Management Information Systems (MIS) or Business Information Systems (BIS). Contact an instructor of such a course and discuss the issue of using data structures to manage information. How are data structures presented to the classes? What are some typical real-world problems?

    Give an oral report of your discussion to your class. Compare and contrast the instructor's presentations with those provided in your own class. Use charts with transparencies as part of your presentation.

24. Select an unworked problem from the previously listed programming problems for this chapter. Construct a structure chart and write all documentary information necessary for this problem. Do not write code. When finished, have a classmate read your documentation to see if precisely what is to be done is clear.

Sorting and Merging

The previous chapters have presented techniques for working with structured variables. In particular, you have seen how to sort lists in either ascending or descending order, search lists for some specific value, and merge lists that may or may not be sorted. You have also seen how to use recursion. In this chapter, we will examine several additional techniques for working with structured variables.

Unfortunately, this chapter cannot answer all of the questions associated with sorting and merging. This text—as with most beginning courses—defers more extensive treatment and examination of other methods and their relative efficiency to later programming courses. A list of suggestions for further reading is included at the end of this chapter.

■ 14.1
Sorting Algorithms

OBJECTIVES

- to understand the algorithm for an insertion sort
- to be able to use an insertion sort in a program
- to understand the algorithm for a bubble sort
- to be able to use a bubble sort in a program
- to understand the algorithm for a quick sort
- to be able to use a quick sort in a program

Several algorithms are available for sorting elements in arrays and files. We have worked with the selection sort since Chapter 10. Three other sorting methods commonly used in programming texts are the *insertion sort*, the *bubble sort*, and the *quick sort*. All of these sorts work relatively well for sorting small lists of elements.

However, when large data bases need to be sorted, a direct application of an elementary sorting process usually requires a great deal of computer time. Thus, some other sorting method is needed. This might involve using a different algorithm or dividing the lists into smaller parts, sorting these parts, and then merging the lists back together. In more advanced courses, you will examine the relative efficiency of sorts and methods for handling large data bases. For now, let's consider these three sorting methods.

Insertion Sort

The purpose of a sort is to produce an array of elements sorted in either ascending or descending order. These elements will normally be read from an input file into an array. Let's now see how an insertion sort arranges numbers in ascending order in an unsorted array.

The main principles of an insertion sort are:

1. Put the first K elements of an array in order.
2. Move the K + 1 element into Temp.
3. Move the sorted elements (1 to K) down, one at a time, until the value in Temp can be placed in order in the previously sorted portion of the array.

To illustrate how this works, consider the array of integers

A

| 4 |
| 2 |
| 0 |
| 15 |
| 8 |

The first step is to put the value from A[2] into Temp by

```
Temp := A[2];
```

This produces

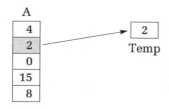

where the shaded cell can be thought of as waiting to receive a value. The value in Temp is then compared to values in the array before A[2]. Since A[1] > A[2], the value in A[1] is "moved down" to produce

A

| 4 |
| 4 |
| 0 |
| 15 |
| 8 |

2
Temp

Since we are at the top of the array, the value in Temp is placed in A[1] to yield

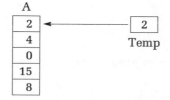

During the next pass, the value of A[3] is put into Temp and we have

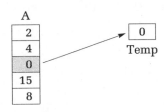

This value is compared to those above it. As long as Temp is less than an array element, the array element is shifted down. This process produces

A

| 2 |
| 2 |
| 4 |
| 15 |
| 8 |

0
Temp

At this stage, the value in Temp is inserted into the array to produce the partially sorted array

A

| 0 |
| 2 |
| 4 |
| 15 |
| 8 |

At the start of the next pass, Temp receives the value in A[4] to yield

A

| 0 |
| 2 |
| 4 |
| 15 |
| 8 |

15
Temp

When the value in Temp is compared to A[3], the process terminates because Temp > A[3]. Thus, using the partially sorted arrays improves the efficiency of the sort. On the last pass, Temp receives the value from A[5] and we have

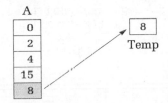

Since Temp < A[4], we next get

<pre>
      A
  ┌──────┐
  │ 0   │   ┌──────┐
  ├──────┤   │ 8   │
  │ 2   │   └──────┘
  ├──────┤   Temp
  │ 4   │
  ├──────┤
  │ 15 │ (shaded)
  ├──────┤
  │ 15 │
  └──────┘
</pre>

At this stage, Temp > A[3] so we insert the value of Temp into A[4] to produce the sorted array

<pre>
      A
  ┌──────┐
  │ 0   │
  ├──────┤
  │ 2   │
  ├──────┤
  │ 4   │
  ├──────┤
  │ 8   │
  ├──────┤
  │ 15 │
  └──────┘
</pre>

In summary, the idea of an insertion sort is to

1. Remove an element (K + 1) from the array.
2. Slide the previously sorted elements down the array until a position is found for the new element.
3. Insert the element in its proper position.
4. Continue until the array is sorted.

A procedure for the insertion sort is

```
PROCEDURE InsertionSort (VAR List : SortArray;
                         ListLength : integer);

{  Given:    An array List with entries in locations 1    }
{                  through ListLength                      }
{  Task:     Apply insertion sort logic to List           }
{  Return:   The array List with entries sorted in        }
{                  ascending order                         }

VAR
  Index, K : integer;
  Temp : ElementType;
  Done : boolean;

BEGIN
  FOR Index := 2 TO ListLength DO
    BEGIN
      Temp := List[Index];
      K := Index;
      Done := false;
      WHILE (K >= 2) AND (NOT Done) DO
        IF Temp < List[K-1] THEN
          BEGIN                              {  Move elements down  }
            List[K] := List[K-1];
            K := K-1
          END
```

```
          ELSE
             Done := true;  {  Found position for insertion  }
          List[K] := Temp                {   Insert into array  }
       END  {  of FOR loop  }
END;  {  of PROCEDURE InsertionSort  }
```

This procedure is called from the main program by

```
InsertionSort (UnsortedList, Length);
```

As expected, records can be sorted by examining some key field and then assigning the entire record accordingly. Thus, if an array type is

```
TYPE
   .
   .
   .
   StudentInfo = RECORD
                   Name : String20;
                   Score : integer
                 END;  {  of RECORD StudentInfo  }
   List = ARRAY [1..ListLength] OF StudentInfo;
```

and the array is to be sorted according to student scores, the field comparison in **PROCEDURE** InsertionSort could be

```
IF Temp.Score < List[K-1].Score
```

Bubble Sort

The sorting algorithm commonly referred to as a bubble sort also rearranges the elements of an array until they are in either ascending or descending order. Like the selection sort, an extra array is not used. Basically, a bubble sort starts at the top of an array and compares two consecutive elements of the array. If they are in the correct order, the next pair is compared. If they are not in the correct order, they are switched and the next pair compared. When this is done for the entire array, one pass has been made and the correct element is in the last position.

Starting at the top each time, successive passes through the array are made until the array is sorted. Two items should be noted here.

1. A flag is needed to indicate whether or not an exchange was made during the pass through the array. If none was made, the array is sorted.
2. Since each pass filters the largest (or smallest) element to the bottom, the length of what remains to be sorted can be decreased by one after each pass.

To illustrate how this algorithm works, assume the array is

```
  A
┌────┐
│ 12 │
├────┤
│  0 │
├────┤
│  3 │
├────┤
│  2 │
├────┤
│  8 │
└────┘
```

Gene Mapping: Computer Scientists Examine Problems of Genome Project

Deciphering the human genome is much like trying to read the instructions on a computer disk filled with programs written in the zeros and ones of electronic code—without knowing the programming language.

That was the message from molecular biologists to computer scientists at a meeting sponsored by the National Research Council. The biologists hope to involve the computer scientists in the U.S. Human Genome Project, a 15-year, $3-billion effort to identify and locate the information contained in human chromosomes.

Computer scientists, with their experience in managing information and using arcane programming languages to store data and convey instructions, could be particularly valuable in helping to read and organize the three billion "letters" that make up the human genetic code, the biologists said.

"The entire program for making *me* is about 10 to the 10 bits," (about 10 trillion pieces of information) said Gerald J. Sussman, a professor of electrical engineering and computer science at the Massachusetts Institute of Technology. "It is no bigger than the U.S. Tax Code, or the design documents for the U.S. space shuttle." Figuring out what the program is, he said, is a computer-science problem.

Biologists said they needed computer scientists to:

Design easy-to-use data bases that can handle the millions of pieces of information that need to be correlated to fully understand genetics—and life.

Design computer networks that will allow biologists to share information conveniently.

Create procedures that will allow biologists to analyze information pulled from laboratory experiments.

Write programs that will let biologists simulate the formation and development of proteins.

The first pass through the array produces

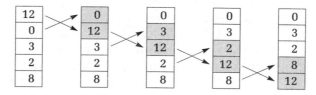

Since an exchange was made, we need to make at least one more pass through the array. However, the length is decreased by one because there is no need to compare the last two elements. A second pass produces

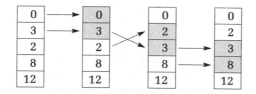

At this stage, the array is sorted, but since an exchange was made, the length is decreased by one and another pass is made. Since no exchange is made during this third pass, the sorting process is terminated.

The algorithm for a bubble sort can be coded in a procedure as follows:

```
PROCEDURE BubbleSort (VAR ListName : List;
                      Length : integer);

VAR
   ExchangeMade : boolean;
   J, Temp : integer;
```

```
BEGIN
  ExchangeMade := true;
  Length := Length - 1;
  WHILE ExchangeMade DO
    BEGIN
      ExchangeMade := false;
      FOR J := 1 TO Length DO
        IF ListName[J] > ListName[J+1] THEN
          BEGIN { Exchange values }
            Temp := ListName[J];
            ListName[J] := ListName[J+1];
            ListName[J+1] := Temp;
            ExchangeMade := true
          END;
      Length := Length - 1 { Decrement length }
    END { of WHILE...DO }
END; { of PROCEDURE BubbleSort }
```

This procedure is called from the main program by

```
BubbleSort (ListName, Length);
```

where ListName is the name of the array to be sorted and Length is the number of elements in the array.

Quick Sort

One of the fastest sorting techniques available is the quick sort. It uses recursion and is based on the idea of separating a list of numbers into two parts. One part contains the numbers smaller than some number in the list and the other contains numbers larger than the number. Thus, if an unsorted array originally contains

14	3	2	11	5	8	0	2	9	4	20
A[1]	A[2]				A[6]					A[11]

we would select the element in the middle position, A[6], and then pivot on the value in A[6], which is 8 in our illustration. Our process would then put all values less than 8 on the left side and all values greater than 8 on the right side. This first subdividing produces

Pivot
↓

4	3	2	2	5	0	8	11	9	14	20
A[1]										A[11]

Now, each sublist is subdivided in the same manner. This process continues until all sublists are in order. The array is then sorted. This is a recursive process.

Before writing a procedure for this sort, let's examine how it works. First, why do we choose the value in the middle position? Ideally, we would like to pivot on the median of the list. However, it is not efficient to find this value first, so we choose the value in the middle as a compromise. The index of this value is found by (First + Last) **DIV** 2 where First and Last are the indices of the initial and final array elements. We then identify a LeftArrow and RightArrow on the far left and far right respectively. This can be envisioned as

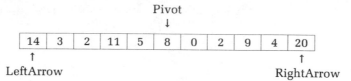

where LeftArrow and RightArrow represent the respective indices of the array components. Starting on the right, the RightArrow is moved left until a value less than or equal to the pivot is encountered. This produces

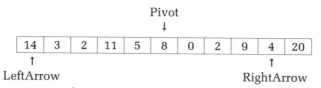

In a similar manner, LeftArrow is moved right until a value greater than or equal to the pivot is encountered. This is the situation just encountered. Now the contents of the two array components are switched to produce

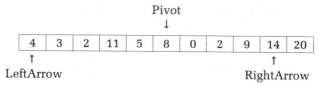

We continue by moving RightArrow left to produce

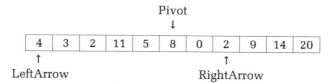

and moving LeftArrow right yields

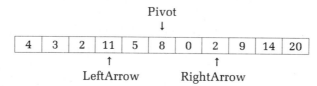

These values are exchanged to produce

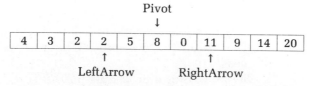

This process stops when LeftArrow > RightArrow is **true**. Since this is still **false** at this point, the next RightArrow move produces

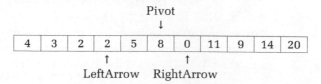

and the LeftArrow move to the right yields

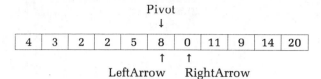

Since LeftArrow < Pivot is **false,** LeftArrow stops moving and an exchange is made to produce

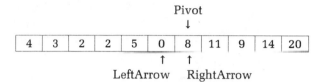

Notice that the pivot, 8, has been exchanged to occupy a new position. This is acceptable because Pivot is the value of the component, not the index. As before, RightArrow is moved left and Left Arrow is moved right to produce

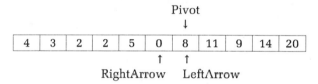

Since RightArrow < LeftArrow is **true,** the first subdividing is complete. At this stage, numbers smaller than Pivot are on the left side and numbers larger than Pivot are on the right side. This produces two sublists that can be envisioned as

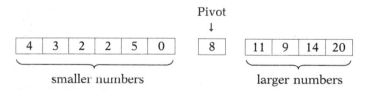

Each sublist can now be sorted by the same procedure. This would require a recursive call to the sorting procedure. In each case, the array is passed as a variable parameter together with the right and left indices for the appropriate sublist. A procedure for this sort is

```
PROCEDURE QuickSort (VAR Num : List;
                         Left, Right : integer);

  VAR
     Pivot, Temp, LeftArrow, RightArrow : integer;

  BEGIN
     LeftArrow := Left;
     RightArrow := Right;
     Pivot := Num[(Left + Right) DIV 2];
     REPEAT
        WHILE Num[RightArrow] > Pivot DO
          RightArrow := RightArrow - 1;
        WHILE Num[LeftArrow] < Pivot DO
          LeftArrow := LeftArrow + 1;
        IF LeftArrow <= RightArrow THEN
```

```
            BEGIN
              Temp := Num[LeftArrow];
              Num[LeftArrow] := Num[RightArrow];
              Num[RightArrow] := Temp;
              LeftArrow := LeftArrow + 1;
              RightArrow := RightArrow - 1
            END  {  of switching elements and then moving arrows  }
          UNTIL RightArrow < LeftArrow;
          IF Left < RightArrow THEN
            QuickSort (Num, Left, RightArrow);
          IF LeftArrow < Right THEN
            QuickSort (Num, LeftArrow, Right)
       END;  {  of PROCEDURE QuickSort  }
```

A complete interactive program to illustrate the use of quick sort follows. The design for this program is

1. Fill the array
2. Sort the numbers
3. Print the list

The complete program is

```
PROGRAM UseQuickSort (input, output);

{  This  program  illustrates  the  quick  sort  as  a sorting  }
{  algorithm.  The array elements are successively  subdivided  }
{  into "smaller" and "larger" elements in parts of the array.  }
{  Recursive calls are made to the PROCEDURE QuickSort.         }

CONST
  MaxLength = 30;

TYPE
  List = ARRAY [1..MaxLength] OF integer;

VAR
  Num : List;
  First, Last, Length : integer;

{************************************************************** }

PROCEDURE FillArray (VAR Num : List;
                     VAR Length : integer);

  {  Given:   Nothing                                            }
  {  Task:    Read numbers entered from the keyboard into the    }
  {             array Num                                        }
  {  Return:  An array of numbers, Num, and number of elements   }
  {             in the array                                     }

  VAR
    Index : integer;

  BEGIN
    Index := 0;
    REPEAT
      Index := Index + 1;
      write ('Enter an integer, -999 to quit.   ');
      readln (Num[Index])
    UNTIL Num[Index] = -999;
    Length := Index - 1
  END;  {  of PROCEDURE FillArray  }
```

```
{ ***************************************************************** }

   PROCEDURE QuickSort (VAR Num : List;
                        Left, Right : integer);

     {  Given:    An unsorted array of integers and array length    }
     {  Task:     Sort the array                                    }
     {  Return:   A sorted array of integers                        }

     VAR
       Pivot, Temp, LeftArrow, RightArrow : integer;

     BEGIN
       LeftArrow := Left;
       RightArrow := Right;
       Pivot := Num[(Left + Right) DIV 2];
       REPEAT
         WHILE Num[RightArrow] > Pivot DO
           RightArrow := RightArrow - 1;
         WHILE Num[LeftArrow] < Pivot DO
           LeftArrow := LeftArrow + 1;
         IF LeftArrow <= RightArrow THEN
           BEGIN
             Temp := Num[LeftArrow];
             Num[LeftArrow] := Num[RightArrow];
             Num[RightArrow] := Temp;
             LeftArrow := LeftArrow + 1;
             RightArrow := RightArrow - 1
           END  {  of IF...THEN  }
       UNTIL RightArrow < LeftArrow;
       IF Left < RightArrow THEN
         QuickSort (Num, Left, RightArrow);
       IF LeftArrow < Right THEN
         QuickSort (Num, LeftArrow, Right)
     END;  {  of PROCEDURE QuickSort  }

{ ***************************************************************** }

   PROCEDURE PrintList (VAR Num : List;
                        Length : integer);

     {  Given:    A sorted array of numbers and array length        }
     {  Task:     Print the numbers                                 }
     {  Return:   Nothing                                           }

     VAR
       Index : integer;

     BEGIN
       writeln;
       writeln ('The sorted list is:');
       writeln;
       FOR Index := 1 TO Length DO
         writeln (Num[Index])
     END;  {  of PROCEDURE PrintList  }

{ ***************************************************************** }

   BEGIN  {  Main program  }
     FillArray (Num, Length);
     QuickSort (Num, 1, Length);
     PrintList (Num, Length)
   END.  {  of main program  }
```

A sample run of this program using the previous data produces

```
Enter an integer, -999 to quit.   14
Enter an integer, -999 to quit.   3
Enter an integer, -999 to quit.   2
Enter an integer, -999 to quit.   11
Enter an integer, -999 to quit.   5
Enter an integer, -999 to quit.   8
Enter an integer, -999 to quit.   0
Enter an integer, -999 to quit.   2
Enter an integer, -999 to quit.   9
Enter an integer, -999 to quit.   4
Enter an integer, -999 to quit.   20
Enter an integer, -999 to quit.   -999

The sorted list is:

0
2
2
3
4
5
8
9
11
14
20
```

Exercises 14.1

1. Modify the insertion sort so that it sorts numbers from an input file rather than from an array. Explain why **PROCEDURE** InsertionSort inserts the first element of the unsorted list into the first position of the sorted list.

2. The array

17
0
3
2
8

   requires five exchanges of elements when sorted using a bubble sort. Since each exchange requires 3 assignment statements, there are 15 assignments for elements in the array. Sort the same array using the insertion sort and determine the number of assignments made.

3. Modify the insertion sort by including a counter that counts the number of assignments of array elements made during a sort.

4. Using the modification in Exercise 3, sort lists of differing lengths that contain randomly generated numbers. Display the results of how many assignments were made for each sort on a graph similar to Figure 14.1. (Use lists whose lengths are multiples of ten.)

5. Modify both the bubble sort and selection sort (from Chapter 10) to include counters for the number of assignments made during a sort.

6. Use the modified version of all three sorts to examine their relative efficiency; that is, run them on arrays of varying lengths and plot the results on a graph. What are your conclusions?

FIGURE 14.1
Array length

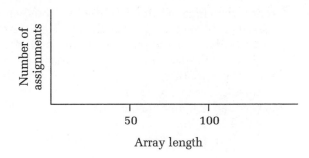

7. Write a short program to read numbers into an array, sort the array, print the sorted numbers, and save the sorted list for later use by some other program.

8. Modify all sorts to sort from high to low rather than low to high.

9. Sorting parallel arrays is a common practice (for example, an array of names and a corresponding array of scores on a test). Modify the insertion sort, bubble sort, and quick sort so that you can sort a list of names and test scores.

10. Write a procedure Exchange for the bubble sort to exchange the values of array components. Then rewrite the bubble sort using **PROCEDURE** Exchange.

11. Suppose you are using a program that contains an array of records in which each record is defined by

```
TYPE
    .
    .
    .
CustomerInfo = RECORD
                  Name : String20;
                  AmountDue : real
               END;
```

Use the bubble sort to sort (and then print) the records alphabetically.

Re-sort the array by the field AmountDue. Print a list ordered by AmountDue where anyone with an amount due of more than $100 will be designated with a triple asterisk'***'.

12. Explain how an array of records with a key field, Name, can be sorted using a quick sort.

13. Modify **PROCEDURE** QuickSort to use the first element in an array as the pivot rather than the middle element.

■ ■ ■ ■

■ 14.2
Merging Algorithms

OBJECTIVES
- to be able to merge two sorted files
- to be able to merge two sorted arrays
- to be able to sort large files or arrays by a sort-merge
- to be able to update an existing sorted file by sorting a new file and then merging it with the existing file

Two-Way Merge

It is often necessary to merge two sorted files or arrays to produce a single file or array. For example, you may wish to update a mailing list that has been sorted by customer name with names to be added to the list. If the names to be added are sorted alphabetically in a file, you need to merge two sorted files. One specific instance of using such a merge was given in Section 13.3 when a new file was merged with a master file to produce an updated master file. We now examine some more general versions of merging.

The process of merging two sorted lists is referred to as a *two-way merge* and requires a third data structure (a file or an array). Assume we are to merge two files of integers—the previously sorted files File1 and File2 —and produce the merged file FinalFile. The idea of this merge is not too difficult. Essentially, you compare elements at the top of each file and assign the higher (or the lower, if you are sorting from low to high) to FinalFile. You then compare the nonassigned element to the next element in the other file and repeat the process. You continue in this manner until the end of one file is reached. Then you sequentially assign all elements remaining in the other file to FinalFile.

A pseudocode development for this is

1. Open all files appropriately
2. **WHILE NOT** at end of either file **DO**
    2.1 **IF** File1 element > File2 element **THEN**
        2.1.1 assign File1 element to FinalFile
        2.1.2 move pointer to next element in File1
        ELSE
        2.1.3 assign File2 element to FinalFile
        2.1.4 move pointer to next element in File2
3. Assign remainder of File1
4. Assign remainder of File2

If we now assume File1, File2, and FinalFile are files of integers and File1 and File2 are sorted, the code for a two-way merge is

```
reset (File1);
reset (File2);
rewrite (FinalFile);
WHILE NOT eof(File1) AND NOT eof(File2) DO
  BEGIN
    IF File1^ > File2^ THEN
      BEGIN
        FinalFile^ := File1^;
        get (File1)
      END
    ELSE
      BEGIN
        FinalFile^ := File2^;
        get (File2)
      END;
    put (FinalFile)
  END;

{ Now assign the rest of the unused file. Only one
  of the following will actually be executed.  }

WHILE NOT eof(File1) DO
  BEGIN
    FinalFile^ := File1^;
    put (FinalFile);
    get (File1)
  END;

WHILE NOT eof(File2) DO
  BEGIN
    FinalFile^ := File2^;
    put (FinalFile);
    get (File2)
  END;
```

Sort-Merge

Large files or arrays present special problems when they need to be sorted. The algorithms we have studied thus far are relatively inefficient when it comes to sorting a long list. To illustrate how the inefficiency increases as lists get longer, consider a worst-case situation in an array of components that is to be sorted high to low using a bubble sort. This worst-case scenario means they are ordered from low to high as illustrated.

A

1
2
3
4
5
6
7
8

This array will be sorted using (8 * 7) / 2 or 28 comparisons, which is the maximum required for an array of length 8. If the array to be sorted was of length 16, the maximum number of comparisons would be (16 * 15) / 2 or 120.

Since the number of comparisons increases so rapidly for progressively longer lists, a preferred method of sorting is to subdivide the list, sort the shorter lists, and then merge to get a single sorted list. To illustrate, let's continue the example of sorting an array with 16 elements. As shown, a bubble sort applied to the array requires at most 120 comparisons. Now, if we divide the array in half, sorting each half will require at most 28 comparisons. These two arrays can then be merged using at most 16 (8 + 8) comparisons. Thus, by subdividing, sorting, and then merging, an array of length 16 can be sorted using at most 72 comparisons rather than 120.

For longer arrays, the problem is even more critical. For example, using an array of length 1,000, a bubble sort requires (1000 * 999) / 2, or 499,500 comparisons. If this is halved, each half sorted, and the sorted results merged, it requires at most (500 * 499) / 2 + (500 * 499) / 2 + 1000, or 250,500 comparisons.

It is easy to see that this process of divide-and-conquer can be extended to each of the smaller arrays. To illustrate the efficiency of successively dividing lists to be sorted, suppose we originally have an array containing 1,024 items. If we subdivide until we get 128 lists of 8 items each, sort each list of 8 items, and then merge pairs of lists until we get a single sorted list, this process would require a maximum of 10,752 comparisons. A bubble sort on the original list would require a maximum of (1024 * 1023) / 2, or 523,776 comparisons.

The process of repeatedly subdividing a long list, sorting shorter lists, and then merging to obtain a single sorted list is referred to as *sort-merge*. A sort-merge can be done by recursion. In this form, subdivisions are performed until each list contains one element. These single-element lists are then merged to achieve the desired result.

To illustrate this recursive sort-merge, let's write a procedure Merge to merge two parts of a global array A. The parts must be consecutive in the array and each part must already be sorted. This procedure is called by sending the index of the initial value and the index of the final value for each of the two portions that are to be merged. Our procedure merges them to form a single sorted portion of the array. Such a procedure is

```
PROCEDURE Merge (AInit, AFinal, BInit, BFinal : integer);

  VAR
    I, J, K, L : integer;
    NewList : ArrayType;

  BEGIN
    L := AInit;
    J := AInit;
    K := BInit;
    WHILE (J <= AFinal) AND (K <= BFinal) DO
      BEGIN
        IF A[J] < A[K] THEN
          BEGIN
            NewList[L] := A[J];
            J := J + 1
          END
        ELSE
          BEGIN
            NewList[L] := A[K];
            K := K + 1
          END;
        L := L + 1
      END;

  {  Now merge remainder of array  }

    FOR I := J TO AFinal DO
      BEGIN
        NewList [L] := A[I];
        L := L + 1
      END;
    FOR I := K TO BFinal DO
      BEGIN
        NewList[L] := A[I];
        L := L + 1
      END;
    FOR I := AInit TO BFinal DO
      A[I] := NewList[I];
  END;  {  of PROCEDURE Merge  }
```

With this procedure available, a recursive version of a sort-merge is

```
PROCEDURE SortMerge (First, Last : integer);

  VAR
    Mid : integer;

  BEGIN
    IF Last - First >0 THEN
      BEGIN
        Mid := (First + Last) DIV 2;
        SortMerge (First, Mid);
        SortMerge (Mid + 1, Last);
        Merge (First, Mid, Mid+1, Last)
      END
  END;  {  of PROCEDURE SortMerge  }
```

This is a relatively elegant version of a sort-merge. Unfortunately, it is not recommended for practical use. For long lists, several recursive calls to Sort-

Merge are inefficient. A more practical method is to write a nonrecursive version and stop subdividing lists at some predetermined length. A specific example using a length of eight is left as an exercise.

Sort-Merge with Files

We close this section with a discussion of a problem encountered by programmers who work with files. Large data bases (mailing lists, for example) are frequently stored in a file of records where the records are sorted according to some key field. As previously noted, this file is often referred to as the MasterFile or OldFile.

Periodically, this original file needs to be updated by adding more records. It is not unusual for these additional records to be entered into a new file (NewFile) in a random order. The problem of updating the master file is solved by sorting NewFile and merging it with the original to form a new MasterFile. This process is so standard that many programmers automatically think this is what is meant by the phrase "sort-merge." However, the phrase is not well defined and the process is also known by other names, for example, sequential update.

Exercises 14.2

1. Verify the worst-case possibility for sorting an array of 16 integers using a bubble sort. The array is in reverse order of the way it is to be sorted. Use a counter to count the number of comparisons.

2. Using the same array as in Exercise 1, sort each half with a bubble sort and then merge the two halves to get a sorted list. Again, use counters to count the number of comparisons made in both sorts and the merge. Compare your results with the results from Exercise 1.

3. Write a test program to implement the two-way merge for two arrays.

4. Using the procedure Merge of this section, write a program to implement the recursive procedure SortMerge.

5. Write a nonrecursive sort-merge to subdivide an array into subarrays of length eight, sort each subarray, and then merge the sorted subarrays to get a single sorted array.

■ ■ ■ ■

RUNNING AND DEBUGGING TIPS

1. Sorting large files or long arrays can be very time consuming. Depending on the number of elements to be processed, use some form of divide-and-conquer; that is, divide the list, sort the elements, and then merge them. Very large data bases may require several subdivisions and subsequent merges.

2. When sorting records using a key field, be careful to compare only the key field and then exchange the entire record accordingly.

■ Summary

Key Terms

bubble sort	quick sort	two-way merge
insertion sort	sort-merge	

Key Concepts

■ An insertion sort creates a sorted array from an unsorted array by starting with an empty array and inserting elements one at a time in their respective order.

- A bubble sort sorts an array by comparing consecutive elements in the array and exchanging them if they are out of order; several passes through the array are made until the list is sorted.
- A quick sort is one of the fastest sorting techniques available. It uses recursion and is based on the idea of separating a list into two parts.
- A two-way merge is used to merge two sorted lists to form a single sorted list.
- A sort-merge is a process whereby a long unsorted list is subdivided, the parts are sorted, and these are merged to form a sorted list.

■ Suggestions for Further Reading

Sorting and merging are subjects of numerous articles and books. This chapter provided some samples of each. For variations and improvements on what is included here as well as other techniques, the interested reader is referred to the following books which many consider to be classics in the field.

Baase, Sara. "Sorting." Chapter 2 in *Computer Algorithms: Introduction to Design and Analysis*. Reading, Mass.: Addison-Wesley Publishing Co., 1978.

Gear, William. *Applications and Algorithms in Engineering and Science*. Chicago: Science Research Associates, 1978.

Horowitz, Ellis, and Sartaz Sahmi. "Divide and Conquer." Chapter 3 in *Fundamentals of Computer Algorithms*. Potomac, Md.: Computer Science Press, 1978.

Knuth, Donald. *The Art of Computer Programming*. Vol. 3, *Sorting and Searching*. Reading, Mass.: Addison-Wesley Publishing Co., 1975.

■ Programming Problems and Projects

■ 1. Write a program to update a mailing list. Assume you have a sorted master file of records where each record contains a customer's name, address, and expiration code. Your program should input a file of new customers, sort the file, and merge the file with the master file to produce a new master.

■ 2. Assume that Readmore Public Library (Problems 6 and 7, Chapter 12) has information about books on their shelves stored in a file of records named OldFile. Information about a new shipment of books is contained in the data file. Both files are sorted alphabetically by book title. Write a program to be used to update OldFile. For each book in the input file, your program should search the existing file to see if the additional book is a duplicate. If it is, change a field in the record to indicate that an additional copy has been obtained. If it is not a duplicate, insert the record in sequence in the file.

3. The Bakerville Manufacturing Company has to lay off all employees who started working after a certain date. Write a program to
   a. Input a termination date.
   b. Search an alphabetical file of employee records to determine who will get a layoff notice.
   c. Create a file of employee records for those who are being laid off.
   d. Update the master file to contain only records of current employees.
   e. Produce two lists of those being laid off, one alphabetical and one by hiring date.

4. The Bakerville Manufacturing Company (Problem 3) has achieved new prosperity and can rehire ten employees who were recently laid off. Write a program to
   a. Search the file of previously terminated employees to find the ten with the most seniority.
   b. Delete those ten records from the file of employees who were laid off.

   c. Insert the ten records alphabetically into the file of current employees.

   d. Print four lists as follows:
- i. an alphabetical list of current employees.
- ii. a seniority list of current employees.
- iii. an alphabetical list of employees who were laid off.
- iv. a seniority list of employees who were laid off.

5. The Shepherd Lions Club sponsors an annual cross-country race for area schools. Write a program to
   a. Create an array of records for the runners; each record should contain the runner's name, school, identification number, and time (in a seven-character string, such as 15:17:3).
   b. Print an alphabetical listing of all runners.
   c. Print a list of schools entered in the race.
   d. Print a list of runners in the race ordered by school name.
   e. Print the final finish order by sorting the records according to the order of finish and printing a numbered list according to the order of finish.

6. Form a team of students (three or four) to identify some local business that has not yet computerized its customer records. The team should have a discussion with the owner or manager to determine how the customer records are used. After talking with the owner or manager, the team should design an information processing system for the business. The system should include complete specifications for the design. Particular attention should be paid to searching and sorting.

   The team should then give an oral presentation to the class and use appropriate charts and diagrams to illustrate their design.

CHAPTER

15

Sets

We have thus far investigated the structured variables, arrays, records, and files. These are structured because, when declared, a certain structure is reserved to subsequently hold values. In an array, a predetermined number of elements all of the same type can be held. A record contains a predetermined number of fields that can hold elements of different types. A file is somewhat like an array but the length is not predetermined and elements must be accessed sequentially.

Another structured data type available in Pascal is a *set*. Since the implementation of sets varies greatly from system to system, you need to check statements and examples in this chapter on your system.

The goal of this chapter is to enable you to use sets when writing programs to solve problems. One fairly common use for sets is to guard against an inadvertent keystroke when users are working with interactive programs. But before you can use sets in a program, you must understand certain fundamentals. In particular, you must be able to properly define sets and use set operations.

■ 15.1
Declarations and Terms

Basic Idea and Notation

A set in Pascal is a structured data type consisting of a collection of distinct elements from an indicated base type (which must be ordinal type). Sets in Pascal are defined and used in a manner consistent with the use of sets in mathematics. A set type is defined by

```
TYPE
    ⟨type name⟩ = SET OF ⟨base type⟩;
```

A set variable is then declared by

```
VAR
    ⟨variable name⟩ : ⟨type name⟩;
```

In a program working with characters of the alphabet, you might have

```
TYPE
  Alphabet = SET OF 'A'..'Z';
VAR
  Vowels, Consonants : Alphabet;
```

In a similar fashion, if your program analyzes digits and arithmetic symbols, you might have

```
TYPE
  Units = SET OF 0..9;
  Symbols = SET OF '*'..'/';  {  Arithmetic symbols  }
VAR
  Digits : Units;
  ArithSym : Symbols;
```

In these examples, Alphabet, Units, and Symbols are set types. Vowels, Consonants, Digits, and ArithSym are set variables.

⊤ A set can contain elements; these elements must be of the defined base type, which must be an ordinal data type. Most implementations of Pascal limit the maximum size of the base type of a set. This limit is such that a base type of **integer** is not allowed. Often the limit is at least 128 so base types of **char** and subranges of **integer** within 0..127 can usually be used.

Assignments to Sets

Once a set variable has been declared, it is undefined until an assignment of values is made. The syntax for assigning is

⟨set name⟩ := [⟨values⟩];

For example, we can have

```
Vowels := ['A', 'E', 'I', 'O', 'U'];
Consonants := ['B'..'D', 'F'..'H', 'J'..'N', 'P'..'T',
               'V'..'Z'];
Digits := [0..9];
ArithSym := ['+', '-', '*', '/'];
```

Notice that the assigned values must be included in brackets and must be of the defined base type. Appropriate values depend on the character set being used. Also, subranges of the base type can be used; thus,

```
Consonants := ['B'..'D'];
```

is the same as

```
Consonants := ['B', 'C', 'D'];
```

It is also possible to have set constants. Just as 4, 'H', and −56.20 are constants, [2,4,6] is a constant. In the previous example, this could have been caused by

```
Digits := [2,4,6];
```

As mentioned, sets are structured data types because, in a sense, they can be thought of as containing a list of elements. However, in listing the elements, note that each element can be listed only once and order makes no difference; thus, [2,4,6] is the same as [4,2,6].

Other Terminology

Once a value of the base type has been assigned to a set, it is an *element of the set*. Thus, if we have

```
Digits := [2,4,6];
```

2, 4, and 6 are elements of Digits. Testing membership in a set is discussed in the next section.

As in mathematics, any set that contains all possible values of the base type is called the *universal set*. In

```
Digits := [0..9];
```

Fractal Geometry and Benoit Mandelbrot

Fractal geometry as a serious mathematical endeavor began [in about 1975] with the pioneering work of Benoit B. Mandelbrot, a Fellow of the Thomas J. Watson Research Center, IBM Corporation. Fractal geometry is a theory of geometric forms so complex they defy analysis and classification by traditional Euclidean means. Yet fractal shapes occur universally in the natural world. Mandelbrot has recognized them not only in coastlines, landscapes, lungs, and turbulent water flow but also in the chaotic fluctuation of prices on the Chicago commodity exchange.

Though Mandelbrot's first comprehensive publication of fractal theory took place in 1975, mathematicians were aware of some of the basic elements during the period from 1875 to 1925. However, because mathematicians at that time thought such knowledge of "fractal dimension" deserved little attention, their discoveries were left as unrelated odds and ends. Also, the creation of fractal illustrations—a laborious and nearly impossible task at the turn of the twentieth century—can now be done quickly and precisely using computer graphics. (Even personal computers can now be used to generate fractal patterns with relative ease.)

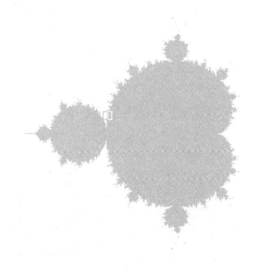

The picture on the left shows an enlargement of the area of the Mandelbrot set shown as a square in the picture on the right.

Source: From *For All Practical Purposes: Introduction to Contemporary Mathematics.* By Consortium for Mathematics and Its Applications. Copyright © 1991 by COMAP, Inc. Reprinted by permission of W.H. Freeman and Company.

Digits is a universal set. It is also possible to consider a set constant as a universal set. Thus, ['A' . . 'Z'] is a universal set if the **TYPE** definition section contains

```
⟨type name⟩= SET OF 'A'..'Z';
```

If A and B have been declared as sets of the same type and all of the elements of A are also contained in B, A is a *subset* of B. If we have

```
VAR
   A, B : Units;
```

and the assignments

```
A := [1,2,3,4,5];
B := [0..6];
```

have been made, A is a subset of B. Note, however, that B is not a subset of A since B contains two elements (0 and 6) that are not contained in A.

The *empty set,* or *null set,* is the set containing no elements. It is denoted by [ ].

Note that these definitions allow for set theory results of mathematics to hold in Pascal. Some of these follow.

1. The empty set is a subset of every set.
2. If A is a subset of B and B is a subset of C, then A is a subset of C.
3. Every set (of the base type) is a subset of the universal set.

Exercises 15.1

1. Find all errors in the following definitions and declarations. Explain your answers.

   a. ```
      TYPE
         Numbers = SET OF real;
      ```

   b. ```
      TYPE
         Numbers = SET OF integer;
      ```

   c. ```
      TYPE
         Alphabet : SET OF 'A'..'Z';
      ```

   d. ```
      TYPE
         Alphabet = SET OF ['A'..'Z'];
      ```

   e. ```
      TYPE
         Conditions = (Sunny, Mild, Rainy, Windy);
         Weather = SET OF Conditions;
      VAR
         TodaysWeather : Weather;
      ```

2. Write a test program to

   a. Discover if **char** is a permissible base type for a set.

   b. Determine the limitation on the size of the base type for a set.

3. Suppose a set A is declared by

   ```
   TYPE
      Letters = SET OF 'A'..'Z';
   VAR
      A : Letters;
   ```

   a. Show how A can be made to contain the letters of your name.

   b. Assign the letters of the word *PASCAL* to A.
   ```

c. Assuming the assignment

```
A := ['T', 'O', 'Y'];
```

list all elements and subsets of A.

4. Let the sets A, B, and U be declared by

```
TYPE
   Alphabet = SET OF 'A'..'Z';
VAR
   A, B, U : Alphabet;
```

and the assignments

```
A := ['B', 'F', 'J'..'T'];
B := ['O'..'S'];
U := ['A'..'Z'];
```

be made. Indicate whether each of the following is **true** or **false**.

a. [ ] is a subset of B   e. 'B' is a subset of A

b. B is an element of A   f. A is a subset of U

c. B is a subset of A   g. 'O' is an element of A

d. 'B' is an element of A

5. Assume A, B, and U are declared as in Exercise 4. Find and explain all errors in the following assignment statements.

a. `A := 'J'..'O';`   d. `A := ['E', 'I', 'E', 'I', 'O'];`

b. `U := [];`   e. `[] := ['D'];`

c. `B := [A..Z];`   f. `B := ['A'..'T', 'S'];`

6. Let A be a set declared by

```
TYPE
   NumRange = 0..100;
VAR
   A : SET OF NumRange;
   M, N : integer;
```

Indicate if the following are valid or invalid. For those that are valid, list the elements of A. For those that are invalid, explain why.

a. `A := [19];`

b. `A := 19;`

c. ```
M := 80;
N := 40;
A := [M + N, M MOD N, M DIV N];
```

d. ```
M := 10;
N := 2;
A := [M, M * N, M / N];
```

7. Define a set type and declare a set variable to be used for each of the following.

a. Set values consist of colors of the rainbow.

b. Set values consist of class in school (Freshman, Sophomore, Junior, or Senior).

c. Set values consist of fruits.

d. Set values consist of grades for a class.

8. Explain why **SET** is not an enumerated type.

■ ■ ■ ■

■ 15.2
Set Operations and Relational Operators

Set Operations

Pascal provides for the set operations *union, intersection,* and *difference* where, in each case, two sets are combined to produce a single set. If A and B are sets of the same type, these operations are defined as follows:

- The union of A and B is A + B where A + B contains any element that is in A or that is in B.
- The intersection of A and B is A * B where A * B contains the elements that are in both A and B.
- The difference of A and B is A − B where A − B contains the elements that are in A but not in B.

To illustrate, suppose A and B are sets that contain integer values and the assignment statements

```
A := [1..5];
B := [3..9];
```

are made. The values produced by set operations follow.

Set Operation	Values
A + B	[1..9]
A * B	[3,4,5]
A − B	[1,2]
B − A	[6..9]

Multiple operations can be performed with sets and, when such an expression is encountered, the same operator priority exists as with priorities for evaluating arithmetic expressions. Thus, if A and B contain the values previously indicated,

```
A + B - A * B
```

produces

```
[1..5] + [3..9]  -  [1..5] * [3..9]
                            ↓
[1..5] + [3..9]  -        [3,4,5]
        ↓
    [1..9]       -        [3,4,5]
                     ↓
            [1,2,6..9]
```

Relational Operators

Relational operators can also be used with sets in Pascal. These operators correspond to the normal set operators equal, not equal, subset, and superset. In each case, a Boolean value is produced. If A and B are sets, these operators are defined as shown in Table 15.1.

Boolean values associated with some set expressions follow.

Set Expression	Boolean Value
[1,2,3] <= [0..10]	true
[0..10] <= [1,2,3]	false
[0..10] = [0..5, 6..10]	true
[] = ([1,2] - [0..10])	true
[1..5] <> [1..3, 4, 5]	false
[] <= [1,2,3]	true

TABLE 15.1
Set operations

Operator	Relational Expression	Definition
= (Equal)	A = B	A equals B; that is, every element in A is contained in B and every element in B is contained in A.
<> (Not equal)	A <> B	A does not equal B; that is, either A or B contains an element that is not contained in the other set.
<= (Subset)	A <= B	A is a subset of B; that is, every element of A is also contained in B.
>= (Superset)	A >= B	A is a superset of B (B is a subset of A); that is, every element of B is contained in A.

Set Membership

Membership in a set is indicated in Pascal by the reserved word **IN**. The general form is

⟨element⟩ **IN** ⟨set⟩

This returns a value of **true** if the element is in the set and a value of **false** if it is not. To illustrate, suppose A and B are sets and the assignments

```
A := [0..20];
B := [5..10];
```

are made. The values of expressions using **IN** follow.

Expression	Boolean Value
10 IN A	**true**
5 IN (A - B)	**false**
20 IN B	**false**
7 IN (A * B)	**true**
80 DIV 20 IN A * B	?

Note that the last expression cannot be evaluated until priorities are assigned to the operators. Fortunately, these priorities are identical to those used for arithmetic expressions with **IN** on the same level as relational operators. They are shown in Table 15.2.

TABLE 15.2
Operator priorities including set operations

Priority Level	Operators
1	( )
2	**NOT**
3	*, /, **MOD, DIV, AND**
4	+, −, **OR**
5	<, >, <=, >=, =, <>, **IN**

Operations at each level are performed in order from left to right as they appear in an expression. Thus, the expression

```
80 DIV 20 IN A * B
```
produces
```
80 DIV 20 IN A * B
        ↓
   4       IN A * B
                ↓
   4       IN [5..10]
             ↓
         false
```

Exercises 15.2

1. When using sets in Pascal, is $>=$ the logical complement of $<=$? Give an example to illustrate your answer.

2. Let A and B be sets defined such that A := [0 .. 10] and B := [2,4,6,8,10] are valid. Write a test program to show that
   a. A + B = A
   b. A * B = B
   c. A − B = [0,1,3,5,7,9]

3. For each of the following sets A and B, find A + B, A * B, A − B, and B − A.
   a. A := [−3 .. 2,8,10], B := [0 .. 4,7 .. 10]
   b. A := [0,1,5 .. 10,20], B := [2,4,6,7 .. 11]
   c. A := [ ], B := [1 .. 15]
   d. A := [0 .. 5, 10, 14 .. 20], B := [3,10,15]

4. Given the following sets
   A := [0,2,4,6,8,10];
   B := [1,3,5,7,9];
   C := [0 .. 5];
   indicate the values in each of the following sets.
   a. A * B − C
   b. A * (B − C)
   c. A * (B + C)
   d. A * B + A * C
   e. A − B * C
   f. A − (B − (A − B))
   g. A * (B * C)
   h. (A * B) * C

5. Using sets A, B, and C with values assigned as in Exercise 4, indicate whether each of the following is **true** or **false**.
   a. A * B = [ ]   d. A + B <> C
   b. C <= A + B   e. A − B >= [ ]
   c. [5] <= B   f. (A + B = C) **OR** ([] <= B − C)

6. In mathematics, when X is an element of a set A, this is denoted by X ∈ A. If X is not in A, we write X∉A. Let B be a set declared by

   ```
   VAR
     B : SET OF 0..10;
   ```

   Examine the following for validity and decide how Pascal handles the concept of not-an-element-of.
   a. `4 NOT IN B`   d. `NOT (4 IN B)`
   b. `4 NOT (IN B)`   e. `4 IN NOT B`
   c. `NOT 4 IN B`   f. `4 IN (NOT B)`

7. Write a short program to count the number of uppercase vowels in a text file. Your program should include the set type

```
TYPE
   AlphaUppercase = SET OF 'A'..'Z';
```

and set variable VowelsUppercase declared by

```
VAR
   VowelsUppercase : AlphaUppercase;
```

■ ■ ■ ■

■ 15.3
Using Sets

Uses for Sets

Now that we know how to declare sets, assign values to sets, and operate with sets, we need to examine some uses of sets in programs. First, however, we need to note an important limitation of sets: as with other structured variables, sets cannot be read or written directly. However, the two processes—generating a set and printing the elements of a set—are not difficult to code. To illustrate generating a set, suppose you wish to create a set and have it contain all the characters in the alphabet found in a line of text. (For this example we assume that the text file does not contain lowercase letters.) You can declare this set with

```
TYPE
   AlphaSymbols = 'A'..'Z';
   Symbols = SET OF AlphaSymbols;
VAR
   Alphabet : Symbols;
   SentenceChar : Symbols;
   Ch : char;
```

Code to generate the set SentenceChar is

```
Alphabet := ['A'..'Z'];
SentenceChar := [];
WHILE NOT eoln(Data) DO
  BEGIN
    read (Data, Ch);
    IF Ch IN Alphabet THEN
      SentenceChar := SentenceChar + [Ch]
  END;
```

For many examples we assume the text file does not contain lowercase letters. As you will see in the Focus on Program Design section, a slight modification can be made to accommodate both uppercase and lowercase letters. For example, you could use both uppercase and lowercase letters by changing the set definitions to

```
TYPE
   Symbols = SET OF char;
VAR
   UppercaseAlphabet : Symbols;
   LowercaseAlphabet : Symbols;
   Alphabet: Symbols;
```

Alphabet could then be formed in the program by

```
UppercaseAlphabet := ['A'..'Z'];
LowercaseAlphabet := ['a'..'z'];
Alphabet := UppercaseAlphabet + LowercaseAlphabet;
```

or

```
Alphabet := ['A'..'Z', 'a'..'z']
```

The general procedure of getting values into a set is to initialize the set by assigning the empty set and use set union to add elements to the set.

The process of printing values of elements in a set is equally short. Assuming you know the data type of elements in the set, a loop can be used where the loop control variable ranges over values of this data type. Whenever a value is in the set, it is printed. To illustrate, assume the set Sentence-Char now contains all the alphabetical characters from a line of text and you wish to print these characters. Since we know the data type for elements of SentenceChar will be characters in 'A' . . 'Z', we can print the contained values by

```
FOR Ch := 'A' TO 'Z' DO
   IF Ch IN SentenceChar THEN
      write (Ch:2);
writeln;
```

If these two fragments of code are applied to the line of text

```
THIS LINE (OBVIOUSLY MADE UP!) DOESN'T MAKE MUCH SENSE.
```

the output is

```
A B C D E H I K L M N O P S T U V Y
```

Now that you are familiar with how to generate elements in a set and subsequently print contents of a set, let's examine some uses for sets in programs. Specifically, let's look at using sets to replace complex Boolean expressions, protect a program against bad data, protect against invalid **CASE** statements, and aid in interactive programming.

STYLE TIP

Sets with appropriate names are particularly useful for checking data. For example, a typical problem when working with dynamic variables (which are discussed in Chapter 16) is to examine an arithmetic expression for correct form. Thus, 3 + 4 is a valid expression but 3 + * 4 is not. As part of a program that analyzes such expressions, you might choose to define the following sets.

```
TYPE
   ValidDigits = SET OF '0'..'9';
   Symbols = SET OF char;
VAR
   Digits : ValidDigits;
   ValidOperator : Symbols;
   LeftSymbol, RightSymbol : Symbols;
```

These sets can now be assigned values such as

```
Digits := ['0'..'9'];
ValidOperator := ['+', '*', '-', '/'];
LeftSymbol := ['(', '[', '{'];
RightSymbol := [')', ']', '}'];
```

Suppose you are writing a program to analyze responses to questions on a standard machine-scored form. If you want a certain action to take place for every response of A, B, or C, instead of

```
IF (Response='A') OR (Response='B') OR (Response='C') THEN
```

you could have

```
IF Response IN ['A', 'B', 'C'] THEN
       .
       .
       .
```

To demonstrate protecting a program against bad data, suppose you are writing a program to use a relatively large data file. Furthermore, suppose that the data are entered by operators in such a fashion that the first entry on the first line for each customer is a single-digit code. This is followed by appropriate data for the customer. To make sure the code is properly entered, you can define a set ValidSym and assign it all appropriate symbols. Your program design can be

```
read (Sym);
IF Sym IN ValidSym THEN
   BEGIN
      .
      .   (action here)
      .
   END
ELSE
    (error message here)
```

Specifically, a program for printing mailing labels might require a 3, 4, or 5 to indicate the number of lines for the name and address that follow. If you are writing a program that also partially edits the data file, you can have

```
read (NumLines);
IF NumLines IN [3,4,5] THEN
   BEGIN
      .
      .   (process number of lines)
      .
   END
ELSE
    (error message here)
```

The third use of sets is to protect against invalid **CASE** statements. This is especially appropriate for implementations that do not have an **OTHERWISE** option (as discussed in Section 5.5). To illustrate, suppose you are working with a program that uses a **CASE** statement where the selector is a letter grade assigned to students. Without sets, the statement is

```
CASE LetGrade OF
   'A' : ...
   'B' : ...
   'C' : ...
   'D' : ...
   'E' : ...
END;  { of CASE LetGrade }
```

To protect against the possibility of LetGrade being assigned a value not in the **CASE** selector list, sets can be used as follows:

```
IF LetGrade IN ['A'..'E'] THEN
   CASE LetGrade OF
      'A' : ...
      'B' : ...
      'C' : ...
      'D' : ...
      'E' : ...
   END  { of CASE LetGrade }
ELSE
    (error message here)
```

A fourth use of sets is as an aid in writing interactive programs. Frequently a user will be asked to respond by pressing a certain key or keys. For example, a message such as the following may be given:

```
Do you wish to continue?
<Y> or <N> and press <RETURN>.
```

In such cases, two problems may occur. First, the user might use uppercase or lowercase letters for a correct response. Second, the user might inadvertently strike the wrong key. To make this part of the program correct and guard against bad data, you could have a set declared and initialized as

```
GoodResponse := ['Y', 'y', 'N', 'n'];
```

and then use a **REPEAT . . . UNTIL** loop as follows:

```
REPEAT
  writeln ('Do you wish to continue?');
  writeln ('<Y> or <N> and press <RETURN>.');
  readln (Response)
UNTIL Response IN GoodResponse;
```

You could then use a **boolean** variable Continue by first assigning it a value **false** and then follow the **REPEAT . . . UNTIL** loop with

```
Continue := Response IN ['Y', 'y'];
```

Sets with Functions

Sets can be used with subprograms. In general, set types can be used as parameters in much the same way that arrays, records, and files are used. However, when working with functions, sets cannot be returned as values of a function because functions cannot return structured types.

To illustrate using sets with functions, let's consider two examples.

■ **EXAMPLE 15.1**

Let's write a function to determine the cardinality (size or number of elements) of a set. Assuming appropriate **TYPE** definitions, such a function can be

```
FUNCTION Cardinality (S : <set type>) : integer;
  VAR
    Ct : integer;
    X : <base type for set>;
  BEGIN
    Ct := 0;
    FOR X := <initial value> TO <final value> DO
      IF X IN S THEN
        Ct := Ct + 1;
    Cardinality := Ct
  END;
```

initial value . . . final value

If given X in set S, increase cardinality counter.

S

This is called from the main program by

```
SetSize := Cardinality(<set name>);
```

Λ NOTE OF INTEREST

Time Is Cure for Computerphobia

Looking back on an article published in 1985, we see the then-prevalent attitude toward computers. What can make an otherwise stalwart manager break into a cold sweat, reel with dizziness, and suffer waves of nausea? The answer is not the latest version of the flu. It's the computer! As reported in the *Executive Action Series,* published by the Bureau of Business Practice, Waterford, Connecticut, a surprising number of managers fear, distrust, and even hate the computer, some in phobic proportions.

Is there a cure for this phobia that has such a destructive effect on productivity? Time is the answer, say the experts. It takes time to overcome computerphobia. A gradual introduction to computer technology is essential. Companies that provide both private instruction to managers and the time to master simple programming have more personnel regularly using their terminals. Confidence and motivation grow as managers successfully master simple computer tasks.

Computerphobia may be slowly decreasing over the years. There is now a growing interest in the concept of Executive Information Systems (EIS), systems designed specifically to meet the unique needs of high-level managers. They focus on communications, unstructured decision-making situations, and related areas that are part of executives' jobs. As these technologies develop, managerial computerphobia decreases and use of technology increases.

■ **EXAMPLE 15.2**

For our second example, let's consider a function to find the maximum (largest ordinal) element of a set. This would typically be applied to a set whose elements are in some subrange of the integers. If not, however, you can easily modify the function by considering the ordinals of set elements.

```
FUNCTION MaxElement (S : <set type>) : <base type>;
  VAR
    Temp : <base type>;
    X : <base type>;
  BEGIN
    IF S = [] THEN
      BEGIN
        writeln ('You are working with an empty set!':40);
        MaxElement := <initial value>
      END
    ELSE
      BEGIN
        Temp := <initial value>;
        FOR X := <initial value> TO <final value> DO
          IF (X IN S) AND (X > Temp) THEN
            Temp := X;
          MaxElement := Temp
      END  {  of ELSE option  }
  END; {  of FUNCTION MaxElement  }
```

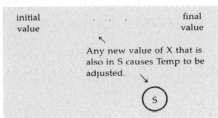

initial   · · ·   final
value   value

Any new value of X that is also in S causes Temp to be adjusted.

S

This is called from the main program by

```
Largest := MaxElement (<set name>);
```

Sets with Procedures

As you recall, sets cannot be returned as values of a function. However, when a program requires a set to be returned from a subprogram, the set can be used as a variable parameter with a procedure. In this manner, sets can either be generated or modified with subprograms. The Focus on Program Design section at the end of this chapter illustrates such a use.

Exercises 15.3

1. Modify the function MaxElement used in Example 15.2 to find the character in a line of text that is latest in the alphabet. Use this function with the Focus on Program Design code presented at the end of this chapter.

2. Write a test program to create a set containing all the consonants from a line of text. Your program should also print all elements in the set.

3. Write a short program to reproduce a text file where every vowel is replaced by an asterisk.

4. Modify the code used to find all the alphabet characters in a line of text so that a complete text file can be analyzed rather than just one line.

5. Write a program to simulate arithmetic indicated in a text file. The arithmetic expression should always be of the form digit-symbol-digit (9 + 8) where all digits and symbols are given as data of type **char**. Your program should protect against bad operation symbols, bad digits (actually nondigits), and division by zero.

6. To illustrate how sets can be used to protect against invalid values for **CASE** selectors, write a short program that uses a **CASE** statement. Run it with an invalid **CASE** selector value. Change the program so the **CASE** statement is protected by using a set. Rerun the program with the same invalid selector.

7. Write a Boolean function to analyze an integer between $-9,999$ and $9,999$ which returns the value **true** if the integer contains only odd digits (1,731) and **false** otherwise.

8. Write a function that returns the length of a string passed to the function as a packed array. Punctuation marks and internal blanks should add to the string length. Blanks at the beginning or end should not.

■ ■ ■ ■

**FOCUS ON
PROGRAM DESIGN**

The sample program for this chapter illustrates a use of sets. In particular, a set is used as a variable parameter in a procedure. The specific problem is to write a program to determine the alphabetical characters used in a line of text. Output from the program is an echo print of the text line, a list of letters in the text, and the number of distinct letters used in the line.

A first-level pseudocode development for this problem is

1. Get the characters
2. Print the characters
3. Determine the cardinality of the set
4. Print a closing message

A structure chart for this program is given in Figure 15.1.

FIGURE 15.1
Structure chart for **PROGRAM**
SymbolCheck

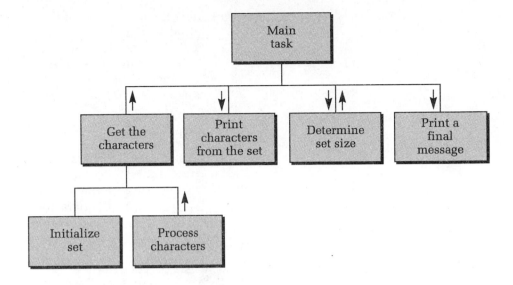

Module specifications for the main modules are

1. GetLetters Module
   Data received: None
   Information returned: A set of letters from a sentence
   Logic: Initialize the set.
          Add (union) distinct letters from a line of text.

2. PrintSet Module
   Data received: A set of letters
   Information returned: None
   Logic: Use a **FOR** loop to scan the alphabet and print the letters con-
          tained in the set.

3. Cardinality Module
   Data received: A set of letters
   Information returned: The cardinality of the set
   Logic: Use a function to count the number of distinct elements in a set.

4. PrintMessage Module
   Data received: Cardinality of the set
   Information returned: None
   Logic: Print a message indicating the set size.

A refinement of the pseudocode produces

1.   Get the characters
      1.1   initialize set
      1.2 **WHILE NOT eoln DO**
          1.2.1   process a character
2.   Print the characters
      2.1 **FOR** Ch := 'A' **TO** 'z' **DO**
           IF Ch is in the set **THEN**
             print Ch

   3.   Determine the cardinality of the set
      3.1   initialize counter to 0
      3.2   **FOR** Ch := 'A' **TO** 'z' **DO**
             IF Ch is in the set **THEN**
                increment counter
      3.3   assign count to function name
   4.   Print a closing message

Step 1.2.1 could be refined to

     1.2.1   process a character
         1.2.1.1   read a character
         1.2.1.2   write a character (echo print)
         1.2.1.3   **IF** character is in the alphabet **THEN**
                   add it to the set of characters

The main program is

```
BEGIN  {  Main program  }
  GetLetters (SentenceChar);
  PrintSet (SentenceChar);
  SetSize := Cardinality(SentenceChar);
  PrintMessage (SetSize)
END.  {  of main program  }
```

A complete program for this is

```
PROGRAM SymbolCheck (input, output, Data);

{  This program illustrates working with sets.  It reads a line }
{  of text and  determines the  number of  distinct letters in  }
{  that line.  Output  includes  the  distinct letters  and the }
{  set cardinality.  Information for this program is stored in   }
{  the text file Data.                                          }

CONST
  Skip = ' ';

TYPE
  AlphaSymbols = SET OF char;

VAR
  SentenceChar : AlphaSymbols;      {  Set of possible letters  }
  SetSize : integer;                {  Cardinality of the set   }
  Data : text;                      {  Data file                }


{******************************************************************* }


PROCEDURE GetLetters (VAR SentenceChar : AlphaSymbols);

  {  Given:    Nothing                                            }
  {  Task:     Read characters from the text file, Data; echo     }
  {            print them; store the alphabetical                 }
  {            characters in a set                                }
  {  Return:   The set of letters contained in the line of        }
  {            text                                               }

  VAR
    Ch : char;
    Alphabet : AlphaSymbols;
```

1

```
      BEGIN
        SentenceChar := [];
        Alphabet := ['A'..'Z'] + ['a'..'z'];
        writeln (Skip:10, 'The line of text is below:');
        writeln; write (Skip:10);
        WHILE NOT eoln(Data) DO
          BEGIN
            read (Data, Ch);
            write (Ch);                              {  echo print  }
            IF Ch IN Alphabet THEN
              SentenceChar := SentenceChar + [Ch]
          END;  { of WHILE NOT eoln(Data)  }         {  of one line  }
        writeln
      END;  {  of PROCEDURE GetLetters  }
```

```
{*****************************************************************}
```

```
PROCEDURE PrintSet (SentenceChar : AlphaSymbols);

  {  Given:    A set of characters                                }
  {  Task:     Print all characters in the set                    }
  {  Return:   Nothing                                            }

  VAR
    Ch : char;

  BEGIN
    writeln (Skip:10, 'The letters in this line are:');
    writeln; write (Skip:10);
    FOR Ch := 'A' TO 'z' DO
      IF Ch IN SentenceChar THEN
        write (Ch:2);
    writeln
  END;  {  of PROCEDURE PrintSet  }
```

```
{*****************************************************************}
```

```
FUNCTION Cardinality (SentenceChar : AlphaSymbols) : integer;

  {  Given:    A set of characters                                }
  {  Task:     Determine the number of characters in the set      }
  {  Return:   The set size (cardinality)                         }

  VAR
    Ct : integer;
    X : char;

  BEGIN
    Ct := 0;
    FOR X := 'A' TO 'z' DO
      IF X IN SentenceChar THEN
        Ct := Ct + 1;
    Cardinality := Ct
  END;  {  of FUNCTION Cardinality  }
```

```
{*****************************************************************}
```

```
PROCEDURE PrintMessage (SetSize : integer);

  {  Given:    The cardinality of the set                         }
  {  Task:     Print a closing message                            }
  {  Return:   Nothing                                            }
```

```
    BEGIN
      write (Skip:10);
      writeln ('There are', SetSize:3, ' letters in this sentence.')
    END;  {  of PROCEDURE PrintMessage  }

{ ***************************************************************** }

BEGIN  {  Main program  }
  reset (Data);
  GetLetters (SentenceChar);
  PrintSet (SentenceChar);
  SetSize := Cardinality(SentenceChar);
  PrintMessage (SetSize)
END.  {  of main program  }
```

When this program is run on the line of text

```
The numbers -2, 5, 20 and symbols '?', ':' should be ignored.
```

The output is

```
The line of text is below:

The numbers -2, 5, 20 and symbols '?', ':' should be ignored.

The letters in this line are:

  T a b d e g h i l m n o r s u y

There are   16 letters in this sentence.
```

RUNNING AND DEBUGGING TIPS

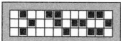

1. When defining a set type, do not use brackets in the definition; thus, the following is incorrect

   ```
   TYPE
     Alphabet = SET OF ['A'..'Z'];
   ```

   The correct form is

   ```
   TYPE
     Alphabet = SET OF 'A'..'Z';
   ```

2. Remember to initialize a set before using it in the program. Declaring a set does not give it a value. If your declaration is

   ```
   VAR
     Vowels : Alphabet;
   ```

   the program should contain

   ```
   Vowels := ['A', 'E', 'I', 'O', 'U'];
   ```

3. Attempting to add an element to a set rather than a set to a set is a common error. If you wish to add 'D' to the set ['A', 'B', 'C'], you should write

   ```
   ['A', 'B', 'C'] + ['D']
   ```

   rather than

   ```
   ['A', 'B', 'C'] + 'D'
   ```

   This is especially a problem when the value of a variable is to be added to a set.

   ```
   ['A', 'B', 'C'] + Ch;
   ```

   should be

   ```
   ['A', 'B', 'C'] + [Ch];
   ```

4. Avoid confusing arrays and array notation with sets and set notation.

5. Certain operators (+, −, and *) have different meanings when used with sets.

■ Summary

Key Terms

difference	intersection	union
element of a set	set	universal set
empty (null) set	subset	

Keywords

IN	**SET**

Key Concepts

- A **SET** in Pascal is a structured data type that consists of distinct elements from an indicated base type; sets can be declared by

```
TYPE
  Alphabet = SET OF char;
VAR
  Vowels : Alphabet;
  GoodResponse : Alphabet;
```

In this definition and declaration, Alphabet is a **SET** type and Vowels and Good-Response are set variables.

- Values must be assigned to a set; thus, we could have

```
Vowels := ['A', 'E', 'I', 'O', 'U'];
GoodResponse := ['Y', 'y', 'N', 'n'];
```

- When listing elements in a set, order makes no difference and each element may be listed only once.
- Standard set operations in Pascal are defined to be consistent with set operations of mathematics; to illustrate, if

```
A := [1,2,3,4];
```

and

```
B := [3,4,5];
```

the union, intersection, and difference of these sets are as follows:

Term	Expression	Value
Union	A + B	[1..5]
Intersection	A * B	[3,4]
Difference	A − B	[1,2]
	B − A	[5]

- Set membership is denoted by using the reserved word **IN**. Such an expression returns a Boolean value; thus, if

```
A := [1,2,3,4];
```

we have

Expression	Value
2 IN A	**true**
6 IN A	**false**

- he relational operators ($<=$, $>=$, $<>$, and $=$) can be used with sets forming boolean expressions and returning values consistent with expected subset and t equality relationships; to illustrate, if

```
A := [1,2,3];
B := [0..5];
C := [2,4];
```

we have

Expression	Value
A <= B	true
B <= C	false
B >= C	true
A = B	false
B <> C	true

- Priority levels for set operations are consistent with those used for arithmetic expressions; they are

Priority Level	Operation
1	( )
2	**NOT**
3	$*$, /, **MOD, DIV, AND**
4	$+$, $-$, **OR**
5	$<$, $>$, $<=$, $>=$, $<>$, $=$, **IN**

- Sets cannot be used with **read** or **write**; however, you can generate a set by initializing the set, assigning the empty set, and using set union to add elements to the set. For example, a set of characters in a text line can be generated by

```
S := [];
WHILE NOT eoln DO
  BEGIN
    read (Ch);
    S := S + [Ch]
  END;
```

This set can be printed by

```
FOR Ch := <initial value> TO <final value> DO
  IF Ch IN S THEN
    write (Ch:2);
```

- Four uses for sets in programs are to replace complex Boolean expressions, to protect a program (or segment) from bad data, to protect against invalid **CASE** statements, and to aid in interactive programming.
- Sets can be used as parameters with subprograms.
- Sets cannot be returned as the value of a function.
- Sets can be generated or modified through subprograms by using variable parameters with procedures.

■ Programming Problems and Projects

Each of the following programming problems can be solved with a program using sets. Hints are provided to indicate some of the uses; you may, of course, find others.

1. Write a program to be used to simulate a medical diagnosis. Assume the following symptoms are coded as indicated.

Symptom	Code
Headache	1
Fever	2
Sore throat	3
Cough	4
Sneeze	5
Stomach pain	6
Heart pain	7
Muscle pain	8
Nausea	9
Back pain	10
Exhaustion	11
Jaundice	12
High blood pressure	13

Furthermore, assume each of the following diseases is characterized by the symptoms as indicated.

Disease	Symptoms
Cold	1,2,3,4,5
Flu	1,2,6,8,9
Migraine	1,9
Mononucleosis	2,3,11,12
Ulcer	6,9
Arteriosclerosis	7,10,11,13
Appendicitis	2,6

Your program should accept as input a person's name and symptoms (coded) and provide a preliminary diagnosis. Sets can be used for
a. Bad data check
b. Symptoms = 1 .. 13;
   Disease = **SET OF** Symptoms;
c. Cold, Flu, Migraine, Mononucleosis, Ulcer, Arteriosclerosis, Appendicitis : Disease;

2. Write a program to serve as a simple text analyzer. Input is any text file. Output should be three histograms: one each for vowel frequency, consonant frequency, and other symbol frequency. Your program should use a set for vowels, one for consonants, and a third for other symbols.

3. Typists often complain that the standard QWERTY keyboard

Q W E R T Y U I O P
A S D F G H J K L ;
Z X C V B N M , . /
space bar

is not efficient. As you can see, many frequently used letters (E, T, N, R, and I) are not on the middle row. A new keyboard, the Maltron keyboard, has been proposed. Its design is

$$Q\ P\ Y\ C\ B\ V\ M\ U\ Z\ L$$
$$A\ N\ I\ S\ F\ E\ D\ T\ H\ O\ R\ ;\ :\ .$$
$$J\ G\ W\ K\ X$$
space bar

Write a program to analyze a text file to see how many jumps are required by each keyboard. For purposes of this program, a jump will be any valid symbol not on the middle row. Output should include the number of valid symbols read and the number of jumps for each keyboard.

4. Write a program to serve as a simple compiler for a Pascal program. Your compiler should work on a program that uses only single-letter identifiers. Your compiler should create a set of identifiers, make sure identifiers are not declared twice, make sure all identifiers on the left of an assignment are declared, and make sure there are no type mismatch errors. For purposes of your compiler program, assume as follows:

a. Variables are declared between **VAR** and **BEGIN**; for example,

```
VAR
  X, Y : real;
  A, B, C : integer;
  M : char;
BEGIN
```

b. Each program line is a complete Pascal statement.

c. The only assignments are of the form X := Y;. Output should include the program line number and an appropriate error message for each error. Run your compiler with several short Pascal programs as text files. Compare your error list with that given in Appendix 5.

5. A number in exponential notation preceded by a plus or minus sign may have the form

Sign	Positive integer	Decimal	Positive integer	E	Sign	Exponent (three digits)

For example, $-45.302E+002$ is the number -4530.2. If the number is in standard form, it will have exactly one digit on the left side of the decimal $(-4.5302E+003)$.

Write a program to read numbers in exponential form from a text file, one number per line. Your program should check to see if each number is in proper form. For those that are, print out the number as given and the number in standard form.

6. Write a program to analyze a text file for words of differing length. Your program should keep a list of all words of length one, two, . . ., ten. It should also count the number of words whose length exceeds ten.

A word ends when one alphabetical character is followed by a character not in the alphabet or when an end-of-line is reached. All words start with letters (7UP is not a word). Your output should be an alphabetized list for each word length. It should also include the number of words whose length exceeds ten characters. An apostrophe does not add to the length of a word.

7. The Falcon Manufacturing Company (Problem 22, Chapter 11; Problem 17, Chapter 12; Problems 12–16, Chapter 13) wants a computerized system to check if a customer is approved for credit. A customer number should be entered from the keyboard, with the program printing the credit limit for the customer if credit has been approved, and "No credit" if it has not. Each line of a text file contains a customer number and the credit limit. Valid customer numbers range from 100 to 999, and credit limits are $100, $300, $500, $1000, and unlimited credit.

8. Write a program in which you read a text file and print out the number of times a character in the file matches a character in your name.

9. The Court Survey Corporation wishes to conduct a poll by sending questionnaires to men and women between 25 and 30 years of age living in your state or any state adjacent to it. A text file containing names, street addresses, cities, states, zip codes, and ages is to be read, with the program printing the names and addresses of those persons matching the criteria.

10. Write a program to test your ESP and that of a friend. Each of you should secretly enter ten integers between 1 and 100. Have the program check each list and print the values that are in both lists and the number of values that are in both lists.

11. Modify Problem 22 from Chapter 10 (the Wellsville Wholesale Company commission problem) to define the sales ranges as sets. Use these sets to verify input and determine the proper commission rate.

12. The Ohio Programmers' Association offices are in a large building with five wings lettered A through E. The office numbers in the wings are as follows:

Wing	Rooms
A	100–150 and 281–300
B	151–190 and 205–220
C	10–50 and 191–204
D	1–9 and 51–99
E	221–280 and 301–319

Write a program for the receptionist, Miss Lovelace, so that she can enter an office number from the keyboard and then have the computer print the wing in which the office is located.

13. Not all programming languages include sets as a data structure. Examine several other languages to determine what data structures they include. Prepare a chart that compares and contrasts the data structures of Pascal (arrays, records, files, and sets) with the data structures of other languages. Give an oral presentation of your results to the class.

14. Select an unworked problem from the programming problems previously listed for this chapter. Construct a structure chart and write all documentary information necessary for the problem. Do not write code. When you are finished, have a classmate read your documentation to see if precisely what is to be done is clear.

Dynamic Variables and Data Structures

Material in the previous fifteen chapters has focused almost exclusively on *static variables,* characteristics of which include:

1. Their size (array length, for example) is fixed at compilation time.
2. A certain amount of memory is reserved for each variable and this memory is retained for the declared variables as long as the program or subprogram in which the variable is defined is active.
3. They are declared in a variable declaration section.
4. The structure or existence of a variable cannot be changed during a run of the program (two exceptions are the length of a file and records with variant parts).

A disadvantage of using only static variables and data structures is that the number of variables needed in a program must be predetermined. Thus, if you are working with an array and you anticipate needing a thousand locations, you would define

```
<name> = ARRAY [1..1000] OF <base type>;
```

This creates two problems. You may overestimate the length of the array and use only part of it; therefore memory is wasted. Or you may underestimate the necessary array length and be unable to process all the data until the program is modified.

Fortunately, Pascal solves these problems with the use of *dynamic variables.* Some of their characteristics follow.

1. Dynamic variable types are defined in the **TYPE** section.
2. Memory for dynamic variables is created as needed and returned when not needed during the execution of a program; therefore, unneeded memory is not wasted and you are limited only by the available memory.

3. A new (and significant) technique must be developed to form a list of dynamic variables; these lists are referred to as *dynamic structures.*

4. In some instances, working with dynamic structures can be slower than working with static structures; in particular, direct access of an array element has no analogue.

5. A significantly different method of accessing values stored in dynamic variables must be developed since memory locations are not predetermined.

A complete development of dynamic variables and data structures is left to other courses in computer science. However, when finished with this chapter, you should have a reasonable understanding of dynamic variables and data structures, and be able to use them in a program. We carefully develop one type of dynamic data structure (linked list) and then introduce three others: stack, queue, and binary tree.

You may find this material somewhat difficult. If so, do not get discouraged. Two reasons for the increased level of difficulty are that some of the work is not intuitive, and the level of abstraction is different from that of previous material. Therefore, as you work through this chapter, you are encouraged to draw several diagrams and write several short programs to help you understand concepts. Also you may need to reread the chapter or particular sections to grasp the mechanics of working with dynamic variables.

■ 16.1
Pointer Variables

Computer Memory

Computer memory can be envisioned as a sequence of memory locations depicted as in Figure 16.1(a). An area where a value can be stored is called a memory location. When a variable is declared in the variable declaration section of a program, a memory location is reserved during execution of that program block. This memory location can be accessed by a reference to the variable name and only data of the declared type can be stored there. Thus, if the declaration section is

```
VAR
   Sum : integer;
```

you can envision it as shown in Figure 16.1(b). If the assignment

```
Sum := 56;
```

is made, we have the arrangement shown in Figure 16.1(c).

Each memory location has an *address*. This is an integer value that the computer must use as a reference to the memory location. When static variables (such as Sum) are used, the address of a memory location is used indirectly by the underlying machine instruction. However, when dynamic variables are used, the address is used directly as a reference or pointer to the memory location.

The *value* that is the address of a memory location must be stored somewhere in memory. In Pascal, this is stored in a *pointer variable*. A pointer variable (frequently denoted as Ptr) is a variable of a predefined type that is used to contain the address of a memory location. To illustrate, assume Ptr has been declared as a pointer variable. If 56 is stored in a memory location whose address is 11640, we can envision it as shown in Figure 16.1(d).

FIGURE 16.1(a)
Computer Memory

FIGURE 16.1(b)
Variable location in memory

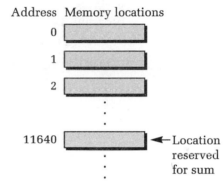

FIGURE 16.1(c)
Value in variable Sum

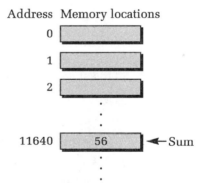

FIGURE 16.1(d)
Relationship between pointer
and memory location

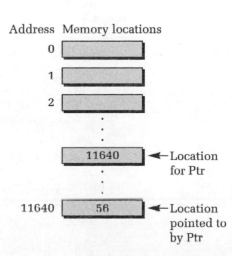

Working with Pointer and Dynamic Variables

T Pointer variables are declared by using a caret (∧) or an up arrow (↑) in front of the type name. Thus,

```
TYPE
  Ages = 0..120;
  PointerToAges = ^Ages;
VAR
  Ptr : PointerToAges;
```

declares Ptr as a pointer variable. Ptr cannot be assigned values of type Ages; Ptr can only contain addresses of locations whose values are of type Ages.

Once this declaration has been made, a dynamic variable can be created. A dynamic variable, designated as Ptr∧, is a variable accessed by a pointer variable; a dynamic variable is not declared in the declaration section of a program. Using the standard procedure **new** with a pointer variable as

```
new (Ptr);  {  This initializes a value for Ptr  }
```

creates the dynamic variable Ptr∧. This can be illustrated by

The pointer variable followed by a caret (or an up arrow) is always the identifier for a dynamic variable. We usually read Ptr∧ as the object (variable) pointed to by Ptr.

To illustrate the relationship between pointer variables and dynamic variables, assume the previous declaration and the code

```
new (Ptr);
Ptr^ := 56;
```

This stage can be envisioned as

where Ptr contains the address of Ptr∧.

Dynamic variables can be destroyed by using the standard procedure **dispose.** Thus, if you no longer need the value of a dynamic variable Ptr∧, then

```
dispose (Ptr);
```

causes the pointer variable Ptr to no longer contain the address for Ptr∧. In that sense, Ptr∧ does not exist because nothing is pointing to it. This location has been returned to the computer for subsequent use.

Since pointer variables contain only addresses of memory locations, they have limited use in a program. Pointer variables of the same type can be used only for assignments and comparison for equality. They cannot be used with **read, write,** or any arithmetic operation. To illustrate, assume we have the definition and declaration

```
TYPE
  Ages = 0..120;
VAR
  Ptr1, Ptr2 : ^Ages;
```

Then
```
new (Ptr1);
new (Ptr2);
```
create the dynamic variables Ptr1^ and Ptr2^. If the assignments
```
Ptr1^ := 50;
Ptr2^ := 21;
```
are made, we can envision this as

The expression Ptr1 = Ptr2 is then **false** and Ptr1 <> Ptr2 is **true.** If the assignment
```
Ptr1 := Ptr2;
```
is made, we can envision

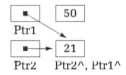

Then Ptr1 = Ptr2 is **true** and Ptr1 <> Ptr2 is **false.**

STYLE TIP

■ ■ ■ ■ ■ ■ ■ ■ ■ ■

> Ptr or some identifier containing Ptr (for example, DataPtr) is frequently used when declaring pointer variables. This reinforces the difference between working with a pointer variable (Ptr) and a dynamic variable (Ptr^).

Notice that in this last illustration, 50 no longer has anything pointing to it. Thus, there is now no way to access this value. Since we did not use **dispose,** the location has not been returned for subsequent reuse. Therefore, you should be careful to use **dispose** when necessary or you could eventually run out of memory.

Dynamic variables can be used in any context used by static variables of the same type. To illustrate, assume the previous declarations for Ptr1 and Ptr2. If appropriate values (50 and 21) are in a data file, the segment
```
new (Ptr1);
new (Ptr2);
read (Ptr1^, Ptr2^);
writeln ('The average of', Ptr1^:5, ' and', Ptr2^:5,
        ' is', (Ptr1^ + Ptr2^) / 2:6:2);
```
produces
```
The average of   50 and   21 is 35.50
```

Defining and Declaring Pointer Variables

The previous definition and declarations of pointer types and pointer variables are relatively uncomplicated; however, in actual practice, pointer types and variables are a bit more complex. For example, in the next section we will define a dynamic variable as a record type where one of the fields in the record type is a pointer of the same type. Thus, you can have

```
TYPE
   String20 = PACKED ARRAY [1..20] OF char;
   DataPtr = ^StudentInfo;
   StudentInfo = RECORD
                     Name: String20;
                     Next : DataPtr
                  END; { of RECORD StudentInfo }
VAR
   Student : DataPtr;
```

Notice that DataPtr makes a reference to StudentInfo before StudentInfo is defined. StudentInfo then contains a field of type DataPtr. In this instance, Pascal makes an exception to the rule that forbids using something before it is defined. Specifically, the following exception is permitted: Pointer type definitions may precede definitions of their reference types. The reverse is not true. That is, a structure may not contain a field or component of a pointer type that has not yet been defined. You will frequently want each record to point to another record. Using a record definition with one field for a pointer permits this.

Another note about working with pointers should be mentioned here. The reserved word **NIL,** whose value is the null pointer that does not point to anything, can be assigned to a pointer variable. Thus, you could have

```
new (Student);
Student^.Next := NIL;
```

This allows pointer variables to be used in Boolean expressions and is needed in later work. For example, if you are forming a list of dynamic

---

A NOTE OF INTEREST

Object-Oriented Programming

Object-oriented development is becoming increasingly important as a method to manage large and complex software systems. Object-oriented concepts are natural extensions of proper structured programming. If structured programming principles have been emphasized, the basic object-oriented idea of encapsulation then follows logically.

Components of object-oriented programs are

Object. The object in object-oriented programming includes the basic data or data structure and related procedures and functions required to keep the object complete. This makes the object like an abstract data type.

Method. A method is a procedure or function that becomes part of the object. It provides the abstraction to the object's data.

Encapsulation. The combining of data structure and methods is called encapsulation. If encapsu-

lation is performed correctly, the user of the object should never need to access the data of the object directly. Procedure and function headers are added to type definitions to describe encapsulation of the methods. The type definitions become the interface to the unit.

The idea of a data structure being linked with its procedures has been a standard practice in creating abstract data types for years and is not a new concept created by object-oriented languages. What *is* new and exciting is what can now be done with the object. Other objects can inherit those same procedures and functions, and those same procedures and functions can easily be altered, if the need arises, without having to rewrite the whole unit. In fact, you need only use the unit and create new methods and data items or rename the existing methods in order to create new objects.

variables where each dynamic variable contains a pointer variable for pointing to the next one, you can use **NIL** as a way to know when you are at the end of a list. This idea and that of pointer type definitions are fully developed in the next section.

Exercises 16.1

1. Discuss the difference between static and dynamic variables.

2. Write a test program to declare a single pointer variable whose associated dynamic variable can have values in the subrange 0 . . 50 and then

   a. Create a dynamic variable, assign the value 25, and print the value.

   b. Create another dynamic variable, assign the value 40, and print the value.

   At this stage of your program, where is the value 25 stored?

3. Illustrate the relationship between pointer variables and dynamic variables produced by

```
TYPE
  Ptr = (Red, Yellow, Blue, Green);
VAR
  Ptr1, Ptr2 : ^Ptr;
BEGIN
  new (Ptr1);
  new (Ptr2);
  Ptr1^ := Blue;
  Ptr2^ := Red
END.
```

4. Assume the **TYPE** and **VAR** sections are given as in Exercise 3. Find all errors in the following.

   a. `new (Ptr1^);`

   b. `new (Ptr2);`
   `Ptr2 := Yellow;`

   c. `new (Ptr1);`
   `new (Ptr2);`
   `Ptr1^ := Red;`
   `Ptr2^ := Ptr1^;`

   d. `new (Ptr1);`
   `new (Ptr2);`
   `Ptr1^ := Red;`
   `Ptr1^ := Ptr2^;`

   e. `new (Ptr1);`
   `new (Ptr2);`
   `Ptr1^ := Red;`
   `Ptr2^ := Ptr1;`

5. Assume pointer variables are declared in the variable declaration section as

```
VAR
  RealPtr1, RealPtr2 : ^real;
  IntPtr1, IntPtr2 : ^integer;
  BoolPtr1, BoolPtr2 : ^boolean;
```

   Indicate if the following are valid or invalid references. Give an explanation for each invalid reference.

   a. `IntPtr1 := IntPtr1 + 1;`

   b. `writeln (RealPtr2:30:2);`

   c. `writeln (BoolPtr1^:15, IntPtr1^:15, RealPtr1^:15:2);`

   d. `IF IntPtr1 < IntPtr2 THEN`
   `   writeln ('All done');`

e. `IF BoolPtr NOT NIL THEN`
     `   new (BoolPtr2);`

f. `IF RealPtr1 <> RealPtr2 THEN`
     `   writeln (RealPtr1^:15:2, RealPtr2^:15:2);`

g. `IF BoolPtr2 THEN`
     `   new (BoolPtr1);`

h. `IF BoolPtr2^ THEN`
     `   new (BoolPtr1);`

6. Assume the declarations of Exercise 5. What is the output from the following fragment of code?

```
new (IntPtr1);
new (IntPtr2);
new (RealPtr1);
new (BoolPtr1);
IntPtr1^ := 95;
IntPtr2^ := 55;
RealPtr1^ := (IntPtr1^ + IntPtr2^) / 2;
BoolPtr1^ := true;
WHILE BoolPtr1^ DO
  BEGIN
    writeln (RealPtr1^:20:2);
    RealPtr1^ := RealPtr1^ - 5;
    IF RealPtr1^ < 0 THEN
      BoolPtr1^ := false
  END;
```

■ ■ ■ ■

■ 16.2
Linked Lists

OBJECTIVES
- to understand why a linked list is a dynamic data structure
- to be able to create a linked list
- to understand how pointers are used to form a linked list
- to be able to print data from a linked list

A *linked list* can be implemented as a dynamic data structure and can be thought of as a list of data items where each item is linked to the next one by means of a pointer. Such a list can be envisioned as follows:

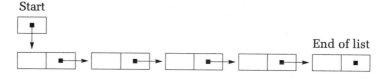

Items in a linked list are called *components* or *nodes*. These lists are used like arrays; that is, data of the same type can be stored in each node. As shown in the previous illustration, each node of a linked list can store certain data as well as point to the next node. Consequently, a record is used for each node where one field of the record is reserved for the pointer. If names of students are to be stored in such a list, we can use the record definition from Section 16.1 as follows:

```
TYPE
  String20 = PACKED ARRAY [1..20] OF char;
  DataPtr = ^StudentInfo;
  StudentInfo = RECORD
                  Name : String20;
                  Next : DataPtr
                END;  {  of RECORD StudentInfo  }
```

Thus, we can envision a list of names as

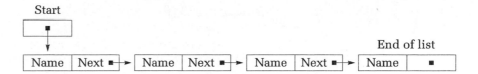

Creating a Linked List

When creating a linked list, you need to be able to identify the first node, the relationship (pointer) between successive nodes, and the last node. Pointers are used to point to both the first and last node. An auxiliary pointer is also used to point to the newest node. The pointer to the first node (Start) is not changed unless a new node is added to the beginning of the list. The other pointers change as the linked list grows. When you have created such a list, the last node is usually designated by assigning **NIL** to the pointer. To illustrate, let's see how a linked list to hold five names can be formed. Using the **TYPE** definition section

```
TYPE
   String20 = PACKED ARRAY [1..20] OF char;
   DataPtr = ^StudentInfo;
   StudentInfo = RECORD
                      Name : String20;
                      Next : DataPtr
                 END; {  of RECORD StudentInfo  }
```

and the variable declaration section

```
VAR
   Start, Last, Ptr : DataPtr;
```

we can generate the desired list by

```
BEGIN
   new (Start);
   Ptr := Start; {  Pointer to first node  }
   FOR J := 1 TO 4 DO
     BEGIN
       new (Last);
       Ptr^.Next := Last;
       Ptr := Last
     END;
   Ptr^.Next := NIL;
```

Let's now examine what happens when this segment of code is executed.

```
new (Start);
```

STYLE TIP
■ ■ ■ ■ ■ ■ ■ ■ ■ ■ ■ ■

When working with linked lists, the identifier Next is frequently used as the name of the field in the record that is the pointer variable. This is to remind you that you are pointing to the next record. It makes code such as

```
P := P^.Next;
```

more meaningful.

causes

```
    Ptr := Start;
```
produces

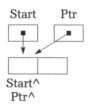

Now that we have started our list, the first pass through the **FOR** loop produces results as shown in Table 16.1. In a similar fashion, the second time

TABLE 16.1
Adding a second node to a linked list

Code	Result
`new (Last);`	Start Ptr Last
`Ptr^.Next := Last;`	Start Ptr Last
`Ptr := Last;`	Start Ptr Last

through the loop causes the list to grow as shown in Table 16.2. As you can see, each pass through the body of the **FOR** loop adds one element to the

TABLE 16.2
Adding a third node to a linked
list

Code	Result
	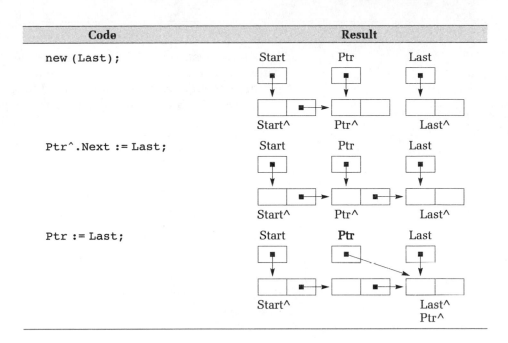

linked list and causes both Ptr and Last to point to the last node of the list. After the loop has been executed four times, we have the following list:

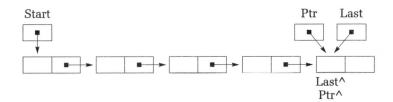

At this stage, the loop is exited and

    Ptr^.Next := NIL;

produces

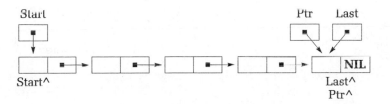

Now when we process the list, we can check the field name Next to determine when the end of the list has been reached. In this sense, **NIL** is used in a manner similar to **eof** with files.

Let's now create a linked list that can be used to simulate a deck of playing cards. We need 52 nodes, each of which is a record with a field for the suit (club, diamond, heart, or spade); a field for the number (1 to 13); and a field for the pointer. Such a record can be defined as

```
TYPE
   Pointer = ^Card;
   Suits = (Club, Diamond, Heart, Spade);
   Card = RECORD
             Suit : Suits;
             Num : 1..13;
             Next : Pointer
          END;  {  of RECORD Card  }
```

As before, we need three pointer variables; they can be declared as

```
VAR
   Start, Last, Ptr : Pointer;
```

If an ace is represented by the number 1, we can start our list by

```
BEGIN
   new (Start);
   Start^.Suit := Club;
   Start^.Num := 1;
   Ptr := Start;
   Last := Start;
```

This beginning is illustrated by

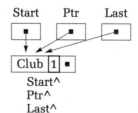

We can then generate the rest of the deck by

```
FOR J := 2 TO 52 DO
   BEGIN
     new (Last);
     IF Ptr^.Num = 13 THEN  {  Start a new suit  }
       BEGIN
         Last^.Suit := succ(Ptr^.Suit);
         Last^.Num := 1
       END
     ELSE  {  Same suit, next number  }
       BEGIN
         Last^.Suit := Ptr^.Suit;
         Last^.Num := Ptr^.Num + 1
       END;
     Ptr^.Next := Last;
     Ptr := Last
   END;
 Ptr^.Next := NIL;
```

The first time through this loop we have

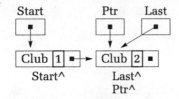

This loop is processed all 51 times and then exited so that when

```
Ptr^.Next := NIL;
```

is executed, we have the list shown in Figure 16.2.

FIGURE 16.2
A linked list simulating a deck
of cards

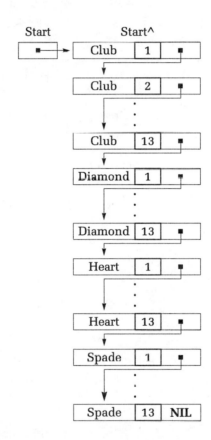

Printing from a Linked List

Thus far, we have seen how to create a dynamic structure and assign data to
components of such a structure. We conclude this section with a look at how
to print data from a linked list.

The general idea is to start with the first component in the list, print the
desired information, and then move sequentially through the list until the
last component **(NIL)** is reached. There are two aspects of this algorithm that
need to be examined. First, the loop control depends on examining the
current record for the value of **NIL** in the pointer field. If P is used to denote
this field, we have

```
WHILE P <> NIL DO
  BEGIN
       .
       .
       .
  END;
```

Second, the loop increment is to assign the pointer (P) used as a loop control variable the value of the Next field of the current record. To illustrate, assume we have the definitions and declarations used previously to form a list of student names. If we declare the variable P by

```
VAR
  P : DataPtr;
```

we can then print the names by

```
BEGIN  {  Print names in list  }
  P := Start;
  WHILE P <> NIL DO
    BEGIN
      writeln (P^.Name:40);
      P := P^.Next
    END
END;  {  of printing names  }
```

In general, printing from a linked list is done with a procedure. When a procedure is used, only the external pointer (Start, in our examples) needs to be used as a parameter. To illustrate, a procedure to print the previous list of names is

```
PROCEDURE PrintNames (Start : DataPtr);
  VAR
    P : DataPtr;
  BEGIN
    P := Start;
    WHILE P <> NIL DO
      BEGIN
        writeln (P^.Name:40);
        P := P^.Next
      END
  END;  {  of PROCEDURE PrintNames  }
```

This would be called from the main program by

```
PrintNames (Start);
```

Exercises 16.2

1. Discuss the differences and similarities between arrays and linked lists.

2. Write a test program to transfer an unknown number of integers from a data file into a linked list and then print the integers from the linked list.

3. Write a procedure to be used with the test program in Exercise 2 to print the integers.

4. Explain why a linked list is preferable when you are getting an unknown number of data items from a data file.

5. Suppose you are going to create a linked list of records where each record in the list should contain the following information about a student: name, four test scores, ten quiz scores, average, and letter grade.

   a. Define a record to be used for this purpose.

   b. What pointer type(s) and pointer variable(s) are needed?

   c. Assume the data for each student is on one line in the data file as

| Smith Mary | 97 98 85 90 9 8 7 10 6 9 10 8 9 7 ▮ |

    i. Show how to get the data for the first student into the first component of a linked list.

   ii. Show how to get the data for the second student into the second component.

6. Why are three pointers (Start, Last, Ptr) used when creating a linked list?

7. Consider the definitions and declarations

```
TYPE
  P = ^Node;
  Node = RECORD
            Num : integer;
            Next : P
         END;
VAR
  A, B, C : P;
```

a. Show how the schematic

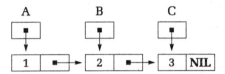

    would be changed by each of the following:

    i. `A := A^.Next;`
   ii. `B := A;`
  iii. `C := A^.Next;`
   iv. `B^.Num := C^.Num;`
    v. `A^.Num := B^.Next^.Num;`
   vi. `C^.Next := A;`

b. Write one statement to change

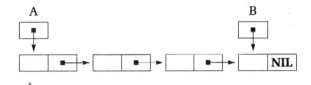

to

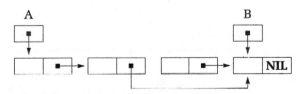

8. Assume the definitions and declarations in Exercise 7. Indicate the output for each of the following:

```
a. new (A);
   new (B);
   A^.Num := 10;
   B^.Num := 20;
   B := A;
   A^.Num := 5;
   writeln (A^.Num, B^.Num);
```

```
b. new (C);
   C^.Num := 100;
   new (B);
   B^.Num := C^.Num MOD 8;
   new (A);
   A^.Num := B^.Num + C^.Num;
   writeln (A^.Num, B^.Num, C^.Num);
c. new (A);
   new (B);
   A^.Num := 10;
   A^.Next := B;
   A^.Next^.Num := 100;
   writeln (A^.Num, B^.Num);
```

9. Write a function Sum to sum the integers in a linked list of integers. Show how it is called from the main program.

■ ■ ■ ■

■ 16.3
Working with Linked Lists

OBJECTIVES

- to be able to insert an element into a linked list
- to be able to delete an element from a linked list
- to be able to update an ordered linked list
- to be able to search a linked list for an element

In this section, we examine some of the basic operations required when working with linked lists. Working with a list of integers, we see how to create a sorted list by inserting elements. We then update a linked list by searching it for a certain value and deleting that element from the list.

The following **TYPE** definition is used for most of this section.

```
TYPE
   DataPtr = ^Node;
   Node = RECORD
             Num : integer;
             Next : DataPtr
          END;
```

Since most of the operations we examine will be used later, procedures are written for them.

Inserting an Element

The dynamic nature of a linked list implies that we are able to insert an element into a list. The three cases considered are inserting an element at the beginning, in the middle, and at the end.

The procedure for inserting at the beginning of a list is commonly called *push*. Before writing code for this procedure, let's examine what should be done with the nodes and pointers. If the list is illustrated by

When working with linked lists of records, Node is frequently used as the record identifier. This facilitates readability of program comments. Thus, comments such as "Get new node," "Insert a node," and "Delete a node" are meaningful.

and we wish to insert

at the beginning, we need to get a new node by

```
new (P);
```

assign the appropriate value to Num

```
P^.Num := 3;
```

and reassign the pointers to produce the desired result. After the first two steps, we have the list

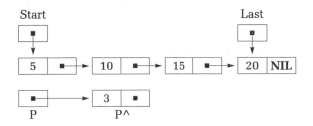

```
P^.Next := Start;
```

yields the list

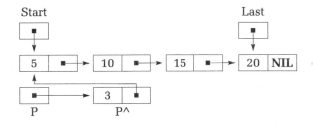

Then

```
Start := P;
```

yields the following, in which the Push is now complete.

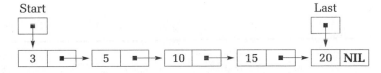

A procedure for this can now be written as

```
PROCEDURE Push (VAR Start : DataPtr;
                    NewNum : integer);
  VAR
    P : DataPtr;
  BEGIN
    new (P);              { Get another node      }
    P^.Num := NewNum;     { Assign the data value }
    P^.Next := Start;     { Point to the first node }
```

```
        Start := P;             {  Point to new first node  }
        IF Start^.Next = NIL THEN
          Last := Start          {  For a list with only one node  }
    END;
```

This procedure can be called from the main program by

```
    Push (Start, 3);
```

A note of caution is in order. This procedure is written assuming there is an existing list with **NIL** assigned to the pointer in the final node. If this is used as the first step in creating a new list, the assignment

```
    Start := NIL;
```

must be previously made.

The basic idea for inserting a node somewhere in a linked list other than at the beginning or end is: get a new node, find where it belongs, and put it in the list. In order to do this, we must start at the beginning of a list and search it sequentially until we find where the new node belongs. When we next change pointers to include the new node, we must know between which pair of elements in the linked list the new node is to be inserted. Thus, if

is to be inserted in an ordered linked list such as

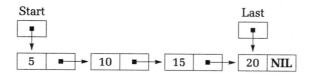

we need to know that the link

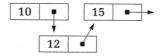

is in the list. Once this pair has been identified, the pointers will be changed to produce

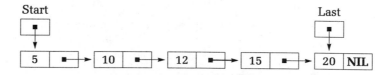

so that the new list with the new node inserted will be

Start   Last

5 → 10 → 12 → 15 → 20 NIL

Let's now see how this can be done. We can get a new node by

```
    new (P);
    P^.Num := NewNum;  {  where NewNum has the value 12  }
```

In order to find where it belongs, we need two pointer variables to keep track of successive pairs of elements as we traverse the list. Assume Before and Ptr have been appropriately declared. Then

```
Ptr := Start;
WHILE (Ptr <> NIL) AND (Ptr^.Num < NewNum) DO
  BEGIN
    Before := Ptr;
    Ptr := Ptr^.Next
  END;
```

will search the list for the desired pair. (This assumes the node to be inserted is not at the beginning of the list.) Using the previous numbers, when this loop is completed we have the arrangement

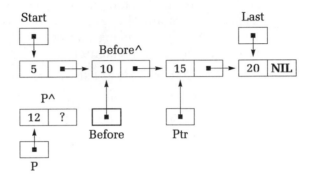

We can put the new node in the list by reassigning the pointers

```
P^.Next := Ptr;
Before^.Next := P;
```

The list can then be envisioned as

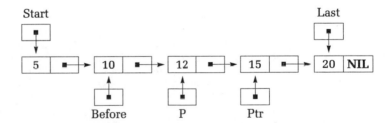

When this code is written together, we have

```
PROCEDURE InsertMiddle (Start : DataPtr;
                        NewNum : integer);
  VAR
    P, Ptr, Before : DataPtr;
  BEGIN

  { Get a new node }

    New (P);
    P^.Num := NewNum;

  { Find where it belongs }

    Ptr := Start;
    WHILE (Ptr <> NIL) AND (Ptr^.Num < NewNum) DO
```

```
BEGIN
  Before := Ptr;
  Ptr := Ptr^.Next
END;

{  Insert the new node  }

  P^.Next := Ptr;
  Before^.Next := P
END; {  of PROCEDURE InsertMiddle  }
```

It can be called from the main program by

```
InsertMiddle (Start, 12);
```

The next problem to consider when inserting a node is how to insert it at the end of the list. In the previous code, when Ptr is **NIL,** a reference to Ptr^ causes an error and thus cannot be used for inserting at the end. This problem can be solved by using a Boolean variable, Looking, initializing it to **true,** and changing the loop control to

```
WHILE (Ptr <> NIL) AND Looking DO
```

The body of the loop then becomes the **IF . . . THEN . . . ELSE** statement

```
IF Ptr^.Num > NewNum THEN
  Looking := false
ELSE
  BEGIN
    Before := Ptr;
    Ptr := Ptr^.Next
  END;
```

The loop is followed by the statement

```
P^.Next := Ptr;
```

Thus, we have

```
new (P);
P^.Num := NewNum;
Ptr := Start;
Looking := true;
WHILE (Ptr <> NIL) AND Looking DO
  IF Ptr^.Num > NewNum THEN
    Looking := false
  ELSE
    BEGIN
      Before := Ptr;
      Ptr := Ptr^.Next
    END;
P^.Next := Ptr;
Before^.Next := P;
Last := P;
```

To see how this permits insertion at the end of a list, suppose NewNum is 30 and the list is

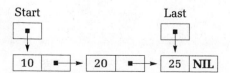

The initialization produces the list illustrated in Figure 16.3(a). Since Ptr <> **NIL** and Looking is **true,** the loop would be entered. Ptr^.Num > NewNum (10 > 30) is **false,** so the **ELSE** option is exercised to produce the list shown in Figure 16.3(b). At this stage, Ptr <> **NIL** and Looking is still **true,** so the loop is entered again. Ptr^.Num > NewNum (20 > 30) is **false,** so the **ELSE** option produces the list illustrated in Figure 16.3(c) Since Ptr is not yet **NIL,** Ptr <> **NIL** and Looking is **true,** the loop is entered, Ptr^.Num > NewNum is **false,** so the **ELSE** option produces the list shown in Figure 16.3(d) Now the condition Ptr <> **NIL** is **false,** so control is transferred to

```
P^.Next := Ptr;
```

FIGURE 16.3(a)
Getting a new node for a linked list

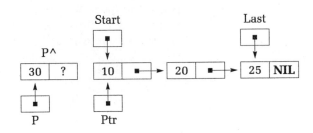

FIGURE 16.3(b)
Positioning Before and Ptr

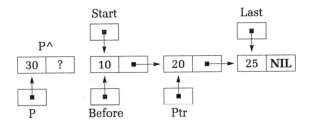

FIGURE 16.3(c)
Moving Before and Ptr

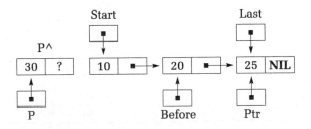

FIGURE 16.3(d)
Before and Ptr ready for insertion

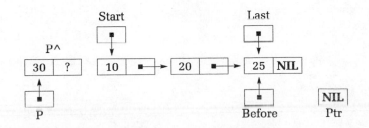

When this and the two lines of code following it are executed, we get the arrangement shown in Figure 16.3(e)

FIGURE 16.3(e)
Insertion at end of linked list is complete

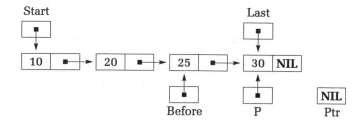

One final comment is in order. A slight modification of this procedure accommodates inserting at the beginning of a list. You may choose to reserve Push for this purpose. However, if you want a single procedure that will insert anywhere in a linked list, it is

```
PROCEDURE Insert (VAR Start, Last : DataPtr;
                       NewNum : integer);
   VAR
     P, Ptr, Before : DataPtr;
     Looking : boolean;
   BEGIN

   {  Initialize  }
   new (P);
   P^.Num := NewNum;
   Before := NIL;
   Ptr := Start;
   Looking := true;

   {  Check for empty list  }
   IF Start = NIL THEN
     BEGIN
       P^.Next := Start;
       Start := P
     END
   ELSE
     BEGIN  {  Now start the loop  }
       WHILE (Ptr <> NIL) and Looking DO
         IF Ptr^.Num > NewNum THEN
           Looking := false
         ELSE
           BEGIN
             Before := Ptr;
             Ptr := Ptr^.Next
           END;

       {  Now move the pointers  }
       IF Looking THEN
         Finish := Ptr;
       P^.Next := Ptr;

       {  Check for insert at beginning  }
       IF Before = NIL THEN
         Start := P
       ELSE
         Before^.Next := P
     END
   END;  {  of PROCEDURE Insert  }
```

To illustrate how **PROCEDURE** Insert can be used to create a linked list of integers sorted from high to low, let's develop a short program to read integers from a data file, create a linked list sorted from high to low, and print contents of components in the linked list. A first-level pseudocode development of this is

1. Create the list
2. Print the list

Step 1 can be refined to

1. Create the list
   1.1 create the first node
   1.2 **WHILE NOT eof DO**
         insert in the list

Using procedures for inserting an element and printing the list, a program is

```
PROGRAM LinkListPrac (input, output);

{  This program is a first illustration of using linked lists.  }
{  It creates a sorted linked list from an unsorted data  file  }
{  and then prints the contents  of the  list.  Procedures are  }
{  used to                                                      }
{                                                               }
{        (1)  insert into the list                              }
{        (2)  print the list                                    }

TYPE
  DataPtr = ^Node;
  Node = RECORD
           Num : integer;
           Next : DataPtr
         END;  {  of RECORD Node  }

VAR
  Number : integer;    {  Number to be inserted                 }
  Start,               {  Pointer for the beginning of the list }
  Finish : DataPtr;    {  Pointer for the end of the list        }

{*************************************************************** }

PROCEDURE Insert (VAR Start, Finish : DataPtr;
                  Number : integer);

{  Given:   A linked list and number to be inserted in order  }
{  Task:    Insert the number in numerical order in the       }
{               linked list                                   }
{  Return:  Nothing                                           }

  VAR
    P, Ptr, Before : DataPtr;
    Looking : boolean;

  BEGIN

    {  Initialize  }

    new (P);
    P^.Num := Number;
    Before := NIL;
```

```
            Ptr := Start;
            Looking := true;

            {  Now start the loop  }

            WHILE (Ptr <> NIL) AND Looking DO
              IF Ptr^.Num > Number THEN
                Looking := false
              ELSE
                BEGIN
                  Before := Ptr;
                  Ptr := Ptr^.Next
                END;  {  of ELSE option  }

            {  Now move the pointers  }

            IF Looking THEN
              Finish := Ptr;
            P^.Next := Ptr;

            {  Check for insert at beginning  }

            IF Before = NIL THEN
              Start := P
            ELSE
              Before^.Next := P
          END;  {  of PROCEDURE Insert  }

{****************************************************************** }

PROCEDURE PrintList (Start : DataPtr);

  {  Given:   A pointer to the start of a linked list          }
  {  Task:    Print numbers from nodes of the linked list      }
  {  Return:  Nothing                                          }

  VAR
    P : DataPtr;

  BEGIN
    writeln;
    P := Start;
    WHILE P <> NIL DO
      BEGIN
        writeln (P^.Num);
        P := P^.Next
      END  {  of WHILE loop  }
  END;  {  of PROCEDURE PrintList  }

{****************************************************************** }

BEGIN  {  Main program  }

{  Start the list  }

  new (Start);
  readln (Number);
  Start^.Num := Number;
  Start^.Next := NIL;
  new (Finish);
  Finish := Start;                        {  List has only one node  }

{  Now create the remainder of the list  }
```

```
    WHILE NOT eof DO
      BEGIN
        readln (Number);
        Insert (Start, Finish, Number)
      END;  {  of WHILE NOT eof  }
    PrintList (Start)
END.  {  of main program  }
```

When this program is run on the data file

the output is

```
-10
  0
  2
 42
 45
 52
 78
 86
 91
 99
100
```

Deleting a Node

A second standard operation when working with linked lists is that of deleting a node. Let's first consider the problem of deleting the first node in a list. This process is commonly called *pop*. Before writing code for this procedure, however, let's examine what should be done with the pointers.

Deleting the first node essentially requires a reversal of the steps used when inserting a node at the beginning of a list. If the list is

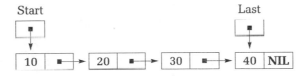

and you wish to produce a list as in

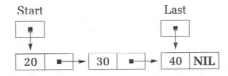

you might think that

```
Start := Start^.Next;
```

would accomplish this. Not true. There are two problems with this method. First, you may—and probably will—want the value of some data fields returned to the main program. Thus, the appropriate fields need their values assigned to variable parameters. A second problem with this method is that the first node has not been returned to the computer for subsequent reuse.

Since one of the advantages of using dynamic variables is not wasting unused storage, the procedure **dispose** should be used with this node.

We can now write a procedure to delete the first node. Assuming the data value is to be returned to the main program, the procedure is

```
PROCEDURE Pop (VAR Start : DataPtr;
               VAR Number : integer);
  VAR
    P : DataPtr;
  BEGIN
    P := Start;              { Use a temporary pointer      }
    Number := P^.Num;        { Return value to main program }
    Start := Start^.Next;    { Move start to next node       }
    dispose (P)              { Return P^ for later use       }
END;  { of PROCEDURE Pop  }
```

The next kind of deletion we examine is when the list is searched for a certain key value and the node containing this value is to be removed from the linked list. For example, if the list contains records for customers of a company, you might want to update the list when a former customer moves away. To illustrate the process, suppose the list is

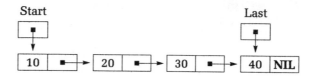

and you wish to delete

The new list is

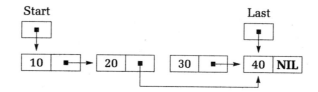

and the node deleted can be returned using **dispose** to produce

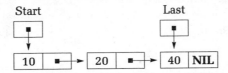

Our method of doing this uses two temporary pointers. One pointer searches the list for the specified data value and, once it is located, the second pointer points to it so we can use **dispose** to return it for subsequent use. If Before and P are the temporary pointers, the code is

```
BEGIN
  Before := Start;
  WHILE Before^.Next^.Num <> NewNum DO
    Before := Before^.Next;
  P := Before^.Next;
  Before^.Next := P^.Next;
  dispose (P)
END;
```

Let's now see how this deletes

```
30  ■
```

from the previous list.

```
Before := Start;
```

yields the list

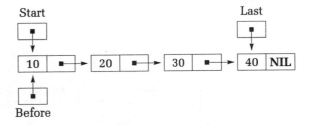

At this stage, NewNum is 30 and Before^.Next^.Num is 20. Since these are not equal, the pointer Before is moved by

```
Before := Before^.Next;
```

Thus, we have the list

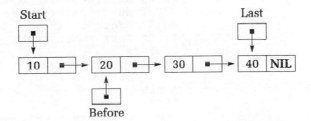

Now Before^.Next^.Num = NewNum (30); so the **WHILE** loop is exited.

```
P := Before^.Next;
```
produces the list

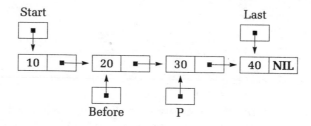

```
Before^.Next := P^.Next;
```
yields the list

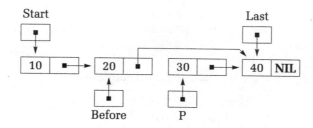

Finally, **dispose** (P); returns the node, so we have

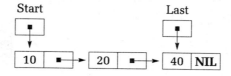

This process can be combined with deleting the first node to produce the following procedure.

```
PROCEDURE Delete (VAR Start : DataPtr;
                     Number : integer);
  VAR
    Before, P : DataPtr;
  BEGIN
    IF Number = Start^.Num THEN
      Pop (Start, Number)
    ELSE
      BEGIN
        Before := Start;
        WHILE Before^.Next^.Num <> Number DO
          Before := Before^.Next;
        P := Before^.Next;
        IF P^.Next = NIL THEN                    {  Reset Last  }
          BEGIN
            Last := Before;
            Last^.Next := NIL
          END
        ELSE
          Before^.Next := P^.Next;
        dispose (P)
      END
  END; {  of PROCEDURE Delete  }
```

This procedure can now be used to delete any node from a linked list. However, it will produce an error if no match is found. A modification to protect against this possibility is left as an exercise.

Exercises 16.3

1. Illustrate how **PROCEDURE** Insert works when inserting a node in the middle of a linked list.

2. Write a test program to see what happens when Ptr is **NIL** and a reference is made to Ptr^.

3. Revise **PROCEDURE** Insert so that it calls **PROCEDURE** Push if a node is to be inserted at the beginning of a list.

4. Modify **PROCEDURE** Delete to protect against the possibility of not finding a match when the list is searched.

5. Modify **PROCEDURE** Pop so that no data value is returned when Pop is called.

6. Write a complete program to allow you to
   a. Create a linked list of records where each record contains a person's name and an amount of money donated to a local fund-raising group; the list should be sorted alphabetically.
   b. Use the linked list to print the donor names and amounts.
   c. Read a name that is to be deleted and then delete the appropriate record from the list.
   d. Print the revised list.

7. Modify **PROCEDURE** Delete to delete the nth node rather than a node with a particular data value. For example, you might be asked to delete the fifth node.

8. Write a procedure to copy the integers in a linked list of integers into a file of integers.

9. Write a complete program that uses a linked list to sort a file of integers. Your program should create a sorted list, print the list, and save the sorted list for later use.

10. Write a procedure to delete duplicate records. Assume an ordered list.

■ ■ ■ ■

■ 16.4
Other Dynamic Data Structures

OBJECTIVES

- to understand why a stack is a dynamic data structure
- to understand how to use a stack in a program
- to understand why a queue is a dynamic data structure
- to understand how to use a queue in a program
- to understand why a binary tree is a dynamic data structure
- to be able to create a binary search tree
- to be able to search a binary search tree

In this final section, we briefly examine some additional dynamic data structures: stacks, queues, and binary trees. All of these data structures have significant computer-oriented applications.

We used stacks in our earlier work with recursion. As you will recall, each recursive call added something to a stack until a stopping state was reached. Stacks are also used when evaluating arithmetic expressions containing parentheses; partial computations are put "on hold" until needed later in the process.

Queues are used when data do not arrive in an orderly manner. A typical setting would be allocating priorities to computer users in a time-sharing system. Another example of a queue is a single waiting line for multiple service windows, such as you might find at an airport or a bank.

Trees are used in programs where a series of yes/no questions can be used with the data. Examples include sorting, computer games, and data that can be stored in the form of a matrix.

In this section, the concepts behind stacks, queues, and binary trees and their elementary use are emphasized as an introduction to these dynamic data structures. A suggested reading list is included for those wishing a more detailed development.

Stacks

A stack can be implemented as a dynamic data structure in which access can be made from only one end. You can think of a stack as paper in a copying machine or trays at a cafeteria (as mentioned in the discussion on recursion in Chapter 8). In both cases, the last one in will be the first one out; that is, you put items in, one at a time, at the top and you remove them, one at a time, from the top. This last-in, first-out order is referred to as *LIFO;* stacks are therefore often termed LIFO structures.

A stack can be envisioned as follows:

E
D
C
B
A

In this illustration, item E is considered the top element in the stack.

The two basic operations needed for working with a stack are inserting an element to create a new stack top (Push) and removing an element from the top of the stack (Pop). If a stack is represented by a linked list, Push and Pop are merely "insert at the beginning" and "delete from the beginning" as developed in Section 16.3.

To illustrate the use of a stack in a program, let's consider a program that will check an arithmetic expression to make sure that parentheses are correctly matched (nested). Our program considers

```
(3 + 4 * (5 MOD 3))
```

to make sure that the number of left parentheses matches the number of right parentheses. A first-level pseudocode for this problem is

1. Read a character
2. **IF** it is a "(" **THEN**
   Push it onto the stack
3. **IF** it is a ")" **THEN**
   Pop the previous "("
4. Check for an empty stack

The growing and shrinking of the stack can be illustrated as shown in Table 16.3.

Two points need to be made concerning this program. First, since the stack is represented by a linked list, the illustration could have been

Stack

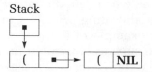

Second, before Pop is used on a stack, a check must be made to make sure the stack is not already empty. Thus, the previous procedure Pop will be re-

TABLE 16.3
Using a stack

Stack Before Read	Character Read	Stack After Character Processed
S (empty)	(	(S — Stack top
(S	*3b̷+b̷4b̷*b̷	(S — Stack top
(S	(	((S — Stack top
((S	5b̷MODb̷3	((S — Stack top
((S	)	(S — Stack top
(S	)	S — Stack top

*b̷ represents a blank space.

placed by PopAndCheck in which a suitable error message will appear if we try to pop an empty stack.

Let's now prepare code for the previous problem. The following definitions are used

```
TYPE
  DataPtr = ^Node;
  Node = RECORD
            Sym : char;
            Next : DataPtr
         END;
VAR
  Stack : DataPtr;
```

PROCEDURE Push is

```
PROCEDURE Push (VAR Stack : DataPtr;
                    Symbol : char);
  VAR
    P : DataPtr;
  BEGIN
    new (P);
    P^.Sym := Symbol;
    P^.Next := Stack;
    Stack := P
  END; { of PROCEDURE Push }
```

PROCEDURE PopAndCheck is

```
PROCEDURE PopAndCheck (VAR Stack : DataPtr);
  VAR
    P : DataPtr;
  BEGIN
    IF Stack = NIL THEN       {  Check for empty stack  }
      writeln ('The parentheses are not correct.':40)
    ELSE
      BEGIN  {  Pop the stack  }
        P := Stack;
        Stack := Stack^.Next;
        dispose (P)
      END
  END;  {  of PROCEDURE PopAndCheck  }
```

With these two procedures, the main body of a program that examines an expression for correct use of parentheses is

```
BEGIN  {  Main program  }
  Stack := NIL;
  WHILE NOT eoln DO
    BEGIN
      read (Symbol);
      IF Symbol = '(' THEN
        Push (Stack, Symbol);
      IF Symbol = ')' THEN
        PopAndCheck (Stack)
    END;

  {  Now check for an empty stack  }

  IF Stack <> NIL THEN
    writeln ('The parentheses are not correct.':40)
END.  {  of main program  }
```

Several modifications of this short program are available and are suggested in the exercises at the end of this section.

Queues

A *queue* can be implemented as a dynamic data structure in which access can be made from both ends. Elements are entered from one end (the rear) and removed from the other end (the front). This first-in, first-out order is referred to as *FIFO;* queues are termed FIFO structures. A queue is like a waiting line. Think of people standing in line to purchase tickets: each new customer enters at the rear of the line and exits from the front. A queue implemented as a linked list can be illustrated as

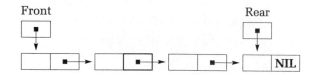

Front   Rear

Basic operations needed for working with queues are remove an element from the front of the list and insert an element at the rear of the list. If we use the definitions

```
TYPE
  DataPtr = ^Node;
  Node = RECORD
            Num : integer;
            Next : DataPtr
         END;
```

we can use variables declared by

```
VAR
  Front, Rear : DataPtr;
```

when working with such a structure.

Removing an element from the front of a queue is similar to **PROCEDURE** PopAndCheck used with a stack. The only difference is that after an element has been removed, if the queue is empty, Rear must be assigned the value **NIL.** A procedure for removing from the front of a queue follows. Here it is assumed that the value of the element removed is to be returned to the main program via a variable parameter.

```
PROCEDURE Remove (VAR Front, Rear : DataPtr;
                  VAR Number : integer);
  VAR
    P : DataPtr;
  BEGIN
    IF Front = NIL THEN    {  Check for empty queue  }
      writeln ('The queue is empty.':40)
    ELSE
      BEGIN    {  Pop the queue  }
        P := Front;
        Front := Front^.Next;
        Number := P^.Num;
        dispose (P)
      END;
    IF Front = NIL THEN   {  Set pointers for empty queue  }
      Rear := NIL
  END;  {  of PROCEDURE Remove  }
```

This procedure is called from the main program by

```
Remove (Front, Rear, Number);
```

A procedure to insert an element at the rear of a queue (assuming there is at least one element in the queue) is similar to the procedure given in the previous section for inserting at the end of a linked list. You are asked to write the code as an exercise.

Trees

A *tree* can be implemented as a dynamic data structure consisting of a special node called a *root* that points to zero or more other nodes, each of which points to zero or more other nodes, and so on. In general, a tree can be visualized as illustrated in Figure 16.4. The root of a tree is its first, or top node. *Children* are nodes pointed to by an element, a *parent* is the node that is pointing to its children, and a *leaf* is a node that has no children.

Applications for trees include compiler programs, artificial intelligence, and game-playing programs. In general, trees can be applied in programs that call for information to be stored such that it can be retrieved rapidly. As illustrated in Figure 16.4, pointers are especially appropriate for implement-

FIGURE 16.4
The general structure of a tree

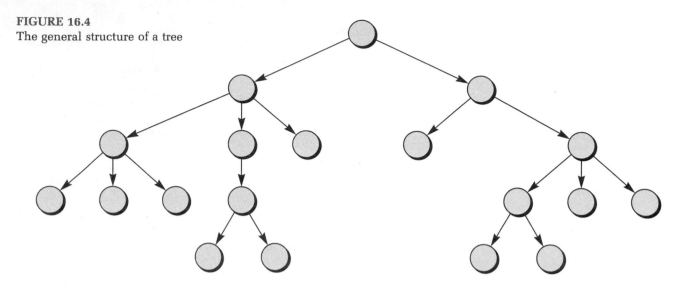

ing a tree as a dynamic data structure. An external pointer is used to point to the root and each parent uses pointers to point to its children. A more detailed tree is illustrated in Figure 16.5.

FIGURE 16.5
Using pointers to create a tree

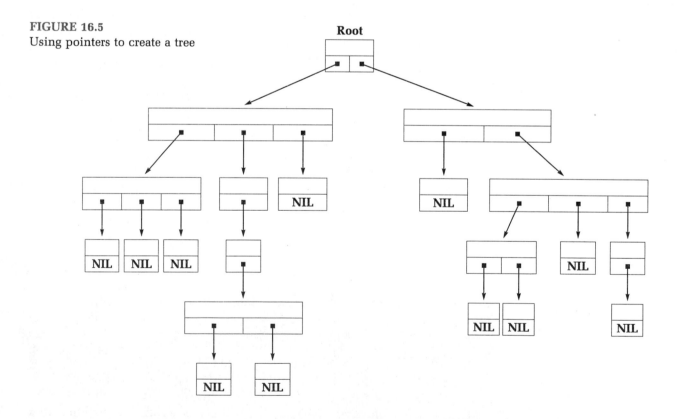

Binary Trees. From this point on, we restrict our discussion of trees to binary trees. A *binary tree* is a tree such that each node can point to at most two children. A binary tree is illustrated in Figure 16.6.

FIGURE 16.6
A binary tree

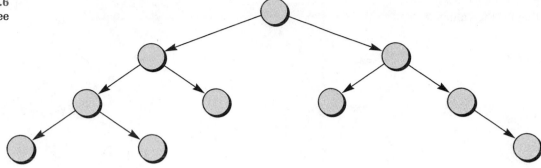

If a binary tree is used to store integer values, a reasonable definition for the pointer type is

```
TYPE
   Pointer = ^TreeNode;
   TreeNode = RECORD
                 Info : integer;
                 RightChild : Pointer;
                 LeftChild : Pointer
              END;
```

A particularly important kind of binary tree is a *binary search tree*. A binary search tree is a binary tree formed according to the following rules:

1. The information in the key field of any node is greater than the information in the key field of any node of its left child and any children of the left child.
2. The information in the key field of any node is less than the information in the key field of any node of its right child and any children of the right child. Figure 16.7 illustrates a binary search tree.

FIGURE 16.7
A binary search tree

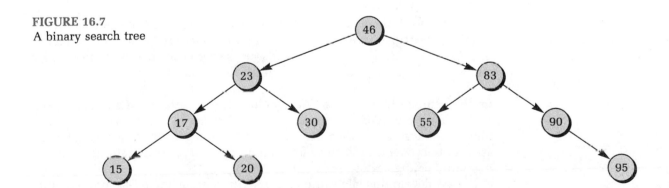

The reference to "search" is used because such trees are particularly efficient when searching for a value. To illustrate, suppose we wish to see whether or not 30 is in the tree. At each node, we check to see if the desired value has been found. If not, we determine on which side to continue looking until either a match is found or the value **NIL** is encountered. If a match is not found, we are at the appropriate node for adding the new value (creating a child). As we search for 30, we traverse the tree via the path indicated by heavier arrows. Notice that after only two comparisons (<46, >23), the desired value has been located, as illustrated in Figure 16.8.

FIGURE 16.8
Searching a tree for the value 30

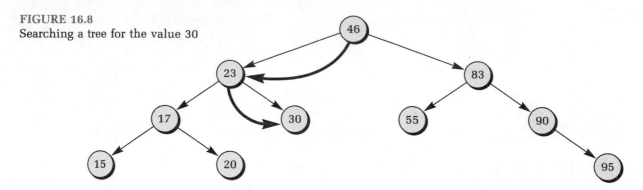

Suppose we now search the tree for the value 65. The path (again indicated by heavier arrows) is shown in Figure 16.9. At this stage, the right child is **NIL** and the value has not been located. It is now relatively easy to add the new value to the tree.

FIGURE 16.9
Searching a tree for the value 65

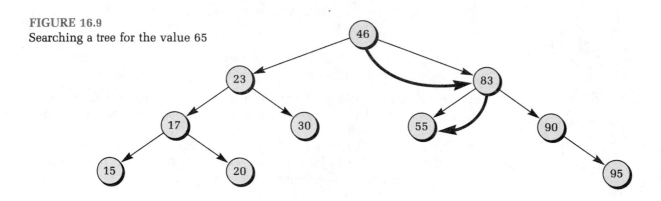

Binary search trees can be used to store any data that can be ordered. For example, the registrar of a university might want to quickly access the record of a particular student. If the records are stored alphabetically by student name in a binary search tree, quick retrieval is possible.

Implementing Binary Trees. We conclude this chapter with a relatively basic implementation of binary search trees: a program to create a binary search tree from integers in a data file. We print the integers in order using a variation of the general procedure for searching a tree. The operations of inserting and deleting nodes are left as exercises.

Before developing algorithms and writing code for these implementations, we need to discuss the recursive nature of trees. (You may wish to reread Section 8.4 at this time.) When you move from one node to a right or left child, you are (in a sense) at the root of a subtree. Thus, the process of traversing a tree is

1. **IF** LeftChild <> **NIL THEN**
    traverse left branch
2. Take desired action
3. **IF** RightChild <> **NIL THEN**
    traverse right branch

Steps 1 and 3 are recursive; each return to them saves values associated with the current stage together with any pending action. If the desired action is to print the values of nodes in a binary search tree, step 2 is

2. Print the value

and when this procedure is called, the result is to print an ordered list of values contained in the tree. If we use the previous definitions

```
TYPE
  Pointer = ^TreeNode;
  TreeNode = RECORD
               Info : integer;
               RightChild : Pointer;
               LeftChild : Pointer
             END;
```

a procedure for printing is

```
PROCEDURE PrintTree (T : Pointer);
  BEGIN
    IF T = NIL THEN
      {  do nothing  }
    ELSE
      BEGIN
        PrintTree (T^.LeftChild);
        writeln (T^.Info);
        PrintTree (T^.RightChild)
      END
  END  {  of PROCEDURE PrintTree  }
```

This procedure is called from the main program by

```
PrintTree (Root);
```

Notice how the recursive nature of this procedure provides a simple, efficient way to inspect the nodes of a binary search tree.

The process of creating a binary search tree is only slightly longer than that for printing. A first-level pseudocode is

1. Initialize root to **NIL**
2. **WHILE NOT eof DO**
    2.1 get a number
    2.2 add a node

A recursive procedure can be used to add a node. An algorithm for this is

    2.2 add a node
         2.2.1 if the current node is **NIL,** store the value and stop
         2.2.2 if the new value is less than the current value, point to the left child and add the node to the left subtree
         2.2.3 if the new value is greater than the current value, point to the right child and add the node to the right subtree

Note that the recursive procedure to add a node adds only nodes containing distinct values. A slight modification—left as an exercise—allows duplicate values to be included. A procedure for adding a node to a binary search tree is

```
PROCEDURE AddNode (VAR Node : Pointer;
                       Number : integer);
  BEGIN
    IF Node = NIL THEN {  Add a new node  }
```

```
        BEGIN
          new (Node);
          Node^.Info := Number;
          Node^.LeftChild := NIL;
          Node^.RightChild := NIL
        END
      ELSE IF Number < Node^.Info THEN
        AddNode (Node^.LeftChild, Number)
      ELSE
        AddNode (Node^.RightChild, Number)
    END;  {  of PROCEDURE AddNode  }
```

A complete program to read unordered integers from a data file, create a binary search tree, and then print an ordered list is as follows:

```
PROGRAM TreePrac (input, output);

{  This program illustrates working with a binary tree.  Note    }
{  the recursion used in AddNode and PrintTree.  Input is  an    }
{  unordered list of integers.  Output  is a sorted list of      }
{  integers that is printed from a binary search tree.           }

TYPE
  Pointer = ^TreeNode;
  TreeNode = RECORD
                Info : integer;
                RightChild : Pointer;
                LeftChild : Pointer
             END;  {  of RECORD TreeNode  }

VAR
  Root : Pointer;          {  Pointer to indicate the tree root  }
  Number : integer;        {  Integer read from the data file    }

{*****************************************************************}

PROCEDURE AddNode (VAR Node : Pointer;
                       Number : integer);

  {  Given:   The root of a binary tree and a number             }
  {  Task:    Insert the number in the binary tree               }
  {  Return:  Nothing                                            }

  BEGIN
    IF Node = NIL THEN                        {  Add a new node  }
      BEGIN
        new (Node);
        Node^.Info := Number;
        Node^.LeftChild := NIL;
        Node^.RightChild := NIL
      END
    ELSE IF Number < Node^.Info THEN    {  Move down left side   }
      AddNode (Node^.LeftChild, Number)
    ELSE                                {  Move down right side   }
      AddNode (Node^.RightChild, Number)
  END;  {  of PROCEDURE AddNode  }

{*****************************************************************}

PROCEDURE PrintTree (Node : Pointer);

  {  Given:   The root of a binary tree                          }
  {  Task:    Print numbers in order from nodes of the binary    }
  {                    tree                                      }
  {  Return:  Nothing                                            }
```

```
        BEGIN
          IF Node = NIL THEN
            {  do nothing  }
          ELSE
            BEGIN
              PrintTree (Node^.LeftChild);
              writeln (Node^.Info);
              PrintTree (Node^.RightChild)
            END
        END;  {  of PROCEDURE PrintTree  }

{****************************************************************** }

BEGIN  {  Main program  }
  new (Root);
  Root := NIL;
  WHILE NOT eof DO
    BEGIN
      readln (Number);
      AddNode (Root, Number)
    END;  {  of WHILE NOT eof  }
  PrintTree (Root)
END.  {  of main program  }
```

When this is run on the data file

```
16  8  -5  20  30  101  0  10  18  ■
```

the output is

```
-5
0
8
10
16
18
20
30
101
```

Exercises 16.4

1. Using the program for checking parentheses (at the beginning of this section), illustrate how the stack grows and shrinks when the following expression is examined.

   ```
   (5 / (3 - 2 * (4 + 3) - (8 DIV 2)))
   ```

2. Write a test program to check an arithmetic expression for correct nesting of parentheses.

3. Modify the program in Exercise 2 so that several expressions may be examined; then give more descriptive error messages. Finally, include a **SET** for the parentheses symbols "(" and ")".

4. Write a program that utilizes a stack to print a line of text in reverse order.

5. Stacks and queues can also be implemented using arrays rather than linked lists. With this in mind,

   a. Give appropriate definitions and declarations for using arrays for these data structures.

   b. Rewrite all procedures using array notation.

6. Write a procedure for inserting an element at the rear of a queue. Illustrate changes made in the linked list when such a procedure is executed.

7. Write a program that uses a stack to check an arithmetic expression for correct use of parentheses "( )," brackets "[ ]," and braces "{ }."

8. Indicate which of the following are binary search trees. Explain what is wrong with those that are not.

a.

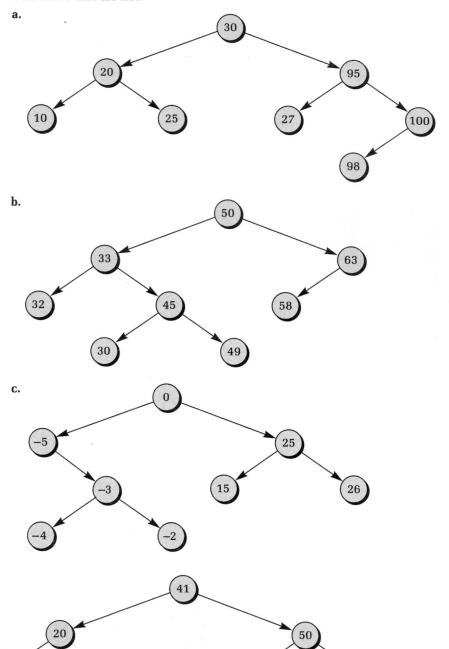

b.

c.

d.

9. Modify **PROCEDURE** AddNode to include the possibility of having nodes equal in value.

10. Write a procedure to allow you to insert a node in a binary search tree.

11. Write a function to search a binary search tree for a given value. The function should return **true** if the value is found and **false** if it is not found.

12. Write a procedure to allow you to delete a node from a binary search tree.

13. Illustrate what binary search tree is created when **PROGRAM** TreePrac is run using the data file

25 14 −3 145 0 98 81 73 85 92 56 21 ■

■ ■ ■ ■

RUNNING AND DEBUGGING TIPS

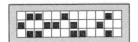

1. Be careful to distinguish between a pointer and its associated dynamic variable. Thus, if Ptr is a pointer, the variable is Ptr∧.

2. When a dynamic variable is no longer needed in a program, use **dispose** so that the memory location can be reallocated.

3. After using **dispose** with a pointer, its referenced variable is no longer available. If you use **dispose** (Ptr), then Ptr∧ does not exist.

4. Be careful not to access the referenced variable of a pointer that is **NIL.** Thus, if the assignment

```
Ptr := NIL;
```

is made, a reference to Ptr∧.Info results in an error.

5. When using pointers with subprograms, be careful to pass the pointer, not the referenced variable, to the subprogram.

6. When creating dynamic data structures, be careful to initialize properly by assigning **NIL** where appropriate and keep track of pointers as your structures grow and shrink.

7. Operations with pointers require that they be of the same type. Thus, exercise caution when comparing or assigning them.

8. Values may be lost when pointers are inadvertently or prematurely reassigned. To avoid this, use as many auxiliary pointers as you wish. This is better than trying to use one pointer for two purposes.

■ **Summary**

Key Terms

address (of a memory location)	FIFO	push
	leaf	queue
binary search tree	LIFO	root
binary tree	linked list	static variable
children	node	tree
component (of a linked list)	parent	value (of a memory location)
	pointer variable	
dynamic structure	pop	
dynamic variable		

Keywords

dispose	**new**	**NIL**

Key Concepts

- Values are stored in memory locations; each memory location has an address.
- A pointer variable is one that contains the address of a memory location; pointer variables are declared by

```
TYPE
  AgeRange = 0..99;
VAR
  Ptr : ^AgeRange;
```

where the caret (^) or up arrow (↑) is used before the predefined data type.

- A dynamic variable is a variable that is referenced through a pointer variable; dynamic variables can be used in the same context as any other variable of that type, and they are not declared in the variable declaration section. In the declaration

```
TYPE
  AgeRange = 0..99;
VAR
  Ptr : ^AgeRange;
```

the dynamic variable is Ptr^ and is available after **new** (Ptr) is executed.

- Dynamic variables are created by

```
new (Ptr);
```

and destroyed (memory area made available for subsequent reuse) by

```
dispose (Ptr);
```

- Assuming the definition

```
TYPE
  AgeRange = 0..99;
VAR
  Ptr : ^AgeRange;
```

the relationship between a pointer and its associated dynamic variable is illustrated by the code

```
new (Ptr);
Ptr^ := 21;
```

which can be envisioned as

Ptr   Ptr^

- The only legal operations on pointer variables are assignments and comparison for equality.
- **NIL** can be assigned to a pointer variable; this is used in a Boolean expression to detect the end of a list.
- Dynamic data structures differ from static data structures in that they are modified during the execution of the program.
- A linked list is a dynamic data structure formed by having each component contain a pointer that points to the next component; generally, each component is a record with one field reserved for the pointer.
- A node is a component of a linked list.
- When creating a linked list, extra pointers are needed to keep track of the first, last, and newest component.
- When creating a linked list, the final component should have **NIL** assigned to its pointer field.
- Printing from a linked list is accomplished by starting with the first component in the list and proceeding sequentially through the list until the last component is reached; a typical procedure for printing from a linked list is

```
PROCEDURE Print (First : DataPtr);
  VAR
    P : DataPtr;
  BEGIN
    P := First;
    WHILE P <> NIL DO
      BEGIN
        writeln (P^.<field name>);
        P := P^.Next
      END
  END;  {  of PROCEDURE Print  }
```

- Inserting a node in a linked list should consider three cases: insert at the beginning, insert in the middle, and insert at the end.
- Inserting at the beginning of a linked list is used frequently and is referred to as Push; one version of this is

```
PROCEDURE Push (VAR Start : DataPtr;
                    NewNum : integer);
  VAR
    P : DataPtr;
  BEGIN
    new (P);
    P^.New := NewNum;
    P^.Next := Start;
    Start := P
  END;  {  of PROCEDURE Push  }
```

- Searching an ordered linked list to see where a new node should be inserted is accomplished by

```
Ptr := Start;
WHILE Ptr^.Num < NewNum DO
  BEGIN
    Before := Ptr;
    Ptr := Ptr^.Next
  END;
```

- In deleting a node from a linked list, one should be able to delete the first node or search for a particular node and then delete it.
- Deleting the first node is referred to as Pop; one version is

```
PROCEDURE Pop (VAR Start : DataPtr;
                   VAR NewNum : integer);
  VAR
    P : DataPtr;
  BEGIN
    P := Start;
    NewNum := P^.Num;
    Start := Start^.Next;
    dispose (P)
  END;  {  of PROCEDURE Pop  }
```

- When a node is deleted from a linked list, it should be returned for subsequent use; this is done by using the standard procedure **dispose.**
- A stack is a dynamic data structure where access can be made from only one end; stacks are referred to as LIFO (last-in, first-out) structures.
- A queue is a dynamic data structure where access can be made from both ends; queues are referred to as FIFO (first-in, first-out) structures.
- A tree is a dynamic data structure consisting of a special node (called a root) that points to zero or more other nodes, each of which points to zero or more other nodes, and so on. Trees are represented symbolically as

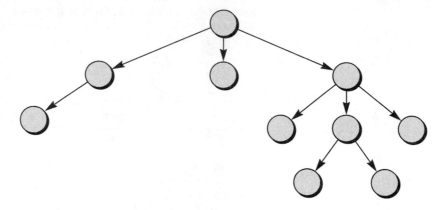

- A root is the first or top node of a tree.
- Trees are particularly useful in programs that use data that can be ordered and that need to be retrieved quickly.
- Binary trees are trees where each node points to at most two other nodes; parent, right child, and left child are terms frequently used when working with binary trees. An illustration of a binary tree is

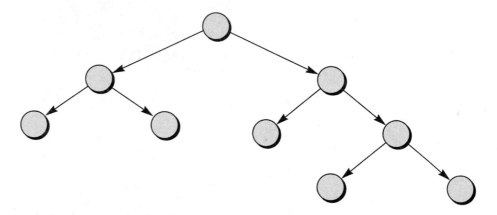

- Binary search trees are binary trees in which the information in any node is greater than the information in any node of its left child and any children of the left child and the information in any node is less than the information in any node of its right child and any children of the right child. An illustration of a typical binary search tree is

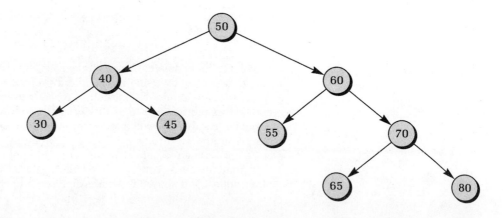

■ Recursive procedures can be used when working with trees; to illustrate, the values in the nodes of a binary search tree can be printed (sequentially) with the following procedure:

```
PROCEDURE PrintTree (T : Pointer);
  BEGIN
    IF T = NIL THEN
      {  do nothing  }
    ELSE
      BEGIN
        PrintTree (T^.LeftChild);
        writeln (T^.Info);
        PrintTree (T^.RightChild)
      END
  END  {  of PROCEDURE PrintTree  }
```

■ Suggestions for Further Reading

Nance, Douglas W., and Thomas L. Naps *Introduction to Computer Science: Programming, Problem Solving, and Data Structures, 2nd Edition.* St. Paul, Minnesota: West Publishing Company, 1992.

Naps, Thomas L., and Bhagat Singh. *Program Design with Pascal: Principles, Algorithms, and Data Structures.* St. Paul, Minnesota: West Publishing Company, 1988.

Naps, Thomas L., and Douglas W. Nance, *Introduction to Computer Science: Programming, Problem Solving, and Data Structures, 2nd Alternate edition.* St. Paul, Minnesota: West Publishing Company, 1992.

Thomas L. Naps. *Introduction to Data Structures and Algorithm Analysis,* 2nd Edition. St. Paul, Minnesota: West Publishing Company, 1992.

■ Programming Problems and Projects

1. Creating an index for a textbook can be accomplished by a Pascal program that uses dynamic data structures and works with a text file. Assume that input for a program is a list of words to be included in an index. Write a program that scans the text and produces a list of page numbers indicating where each word is used in the text.

2. One of the problems faced by businesses is how best to manage their lines of customers. One method is to have a separate line for each cashier or station. Another is to have one feeder line where all customers wait and the customer at the front of the line goes to the first open station. Write a program to help a manager decide which method to use by simulating both options. Your program should allow for customers arriving at various intervals. The manager wants to know the average wait in each system, average line length in each system (because of its psychological effect on customers), and the longest wait required.

3. Write a program to keep track of computer transactions on a mainframe computer. The computer can process only one job at a time. Each line of input contains a user's identification number, a starting time, and sequence of integers representing the duration of each job.

   Assume all jobs are run on a first-come, first-served basis. Your output should include a list of identification numbers, the starting and finishing times for each job, and the average waiting time for a transaction.

4. Several previous programming problems have involved keeping records and computing grades for students in some class. If linked lists are used for the students' records, such a program can be used for a class of 20 students or a class of 200 students. Write a recordkeeping pro-

gram that utilizes linked lists. Input is from an unsorted data file. Each student's information consists of the student's name, ten quiz scores, six program scores, and three examination scores. Output should include:

a. A list, alphabetized by student name, incorporating each student's quiz, program, and examination totals; total points; percentage grade; and letter grade.

b. Overall class average.

c. A histogram depicting class averages.

5. Modify the program you developed for Readmore Public Library (Problem 6 and 7, Chapter 12 and Problem 2, Chapter 14) to incorporate a dynamic data structure. Use a linked list to solve the same problem.

6. Mailing lists are frequently kept in a data file sorted alphabetically by customer name. However, when they are used to generate mailing labels for a bulk mailing, they must be sorted by zip code. Write a program to input an alphabetically sorted file and produce a list of labels sorted by zip code. The data for each customer are

a. Name.

b. Address, including street (plus number), city, two-letter abbreviation for the state, and zip code.

c. Expiration information, including the month and year.

Use a binary tree to sort by zip code. Your labels should include some special symbol for all expiring subscriptions. (See Problem 1, Chapter 14.)

7. Linked lists, stacks, and queues can be presented by using either dynamic variables or static variables (arrays). Talk with a computer science instructor who prefers the dynamic variable approach and with one who prefers the static variable approach. List the advantages and disadvantages of each method. Give an oral report to your class summarizing your conversations with the instructors. Create a chart to use as part of your presentation.

☷ Appendixes

Appendix 1
Reserved Words

The following words have predefined meanings in standard Pascal and cannot be changed. Each of these, except **GOTO** and **LABEL,** have been developed in the text. These statements are discussed in Appendix 7.

AND	**END**	**MOD**	**REPEAT**
ARRAY	**FILE**	**NIL**	**SET**
BEGIN	**FOR**	**NOT**	**THEN**
CASE	**FORWARD**	**OF**	**TO**
CONST	**FUNCTION**	**OR**	**TYPE**
DIV	**GOTO**	**PACKED**	**UNTIL**
DO	**IF**	**PROCEDURE**	**VAR**
DOWNTO	**IN**	**PROGRAM**	**WHILE**
ELSE	**LABEL**	**RECORD**	**WITH**

Appendix 2
Standard Identifiers

The standard identifiers for constants, types, files, functions, and procedures are set forth in this appendix. All have predefined meanings that could (but probably should not) be changed in a program. Summary descriptions are given for the functions and procedures.

Constants	Types	Files
false	**boolean**	**input**
maxint	**char**	**output**
true	**integer**	
	real	
	text	

Functions

Function	Parameter Type	Result Type	Value Returned
abs(x **)**	**integer** **real**	**integer** **real**	Absolute value of x
arctan(x **)**	**integer** **real**	**real**	Arctangent of x (radians)
chr(a **)**	**integer**	**char**	Character with ordinal a
cos(x **)**	**integer** **real**	**real**	Cosine of x (radians)
eof(F **)**	**file**	**boolean**	End-of-file test for F
eoln(F **)**	**file**	**boolean**	End-of-line test for F
exp(x **)**	**integer** **real**	**real** **real**	e^x
ln(x **)**	**integer** (positive) **real** (positive)	**real**	Natural logarithm of x
odd(a **)**	**integer**	**boolean**	Tests for a an odd integer
ord(x **)**	nonreal scalar	**integer**	Ordinal number of x
pred(x **)**	nonreal scalar	same as x	Predecessor of x

Functions (continued)

Function	Parameter Type	Result Type	Value Returned
round(*x*)	real	integer	Rounds off *x*
sin(*x*)	integer real	real	Sine of *x*
sqr(*x*)	integer real	integer real	Square of *x*
sqrt(*x*)	integer real	real	Square root of *x*
succ(*x*)	nonreal scalar	same as *x*	Successor of *x*
trunc(*x*)	real	integer	Truncated value of *x*

Procedures

Procedure Call	Purpose of Procedure
dispose (Ptr)	Returns variable referenced by Ptr to available space list
get (F)	Advances the file pointer for the file F and assigns the new value to F∧
new (Ptr)	Creates a variable of the type referenced by Ptr and stores a pointer to the new variable in Ptr
pack (U, J, P)	Copies unpacked array elements from U into the packed array P; copying starts with P[1] := U[J]
page (F)	Starts printing the next line of text F at the top of a new page
put (F)	Appends the current value of F to the file F
read (F, ⟨variable list⟩)	Reads values from file F into indicated variables; if F is not specified, **input** is assumed
readln (F, ⟨variable list⟩)	Executes the same as **read** and then advances the file pointer to the first position following the next end-of-line marker
reset (F)	Resets the pointer in file F to the beginning for the purpose of reading from F
rewrite (F)	Resets the pointer in file F to the beginning for the purpose of writing to F
unpack (P, U, J)	Copies packed array elements from P into the unpacked array U; copying starts with U[J] := P[1]
write (F, ⟨parameter list⟩)	Write values specified by parameter list to the text file F; if F is not specified, **output** is assumed
writeln (F, ⟨parameter list⟩)	Executes the same as **write** and then places an end-of-line marker in F

Appendix 3
Syntax Diagrams

Syntax diagrams in this appendix are listed in the following order:

```
Program
      Identifier
      File List
Declarations and Definitions
      Label Declaration
      Constant Definition
      Type Definition
            Type
                        Enumerated Type
                        Subrange Type
                        Pointer Type
                        Array Type
                        Record Type
                              Field List
                                          Fixed Part
                                    Variant Part
                                          Variant Description
                        File Type
                        Set Type
      Variable Declaration
      Procedure and Function Declarations
            Formal Parameter List
Body
      Compound Statement
            Statement
                  Assignment Statement
                        Expression
                              Term
                                    Factor
                                          Variable
                                          Set Value
                  Boolean Expression
            read or readln Statement
            write or writeln Statement
```

```
Procedure Statement
IF Statement
CASE Statement
     Case Label
WHILE Statement
REPEAT Statement
FOR Statement
WITH Statement
GOTO Statement
Empty Statement
```

Program

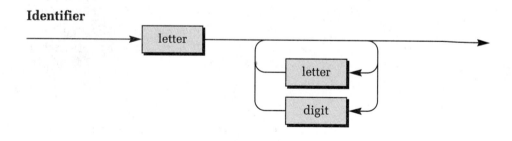

Identifier

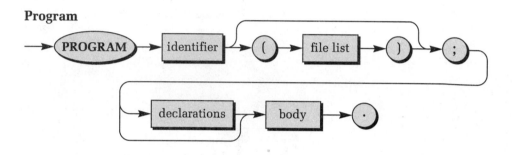

File List

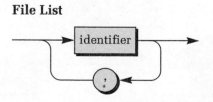

Declarations and Definitions

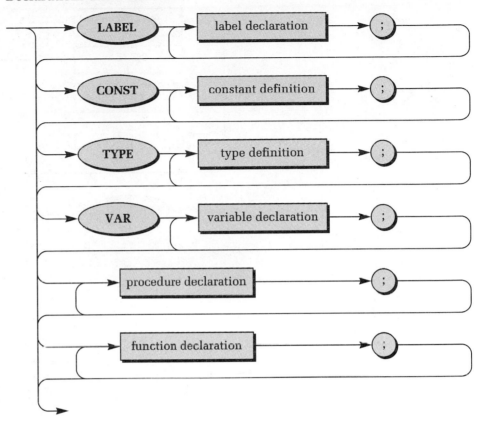

Label Declaration

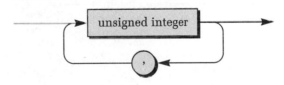

Constant Definition

Type Definition

Type

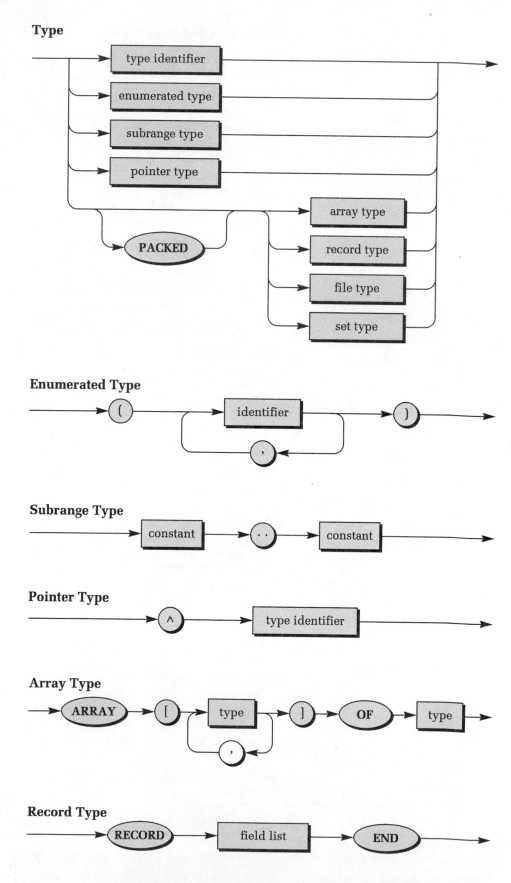

Enumerated Type

Subrange Type

Pointer Type

Array Type

Record Type

Field List

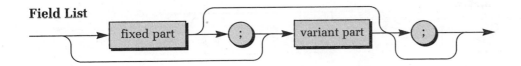

Fixed Part

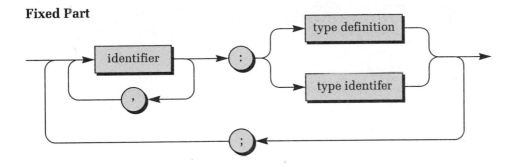

Variant Part

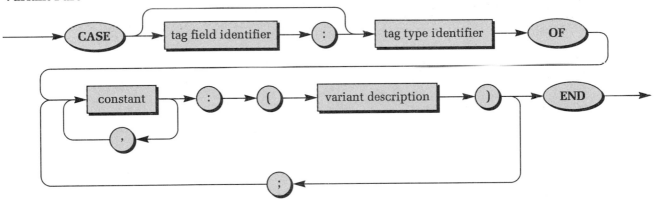

Variant Description

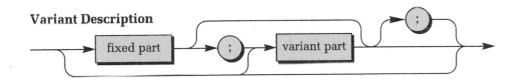

File Type

Set Type

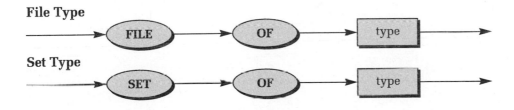

Variable Declaration

Procedure and Function Declarations

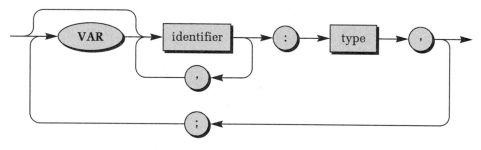

Formal Parameter List

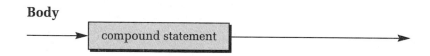

Body

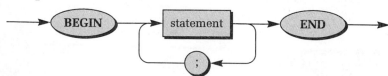

Compound Statement

Statement

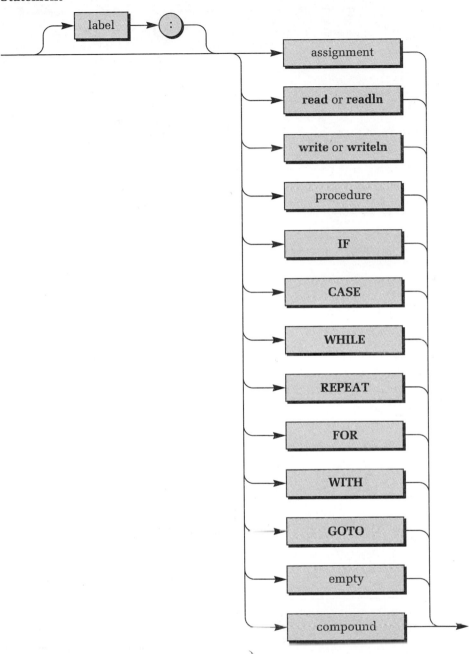

Assignment Statement

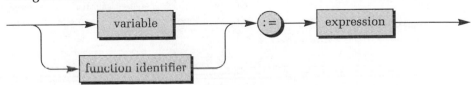

Expression

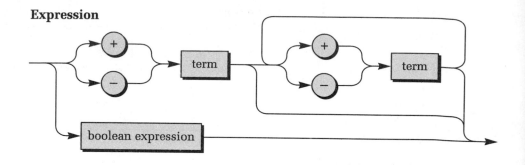

Term

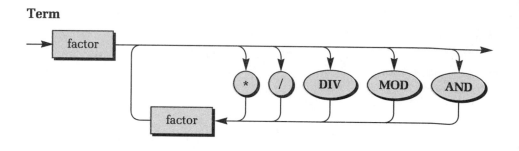

Factor

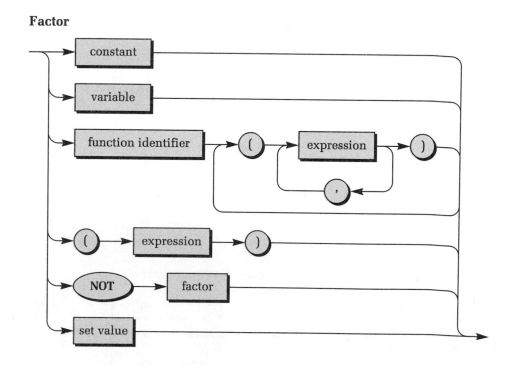

Variable

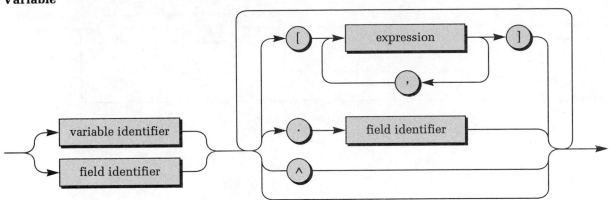

Set Value

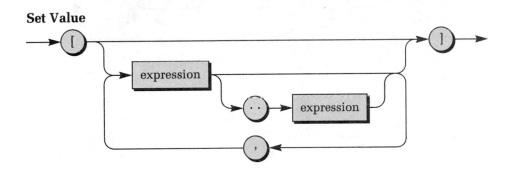

Boolean Expression

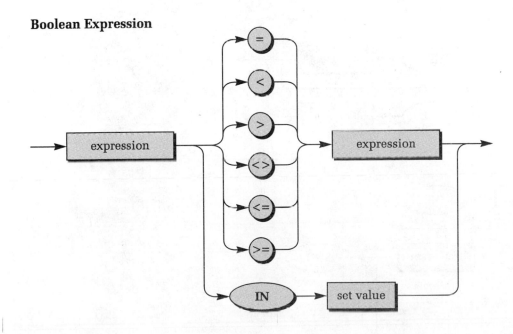

read or readln Statement

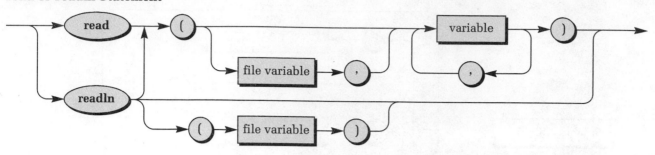

write or writeln Statement

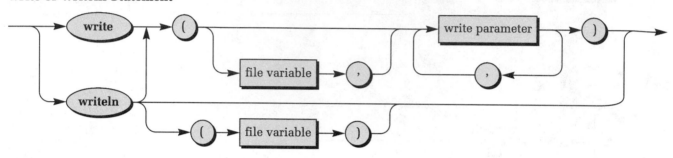

Procedure Statement

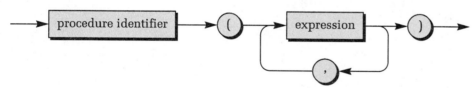

IF Statement

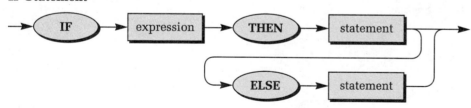

CASE Statement

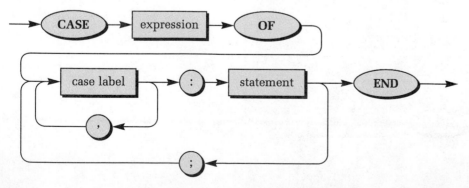

Case Label

WHILE Statement

REPEAT Statement

FOR Statement

WITH Statement

GOTO Statement

Empty Statement

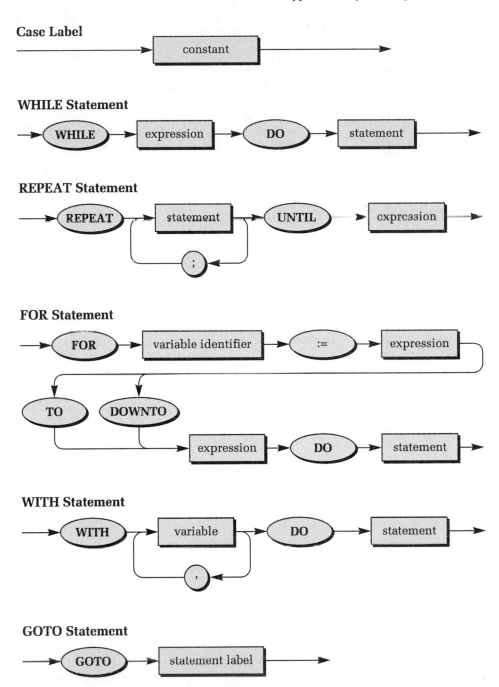

Appendix 4
Character Sets

The two tables included here show the ordering of two common character sets. Note that only printable characters are shown for each set. Ordinals without character representations either do not have standard representation, or they are associated with unprintable control characters. In each list, the blank is denoted by "ƀ".

The American Standard Code for Information Interchange (ASCII)

Left Digit(s)	Right Digit									
	0	1	2	3	4	5	6	7	8	9
3			ƀ	!	"	#	$	%	&	'
4	(	)	*	+	,	−	.	/	0	1
5	2	3	4	5	6	7	8	9	:	;
6	<	=	>	?	@	A	B	C	D	E
7	F	G	H	I	J	K	L	M	N	O
8	P	Q	R	S	T	U	V	W	X	Y
9	Z	[	\	]	^	_	`		a	b	c
10	d	e	f	g	h	i	j	k	l	m
11	n	o	p	q	r	s	t	u	v	w
12	x	y	z	{	|	}	~			

*Codes less than 32 or greater than 126 are nonprintable.

The Extended Binary Coded Decimal Interchange Code (EBCDIC)

Left Digit(s)	Right Digit									
	0	1	2	3	4	5	6	7	8	9
6					þ					
7					¢	.	<	(	+	|
8	&									
9	!	$	*	)	;	¬	-	/		
10							^	,	%	—
11	>	?								
12			:	#	@	'	=	"		a
13	b	c	d	e	f	g	h	i		
14						j	k	l	m	n
15	o	p	q	r						
16			s	t	u	v	w	x	y	z
17								\	{	}
18	[	]								
19				A	B	C	D	E	F	G
20	H	I								J
21	K	L	M	N	O	P	Q	R		
22							S	T	U	V
23	W	X	Y	Z						
24	0	1	2	3	4	5	6	7	8	9

*Codes not listed in this table are nonprintable.

Appendix 5 Compiler Error Messages

The following are typical error messages used by a compiler to identify compilation errors. Such errors will be identified by number with appropriate messages produced at the bottom of a compilation listing. Different compilers produce different error messages.

```
 1   ERROR IN SIMPLE TYPE.
 2   IDENTIFIER EXPECTED.
 3   'PROGRAM' EXPECTED.
 4   ')' EXPECTED.
 5   ' ' EXPECTED.
 6   UNEXPECTED SYMBOL.
 7   ERROR IN PARAMETER LIST.
 8   'OF' EXPECTED.
 9   '(' EXPECTED.
10   ERROR IN TYPE.
11   '[' EXPECTED.
12   ']' EXPECTED.
13   'END' EXPECTED.
14   ';' EXPECTED.
15   INTEGER CONSTANT EXPECTED.
16   '=' EXPECTED.
17   'BEGIN' EXPECTED.
18   ERROR IN DECLARATION PART.
19   ERROR IN FIELD-LIST.
20   ',' EXPECTED.
21   '..' EXPECTED.

40   VALUE PART ALLOWED ONLY IN MAIN PROGRAM.
41   TOO FEW VALUES SPECIFIED.
42   TOO MANY VALUES SPECIFIED.
43   VARIABLE INITIALIZED TWICE.
44   TYPE IS NEITHER ARRAY NOR RECORD.
45   REPETITION FACTOR MUST BE GREATER THAN ZERO.
```

```
50    ERROR IN CONSTANT.
51    ':=' EXPECTED.
52    'THEN' EXPECTED.
53    'UNTIL' EXPECTED.
54    'DO' EXPECTED.
55    'TO' OR 'DOWNTO' EXPECTED.
57    'FILE' EXPECTED.
58    ERROR IN FACTOR.
59    ERROR IN VARIABLE.
60    FILE TYPE IDENTIFIER EXPECTED.

101   IDENTIFIER DECLARED TWICE.
102   LOWBOUND EXCEEDS HIGHBOUND.
103   IDENTIFIER IS NOT OF APPROPRIATE CLASS.
104   IDENTIFIER NOT DECLARED.
105   SIGN NOT ALLOWED.
106   NUMBER EXPECTED.
107   INCOMPATIBLE SUBRANGE TYPES.
108   FILE NOT ALLOWED HERE.
109   TYPE MUST NOT BE REAL.
110   TAGFIELD TYPE MUST BE SCALAR OR SUBRANGE.
111   INCOMPATIBLE WITH TAGFIELD TYPE.
112   INDEX TYPE MUST NOT BE REAL.
113   INDEX TYPE MUST BE SCALAR OR SUBRANGE.
114   BASE TYPE MUST NOT BE REAL.
115   BASE TYPE MUST BE SCALAR OR SUBRANGE.
116   ERROR IN TYPE OF STANDARD PROCEDURE PARAMETER.
117   UNSATISFIED FORWARD REFERENCE.
119   FORWARD DECLARED; REPETITION OF PARAMETER LIST NOT ALLOWED.
120   FUNCTION RESULT TYPE MUST BE SCALAR, SUBRANGE, OR POINTER.
121   FILE VALUE PARAMETER NOT ALLOWED.
122   FORWARD DECLARED FUNCTION; REPETITION OF RESULT TYPE NOT
      ALLOWED.
123   MISSING RESULT TYPE IN FUNCTION DECLARATION.
124   FIXED-POINT FORMATTING ALLOWED FOR REALS ONLY.
125   ERROR IN TYPE OF STANDARD FUNCTION PARAMETER.
126   NUMBER OF PARAMETERS DOES NOT AGREE WITH DECLARATION.
127   INVALID PARAMETER SUBSTITUTION.
128   PARAMETER PROCEDURE/FUNCTION IS NOT COMPATIBLE WITH
      DECLARATION.
129   TYPE CONFLICT OF OPERANDS.
130   EXPRESSION IS NOT OF SET TYPE.
131   TESTS ON EQUALITY ALLOWED ONLY.
132   '<' AND '>' NOT ALLOWED FOR SET OPERANDS.
133   FILE COMPARISON NOT ALLOWED.
134   INVALID TYPE OF OPERAND(S).
135   TYPE OF OPERAND MUST BE BOOLEAN.
136   SET ELEMENT MUST BE SCALAR OR SUBRANGE.
137   SET ELEMENT TYPES NOT COMPATIBLE.
138   TYPE OF VARIABLE IS NOT ARRAY.
139   INDEX TYPE IS NOT COMPATIBLE WITH DECLARATION.
140   TYPE OF VARIABLE IS NOT RECORD.
141   TYPE OF VARIABLE MUST BE FILE OR POINTER.
142   INVALID PARAMETER SUBSTITUTION.
143   INVALID TYPE OF LOOP CONTROL VARIABLE.
144   INVALID TYPE OF EXPRESSION.
145   TYPE CONFLICT.
146   ASSIGNMENT OF FILES NOT ALLOWED.
147   LABEL TYPE INCOMPATIBLE WITH SELECTING EXPRESSION.
148   SUBRANGE BOUNDS MUST BE SCALAR.
149   INDEX TYPE MUST NOT BE INTEGER.
150   ASSIGNMENT TO THIS FUNCTION IS NOT ALLOWED.
151   ASSIGNMENT TO FORMAL FUNCTION IS NOT ALLOWED.
```

```
152   NO SUCH FIELD IN THIS RECORD.
155   CONTROL VARIABLE MUST NOT BE DECLARED ON AN INTERMEDIATE
      LEVEL.
156   MULTIDEFINED CASE LABEL.
157   RANGE OF CASE LABELS IS TOO LARGE.
158   MISSING CORRESPONDING VARIANT DECLARATION.
159   REAL OR STRING TAGFIELDS NOT ALLOWED.
160   PREVIOUS DECLARATION WAS NOT FORWARD.
161   MULTIPLE FORWARD DECLARATION.
164   SUBSTITUTION OF STANDARD PROCEDURE/FUNCTION NOT ALLOWED.
165   MULTIDEFINED LABEL.
166   MULTIDECLARED LABEL.
167   UNDECLARED LABEL.
168   UNDEFINED LABEL IN THE PREVIOUS BLOCK.
169   ERROR IN BASE SET.
170   VALUE PARAMETER EXPECTED.
172   UNDECLARED EXTERNAL FILE.
173   FORTRAN PROCEDURE OR FUNCTION EXPECTED.
174   PASCAL PROCEDURE OR FUNCTION EXPECTED.
175   MISSING FILE 'INPUT' IN PROGRAM HEADING.
176   MISSING FILE 'OUTPUT' IN PROGRAM HEADING.
177   ASSIGNMENT TO FUNCTION ALLOWED ONLY IN FUNCTION BODY.
178   MULTIDEFINED RECORD VARIANT.
179   X-OPTION OF ACTUAL PROCEDURE/FUNCTION DOES NOT MATCH
      FORMAL DECLARATION.
180   CONTROL VARIABLE MUST NOT BE FORMAL.
181   ARRAY SUBSCRIPT CALCULATION TOO COMPLICATED.
182   MAGNITUDE OF CASE LABEL IS TOO LARGE.
183   SUBRANGE OF TYPE REAL IS NOT ALLOWED.

198   ALTERNATE INPUT NOT FOUND.
199   ONLY ONE ALTERNATE INPUT MAY BE ACTIVE.

201   ERROR IN REAL CONSTANT DIGIT EXPECTED.
202   STRING CONSTANT MUST BE CONTAINED ON A SINGLE LINE.
203   INTEGER CONSTANT EXCEEDS RANGE.
204   8 OR 9 IN OCTAL NUMBER.
205   STRINGS OF LENGTH ZERO ARE NOT ALLOWED.
206   INTEGER PART OF REAL CONSTANT EXCEEDS RANGE.
207   REAL CONSTANT EXCEEDS RANGE.

250   TOO MANY NESTED SCOPES OF IDENTIFIERS.
251   TOO MANY NESTED PROCEDURES AND/OR FUNCTIONS.
255   TOO MANY ERRORS ON THIS SOURCE LINE.
256   TOO MANY EXTERNAL REFERENCES.
259   EXPRESSION TOO COMPLICATED.
260   TOO MANY EXIT LABELS.
261   TOO MANY LARGE VARIABLES.
262   NODE TO BE ALLOCATED IS TOO LARGE.
263   TOO MANY PROCEDURE/FUNCTION PARAMETERS.
264   TOO MANY PROCEDURES AND FUNCTIONS.

300   DIVISION BY ZERO.
302   INDEX EXPRESSION OUT OF BOUNDS.
303   VALUE TO BE ASSIGNED IS OUT OF BOUNDS.
304   ELEMENT EXPRESSION OUT OF RANGE.

350   ONLY THE LAST DIMENSION MAY BE PACKED.
351   ARRAY TYPE IDENTIFIER EXPECTED.
352   ARRAY VARIABLE EXPECTED.
353   POSITIVE INTEGER CONSTANT EXPECTED.

397   PACK AND UNPACK ARE NOT IMPLEMENTED FOR DYNAMIC ARRAYS.
398   IMPLEMENTATION RESTRICTION.
```

Appendix 6
Turbo Pascal Notes

This text is written using standard Pascal. The decision to use standard Pascal rather than some other version was made for three reasons.

1. Standard Pascal is still frequently used at many colleges and universities.
2. Although many different versions of Pascal are available, no single one is dominant.
3. Standard Pascal is the easiest version from which to adapt if some other version is being used.

Recently, however, Turbo Pascal has begun to grow rapidly in popularity. Turbo's popularity is a function of the increasing use of personal computers, good compiler programs, and Turbo's relatively low cost.

The third edition of this text has responded to the increasing use of Turbo Pascal by expanding this appendix on Turbo Pascal. Here, reference is made to parts of the text where specific differences occur between standard and Turbo Pascal. These differences are explained in some detail.

Using a properly formatted disk containing Turbo Pascal, boot the system. When the prompt appears, enter 'TURBO' and press ⟨RETURN⟩. Next enter 'Y' or 'N' for error messages. At this stage, several options are available. Enter 'W' and you will be asked to enter a work file name. Enter 'Prac1' and press ⟨RETURN⟩. Then enter 'E' and you will be in the edit mode ready to write a program.

To see how the compiler works, input the following sample program. Enter this program exactly as written—complete with the error!

```
PROGRAM Practice;
  VAR
    A, B, Sum : integer;
  BEGIN
    A := 20
    B := 30;
    Sum := A + B;
    writeln ('Sum is', Sum:5)
  END.
```

A.21

Exit the edit mode by pressing Ctrl-K-D. Enter 'C' to compile the program. The error message

```
"Error 85: ';' expected. Press <Esc>"
```

appears. Press ⟨Esc⟩ and you will be returned to the program in the edit mode with the cursor under the 'B' of B := 30;. Move the cursor to where the missing semicolon belongs (after 20), enter the semicolon, and press Ctrl-K-D to exit. Compile again by entering 'C'. You now have an error-free program and can run it by entering 'R'.

You can save the program by entering 'S'. It will be saved as PRAC1.PAS. You can then exit by pressing 'Q'. Prac1 is now a permanent file. If you need to use it again, enter 'TURBO' and type in 'Prac1' when a work file name is requested.

Versions 5.0 and 6.0 have significantly different environments. After leaving the edit mode, menus are available for running and compiling. You run and/or compile a program by selecting the appropriate menu choice. A little practice with these menus should make you comfortable with their use.

The remainder of this appendix consists of specific page references in bold type, followed by appropriate comments. Turbo logos, (shown to the left), are used throughout the text to indicate a reference to this appendix.

Turbo Notes

Page 30: Turbo does not require a file list with the program heading.

```
PROGRAM <name>;
```

is sufficient.

Page 38: maxint is 32767. Most versions of Turbo also include the integer data types **byte, word, shortint,** and **longint.** For those versions, the constant **longmaxint** is 2147483647.

Page 38: Most versions of Turbo also include the real data types **single, double, extended,** and **comp: single** is a floating point type with a range of $1.5 * 10^{-45}$ to $3.4 * 10^{38}$ (positive and negative); **double** is a floating point type with a range of $5.0 * 10^{-324}$ to $1.7 * 10^{308}$ (positive and negative); **extended** is a floating point type with a range from $3.4 * 10^{-4932}$ to $1.1 * 10^{4932}$ (positive and negative); and **comp** is an integral type with a range from $-9.2 * 10^{18}$ to $9.2 * 10^{18}$.

Page 39: string data types may be defined. For an explanation and illustration of declaring and using strings, see the comment for page 458.

Page 39: Default output is to the monitor. Output can be directed to the printer by using lst (short for list) within a **writeln** statement. Thus,

```
writeln ('Hello');
```

goes to the screen and

```
writeln (lst, 'Hello');
```

outputs to the printer.

In later versions of Turbo, the use of lst to send output to the printer is only available by linking a library procedure to your program. lst is defined in the unit, Printer, and is linked by:

```
Uses Printer;
```

following the program header. Using lst, however, is not practical while debugging.

For ease in directing output between the CRT and printer, Marilyn Jussel, Kearney State College, suggests a standard procedure that allows one to select output destination without changing code. While debugging, the output goes to the screen; otherwise the output goes to the printer.

The version that requires the library unit CRT is

```
Uses CRT

PROCEDURE Output_To_Where;

  VAR
    OutFile : text;
    Choice : char;

  BEGIN

    writeln ('Do you want printer output?');
    write ('Please enter choice (Y or N)');
    readln (Choice);
    IF (upcase(Choice) = 'Y') THEN
      assign (OutFile, 'prn')
    ELSE
      AssignCRT (OutFile);  {  Procedure defined in Unit CRT  }
    rewrite (OutFile)

  END;  {  of PROCEDURE Output_To_Where  }
```

The second version does not require a library unit. The only change to the code is the line following **ELSE**.

```
    assign (OutFile, 'con');
```

The distinction should be made that on the screen the command

```
    writeln;
```

gives a blank line, but on the printer the programmer must include the output file name:

```
    writeln (OutFile);
```

Page 40: There is no default field width. Thus

```
    writeln (100, 87, 95);
```

produces

```
    1008795
```

Page 42: The last line of output for Example 2.1 is

```
    Pittsburgh, PA15238
```

Page 45: The same table is produced using Turbo.
Page 53: The **MOD** operator returns the remainder obtained by dividing its two operands; that is

```
    i MOD j = i - (i DIV j) * j
```

The sign of the result of **MOD** is the same as the sign of i. An error occurs if j is zero. To better illustrate the difference, consider the expression -17 **MOD** 3. In standard Pascal, the result is 1; in Turbo Pascal, the result is -2.
Page 56:

```
    writeln (maxint + 1);
```

produces

```
    -32768
```

Page 66: The standard file **input** is not required as part of the heading. When omitted, the default input file is the keyboard.
Page 68: Interactive programs should use **readln** rather than **read**. In order for **read** to be used in an interactive program, a compiler directive ({$B-}) should be used. This, however, restricts editing. For best results, use separate **readln**s for character data.

Page 74: Reading character data using **readln** presents no problems. However, if characters are mixed with numbers, each number must be followed by a blank, tab, or carriage return. Thus,

```
23-A
```

is not allowed. It should be entered as

```
23 A
```

If you wish to symbolically enter the fraction 2/3, it would have to be 2 /3 or 2 / 3.

Page 116: The error message is

```
Run-time error 04, PC=2CEA
Program aborted
```

Page 118: The Turbo compiler is especially helpful for debugging. After listing an error message (see the previous note), it continues with directions for subsequent action. For example, the full screen message for division by zero of the previous note is

```
Run-time error 04, PC=2CEA
Program aborted

Searching
7 lines

Run-time error position found. Press <Esc>
```

When the ⟨Esc⟩ key is pressed, the editor is automatically reentered and the cursor is located at the position where execution was halted.

Page 120: No error message is produced. The default value for variables is zero. Thus, A + B has the value 10 + 0 and the Average is 5.0.

Page 144: Output in Turbo is **true.**

Page 145: eoln and **eof** should be used only when reading from text files (see Turbo note for page 381). Both functions work if the file is a logical device. **eoln** is **true** if the character read is a ⟨RETURN⟩ or if **eof** is **true. eof** is **true** if the character read is a Ctrl-Z. However, when getting input interactively, it is preferable to use Boolean flags other than **eoln** and **eof.**

Page 183: ELSE is optional inside a **CASE** statement.

Page 184: Turbo Pascal does not include an **OTHERWISE** option for a **CASE** statement. However, an equivalent **ELSE** option is available. Syntax for the **ELSE** option is

```
CASE ⟨selector⟩ OF
  ⟨label 1⟩ : ⟨statement 1⟩;
      .
      .
      .
  ⟨label 2⟩ : ⟨statement n⟩
ELSE
  BEGIN
    ⟨statement 1⟩;
        .
        .
        .
    ⟨statement m⟩
  END {    of ELSE option    }
END {    of CASE statement    }
```

Page 211: All variables are initialized to zero as a default setting. When a loop has been exited, the loop index retains the last assigned value.

Page 226: See Turbo note for page 145.
Page 228: See Turbo note for page 145.
Page 381: Text files are written using the Turbo editor. You can create a data disk by using the Turbo editor in the same way as you would write a program. However, instead of program lines, you enter appropriate lines of data. When finished, you exit the editor and save the file on the disk by entering 'S'.

When this is saved on the disk, it would be listed in the directory as DATA1.PAS (unless some other designator is specified). You can then use the data file by declaring a file of type **text** in the variable declaration section. The file name does not have to be listed in the program heading. Thus, you could have

```
PROGRAM UseData;
VAR
   DataFile : text;
```

Within the program you must then assign the file name on the directory to the declared file. This can be accomplished by

```
assign (DataFile, 'DATA.PAS');
reset (DataFile);
```

Notice that DataFile is **reset** to guarantee the pointer is at the beginning of the file. At this stage, you can use **read** or **readln** to get input from the text file DataFile. You can accomplish this by including the file name in the **read** or **readln** command. Thus, you might have

```
WHILE NOT eof(DataFile) DO
   BEGIN
      readln (DataFile, Num);
      writeln (Num)
   END;
```

When you finish reading from a text file, you should close it with a **close** command. In the previous example, this would be

```
close (DataFile);
```

eoln and **eof** can be used with text files. The text file must be included as an argument. Thus, you might have statements such as

```
WHILE NOT eof(Data);
```

or

```
WHILE NOT eoln(Data);
```

When reading from a text file, you must include the file name as an argument. Typical statements are

```
   read (Data, ⟨variables here⟩);
or
   readln (Data, ⟨variables here⟩);
```

Page 382: See Turbo for Page 381.
Page 402: Subrange limits may be ignored. Assignment of a value outside the specified range will not cause a compilation error. However, since you cannot predict what value will be stored, you should not use subranges as a form of program protection. This can lead to program crashes caused by inappropriate values.
Page 458: A **string** data type is available in Turbo Pascal. Correct syntax is

```
VAR
   Name : string;
```

or

```
VAR
  Name : string[n];
```

for early versions of Turbo where *n* specifies the string length (from 1 through 255). With this declaration, you could have a statement such as

```
readln (Data, Score, Name);
```

as part of a program. There are several string functions and procedures available in Turbo. They include **delete, insert, str, concat(+), copy, length, pos, val,** and **numstr.** Students working in a Turbo environment are encouraged to become familiar with each of these.

Page 459: All variables are automatically packed in Turbo. Thus, packed arrays need not be declared and procedures **pack** and **unpack** have no effect. (For a discussion of **pack** and **unpack,** see Appendix 8.)

Page 460: For the first reference, see Turbo note for page 458. In Turbo, the length of a string variable is dynamic. The actual length is determined by the current string value assigned to that variable. Therefore, even though Name may be declared as string[20], if Name is assigned 'Sue', its length will be 3.

Page 461: See Turbo note for page 458.

Page 502: Since **string** is a data type available in Turbo Pascal, packed arrays of characters are not needed. An array of **strings** can be thought of as a one-dimensional array.

Page 544: Loops are not needed for reading names when using a **string** data type. The code on this page could be replaced by

```
WITH Student DO
  BEGIN
    read (Data, Name);
    FOR J := 1 TO 3 DO
      read (Data, Score[J];
    readln (Data);
    Average := (Score[1] + Score[2] + Score[3] / 3
  END;
```

Page 545: See Turbo note for page 544.
Page 548: See Turbo note for page 544.
Page 549: See Turbo note for page 544.
Page 589: File names are not required as part of a program heading. If information is stored in a binary file named DATA, it is listed in the directory as DATA.PAS. Assuming such a file of integers exists, the following program illustrates how the data can be accessed.

```
PROGRAM UseData;
VAR
  DataFile : FILE OF integer;
  Num : integer;
BEGIN
  assign (DataFile, 'DATA.PAS');
  reset (DataFile);
  WHILE NOT eof(DataFile) DO
    BEGIN
      read (DataFile, Num);
      writeln (Num)
    END;
  close (DataFile)
END.
```

The effect of this program is to print the integers in DATA.PAS to the screen.

Turbo Pascal permits random access of binary files. Using the procedure **seek,** a particular file component can be located by

```
seek (<file name>, <position - 1>);
```

The component can then be obtained by

```
read (<file name>, <component>);
```

Random access files can be opened for reading **(read)** and writing **(write)** at the same time. Thus, if you are updating a file, after processing a component, you reposition the pointer by

```
seek (<file name>, <position - 1>);
```

and then **write** the updated component to the file by

```
write (<file name>, <component>):
```

When you are finished, you should close the file by

```
close (<file name>);
```

Page 593: Files in Turbo may be created in two ways. Files of type **text** are created by using the Turbo editor with an appropriately named data file. Both numeric and nonnumeric data may be entered in a text file. Both **read** and **readln** may be used when retrieving data from a text file.

Binary files must be created from a program by writing to a defined file. A sample program that creates a binary file of integers from a text file follows.

```
PROGRAM FilePrac;

VAR
  Num : integer;           {  Integers moved between files  }
  NewFile : FILE OF integer; {  Binary file of integers        }
  OldFile : text;          {  Existing text file             }

BEGIN

  assign (OldFile, 'INTDATA.PAS');
  assign (NewFile, 'NEWDATA.PAS');
  reset (OldFile);
  rewrite (NewFile);
  writeln ('OldFile', 'Values to NewFile':29);
  writeln ('-------', '-----------------':29);
  WHILE NOT eof(OldFile) DO
    BEGIN
      readln (OldFile, Num);   {  read from the text file    }
      write (Num);             {  display the number          }
      Num := Num * 10;
      writeln (Num:20);        {  display the new number      }
      write (NewFile, Num)     {  write to the binary file    }
    END;
  close (OldFile);
  close (NewFile);
  reset (NewFile);
  writeln;

  {  Now display contents of the binary file.                 }

  writeln ('Values from NewFile');
  writeln ('-------------------');
  WHILE NOT eof(NewFile) DO
    BEGIN
      read (NewFile, Num);
      writeln (Num)
    END;
  close (NewFile)

END.  {  of main program  }
```

Output from this program is

```
            OldFile                 Values to NewFile
            -------                 -----------------
            2                       20
            4                       40
            6                       60
            8                       80
            10                      100


            Values from NewFile
            -------------------
            20
            40
            60
            80
            100
```

Page 594: get and **put** are not used in Turbo Pascal. All files are accessed using **read, readln, write,** or **writeln.** This simplifies working with files since you no longer must work with file windows and buffer variables.

Page 598: There are no internal files in Turbo Pascal.

Page 606: The following program is included as a sample of creating a file of records in Turbo. Specifically, it creates a file of records for Programming Problem 9 from Chapter 13.

```
PROGRAM CreateDataFile;

TYPE
  Flight = RECORD
              FlightNumber : integer;
              ETA : 0..2400;
              ETD : 0..2400;
              Orig, Dest : string[15]
           END;  { of RECORD }

VAR
  FlightFile : FILE OF Flight;
  FlightRec : Flight;
  MoreData : boolean;
  Continue : char;

BEGIN

  assign (FlightFile, 'NewFile.pas');
  rewrite (FlightFile);
  MoreData := true;
  WHILE MoreData DO     { Get one flight record }
    BEGIN
      WITH FlightRec DO
        BEGIN
          ClrScr;
          writeln ('Enter a data line');
          writeln ('Origin        *Destination  * ETA   ETD    Flight Num');
          readln (Orig, Dest, ETA, ETD, FlightNumber)
        END;
      write (FlightFile, FlightRec);    { write one record to the file }
      write ('Continue? y or n   ');
      readln (Continue);
      MoreData := (Continue = 'y') OR (Continue = 'Y')
    END; { of getting data  }
  close (FlightFile);
  reset (FlightFile);     { Print contents of the binary file }

  { Display contents of the binary file  }
```

```
   WHILE NOT eof(FlightFile) DO
     BEGIN
       read (FlightFile, FlightRec);
       WITH FlightRec DO
         writeln (Orig:12, Dest:12, ETA:5, ETD:5, FlightNumber:5)
     END

END.  {  of PROGRAM  }
```

A sample run of this program produces the binary file

```
   Detroit        Chicago         752  756  521
   Chicago        Tampa          1157  857  911
```

Page 648: The maximum number of elements in a set is 256, and the ordinal values of the base type must be within the range 0 through 255.

Page 679: Turbo Pascal uses a caret (^) rather than an up arrow (↑) for pointer variables.

Appendix 7
GOTO Statement

In your work with computers, you may have heard of a **GOTO** statement. It is another statement in Pascal that allows a programmer to transfer control within a program. The **GOTO** statement has the effect of an immediate unconditional transfer to an indicated designation. You should not use **GOTO** statements in a Pascal program, but for the sake of completeness, you should be aware of their existence and how they work.

Early programming languages needed a branching statement; therefore, both FORTRAN and BASIC were designed using a **GOTO** statement for branching. Subsequent languages, particularly Pascal, included more sophisticated branching and looping statements. These statements led to an emphasis on structured programming, which is easier to design and read. If you are a beginning programmer and have not used the **GOTO** statement in another language, you should continue to develop your skills without including this statement. If you have already written programs in a language that uses **GOTO** statements, you should still attempt to write all Pascal programs without **GOTO** statements.

One instance in which **GOTO** statements might be appropriate is in making a quick exit from some part of the program. For example, if you are getting data from somewhere within a program and you have a check for valid data, your design could include a program segment such as

```
read data
IF (<bad data>) THEN
  BEGIN
    <write error message>;
    GOTO <end of program>
  END
ELSE
  <process data>
```

With the previous admonitions against using **GOTO** statements in mind, we will now briefly examine the form, syntax, and flow of control for these statements.

GOTO statements require the use of numerically labeled statements. Thus, your program could contain

```
LABEL
  <label 1>,
  <label 2>;
    .
    .
    .
GOTO 100;
    .
    .
    .
100: <program statement>;
    .
    .
    .
```

All labels must be declared in a label declaration section that precedes the constant definition section in a program. Each label can only be used for a single program statement. The form for the label declaration section is

> **LABEL**
>   ⟨label 1⟩,
>   ⟨label 2⟩,
>   .
>   .
>   .
>   ⟨label *n*⟩;

Correct form for a **GOTO** statement is

> **GOTO** ⟨numerical label⟩;

where numerical label is an integer from 1 to 9999 inclusive. Declared labels are then used with appropriate statements in a program. Proper syntax for labeling a statement is

> ⟨label⟩ : ⟨program statement⟩;

Consider the fragment

```
BEGIN
  read (Num);
  IF Num < 0 THEN
    GOTO 100
  ELSE
    Sum := Sum + Num;
       .
       .
       .
  100: writeln ('Data include a negative number,':40)
END.
```

In this instance, when a negative number is encountered as a data item, an appropriate message is printed and the program is terminated.

GOTO statements permit you to immediately transfer out of any control structure. As stated, we recommend you avoid the use of this statement whenever possible. However, if you must use it, use it only for an immediate exit from some point in the program; never use it to construct a loop in Pascal.

⊞ Appendix 8 Packing and Unpacking

The basic trade-off between working with arrays and packed arrays is that packed arrays require less memory but more time to access individual components. It is possible to facilitate working with packed and unpacked arrays (arrays that are not packed) by using assignment loops. For example, consider the following declarations.

```
TYPE
   String10 = PACKED ARRAY [1..10] OF char;
   Aray10 = ARRAY [1..10] OF char;
VAR
   PakName : String10;
   UnpakName : Aray10;
```

We now have reserved memory for

PakName

and

UnpakName

	UnpakName[1]
	UnpakName[2]
	UnpakName[3]
	UnpakName[4]
	UnpakName[5]
	UnpakName[6]
	UnpakName[7]
	UnpakName[8]
	UnpakName[9]
	UnpakName[10]

Now suppose that UnpakName contains the name 'John Smith'.

UnpakName

'J'
'o'
'h'
'n'
'S'
'm'
'i'
't'
'h'

and we wish to put the characters into a packed array for storage, sorting, or writing. This could be accomplished by

```
FOR J := 1 TO 10 DO
   PakName [J] := UnpakName[J];
```

and would produce the following:

PakName

'J'	'o'	'h'	'n'	''	'S'	'm'	'i'	't'	'h'

This string can still be accessed as one packed array variable.

A **FOR** loop could also be used to transfer elements from a packed array to an unpacked array, but Pascal does provide standard procedures for both of these processes. An array can be packed by

```
pack (UnpackedArray, J, PackedArray);
```

This fills all of PackedArray with elements of UnpackedArray, starting with UnpackedArray [J]. An array can be unpacked by

```
unpack (PackedArray, UnpackedArray, K);
```

This copies all elements of PackedArray into UnpackedArray, putting the first element in UnpackedArray [K]. For these procedures, PackedArray and UnpackedArray do not have to be of the same length and K may be a constant or expression. Unfortunately, **pack** and **unpack** are difficult to use. Therefore, since **FOR** loops can accomplish the same results and are about as efficient, you would do well to use them if you wish to transfer between packed and unpacked arrays.

⊞ Glossary

abstract data type (ADT) A form of abstraction that arises from the use of defined types. An ADT consists of a class of objects, a defined set of properties of those objects, and a set of operations for processing the objects.

accumulator A variable used for the purpose of summing successive values of some other variable.

actual parameter A variable or expression contained in a procedure or function call and passed to that procedure or function. *See also* **formal parameter.**

address Often called address of a memory location, this is an integer value that the computer can use to reference a location. *See also* **value.**

algorithm A finite sequence of effective statements that, when applied to the problem, will solve it.

application software Programs designed for a specific use.

argument A value or expression passed in a function or procedure call.

arithmetic/logic unit (ALU) The part of the central processing unit (CPU) that performs arithmetic operations and evaluates expressions.

array A structured variable designed to handle data of the same type.

array index The relative position of the components of an array.

array of records An array whose component type is a record.

ASCII collating sequence The American Standard Code for Information Interchange ordering for a character set.

assembly language A computer language that allows words and symbols to be used in an unsophisticated manner to accomplish simple tasks.

assertion Special comments used with selection and repetition that state what you expect to happen and when certain conditions will hold.

assignment statement A method of putting values into memory locations.

batch input Input for a program being run in batch mode. Also referred to as stream input.

batch processing A technique of executing the program and data from a file that has been created. User interaction with the computer is not required during execution. Also referred to as stream input.

BEGIN ... END block The segment of code between **BEGIN** and **END** that, when a compound statement is executed within a program, is treated as a single statement.

binary digit A digit, either 0 or 1, in the binary number system. Program instructions are stored in memory using a sequence of binary digits. Binary digits are called bits.

binary search The process of examining a middle value of a sorted array to see which half contains the value in question and halving until the value is located.

binary search tree A binary tree such that (1) the information in the key field of any node is greater than the information in the key field of any node of its left child and any of its children and (2) the information in the key field of any node is less than the information in the key field of any node of its right child and any of its children.

binary tree A tree such that each node can point to at most two children.

bit *See* **binary digit.**

block A program in Pascal can be thought of as a heading and a block. The block contains an optional declaration part and a compound statement. The block structure for a subprogram is a subblock. *See also* **subblock.**

Boolean expression An expression whose value is either true or false. *See also* **compound Boolean expression** and **simple Boolean expression.**

bottom-up testing Independent testing of modules.

bubble sort Rearranges elements of an array until they are in either ascending or descending order. Consecutive elements are compared to move (bubble) the elements to the top or bottom accordingly during each pass. *See also* **index sort, insertion sort, quick sort,** and **selection sort.**

buffer variable The actual vehicle through which values are passed to or from a file component.

built-in function *See* **standard function.**

bus A group of wires imprinted on a circuit board to facilitate communication between components of a computer.

byte A sequence of bits used to encode a character in memory. *See also* **word.**

call Any reference to a subprogram by an executable statement. Also referred to as invoke.

central processing unit (CPU) A major hardware component that consists of the arithmetic/logic unit (ALU) and the control unit.

character set The list of characters available for data and program statements. *See also* **collating sequence.**

children Nodes pointed to by an element in a tree.

code (writing) The process of writing executable statements that are part of a program to solve a problem.

cohesive subprogram A subprogram designed to accomplish a single task.

collating sequence The particular order sequence for a character set used by a machine. *See also* **ASCII** and **EBCDIC.**

comment A nonexecutable statement used to make a program more readable.

compatible type Variables that have the same base type. A value parameter and its argument must be of compatible type. *See also* **identical type.**

compilation error An error detected when the program is being compiled. A complete list of compilation error messages is set forth in Appendix 5. *See also* **design error, logic error, run-time error,** and **syntax error.**

compiler A computer program that automatically converts instructions in a high-level language to machine language.

component of a file One element of the file data type.

component of a linked list *See* **node.**

component of an array One element of the array data type.

compound Boolean expression Refers to the complete expression when logical connectives and negation are used to generate Boolean values. *See also* **Boolean expression** and **simple Boolean expression.**

compound statement Uses the reserved words **BEGIN** and **END** to make several simple statements into a single compound statement.

conditional statement *See* **selection statement.**

constant The contents of a memory location whose contents cannot be changed in the body of the program.

constant definition section The section where program constants are defined for subsequent use.

control structure A structure that controls the flow of execution of program statements.

control unit The part of the central processing unit (CPU)

that controls the operation of the rest of the computer.

counter A variable used to count the number of times some process is completed.

data The particular characters that are used to represent information in a form suitable for storage, processing, and communication.

data abstraction The separation between the conceptual definition of a data structure and its eventual implementation.

data type A formal description of the set of values that a variable can have.

data validation The process of examining data prior to its use in a program.

debugging The process of eliminating errors or "bugs" from a program.

declaration section The section used to declare (name) all symbolic constants, data types, variables, and subprograms that are necessary to the program.

decrement To decrease the value of a variable.

design error An error such that a program runs, but unexpected results are produced. Also referred to as a logic error. *See also* **compilation error, run-time error,** and **syntax error.**

difference The difference of set A and set B is A − B where A − B contains the elements that are in A but not in B. *See also* **intersection, subset,** and **union.**

dynamic structure A data structure that may expand or contract during execution of a program.

dynamic variable Frequently designed as Ptr^ or Ptr↑, a dynamic variable is a variable accessed by a pointer variable.

EBCDIC collating sequence The Extended Binary Coded Decimal Interchange Code ordering for a character set.

echo checking A debugging technique in which values of variables and input data are displayed during program execution.

effective statement A clear, unambiguous instruction that can be carried out.

element of an array *See* **component of an array.**

element of a set A value that has been assigned to a set.

empty set A set containing no elements. Also called a null set.

empty statement A semicolon used to indicate that no action is to be taken. Also referred to as a null statement.

encapsulation The process of hiding implementation details of a subprogram.

end-of-file marker (eof) A special marker inserted by the machine to indicate the end of the data file. In this text it is represented by a black square (■).

end-of-line marker (eoln) A special marker inserted by the machine to indicate the end of a line in the data. In this text it is represented by a black column (▌).

entrance controlled loop *See* **pretest loop.**

enumerated data type A data type that is defined in the **TYPE** definition section by the programmer. Also referred to as user-defined data type.

error *See* **compilation error, design error, logic error, run-time error,** and **syntax error.**

executable section Contains the statements that cause the computer to do something. Starts with the reserved word **BEGIN** and concludes with the reserved word **END.**

executable statement The basic unit of grammar in Pascal consisting of valid identifiers, standard identifiers, reserved words, numbers, and/or characters, together with appropriate punctuation.

execute To perform a program step-by-step.

exit controlled loop *See* **posttest loop.**

exponential form *See* **floating point.**

extended IF statement Nested selection where additional IF . . . THEN . . . ELSE statements are used in the **ELSE** option. *See also* **nested IF statement.**

external file A file used to store data in secondary storage between runs of a program. *See also* **internal file.**

field width The phrase used to describe the number of columns used for various output. *See also* **formatting.**

field A component of a record.

FIFO *See* **queue.**

file A data structure that consists of a sequence of components all of the same type.

file window A term used in this book, though not designated by Pascal, to indicate an imaginary window through which values of a file component can be transferred.

fixed repetition loop A loop used when it is known in advance the number of times a segment of code needs to be repeated. **FOR . . . TO . . . DO** is a fixed repetition loop. Also referred to as an iterated loop.

fixed parts Fields in a record that exist for all records of a particular type. *See also* **variant part.**

fixed point A method of writing decimal numbers where the decimal is placed where it belongs in the number. *See also* **floating point.**

floating point A method for writing numbers in scientific notation to accommodate numbers that may have very large or very small values. Exactly one nonzero digit must appear on the left of the decimal. *See also* **fixed point.**

FOR loop A fixed repetition loop causing a fragment of code to be executed a predetermined number of times. **FOR . . . TO . . . DO** and **FOR . . . DOWNTO . . . DO** are **FOR** loops.

formal parameter A variable, declared and used in a procedure or function declaration, that is replaced by an actual parameter when the procedure or function is called.

formatting Designating the desired field width when printing integers, reals, Boolean values, and character strings. *See also* **field width.**

forward reference A method by which a subprogram can call another subprogram that appears later in the declaration section.

function *See* **standard function** and **user-defined function.**

global identifier An identifier that can be used by the main program and all subprograms in a program.

global variable *See* **global identifier.**

hardware The actual computing machine and its support devices.

high-level language Any programming language that uses words and symbols to make it relatively easy to read and write a program. *See also* **assembly language** and **machine language.**

higher-dimensional array An array of more than two dimensions.

identical type Variables that are declared with the same type identifier. A variable parameter and its argument must be of identical type. *See also* **compatible type.**

identifiers Words that must be created according to a well-defined set of rules but can have any meaning subject to these rules. *See also* **standard identifiers.**

index *See* **array index** or **loop index.**

index sort Sorting an array by ordering the indices of the components rather than exchanging the components.

index type The data type used for specifying the range for the index of an array. The index type can be any ordinal data type that specifies an initial and final value.

infinite loop A loop in which the controlling condition is not changed in such a manner to allow the loop to terminate.

input Data obtained by a program during its execution. *See also* **batch input** and **interactive input.**

input assertion A precondition for a loop.

input device A device that provides information to the computer. Typical devices are keyboards, disk drives, card readers, and tape drives. *See also* **I/O device** and **output device.**

insertion sort Sorts an array of elements in either ascending or descending order. Starts with an empty array and inserts elements one at a time in their proper order. *See also* **bubble sort, index sort, quick sort,** and **selection sort.**

integer arithmetic operations Operations allowed on data of type **integer.** This includes the operations of addition, subtraction, multiplication, **MOD,** and **DIV** to produce integer answers.

interactive input A method of getting data into the program from the keyboard. User interaction is required during execution.

interface A formal statement of how communication occurs between subprograms, the main driver, and other subprograms.

internal file A file, also called a temporary or scratch file, that is used for processing only and not saved in secondary storage. *See also* **external file.**

intersection The intersection of set A and set B is A * B where A * B contains the elements that are in both A and B. *See also* **difference, subtest,** and **union.**

invariant expression An assertion that is true before the loop and after each iteration of the loop.

invoke *See* **call.**

I/O device Any device that allows information to be transmitted to or from a computer. *See also* **input device** and **output device.**

iterated loop *See* **fixed repetition loop.**

keywords Either reserved words or predefined identifiers.

leaf In a tree, a node that has no children.

length (of an array) The number of components of an array.

LIFO *See* **stack.**

linear search *See* **sequential search.**

linked list A list of data items where each item is linked to the next one by means of a pointer.

local identifier An identifier that is restricted to use within a subblock of a program.

local variable *See* **local identifier.**

logic error *See* **design error.**

logical operator Either logical connective (**AND, OR**) or negation (**NOT**).

loop index Variable used for control values in a **FOR** loop.

loop invariant An assertion that expresses a relationship between variables that remain constant throughout all iterations of the loop.

loop variant An assertion whose truth changes between the first and final execution of the loop.

loop verification The process of guaranteeing that a loop performs its intended task.

loops Program statements that cause a process to be repeated. *See also* **FOR loop, REPEAT . . . UNTIL loop,** and **WHILE . . . DO loop.**

low-level language *See* **assembly language.**

machine language The language used directly by the computer in all its calculations and processing.

main block The part of a program consisting of both the declaration and executable sections.

main driver The main program when subprograms are used to accomplish specific tasks.

main memory Memory contained in the computer. *See also* **memory** and **secondary memory.**

main unit The main unit contains the central processing unit (CPU) and the main (primary) memory; it is hooked to an input device and an output device.

mainframe Large computers typically used by major companies and universities. *See also* **microcomputer** and **minicomputer.**

master file An existing external file.

maxint The largest integer constant available to a particular system.

memory The ordered sequence of storage cells that can be accessed by address. Instructions and variables of an executing program are temporarily held here. *See also* **main memory** and **secondary memory.**

memory location A storage cell that can be accessed by address. *See also* **memory.**

merge The process of combining lists. Typically refers to files or arrays.

microcomputer A personal computer with relatively limited memory, generally used by one person at a time. *See also* **mainframe** and **minicomputer.**

minicomputer A small version of a mainframe computer. It can be used by several people at once. *See also* **mainframe** and **microcomputer.**

mixed-mode Expressions containing data of both **integer** and **real** types; the value will be given as a real and not as an integer.

modular development The process of developing an algorithm using modules. *See also* **module.**

modularity The property possessed by a program which is written using modules.

module An independent unit that is part of a larger development. Usually a procedure or function. *See also* **modular development.**

module specifications A description of data received, information returned, and logic used in the module.

negation The use of the logical operator **NOT** to negate the Boolean value of an expression.

nested IF statement A selection statement used within another selection statement. *See also* **extended IF statement.**

nested loop A loop as one of the statements in the body of another loop.

nested record A record as a field in another record.

nested selection Any combination of selection statements within selection statements. *See also* **selection statement.**

node One data item in a linked list.

null set *See* **empty set.**

null statement *See* **empty statement.**

object code *See* **object program.**

object program The machine code version of the source program.

opened for reading Positions a pointer at the beginning of a file for the purpose of reading from the file.

opened for writing Positions a pointer at the beginning of a file for the purpose of writing to the file.

opening a file Positions a pointer at the beginning of a file. *See also* **opened for reading, opened for writing.**

operating system A large program that allows the user to communicate with the hardware.

ordinal data type A data type ordered in some association with the integers; each integer is the ordinal of its associated character.

output Information that is produced by a program.

output assertion A postcondition for a loop.

output device A device that allows you to see the results of a program. Typically it is a monitor or printer. *See* **input device** and **I/O device.**

overflow In arithmetic operations, a value may be too large for the computer's memory location. A meaningless value may be assigned or an error message may result. *See also* **underflow.**

packed array An array that has had data placed in consecutive bytes.

parallel arrays Arrays of the same length but with different component data types.

parameter *See* **argument.**

parameter list A list of parameters. An actual parameter list is contained in the procedure or function call. A formal parameter list is contained in the procedure or function heading.

parent In a tree, the node that is pointing to its children.

passed by reference When variable parameters are used in subprograms.

peripheral memory *See* **secondary memory** and **memory.**

pointer variable Frequently designated as Ptr, a pointer variable is a variable that contains the address of a memory location. *See also* **address** and **dynamic variable.**

pop A procedure to delete a node from a linked list.

postcondition An assertion written after a segment of code.

posttest loop A loop where the control condition is tested after the loop is executed. **REPEAT . . . UNTIL** is a posttest loop. Also referred to as an exit controlled loop.

precondition An assertion written before a particular statement.

pretest condition A condition that controls whether the body of the loop is executed before going through the loop.

pretest loop A loop where the control condition is tested before the loop is executed. **WHILE . . . DO** is a pretest loop. Also referred to as an entrance controlled loop.

primary memory *See* **main memory** and **memory.**

procedural abstraction The process of considering only what a procedure is to do rather than details of the procedure.

procedure A subprogram designed to perform a specific task as part of a larger program. Procedures are not limited to returning a single value to the main program.

program A set of instructions that tells the machine (the hardware) what to do.

program heading The first statement of any Pascal program; it must contain the reserved word **PROGRAM.**

program proof An analysis of a program that attempts to verify the correctness of program results.

program protection A method of using selection statements to guard against unexpected results.

program walk-through The process of carefully following, using pencil and paper, steps the computer uses to solve the problem given in a program. Also referred to as trace.

programming language Formal language that computer scientists use to give instructions to the computer.

prompt A marker on the terminal screen that requests input data.

protection *See* **program protection.**

pseudocode A stylized half-English, half-code language written in English but suggesting Pascal code.

push A procedure for adding a node to the beginning of a linked list.

queue A dynamic data structure where elements are entered from one end and removed from the other end. Referred to as a FIFO (first-in, first-out) structure.

quick sort A relatively fast sorting technique that uses recursion. *See also* **bubble sort, insertion sort,** and **selection sort.**

reading from a file Retrieving data from a file.

real arithmetic operations Operations allowed on data of type **real.** This includes addition, subtraction, multiplication, and division.

record A data structure that is a collection of fields that may be treated as a whole or that will allow you to work with individual fields.

recursion The process of a subprogram calling itself. A clearly defined stopping state must exist. Any recursive subprogram can be rewritten using iteration.

recursive step A well-defined step that leads to the stopping state in the recursive process.

recursive subprogram *See* **recursion.**

relational operator An operator used for comparison of data items of the same type.

REPEAT . . . UNTIL loop A posttest loop examining a Boolean expression after causing a fragment to be executed. *See also* **FOR loops, loops,** and **WHILE . . . DO loop.**

repetition *See* **loops.**

reserved words Words with have predefined meanings that cannot be changed. They are highlighted in text by capital boldface print; a list of Pascal reserved words is set forth in Appendix 1.

return type The data type for a function name.

robust The state in which a program is completely protected against all possible crashes from bad data and unexpected values.

root The first or top node in a tree.

run-time error Error detected when, after compilation is completed, an error message results instead of the correct output. *See also* **compilation error, design error, logic error,** and **syntax error.**

scope of identifier The largest block in which the identifier is available.

scratch file *See* **internal file.**

secondary memory device An auxiliary device for memory, usually a disk or magnetic tape. *See also* **main memory** and **memory.**

selection sort A sorting algorithm that sorts the components of an array in either ascending or descending order. This process puts the smallest or largest element in the top position and repeats the process on the remaining array components. *See also* **bubble sort, index sort, insertion sort,** and **quick sort.**

selection statement A control statement that selects some particular logical path based on the value of an expression. Also referred to as conditional statement.

self-documenting code Code that is written using descriptive identifiers.

sentinel value A special value that indicates the end of a set of data or of a process.

sequential algorithm *See* **straight-line algorithm.**

sequential search The process of searching a list by examining the first component and then examining successive components in the order in which they occur. Also referred to as linear search.

set A structured data type that consists of a collection of distinct elements from an indicated base type (which must be ordinal).

side effect An unintentional change in a variable which is the result of some action taken in a program.

simple Boolean expression An expression where two numbers or variable values are compared using a single relational operator. *See also* **Boolean expression** and **compound Boolean expression.**

software Programs that make the machine (the hardware) do something, such as word processing, data-base management, or games.

software engineering The process of developing and maintaining large software systems.

software system life cycle The process of development, maintenance, and demise of a software system. Phases include analysis, design, coding, testing/verification, maintenance, and obsolescence.

sort-merge The process of repeatedly subdividing a long list, sorting shorter lists, and then merging to obtain a single sorted list.

source program A program written by a programmer. *See also* **system program.**

stack A dynamic data structure where access can be made from only one end. Referred to as a LIFO (last-in, first-out) structure.

standard function A built-in function available in most versions of Pascal.

standard identifiers Predefined words whose meanings can be changed if needed. Standard identifiers are highlighted in text by lowercase boldface print; a list of Pascal standard identifiers is set forth in Appendix 2.

standard simple types The predefined data types **integer, real, char,** and **boolean.**

static variable A variable whose size (for example, array length) is fixed at compilation time. A certain memory area is reserved for each variable, and these locations are retained for the declared variables as long as the program or subprogram in which the variable is defined is active.

stepwise refinement The process of repeatedly subdividing tasks into subtasks until each subtask is easily accomplished. *See also* **structured programming** and **top-down design.**

stopping state The well-defined termination of a recursive process.

straight-line algorithm Also called sequential algorithm, this algorithm consists of a sequence of simple tasks.

stream input *See* **batch input.**

string An abbreviated name for a string constant.

string constant One or more characters used as a constant in a program.

string data type A data type which permits a sequence of characters. This is not available in standard Pascal, but can be simulated using a packed array of characters.

structure chart A graphic method of indicating the relationship between modules when designing the solution to a problem.

structured programming Programming that parallels a solution to a problem achieved by top-down design. *See also* **stepwise refinement** and **top-down design.**

stub programming A no-frills, simple and often incomplete version of a final program.

subblock A block structure for a subprogram. *See also* **block.**

subprogram A program within a program. Procedures and functions are subprograms.

subrange The defined subset of values of an existing ordinal data type.

subscript *See* **array index** or **loop index.**

subset Set A is a subset of set B if all the elements in A are also in B. *See also* **difference, intersection,** and **union.**

syntax The formal rules governing construction of valid statements.

syntax diagramming A method to formally describe the legal syntax of language structures; syntax diagrams are set forth in Appendix 3.

syntax error An error in spelling, punctuation, or placement of certain key symbols in a program. *See also* **compilation error, design error, logic error,** and **run-time error.**

system program A special program used by the computer to activate the compiler, run the machine code version, and cause output to be generated. *See also* **source program.**

systems software The programs that allow users to write and execute other programs, including operating systems such as DOS.

tag field A field used in defining variant records. Values of the tag field determine the variant record structure.

temporary file *See* **internal file.**

test program A short program written to provide an answer to a specific question.

text file A file of characters that is divided into lines.

top-down design A design methodology for solving a problem whereby you first state the problem and then proceed to subdivide the main task into major subtasks. Each subtask is then subdivided into smaller subtasks. This process is repeated until each remaining subtask is easily solved. *See also* **stepwise refinement** and **structured programming.**

trace *See* **program walk-through.**

transaction file A file containing changes to be made in a master file.

tree A dynamic data structure consisting of a special node (a root) that points to zero or more other nodes, each of which point to zero or more other nodes, and so on.

two-dimensional array An array in which each element is accessed by a reference to a pair of indices.

two-way merge The process of merging two sorted lists.

type *See* **data type.**

underflow If a value is too small to be represented by a computer, the value is automatically replaced by zero. *See also* **overflow.**

union The union of set A and set B is A + B where A + B contains any element that is in A or that is in B. *See also* **difference, intersection,** and **subset.**

universal set Any set that contains all possible values of the base type.

unpacked array An array in which data are not in consecutive bytes.

user-defined data type *See* **enumerated data type.**

user-defined function A subprogram (function) written by the programmer to perform a specific task. Functions return one value when called.

user-friendly A phrase used to describe an interactive program with clear, easy-to-follow messages for the user.

value Often called value of a memory location. Refers to the value of the contents of a memory location. *See also* **address.**

value parameter A formal parameter that is local to a subprogram. Values of these parameters are not returned to the calling program.

variable A memory location, referenced by an identifier, whose value can be changed during a program.

variable condition loop A repetition statement in which the loop control condition changes within the body of the loop.

variable declaration section The section of the declaration section where program variables are declared for subsequent use.

variable dictionary A listing of the meaning of variables used in a program.

variable parameter A formal parameter that is not local to a subprogram. Values of these parameters are returned to the calling program.

variant part The part of a record structure in which the number and type of fields can vary. *See also* **fixed part.**

WHILE . . . DO loop A pretest loop examining a Boolean expression before causing a fragment to be executed.

word A unit of memory consisting of one or more bytes. Words can be addressed.

writing to a file The process of entering data to a file.

Answers to Selected Exercises

This section contains answers to selected exercises from the exercise sets at the end of each section. In general, answers to odd numbered problems are given.

CHAPTER 2

Section 2.1

1. a. and c. are effective statements.

   b. is not effective because you cannot determine when to perform the action.

   d. is not effective because there is no smallest positive fraction.

   e. is not effective because you cannot determine in advance which stocks will increase in value.

3. a. 1. Select a topic
      2. Research the topic
      3. Outline the paper
      4. Refine the outline
      5. Write the rough draft
      6. Read and revise the rough draft
      7. Write the final paper

   c. 1. Get a list of colleges
      2. Examine criteria (programs, distance, money, and so on)
      3. Screen to a manageable number

      4. Obtain further information
      5. Make a decision

5. a. First-level development
      1. Get information for first employee
      2. Perform computations for first employee
      3. Print results for first employee
      4. ⎫
      5. ⎬ repeat for second employee
      6. ⎭

   Second-level development
      1. Get information for first employee
         1.1 get hourly wage
         1.2 get number of hours worked
      2. Perform computations for first employee
         2.1 compute gross pay
         2.2 compute deductions
         2.3 compute net pay
      3. Print results for first employee
         3.1 print input data
         3.2 print gross pay
         3.3 print deductions
         3.4 print net pay
      4. ⎫
      5. ⎬ repeat for second employee
      6. ⎭

   Third-level development
      1. Get information for first employee
         1.1 get hourly wage
         1.2 get number of hours worked
      2. Perform computations for first employee
         2.1 compute gross pay
         2.2 compute deductions
            2.2.1 federal withholding
            2.2.2 state withholding
            2.2.3 social security
            2.2.4 union dues
            2.2.5 compute total deductions
         2.3 compute net pay
            2.3.1 subtract total deductions from gross
      3. Print results for first employee
         3.1 print input data
            3.1.1 print hours worked
            3.1.2 print hourly wage
         3.2 print gross pay
         3.3 print deductions
            3.3.1 print federal withholding
            3.3.2 print state withholding
            3.3.3 print social security
            3.3.4 print union dues
            3.3.5 print total deductions

second em-

ways to solve this problem, one of which

1. Ge... umbers as input
2. Put them in order - Small, Large
3. Check for a divisor
   3.1 **IF** Small is a divisor of Large **THEN**
       3.1.1 GCD is Small
       ELSE
       3.1.2 Decrease Small until a common divisor is found
4. Print the results
   3.1.2 can be further refined as
   3.1.2 Decrease Small until a common divisor is found
       3.1.2.2 **REPEAT**
               IF GCDCandidate is a common divisor **THEN**
               GCD is GCDCandidate
               ELSE
               Decrease GCDCandidate by 1
               UNTIL a common divisor is found

Section 2.2

3. a., b., and e. are valid; however, a semicolon must be used between the heading in **a.** and the next line of code.

   c. does not begin with the reserved word **PROGRAM.**

   d. is missing an identifier for the program name.

   f. and g. use improper identifiers for the program name.

5. A typical constant definition statement is

```
CONST
   Name = 'Julie Adams';
   Age = 18;
   BirthDate = 'November 10, 1973';
   Birthplace = 'Carson City, MI';
```

Section 2.3

1. a., d., e., and g. are valid.

   b. has a decimal.

   c. has a comma.

   f. is probably larger than **maxint**

3. a. 1.73E2

   b. 7.43927E11

   c. $-2.3E-8$

   d. 1.4768E1

   e. $-5.2E0$

5. a. and d. are **integers.**

   b., c., and g. are **reals.**

   e. and f. are string constants.

7. a.
```
writeln ('Score':14);
writeln ('-----':14);
writeln (86:13);
writeln (82:13);
writeln (79:13);
```

CHAPTER 3

Section 3.1

1. a. 11

   b. -41

   c. 3

   d. 24

   e. 126

   f. 63

   g. 48

   h. 140

   i. 1

   j. 7

3. a. and b. are valid, type **integer.**

   c., e., f., g., h., and i are valid, type **real.**

   d. and j. are invalid.

5. Output will vary according to local implementation.

Section 3.2

1. a., b., e., f., and h. are valid assignment statements.

   c. is invalid. A real cannot be assigned to an integer variable.

   d. is invalid. An operand cannot be on the left of an assignment statement.

   g. is invalid. IQ/3 is a real.

3. a.

3	-5
A	B

   b.

26	31
A	B

   c.

-3	-5
A	B

   d.

9	9
A	B

5.
Sex	M
Age	23
Height	73 inches
Weight	186.5 lbs

7. column 11
```
***************************
*                         *
*   Name     Age    Sex   *
*   ----     ---    ---    *
*                         *
*   Jones    21     M     *
*                         *
***************************
```

9.　　　　　column 10
　　　　　　　↓
```
            This  reviews string formatting.
     When a letterAis used,
            Oops! I forgot to format.
            When a letter A is used,
            it is a string of length one.
```

Section 3.3

1. The file name **input.**

5. a. 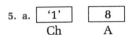　　　

b. 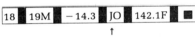　　　

c. All variables unassigned　　　

d. All variables unassigned　　　

e.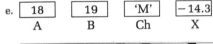

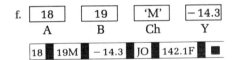

f.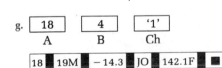

g.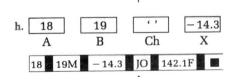

h.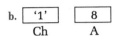

Section 3.4

3.
```
   CPS 150                 TEST #2
   ------------------------------------
   Total points           100
   My score                93
   Class average          82.3
```

Section 3.5

1. a. 15.2　　　　　　　d. 36

b. 14　　　　　　　　e. −4.5

c. 0　　　　　　　　　f. −11.98

3. **a.** `sqrt(A*A+B*B)`

   b. `(-B + sqrt(B*B-4*A*C)) / (2 * A)`
   and
   `(-B - sqrt(B*B-4*A*C)) / (2 * A)`

5. `(round(10*X)) / 10.0`

7. **a.** `-4.30   4.30   -4   -4`

   b. `4` (depends on character set—65 in ASCII)

   c. Depends on character set

9. **a.** `Uppercase := chr(ord(LowerCase) - ord('a') + ord('A'));`

   b. `IntValue := ord(Digit) - ord('0');`

CHAPTER 4

Section 4.1

1. **a.** `Total := Test1 + Test2 + Test3 + Test4;`

   b. `Average := Total / 4;`

   c. `TotalIncome := Salary + Tips;`

   d. `Time := Distance / Rate;`

   e. `Grade := TotalPoints / 6;`

   f. `writeln (Name:20, TotalPoints:10, Grade:5);`

   g. `writeln (NumberAttending:5, TicketPrice:10:2,`
   `        TotalReceipts:10:2);`

3.
```
PROGRAM BoxVolume (output);
CONST
   Skip = '';
VAR
   Length, Width, Height, Volume : integer;
BEGIN
   Length := 8;
   Width := 3;
   Height := 2;
   Volume := Length * Width * Height;
   writeln (Skip:10, 'Length =', Length:10);
   writeln (Skip:10, 'Width =', Width:10);
   writeln (Skip:10, 'Height =', Height:10);
   writeln;
   writeln (Skip:10, 'Volume =', Volume:10)
END.
```

7. **a., b., c., e.,** and **h.** are acceptable.

   d. is not correctly stated.

   f. is valid but should have consistent comment closings

   g. should have consistent comment starts.

Section 4.2

1. There should be a semicolon after Y in the first line. '=' should be replaced by ':=' in the second line. The correct code is

```
X := 3 * Y;
Y := 4 - 2 * Z;
writeln (X, Y);
```

3. The added semicolons are circled for your convenience.

```
PROGRAM ExerciseThree (output);

CONST
  Name = 'Jim Jones';
  Age = 18;

VAR
  Score : integer;

BEGIN
  Score := 93;
  writeln ('Name':13, Name:15);
  writeln ('Age':12, Age:16);
  writeln ('Score':14, Score:14)
END.
```

5. The misspelled keywords (with the correct spelling) follow.

PROGRRAM	(should be PROGRAM)
reals	(should be real)
chr	(should be char)
interger	(should be integer)
writln	(should be writeln)

7. Statements a. and e. are valid. The reasons the others are invalid follow.

   b. The operand (+) is on the left of an assignment statement.

   c. C has not been declared.

   d. Wage should be spelled Wages.

   f. Hours has not been declared.

   g. CourseName can only be assigned a single character.

   h. A value cannot be assigned to a constant.

   i. A real cannot be assigned to an intogor.

9. Errors are circled.

```
PROGRAM Errors (output(;          should be )


(***********************************)
(*                               *)
(*   There are thirteen errors.   $)     should be *
(*                               *)
(***********************************        ) missing


VAR
  Day : char;
  Percent : real              ; missing
  A, B ; int;               ; should be : and int should be integer

BEGIN (   Main program   )   ( ) should be { } or (* ... *)
  Day = 'M';                 should be :=
  Percentage := 72 / 10;     should be Percent
  A := 5;
  B := A * 3.2;              B is of type integer
  writln (A, B:20);          should be writeln
  writeln (Day:10:2);        incorrect formatting
  writeln (A+B:8, Percent:18)
END                          . missing
```

Section 4.3

1.

Value of A	Value of B	Value of C
33	undefined	undefined
33	−2	undefined
28	−2	undefined
28	28	undefined
28	28	30
28	28	30
28	28	1
29	28	1

3.

Code with Errors

```
Max = 100.0 : real;
A, Sum : integer
A := 86.0;
A + Sum := Sum
writeln (Sum:15:2)
```

Corrected Code

```
Max = 100.0;
A, Sum : integer;
A := 86;
Sum := A + Sum;
writeln (Sum:15)
```

Code with Errors

```
PROGRAM Compile Errors (output);
B := A - 10;
writeln ('The value of A is : 20, A:6);
```

Corrected Code

```
PROGRAM CompileErrors (output);
A := A - 10:   (B is not declared)
writeln ('The value of A is':20, A:6);
```

5. The following changes would be needed.

   a. underline Donations.

   b. skip a line before 100.00.

   c. print dollar signs.

   d. skip a line before total.

   e. print Total.

CHAPTER 5

Section 5.1

1.
```
true true  false
           false
```

3. Only c. and f. are valid.

5. a., b., d., and g. are **true**.

   c., e., and f. (which compare as reals) are **false**.

7. a., b., and c. are **true**.

   d. and e. are **false**.

Section 5.2

1. a. 10   5

   b. no output

   c. 5   B has no value

   d. 10   5

   e. 15   4
      15   4

   f. 10   5

3. a. should be
```
IF A = 10 THEN ...
```
   b. `3 < X < 10`
   cannot be evaluated. This should be
```
(3 < X) AND (X < 10)
```
   c. This expression needs a **BEGIN** ... **END** to be consistent with indenting. It should be
```
IF A > 0 THEN
  BEGIN
    Count := Count + 1;
    Sum := Sum + A
  END;
```
   d. `IF Ch = 'A' OR 'B' THEN`
   should be
```
IF (CH = 'A') OR (CH = 'B') THEN
```

5. Yes.

9.
```
BEGIN
   readln (Num1, Num2, Num3);
   Total := Total + Num1 + Num2 + Num3;
   writeln (Num1:5, Num2:5, Num3:5);
   writeln;
   writeln (Total)
END;
```

11.
```
read (Ch1, Ch2, Ch3);
IF (Ch1 <= Ch2) AND (Ch2 <= Ch3) THEN
   writeln (Ch1, Ch2, Ch3);
```
   This can also be written as
```
read (Ch1, Ch2, Ch3);
IF Ch1 <= Ch2 THEN
   IF Ch2 <= Ch3 THEN
      writeln (Ch1, Ch2, Ch3);
```

Section 5.3

1. a. −14   14

   b. 50   25
      1   75

   c. 10   5
      5   0

3. a. Since the intent appears to be a statement that counts characters other than periods, a **BEGIN** ... **END** block should be included in the **IF ... THEN** option.
```
IF Ch <> '.' THEN
  BEGIN
    CharCount := CharCount + 1;
    writeln (Ch)
  END
ELSE
  PeriodCount := PeriodCount + 1;
```

b. The semicolon between **END** and **ELSE** should be omitted.

c. Technically this fragment will run. However, since it appears that OldAge := OldAge + Age is to be included in the **ELSE** option, the programmer probably meant

```
ELSE
  BEGIN
    OldCount := OldCount + 1;
    OldAge := OldAge + Age
  END;
```

Section 5.4

	X	Y
1. a.	38.15	763.0
b.	-21.0	21.0
c.	600.0	1200.0
d.	3000.0	9000.0

3. a.
```
IF Ch = 'M' THEN
   IF Sum > 1000 THEN
      X := X + 1
   ELSE
      X := X + 2
ELSE IF Ch = 'F' THEN
   IF Sum > 1000 THEN
      X := X + 3
   ELSE
      X := X + 4;
```

b.
```
read (Num);
   IF Num > 0 THEN
      IF Num <= 10000 THEN
         BEGIN
            Count := Count + 1;
            Sum := Sum + Num
         END
      ELSE
         writeln ('Value out of range':27)
   ELSE
      writeln ('Value out of range':27);
```

c.
```
IF A > 0 THEN
   IF B > 0 THEN
      writeln ('Both positive':22)
   ELSE
      writeln ('Some negative':22)
ELSE
   writeln ('Some negative':22);
```

d.
```
IF C <= 0 THEN
   IF A > 0 THEN
      IF B > 0 THEN
         writeln ('Option one':19)
      ELSE
         writeln ('Option two':19)
   ELSE
      writeln ('Option two':19)
ELSE
   writeln ('Option one':19);
```

5.
```
IF Average < 90 THEN
   IF Average < 80 THEN
      IF Average < 70 THEN
         IF Average < 55 THEN
               Grade := 'E'
         ELSE Grade := 'D'
      ELSE Grade := 'C'
   ELSE Grade := 'B'
ELSE Grade := 'A' ;
```

This could be written using sequential **IF . . . THEN** statements. For example,

```
IF (Average <= 100) AND (Average >= 90) THEN
   Grade := 'A' ;
IF (Average < 90) AND (Average >= 80) THEN
   Grade := 'B' ;
      .
      .
      .
```

The disadvantage of this method is that each Boolean expression of each statement will always be evaluated. This is relatively inefficient.

7.

8	13	104
A	B	C

Section 5.5

3.
```
IF ((Age DIV 10) > 10) OR ((Age DIV 10) < 1) THEN
   writeln ('Value of age is', Age)
ELSE
   .
   . (CASE statement here)
   .
```

5. a.
```
5          3              125
```
  b.
```
You have purchased    Super Unleaded gasoline
```
  c.
```
3        -3
```
  d.
```
5        10            -5
```

7. Assume there is a variable ClassType. The design of the fragment to compute fees is

```
read (ClassType);
CASE ClassType OF
   'U' :⎫
   'G' :⎬ (list options here)
   'F' :⎬
   'S' :⎭
END;  { of CASE }
```

CHAPTER 6

Section 6.2

1. a.
```
*
  *
    *
      *
        *
          *
```

b.
```
 1 :        9
 2 :        8
 3 :        7
 4 :        6
 5 :        5
 6 :        4
 7 :        3
 8 :        2
 9 :        1
10 :        0
```

c.
```
**    2
**    3
**    4
**    5
**    6
**    7
**    8
**    9
**   10
**   11
**   12
**   13
**   14
**   15
**   16
**   17
**   18
**   19
**   20
```

d.
```
 1
 2
 3
 4
 5
 6
 7
 8
 9
10
11
12
13
14
15
16
17
18
19
20
21
```

3. a.
```
FOR J := 1 TO 4 DO
   writeln ('*':10);
```

b.
```
FOR J := 1 TO 8 DO
   writeln ('***':J+5);
```

c.
```
writeln ('*':10);
FOR J := 1 TO 3 DO
   writeln ('*':10-J, '*':2*J);
writeln ('**** ****':14);
FOR J := 1 TO 2 DO
   writeln ('* *':11);
writeln ('***':11);
```

d. This is a "look ahead" problem that can be solved by a loop within a loop. This idea is developed in Section 6.6.

```
FOR J := 5 DOWNTO 1 DO
  BEGIN
    write (' ':(6-J)); {  Indent a line  }
    FOR K := 1 TO (2*J-1) DO {  Print a line  }
      write ('*');
    writeln
  END;
```

5. a.
```
FOR J := 1 TO 5 DO
   write (J:3);
FOR J := 5 DOWNTO 1 DO
   write (6-J:3);
```

b.
```
FOR J := 1 TO 5 DO
   writeln ('*':J);
FOR J := 5 DOWNTO 1 DO
   writeln ('*':(6-J));
```

7.
```
FOR J := 2 TO 10 DO
   writeln (12-J:12-J);
```

9. The key loop in this program will be
something like

```
FOR J := -10 TO 10 DO
   BEGIN
      Num := 5*J;
      writeln (Num:10, Num * Num:10, Num * Num * Num:10)
   END;  {  of printing the chart  }
```

Section 6.3

3. a.
```
1
2
3
4
5
6
7
8
9
10
```

b.
```
1      0
2      1
3      2
4      1
5      2
```

c. 54   50

d.
```
The partial sum is     1
The partial sum is     3
The partial sum is     6
The partial sum is    10
The partial sum is    15

The count is     5
```

e.   96.00   2.00

5. a. A 18 -14.3B

b. A 18 -14.3B C 21 10.0D E 19 -11.5F

c. same as b.

d. same as a.

e.
```
A 18 -14.3 B
C 21 10.0 D
E 19 -11.5 F
```

7.
```
Ch is  X    eoln is  false    eof is   false
Ch is  Y    eoln is  false    eof is   false
Ch is  Z    eoln is  false    eof is   false
Ch is  b    eoln is  false    eof is   false
Ch is  1    eoln is  false    eof is   false
Ch is  3    eoln is  true     eof is   false
Ch is  b    eoln is  false    eof is   false
Ch is  A    eoln is  false    eof is   false
Ch is  B    eoln is  false    eof is   false
Ch is  C    eoln is  false    eof is   false
Ch is  b    eoln is  false    eof is   false
```

```
Ch is 2   eoln is   false   eof is   false
Ch is 1   eoln is   false   eof is   false
Ch is b   eoln is   true    eof is   false
Ch is M   eoln is   false   eof is   false
Ch is N   eoln is   false   eof is   false
Ch is O   eoln is   false   eof is   false
Ch is b   eoln is   false   eof is   false
Ch is 2   eoln is   false   eof is   false
Ch is 5   eoln is   true    eof is   false
Ch is b   eoln is   true    eof is   true
```

Section 6.4

```
3. a. 1    9
      2    8
      3    7
      4    6
      5    5
      6    4

   b.    2
         4
         8
        16
        32
        64
       128

   c. 1
      2
      3
      4
      5
      6
      7
      8
      9
     10

   d. 1    0
      2    1
      3    2
      4    1
      5    2
```

5. a. A 18 -14.3B

b. A 18 -14.3B C 21 10.0D 3 19 -11.5F

c. Same as a.

d. Same as b.

```
e. A 18    -14.3   B
   C 21 10.0 D
   3 19    -11.5  F
```

```
7. read (Num);
   IF Num < 10000 THEN
      BEGIN
         PowerOfNum := Num;
         REPEAT
            writeln (PowerOfNum);
            PowerOfNum := PowerOfNum * Num
         UNTIL PowerOfNum > 10000
      END;
```

Section 6.5

3. The loop in Exercise **2c.** can be re-written in each of the following ways.

```
   i. WHILE X < 4.0 DO
         BEGIN
            writeln (X:20:2);
            X := X + 0.5
         END;
  ii. FOR J := 1 TO 8 DO
         BEGIN
            writeln (X:20:2);
            X := X + 0.5
         END;
 iii. FOR J := 8 DOWNTO 1 DO
         BEGIN
            writeln (X:20:2);
            X := X + 0.5
         END;
```

5. Since the condition 6 < 5 is **false**, the loop will not be entered. In a **RE-PEAT ... UNTIL** loop, the loop body is always executed at least once before the Boolean expression controlling the loop is evaluated.

Section 6.6

```
3. a. FOR K := 1 TO 5 DO
         BEGIN
            write (' ':K);
            FOR J := K TO 5 DO
               write ('*');
            writeln
         END;

   c. FOR K := 1 TO 7 DO
         IF K < 5 THEN
            BEGIN
               FOR J := 1 TO 3 DO
                  write ('*');
               writeln
            END
         ELSE
            BEGIN
               FOR J := 1 TO 5 DO
                  write ('*');
               writeln
            END;
```

```
5. 4   4   4   4
   5   5   5   5
   6   6   6   6
   7   7   7   7

   5   5   5
   6   6   6
   7   7   7

   6   6
   7   7
```

Section 6.7

1. a. This is an infinite loop.

   b. The loop control variable, K, is unassigned once the **FOR . . . TO** loop is exited. Thus, the attempt to use K in the expression K **MOD** 3 = 0 may result in an error.

3.
```
Count := 0;
Sum := 0.0;
WHILE NOT eof DO
  BEGIN
    readln (Num);
    IF Num > 0.0 THEN
      BEGIN
        Count := Count + 1;
        Sum := Sum + Num
      END
  END;  {  of WHILE...DO loop  }
```

5. The program fragment necessary for this task is a modification of Example 6.26.

```
WHILE NOT eof DO  {  Process one line  }
  BEGIN
    write (' ':10);
    WHILE NOT eoln DO  {  Process 1 character  }
      BEGIN
        read (ch);
        IF Ch <> ' ' THEN
          write (Ch)
      END;
    readln;  {  Advance the pointer  }
    writeln
  END;  {  of WHILE NOT eof  }
```

CHAPTER 7

Section 7.2

1. A procedure is a subprogram. As such it is contained within a complete program. It is headed by the reserved word **PROCEDURE** and has a semicolon after the last **END** rather than a period. A program is headed by the reserved word **PROGRAM** and has a period after the last **END**.

3.
```
PROCEDURE PrintHeading;
  CONST
    Splats = '******************************';
    Edge = '*                            *';
    Name = 'John J. Smith';
    Date = 'September 15, 1992';
  BEGIN
    writeln (Skip:20, Splats);
    writeln (Skip:20, Edge);
    writeln (Skip:20 '*', Skip:5, Name, Skip:10, '*');
    writeln (Skip:20 '*', Skip:5, Date, Skip:5, '*');
    writeln (Skip:20, Edge);
    writeln (Skip:20, Splats)
  END;  {  of PROCEDURE PrintHeading  }
```

5. a. Suppose you want the heading to be

```
              R & R Produce Company
              ---------------------

Items Purchased        Price per Item     Total per Item
---------------        --------------     --------------
```

   A procedure for this is

```
PROCEDURE PrintHeading;
  CONST
    Skip = ' ';
  BEGIN
    writeln;
    writeln (Skip:20, 'R & R Produce Company');
    writeln (Skip:20, '---------------------');
    writeln;
    write (Skip:5, 'Items Purchased');
    write (Skip:5, 'Price per Item');
```

```
        writeln (Skip:5, 'Total per Item');
        write (Skip:5, '----------------');
        write (Skip:5, '--------------');
        writeln (Skip:5, '--------------');
        writeln
    END;
```

Section 7.3

3. a. A and B are variable parameters. X is a value parameter.

b. A and X are variable parameters. B and Ch are value parameters.

c. X, Y, and Z are variable parameters. A, B, and Ch are value parameters.

5. a. `Prob5 (Num1, Num2, Letter);`

b. `PrintHeader;`

c. `FindMax (Num1, Num2, Max);`

d. `Switch (Num1, Num2);`

e. `SwitchAndTest (Num1, Num2, Flag);`

Section 7.4

3. c. and d. are valid.

a. is invalid. The data type for what will be returned to the calling program must be listed.

`FUNCTION RoundTenth (X : real) : real;`

b. is invalid. Data types must be listed for X and Y.

e. is invalid. The comma following **char** should be a semicolon.

5. a.
```
FUNCTION MaxOfTwo (X, Y : real) : real;
    BEGIN
        IF X > Y THEN
            MaxOfTwo := X
        ELSE
            MaxOfTwo := Y
    END;
```

f.
```
FUNCTION MultOf5 (A : integer) : boolean;
    BEGIN
        IF A MOD 5 = 0 THEN
            MultOf5 := true
        ELSE
            MultOf5 = false
    END;
```

7.
```
FUNCTION Factorial (N : integer) : integer;
    VAR
        Fact, J : integer;
    BEGIN
        Fact := 1;
        FOR J := 1 TO N DO
            Fact := Fact * J;
        Factorial := Fact
    END;
```

7. b.
```
PROCEDURE MaxAndAver (X, Y, Z : real;
                      VAR Max, Aver : real);
    BEGIN
        Max := X;
        IF Y > Max THEN
            Max := Y;
        IF Z > Max THEN
            Max := Z;
        Aver := (X + Y + Z) / 3.0
    END;
```

9. There are several reasonably short methods of writing such a function. If we assume the main program checks for a valid symbol, one such function is

```
FUNCTION Arithmetic (Operand : char;
                     N1, N2 : integer) : integer;
  BEGIN
    IF Operand = '+' THEN
      Arithmetic := N1 + N2
    ELSE
      Arithmetic := N1 * N2
  END;  {  of FUNCTION Arithmetic  }
```

CHAPTER 8

Section 8.1

7. Identifiers for this program are represented schematically by the figure at right.

9. 10
   20
   10
   30
   30

11. a. Average cannot be used as a procedure name since it has already been declared as an identifier with scope that includes that procedure.

   b. No errors. The variables declared in the procedure heading are local to it.

   c. No errors.

13. The main program is trying to access an identifier that is not available. The line

```
writeln (X1:20:2);
```

   in the main program is inappropriate because the scope of X1 is **PROCEDURE** Sub1.

Section 8.2

1. a. variable parameters

   b. variable parameters

   c. value parameters

PROGRAM Practice

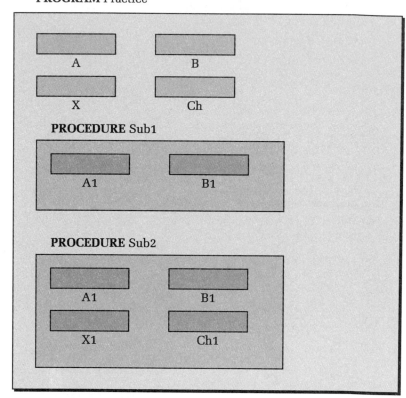

3. The pseudocode design indicates procedures could be written for

   1. Initialize variables   `Initialize (<parameter list>);`
   2. Print a heading   `PrintHeading;`
      3.1 get new data   `GetData (<parameter list>);`
   4. Print results   `PrintResults (<parameter list>);`

Until more is known about the problem, step 3.2 (perform computations) cannot be determined. However, if we assume a function (Compute) is written for this, a main program could be

```
BEGIN  {  Main program  }
  Initialize (<variable list>);
  PrintHeading;
  Flag := true;
  Count := 0;
  WHILE Flag = true DO
    BEGIN
      GetData (<variable list>);
      NewValue := Compute(<variable list>);
      Count := Count + 1;
      IF (<check condition>) THEN
        Flag := false
    END;  {  of WHILE...DO  }
  PrintResults (<variable list>)
END.  {  of main program  }
```

Section 8.3

5. A schematic representation is shown at right.

X, Y, and Ch can be used in all sub-blocks of ExerciseFive.

X1, Ch1, and J declared in **PROCEDURE** A can be used in all sub-blocks of **PROCEDURE** A but cannot be used in **PROCEDURE** B or ExerciseFive.

M and Y1 can be used only in **FUNCTION** Inner.

X1 and Ch2, declared in **PROCEDURE** B, can be used only in **PROCEDURE** B.

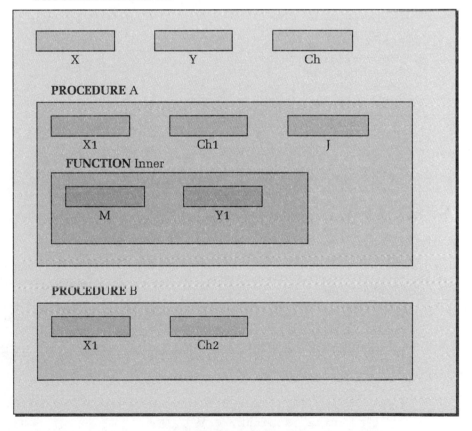

PROGRAM ExerciseFive

7. a. A schematic representation is shown at right.

   A, B, and Num are available to all blocks. A1, B1, Prod and K are available to MaxPower and Sort. A2, B2, and Temp are available only to Sort.

   b. 243

   c. This function performs the task of computing A to the power of B (A^B) where A is the smaller of the two positive integers A and B.

Section 8.4

1. There is no stopping state.

3. a. i. Y = 9.0
       ii. Y = 8.0
      iii. Y = 256.0
       iv. Y = 1.0

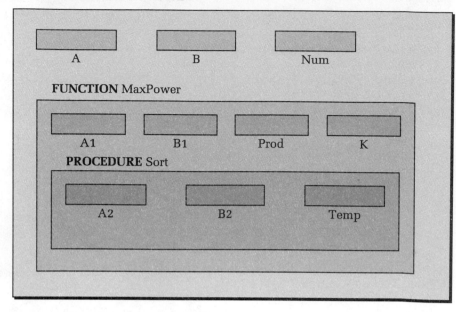

PROGRAM ExerciseSeven

A B Num

FUNCTION MaxPower

A1 B1 Prod K

PROCEDURE Sort

A2 B2 Temp

5.
```
FUNCTION IterFactorial (N : integer) : integer;
  VAR
    PartialProduct,
    NextFactor : integer;
  BEGIN
    PartialProduct := 1;
    FOR NextFactor := 2 TO N DO
      PartialProduct := PartialProduct * NextFactor;
    IterFactorial := PartialProduct
  END;  {  of FUNCTION IterFactorial  }
```

CHAPTER 9

Section 9.1

3. The variables should be formatted so the integers will be separated by blanks. You should check your answers to Exercises 5–7 on your computer due to possible differences in reading text files.

11.
```
PROGRAM DeleteBlanks (input, output, NoBlank);
  VAR
    NoBlank : text;
    Ch :char;
  BEGIN
    rewrite (NoBlank);  {  Open for writing  }
    WHILE NOT eof DO
      BEGIN
        WHILE NOT eoln DO
          BEGIN
            read (Ch);
            IF Ch <> ' ' THEN
              write (NoBlank, Ch)
          END;  {  of WHILE NOT eoln  }
        readln;
        writeln (NoBlank)
      END  {  of WHILE NOT eof  }
  END.  {  of main program  }
```

Section 9.2

3. **a.** Jane is listed in both types Names and People.

   b. Red is listed twice in type Colors.

   c. Parentheses are needed around the values. Thus, it should be
   ```
   TYPE
      Letters = (A, C, E);
   ```

5. **a.**, **d.**, and **e.** are valid.

   b. is invalid; Tues + Wed is not defined.

   c. is valid (but a poor choice).

   f. is invalid; you cannot **write** user-defined values.

   g. is invalid; you cannot **read** user-defined ordinals.

   h. is invalid; the operation Tues + 1 is not defined.

Section 9.3

1. **a.** The definition is invalid; 10 . . 1 is not a subrange of existing ordinal data type.

   b. Bases and Double are valid. Score is invalid because Second . . Home is not a subrange.

   c. All definitions and declarations are valid. However,
   ```
   Hue := Blue
   ```
   is an invalid use because Blue is not in the subrange defined for Stripes.

   d. The definitions are invalid because the type Days must be defined before the subrange Weekdays.

   e. All definitions and declarations are valid, but
   ```
   Score2 := Score1 + 5
   ```
   will produce a run-time error because the intended value (65) is not in the defined subrange.

3. **a.** Dependents usually refers to the number of single-family dependents for tax purposes. Twenty is a reasonable maximum.

   b. Assuming hours worked in one week, 0 to 60 is a reasonable range.

   c. The subrange was chosen for a maximum score of ten. This would vary for other maximum scores.

   d. The subrange could be used if the total points were a maximum of 700. This might be used in some grading programs.

5. **a.** and **b.** are compatible. The base type is ChessPieces.

   c. and **f.** are incompatible.

   d. and **e.** are compatible. The base type is **integer**.

Section 9.4

1. **a.** Oak

   b. Cotton

   c. 2

   d. Invalid

   e. 3

   f. Invalid

   g. 0

3. **a.** 'D'

   b. 10

   c. 'O'

   d. Invalid; addition of characters is not defined.

   e. Invalid; **pred**('K') is a character; thus, the operation, '+', is not defined.

   f. 'Z'

5. **a.**
   ```
   Weekend
   Weekday
   Weekday
   Weekday
   Weekday
   ```

   b. For a **WHILE** loop, you could use the Boolean expression **WHILE** Day < Sat **DO.**
   ```
   Day := Sun;
   WHILE Day < Sat DO
      BEGIN
         .
         .      (body of loop here)
         .
      END;
   ```
   A **FOR** loop could be controlled by the Boolean expression
   ```
   FOR Day := Sun TO Fri DO
      BEGIN
         .
         .      (body of loop here)
         .
      END;
   ```

c. This can be accomplished by using ordinal values. For example, if OrdValue has been declared, the loop could be

```
OrdValue := 0;
  REPEAT
    CASE OrdValue OF
       0        : (action here)
      1,2,3,4,5 :
    END;  {  of CASE OrdValue  }
    OrdValue := OrdValue + 1
  UNTIL OrdValue = 6;
```

d. The last value (Sat) is not being considered. This could be altered by using a **FOR** loop and including Sat or using a variable control loop and adding a **writeln** statement such as

```
writeln ('Weekend':20);
```

outside the loop.

7. Assume variables MonthNum and Month have been appropriately declared. A function could be

```
FUNCTION Month (MonthNum : integer) : MonthName;
  BEGIN
    CASE MonthNum OF
       1  : Month := Jan;
       2  : Month := Feb;
           .
           .
           .
      12 : Month := Dec
    END {  of CASE MonthNum  }
  END; {  of FUNCTION Month  }
```

CHAPTER 10

Section 10.1

1. a.
```
TYPE
  ScoreList = ARRAY [1..35] OF integer;
VAR
  Score : ScoreList;
```

   b.
```
TYPE
  PriceList = ARRAY [1..20] OF real;
VAR
  CarCost : PriceList;
```

   c.
```
CONST
  NumQuestions = 50;
TYPE
  AnswerList = ARRAY [1..NumQuestions] OF char;
VAR
  Answer : AnswerList;
```

   Note: It is possible to use an array of element type **boolean** here.

   d.
```
TYPE
  GradeList = Array [1..6] OF char;
VAR
  Grade : GradeList;
```

3. a. There is no error if Hours has been defined as a constant.

   b. No error.

   c. No index range has been given for the array.

   d. The index range should be [1 .. 10] rather than [1 **TO** 10].

   e. The index range is not appropriate; something like **ARRAY** [⟨index range⟩] **OF boolean** should be used.

   f. [1 ... 5] should be [1 .. 5].

5. a.
```
TYPE
   LetterList = ARRAY [1..100] OF 'A'..'Z';
VAR
   Letter : LetterList;
```
   b.
```
TYPE
   Name = ARRAY [1..30] OF char;
VAR
   CompanyName : Name;
```
   c.
```
TYPE
   ScoreList = ARRAY [30..59] OF real;
VAR
   Score : ScoreList;
```

7.

a. Money

183.25	Money[1]
10.04	Money[2]
17.32	Money[3]

b. Money

10.04	Money[1]
19.26	Money[2]
17.32	Money[3]

c. Money

19.26	Money[1]
10.04	Money[2]
2.68	Money[3]

Section 10.2

1. a. **List**

0	List[1]
0	List[2]
1	List[3]
1	List[4]
1	List[5]

c. Answer

false	Answer[1]
true	Answer[2]
false	Answer[3]
true	Answer[4]
false	Answer[5]
true	Answer[6]
false	Answer[7]
true	Answer[8]
false	Answer[9]
true	Answer[10]

b. List

5	List[1]
6	List[2]
7	List[3]
8	List[4]
9	List[5]

Score

1	Score[1]
2	Score[2]
2	Score[3]
2	Score[4]
3	Score[5]

   d. The contents of this array depend on the character set being used.

3. The section counts the number of scores greater than 90.

5. TYPE
```
   ListOfLetters = ARRAY [1..20] OF char;
VAR
   Letter : ListOfLetters;
```
A **FOR** loop could be used as follows:
```
FOR J := 1 TO 20 DO
   read (Letter[J]);
```

7.
```
FOR J := 1 TO 100 DO
   A[J] := 0.0;
```

9. a. JOHN SMITH

   b. SMITH, JOHN

   c. HTIMS NHOJ

11.
```
writeln ('Test Number', 'Score':10);
writeln ('-----------', '-----':10);
writeln;
FOR J := 1 TO 50 DO
   writeln ('<':4, J:2, '>', TestScore[J]:11);
```

Section 10.3

1. a. after one pass   after two passes

−20
10
0
10
8
30
−2

−20
−2
0
10
8
30
10

   b. Three exchanges are made.

3. A high to low sort is achieved by changing
```
IF A[K] < A[Index] THEN
```
to
```
IF A[K] > A[Index] THEN
```

Section 10.4

1. a. is valid; it can be called by
```
NewList (List1, Aray);
```

   b. is invalid; a semicolon is needed after Row.

   c. is invalid; array declaration cannot be included in the heading.

   d. is valid; can be called by
```
NewList (List1, List2);
```

   e. is invalid; Column cannot be used as a variable name.

   f. is invalid; array declaration cannot be included in the heading.

   g. is invalid; Name is not a data type.

   h. is valid; can be called by
```
Surnames (Name1, Name2);
```

i. is invalid; Name is not a data type.

j. is valid; can be called by

```
Table (List1, List2);
```

3. **a.** `PROCEDURE OldList (X: Row;`
                       `Y : Column);`

   b. `PROCEDURE ChangeList (X : Row;`
                              `N : String20;`
                              `D : Week);`

   c. This call is inappropriate because the data type for A and B has not been defined in the **TYPE** section.

   d. This call is inappropriate because the argument, String20, is a data type rather than a variable.

5. **a.** List1   List2

List1	List2
1	0
4	0
9	0
16	0
25	0
36	0
49	0
64	0
81	0
100	0

Section 10.5

1. **a.**, **c.**, **d.**, and **f** are valid; **true.**
   b. and **e.** are invalid.

3. **a.** `To err is human. Computers do not forgive.`

   b. `To err is human. Computers do not forgive.`
      `There are 15 blanks.`

   c. `    To err is human.                    *********`
                    `↑      (20 blanks)`
                `(position 18)`

   d. `To err is human. Computers do not forgive.`
              `.evigrof ton od sretupmoC .namuh si rre oT`
      `(8 blanks)`

5. `MCount := 0;`
   `FOR J := 1 TO 100 DO`
   `   IF Message[J] = 'M' THEN`
   `      MCount := MCount + 1;`

Section 10.6

1. `FOR J := 1 TO Length DO`
   `   IF Num = A[J] THEN`
   `      writeln (Num, ' is in position', J:5);`

3. The value of Index in the loop can be used as a counter.

5.   a. `Num = 18`

	First	Last	Mid	A[Mid]	Found
Before loop	1	5	Undefined	Undefined	**false**
After first pass	1	2	3	37	**false**
After second pass	1	2	1	18	**true**

c. `Num = 76`

	First	Last	Mid	A[Mid]	Found
Before loop	1	5	Undefined	Undefined	**false**
After first pass	4	5	3	37	**false**
After second pass	4	3	4	92	**false**

Since First > Last, the loop will be exited and an appropriate message should be printed.

7.   Algorithmic developments for this problem follow.

a. 1. Copy file components into an array
   2. Get number to look for
   3. Search sequentially for a match

c. 1. Copy file components into an array
   2. Get new number
   3. Use a binary search until Last < First
   4. Assign First to Position
   5. Move array components ahead one from Position to the end of the list

```
FOR J := Length DOWNTO Position DO
   A[J + 1] := A[J];
```
   6. Assign new number to

```
A[Position];
```

9.   There will be a maximum of five passes.

CHAPTER 11

Section 11.1

1.   a. `DrugPrice = ARRAY [1..4, 1..5] OF real;`
        `DrugPrice = ARRAY [1..4] OF ARRAY [1..5] OF real;`

     b. `Grade = ARRAY [1..20, 1..6] OF char;`
        `Grade = ARRAY [1..20] OF ARRAY [1..6] OF char;`

     c. `QuizScore = ARRAY [1..30, 1..12] OF integer;`
        `QuizScore = ARRAY [1..30] OF ARRAY [1..12] OF integer;`

3. a.   ShippingCost

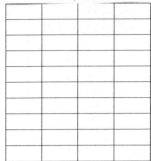

40 locations available

GradeBook

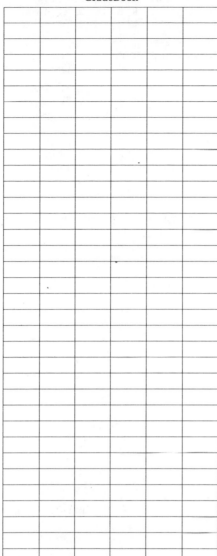

210 locations available

b.   A

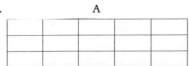

15 locations available

c.   Schedule

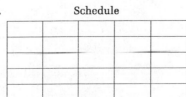

25 locations available

d.   AnswerSheet

(grid table — 250 locations available)

250 locations available

5. a.
```
FOR J := 1 TO 3 DO
  FOR K := 1 TO 6 DO
    A[J,K] := 2 * J + K;
```
   b.
```
FOR J := 1 TO 3 DO
  FOR K := 1 TO 6 DO
    A[J,K] := 0;
```
   c.
```
FOR J := 1 TO 3 DO
  FOR K := 1 TO 6 DO
    A[J,K] := 2 * J;
```

7.
```
TYPE
  String20 = PACKED ARRAY [1..20] OF char;
  NameList = ARRAY [1..50] OF String20;
VAR
  Name: NameList;

FOR J := 1 TO 50 DO              {  Loop to get data  }
  BEGIN
    FOR K := 1 TO 20 DO          {  Read one line  }
      read (Name[J,K];
    readln
  END;
```

9. a.
```
FOR J := 1 TO 4 DO
  BEGIN
    MinRow[J] := Table[J,1];
    FOR K := 2 TO 5 DO
      IF Table[J,K] < MinRow[J] THEN
        MinRow[J] := Table [J,K]
  END;
```
   c.
```
Total := 0;
FOR J := 1 TO 4 DO
  FOR K := 1 TO 5 DO
    Total := Total + Table[J,K];
```

11. a.
```
TYPE
  Table = ARRAY [1..3, 1..8] OF integer;
```
   b.
```
PROCEDURE Replace (VAR A : Table);
  VAR
    J, K : integer;
  BEGIN
    FOR J := 1 TO 3 DO
      FOR K := 1 TO 8 DO
        IF A[J,K] < 0 THEN
          A[J,K] := 0
  END:  {  of PROCEDURE Replace  }
```
   c. **PROCEDURE** Replace of **b.** could be called by

```
Replace (Table3X5);
```

13. a. Reading values into A and B depends on how data are arranged in the data file.

   b.
```
FOR H := 1 TO M DO
  FOR J := 1 TO P DO
    BEGIN
      Sum := 0;
      FOR K := 1 TO N DO
        Sum := Sum + A[H,K] * B[K,J];
      C[H,J] := Sum
    END;
```

Section 11.2

1. **a.** This prints an alphabetical listing of the states whose first letter is *O*.

   b. This prints every fifth state in reverse alphabetical order.

   c. This lists the first two letters of each state.

   d. This counts all occurrences of the letter *A* in the names of the states.

3. Assume the number of data lines is in NumLines.

   a.
```
FOR J := 1 TO NumLines DO
   BEGIN
      read (Name[J,1]);
      K := 1;
      WHILE Name[J,K] <> '*' DO
        BEGIN
           K := K + 1;
           read (Name[J,K])
        END;
      Length := K;
      FOR K := Length TO 20 DO
        Name [J,K] := ' ';
      readln
   END;
```

   c.
```
FOR J := 1 TO NumLines Do
   BEGIN
      FOR J := 1 TO 20 DO
         read (Name[J,K]);
      readln
   END;
```

Section 11.3

1. **a.** These declarations are not appropriate because Names is an array of 10 elements while Amounts is an array of 15 elements.

   b. These are appropriate because both Table and Names represent an array of size 12 × 10.

3. **b.** Assume an array type is defined as

```
TYPE
   GradeCount = ARRAY ['A'..'E'] OF integer;
```
If Count is a variable of type GradeCount, the frequency of each grade can be determined by

```
FOR Ch := 'A' TO 'E' DO  {  Initialize  }
   Count[Ch] := 0;
FOR J := 1 TO ListLength DO
   CASE Grade[J] OF
      'A' : Count['A'] := Count['A'] + 1;
      'B' : Count['B'] := Count['B'] + 1;
      'C' : Count['C'] := Count['C'] + 1;
      'D' : Count['D'] := Count['D'] + 1;
      'E' : Count['E'] := Count['E'] + 1
   END;  {  of CASE Grade[J]  }
```

Section 11.4

1. a. 2 * 3 * 10 = 60

   b. 6 * 3 * 4 = 72

   c. 3 * 2 * 11 = 66

   d. 4 * 10 * 15 = 600

3. ```
   TYPE
      Floor = 1..4;
      Wing = 1..5;
      Room = 1..20;
      FloorPlan = ARRAY [Floor, Wing, Room] OF char;
   VAR
      RoomType : FloorPlan;
   ```

5. There are 10 schools, 12 sports and 2 genders. Thus, there are 10*12*2 (240) memory locations reserved.

7. a.
   ```
   {  initialize to zero  }
   FOR School := 'A' TO 'J' DO
     NumGrants[School] := 0;
   FOR School := 'A' TO 'J' DO  {  consider each school  }
     FOR Sport := Baseball TO Wrestling DO  {  consider each sport  }
       FOR Gender := Male TO Female DO  {  consider each gender  }
         NumGrants[School] := NumGrants[School] +
                              Grants[School, Sport, Gender];
   ```

CHAPTER 12

Section 12.1

5. a. Employee

b. House
   ```

c. PhoneListing

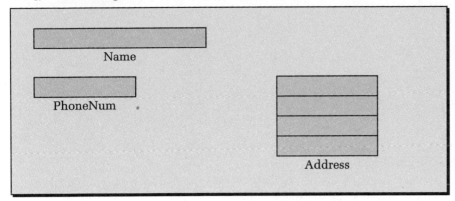

7. a.   `Info : RECORD`

should be

     `Info = RECORD`

and

     `Name = PACKED`

should be

     `Name : PACKED`

b. Member is used as both a variable and a data type.

c.   `IQ = 50..200`

should be

     `IQ : 50..200`

Section 12.2

1. a., c., and d. are valid.

b. is invalid; Cust2 and Cust3 are not of identical type.

e. is valid but demonstrates a poor practice. For better readability, you should always determine precisely which fields are being used.

3. a. The three different methods you could use are

(1) `Employee2 := Employee1;`

(2)
```
WITH Employee2 DO
    BEGIN
      Name := Employee1.Name;
      SSN := Employee1.SSN;
      Age := Employee1.Age;
      HourlyWage := Employee1.HourlyWage;
      Volunteer := Employee1.Volunteer
    END;  {  of WITH...DO  }
```

(3)
```
WITH Employee1 DO
    BEGIN
      Employee2.Name := Name;
      Employee2.SSN := SSN;
      Employee2.Age := Age;
      Employee2.HourlyWage := HourlyWage;
      Employee2.Volunteer := Volunteer
    END;  {  of WITH...DO  }
```

b. Did you consider

```
WITH Employee2 DO
  BEGIN
    Temp := HoursWorked;
    Employee2 := Employee1;
    HoursWorked := Temp
  END;
```

5.
```
FUNCTION Grade (Pts : integer) : char;
  VAR
    Percent : real;
  BEGIN
    Percent := Pts / 5;  {  Compute percent  }
    IF Percent < 60 THEN
      Grade := 'E'
    ELSE IF Percent < 70 THEN
      Grade := 'D'
    ELSE IF Percent < 80 THEN
      Grade := 'C'
    ELSE IF Percent < 90 THEN
      Grade := 'B'
    ELSE
      Grade := 'A'
  END;
```

This can be called by

```
With Student DO
  LetterGrade := Grade(TotalPts);
```

Section 12.3

1. a. See figure at right.

   b. i, iii, iv, viii, ix, and x are valid references

   ii, v, vi, and vii are invalid references

3.
```
TYPE
    String20 = PACKED ARRAY [1..20] OF char;
    Status = ('S', 'M', 'W', 'D');
    NumKids = 0..15;
    FamilyRec = RECORD
                    MaritalStatus : Status;
                    Children : NumKids
                END;  {  of FamilyRec  }
    AddressRec = RECORD
                    Street : String 20;
                    City : String20;
                    State : PACKED ARRAY [1..2] OF char;
                    ZipCode : integer
                END;  {  of AddressRec  }
    CustomerInfo  = RECORD
                    Name : String20;
                    Address : AddressRec;
                    SSN : PACKED ARRAY [1..11] OF char;
                    AnnualIncome : real;
                    FamilyInfo : FamilyRec
                END;  {  of CustomerInfo  }
  VAR
    Customer : CustomerInfo;
```

```
5. CONST
     SquadSize = 15;
   TYPE
     String20 = PACKED ARRAY[1..20] OF char;
     AgeRange = 15..25;
     HeightRange = 70..100;
     WeightRange = 100..300;
     PlayerInfo = RECORD
                    Name : String20;
                    Age : AgeRange;
                    Height : HeightRange;
                    Weight : WeightRange;
                    ScoringAv : real;
                    ReboundAv : real
                  END; {  of PlayerInfo  }
     PlayerList = ARRAY [1..SquadSize] OF PlayerInfo;
   VAR
     Player : PlayerList;
```

7. a. Student

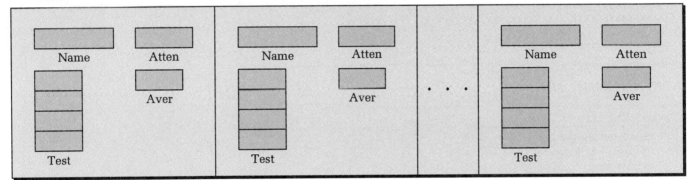

b. This function computes the test average for one student. It could be called by

```
WITH Student[K] DO
  Aver := GuessWhat(Test);
```

c. Format and headings will vary according to personal preference. However, your procedure should include

```
WITH St DO  {  Printout for St  }
  BEGIN
     .
     .
     .
     write ('Your attendance was ');
     CASE Atten OF
       Excellent : writeln ('excellent.');
       Average   : writeln ('average.');
       Poor      : writeln ('poor.')
     END; {  of CASE  }
     .
     .
     .
  END;  {  of WITH...DO  }
```

Section 12.4

3. a. The type TagType for the tag field Tag has not been defined.

   b. There is no value listed for the C of the tag field.

   c. There is a syntax error. A semicolon is needed between **boolean** and **CASE**. A type has not been given for the tag field. It should be

   ```
   CASE Tag : TagType OF
   ```

   d. Only one variant part can be defined in a record.

5. a. Figure

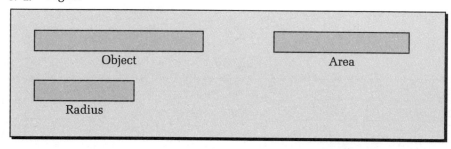

   b. Figure

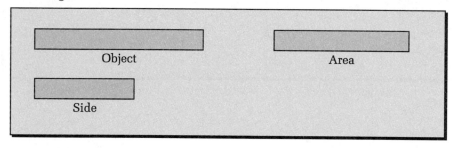

   c. Figure

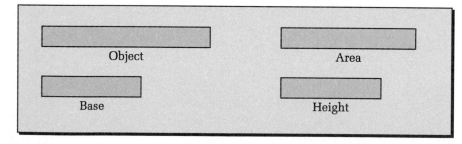

7.
```
PubType = (Book, Article);
DataRange = 1600..2000;
PublicationInfo = RECORD
                Author : String30;
                Title : String30;
                Date : DataRange;
                CASE Pub : PubType OF
                   Book    : (Publisher : String30;
                              City : String30);
                   Article : (JournalName : String30;
                              VolumeNumber : integer)
            END;
```

CHAPTER 13

Section 13.1

3. a. is valid; the component type is an integer in the subrange 0 .. 120

    b. is invalid; no file type has been defined.

    c. is invalid; component type for a file cannot be another file.

    d. is invalid; the expression **FILE**[1 .. 100] has no meaning.

    e. is valid; the component type is **integer.**

5.
```
TYPE
    String20 = PACKED ARRAY [1..20] OF char;
    AddressType = ARRAY [1..3] OF String20;
    GenderType = (M, F);
    PatientInfo = RECORD
                      Name : String20;
                      Address : AddressType;
                      Height : 0..200;
                      Weight : 0..300;
                      Age : 0..120;
                      Gender : GenderType;
                      InsuranceCo : String20
                  END;  {  of PatientInfo  }
    PatientFile = FILE OF PatientInfo;
VAR
    Patient : PatientFile;
```

Section 13.2

3.
```
TYPE
    FileType = FILE OF 0..100;
VAR
    SevenMult : FileType;
```

A fragment of code for this problem is

```
rewrite (SevenMult);  {  Open the file  }
Num := 1;
Sevens := 7;
WHILE Sevens < 100 DO
  BEGIN
    SevenMult^ := Sevens;
    put (SevenMult);
    Num := Num + 1;
    Sevens := 7 * Num
  END;  {  of WHILE...DO  }
```

5. Using **get** we have

```
reset (FivesFile);
A := FivesFile^;
get (FivesFile);
B := FivesFile^;
get (FivesFile);
C := FivesFile^;
get (FivesFile);
D := FivesFile^;
```

Using **read** we have

```
reset (FivesFile);
read (FivesFile, A);
read (FivesFile, B);
read (FivesFile, C);
read (FivesFile, D);
```

7. The **reset** procedure opens a file so that values may be read from the file. Contents of the file are not altered by this command. When **reset**(⟨file name⟩) is executed, the value of the first component is copied into the buffer variable.

   The **rewrite** procedure opens a file so that values may be written to the file. When **rewrite**(⟨file name⟩) is executed, any previous contents are lost.

9. a. The **reset** procedure opens the file for reading from the file, and **put** is used to write to the file. It appears that

   ```
   reset(File1);
   ```

   should have been

   ```
   rewrite(File1);
   ```

   b. No errors.

   c. The buffer variable is not properly written.

   ```
   File1 := 10 * J;
   ```

   should be

   ```
   File1^ := 10 * J;
   ```

d. This loop will execute, but nothing happens. In order to put the values into File1, the loop should be

   ```
   FOR J := 1 TO 5 DO
     BEGIN
       File1^ := J * 10;
       put (File1)
     END;
   ```

e. The files are mixed up. It appears that the intent is to copy the contents of File1 into File2.

f. No errors. This is a correct version of a problem similiar to that posed in

11. The output is

   ```
   -17
   -4
   ```

   The files contain the following values.

8	−17	0	−4	21

   OldFile

8	0	21

   NewFile

Section 13.3

1. b.
```
TYPE
    String20 = PACKED ARRAY [1..20] OF char;
    BookInfo = RECORD
                  Author : String20;
                  Title : String20;
                  StockNumber : integer;
                  Price : real;
                  Quantity : 0..500
               END;  {  of RECORD BookInfo  }
    BookFile = FILE OF BookInfo;
VAR
    Book : BookFile;
```

3. a.
```
TYPE
    String20 = PACKED ARRAY [1..20] OF char;
    QuizList = ARRAY [1..10] OF 0..10;
    TestList = ARRAY [1..4] OF 0..100;
    StudentRec = RECORD
                  Name : String20;
                  Number : integer;
                  Quiz : QuizList;
                  Test : TestList
               END;  {  of RECORD StudentRec  }
    StudentFile = FILE OF StudentRec;
VAR
    Student : StudentFile;
```

b.
```
PROCEDURE GetData (VAR St : StudentFile);
   VAR
      J : integer;
   BEGIN
      rewrite (St);         {  Open St for writing  }
      WHILE NOT eof(input) DO
        BEGIN
          WITH St^ DO  {  Get data for one student  }
            BEGIN
              FOR J := 1 TO 20 DO
                read (Name[J];  {  Get a name  }
              read (Number);        {  Get student ID  }
              FOR J := 1 TO 10 DO
                read (Quiz[J]);  {  Get quiz scores  }
              FOR J := 1 TO 4 DO
                read (Test[J]  {  Get test scores  }
            END;  {  of WITH...DO  }
          readln;
          put (St)  {  Move data to file  }
        END  {  of WHILE NOT eof  }
   END;  {  of PROCEDURE GetData  }
```

c. The basic design for this task is
to

(1) Transfer records to an array
(2) Sort the array
(3) Transfer records from the array back to the file

Assuming suitable definitions and declarations have been made, a procedure for this is

```
PROCEDURE SortFile (VAR St : StudentFile);
   VAR
      Temp : StudentRec;
      J, K, Length, Index : integer;
      TempList : ARRAY [1..MaxSize] OF StudentRec;
   BEGIN
      reset (St);
      J := 0;
      WHILE NOT eof(St) DO  {  Copy to array  }
        BEGIN
          J := J + 1;
          TempList[J] := St^;
          get (St)
        END;
      Length := J;

   {  Now sort the array  }

      FOR J := 1 TO Length-1 DO
        BEGIN
          Index := J;
          FOR K := J + 1 TO Length DO
            IF TempList[K].Name < TempList[Index].Name THEN
              Index := K;
          IF Index <> J THEN
            BEGIN
              Temp := TempList[Index];
              TempList[Index] := TempList[J];
              TempList[J] := Temp
            END  {  of exchange  }
        END;  {  of one pass  }
```

```
            {  Now copy back to the file  }

            rewrite (St);
            FOR J := 1 TO Length DO
              BEGIN
                St^ := TempList[J];
                put (St)
              END
            END;  { of PROCEDURE SortFile  }
```

CHAPTER 14

Section 14.1

1.
```
PROCEDURE InsertionSort (VAR B : List);
  VAR
    Num, Index, N : integer;
    Found : boolean;
  BEGIN
    NewLength := 0;
    WHILE NOT eof DO
      BEGIN
        Index := 1;
        Found := false;
        readln (Num);
        WHILE NOT Found AND (Index <= NewLength) DO
          IF Num < B[Index] THEN
            Found := true
          ELSE
            Index := Index + 1;
        FOR N := NewLength DOWNTO Index DO
          B[N+1] := B[N];
        B[Index] := Num;
        NewLength := NewLength + 1
      END  { of WHILE NOT eof  }
  END;  { of PROCEDURE InsertionSort  }
```

3. Change
```
FOR N := NewLength DOWNTO Index DO
  B[N+1] := B[N];
B[INDEX] := A[J];
```

to
```
FOR N := NewLength DOWNTO Index DO
  BEGIN
    B[N+1] := B[N];
    Count := Count + 1
  END;
B[Index] := A[J];
Count := Count + 1;
```

5. The bubble sort modification is
```
BEGIN  { Exchange values  }
  Temp := A[J];
  A[J] := A[J+1];
  A[J+1] := Temp;
  ExchangeMade := true;
  Count := Count + 3  { Counter here  }
END;
```

9. Assume the arrays are A and B. The bubble sort change is then

```
BEGIN  {  Exchange values  }
  TempA := A[J];
  TempB := B[J];
  A[J] := A[J+1];
  B[J] := B[J+1];
  A[J+1] := TempA;
  B[J+1] := TempB;
  ExchangeMade := true
END;  {  of exchanging values  }
```

Section 14.2

1. Modify the code for a bubble sort by

```
FOR J := 1 TO Length DO
  BEGIN
    Count := Count + 1;  {  Counter here  }
    IF A[ J] > A[J+1] THEN
      BEGIN
        .
        .
        .
      END;
```

CHAPTER 15

Section 15.1

1. a. **real** is not an ordinal data type.

   b. **integer** will exceed maximum size for a set.

   c. : should be =.

   d. Brackets should not be used.

   e. No errors.

3. a. `A := ['J', 'I', 'M'];`

   b. `A := ['P', 'A', 'S', 'C', 'L'];`

   c. The elements are 'T', 'O', and 'Y'. The eight subsets are [ ], ['T'], ['O'], ['Y'], ['T', 'O'], ['T', 'Y'], ['O', 'Y'], ['T', 'O', 'Y']

5. a. Brackets are needed, as

   `A := ['J'..'O']`

   b. No errors.

   c. Single quotations marks are needed, as

   `B := ['A'..'Z'];`

   d. 'E' and 'I' are listed more than once.

   e. [ ] is not a set variable.

   f. Since 'S' is in the subrange 'A' .. 'T', it is listed more than once.

7. a.
```
TYPE
   Hues = (Red, Orange, Yellow, Green, Blue, Indigo, Violet);
   RainbowSet = SET OF Hues;
VAR
   Rainbow : RainbowSet;
```

c.
```
Type
   SomeFruits = (Apple, Orange, Banana, Grape, Pear, Peach,
                 Strawberry);
   FruitSet = SET OF SomeFruits;
VAR
   Fruit : FruitSet;
```

Section 15.2

1. No. When $A = B$, both $A \geq B$ and $A \leq B$ are **true.**

3. a. $A + B = [-3..4, 7..10]$
   $A * B = [0,1,2,8,10]$
   $A - B = [-3,-2,-1]$
   $B - A = [3,4,7,9]$

   c. $A + B = B$
   $A * B = A$
   $A - B = A$
   $B - A = B$

5. All of these are **true.**

7. Code for this is
```
VowelsUppercase := ['A', 'E', 'I', 'O', 'U'];
VowelCount := 0;
WHILE NOT eof DO
  BEGIN
    read(Ch);
    IF Ch IN VowelsUppercase THEN
      VowelCount := VowelCount + 1
  END;
```

Section 15.3

3. Modify **PROGRAM** Delete-Blanks presented in Section 9.1, Example 9.4, by changing
```
IF Ch = ' ' THEN
  Ch := '*';
```
   to
```
IF Ch IN Vowels THEN
  write '*'
ELSE
  write (Ch);
```

7.
```
FUNCTION AllOddDigits (Num : integer) : boolean;
   TYPE
     Digits = SET of 0..9;
   VAR
     EvenDigits : Digits;
     NumDigits, J, Digit : integer;
   BEGIN
     EvenDigits := [0,2,4,6,8,10];
     IF Num DIV 1000 = 0 THEN   {  Num < 1000  }
       IF Num DIV 100 = 0 THEN  {  Num < 100  }
         IF Num DIV 10 = 0 THEN  {  Num < 10  }
```

```
        NumDigits := 1
      ELSE NumDigits := 2
    ELSE NumDigits := 3
  ELSE NumDigits := 4;
  AllOddDigits := true;
  FOR J := 1 TO NumDigits DO
    BEGIN
      Digit := abs(Num MOD 10);
      IF Digit IN EvenDigits THEN
        AllOddDigits := false;
      Num := Num DIV 10
    END   {  of FOR loop   }
END;  {  of FUNCTION AllOddDigits   }
```

CHAPTER 16

Chapter 16.1

3.

5.   c., f., and h. are valid.

a. is invalid; IntPtr1 + 1 is not allowed.

b. is invalid; pointers cannot be used with **writeln.**

d. is invalid; < is not a valid comparison for pointers.

e. is invalid;

```
BoolPtr NOT NIL
```

should be

```
BoolPtr2 <> NIL
```

g. is invalid; BoolPtr2 is not a Boolean expression.

Section 16.2

3.   Assume the file name is Num. A procedure is then

```
PROCEDURE PrintNumbers (First : DataPtr);
  VAR
    P : DataPtr;
  BEGIN
    P := First;
    WHILE P <> NIL DO
      BEGIN
        writeln (P^.Num);
        P := P^.Next
      END
  END;  {  of PROCEDURE PrintNumbers   }
```

and is called by

```
PrintNumbers (Start);
```

5.   a. TYPE

```
    String20 = PACKED ARRAY [1..20] OF char;
    TestList = ARRAY [1..4] OF 0..100;
    QuizList = ARRAY [1..10] OF 0..10;
```

```
DataPtr = ^StudentInfo;
StudentInfo = RECORD
                   Name : String20;
                   Test : TestList;
                   Quiz : QuizList;
                   Average : real;
                   Grade : char;
                   Next : DataPtr
                   END;  {  of RECORD StudentInfo  }
VAR
   Student : DataPtr;
```

b. The pointer variable is Student. The pointer type is DataPtr.

c. Assume Start, Ptr, and Last have been declared to be of type DataPtr. Data for the first student can then be obtained by

```
new (Start);
Ptr := Start;
Last := Start;
WITH Start^ DO
  BEGIN
    FOR J := 1 TO 20 DO
      read (Name[J]);
    FOR J := 1 TO 4 DO
      read (Test[J]);
    FOR J := 1 TO 10 DO
      read (Quiz[J]);
    Next := NIL
  END;
readln;
```

Data for the second student can be obtained by

```
new (Last);
Ptr^.Next := Last;
Ptr := Last;
WITH Last^ DO
  BEGIN
    FOR J := 1 TO 20 DO
      read (Name[J]);
    FOR J := 1 TO 4 DO
      read (Test[J]);
    FOR J := 1 TO 10 DO
      read (Quiz[J])
  END;
readln;
Ptr^.Next := NIL;
```

7. a. Working from the original

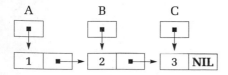

each time, we get

Code	Result

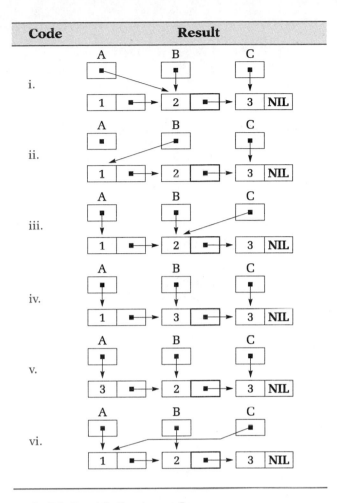

i.

ii.

iii.

iv.

v.

vi.

b. `A^.Next^.Next := B;`

9. Assume the linked list has been declared and values read into the field Num for each component of the list. Furthermore, assume Start is the pointer to the first node. A function for summing is then

```
FUNCTION Sum (First : DataPtr) : integer;
  VAR
    Total : integer;
    P : DataPtr;
  BEGIN
    Total := 0;
    P := First;
    WHILE P <> NIL DO
      BEGIN
        Total := Total + P^.Num;
        P := P^.Next
      END;
    Sum := Total
  END; { of FUNCTION Sum }
```

Section 16.3

1. Assume the original list can be envisioned as

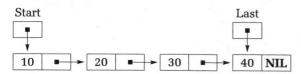

and you wish to insert 25 into the list. The initialization produces

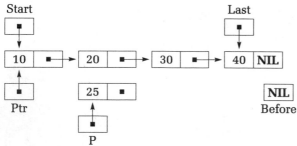

Since the loop is not empty, the **WHILE ... DO** loop will be executed until we have

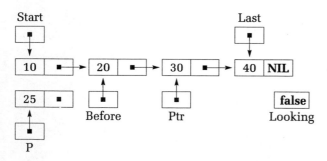

The pointers are then moved to obtain

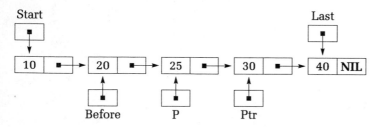

3. The new code is

```
IF Before = NIL THEN
   Push (Start, NewNum)       {  Call to Push  }
ELSE
   Before^.Next := P;
```

5. The heading becomes

```
PROCEDURE Pop (VAR Start : DataPtr);
```

and the line

```
NewNum := P^.Num
```

should be deleted.

7.
```
PROCEDURE Delete (VAR Start : DataPtr;
                      Position : integer);
   VAR
     Before, P : DataPtr;
   BEGIN
     IF Position = 1 THEN
       Pop (Start, Start^.Num)
     ELSE
       BEGIN
         Before := Start;
         FOR J := 1 TO (Position - 2) DO
           Before := Before^.Next;
         P := Before^.Next;
         Before^.Next := P^.Next;
         dispose (P)
       END  {  of ELSE option  }
   END;  {  of modified PROCEDURE Delete  }
```

Section 16.4

1. Illustrating only the parentheses, you get

S

Character Read	New Stack
"("	(
"("	((
"("	(((
")"	((
"("	(((
")"	((
")"	(
")"	

5. a.
```
CONST
  MaxStack = <value>;
TYPE
  Stack = RECORD
            Item : ARRAY [1..MaxStack] OF <data type>;
            Top : 0..MaxStack
          END;
VAR
  S : Stack;
```

b. Push becomes

```
PROCEDURE Push (VAR S : Stack;
                    X : integer);
  BEGIN
    IF S.Top = MaxStack THEN
      writeln ('Stack overflow')
    ELSE
      BEGIN
        S.Top := S.Top + 1;
        S.Item[S.Top] := X
      END
  END; {  of PROCEDURE Push  }
```

PopAndCheck becomes

```
PROCEDURE PopAndCheck (VAR S : Stack;
                       VAR X : integer;
                       VAR Underflow : boolean);
  BEGIN
    IF Empty(S) THEN  {  Check for empty stack  }
    Underflow := true
    ELSE
      BEGIN
        Underflow := false;
        X := S.Item[S.Top];
        S.Top := S.Top - 1
      END  {  of ELSE option  }
  END; {  of PROCEDURE PopAndCheck  }
```

9. Change the **ELSE** option to

```
ELSE IF Num = Node^.Info THEN
  writeln (Num, 'is a duplicate value.')
ELSE IF Num < Node^.Info THEN
  AddNode (Node^.LeftChild, Num)
ELSE
  AddNode (Node^.RightChild, Num)
```

11.
```
FUNCTION Search (Node : Pointer;
                 NewNum : integer) : boolean;
  VAR
    Found : boolean;
    Current : Pointer;
  BEGIN
    Current := Node;
    Found := false;
    WHILE (Current <> NIL) AND NOT Found Do
      IF Current^.Num = NewNum THEN
        Found := true
      ELSE IF Current^.Num < NewNum THEN
        Current := Current^.RightChild
      ELSE
        Current := Current^.LeftChild;
    Search := Found
  END;  {  of FUNCTION Search  }
```

13.

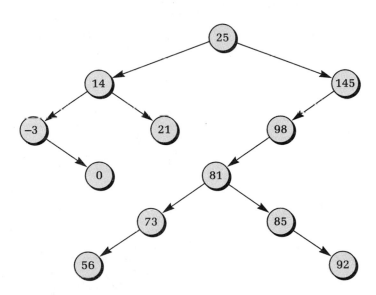

▦ Index

Credits

PHOTOS

Figures 1.4, 1.5a, 1.5b, 1.5c, and 1.6b: Courtesy of IBM Corporation

Figures 1.5d and 1.6a: Courtesy of Apple Computer, Inc.

Figure 1.8: Robert Barclay.

NOTES OF INTEREST

Page 11: Data Loss on Floppy Disks

Reprinted with permission from *Information Systems in Business: An Introduction*, p. 230, by James O. Hicks, Jr. Copyright © 1990 by West Publishing Company. All rights reserved. Permission for figure is credited to Verbatim Corporation, 1200 W WT Harris Blvd., Charlotte, NC 28213.

Page 13: Why Learn Pascal?

Reprinted with permission from "Pascal," by T. Woteki and A. Freiden, published in the September 1983 issue of *Popular Computing* magazine. © McGraw-Hill, Inc., New York. All rights reserved.

Page 22: Software Verification

From Ivars Peterson, "Finding Fault: The Formidable Task of Eradicating Software Bugs," SCIENCE NEWS, February 16, 1991, Vol. 139. Reprinted with permission from SCIENCE NEWS, the weekly newsmagazine of science. Copyright © 1991 by Science Services, Inc. Photo courtesy of Ontario Hydro.

Page 35: Blaise Pascal

Adapted from William Dunham, *Journey Through Genius: The Great Theorems of Mathematics,* John Wiley & Sons, 1990. Photos: Courtesy of IBM Corporation.

Page 71: Ethics and Computer Science

From the *Minneapolis Star/Tribune,* October 14, 1990, The Washington Post reprinted with permission.

Page 78: Defined Constants and Space Shuttle Computing, *Communications of the ACM* 27, No. 9 (September 1984): 880. Copyright 1984, Association for Computing Machinery, Inc. Reprinted by permission of Association for Computing Machinery, Inc.

Page 84: Herman Hollerith

Reprinted by permission for *Introduction to Computers with BASIC,* pp. 27–28, by Fred G. Harold. Copyright © 1984 by West Publishing Company. All rights reserved. Photos courtesy of IBM Corporation.

Page 104: Communication Skills Needed

From P. Jackowitz, R. Plishka, J. Sidbury, J. Hartman, and C. White, ACM Press *SIGCSE Bulletin* 22, No. 1, (February, 1990). Copyright 1991, Association for Computing Machinery, Inc. Reprinted by permission of Association for Computing Machinery, Inc.

Page 119: A Software Glitch

From Ivars Peterson, "Finding Fault: The Formidable Task of Eradicating Software Bugs," SCIENCE NEWS, February 16, 1991, Vol. 139. Reprinted with permission from SCIENCE NEWS, the weekly newsmagazine of science. Copyright 1991 by Science Services, Inc.

Pages 127 and 133: Debugging or Sleuthing

From J. Bentley, *Communications of the ACM* 28, No. 2 (February 1985): 139. Copyright 1985, Association for Computing Machinery, Inc. Reprinted by permission of Association for Computing Machinery, Inc.

Page 151: George Boole

Adapted from William Dunham, *Journey Through Genius: The Great Theorems of Mathematics,* John Wiley & Sons, 1990. Photo: The Bettmann Archive.

Page 166: Artificial Intelligence

Reprinted by permission from *The Mind Tool,* Fifth Ed., pp. 394–398, by Neill Graham. Copyright © 1989 by West Publishing Company. All rights reserved.

Page 219: Charles Babbage

Reprinted by permission from *Introduction to Computers with BASIC,* pp. 24–26, by Fred G. Harold. Copyright © 1984 by West Publishing Company. All rights reserved. Photos courtesy of IBM Corporation.

Page 229: Ada Augusta Byron

Reprinted by permission from *Introduction to Computers with BASIC,* pp. 26–27, by Fred G. Harold. Copyright © 1984 by West Publishing Company. All rights reserved. Photo: The Bettmann Archive.

Page 261: A Digital Matter of Life and Death

From Ivars Peterson, "A Digital Matter of Life and Death," SCIENCE NEWS, March 12, 1988, Vol. 133. Reprinted with permission from SCIENCE NEWS, the weekly newsmagazine of science. Copyright 1988 by Science Services, Inc.

Page 308: Computer Ethics: Hacking and Other Intrusions

Reprinted by permission from *Computers Under Attack: Intruders, Worms, and Viruses,* pp. 150–155, edited by Peter J. Denning, Article 7, "The West German Hacker Incident and Other Intrusions," by Mel Mandell. Copyright 1990, Association for Computing Machinery, Inc.

Page 342: Niklaus Wirth: Pascal to Modula-2

Adapted from Nicklaus Wirth, Programming Language Design to Computer Construction, 1984 Turing Award Lecture, *Communications of the ACM,* 28, No. 2 (February 1985).

Page 398: Career Opportunities in Computer Science

From Carol Wilson, Western Kentucky University, Bowling Green, Kentucky, 1991.

Page 408: Computer Ethics: Viruses

From Philip J. Hilts, Science Lab, in *The Washington Post National Weekly Edition,* May 23–29, 1988. Reprinted by permission of The Washington Post.

Page 427: Monolithic Idea: Invention of the Integrated Circuit

Adapted from T. R. Reid, "The Chip," *Science,* February 1985, pp. 32–41.

Page 442: Too Few Women in the Computer Science Pipeline?

From Carol Wilson, Western Kentucky University, Bowling Green, Kentucky, 1991.

Page 499: The Next Decade: What the Future Holds

From Daniel E. Kinnaman, "The Next Decade: What the Future Holds," *Technology & Learning* 11, No. 1 (September 1990). Reprinted by permission of *Technology & Learning* © 1990, Peter Li, Inc.

Page 509: Computer Ethics: Worms

Reprinted by permission from *Computers Under Attack: Intruders, Worms, and Viruses,* pp. 191 and 265, edited by Peter J. Denning, Article 9, "Computer Security in the Business World," by Maurice V. Wilkes; and Article 16, "The 'Worm' Programs— Early Experience with a Distributed Computation," by John F. Shoch and Jon A. Hupp. Copyright 1990, Association for Computing Machinery, Inc.

Page 552: Using Key Fields in Records

From David Gifford and Alfred Spector: "The TWA Reservations System: An Interview with Carol Flood and Ted Celentio," *Communications of the ACM* 17, No. 7 (July 1984): 650–657, Copyright 1984, Association for Computing Machinery, Inc. Reprinted by permission of Association for Computing Machinery, Inc.

Page 560: Impact of Computers on Art

From Dana J. Lamb, "The Impact of the Computer on the Arts," *Academic Computing,* April, 1989, pp. 22–24. Reprinted by permission from Academic Computing.

Page 574: Artist of Interface

From Ron Wolf, "Artist a Go-Between for Users, Computers," *The Chicago Tribune,* June 10, 1990. Reprinted by permission from Knight-Ridder Tribune News.

Page 592: Relational Databases

From William D. Nance, Management Information Systems, San Jose State University, San Jose, California, 1991.

Page 600: Backup and Recovery of Data

From William D. Nance, Management Information Systems, San Jose State University, San Jose, California, 1991.

Page 610: History Stuck on Old Computer Tapes

From the *Minneapolis Star/Tribune,* "30 Years of History Stuck on Old Computer Tapes," January 2, 1991. Reprinted by permission of the Associated Press.

Page 632: Gene Mapping Computer Scientists Examine Problems of Genome Project

From *The Chronicle of Higher Education,* May 9, 1990. Reprinted by permission of The Chronicle of Higher Education.

Page 649: Fractal Geometry and Benoit Mandlebrot Figure from *Integrated Computer Graphics,* p. 128, by Bruce Mielke. Copyright © 1991 by West Publishing Company.

Page 659: Time Is Cure for Computerphobia

Electronic Education 4, No. 6 (March/April, 1985), "Around the Circuit—Time Is Cure for Computerphobia."

Page 676: Object-Oriented Programming

Adapted from "Starting with the Basics of Object-Oriented Programming Using Turbo Pascal 5.5," by Captain Byron B. Thatcher, in *Interface: The Computer Education Quarterly* 12, Issue 4 (1990): 15–18.

Page 696: Using Pointers

From Nazim H. Madhavji, "Visibility Aspects of Programmed Dynamic Data Structures," *Communications of the ACM* 27, no. 8 (August 1984): 766. Copyright 1984, Association for Computing Machinery, Inc. Reprinted by permission of Association for Computing Machinery, Inc.